The
INTERNATIONAL CRITICAL COMMENTARY
on the Holy Scriptures of the Old and New Testaments

GENERAL EDITORS

G. I. DAVIES, F.B.A.

Professor of Old Testament Studies in the University of Cambridge
Fellow of Fitzwilliam College

AND

G. N. STANTON, Hon. D.D.

Lady Margaret's Professor of Divinity in the University of Cambridge
Fellow of Fitzwilliam College

CONSULTING EDITORS

J. A. EMERTON, F.B.A.

Emeritus Regius Professor of Hebrew in the University of Cambridge
Fellow of St John's College, Cambridge
Honorary Canon of St George's Cathedral, Jerusalem

AND

C. E. B. CRANFIELD, F.B.A.

Emeritus Professor of Theology in the University of Durham

FORMERLY UNDER THE EDITORSHIP OF

S. R. DRIVER
A. PLUMMER
C. A. BRIGGS

COLOSSIANS AND PHILEMON

A CRITICAL AND EXEGETICAL COMMENTARY

ON

COLOSSIANS AND PHILEMON

BY

R. McL. WILSON

Emeritus Professor of Biblical Criticism in the University of St Andrews

T&T CLARK INTERNATIONAL
A Continuum imprint
LONDON • NEW YORK

T&T Clark International
A Continuum imprint

The Tower Building
11 York Road
London SE1 7NX

15 East 26th Street
New York, NY 10010
USA

www.tandtclark.com

British Library Cataloguing-in-Publication Data
A catalogue record for this book is available from the British Library

ISBN: 0 567 04471 8

Typeset by Data Standards Ltd, Frome, Somerset, UK
Printed and bound in Great Britain by MPG Books Ltd, Cornwall

For Enid
In Loving Memory

CONTENTS

PREFACE

Commentators, and reviewers, often ask whether 'yet another' commentary is really necessary for this book or that, a question that only becomes more pressing when a reviewer can begin by observing that according to its bibliography the book he is dealing with is the sixth on Colossians and the fifth on Philemon within the current decade.[1] Do we really need 'yet another'?

Unfortunately the answers suggested are not always very satisfactory. It is, of course, obvious that if there is to be a series on the New Testament, then every book should find its place, either in its own right or in association with others, as with the Letters of John or the Pastorals. This, however, does not answer the question, but merely pushes it a stage further back: is the series really necessary? Again, it is obvious that the circumstances of today are not those of our predecessors. Much has changed since they wrote, in the outlook, attitudes and beliefs of contemporary society and in the world of scholarship itself, through new discoveries or the application of new methods. So commentaries for our modern age must be written to meet the needs of our time. But does that mean that commentaries of a bygone age are now worthless? Over forty years ago, Martin Albertz observed that the works of Zahn were heedlessly pushed aside by the younger generation of New Testament scholars, and even Harnack was forgotten: 'Hören kann man fast nur noch auf die Menschen seiner Zeit und der Generation vorher' (It is almost as if one can only listen to the people of one's own time and the generation before it).[2] In point of fact, a commentator today is building upon the work of those who went before him. One can still learn much from Lightfoot—or from Calvin, to name but two.

The beginnings of an answer begin to emerge when we consider the nature of a commentary, and its purpose. Many years ago, when the question came up in conversation, a colleague said, 'What *we* want to know is what *you* think.' A commentary is normally the work of an individual, or sometimes the fruit of a collaboration between two scholars; it is not very often the work of a committee. This means that it carries the marks of that individual scholar's judgement and

---

[1] C. F. D. Moule, reviewing J. D. G. Dunn's *Colossians and Philemon, JTS* 48 (1997) 202. On the reading and writing of commentaries cf. E. Best's article under that title, *ExpT* 107 (1996) 358–62.

[2] *Die Botschaft des Neuen Testaments,* ii (1957), 12. Best notes 'a distressing symptom in much modern academic writing of concentrating only on what has been written in the past ten or twenty years. Some modern commentaries, indeed, appear to be commentaries on the commentaries, monographs and articles written in the last few years rather than commentaries on the text!' ('The Reading and Writing of Commentaries', 358). Cf. also M. Hengel, 'Aufgaben' (NTS 40, 1994, 321–57).

experience, reflects his study of the text and his knowledge of the subject. His opinions may or may not be widely shared, but he is entitled to give voice to his views, provided he has done the necessary spadework and has something to say, with the necessary evidence to back his judgements.

A second point relates to the readership for which the commentary is intended. For a non-specialist clientele much in the way of technical detail which would be essential for an 'academic' commentary may have to be omitted as irrelevant for potential readers. Not many readers nowadays are competent in Greek, and a commentary designed for the man or woman in the street or in the pew may have to avoid any reference to that language. For one accustomed to referring to his Greek New Testament rather than to some English version, the writing of such a commentary can be an exacting task![3]

As to the writing of commentaries, there are various possibilities. One might, for example, begin by reading every existing commentary, every monograph relating to the subject, every book or article, feeding the data into a computer as one proceeds, and then write up all the material, with all the information duly slotted in and all the references duly recorded. Such a commentary could be a veritable mine of information; it could also be quite intolerably dull. It can be tedious in the extreme to find strings of names on this side or that, to indicate which among earlier scholars has supported or opposed some point of view, with a set of notes at the bottom of the page (or worse, in endnotes) simply supplying references that may never be followed up. In that connection, incidentally, a book once sent for review contained the statement, 'Die vorliegende Arbeit beabsichtigt, sämtliche Abhandlungen über (das Thema), die im deutschen, französischen, angloamerikanischen, niederländischen, italienischen und spanischen Sprachraum erschienen sind, zu berücksichtigen und kritisch zu würdigen', which I took to be a statement of intent—to provide a comprehensive coverage and critical evaluation of all the literature on the subject published in the German, French, British and American, Dutch, Italian and Spanish areas. Having some slight knowledge of the subject, the fruit of over thirty years' experience, I knew this to be rather a large order, so I made some checks: of the authors listed in the bibliography, some fifty were never mentioned in the notes; 68 were indeed cited, but many of them only once. That author relied largely on just three earlier scholars, in one case following his authority so slavishly as to

---

[3] Many years ago, a publisher put out an English translation of a commentary, with the following note on the jacket: 'Knowledge of Greek is not essential; Greek words are transliterated into English letters, and generally are at once translated.' Opposite his preface, the author had placed a quotation from Luther, urging the study of the ancient languages: 'without the knowledge of languages we can scarcely preserve the Gospel'. The first three pages, moreover, contained three words or phrases in Hebrew script!

reproduce a manifest printing error. In the light of that, I make no
such far-reaching claims![4]

Ernst Haenchen in several of his books[5] tells how he once had to
go to Switzerland for health reasons. At the time, it was forbidden to
take books across the frontier, and it was only when he reached the
stage of convalescence that he discovered he had brought his Nestle
with him. 'This was all I had when I began to occupy the time of my
convalescence with some serious work. That was a great blessing. For
when I now sought to penetrate more deeply into Acts, I was not led
astray by any secondary literature which was primarily interested in
Luke's sources.' The first task was to decide for himself what the
author had meant to say to his readers. This did not mean complete
disregard for the secondary literature, but its turn came later.

That would seem to be the right approach—to form one's own
opinion first, then check the secondary literature to find out what
other views have been advanced, and where necessary make the
appropriate adjustments. In the present case that was not entirely
possible, for I had lectured on Colossians for several years before
starting work on this commentary. My notes, based on a few selected
earlier commentaries and occasionally updated from further reading,
formed the starting point for this volume, but the whole has been
worked over afresh and the coverage of the literature greatly
extended. Unfortunately, each new book or article seems to produce
its own crop of references, not all of which have been readily
accessible. As indicated above, I make no claim to have read
everything, but one must call a halt somewhere!

A further point relates to parallels: it is of course important to note
parallel passages, which may provide a clue to interpretation, or in
some cases point to a relationship, although in some of these cases
the nature of that relationship may not be entirely clear. Many years
ago, E. Earle Ellis wrote, 'Because of its emphasis on placing
Scripture in its historical environment modern biblical scholarship
has often tended to convert parallels into influences and influences
into sources' (*St Paul's Use of the OT*, 82; see the entire paragraph).
We have to ask what the parallels signify. Are they merely parallels in
terminology, such as are almost bound to occur when two authors
are dealing with the same subject? Or do they indicate that one

[4] My discussion of the Colossian 'hymn' had already been completed before the
publication of C. Stettler's *Der Kolosserhymnus* (2000). To engage with it in any detail
would have meant a considerable expansion of an already lengthy section. I have
therefore confined myself to a general reference—which is not intended in disparagement of this book. Most of my Nag Hammadi references had already been identified
before I had access to Evans, Webb and Wiebe, *Nag Hammadi Texts and the Bible*
(1993). References drawn from this volume are duly acknowledged (as *NHTB*). In
general, I have referred to dictionaries and reference works available to me, although
some of them are now antiquated; the reader may replace them with more modern
works. A third edition of the *Greek–English Lexicon* (BAGD), revised by F. W.
Danker, has now been published; cf. the review by J. L. North in *JTS* 54 (2003), 271–
80.
[5] For example, in his preface to *The Acts of the Apostles* (ET 1971).

author has been influenced by the other? Are they such as to suggest that one author is indebted to the other, or do they indicate only that both are drawing on some common source? There are at least four different possibilities, and it may be hazardous to adopt one without further consideration. Even when it is likely that there is some dependence, it is sometimes difficult in the extreme to determine who is drawing upon the other.

In that connection there is another problem: how far should one go in accumulating parallels? Ideally, of course, the commentator should identify the parallels for himself, but many of them have long been known, and listed by his predecessors. To list his source in every case would be tedious for the reader (X compares such and such a text; Y adds some others; Z still more!); but simply to combine the lists would be less than honest, and convey the impression of much wider learning than the author actually possesses (a reviewer once remarked that most of an author's references seemed to be to secondary sources—not realizing that that author was trying to avoid that pretence!). In the present case, the parallels in the Dead Sea Scrolls have been very fully listed by Lohse. Since Qumran is not a field with which I am familiar, I have taken over only a few, with due acknowledgement.

In a sense, there cannot be too many commentaries, for each is the fruit of one man's knowledge and experience, written to meet the needs of a particular group of readers. The reader should have a choice, and be allowed to exercise his or her own judgement. The task of the commentator is to provide his readers with the necessary information, indicating the problems and at least some of the solutions that have been suggested, with some pointers to a critical assessment of their value. The commentator of course has his own point of view, his own opinions, but a commentary is no place for dogmatism, or for promoting a particular theory.

At various points in the volume (e.g. pp. 65–66) there are passages in small type, which the reader might wish to skip as secondary to the main purpose, which is interpretation of the text.

The editors and the publisher have been very patient, waiting for a book which has taken far longer to write than was imagined at the outset. As already noted, at least part of the delay has been due to the fact that every book or article consulted seemed to offer a fresh set of references demanding to be checked. Moreover, the writing of a commentary entailed at some points a complete reconsideration of opinions previously held. I can only apologize to friends and colleagues for overlooking relevant points that might have called for mention; but one cannot remember everything! Professor G. N. Stanton, New Testament editor for the series, has made some judicious comments, which have been duly taken into account, but responsibility for any flaws of course remains with me.

In the production of a book, an important but often unacknowledged part is played behind the scenes, by the editorial staff, the printers, the proof-readers, without whose efforts the quality of the work would be much the poorer. From long experience, as author and editor and reviewer, I know the difference it can make, and am happy to make due acknowledgement of the contribution made by Philip Law and Sarah Douglas and their staff at T&T Clark.

I had it in mind to dedicate this book to my wife, who should have had one many a long year ago. Sadly, it must now be dedicated to her memory: she died on Christmas Day, 2003. Never merely a meek and submissive wife, she was a good companion and a supportive partner through all the years of our married life, and possessed of a real flair for getting on with other people, no matter who they might be. Some verses in the last chapter of Proverbs are not relevant (Enid never had a staff of servants to do her bidding, nor did she ever purchase a vineyard with the fruit of her labours!), but reading the passage again, as I have done often in recent months, I can only say that I was privileged to have a very capable wife, truly more precious than jewels. I am now beyond the stage of merely grieving, and look back on the years of our married life with proud thanksgiving.

ABBREVIATIONS

AB	Anchor Bible
ABD	*Anchor Bible Dictionary*, ed. D. N. Freedman (New York, 1992)
AnBib	Analecta biblica
ANRW	*Aufstieg und Niedergang der römischen Welt*, ed. H. Temporini and W. Haase (Berlin, 1972–)
AThANT	Abhandlungen zur Theologie des Alten und Neuen Testaments
AV	Authorized Version
BAGD	W. Bauer, W. F. Arndt, F. W. Gingrich and F. W. Danker, *Greek–English Lexicon of the New Testament* (Chicago and London, 1979)
BCNH	Bibliothèque Copte de Nag Hammadi
Beg.	*The Beginnings of Christianity*, ed. F. J. Foakes Jackson and Kirsopp Lake, 5 vols (London, 1920–33)
BHTh	Beiträge zur historischen Theologie
BJRL	*Bulletin of the John Rylands Library*
BZNW	Beihefte zur Zeitschrift für die neutestamentliche Wissenschaft
CRAIBL	*Comptes rendus de l'Académie des inscriptions et belles-lettres*
DAC	*Dictionary of the Apostolic Church*, ed. J. Hastings, 2 vols (Edinburgh, 1915, 1918)
EGT	*Expositor's Greek Testament*, ed. W. R. Nicoll, 5 vols (London, 1903–10)
EncBib	*Encyclopaedia Biblica*, ed. T. K. Cheyne and J. S. Black (London, 1914)
EKKNT	Evangelisch-Katholischer Kommentar zum Neuen Testament
ET	English translation
ExpT	*Expository Times*
FRLANT	Forschungen zur Religion und Literatur des Alten und Neuen Testaments
FS	Festschrift
HDB	*A Dictionary of the Bible*, ed. J. Hastings, 5 vols (Edinburgh, 1900–04)
HNT	Handbuch zum Neuen Testament
HTR	*Harvard Theological Review*
IBS	*Irish Biblical Studies*
ICC	The International Critical Commentary
JBL	*Journal of Biblical Literature*
JJS	*Journal of Jewish Studies*
JR	*Journal of Religion*

JSNT	*Journal for the Study of the New Testament*
JSNTSS	Journal for the Study of the New Testament, Supplement Series
JTS	*Journal of Theological Studies*
KEK	Kritisch-exegetischer Kommentar über das Neue Testament
LSJ	H. C. Liddell, R. Scott and H. S. Jones, *Greek–English Lexicon*, 5 edn (Oxford, 1968)
LXX	Septuagint
NA²⁷	B. Aland, K. Aland *et al.* (eds), in succession to Eberhard and Erwin Nestle, *Novum Testamentum Graece*, 27th edn (Stuttgart, 1993)
NCB	New Century Bible
NEB	New English Bible
NHLE	*The Nag Hammadi Library in English*
NHMS	Nag Hammadi and Manichaean Studies
NHS	Nag Hammadi Studies
NHTB	*The Nag Hammadi Texts and the Bible*
NovTest	*Novum Testamentum*
NovTest Supp	*Novum Testamentum*, Supplements
NRSV	New Revised Standard Version
NTS	*New Testament Studies*
ODCC	*The Oxford Dictionary of the Christian Church*, ed. F. L. Cross and E. A. Livingstone, 3rd edn (Oxford, 1997)
PCG	W. L. Knox, *St Paul and the Church of the Gentiles* (Cambridge, 1939)
PCJ	W. L. Knox, *St Paul and the Church of Jerusalem* (Cambridge, 1925)
PG	*Patrologia Graeca*, ed. J.-P. Migne, 166 vols (Paris, 1857–83)
PL	*Patrologia Latina*, ed. J.-P. Migne, 221 vols (Paris, 1844–65)
POx	Papyrus Oxyrynchus
PRJ	W. D. Davies, *Paul and Rabbinic Judaism* (London, 1948)
RAC	*Reallexikon für Antike und Christentum*
RB	*Revue Biblique*
RGG	*Religion in Geschichte und Gegenwart*
RSV	Revised Standard Version
RV	Revised Version
Schürer	E. Schürer, *History of the Jewish People in the Age of Jesus Christ*, English edn revd G. Vermes and F. Millar (Edinburgh 1973–86)
SEÅ	*Svensk exegetisk årsbok*
SJT	*Scottish Journal of Theology*
SNTSMS	Society for New Testament Studies Monograph Series
ST	*Studia Theologica*

TLZ	*Theologischer Literaturzeitung*
TRE	*Theologische Realenzyklopädie*
TU	Texte und Untersuchungen
TWNT	*Theologisches Wörterbuch zum Neuen Testament*, ed. G. Kittel and G. Friedrich, 11 vols (Stuttgart, 1932–79); ET *Theological Dictionary of the New Testament*, tr. G. W. Bromiley (Grand Rapids, 1964–73)
UBS	United Bible Societies
VigChr	*Vigiliae Christianae*
v.l.	*varia lectio* (variant reading)
WUNT	Wissenschaftliche Untersuchungen zum Neuen Testament
ZNW	*Zeitschrift für die neutestamentliche Wissenschaft*
ZTK	*Zeitschrift für Theologie und Kirche*

BIBLIOGRAPHY

No attempt has been made at complete coverage. Cf. Lohse, 210–19, and for Philemon the bibliographies in Fitzmyer. K. Staab's *Pauluskommentare aus der griechischen Kirche* (1933) was not available to me.

I. Commentaries
Except where specifically noted, the following deal with both Colossians and Philemon.

Patristic
Chrysostom, PG 62, 299–302 (Col.), 701–20 (Philem.).
John the Deacon (pseudo-Jerome), PL 30, 891–902 (Col.), 945–46 (Philem.); also in A. Souter (ed.), *Cambridge Texts and Studies* IX, vol. ii, (Cambridge, 1926), 451–73 (Col.), 536–39 (Philem.). Souter claims it to be an interpolated version of a commentary by Pelagius.
Oecumenius, PG 119, 9–56 (Col.), 262–72 (Philem.).
Theodore of Mopsuestia, *Theodori episcopi Mopsuesteni in epistolas B. Pauli commentarii*, ed. H. B. Swete, i (Cambridge, 1880), 253–312 (Col.); ii (Cambridge, 1882), 258–85 (Philem.).
Theodoret, PG 82, cols 591–628 (Philem. 871–78).

Sixteenth to Eighteenth Centuries
Bengel, J. A., *Gnomon Novi Testamenti* (3rd edn 1773, repr. London, 1862), 733–46, (Col.), 800–02 (Philem.).
Calvin, J., *Commentaries on Philippians, Colossians and Thessalonians*, tr. J. Pringle, Calvin Translation Society (Edinburgh, 1851), 132–232.
—*Commentaries on Timothy, Titus and Philemon*, tr. W. Pringle, Calvin Translation Society (Edinburgh, 1856).
—*The Epistles of Paul the Apostle to the Galatians, Ephesians, Philippians and Colossians*, tr. T. H. L. Parker (Edinburgh, 1965), 297–362.
—*The Second Epistle of Paul to the Corinthians, The Epistles of Paul to Timothy, Titus and Philemon*, tr. T. A. Smail (Edinburgh, 1964), 393–401.
Melanchthon, P., *Paul's Letter to the Colossians*, tr. D. C. Parker (Sheffield, 1989).

Modern Works
Aletti, J. N., *Epître aux Colossiens*, Etudes Bibliques, n.s. 20 (Paris, 1993).

Barclay, J. M. G., *Colossians and Philemon*, New Testament Guides (Sheffield, 1997).
Barth, M., *Colossians: A New Translation with Introduction and Commentary*, AB 34B (New York, 1994).
—*The Letter to Philemon: A New Translation with Notes and Commentary* (Grand Rapids, 2000).
Collanges, J. F., *L'Epître à Philémon* (Geneva, 1987).
Dibelius, M., *An die Kolosser, Epheser, an Philemon*, HNT (Tübingen, 1927; 3rd edn 1953, ed. H. Greeven).
Dodd, C. H., *Abingdon Bible Commentary* (London, 1929), 1250–62 (Col.), 1292–94 (Philem.).
Dunn, J. D. G., *The Epistles to the Colossians and to Philemon* (Carlisle, 1996).
Fitzmyer, J. A., *The Letter to Philemon*, AB 34C (New York, 2000).
Furnish, V. P., *Interpreter's One-Volume Commentary on the Bible* (Nashville and New York, 1971), 856–64, (Col.), 894–96 (Philem.).
Gnilka, J., *Der Kolosserbrief* (Freiburg, Basel and Vienna, 1980).
—*Der Philemonbrief* (Freiburg, Basel and Vienna, 1982).
Hartman, L., *Kolosserbrevet*, Kommentar till Nya Testamentet 12 (Uppsala, 1985).
Hübner, H., *An Philemon, an die Kolosser, an die Epheser*, HNT 12 (Tübingen, 1997).
Lightfoot, J. B., *The Epistles of St Paul: Colossians and Philemon* (London, 1875; 3rd edn 1879, 4th edn 1892).
Lindemann, A., *Der Kolosserbrief*, Zürcher Bibelkommentare (Zurich, 1983).
Lohmeyer, E., *Die Briefe an die Philipper, an die Kolosser und an Philemon*, KEK IX (Göttingen, 1930; 13th edn 1964).
Lohse, E., *Colossians and Philemon* (Philadelphia, 1971, repr. 1975; ET of *Die Briefe an die Kolosser und an Philemon*, KEK (Göttingen, 1968).
Martin, G. C., *Ephesians, Colossians, Philemon, Philippians*, Century Bible (London, n.d.).
Martin, R. P., *Ephesians, Colossians and Philemon*, Interpretation (Louisville, Ky., 1991).
Moule, C. F. D., *The Epistles to the Colossians and Philemon*, Cambridge Greek Testament Commentary (Cambridge, 1957).
—*Peake's Commentary on the Bible*, revd edn (London, 1962), 990–95.
Moule, H. G. C., *The Epistles to the Colossians and Philemon*, Cambridge Bible for Schools and Colleges (Cambridge, 1893).
O'Brien, P. T., *Colossians and Philemon*, Word Commentaries 44 (Waco, Tex., 1982).
Oesterley, W. O. E., *Philemon*, EGT, iv (London, 1910).
Peake, A. S., *Colossians*, EGT, iii (London, 1903).
Pfammatter, J., *Epheserbrief; Kolosserbrief* (Würzburg, 1987).
Pokorný, P., *Colossians* (Peabody, Mass., 1991; ET of *Der Brief des Paulus an die Kolosser*, Theol. Handkommentar zum NT (Berlin, 1987).

Radford, L. B., *The Epistles to the Colossians and Philemon*, (London, 1931).

Schweizer, E., *Der Brief an die Kolosser* (Zurich, 1976, 2nd edn 1980: ET London, 1982).

Scott, E. F., *The Epistles to the Colossians, to Philemon and to the Ephesians*, Moffatt Commentary (London, 1930, repr. 1942).

Stuhlmacher, P., *Der Brief an Philemon*, 2nd edn, EKKNT xviii (Zurich, 1981).

Wall, R. W., *Colossians and Philemon*, IVP New Testament Commentary Series (Downers Grove, Ill., 1993).

Williams, A. L., *The Epistles to the Colossians and Philemon*, Cambridge Greek Testament Commentary (Cambridge, 1928).

Wright, N. T., *Colossians and Philemon*, Tyndale Commentaries (Leicester and Grand Rapids, 1986).

II. Other Literature

Aland, B. (ed.), *Gnosis*, FS Hans Jonas (Göttingen, 1978).

Aletti, J. N., *Colossiens 1, 15–20, genre et exégèse du texte; fonction de la thématique sapientielle*, AnBib 91 (Rome, 1981).

Allan, J. A., "The 'in Christ' Formula in Ephesians", *NTS* 5 (1958/59), 54–62.

—"The 'in Christ' Formula in the Pastoral Epistles", *NTS* 10 (1963/64), 115–121.

Allenbach, J., et al., *Biblia Patristica. I: Des origines à Clément d'Alexandrie et Tertullien* (Paris, 1975).

Andresen, C., and Klein, G. (eds), *Theologia crucis—signum crucis*, FS E. Dinkler (Tübingen, 1979).

Arnold, C. E., 'Colossae', *ABD*, i. 1089.

—*The Colossian Syncretism: The Interface between Christianity and Folk Belief at Colossae*, WUNT 2. Reihe 77 (Tübingen, 1995).

—'Returning to the Domain of the Powers: STOICHEIA as Evil Spirits in Galatians 4.3, 9', *NovTest* 38 (1996), 55–76.

—*Ephesians: Power and Magic*, SNTSMS 63 (Cambridge, 1989).

Attridge, H. W. (ed.), *Nag Hammadi Codex I*, NHS 22 (Leiden, 1985) (texts & translations); NHS 23 (notes).

Baggott, L. J., *A New Approach to Colossians* (London, 1961).

Barbour, R. S., 'Salvation and Cosmology: The Setting of the Epistle to the Colossians', *SJT* 20 (1967), 257–71.

Barc, B. (ed.), *Colloque international sur les textes de Nag Hammadi*, BCNH, section 'Etudes' 1 (Quebec City, 1981).

Barclay, J. M. G., 'Paul, Philemon and the Dilemma of Christian Slave-Ownership', *NTS* 37 (1991), 161–86.

Barrett, C. K., *The Acts of the Apostles*, ICC, 2 vols (Edinburgh, 1994, 1998).

—*The Epistle to the Romans* (London, 1957).

—*From First Adam to Last* (London, 1962).

—'Pauline Controversies in the Post-Pauline Period', *NTS* 20 (1974), 229–45.

—'Shaliaḥ and Apostle', in Barrett *et al.* (eds), *Donum Gentilicium*, 88–102.

Barrett, C. K., Bammel, E. and Davies, W. D., *Donum Gentilicium*, FS Daube (Oxford, 1978).

Bartchy, S. S.,'Philemon', *ABD*, v. 305–10.

—'Slavery', *ABD*, vi. 65–73.

Bauckham, R.,'Pseudo-Apostolic Letters', *JBL* 107 (1988), 469–94.

Bauer, W., *Rechtgläubigkeit und Ketzerei im ältesten Christentum* (Tübingen, 1934; 2nd edn 1964, ET *Orthodoxy and Heresy in Earliest Christianity,* Philadelphia, 1971).

Baur, F. C., *Paul the Apostle of Jesus Christ* (ET London, 1875).

Beasley-Murray, P., 'Colossians 1:15–20: An Early Christian Hymn Celebrating the Lordship of Christ', in Hagner and Harris (eds), *Pauline Studies*, 169–83.

Belleville, L., 'Ἰουνιαν . . . ἐπισημοι ἐν τοῖς ἀποστόλοις', NTS 51 (2005), 231–49.

Benoit, P., 'L'hymne christologique de Col 1, 15–20; jugement critique sur l'état de recherches', *Christianity, Judaism and other Greco-Roman Cults*, FS M. Smith (Leiden, 1975), i. 226–63.

—'Ἅγιοι en Colossiens 1.12: hommes ou anges?', in Hooker and Wilson (eds), *Paul and Paulinism*, 83–101.

—'Qumrân et le Nouveau Testament', *NTS* 7 (1960/61) 276–96 (ET in O'Connor and Charlesworth (eds), *Paul and the Dead Sea Scrolls*, 1–30).

Best, E., *Ephesians*, New Testament Guides (Sheffield, 1993).

—*Ephesians*, ICC (Edinburgh, 1998).

—*Essays on Ephesians* (Edinburgh, 1997).

—'The Haustafel in Ephesians (Eph. 5.22—6.9)', *IBS* 16 (1994), 146–60 (repr. in Best, *Essays on Ephesians*, 189–203).

—*One Body in Christ* (London, 1955).

—'Paul's Apostolic Authority—?', *JSNT* 27 (1986), 3–25 (repr. in Best, *Essays on Ephesians*, 25–49).

—'The Reading and Writing of Commentaries', *ExpT* 107 (1996), 358–62.

—'Recipients and Title of the Letter to the Ephesians: Why and When the Designation "Ephesians"?', *ANRW* II. 25.4, 3247–79.

—'Who Used Whom? The Relationship of Ephesians and Colossians', *NTS* 43 (1997), 72–96.

Bianchi, U. (ed.), *Le Origini dello Gnosticismo*, Numen Suppl. 12 (Leiden, 1967).

Birdsall, J. N., 'Πρεσβύτης in Philemon 9: A Study in Conjectural Emendation', *NTS* 39 (1993), 625–30.

Bjerkelund, C. J., *Parakalô* (Oslo, 1967).

Bockmuehl, M. N. A., *Revelation and Mystery in Ancient Judaism and Pauline Christianity*, WUNT 2. Reihe 36 (Tübingen, 1990; American edn Grand Rapids, 1997).

Böhlig, A., and Wisse, F., *Zum Hellenismus in den Schriften von Nag Hammadi*, Göttinger Orientforschungen VI, Reihe. vol. ii (Wiesbaden, 1975).

Boobyer, G. H., *'Thanksgiving' and the 'Glory of God' in Paul* (Leipzig, 1929).

Booth, K. N., '"Deficiency": A Gnostic Technical Term', *Studia Patristica* xiv, ed. E. A. Livingstone, TU 117 (Berlin, 1976), 191–202.

Borchert, G. L., *Paul and his Interpreters: An Annotated Bibliography* (Madison, Wisc., 1985).

Bornkamm, G., 'Die Häresie des Kolosserbriefs', *TLZ* 73 (1948), 11–20; ET in Francis and Meeks (eds), *Conflict at Colossae*, 123–45.

—'"Die Hoffnung" im Kolosserbrief—Zugleich ein Beiträg zur Frage der Echtheit des Briefes', *Studien zum Neuen Testament und zur Patristik*, FS Klostermann, TU 77 (Berlin, 1961), 59–64.

Bouttier, M., 'Complexio Oppositorum: Sur les formules de I Cor. xii.13; Gal. iii.26-28; Col. iii.10, 11', *NTS* 23 (1977), 1–19.

—*En Christ: Etude d'exégèse et de théologie paulinienne* (Paris, 1962).

—*L'épître de saint Paul aux Ephésiens*, Commentaire du Nouveau Testament IXb (Geneva, 1991).

Braun, H., *Qumran und das Neue Testament,* 2 vols (Tübingen, 1966).

Brockington, L. H., 'The Septuagintal Background to the New Testament Use of ΔΟΞΑ', in Nineham (ed.), *Studies in the Gospels,* 1–8.

Brox, N., *Falsche Verfasserangaben* (Stuttgart, 1975).

Bruce, F. F., 'The "Christ-Hymn" of Col 1, 15–20', *SEÅ* 49 (1984), 99–111.

—'The Colossian Heresy', *SEÅ* 49 (1984), 195–208.

—'Jews and Christians in the Lycus Valley', *Bibliotheca Sacra* 141 (1984), 3–15.

—'St Paul in Rome 2: The Epistle to Philemon', *BJRL* 48 (1965/66), 81–97.

—'St Paul in Rome 3: The Epistle to the Colossians', *BJRL* 48 (1965/66), 268–85.

Bujard, W., *Stilanalytische Untersuchungen zum Kolosserbrief* (Göttingen, 1973).

Bultmann, R., *Primitive Christianity in its Contemporary Setting* (ET London, 1956).

—*Theologie des Neuen Testaments* (Tübingen, 1948–53; 5th edn 1965; ET London, 1952, 1955).

—*Gnosis,* tr. J. R. Coates (from TWNT) (London, 1952).

Burer, M., and Wallace, D. B., 'Was Junia Really an Apostle? A Re-examination of Rom 16.7', *NTS* 47 (2001), 76–91.

Burger, C., *Schöpfung und Versöhnung: Studien zum liturgischen Gut im Kolosser- und Epheserbrief* (Neukirchen, 1975).

Burnet, R., 'Pourquoi avoir écrit l'insipide épître aux Laodicéens?', *NTS* 48 (2002), 132–41.

Campbell, D. A., 'The Scythian Perspective in Col 3.11: A Response to Troy Martin', *NovTest* 39 (1997), 81–84.

—'Unravelling Colossians 3.11b', *NTS* 42 (1996), 120–32.

Carr, W., *Angels and Principalities*, SNTSMS 42 (Cambridge, 1981).

Chadwick, H., 'All Things to All Men', *NTS* 1 (1954/55), 270–75.

Collins, R. F., *Letters that Paul Did Not Write* (Wilmington, Del., 1988).

Conzelmann, H., *An Outline of the Theology of the New Testament* (ET London, 1969).

—'Paulus und die Weisheit', *NTS* 12 (1965/66), 231–44.

—'Die Schule des Paulus', in Andresen and Klein (eds), *Theologia crucis—signum crucis*, 85–96.

Coppens, J., '"Mystery" in the Theology of Saint Paul and its parallels at Qumran', in O'Connor and Charlesworth (eds), *Paul and the Dead Sea Scrolls*, 132–58.

Cothenet, E., 'La tradition selon Jude et 2 Pierre', *NTS* 35 (1989), 407–20.

Coutts, J., 'The Relationship of Ephesians and Colossians', *NTS* 4 (1957/58), 201–07.

Craddock, F. B., ' "All Things in Him": A Critical Note on Col. i.15-20', *NTS* 12 (1965/66), 78–80.

Cranfield, C. E. B., 'Dying with Christ and Being Raised with Christ', *Metanoia* 2 (1992), 99–102.

—*The Epistle to the Romans*, 2 vols (Edinburgh, 1975, 1979).

—'Romans 6.1–14 Revisited', *ExpT* 106 (1994/95), 40–43.

—'Some Human Relationships (Col 3:18—4.1)', *ExpT* 104 (1992/93), 305–07.

Cross, F. L., (ed.), *The Jung Codex* (London, 1955).

Crouch, J. E., *The Origin and Intention of the Colossian Haustafel*, FRLANT 109 (Göttingen, 1972).

Dahl, N. A., 'Christ, Creation and the Church', in Davies and Daube (eds), *The Background of the New Testament and its Eschatology*, 422–43; repr. in Dahl, *Jesus in the Memory of the Early Church*, 120–40.

—'Form-Critical Observations on Early Christian Preaching', in Dahl, *Jesus in the Memory of the Early Church*, 30–36.

—*Jesus in the Memory of the Early Church* (Minneapolis, 1976).

Daniélou, J., *Théologie du judéo-christianisme* (Tournai, 1958).

Daniels, B. L., and Suggs, M. J. (eds), *Studies in the History and Text of the New Testament*, FS Clark, Studies and Documents 29 (Salt Lake City, 1967).

Davies, W. D., *Christian Origins and Judaism* (London, 1962).

—*Jewish and Pauline Studies* (London, 1984).

—*Paul and Rabbinic Judaism* (London, 1948).

Davies, W. D., and Daube, D. (eds), *The Background of the New Testament and its Eschatology*, FS Dodd (Cambridge, 1964).

Deichgräber, R., *Gotteshymnus und Christushymnus in der frühen Christenheit* (Göttingen, 1967).

Deissmann, G. A., *Bible Studies* (ET Edinburgh, 1903).

—*Light from the Ancient East* (ET London, 1927).

—*Paul: A Study in Social and Religious History* (ET London, 1926).

de Jonge, M., 'The Earliest Christian Use of Christos: Some Suggestions', *NTS* 32 (1986), 321–43.

DeMaris, R. E., *The Colossian Controversy: Wisdom in Dispute at Colossae* (Sheffield, 1994).
Dibelius, M., 'The Isis Initiation of Apuleius and Related Initiatory Rites', in Francis and Meeks (eds), *Conflict at Colossae*, 61–121 (ET of 'Die Isisweihe bei Apuleius und verwandte Initiations-Riten' (SB Heidelberg, 1917)).
Dodd, C. H., *The Bible and the Greeks* (London, 1935).
—*The Epistle of Paul to the Romans*, Moffatt Commentary (London, 1932).
—*Gospel and Law* (Cambridge, 1951).
—*The Interpretation of the Fourth Gospel* (Cambridge, 1953).
—*New Testament Studies* (Manchester, 1953).
Doughty, D. J., 'The Priority of ΧΑΡΙΣ', *NTS* 19 (1972/73), 163–80.
Downing, F. G., *Cynics and Christian Origins* (Edinburgh, 1992).
—*Cynics, Paul and the Pauline Churches* (London, 1998).
—'A Cynic Preparation for Paul's Gospel for Jew and Greek, Slave and Free, Male and Female', *NTS* 42 (1996), 454–62.
—'Paul's Drive for Deviants', *NTS* 49 (2003), 360–71.
Drake, A. E., 'The Riddle of Colossians: *Quaerendo invenietis*', *NTS* 41 (1995), 123–44.
Duncan, G. S., 'Chronological Table to Illustrate Paul's Ministry in Asia', *NTS* 5 (1958/59), 43–45.
—'Paul's Ministry in Asia - The Last Phase', *NTS* 3 (1956/57), 211–18.
—*St Paul's Ephesian Ministry* (London, 1929).
—'Were Paul's Imprisonment Epistles written from Ephesus?', *ExpT* 67 (1955/6) 163–66.
Dunn, J. D. G., 'The Colossian Philosophy: A Confident Jewish Apologia', *Biblica* 76 (1995), 153–81.
Ellis, E. E., 'Paul and his Co-workers', *NTS* 17 (1970/71), 437–52.
—*Paul's Use of the Old Testament* (Edinburgh, 1957).
Elliott, J. K., *The Apocryphal New Testament* (Oxford, 1993).
Eltester, F. W., *Eikon im Neuen Testament*, BZNW 23 (Berlin, 1958).
Eltester, W. (ed.), *Judentum, Urchristentum, Kirche*, FS Jeremias, BZNW 26 (Berlin, 1960; 2nd edn 1964).
Eltester, W., and Kettler, F. H., *Apophoreta*, FS Haenchen, BZNW 30 (Berlin, 1964).
Epp, E. J., and MacRae, G. W. (eds), *The New Testament and its Modern Interpreters* (Atlanta, 1989).
Ernst, J., 'Kolosserbrief', *TRE* 19 (1990), 370–76.
—*Pleroma und Pleroma Christi* (Regensburg, 1970).
Esler, P. F., 'Paul and Stoicism: Romans 12 as a Test Case', *NTS* 50 (2004), 105–24.
Evans, C. A., and Hagner, D. A. (eds), *Anti-Semitism and Early Christianity* (Minneapolis, 1993).
Evans, C. A., Webb, R. L., and Wiebe, R. A., *Nag Hammadi Texts and the Bible: A Synopsis and Index*, New Testament Tools and Studies 18 (Leiden, 1993).

Fischer, K.-M., 'Anmerkungen zur Pseudepigraphie im Neuen
  Testament', *NTS* 23 (1977), 76–81.
Foerster, W., 'Abfassungszeit und Ziel des Galaterbriefes', in Eltester
  and Kettler (eds), *Apophoreta*, 135–41.
—'Die Irrlehrer des Kolosserbriefes', in van Unnik, W. C., and van
  der Woude, A. S. (eds), *Studia Biblica et Semitica*, 71–80.
Fossum, J., 'Colossians 1.15–18a in the Light of Jewish Mysticism
  and Gnosticism', *NTS* 35 (1989), 183–201.
—*The Name of God and the Angel of the Lord*, WUNT 36 (Tübingen,
  1985).
Francis, F. O., 'The Background of EMBATEUEIN (Col 2:18) in
  Legal Papyri and Oracle Inscriptions', in Francis and Meeks (eds),
  Conflict at Colossae, 197–218.
—'The Christological Argument in Colossians', in Jervell and Meeks
  (eds), *God's Christ and His People*, 198–208.
—'Humility and Angel Worship in Col 2:18', *Studia Theologica* 16
  (1963), 109–34; repr. in Francis and Meeks (eds), *Conflict at
  Colossae*, 163–95.
Francis, F. O., and Meeks, W. (eds), *Conflict at Colossae* (Missoula,
  Mont. 1975).
Francis, F. O., and Sampley, J. P., *Pauline Parallels*, 2nd edn
  (Philadelphia, 1984).
Friedländer, M., *Der vorchristliche jüdische Gnosticismus* (Göttingen,
  1898; repr. Farnborough, 1972).
Furnish, V. P., 'Colossians', *ABD*, i. 1090–96.
—'On Putting Paul in His Place', *JBL* 113 (1994), 3–17.
—'Pauline Studies', in Epp and MacRae (eds), *The New Testament
  and its Modern Interpreters*, 321–50.
Gamble, H. Y., 'The Canon of the New Testament', in Epp and
  MacRae (eds), *The New Testament and its Modern Interpreters*,
  201–43.
Gasque, W. W., and Martin, R. P. (eds), *Apostolic History and the
  Gospel*, FS Bruce (Exeter, 1970).
Goehring, J. E., Hedrick, C. W., and Sanders, J. T. (eds), *Gnosticism
  and the Early Christian World*, FS Robinson (Sonoma, Calif.,
  1990).
Good, D. J., *Reconstructing the Tradition of Sophia in Gnostic
  Literature* (Atlanta, 1987).
Goppelt, L., *Apostolic and Post-Apostolic Times* (ET Exeter, 1970).
—*Christentum und Judentum im ersten und zweiten Jahrhundert,*
  (Gütersloh, 1954).
Goulder, M. D., 'Colossians and Barbelo', *NTS* 41 (1995), 601–19.
—'The Visionaries of Laodicea', *JSNT* 43 (1991), 16–39.
Grant, R. M., *A Historical Introduction to the New Testament*
  (London, 1963).
Gruenwald, I., 'Knowledge and Vision: Towards a Clarification of
  Two "Gnostic" Concepts in the Light of their Alleged Origins',
  Israel Oriental Studies 3 (1973), 63–107.
—'Jewish Sources for the Gnostic Texts from Nag Hammadi',

Proceedings of the Sixth World Congress of Jewish Studies (Jerusalem, 1977), iii. 45–56.

—'The Problem of the Anti-Gnostic Polemic in Rabbinic Literature', in van den Broek and Vermaseren (eds), *Studies in Gnosticism and Hellenistic Religions*, 171–89.

Gunther, J. J., *St Paul's Opponents and their Background* (Leiden, 1973).

Guthrie, D., 'Acts and Epistles in Apocryphal Writings', in Gasque and Martin (eds), *Apostolic History and the Gospel*, 328–45.

—'The Development of the Idea of Canonical Pseudepigrapha in New Testament Criticism', in Martin (ed.), *Vox Evangelica*, 43–59.

—*New Testament Introduction: The Pauline Epistles* (London, 1961).

Hagner, D. A., and Harris, M. J. (eds), *Pauline Studies*, FS Bruce (Exeter, 1980).

Harrill, J. A., 'The Vice of Slave Dealers in Greco-Roman Society: The Use of a Topos in 1 Timothy 1:10', *JBL* 118 (1999), 97–122.

Hartman, L., 'Humble and Confident: On the So-called Philosophers in Colossae', in *Mighty Minorities?*, FS J. Jervell = *Studia Theologica* 49 (1995), 25–39.

—'On Reading Others' Letters', *HTR* 79 (1986), 137–46.

Hedrick, C. W. (ed.), *Nag Hammadi Codices XI, XII, XIII* (Leiden, 1990).

Hedrick, C. W., and Hodgson, R. (eds), *Nag Hammadi, Gnosticism and Early Christianity* (Peabody, Mass., 1986).

Hegermann, H., *Die Vorstellung vom Schöpfungsmittler im hellenistischen Judentum und Urchristentum*, TU 82 (Berlin, 1961).

Hengel, M., 'Aufgaben der neutestamentlichen Wissenschaft', *NTS* 40 (1994) 321–57.

—'Erwägungen zum Sprachgebrauch von Χριστός bei Paulus und in der "vorpaulinischen" Überlieferung', in Hooker and Wilson (eds), *Paul and Paulinism*, 135–59.

—*Judaism and Hellenism*, 2 vols (ET London, 1974).

Henshaw, T., *New Testament Literature* (London, 1963).

Hill, D., *Greek Words and Hebrew Meanings* (Cambridge, 1967).

Hollenbach, B., 'Col. II.23: Which Things Lead to the Fulfilment of the Flesh', *NTS* 25 (1979), 254–61.

Hooker, M. D., 'Were There False Teachers in Colossae?', in Lindars and Smalley (eds), *Christ and Spirit in the New Testament*, 315–31.

Hooker, M. D., and Wilson, S. G. (eds), *Paul and Paulinism*, FS C. K. Barrett (London, 1982).

Hoppe, R., *Der Triumph des Kreuzes: Studien zum Verhältnis des Kolosserbriefes zur paulinischen Kreuzestheologie*, Stuttgarter Biblische Beiträge 28 (Stuttgart, 1994).

Hunter, A. M., *Interpreting Paul's Gospel* (London, 1954).

—*Paul and his Predecessors*, 2nd edn (London, 1961).

Huppenbauer, H. W., *Der Mensch zwischen zwei Welten* (Zurich, 1959).

Hurst, L. D., *The Epistle to the Hebrews: Its Background of Thought* (Cambridge, 1990).

Hurtado, L. W., *One God, One Lord* (London, 1988).

Hyatt, J. P. (ed.), *The Bible in Modern Scholarship* (Nashville, 1965).

Jeremias, J., 'Chiasmus in den Paulusbriefen', ZNW 49 (1958) 145–56 = ABBA (Göttingen, 1966), 276–90.

Jervell, J., *Imago Dei. Gen 1.26f. im Spätjudentum, in der Gnosis, und in den paulinischen Briefen*, FRLANT NF 58 (Göttingen, 1960).

Jervell, J., and Meeks, W. A. (eds), *God's Christ and His People*, FS Dahl (Oslo, 1977).

Jonas, H., *Gnosis und spätantiker Geist*, 2nd edn (Göttingen, 1954).

—*The Gnostic Religion* (Boston, 1958).

—'Response to G. Quispel's "Gnosticism and the New Testament"', in Hyatt (ed.), *The Bible in Modern Scholarship*, 279–93.

Jülicher, A., and Fascher, E., *Einleitung in das Neue Testament*, 7th edn (Tübingen, 1931).

Kennedy, H. A. A., *St Paul and the Mystery Religions* (London, 1913).

—*The Theology of the Epistles* (London, 1919; repr. 1934).

Kiley, M., *Colossians as Pseudepigraphy*, (Sheffield, 1986).

Kirk, K. E., *The Vision of God* (London, 1931).

Kirkland, A., 'The Beginnings of Christianity in the Lycus Valley', *Neotestamentica* 29 (1995), 109–24.

Knox, J., *Philemon among the Letters of Paul: A New View of its Place and Importance*, 2nd edn (New York and Nashville, 1959).

Knox, W. L., *St Paul and the Church of the Gentiles* (Cambridge, 1939).

— *St Paul and the Church of Jerusalem* (Cambridge, 1925).

Koch, D. A., 'Kollektenbericht, "Wir"-Bericht und Itinerar: Neue (?) Überlegungen zu einem alten Problem', *NTS* 45 (1999), 367–90.

Koester, H., *Ancient Christian Gospels* (London, 1990).

—*Einführung in das Neue Testament* (Berlin, 1980; ET *History and Literature of Early Christianity,* 2 vols (Philadelphia, 1982); references are to this translation).

Koester, H., and Robinson, J. M., *Trajectories through Early Christianity* (Philadelphia, 1971).

Kramer, W., *Christos, Kyrios, Gottessohn* (Zurich and Stuttgart, 1963).

Krause, M. (ed.), *Essays on the Nag Hammadi Texts*, FS Böhlig, NHS 3 (Leiden, 1972).

Kremer, J., *Was an den Leiden Christi noch mangelt*, BBB 12 (Bonn, 1956).

Kümmel, W. G., *Introduction to the New Testament* (London, 1966; ET of P. Feine, J. Behm and W. G. Kümmel, *Einleitung in das Neue Testament* (Heidelberg, 1965; rev edn from 17th German edn (1973), 1975).

Lähnemann, J., *Der Kolosserbrief: Komposition, Situation und Argumentation* (Gütersloh, 1971).

Lampe, P., 'Keine "Sklavenflucht" des Onesimus', *ZNW* 76 (1985), 135–37.

Larsson, E., *Christus als Vorbild*, Acta Seminarii Neotestamentici Upsaliensis xxiii (Uppsala, 1962).

Leaney, A. R. C., 'Conformed to the Image of his Son (Rom. VIII.29)', *NTS* 10 (1963/64), 470–79.

Levinson, J. R., '2 Apoc.Bar. 48:42–52.7 and the Apocalyptic Dimension of Colossians 3:1–6', *JBL* 108 (1989), 93–108.

Lilla, S. R. C., *Clement of Alexandria: A Study in Christian Platonism and Gnosticism* (Oxford, 1971).

Lincoln, A. T., *Paradise Now and Not Yet*, SNTSMS 43 (Cambridge, 1981).

Lincoln, A. T., and Wedderburn, A. J. M., *The Theology of the Later Pauline Letters* (Cambridge, 1993).

Lindars, B., and Smalley, S. S. (eds), *Christ and Spirit in the New Testament*, FS Moule (Cambridge, 1973).

Lindemann, A., 'Die Gemeinde von "Kolossä" ', *Wort und Dienst* 16 (1981), 111–34.

—*Paulus im ältesten Christentum*, BHTh 58 (Tübingen, 1979).

Loader, W. R. G., 'Christ at the Right Hand—Ps. cx.1 in the New Testament', *NTS* 24 (1978), 199–217.

Logan, A. H. B., *Gnostic Truth and Christian Heresy* (Edinburgh, 1996).

Logan, A. H. B., and Wedderburn, A. J. M. (eds), *The New Testament and Gnosis*, FS Wilson (Edinburgh, 1983).

Lohse, E., 'Christologie und Ethik im Kolosserbrief', in Eltester and Kettler (eds), *Apophoreta*, 156–68.

—'Christusherrschaft und Kirche im Kolosserbrief', *NTS* 11 (1964/65), 203–16.

—*The Formation of the New Testament* (ET Nashville, 1981).

—'Pauline Theology in the Letter to the Colossians', *NTS* 15 (1968/69), 211–20.

Lowe, M. F., 'The Critical and the Skeptical Methods in New Testament Research', *Gregorianum* 81 (2000), 693–721.

Lührmann, D., 'Neutestamentliche Haustafeln und antike Ökonomie', *NTS* 27 (1981), 83–97.

Luttenberger, J., 'Der gekreuzigte Schuldschein: Ein Aspekt der Deutung des Todes Jesu im Kolosserbrief', *NTS* 51 (2005), 80–95.

Lyonnet, S., 'L'Epître aux Colossiens (Col 2,18) et les mystères d'Apollon Clarien', *Biblica* 43 (1962), 417–35.

—'L'étude du milieu littéraire et l'exégèse du Nouveau Testament: 4. Les adversaires de Paul à Colosses', *Biblica* 37 (1956), 27–38; ET in Francis and Meeks (eds), *Conflict at Colossae*, 147–61.

—'St Paul et le gnosticisme: la lettre aux Colossiens', in Bianchi (ed.), *Le Origini dello Gnosticismo*, 538–51.

MacDonald, M. Y., *The Pauline Churches*, SNTSMS 60 (Cambridge, 1988).

Macgregor, G. H. C., 'Principalities and Powers: The Cosmic Background of St Paul's Thought', *NTS* 1 (1954/55), 17–28.

MacRae, G. W., 'The Jewish Background of the Gnostic Sophia

Myth', *NovTest* xii, 2, *Essays on the Coptic Gnostic Library* (Leiden, 1970), 86–101.

Maier, J., 'Jüdische Faktoren bei der Entstehung der Gnosis?', in Tröger (ed.), *Alte Testament-Frühjudentum-Gnosis*, 239–58.

Manson, T. W., *The Teaching of Jesus*, 2nd edn (Cambridge, 1939).

Martin R. P. (ed.), *Vox Evangelica* (London, 1962).

Martin, T., 'But Let Everyone Discern the Body of Christ (Col 2:17)', *JBL* 114 (1995), 249–55.

—*By Philosophy and Empty Deceit*, JSNTSS 118 (Sheffield, 1996).

—'Pagan and Judeo-Christian Time-Keeping Schemes in Gal. 4.10 and Col. 2.16', *NTS* 42 (1996), 105–19.

—'The Scythian Perspective in Col 3:11', *NovTest* 37 (1995), 249–61.

Marxsen, W., *Introduction to the New Testament*, (ET Oxford, 1968).

Meade, D. G., *Pseudonymity and Canon: An Investigation into the Relationship of Authorship and Authority in Jewish and Earliest Christian Tradition*, WUNT 39 (Tübingen, 1986; American edn Grand Rapids, 1987).

Meeks, W. A., 'In One Body: The Unity of Humankind in Colossians and Ephesians', in Jervell and Meeks (eds), *God's Christ and his People*, 209–21.

Metzger, B. M., *The Canon of the New Testament* (Oxford, 1987).

—*Index to Periodical Literature on the Apostle Paul* (Leiden, 1970; see also Mills, *An Index to Periodical Literature on the Apostle Paul*).

—'Literary Forgeries and Canonical Pseudepigrapha', *JBL* 91 (1972), 3–24.

—'Methodology in the Study of the Mystery Religions and Christianity', *HTR* 48 (1955), 1–20; repr. in B. M. Metzger, *Historical and Literary Studies* (Leiden, 1968), pp. 1–24.

—'The Punctuation of Rom. 9.5', in Lindars and Smalley (eds), *Christ and Spirit in the New Testament*, 95–112.

—*The Text of the New Testament* (Oxford, 1968).

—*A Textual Commentary on the Greek New Testament* (London and New York, 1971).

Metzger B. M., and Coogan, M. D. (eds), *The Oxford Companion to the Bible* (Oxford, 1993).

Michaelis, W., *Die Gefangenschaft des Paulus in Ephesus* (Gütersloh, 1925).

Mills, W. E., *An Index to Periodical Literature on the Apostle Paul* (Leiden, 1993; see also Metzger, *An Index to Periodical Literature on the Apostle Paul*).

Moffatt, J., *Introduction to the Literature of the New Testament*, 3rd edn (Edinburgh, 1918).

Moritz, T., *A Profound Mystery: The Use of the Old Testament in Ephesians* (Leiden, 1996).

Moule, C. F. D., *An Idiom Book of New Testament Greek* (Cambridge, 1953).

—*The Origin of Christology* (Cambridge, 1977).

—'St Paul and Dualism: The Pauline Conception of the Resurrection', *NTS* 12 (1965/66), 106–23.

Moule, H. C. G., *Colossian Studies* (London, 1902).

Müller, P., *Anfänge der Paulusschule: Dargestellt am zweiter Thessalonicherbrief und am Kolosserbrief*, AThANT 74 (Zurich, 1988).

Mullins, T. Y., 'The Thanksgivings of Philemon and Colossians', *NTS* 30 (1984), 288–93.

Münderlein, G., 'Die Erwählung durch das Pleroma: Bemerkungen zu Kol. i.19', *NTS* 8 (1961/62), 264–76.

Munro, W., 'Col. III.18-IV.1 and Eph. V.21-VI.9: Evidence of a Late Literary Stratum?', *NTS* 18 (1971/72), 434–47.

Munro, W., *Authority in Paul and Peter. The Identification of a Pastoral Stratum in the Pauline Corpus and 1 Peter*, SNTSMS 45 (Cambridge, 1983).

Murphy-O'Connor, J., 'The Essenes and their History', *RB* 81 (1974), 215–44.

—'Qumran and the New Testament', in Epp and MacRae (eds), *The New Testament and its Modern Interpreters*, 55–71 (Pauline literature, 60–61).

—'Truth: Paul and Qumran', in Murphy-O'Connor and Charlesworth (eds), *Paul and the Dead Sea Scrolls*, 179–230.

Murphy-O'Connor, J., and Charlesworth, J. H. (eds), *Paul and the Dead Sea Scrolls* (New York, 1990).

Neugebauer, F., 'Das Paulinische "In Christo"', *NTS* 4 (1957/58), 124–38.

—*In Christus—EN XPIΣTΩI: Eine Untersuchung zum paulinischen Glaubensverständnis* (Göttingen and Berlin, 1961).

Nineham, D. E. (ed.), *Studies in the Gospels* (Oxford, 1955).

Nock, A. D., *Essays on Religion and the Ancient World*, ed. Z. Stewart, 2 vols (Oxford, 1972).

Norden, E., *Agnostos Theos* (Leipzig, 1913; 4th edn Stuttgart, 1956).

O'Brien, P. T., *Introductory Thanksgivings in the Letters of Paul* (Leiden, 1977).

—'Thanksgiving and the Gospel in Paul', *NTS* 21 (1975), 144–55.

—'Thanksgiving within the Structure of Pauline Theology', in Hagner and Harris (eds), *Pauline Studies*, 50–66.

Ollrog, W. H., *Paulus und seine Mitarbeiter* (Neukirchen, 1979).

O'Neill, J. C., 'The Source of the Christology in Colossians', *NTS* 26 (1980), 87–100.

Pearson, B. A., *The Emergence of the Christian Religion* (Harrisburg, Pa., 1997).

—'Friedländer Revisited', *Studia Philonica* 2 (1973), 23–29 (revd version in Pearson, *Gnosticism, Judaism and Egyptian Christianity*, 10–28).

—*Gnosticism, Judaism and Egyptian Christianity* (Minneapolis, 1990).

—'Philo and Gnosticism', in *ANRW* II.21.1 (Berlin and New York, 1984), 295–342.

—'Philo, Gnosis and the New Testament', in Logan and Wedderburn (eds), *The New Testament and Gnosis*, 73–89 (updated in Pearson, *Gnosticism, Judaism and Egyptian Christianity*, 165–82).

—'The Problem of "Jewish Gnostic" Literature', in Hedrick and Hodgson (eds), *Nag Hammadi, Gnosticism and Early Christianity*, 15–35 (revd version in Pearson, *The Emergence of the Christian Religion*, 122–46).

Percy, E., *Die Probleme der Kolosser- und Epheserbriefe* (Lund, 1946).

—'Zu den Problemen des Kolosser- und Epheserbriefes', *ZNW* 43 (1950/51), 178–94.

Petersen, N. R., *Rediscovering Paul* (Philadelphia, 1985).

Pétrement, S., *Le Dieu séparé* (Paris, 1984; ET *A Separate God: The Christian Origins of Gnosticism* (San Francisco, 1990)).

Plisch, U.-K., 'Die Apostolin Junia: Das exegetische Problem in Rom 16.7 im Licht von Nestle-Aland[27] und der sahidischen Überlieferung', *NTS* 42 (1996), 477–78.

Pokorný, P., *The Genesis of Christology* (Edinburgh, 1987).

—'Pseudepigraphie I', *TRE* 27 (1997), 645–55.

Pollard, T. E., 'Colossians 1.12–20: A Reconsideration', *NTS* 27 (1981), 572–75.

Porter, S. E., and Evans, C. A. (eds), *New Testament Text and Language* (Sheffield, 1997).

Quispel, G., *Gnosis als Weltreligion* (Zurich, 1951).

—*Gnostic Studies*, 2 vols (Istanbul, 1974–75).

—'Gnosticism and the New Testament', in Hyatt (ed.), *The Bible in Modern Scholarship*, 252–71.

Rapske, B. M., 'The Prisoner Paul in the Eyes of Onesimus', *NTS* 37 (1991), 187–203.

Reicke, B., 'Caesarea, Rome and the Captivity Epistles', in Gasque and Martin (eds), *Apostolic History and the Gospel*, 277–86.

—'Traces of Gnosticism in the Dead Sea Scrolls?', *NTS* 1 (1954/55), 137–41.

Reinach, T., *Textes d'auteurs grecs et romains relatifs au Judaïsme* (Paris, 1895).

Reumann, J., 'OIKONOMIA-Terms in Paul in Comparison with Lucan *Heilsgeschichte*', *NTS* 13 (1966/67), 147–67.

Richards, E. R., *The Secretary in the Letters of Paul*, WUNT 2/42 (Tübingen, 1991).

Richardson, A., *Introduction to New Testament Theology* (London, 1958).

Riesenfeld, H., 'Faith and Love promoting Hope: An Interpretation of Philemon v.6', in Hooker and Wilson (eds), *Paul and Paulinism*, 251–57.

Robinson, J. A., *St Paul's Epistle to the Ephesians* (London, 1909).

Robinson, J. M., 'Die Hodajot-Formel in Gebet und Hymnus des Frühchristentums', in Eltester and Kettler (eds), *Apophoreta*, 194–235.

—'The Nag Hammadi Library and the Study of the New Testament', in Logan and Wedderburn (eds), *The New Testament and Gnosis*, 1–18.

Robinson, J. M. (genl ed.), *The Nag Hammadi Library in English*, 3rd edn (San Francisco, 1988).

Roller, O., *Das Formular der paulinischen Briefe* (Stuttgart, 1933).

Rowland, C., 'Apocalyptic Visions and the Exaltation of Christ in the Letter to the Colossians', *JSNT* 19 (1983), 73–83.

Rudolph, K., *Gnosis* (ET Edinburgh, 1983; 3rd revd German edn Göttingen, 1990).

—'"Gnosis" and "Gnosticism"—the Problems of their Definition and their Relation to the Writings of the New Testament', in Logan and Wedderburn (eds), *The New Testament and Gnosis*, 21–37.

—'Sophia und Gnosis: Bemerkungen zum Problem "Gnosis und Frühjudentum"', in Tröger (ed.), *Altes Testament–Frühjudentum–Gnosis*, 221–37.

Rusam, D., 'Neue Belege zu den στοιχεῖα τοῦ κόσμου (Gal 4,3.9; Kol 2,8.20)', *ZNW* 83 (1992), 119–25.

Sanders, E. P., 'Literary Dependence in Colossians', *JBL* 85 (1966), 28–45.

Sanders, J. T., 'Nag Hammadi, Odes of Solomon and NT Christological Hymns', in Goehring *et al.* (eds), *Gnosticism and the Early Christian World*, 51–66.

—*The New Testament Christological Hymns,* SNTSMS 15 (Cambridge, 1971).

Sappington, T. J., *Revelation and Redemption at Colossae* (Sheffield, 1991).

Saunders, E. W., 'The Colossian Heresy and Qumran Theology', in Daniels and Suggs (eds), *Studies in the History and Text of the New Testament*, 133–45.

Schenk, W., 'Der Brief des Paulus an Philemon in der neueren Forschung (1945–1987)', *ANRW* II.25.4, 3439–95.

—'Der Kolosserbrief in der neueren Forschung (1945–1985)', *ANRW* II.25.4, 3327–64.

Schenke, G., *Die Dreigestaltige Protennoia*, TU 132 (Berlin, 1984).

Schenke, H. M., 'Nag Hammadi', *TRE* 23 (1994), 731–36.

—'Die neutestamentliche Christologie und der gnostische Erlöser', in Tröger (ed.), *Gnosis und Neues Testament*, 205–29.

—'Die Tendenz der Weisheit zur Gnosis', in Aland (ed.), *Gnosis*, 351–72.

—'Das Weiterwirken des Paulus und die Pflege seines Erbes durch die Paulus-Schule', *NTS* 21 (1975), 505–18.

—'Der Widerstreit gnostischer und kirchlicher Christologie im Spiegel des Kolosserbriefes', *ZTK* 61 (1964), 391–403.

Schenke, H. M., and Fischer, K. M., *Einleitung in die Schriften des Neuen Testaments. I. Die Briefe des Paulus. Schriften des Paulinismus* (Berlin, 1978).

Schmithals, W., *Die Briefe des Paulus in ihrer ursprünglichen Form* (Zurich, 1984).

—'The Corpus Paulinum and Gnosis', in Logan and Wedderburn (eds), *The New Testament and Gnosis*, 107–24.

—*Neues Testament und Gnosis* (Darmstadt, 1984).

—*Paul and the Gnostics* (ET Nashville, 1972).

Schnackenburg, R., 'Apostles Before and During Paul's Time', in Gasque and Martin (eds), *Apostolic History and the Gospel*, 287–303.

Schneemelcher, W., *New Testament Apocrypha*, 2 vols (ET Cambridge 1991, 1993).

Schnelle, U., 'Transformation und Partizipation als Grundgedanken paulinischer Theologie', *NTS* 47 (2001), 58–75.

Schoeps, H. J., *Urgemeinde, Judenchristentum, Gnosis* (Tübingen, 1956).

Scholer, D. M., *Nag Hammadi Bibliography 1948–1969*, NHS 1 (Leiden, 1971).

—*Nag Hammadi Bibliography 1970–1994*, NHMS 32 (Leiden, 1997).

Schrage, W., 'Zur Ethik der neutestamentlichen Haustafeln', *NTS* 21 (1975), 1–22.

Schrage, W. (ed.), *Studien zum Text und zur Ethik des Neuen Testaments*, FS Greeven, BZNW 47 (Berlin, 1986).

Schubert, P., *Form and Function of the Pauline Thanksgivings*, BZNW 20 (Berlin, 1939).

Schürer, E., *History of the Jewish People in the Age of Jesus Christ*, English edn revd G. Vermes and F. Millar (Edinburgh, 1973–86).

Schwanz, P., *Imago Dei als christologisch-anthropologisches Problem in der Geschichte der Alten Kirche von Paulus bis Clemens von Alexandrien* (Halle, 1970).

Schweizer, E., 'Christus und Geist im Kolosserbrief', in Lindars and Smalley (eds), *Christ and Spirit in the New Testament*, 297–313.

—'Slaves of the Elements and Worshippers of Angels: Gal 4:3, 9 and Col 2:8, 18, 20', *JBL* 107 (1988), 455–68.

Scroggs, R., *The Last Adam: A Study in Pauline Anthropology* (Oxford, 1966).

Segal, A. F., 'Hellenistic Magic: Some Questions of Definition', in van den Broek and Vermaseren (eds), *Studies in Gnosticism and Hellenistic Religions*, 349–75.

—'Paul's Thinking about Resurrection in its Jewish Context', *NTS* 44 (1998), 400–19.

Siegert, F., *Nag Hammadi Register*, WUNT 26 (Tübingen, 1982).

Simon, M., *Le christianisme antique et son contexte religieuse*, WUNT 23, 2 vols (Tübingen, 1981).

—'Eléments gnostiques chez Philon', in Bianchi (ed.), *Le Origini dello Gnosticismo* (Leiden, 1967), 359–74 (repr. in Simon, *Le christianisme antique*, 336–53).

Standhartinger, A., 'Colossians and the Pauline School', *NTS* 50 (2004), 572–93.

—*Studien zur Entstehungsgeschichte und Intention des Kolosserbriefs* NovTest Supp 94 (Leiden, 1999).

—'Weisheit in *Joseph und Aseneth* und den paulinischen Briefen', *NTS* 47 (2001), 482–501.
Stanley, C. D., ' "Neither Jew nor Greek": Ethnic Conflict in Graeco-Roman Society', *JSNT* 64 (1996), 101–24.
Stead, G. C., 'The Valentinian Myth of Sophia', *JTS* 20 (1969), 78–104.
Stettler, C., *Der Kolosserhymnus: Untersuchungen zu Form, traditionsgeschichtlichem Hintergrund und Aussage von Kol 1,15–20*, WUNT 131 (Tübingen, 2000).
Still, T.D., 'Eschatology in Colossians: How Realized is it?', *NTS* 50 (2004), 125–38.
Suhl, A., *Paulus und seine Briefe* (Gütersloh, 1975).
Sumney, J. L., *Identifying Paul's Opponents: The Question of Method in 2 Corinthians*, JSNTSS 40 (Sheffield, 1990).
—'Those Who "Pass Judgment": The Identity of the Opponents in Colossians', *Biblica* 74 (1993), 366–88.
Testa, E., 'Gesù pacificatore universale: Inno liturgico della chiesa madre (Col. 1,15–20 + Ef. 2,14–16)', *Studii Biblici Franciscani Liber Annuus* 19 (1969), 5–64.
Thomassen, E. and Painchaud, L., *Le Traité Tripartite*, BCNH 19 (Quebec, 1989).
Thornton, T. C. G., 'Jewish New Moon Festivals, Galatians 4.3-11 and Colossians 2.16', *JTS* 40 (1989), 97–100.
Thrall, M. E., *The Second Epistle to the Corinthians*, ICC, 2 vols (Edinburgh, 1994, 2000).
Thurén, L., 'Hey Jude! Asking for the Original Situation and Message of a Catholic Epistle', *NTS* 43 (1997), 451–65.
Trebilco, P. R., *Jewish Communities in Asia Minor*, SNTSMS 69 (Cambridge, 1991).
Tröger, K. W., 'The Attitude of the Gnostic Religion towards Judaism', in Barc (ed.), *Colloque international sur les textes de Nag Hammadi*, 86–98.
—*Die Gnosis: Heilslehre und Ketzerglaube* (Freiburg, 2001).
—'Gnosis und Judentum', in Tröger (ed.), *Altes Testament–Frühjudentum–Gnosis*, 155–68.
Tröger, K. W. (ed.), *Altes Testament–Frühjudentum–Gnosis*, (Gütersloh, 1980).
—(ed.), *Gnosis und Neues Testament* (Berlin, 1973).
Turner, C. H., 'Greek Patristic Commentaries on the Pauline Epistles', *HDB* v (London, 1904), 484–531.
Uro, R. (ed.), *Thomas at the Crossroads* (Edinburgh, 1998).
Van Broekhoven, H., 'The Social Profiles in the Colossian Debate', *JSNT* 66 (1997), 73–90.
van den Broek, R., 'The Present State of Gnostic Studies', *VigChr* 37 (1983), 41–71.
van den Broek, R., and Vermaseren M. J. (eds), *Studies in Gnosticism and Hellenistic Religions*, FS Quispel (Leiden, 1981).
van der Horst, P. W., 'Observations on a Pauline Expression', *NTS* 19 (1972/73), 181–87.

van Kooten, G. H., *Cosmic Christology in Paul and the Pauline School*, WUNT II/171 (Tübingen, 2003).
van Unnik, W. C., 'Die jüdische Komponente in der Entstehung der Gnosis', *VigChr* 15 (1961), 65–82.
—'Gnosis und Judentum', in Aland (ed.), *Gnosis*, 65–86.
van Unnik, W. C., and van der Woude, A. S., *Studia Biblica et Semitica*, FS Vriezen (Wageningen, Netherlands, 1967).
Vielhauer, P., *Geschichte der urchristlichen Literatur* (Berlin, 1975).
Waldstein, M., and Wisse, F. (eds), *The Apocryphon of John*, synopsis of Codices II 1, III 1 and IV 1 with BG 8502, 2 (Leiden, 1995).
Wedderburn, A. J. M., *Baptism and Resurrection* (Tübingen, 1987).
—'Some Observations on Paul's Use of the Phrases "In Christ" and "With Christ" ', *JSNT* 25 (1985), 83–97 (repr. in Porter and Evans (eds), *New Testament Text and Language,* 145–59).
—'The Theology of Colossians', in Lincoln and Wedderburn, *The Theology of the Later Pauline Letters,* 3–71.
Weidinger, K., *Die Haustafeln: Ein Stück urchristlicher Paränese* (Leipzig, 1928).
Weiss, H. F., 'Gnostische Motive und antignostische Polemik im Kolosser- und im Epheserbrief', in Tröger (ed.), *Gnosis und Neues Testament*, 311–24.
Wendland, P., *Die hellenistisch-römische Kultur: Die urchristlichen Literaturformen*, HNT 1.2, 3 (Tübingen, 1912).
Wickert, U., 'Kleinasien', *TRE* 19 (1990), 244–65.
—'Der Philemonbrief—Privatbrief oder Apostolisches Schreiben?', *ZNW* 52 (1961), 230–38.
Wiles, G. P., *Paul's Intercessory Prayers*, SNTSMS 24 (Cambridge, 1974).
Williams, A. L., 'The Cult of Angels at Colossae', *JTS* 10 (1909), 413–38.
Williams, F. (tr.), *The Panarion of Epiphanius of Salamis*, Book I, NHS 35 (Leiden, 1987).
Wilson, R. McL., 'Anti-Semitism in Gnostic Writings', in Evans and Hagner (eds), *Anti-Semitism and Early Christianity*, 269–89.
—'Ethics and the Gnostics', in Schrage (ed.), *Studien zum Text und zur Ethik des Neuen Testaments*, 440–49.
—*Gnosis and the New Testament* (Oxford, 1968).
—'Gnosis/Gnostizismus II', *TRE* 13 (1985), 535–50.
—*The Gnostic Problem* (London, 1958).
—*The Gospel of Philip* (London, 1962).
—'Philo and Gnosticism', *Studia Philonica Annual* 5 (1993), 84–92.
—'Philo of Alexandria and Gnosticism', *Kairos* 14 (1972), 213–19.
Wilson, W. T., *The Hope of Glory: Education and Exhortation in the Epistle to the Colossians*, NovTest Supp 88 (Leiden, 1997).
Winter, S. C., 'Paul's Letter to Philemon', *NTS* 33 (1987), 1–15.
Wischmeyer, O., 'Agape in der außerchristlichen Antike', *ZNW* 69 (1978), 212–38.

Wisse, F., 'The Epistle of Jude in the History of Heresiology', in Krause (ed.), *Essays on the Nag Hammadi Texts*, 133–43.
—'Die Sextus-Sprüche und das Problem der gnostischen Ethik', in A. Böhlig and F. Wisse, *Zum Hellenismus in den Schriften von Nag Hammadi*, 55–86.
—'The Use of Early Christian Literature as Evidence for Inner Diversity and Conflict', in Hedrick and Hodgson (eds), *Nag Hammadi, Gnosticism and Early Christianity*, 177–90.
Wright, N. T., 'Poetry and Theology in Colossians 1.15-20', *NTS* 36 (1990), 444–68.
Yamauchi, E. M., 'Jewish Gnosticism? The Prologue of John, Mandaean Parallels and the Trimorphic Protennoia', in van den Broek and Vermaseren (eds), *Studies in Gnosticism and Hellenistic Religions*, 467–97.
—*Pre-Christian Gnosticism*, 2nd edn (Grand Rapids, 1983).
Yates, R., 'Colossians 2,14: Metaphor of Forgiveness', *Biblica* 71 (1990), 248–59.
—'Colossians 2.15: Christ Triumphant', *NTS* 37 (1991), 573–91.
—'Colossians and Gnosis', *JSNT* 27 (1986), 49–68.
—'From Christology to Soteriology', *ExpT* 107 (1996), 268–70.
—' "The Worship of Angels" (Col 2.18)', *ExpT* 97 (1985), 12–15.
Zandee, J., 'Die Person der Sophia in der vierten Schrift des Codex Jung', in Bianchi (ed.), *Le Origini dello Gnosticismo*, 203–14.
—*The Teachings of Sylvanus* (Leiden, 1991).

COLOSSIANS

INTRODUCTION

I. COLOSSAE

Colossae[1] was one of a group of three ancient cities in the Lycus valley in Asia Minor, about 100 miles inland from Ephesus. Of the other two, both mentioned at Col. 4.13, one was Hierapolis, later the seat of the bishop Papias, the extant remains of whose writings are included among the works called the Apostolic Fathers (cf. Eusebius, *HE* iii.36 and for Papias' writings *HE* iii.39). According to Eusebius (*HE* iii.31) Philip the Apostle and his two unmarried daughters were buried in Hierapolis, while a third daughter was buried in Ephesus.[2] Hierapolis is mentioned only this once in the New Testament, and its chief claim to fame is perhaps its connection with the Stoic philosopher Epictetus, who was born there (cf. *HDB* i. 379f.; *DAC* i. 565f.).

The second city was Laodicea, city of the 'lukewarm' church of Rev. 3.14–22 (cf. *HDB* iii. 44f.; *DAC* i. 683f.).[3] A letter to Laodicea is mentioned in 4.16, and the injunction there to exchange letters, together with the charge at 4.15 to 'give my greetings to the brothers and sisters in Laodicea' (NRSV), may perhaps point to closer contacts between Colossae and Laodicea than between either and Hierapolis;[4] moreover Laodicea is mentioned at 2.1, but there is no reference to Hierapolis. The Laodicean letter has not survived, although Marcion's canon included Ephesians under this title; the 'Epistle to the Laodiceans' contained in the New Testament

---

References by author's surname and page number alone are to that author's commentary cited in section I of the Bibliography, or to a work mentioned earlier in the context.

[1] On the spelling of the name, see Lightfoot, 16 and n. 4; Lohse 8 n. 23. 'Colossae' appears to be the older form, 'Colassae' a later spelling which has crept into some manuscripts and versions. The citation of P46 and A (in brackets) for the second form in NA27 is due to its appearance in the later subscription (see p. 741 there). Lightfoot after a long discussion puts ἐν Κολοσσαῖς in the text, and 'with more hesitation' πρὸς Κολοσσαεῖς in the superscription. For description of the area and of the three cities see Lightfoot, 1–72; Ramsay, *Cities and Bishoprics of Phrygia* and *The Church in the Roman Empire*; also the relevant articles in *HDB, DAC* and *EncBib*.

[2] Eusebius here quotes Polycrates, bishop of Ephesus *c.* AD 190, but later in the chapter confuses Philip the Apostle with Philip the Evangelist (cf. Acts 21.8f.). For discussion and further literature see Lightfoot, 45 n. 3; P. W. Schmiedel, *EncBib*, 3697–701; H. Cowan, *HDB* iii. 834b–37a; Schneemelcher, *NT Apocrypha*, ii 57–58; revd edn (1993), 23–24. For the association of Philip with Hierapolis in the later *Acts of Philip* see A. de Santos Otero in Schneemelcher, *NT Apocrypha*, ii, ET (1993), 469f.

[3] On this passage cf. C. R. Koester, *NTS* 49 (2003), 407–24.

[4] Lightfoot (69) notes that Laodicea was later the metropolis of the province of Phrygia Pacatiana, with Colossae among its suffragan bishoprics, while Hierapolis belonged to the neighbouring province of Phrygia Salutaris. On Laodicea cf. also Lindemann, 'Gemeinde', 129ff.

INTRODUCTION TO COLOSSIANS

apocrypha is no more than a pastiche made up of extracts from
genuine Pauline letters, especially Philippians.[5]
Colossae itself (cf. *HDB* i. 454; *DAC* i. 226f.; *ABD* i.
1089), the oldest of the three, was a city well known from early antiquity: it
stood on the main trade route between Ephesus and the Euphrates,
and was at one time a place of considerable importance. Herodotus
(vii.30.1) describes it as 'a great city in Phrygia', while Xenophon
(*Anab.* i.2.6) calls it 'prosperous and large'. By the time of Paul,
however, it appears to have declined in significance, probably
through the rise of Laodicea, which became the chief city of the
area, and Hierapolis. Strabo (xii.8.13) speaks of it as a town
(πόλισμα), while Pliny the Elder (*Hist. nat.* v (41) 145) calls it not
urbs but *oppidum*. Unlike the other two cities, the site of Colossae has
never been excavated (cf. Yamauchi, *New Testament Cities in
Western Asia Minor*, Grand Rapids, 1980).

According to Tacitus (*Ann.* xiv. 27), Laodicea was laid prostrate
by an earthquake in AD 60, but recovered entirely by her own
resources (*propriis opibus revaluit*; this provides a telling footnote to
Rev. 3.17). It is not known how far Colossae (some ten miles away)
was affected, but if it was less prosperous at the time it might have
taken longer to recover.[6] It does not seem to have been completely
destroyed, and therefore abandoned, since there are references later,[7]

---

[5] Cf. Schneemelcher, *NT Apocrypha*, ii. 128–32 (rev. ed. (1993) 42–46); J. K. Elliott,
The Apocryphal New Testament (1993), 543–46; Metzger, *The Canon of the New
Testament* 182f., 197, 239–40. The Greek version in the St Andrews ms mentioned by
Metzger (183 n. 51) is Elias Hutter's retroversion (cf. Metzger 239 n. 20) with some
orthographic errors. Moffatt (159) notes that this reference at 4.16 'has given rise to a
swarm of hypotheses', e.g. that this letter is (1) Ephesians (cf. Baur, *Paul*, 43f.;
Lightfoot 37; Deissmann, *Paul*, 24, 73; Goulder, *JSNT* 43 (1991), 16–39), (2) Hebrews,
or (3) a letter from Laodicea to Paul. For the 'maze of conflicting hypotheses' on this
question cf. Lightfoot 340–66, with discussion of the apocryphal letter, the Latin text
and his own Greek translation of it. Cf. also R. Burnet, *NTS* 48 (2002), 132–41. Moritz
(*A Profound Mystery*, 6) thinks it by no means impossible that Marcion's view is
correct.

[6] According to Orosius later (*Adv. Paganos* 7.7), *tres urbes, hoc est Laudicea,
Hierapolis, Colossae, terrae motu conciderunt*. Some (e.g. Pokorný, 19) think this the
same earthquake, but for Lohse (9; cf. Hübner, 14f.) it is not certain that this report
refers to the same event as that recorded by Tacitus, since Laodicea was subject to
earthquakes (cf. Lightfoot, 38 and n. 1); Standhartinger (*Studien*, 11 n. 30) cites T. R. S.
Broughton as listing five occurrences in the space of some two centuries ('Roman Asia
Minor', in T. Frank (ed.), *An Economic Survey of Ancient Rome*, IV (1959), 610); cf.
also *NTS* 50 (2004), 586 n. 59). Lightfoot notes that Eusebius (in terms very similar to
Orosius) places the earthquake after the burning of Rome, which would make the
terminus ante quem for the writing of the letter some years later. We must also allow for
the time it would take for the news to reach Rome.

[7] Pokorný (19), citing Schweizer (*Theologische Berichte* 5 (1976) 171), notes that it is
not attested on coins until the reign of Antoninus Pius (138–61), and concludes that in
the intervening period it 'remained an insignificant village among the ruins'. Cf.
Lindemann, 'Gemeinde', 127ff. Lightfoot, however, notes (44 n. 1) that in all the other
cases of earthquake in the Asiatic cities which Tacitus records, he mentions their
obtaining relief from the Senate or the emperor. Cf. also Wedderburn, *Baptism and
Resurrection*, 70 n. 6.

but in the seventh or eighth century it disappeared from history, being succeeded by Chonae, some three miles further south (Ramsay, *HDB* i. 454b: in 787 Bishop Dionysius took his title from Colossae, but had his home in Chonae; in 870 and 879 Samuel was bishop (later archbishop) of Chonae, and Colossae had become practically forgotten). There is no reference in the letter to this earthquake, which might have some bearing on the date: either the letter was written before the earthquake, or it was sufficiently later for the event to have been forgotten. It is, however, also possible that Colossae simply was not affected, although that is perhaps more doubtful if a city only ten miles away was seriously damaged.[8]

Phrygia was an area in which considerable numbers of Jews had been settled by Antiochus the Great (223–187 BC),[9] which might have relevance for the seemingly Jewish character of some of the 'false teachings' condemned in the letter; but Ramsay observes (*HDB* i. 454b) that there is no evidence for any large-scale settlement of Jews as colonists at Colossae itself, as was the case in some other cities, and 2.13 would seem to suggest that the congregation was predom-

---

[8] If Orosius (n. 6 above) is referring to the same earthquake, that would of course settle the question. Most scholars appear to assume that Colossae was destroyed. Calvin, taking it to have happened 'not long after this epistle was written', sees in the earthquake 'a remarkable mirror of divine judgement': the Colossians had been faithfully instructed in the Gospel, 'but immediately afterwards, Satan had crept in with his tares' (*Epistles of Paul*, 297).

[9] Josephus (*Ant.* xii.149) speaks of 2,000 Jewish families from Mesopotamia and Babylonia. According to Schürer (iii. 1, 17 n. 33) the authenticity of the letter giving instructions for this settlement has often been disputed, but there are no conclusive arguments against it (cf. also P. R. Trebilco, *Jewish Communities in Asia Minor* (1991), 5f.). Schürer notes at a later point (27f.) that the main centres appear to have been Laodicea and Apamea, citing the quantities of gold intended for the Temple which were confiscated in these cities on the orders of Flaccus (see Cicero, *Pro Flacc.* 28) and also a number of Jewish epitaphs found in Hierapolis. On the basis of the passage in Cicero, Lightfoot (20) calculates a population of more than eleven thousand adult freemen for the district of Laodicea, but Trebilco (14) notes, with reference to Apamea, that the amount mentioned need not necessarily have been the contribution for a single year. He does, however, think that there were large Jewish populations in these areas. It is natural to assume that some of these Jews lived in Colossae, as well as in Hierapolis or in Laodicea itself; but Colossae is not mentioned in Schürer's detailed survey of Jewish communities in Asia Minor (iii. 1.17–36), nor does it appear in Trebilco's index. Discussing the tensions between Jew and Greek in Asia Minor, C. D. Stanley (*JSNT* 64 (1996), 101–24) mentions Laodicea, but not Colossae. Barth (14) estimates that there were 'at least 500' tax-paying Jews in Colossae, but does not enter into details. Dunn thinks 'we may have to allow a total Jewish population of Colossae during this period of as many as two or three thousand' (22), which implies 'the presence of (probably) several synagogues' (29). For Moritz (*A Profound Mystery*, 5 n. 15), the lack of evidence of any Jewish presence in Colossae is vital for any attempted explanation of the relationship between Eph. and Col.: he suggests (220) that, having written Col., the same author decided to address other churches in Asia Minor, albeit with a stronger Jewish component.

inantly Gentile.[10] There is certainly a Jewish element in the 'false teaching', as will be seen below, but it appears that there was also an element of a more 'philosophical' nature, and some of the speculations seem to have survived for centuries later. Thus a canon of the Council of Laodicea (c. AD 363) runs: 'It is not right for Christians to abandon the Church of God and go away and invoke angels'.[11] About a century later, Theodoret, commenting on Col. 2.18, says, 'This disease remained long in Phrygia and Pisidia ... and even to the present time oratories [εὐκτήρια] of the holy Michael may be seen among them and their neighbours' (Strahan, DAC i. 227a). Ramsay also notes that in the ninth and tenth centuries 'Michael, the leader of the host of angels, was worshipped as the great saint of Colossae (and of its later representative Chonae)'.

II. THE CHURCH AT COLOSSAE

This was not an area in which Paul himself had worked (cf. 2.1),[12] and we have no detailed information about the foundation of the churches there. The natural inference from the references in Colossians is that it was due to Epaphras (cf. 1.7f.; 4.12f.), who was probably one of Paul's Ephesian converts. The reference to Laodicea and Hierapolis at 4.13 suggests that he had some responsibility for all three cities, and certainly the language Paul uses of him indicates a high regard and esteem: he is Paul's beloved σύνδουλος, a faithful servant of Christ, titles which elsewhere are accorded only to trusted fellow-workers like Tychicus (4.7; cf. Eph. 6.21) and Timothy (1 Thess. 3.2; but cf. Metzger, Text of the NT, 240–42).

There is, of course, the possible alternative that the gospel was carried to these cities by some unknown converts from Paul's mission in Ephesus, but it would seem clear that even in that case Epaphras had taken a prominent part in the life and work of the Christian community there, and there is much to be said for the view that he was responsible for the original evangelizing of the area. This would certainly seem to be the most plausible inference from the evidence available, and indeed several scholars take it more or less for granted.

---

[10] According to Kümmel (1975 edn, 337) there is no sign of a Jewish-Christian element in the church. The observance of feasts, new moon and sabbath (2.16) belongs to the demands of the false teachers (338). It is, however, open to question whether the metaphorical references to circumcision (2.11), and what appear to be allusions to the Mosaic law (2.8, 14), would have been readily intelligible to an entirely non-Jewish audience; but these may reflect the author's background, not that of his readers. At any rate, while the community was probably predominantly Gentile, it would seem unwise to deny the possibility that there was also a Jewish element.

[11] For the canons paralleled in Colossians see Lightfoot, 68f.

[12] W. J. Woodhouse in EncBib, col. 859 remarks that 'it would be unsafe to argue that he had not seen the town itself'; he could have passed through on his third missionary journey (Acts 18.23; 19.1), or visited it during his three years' stay in Ephesus (cf. Acts 19.10). However, Woodhouse concludes that 'the Colossian church was an indirect product of the apostle's activity in Ephesus'.

If the reading ὑπὲρ ἡμῶν is adopted at 1.7, this would imply that he acted on Paul's behalf, as his emissary or representative, but this reading is perhaps not absolutely certain (see Commentary *ad loc.*). From Philem. 23 we learn that he was a fellow prisoner of Paul, from Col. 1.8 that he had told the apostle of the congregation's love, while at 4.12 he sends greetings back to the congregation. On the basis of these statements Kümmel (337f.) infers that he had sought out Paul because of the situation in Colossae, and had willingly shared his imprisonment; when Paul wrote the letter, it was delivered by Tychicus (4.7f.), while Epaphras remained with Paul (4.12f.).

Some of these deductions about the role of Epaphras are, however, no more than inferences from Colossians itself, without other support, and presuppose the authenticity of the letter (on which see below) and also the accuracy of the conclusions which we draw from it. The opening verses of the letter to Philemon might perhaps suggest another possibility: after mention of Philemon himself, Apphia and Archippus, there is added καὶ τῇ κατ᾽ οἶκόν σου ἐκκλησίᾳ (Philem. 2). If the community met in the house of Philemon, that might be because he had been its founder; thus Koester (ii. 135) infers on this basis that 'we can assume that the Christian church in Colossae was founded by Philemon, whom Paul must have converted in Ephesus'. On the other hand, it might mean only that the house of Philemon was the largest or the most suitable for the meetings of the community. Lightfoot (31, 371) thinks of Philemon as converted by Paul at Ephesus, but assigns to him a secondary role in the building up of the community in this area and gives to Epaphras 'the chief glory of preaching the Gospel at Colossae'.

Kümmel incidentally speaks (337) of two house churches at Colossae, the other being that of Nympha (or Nymphas; see Commentary at Col. 4.15); but was the latter not in Laodicea?[13] There is, of course, no reason to believe that there was only one such house church in any community, and in the larger cities it might well have been convenient to have several at strategic points; but we have to remember that we are still dealing with a comparatively early stage in the Christian mission, and cannot simply assume large Christian communities in any given place. Goppelt for example remarks of the second and third generations that 'in Asia the network of churches according to the letters of Revelation i-ii and Ignatius is much more extensive and thicker than at the time of Colossians' (*Apostolic and Post-Apostolic Times*, 114). What matters here is that such problems show the difficulties we face in any historical reconstruction. Lightfoot for example harmonizes Colossians and Philemon, but how solid in fact is the evidence for the role of Epaphras?

With regard to the composition of the Colossian community, it has already been noted that 2.13, with its reference to 'the uncircumcision

---

[13] After listing the greetings of Paul's companions in vv. 10–14, the text continues in v. 15, ἀσπάσασθε τοὺς ἐν Λαοδικείᾳ ἀδελφοὺς καὶ Νύμφαν καὶ τὴν κατ᾽ οἶκον αὐτῆς ἐκκλησίαν (see Commentary *ad loc.*).

of your flesh', seems to suggest a predominantly Gentile membership. There is certainly a Jewish element in the false teaching, but it is not clear whether this was introduced by Jewish Christians or is the result of an imperfect grasp of the Old Testament and of Jewish teaching on the part of Gentiles. Another possible indication of a largely Gentile membership occurs in 1.27: 'to them [i.e. the "saints"] God chose to make known how great among the Gentiles are the riches of the glory of this mystery', and perhaps the strongest sign of all is in 1.21, which speaks of the Colossians as 'you who were once estranged and hostile in mind'. This of course recalls the similar passage in Eph. 2.11–12, but is not elaborated to the same extent: in Ephesians the reference to 'aliens from the commonwealth of Israel and strangers to the covenants of promise' suggests an almost exclusively Gentile membership. Moreover, since Ephesians is probably later than and even dependent on Colossians (see below), it could be dangerous to use it for the interpretation of Colossians. At all events, in view of the probable predominance of Gentiles in the local population and the general character of the false teaching, it is best to think of a largely Gentile Christian community; but the possibility that there were also members of Jewish descent should not be ruled out.

III.   THE LETTER TO THE COLOSSIANS

The problems discussed in this introduction are complicated by the fact that the various questions are interconnected, so that a decision regarding one may affect our judgement of another. Thus Colossians has sometimes been regarded as directed against the Gnostic heresy (or against the Ebionites), and consequently dated to the second century; it therefore could not be an authentic letter of Paul. Subsequent research, however, as will be seen below, has tended to place the origins of the 'Gnostic' movement much earlier, even into the New Testament period if not before, and this argument therefore falls, both in regard to the date and against the authenticity of the letter. The authenticity of Colossians has in fact been strongly maintained by quite a number of scholars.

Again, Colossians is one of a number of letters all ostensibly written by Paul in prison: is it the same captivity in every case, or are we to think of Paul writing from different places of imprisonment during his career? One of the problems here is to find a place for Colossians within the context of what we know of Paul's life and within the development of his theology. There are also questions regarding the relationship of Colossians to other letters, notably Philemon and Ephesians: at 4.10ff. Aristarchus, Mark, Epaphras, Luke and Demas send their greetings, and all five are listed in Philem. 23f. (on these five, see the introduction to Philemon, below); at 4.17 a message is addressed to Archippus, who is named in the address of Philem. 2; the letter to Philemon is a plea for Onesimus, who is named as ἐξ ὑμῶν at Col. 4.9. There are thus close links between Colossians and

Philemon,[14] although the relation of Colossians to Ephesians presents a somewhat more complex problem (see below). All the relevant questions are open to discussion, and the only course is to deal with each in turn and then try to draw the various threads together.

A   Authenticity

The authenticity of Colossians[15] has frequently been called in question, first by Mayerhoff in 1838, who found in the letter a dependence on Ephesians, un-Pauline ideas, and opposition to Cerinthus (Kümmel, 340). F. C. Baur rejected it as directed against the Ebionites and showing affinities with Gnosticism, and therefore belonging to the second century. It is, however, doubtful whether we can be so specific in identifying a particular opponent such as Cerinthus, and in any case further research into Gnosticism has rendered any such argument precarious (see below). In some instances indeed the Gnostics would seem to be quoting from Colossians itself.[16]

C. F. D. Moule (13) finds it 'impossible to doubt that Philemon was written by St Paul, or to doubt the close connexion between Philemon and Colossians' (cf. the points of similarity already noted above). On that basis Colossians too should be recognized as Pauline,[17] and we are left with the problem of trying to fit it into what we know of Paul's career. Nevertheless, that is not the only possibility, as will appear, and the authenticity of Col. continues to be the subject of debate: as Kümmel observes (340), 'Against the oft-repeated assumption of the Pauline origin of Colossians, especially

[14] Cf. Standhartinger, 81–85.
[15] The question is discussed in the commentaries and introductions, with a bewildering variety of opinion, which may be broadly classified into (1) defence of Pauline authorship; (2) rejection; (3) an attempt to preserve some connection with Paul, either by postulating an amanuensis or on the assumption of composition by a disciple during Paul's lifetime; and (4) the view that the letter was written by some later disciple after Paul's death. There is a brief survey of research in Lähnemann (12–27); for a review of recent studies, cf. R. F. Collins, *Letters that Paul Did Not Write* (1988), 175–78. Cf. also, among others, Jülicher, 126ff.; Kümmel (1975 edn), 340ff.; Vielhauer, 196–200; Schenke and Fischer, 165ff.; Koester, ii. 263f.; Barclay, 18–36. DeMaris (*The Colossian Controversy*, 11) sees a steady shift in the scholarly consensus over the past fifteen to twenty years, in favour of pseudonymity. Hübner (10) sees no need to refute the 'authenticity thesis' yet again, and concentrates on theological interpretation.
[16] E.g. Irenaeus *Adv. haer.* i.4.5; *Exc. ex Theod.* 43.3: cf. Col. 1.16; Irenaeus, *Adv. haer.* i.3,4; Hippolytus, *Refut.* viii.13.2. cf. Col. 2.9; Hippolytus *Refut.* viii.10,7: cf. Col. 2.14f. If these references may appear suspect in that the heresiologists could be placing their own allusions in the mouths of their opponents, van Unnik noted (*The Jung Codex*, ed. F. L. Cross (1955), 115) that the author of the *Gospel of Truth* made use of Colossians among other NT writings. Cf. also F. Siegert, *Nag-Hammadi Register* (1982), index pp. 342–43, for allusions to Colossians in some of the Nag Hammadi texts. For references in the early Fathers, cf. Aletti, 20f. (he refers to Gnilka, pp. ix–xii, 'pour une liste quasiment exhaustive').
[17] Peake already refers (491) to 'the close connexion of Colossians with Philemon, which, if genuine, all but guarantees the genuineness of Colossians'. Others, however, (e.g. Schenk, *ANRW* II.25.4, 3338ff.) would claim the similarities as evidence for the use of Philemon by the author of Colossians.

since the work of Dibelius, Lohmeyer and Percy, doubt has been
expressed again recently and in increasing measure' (referring to
Bultmann, Käsemann, Bornkamm and others). He himself, however,
finally concludes (244) that the letter 'is to be regarded as doubtless
Pauline'.[18]
On the other hand H. M. Schenke (in Schenke and Fischer, 165ff.)
is even more confident that it is not authentic. Lohse (180) observes
that 'the thought of Col certainly exhibits Pauline features', but adds
immediately that the differences between Colossians and the
theology of the major Pauline epistles must not be overlooked:
'Pauline theology has undergone a profound change in Col, which is
evident in every section of the letter and has produced new
formulations in Christology, ecclesiology, the concept of the apostle,
eschatology, and the understanding of baptism' (see his detailed
examination at 177–83; cf. also Hoppe, *Triumph*, 12–35). He
therefore concludes that Paul 'cannot be considered to be the direct
or indirect author of Col. Rather a theologian schooled in Pauline
thought composed the letter with the intention of bringing the
Apostle's word to bear on the situation that had arisen in the Asia
Minor communities'.
At this point something should perhaps be said about the question
of pseudepigraphy.[19] For some people the idea of someone writing a
book and putting it under the name of an apostle is quite intolerable,
the more especially where a book accepted into the canon is involved.
Such a practice is for them tantamount to fraud and forgery, and
they cannot bring themselves to believe either that any Christian
could have been guilty of so heinous a crime or that the Church

[18] According to Hübner (9), Kümmel later changed his mind.
[19] See Mark Kiley, *Colossians as Pseudepigraphy* (1986); Guthrie, *NT Introduction*,
282ff. and 'Development'; Kümmel 362f. (with reference to Ephesians); Collins,
Letters that Paul Did Not Write, esp. chs 2 and 7 (for Colossians see ch. 5); Pokorný
14ff.; cf. also Best, *Ephesians*, 10–13. Moffatt, *Introduction* (40ff.) already devotes some
pages to the topic, although with reference to the apocalyptic literature—in regard to
Colossians he concurs (155) with the view that 'neither the language nor the contents of
Col 1–2 render the Pauline authorship impossible'. On pseudo-apostolic letters see R.
Bauckham in *JBL* 107 (1988), 469–94 –'Those whose authenticity could be regarded as
vindicated by this study [Colossians, 1 Peter, Jude] are those which many scholars still
regard as having a reasonable claim to authenticity' (492); according to Goppelt
(*Apostolic and Post-Apostolic Times*, 103) 'the authenticity of Colossians has been
generally acknowledged' (cf. his n. 2), but the 'range of opinions' set out by Collins
(*Letters*, 175–78) presents a very different picture. On the whole question of
pseudepigraphy see also K. Aland, 'The Problem of Anonymity and Pseudonymity
in Christian Literature of the First Centuries', *JTS* n.s. 12 (1961), 39ff.; B. M. Metzger,
'Literary Forgeries and Canonical Pseudepigrapha', *JBL* 91 (1972), 3–24; N. Brox,
Falsche Verfasserangaben (1975); K. M. Fischer, 'Anmerkungen zur Pseudepigraphie
im Neuen Testament', *NTS* 23 (1977), 76–81; L. R. Donelson, *Pseudepigraphy and
Ethical Argument in the Pastoral Epistles* (1986); and particularly D. G. Meade,
Pseudonymity and Canon (1986), who, however, does not discuss Colossians: 'Although
some would want to include Colossians and 2 Thessalonians among the deutero-
Paulines, the arguments are so contested that it would not be methodologically sound
to assume, as we will do with Ephesians and the Pastorals, that their pseudonymity is a
foregone conclusion' (118). Cf. also the articles 'Pseudepigraphie' and 'Pseudonymität'
in *TRE* 27 (1997), 645–55, 659–70, and Standhartinger, *Studien*, 29–59.

would have countenanced anything of the sort. It is, however, open to question whether this is not to transplant a modern attitude, a modern way of thinking, back into the first century, where attitude and outlook in such matters may have been very different.

The fact of the matter is that, as the pages of Eusebius show, a very large number of writings was placed under the names of apostles or other worthies of a bygone age; indeed, pseudepigraphy was by no means uncommon in the ancient world. As H. J. Cadbury put it (*NTS* 5 (1958/59), 94), 'In the first Christian centuries neither moral nor literary standards condemned writing under an assumed name or impersonating a well-known character'. Tertullian tells us (*De Baptismo* 17) that the presbyter who wrote the *Acts of Paul* was removed from office when he confessed, although he said that he did it 'out of love for Paul', and many such works were stigmatized as 'apocryphal'.[20] Where a book was known to be pseudonymous, therefore, the Church in later times certainly did not countenance it; but Colossians has been part of the Corpus Paulinum as far back as we can reach.

We need, however, to consider the situation in which such works were written, their character, and the purpose for which they were written. It is one thing for a document to be attributed to an apostle in order to gain credence for some dubious or even heretical opinion, which would indeed be a fraudulent procedure; but that is not the only possibility. From a modern point of view, all pseudepigraphy could be bluntly classed as forgery, but the evidence from the ancient world makes it necessary to distinguish between dishonest forgery, undertaken for nefarious and malicious ends, and what might be described, paradoxical as it may appear, as honest forgery. Kiley (22f.) cites a passage from the sixth-century writer Olympiodorus, to the effect that Pythagoras did not leave any personal writings, 'saying that one should not leave behind lifeless writings, since they were not able to speak in their defence'; but he did leave 'spirited writings', writings with souls (or life) in them, i.e. disciples. 'His disciples then, having created writings through goodwill, inscribed [them with] the name of Pythagoras. And for this reason all of the writings handed down in the name of Pythagoras are spurious'.[21]

Sometimes a work might be given a pseudonymous ascription out of prudence: in an age of persecution, for example, to avoid

[20] For information about these works, and translations of the more important ones, see W. Schneemelcher, *New Testament Apocrypha*; M. R. James, *The Apocryphal New Testament* (1924, revd edn 1953); J. K. Elliott, *The Apocryphal New Testament* (1993). For bibliography see J. H. Charlesworth, *The New Testament Apocrypha and Pseudepigrapha* (1987).

[21] Collins (*Letters*, 76) notes that Porphyry counts 280 books among the 'authentic' works of Pythagoras, 'but only eighty of these are judged to have come from Pythagoras himself. The rest come from noble men who belong to Pythagoras' circle or his party, or who were heirs to his wisdom.' He adds that Tertullian is often cited as having remarked that 'it is allowable that that which disciples publish should be regarded as their master's work' (*Adv. Marcionem* iv.5; PL 2, 567).

attracting the attention of hostile authorities.[22] Or it may be that the author was honestly and sincerely trying to develop and carry further the teachings of his master, to apply his master's principles in somewhat different circumstances, in the face of some new danger. It is this last possibility that Lohse has in mind. Many years ago W. L. Knox thought of Colossians as written by Paul himself in response to a new situation (*PCG* 146ff.), but this entails problems with regard to location within what we know of Paul's career. Would it really make so much difference if the letter was written not by Paul himself but by a disciple who was trying to develop Paul's ideas to meet that new situation?[23]

The objections raised against the authenticity of the letter relate mainly (1) to language and style, and (2) to matters of content. In regard to vocabulary, there are 34 hapax legomena,[24] and in addition

[22] 'Pseudonymity was a frequent feature in early literature. There was nothing immoral about it; it was simply the equivalent of modern anonymity. It was a mark of humility; the author, being too diffident to write under his own name, took shelter under a better-known name. Incidentally this would help to facilitate the work's wider acceptance, and in times of persecution an added motive would be the precaution of security' (A. W. Argyle, *NTS* 20 (1974), 445).

[23] E. Cothenet (*NTS* 35 (1989), 418f.) writes that 2 Peter, with the Pastorals, is a model of the pseudepigraphic genre, so flourishing in Graeco-Roman and Jewish antiquity. The best example, he says, is provided by the custom, in the rhetorical schools, of making the students write ' "à la manière de", des grands auteurs s'entend!' In the philosophical schools, the disciple, out of respect, placed under his master's name the developments which he brought to the teaching he received. Applying this to the New Testament writings, Cothenet adds that in this period of transition between the apostolic age and the time when the monarchic episcopate became general in the churches, those disciples who felt themselves called to intervene in defence of the apostolic heritage and its application to the circumstances of the time could not do other than take shelter under the patronage of an apostle or an immediate disciple. More than eighty years ago P. Wendland already noted that in the refutation of heresy appeal was readily made to authoritative names (*Die hellenistisch-romische Kultur*, 365). Fischer ('Anmerkungen', 76) claims that in this period (between Paul and *1 Clement*) pseudepigraphy was the only literary form of expression for early Christianity. He draws the conclusion (79) that at this time there was no person or institution possessed of general authority within the Church: he who wished to speak to the world could not do so in his own person, but only under the name of those who possessed an authority rooted in the past. Only as 'Paul' or 'Peter' could one hope to find a hearing.

[24] ἀθυμεῖν (3.21), αἰσχρολογία (3.8), ἀνεψιός (4.10), ἀνταναπληροῦν (1.24), ἀνταπόδοσις (3.24), ἀπεκδύεσθαι (2.15; 3.9), ἀπέκδυσις (2.11), ἀπόχρησις (2.22), ἀρεσκεία (1.10), ἀφειδία (2.23), βραβεύειν (3.15), δογματίζεσθαι (2.20), ἐθελοθρησκεία (2.23), εἰρηνοποιεῖν (1.20), ἐμβατεύειν (2.18), εὐχάριστος (3.15), θεότης (2.9), καταβραβεύειν (2.18), μετακινεῖν (1.23), μομφή (3.13), νεομηνία (2.16), ὁρατός (1.16), παρηγορία (4.11), πιθανολογία (2.4), πλησμονή (2.23), προακούειν (1.5), προσηλοῦν (2.14), πρωτεύειν (1.18), Σκύθης (3.11), στερέωμα (2.5), συλαγωγεῖν (2.8), σωματικῶς (2.9), φιλοσοφία (2.8), χειρόγραφον (2.14). See Lohse's detailed discussion, 84ff. Peake, 488 considers this 'on the whole not an exceptional number'. Similarly Moffatt (154) writes that the vocabulary 'presents no features which necessarily involve a sub-Pauline author'. In his view 'the speculative advance constitutes a more serious difficulty', but some aspects are already implied in the accepted letters, and the advanced Christology 'does not ... represent a position which would have been necessarily impossible for Paul to occupy' (155). Vielhauer (196) notes that the non-Pauline vocabulary carries less weight when we consider that the author in his polemic uses the terminology of his opponents, and in addition cites liturgical material

fifteen words which appear elsewhere in the New Testament but not in Paul (so Kümmel 1966, 240, following Holtzmann; Lohse, 85f., taking Eph., 2 Thess. and the Pastorals as non-Pauline, lists twenty-eight[25]). Over against that, several of Paul's commonest concepts are missing, like δικαιοσύνη, δικαίωσις, νόμος, σωτηρία, ἀποκάλυψις (cf. Kiley 44f.).[26]

In regard to style, there is a heaping up of synonyms, e.g. 'praying and asking, in all spiritual wisdom and understanding' (1.9); 'holy and blameless and irreproachable' (1.12) and of genitive constructions, e.g. ὁ λόγος τῆς ἀληθείας τοῦ εὐαγγελίου (1.5); πᾶν πλοῦτος τῆς πληροφορίας τῆς συνέσεως (2.2); ἡ ἀπέκδυσις τοῦ σώματος τῆς σαρκός (2.11); ἡ πίστις τῆς ἐνεργείας τοῦ θεοῦ τοῦ ἐγείραντος αὐτὸν ἐκ νεκρῶν (2.12). 'The style is cumbersome, verbose, and surfeited to opacity with subordinate clauses, participial and infinitive constructions or substantives with ἐν' (Kümmel, 1966 edn, 241). 1.9–20 and 2.9–15 each form a single sentence—Schenke, 166 adds 1.3–8 and 1.21–23, and remarks, 'So wirkt die Sprache des Kol über weite Partien hin verschwommen'.

The facts are beyond dispute, but their interpretation is quite another matter. Peake (488–89) claims that the contents of ch. 2 would have made even a larger proportion of peculiar words not at all strange, and with regard to the style writes, 'these features may be partially paralleled in the earlier letters; and where they cannot be we may rightly lay stress on the difference in Paul's circumstances and the problems with which he had to deal'. Similarly Kümmel (1975

(1.12–20; 2.10–15); but a considerable number of the terms in question cannot be set aside in this fashion. Lohse (86) observes that 'hapax legomena and unusual expressions appear in considerable numbers in the other Pauline letters', and cites Zahn's collection of the material for Galatians (n. 146). Even so short a letter as Philemon has several, e.g. ἀποτίνω (19), ἄχρηστος (11), ἑκούσιος (14), ὀνίναμαι (20), προσοφείλειν (19).

[25]ἅλας (4.6), ἀπόκεισθαι (1.5), ἀποκρίνεσθαι (4.6), ἀπόκρυφος (2.3), ἀρτύειν (4.6), γεύεσθαι (2.21), δειγματίζειν (2.15), δυναμοῦν (1.11), ἔνταλμα (2.22), ἐξαλείφειν (2.14), ἑορτή (2.16), θιγγάνειν (2.21), θρησκεία (2.18), θρόνος (1.16), ἰατρός (4.14), κλῆρος (1.12), κρατεῖν (2.19), κρύπτειν (3.3), παραλογίζεσθαι (2.4), πικραίνειν (3.19), πλουσίως (3.16), πόνος (4.13), σκιά (2.17), σύνδουλος (1.7; 4.7), συνεστηκέναι (1.17; i.e. the intransitive use—Paul uses συνίστημι transitively), τελειότης (3.14), ὑπεναντίος (2.14) and the phrase τὰ ἄνω (3.1; Paul uses ἄνω without the article. In addition, ten words occur only in Colossians and Ephesians: ἀνθρωπάρεσκος (3.22), ἀποκαταλλάσσειν (1.20, 22), ἀπαλλοτριοῦσθαι (1.21), αὔξησις (2.19), ἀφή (2.19), ὀφθαλμοδουλία (3.22), ῥιζοῦσθαι (2.7), συνεγείρειν (2.12; 3.1), συνζωοποιεῖν (2.13), ὕμνος (3.16). It should be added that with some of these the usage differs between Eph. and Col. Over against these Lohse lists eleven words which appear only in Colossians and the other Pauline letters, not elsewhere in the NT: ἀπεῖναι (2.5), ἑδραῖος (1.23), εἰκῆ (2.18; v.l. in Matt. 5.22), ἐρεθίζειν (3.21), θριαμβεύειν (2.15), ἱκανοῦν (1.12), ἰσότης (4.1), πάθος (3.5), συναιχμάλωτος (4.10), συνθάπτεσθαι (2.12) and φυσιοῦσθαι (2.18); some of these occur in only one letter other than Colossians.

[26]Vielhauer (197) pertinently remarks that it is difficult to explain the absence of the *Rechtfertigungsterminologie* (terms relating to justification): it is particularly striking in a controversy with a teaching and practice which presumed so much on human achievements. Cf. Lohse 86ff.; in matters of style he notes a number of features which can be paralleled in the generally accepted letters, but these usages are not so common in the major letters as in Colossians.

edn, 341) says that 'the different mode of expression is in part
explicable by reason of the strong use of liturgical-hymnic style in
which thanksgiving and prayers are offered in the letters acknowledged as genuine, and in part by reason of the polemical aim of the
letter. The peculiarities of speech and mode of expression are most
evident in those sections ... in which Paul is polemicizing against the
false teaching, or when, with it in view, he sets forth his own ideas in
hymnic form (1:10-20; 2:16-23)'.[27] On the other hand, Colossians
does show 'clear stylistic peculiarities of Paul', which can be
paralleled only in the letters generally acknowledged as authentic:

pleonastic καί after διὰ τοῦτο (1:9) is found in the NT only in Paul
(1 Thess. 2:13; 3:5; Rom. 13:6; cf. also Rom. 9:24 [and Eph. 1:15
borrowing from Col. 1:9]); οἱ ἅγιοι αὐτοῦ in NT only in Col. 1:26;
1 Thess. 3:13; 2 Thess. 1:10; χαρίζεσθαι = forgive, 2:13; 3:13;
otherwise in NT only in 2 Cor. 2:7, 10; 12:13 (and Eph.
4:32 = Col. 3:13); ἐν μέρει, 2:16 = 'with regard to' in NT
otherwise only in 2 Cor. 3:10; 9:3; Col.1:10, πᾶν ἔργον ἀγαθόν,
is found only in Paul in 2 Cor. 9:8; 2 Thess. 2:17 (likewise the
singular ἔργον ἀγαθόν alone in Rom. 2:7; 13:3; Phil. 1:6); on the
other hand, the plural ἔργα ἀγαθά is found only in Eph. 2:10;
1 Tim. 2:10; Acts 9:36 in the NT (Kümmel, 1966 edn, 241; some
modifications in 1975 edn, 341f.; but cf. Schenk, ANRW II.25.4,
3342 n. 51)

Kümmel accordingly concludes that the language and style of
Colossians 'give no cause to doubt the Pauline origin of the Epistle'.[28]
Vielhauer on the other hand (197) thinks the language and style not
exactly favourable to Pauline authorship; for Koester (ii. 263) the
linguistic evidence is 'not fully decisive'. More recently Dunn (35)
speaks of 'the strong likelihood' that the letter comes from a hand
other than Paul's.[29] On Lohse's view we have to think of an author

[27] Pokorný, however, (3) notes that the stylistic differences do not occur only in the
polemic against the false teaching, so that we cannot explain them entirely as
associated with this theme. Sappington (Revelation, 23) notes against G. E. Cannon
(The Use of Traditional Materials in Colossians, (1983)) that 'the stylistic characteristics
uncovered by Bujard are present in "non-traditional" as well as allegedly "traditional"
passages'. For criticism of Kümmel (1965 German edn) cf. Lähnemann, 19–23.
O'Brien (Colossians, p. xlix) considers the differences insufficient to reject Pauline
authorship, and suggests that they are best interpreted as called forth by the
circumstances at Colossae. Aletti likewise, after reviewing the similarities and
differences between Colossians and the major letters (22–25), writes 'avant de déclarer
Col deutéro-paulinienne, il importe de considérer les raisons logiques, liées au projet de
l'épître et à ses necessités internes' (25).
[28] As mentioned above (n. 18), Kümmel later changed his mind.
[29] Later (38) Dunn suggests that the letter was written by Timothy and approved by
Paul, who added the final greeting in 4.18. The reference there to Paul's bonds, he
observes, 'has a particular poignancy': 'perhaps it was the fetters themselves which
made it difficult for Paul to add more than this brief scrawl' (289). This seems at
variance with Acts 28.30–31, where Paul is free to receive all who came to him, and to
preach μετὰ πάσης παρρησίας ἀκωλύτως—but allowance must be made for the
possible apologetic character of Acts.

'thoroughly acquainted with the principal themes of Pauline theology' and 'well versed in the epistles of Paul' (182). Here the apocryphal *Letter to the Laodiceans* already mentioned affords an interesting and instructive comparison: as noted above, that is a pastiche compiled from bits and pieces of the genuine Pauline letters, but in writing Colossians our author 'did not use [Paul's letters] constantly as if to produce a patchwork of individual passages from other epistles. Rather, he responds to the challenge that the "philosophy" presented by applying Pauline theology to this new problem' (Lohse, 182).[30]

A possible alternative, but one that is rather less likely, is the suggestion that Paul made use of the services of an amanuensis: Rom. 16.22 provides clear evidence that he sometimes did, and it has often been suggested that at 1 Cor. 16.21 and Gal. 6.11 he is taking the pen into his own hand for the final words of salutation. (A third case, 2 Thess. 3.17, is open to question since the authenticity of that letter is disputed; Col. 4.18 would add a fourth, if on other grounds we could accept the letter as authentic, but is scarcely proof of authenticity in itself. In both these cases the form is identical to that of 1 Cor. 16.21, ὁ ἀσπασμὸς τῇ ἐμῇ χειρὶ Παύλου, which might conceivably indicate that they were copied from that verse.) This 'secretary theory' would certainly mean that the thought was that of Paul, although the style and language might owe more to the amanuensis;[31] but the fact that he sometimes employed a secretary does not mean that he always did so. In any case we should then have to ask just what the contribution of the secretary was: might Paul not

---

[30] Guthrie in *Apostolic History and the Gospel*, 328–45 examines some apocryphal writings, and notes that 'paradoxically, pseudepigraphic letters are fewer in number than the other types' (338); this, he thinks, 'cannot fail to be highly significant in the examination of pseudepigraphic epistolary hypotheses in New Testament criticism' (345). See also 'Appendix C: Epistolary Pseudepigraphy' in his *Introduction*, 282–94. This position is, however, criticized as 'without justification' by Kümmel (363). There may be fewer pseudepigraphic letters, but that in itself implies that there are some; all the evidence would seem to indicate that in the ancient world pseudepigraphy was not regarded, as it would be today, simply in terms of falsehood, fraud and forgery. Elliott (*The Apocryphal NT*, 537–54) includes in his section on 'Apocryphal Epistles' the texts of the *Letters of Christ and Abgar*, the *Letter of Lentulus*, the *Epistle to the Laodiceans*, the *Correspondence of Paul and Seneca* and a brief description of the *Epistle to the Alexandrians*. A third epistle to the Corinthians is included in the *Acts of Paul*. The *Epistula Apostolorum* (ibid. 555–88) belongs rather with the *Dialogues of the Redeemer*, as does the *Epistula Jacobi Apocrypha* or *Apocryphon of James* from Nag Hammadi (cf. Schneemelcher, *NT Apocrypha* i. 249–84, 285–99), while the *Epistle of Pseudo-Titus* (ibid. ii. 53–74) is a protracted treatise in praise of chastity.

[31] We may recall Origen's comment on Hebrews, as reported by Eusebius (*HE* vi.25.13f.), that 'the thoughts are those of the apostle, but the style and composition belong to someone who recorded the apostolic teachings and as it were noted down what was said by the teacher'. Origen's further remark that 'it was not for nothing that the men of old handed it down as Paul's' may have some relevance to the discussion of pseudepigraphy: he is well aware of the differences in style and language, but clearly values the book, and is prepared to commend those who accept it as Paul's, although his final word is 'Who wrote the epistle, God only knows.' The idea that the work of some disciple should be circulated under Paul's name does not appear to be a matter of great concern to him.

equally well have dictated?[32] We should not allow our judgement to be distorted by the situation in a modern business, where the letter might be signed by the general manager, but actually drafted by some possibly quite junior clerk. It is always dangerous to transport aspects of the modern situation into the ancient world! Lohse (181 n. 10) bluntly says, 'Only embarrassment can have caused the proposal that Paul instructed one of his secretaries to compose the letter'. In his view, if we are to entertain the possibility of another hand at work, it is better to think of 'a theologian decisively influenced by Paul', one who 'acted and decided for himself' (91).[33]

In regard to content, 'Paul' here develops his ideas in such a way as to meet the threat of false teaching. It has been claimed that while in Colossians there is an advance on his earlier thought, it is still within the same general line of development and does not involve any radical departure (although W. L. Knox (*PCG*, 178) writes that 'whether he realised it or not, he had committed the Church to the theology of Nicaea'[34]). On the other hand Vielhauer (197ff.; cf. also Koester ii. 264f.) notes that there are differences in Christology and consequently in ecclesiology, in the conception of the apostolate and of baptism, and finally in eschatology (cf. Lohse, quoted above, p. 10): in Paul the cosmic significance of Christ is subsidiary, whereas in Colossians it is fundamental; in speaking of the Church as the body of Christ, Paul never speaks of Christ as the 'head' as in Col. 1.18; the difficult passage about the ὑστερήματα (1.24) suggests that the sufferings of Christ require to be completed by the apostle, which contradicts Paul's theology of the cross and therefore cannot come from him; Colossians speaks of the baptized as not only buried with

---

[32] C. K. Barrett (*Romans*, 286) refers for 'Paul's custom of dictating his letters' to 1 Cor. 16.21; Gal. 6.11; Col. 4.18; 2 Thess. 3.17; cf. also Best, *1 and 2 Thessalonians*, 347. The clearest evidence is, however, the passage on which Barrett is commenting, Rom. 16.22, on which Best writes in his *Letter of Paul to the Romans* (1967, 177) that 'Paul usually dictated his letters, and Tertius, his secretary, here adds his own greeting'. On that basis it is natural to assume that at the points listed in the other letters Paul is taking over the pen from the amanuensis to add his own personal greetings (Lightfoot, commenting on 4.18, refers to 'the Apostle's general practice'). Dictation to a secretary is, however, one thing; entrusting the actual formulation of a letter to some associate may be quite another. We need to be quite clear as to which we have in mind. On the whole question see Cranfield, *Romans*, 2–4. Cf. also Kümmel, 1975 edn, 251. E. R. Richards has published a dissertation on *The Secretary in the Letters of Paul* (1991); but see the review by H. D. Betz in *JTS* 43 (1992), 618–20. Richards does, however, recognize (23f.) that the secretary could serve different functions, as recorder (i.e. writing to dictation), as editor, as co-author or as composer (in this last case being allowed a considerable freedom).

[33] As indicated above, Paul did on occasion make use of the services of an amanuensis, but this does not mean that he always did so. The weakness of the 'secretary theory' is that it appeals to what is assumed to be 'the Apostle's general practice' in a desperate attempt to preserve some measure of authenticity for the letter, in the face of evidence which seems to point in another direction.

[34] Cf. N. T. Wright ('Poetry', 463): 'Although the writers of the NT did not themselves formulate the doctrine of the Trinity, they bequeathed to their successors a manner of speaking and writing about God which made it, or something very like it, almost inevitable'.

Christ but risen with him (2.12; 3.1), whereas for Paul the resurrection of Christians is still in the future (cf. Rom. 6.4f.). As already noted, the objection based on the character of the false teaching in view depends on the assumption that such theories were not possible in the time of Paul, but the tendency of recent study has been to push back the beginnings of these theories—possibly even into pre-Christian times (see further below).

Thus far, the question of authenticity has been considered almost entirely from the traditional point of view, taking Colossians in and for itself and using Philemon only for supplementary information. This is very natural, since Colossians is after all the longer letter, and, moreover, it is the first of the two in the traditional sequence of the Pauline corpus. This approach, however, leaves at least two questions that are difficult to answer: how to fit Colossians into what we know of Paul's career, and how to explain the preservation of Philemon, a personal letter without any significant doctrinal content, and its inclusion among the Pauline letters. If we reverse the traditional order, it is possible to suggest an explanation for the second question, and perhaps eliminate the first (cf. Schenke, 154ff.). It is after all Philemon that is the commonly accepted letter, Colossians the one that is in dispute. Now if some disciple of Paul knew of the (genuine) letter to Philemon, he might have used it as the basis for the compilation of Colossians when he sought to apply Paul's teachings in a developed form to meet the problems of the new situation with which the Church of his time was confronted. We must then assume that he placed Colossians under Paul's name either out of modesty, or following the fairly common practice by which the teaching of a disciple was fathered upon the original founder of a school of thought, or simply because under Paul's name it would have carried a greater authority than under his own.

In any case it was a genuine letter that provided the stimulus for his writing, and if the two were to be put into circulation together the second would have to be put under Paul's name too. If his opponents were an early 'Gnostic' group, he was in a sense combating them with their own weapons, for the second-century Gnostics later certainly appealed to traditions handed down from the apostolic age, by James for example to Mariamne, or from Paul to Theudas, and so to the Gnostics themselves (cf. Schenke, 168). It might even be that this solution would explain the absence of any mention of the earthquake referred to by Tacitus: if it was common knowledge in Asia Minor, the fact that this letter is addressed to a town so close to the area affected might in itself have alerted readers to its pseudonymous character. But here we are moving into the realms of speculation. For A. J. M. Wedderburn, 'The idea of a later pseudonymous letter written to a city that was in ruins and to a church there that perhaps no longer existed and which Paul had never visited (Col. 2.1) seems too macabre to be likely, especially since the letter makes no mention of this disaster that had overtaken the city' (*Baptism and Resurrection*, 70). His own suggestion is that Colossians 'was written by a close follower of Paul during the apostle's lifetime, perhaps in a situation where Paul's imprisonment (Col. 4.3, 10, 18) meant that he had to leave the composition of the letters to Colossae and to Philemon rather more in the hands of his associates than he had previously been accustomed to do' (ibid. 71).[35] There is, however, yet another possible alternative: that some later disciple, well aware of the earthquake, deliberately avoided any reference to it in order to convey the impression of a letter written in Paul's lifetime, somewhere before AD 60. A city in ruins and a church that no longer existed might have suited his purpose very well, since there would be nobody to expose the pseudonymity;[36] but this again is conjecture.

The latest detailed study of the question is the monograph of Kiley, *Colossians as Pseudepigraphy*. Following the researches of Bujard,[37] and sometimes correcting or refining them, he argues (51ff.) that the style of Colossians is sufficiently different from that of the generally accepted letters to preclude Pauline authorship: 'Bujard has established beyond a reasonable doubt that Paul's authorship of Col is highly unlikely because the letter's grammatical and syntactical characteristics, as well as its rhetorical engagement, are sufficiently divergent from Paul' (59). Kiley further notes (1) the portrayal of the

---

[35] Schweizer before him suggested Timothy (cf. also Ollrog, *Mitarbeiter*, 241; Dunn, 35–39), Suhl Epaphras. According to Collins (*Letters*, 172, 176), the first of these suggestions goes back to Ewald in 1857, the second to Klöpper in 1882. Other scholars have been content to suggest a disciple, without mentioning any name. L. Hartman (*HTR* 79 (1986), 140) finds the idea of 'a rather independent Pauline disciple (why not the co-author, Timothy?)' more natural than the assumption 'that the author cleverly "writes to" a community that does not exist any more—after the earthquake in the Lycus valley in the early sixties—when there would be less chance of being detected!' Against Schweizer's suggestion of a letter written by some disciple while Paul was a prisoner in Ephesus, Hübner (10) cites Lindemann's arguments ('Gemeinde', 115f.) that this would put Col. before Rom., and the assumption that certain passages in Col. were written before corresponding passages in Rom. is highly problematic. Lindemann (114f.) rules out a post-Pauline letter addressed to Colossae, and argues (117ff.) that it was actually intended for Laodicea: the author wanted to convey to his readers the impression that Paul had once, with an eye on Colossae (i.e. about AD 60), taken up a position with regard to a development such as was now appearing in a very similar form in their own community. But cf. Schenk, *ANRW* II.25.4, 3335 n. 27: rather than trying to establish a Pauline authority where no Pauline tradition as yet existed, the author is seeking to claim an existing Pauline authority for his own purposes.

[36] Cf. Pokorný, 20, referring to Lindemann, 'Gemeinde', 128f.: 'addressing a letter, post-dated in the life of the apostle, to a community that has already disappeared, is theoretically the best method to promote a letter as authentic'. On his view, the letter 'was intended for the Christians in the broader region of the province of Asia Minor, but not directly for Colossae' (Pokorný, 21). W. T. Wilson (*The Hope of Glory*, 17) writes, 'The pseudepigrapher's hope, we can imagine, would have been for the Laodicean Christians to recognize in Paul's words for the Colossians (presumably written some years earlier) counsel that was meaningful for the situation currently confronting them.' Lindemann ('Gemeinde', 118) rejects the idea of a wider circle and argues that the problems of a quite specific community are in view.

[37] *Stilanalytische Untersuchungen zum Kolosserbrief* (1973); 'the most comprehensive stylistic study of the undisputed letters vis-à-vis Col now in existence' (Kiley, 129, n. 105; cf. Pokorný, 3). Cf. also the comprehensive summary in Schenk, *ANRW* II.25.4, 3327–38.

Apostle (59–61; cf. Collins, *Letters*, 203–07), (2) the portrayal of and reaction to the heresy (61–65) and (3) the portrayal of other issues affecting the believers (65–69), and claims (73) that the stance taken by Colossians with regard to these issues differentiates it from Paul.

One factor on which he lays considerable stress (46ff.) is the absence of any reference to financial transactions connected with Paul's mission: in the seven letters commonly regarded as authentic (Rom., 1 and 2 Cor., Gal., Phil., 1 Thess., Philem.) 'it is symptomatic or characteristic of all seven that Paul is shown engaged in some kind of financial transaction on behalf of his mission. I suggest that the absence of these transactions in the other six canonical letters bearing Paul's name as author (Col among them) means that they are spurious'. This, however, is perhaps not so strong an argument as he seems to think:[38] for one thing, there might have been reasons to account for this lack of mention; for another, what reference is there to financial transactions relating to Paul's mission in Philemon? Kiley (48) notes that in Philem. 18–19 Paul offers to pay any damages incurred by Onesimus and asks that the latter's debts be debited to himself; but is this a 'financial transaction on behalf of his mission'? The most obvious such transaction is Paul's great collection for the saints in Jerusalem, which certainly has a prominent place in some of these letters; but there is nothing about it in 1 Thessalonians (Kiley, 49 refers to 1 Thess. 2. 9, where Paul speaks of his labours as undertaken to avoid imposing a burden on the community), and in Galatians there is at most the reference to 'remembering the poor' at 2.10, which Duncan for example (*Moffatt Commentary* (1934), 52) takes to refer to the 'famine visit' of Acts 11.29, hence before the launching of the great collection itself (on which see e.g. D. Georgi, *Die Geschichte der Kollekte des Paulus für Jerusalem*, (1965); K. F. Nickle, *The Collection: A Study in Paul's Strategy* (1966)). The agreement with the 'pillars' in Jerusalem was rather the occasion for the launching of the collection. Kiley's suggestion thus appears to stand in need of considerable qualification.

A more serious obstacle in the way of any acceptance of authenticity is the problem of locating the letter within what we know of Paul's career: we require a period of fairly prolonged imprisonment, but probably not the imprisonment during which Philippians was written, at an advanced stage of Paul's life, and at a time when the 'Gnostic' elements, if such they are, could have developed to the point which they appear to have reached; moreover, since there is no mention of the earthquake, it would presumably have to be before AD 60, or at the latest very soon thereafter.[39]

[38] 'Kiley's argument that the lack of reference to financial transactions is suspicious can hardly be taken seriously' (Barclay, *Colossians*, 24).

[39] The best alternative would seem to be Dunn's suggestion of composition by Timothy near the end of Paul's life, which makes Col. a bridge between the major letters and the pseudo-Paulines. Even here, however, there are difficulties: the distance Onesimus would have had to travel, the coincidence that brought him into contact with Paul, and so on. And would Epaphras have travelled all the way to Rome to seek Paul's help in dealing with the 'heresy' in Colossae?

B   Place of writing

Traditionally Colossians is thought to have been written from Rome,[40] as one of the Epistles of the Captivity—the others being Ephesians, Philippians, Philemon and the Pastorals. Of these, the Pastorals are now generally regarded as non-Pauline, at least in their present form. Ephesians, Colossians and Philemon certainly belong together, for various reasons, but it is difficult to imagine Philippians as written at the same time as Colossians.[41] If Colossians too is non-Pauline, the question where it was written does not arise, at least not in the usual form. On the assumption of authenticity, two other suggestions have been made as to the place of writing: (1) that Paul was in Caesarea, and (2) that he was in Ephesus. Either of these would make the letter somewhat earlier, especially the latter; if from Rome, it must have been written about AD 60 or a little later, and in that case the absence of any reference to the earthquake mentioned by Tacitus may create problems. We know from Acts (23.33—26.32) of a long imprisonment in Caesarea while Paul was awaiting trial before Caesar, but the decisive objection to this view is, as Moule (23) points out, 'that Paul must have known, during his imprisonment at Caesarea, that to be released would inevitably mean being lynched by the Jews, and that his one hope of remaining alive was to go to Rome under Roman escort'. Again, as Scott (4) observes, 'at Caesarea, when Paul's thoughts were all turning towards Rome and the West, we cannot conceive of him as planning an immediate return to Asia'.

The case for an Ephesian imprisonment is in some respects rather stronger, and has been argued by G. S. Duncan both in his book

[40] In the subscription added later at the end, some mss have απο Ρωμης (A B¹ P pc), others απο Ρωμης δια Τυχικου και Ονησιμου (075, 1739, 1881 and the Majority text). When 0278 refers to Tychicus alone, it would seem that we have a growing text (P⁴⁶ and other mss omit it altogether), and that the simple προς Κολοσσαεις of ℵ B* C and other mss should have the preference.

[41] 'The letter to the Philippians stands alone' (Lightfoot, *Philippians* (1894), 31f.); he places Philemon early in the Roman captivity and the other three letters late, but lists several authors who take an opposite view. See his discussion of the order of the Captivity Epistles (30–46). Pokorný (4) finds it difficult to place Col. close to Phil., and thinks the latter probably written during the Ephesian imprisonment (5). Ollrog (*Mitarbeiter*, 245) places Col. in an Ephesian imprisonment in AD 53–54, and thinks it probably written by Timothy (219; cf. his discussion at 219–33 and his excursus on the *Abfassungsverhältnisse*, 236ff.). Cf. also Reicke in *Apostolic History and the Gospel*, 278, who remarks that 'the differences between the two groups of letters [i.e. Eph., Col. and Philem. on the one hand, Phil. on the other] suggest different occasions'. He places Phil. in Rome, the others at Caesarea; but against Caesarea as the place of writing for Col. cf. Lohse, 166. T. W. Manson (*BJRL* 1939, repr. in *Studies in the Gospels and Epistles* (1962), 149–67) argues that Philippians was written from Ephesus, but not from prison, between AD 52 and 55. Koester (ii. 131) thinks on the basis of internal evidence that there is 'clearly a preponderance' of evidence in favour of the composition of Philippians and Philemon during an Ephesian imprisonment; he regards Colossians as written by one of Paul's disciples, probably 'not very long after Paul's missionary activity' (ii. 264, 266).

St Paul's Ephesian Ministry and later in a number of articles.[42] The
main arguments are summed up by Scott (4) under five heads:

1. Paul writes in the name of himself and Timothy, his companion
   on the third missionary journey.
2. He mentions a number of men who are with him, and who are all
   associated with that earlier period (but cf. Moule, 24 regarding
   Luke).
3. He refers to future plans, taking it for granted that he will resume
   work in Asia, whereas before he went to Rome he had definitely
   closed his mission in the East.
4. He is in close and frequent touch with Asia and Macedonia, which
   would hardly have been possible in Rome.
5. Onesimus could not have made his way from Colossae to Rome,
   and Paul could not have sent him back such a distance.

Moule (22) adds that the Monarchian Prologues (believed to be
connected with Marcion *c.* AD 150)[43] describe Colossians as written
from Ephesus—but these prologues assign both Philippians and
Philemon to Rome. One question here of course is: how accurate is
this information? The Colossians are said in the Prologues to have
received the word from Archippus, who had accepted the ministry
among them. This is presumably an inference from Col. 4.17, but is
not the only possible interpretation of the verse. Most scholars, as
indicated above, think of Epaphras.

On the other hand we have no clear evidence for an Ephesian
imprisonment, which has to be inferred from indirect allusions, and
as Scott says (5), runaway slaves notoriously made for Rome, where
they were safer from detection than anywhere else. The argument
from the distances is stronger, but Moule (24) points out that travel

---

[42] See Duncan, *St Paul's Ephesian Ministry* (1929); also *ExpT* 67 (1955/6), 163ff.;
NTS 3 (1956/7), 211–18; *NTS* 5 (1958/59), 43–45. Cf. also Michaelis, *Die
Gefangenschaft des Paulus in Ephesus*; other references in Deissmann, *Paul*, 17f.,
Light from the Ancient East, 237f.; Lohse, 166 n. 14. For a critical assessment cf. Dodd,
New Testament Studies, 89–108. Jülicher (134) notes as a major argument against 'the
fashionable transference of Col to an Ephesian imprisonment' that it is one thing to
place so significant a change in Paul's thinking as we find in Colossians and Ephesians
in the last years of Paul's life, but quite another matter to put it shortly after the
Corinthian letters and before Galatians and Romans (cf. Hübner, 10, citing the
arguments of Lindemann, 'Gemeinde', 115f.). It is not possible here to deal in detail
with the problems of Pauline chronology! Francis and Sampley (*Pauline Parallels*)
present a selection of chronological tables on pp. 67, 141, 175, 207 and 223. For earlier
advocates of an Ephesian imprisonment cf. Moffatt, *Introd.*, 169 n. * and App. C, 622–
23. Hoppe (*Triumph*, 6 n. 4) observes that there is no express mention of an Ephesian
imprisonment either in Acts or in Paul himself, but considers it 'more than probable',
referring for detailed discussion to Gnilka, *Phil.* 18–24.

[43] The reference should be to the Marcionite Prologues (*ODCC* 1034), a set of
prologues to the Pauline letters found in mss of the Vulgate and generally recognized as
originating in Marcionite circles. The Monarchian Prologues are prefixed to the
Gospels (*ODCC* 1102).

between Rome and the East was frequent and not so formidable a task as to make the communications implied by these letters impossible. Both he and Scott accordingly adhere to the traditional view. The situation is somewhat different in Philippians, where several journeys are involved. On the other hand it may be observed that it is not only a matter of the distances to be covered, but of the sea crossings: on a small ship, with a limited number of passengers, a runaway slave would run greater risk of detection than in a large city such as Ephesus. Or are we to imagine Onesimus making the whole journey by land, and possibly swimming the Hellespont? We might also ask how he could have found the fare for the sea journey, but runaway slaves notoriously stole some of their masters' property before making their escape, and Philem. 18 offers a hint that this was so in the case of Onesimus.

Another point relates to the nature of the false teaching which is in view in Colossians (on which see below): it is not the Judaizing heresy which Paul assails in Galatians,[44] even if there are some elements common to these two letters; nor can we assume without more ado that it was the same as that opposed in the Corinthian correspondence, where it can further be argued that the opponents of the second letter are a different group from those opposed in the first. It is no longer possible simply to classify Paul's opponents in Corinth as 'Gnostics' without further discrimination; but into this we need not enter. For present purposes the question is: can we reasonably imagine an outbreak of some kind of proto-Gnostic heresy in Colossae, different from that in Corinth, in the period of Paul's Ephesian ministry? It is indeed not impossible that Paul should within a comparatively short span of time have to defend his gospel against three different groups of opponents, but that would seem to indicate that the early Christians were considerably more contentious than we have hitherto believed. On the other hand, these letters are addressed to three different areas, and the problems which arose in the cosmopolitan seaport of Corinth might well have been different from those which affected cities in Asia Minor.

There are, as already noted, some similarities between Colossians and Galatians, which have led scholars in the past to think that the problem was the same in both cases; but there are also differences which must be duly taken into account. We have to think not of abstract 'heresies' but of people in different areas who combined ideas from their own earlier background with their new Christian

---

[44] 'The legal character of this doctrine is clearly reminiscent of the Judaizing requirements imposed by the false teachers of Galatia, but is distinguished from the latter in that the Colossian false teaching is not based on the necessity of keeping the Mosaic law for salvation, but is related to the worship of the στοιχεῖα τοῦ κόσμου ("elemental spirits of the universe").' (E. Lohse, *The Formation of the New Testament* (ET 1981), 89). Dunn, however, (*Biblica* 76, (1995), 179) warns against the danger of assuming that the only challenge had to be of the sort encountered in Galatia.

faith, and sometimes reached conclusions which to others appeared to be detrimental to that faith, and which in a later age were to be denounced as heretical.

On Lohse's view the case for Ephesus is stronger, but in a different way: he thinks it likely that the Pauline school tradition 'was based in Ephesus as the centre of the Pauline mission in Asia Minor, and that it was cultivated and further developed in the circle of the Apostle's students' (181; cf. also Schenke in Schenke and Fischer, *Einleitung*, 233–45).[45] Goppelt (*Apostolic and Post-Apostolic Times*, 103) argues that Paul's imprisonment must have lasted for months, or even years, and that Paul was only in such a situation in Caesarea or Rome, certainly not in Ephesus. He opts for Rome—but do all the Captivity Epistles relate to the same imprisonment?

C Colossians and Ephesians[46]

The relation between Colossians and Ephesians presents a question of considerable complexity. As already noted, there are ten words

[45] On the question of a Pauline 'school', cf. Conzelmann, 'Paulus und die Weisheit', (esp. 233f.), who thinks of a school initially headed by Paul, concerned with the Wisdom tradition, and located in Ephesus; also Conzelmann, 'Die Schule des Paulus'; cf. also Best, *Ephesians*, 36–40. For a detailed discussion, based on 2 Thess. and Col., see Müller, *Anfänge der Paulusschule*. On the development of the Pauline Corpus and the nature of the Pauline 'school' cf. also Schenke, *NTS* 21 (1975), 508–09, 515–17. For a recent survey of the varying theories on this question see Standhartinger, *Studien*, 3–10, and also her article 'Colossians and the Pauline School', *NTS* 50 (2004), 572–93.

[46] On this topic see Moffatt, 375–81; Wendland, *Die hellenistisch-romische Kultur*, 361–64; Guthrie, 103ff.; Kümmel (1975 edn), 358ff.; Pokorný, 7ff.; Barth, 72–114 (with detailed discussion and ample references); Bouttier, *L'épître de saint Paul aux Éphésiens*, 34–35 (with table of parallel passages, 308–09); Wedderburn, *Baptism and Resurrection*, 70–84; Best, *Ephesians* (1993), 22–25, also *NTS* 43 (1997), 72–96 and *Ephesians* (1998), index, *s.v.* According to F. C. Baur (*Paul*, 2), 'The relationship between the two Epistles is certainly striking enough, and by the nearly unanimous judgement of critics and interpreters it is the Epistle to the Ephesians and not that to the Colossians which must be held to be dependent on the other.' Baur refers to de Wette for the view that Eph. is 'nothing but a rhetorical expansion' of Col. In more recent times, Goodspeed, *The Key to Ephesians* (1956), Knox, *Philemon among the Letters of Paul* (revd edn 1959) and Mitton, *The Epistle to the Ephesians, its Authorship, Origin and Purpose* (1951) among others argue for the dependence of Ephesians on Colossians. J. Coutts in *NTS* 4 (1957/58), 201ff. argues for the priority of Ephesians, but has not carried conviction (cf. Lohse 4 n. 2; Merkel, *ANRW* II.25.4, 3217, citing Benoit, 'Rapports littéraires entre les épîtres aux Colossiens et aux Éphésiens', *Neutestamentliche Aufsätze* (1963), 11–22). Cf. also G. Johnston, *The Doctrine of the Church in the New Testament* (1943), 136–40. Some of the passages showing similarity are presented in parallel columns, in English (RV), by G. Currie Martin (App. B, 181–87); he regards both as authentic, considering Col. as intended to correct certain definite errors and meet the circumstances of an individual church, and Eph. as containing the general principles which in Col. find application to local needs. Standhartinger (*Studien*, 53 n. 139) remarks that a quarter of Eph. consists of formulations from Col., and lists a string of parallel passages. Cf. also van Kooten, *Cosmic Christology*, 147–204, who in an appendix (215–89) presents a synopsis to show the adaptation of the structure of Col. by the author of Eph, with the passages drawn from Paul's major letters and from the LXX.

shared by these two letters alone;[47] there are also a further fifteen
which are not found in the other Pauline letters but appear both in
Ephesians and Colossians and in other NT documents.[48] A stronger
indication of some relationship is the fact that they share not only
words but whole phrases, sometimes of considerable length.[49]
Colossians does of course have its 34 hapax legomena, but
Ephesians has several hapax legomena of its own, which only
complicates the problem further. In brief, the two letters are
sufficiently different to be considered independent, yet show such
similarities as to suggest that there must be some connection between
them.[50]

Those who maintain the authenticity of both would claim that the
differences are only such as might have been effected by the same
author, writing while the memory of the earlier letter was still fresh in
his mind. This might hold for Col. 4.7–8, which appears in identical
form at Eph. 6.21–22, prefaced by ἵνα δὲ εἰδῆτε καὶ ὑμεῖς τὰ
κατ᾽ ἐμέ, τί πράσσω. On this view Paul still had the Colossians
passage in mind when he wrote Ephesians, and the καὶ ὑμεῖς means
'you too, in Ephesus'—i.e. as well as the Colossians (the reference to
Onesimus in Col. 4.9 is then naturally dropped as irrelevant); but the
words prefixed could have been intended to convey that impression
by some later writer drawing upon Colossians. Mayerhoff argued
that Colossians was influenced by Ephesians, which presupposes that
Ephesians came first, but this, as Kiley (40) says, is 'a problematic
suggestion' and indeed may well be disproved by these very verses.

At other points there are minor changes only: the substitution of
words (cf. Col. 1.22, παραστῆσαι ὑμᾶς ἁγίους καὶ ἀμώμους καὶ
ἀνεγκλήτους κατενώπιον αὐτοῦ; Eph. 1.4, εἶναι ἡμᾶς ἁγίους καὶ

[47] See above, n. 25.
[48] ᾅδειν (3.16), αἰτεῖσθαι (1.9), ἀπάτη (2.8), αὔξειν (2.19), ἄφεσις (1.14), βλασφημία (3.8), διάνοια (1.21), δόγμα (2.14), θεμελιοῦν (1.23), κατενώπιον (1.22), κατοικεῖν (1.19; 2.9), κράτος (1.11), κυριότης (1.16), σύνδεσμος (2.19; 3.14), ᾠδή (3.16).
[49] E.g. Col. 1.4, καὶ τὴν ἀγάπην ἣν ἔχετε εἰς πάντας τοὺς ἁγίους (cf. Eph. 1.15); Col. 3.16 ψαλμοῖς, ὕμνοις, ᾠδαῖς ἐν χάριτι ᾄδοντες (cf. Eph. 5.19); Col. 3.22 μὴ ἐν ὀφθαλμοδουλίᾳ ὡς ἀνθρωπάρεσκοι (cf. Eph. 6.6). Cf. also Col. 3.18–22 and Eph. 5.22, 25; 6.1, 4, 5: each injunction in the Colossians list is paralleled, in the same order, in Ephesians, but in the latter they are much elaborated. Has Ephesians expanded the Colossians *Haustafel*, or Colossians condensed that of Ephesians? If both draw upon an older tradition, the same questions would apply: which represents the more original version?
[50] 'In certain passages Ephesians reads like the first commentary on Colossians, though admittedly it does more than explicate the thoughts of Colossians: it also expands them into concepts of its own' (Lohse, 4; in a footnote he mentions the possibility that both are dependent on common traditions, used independently in each letter, but considers it more probable that the author of Eph. knew Col.). Hübner (11) regards Eph. as in certain respects something like a second edition of Col., a reworking which develops the theology of Col. into a theology of the Church. But see also Best, *NTS* 43 (1997), 72–96, who notes that sometimes the evidence favours the priority of Col., at others that of Eph.

ἀμώμους κατενώπιον αὐτοῦ; Col. 3.21, οἱ πατέρες, μὴ ἐρεθίζετε τὰ
τέκνα ὑμῶν, ἵνα μὴ ἀθυμῶσιν; Eph. 6.4, οἱ πατέρες, μὴ παροργίζετε
τὰ τέκνα ὑμῶν, ἀλλὰ ἐκτρέφετε αὐτὰ ἐν παιδείᾳ καὶ νουθεσίᾳ
κυρίου) or a change in word order (e.g. Col. 1.10, περιπατῆσαι ἀξίως
τοῦ κυρίου; Eph. 4.1, ἀξίως περιπατῆσαι τῆς κλήσεως ἧς ἐκλήθητε;
Col. 2.13, καὶ ὑμᾶς νεκροὺς ὄντας [ἐν] τοῖς παραπτώμασιν; Eph.
2.1, καὶ ὑμᾶς ὄντας νεκροὺς τοῖς παραπτώμασιν; 2.5, καὶ ὄντας
ὑμᾶς νεκροὺς τοῖς παραπτώμασιν). Such changes might be regarded
as merely stylistic variations by the same author, but in other cases
the same words are used in a different way, e.g. ἀποκαταλλάσσω in
Col. 1.20, 22 of the reconciliation of all things, and the 'alienated'
Colossians, to God, but in Eph. 2.16 of the reconciliation of Jew and
Gentile; παρακαλέω in Col. 2.2; 4.8 in the sense of 'comfort,
encourage' (cf. Eph. 6.22), but in Eph. 4.1 in the sense of 'exhort,
command'. We may add the use of πλήρωμα at Col. 1.19; 2.9 (the
fullness of deity) and Eph. 1.10 (the fullness of the times), 1.23 (of the
Church which is his body), 3.19 (the fullness of God), 4.13 (the
fullness of Christ). At Col. 2.7 ῥιζοῦσθαι is used of the Colossians
being rooted in Christ, at Eph. 3.17 of being 'rooted and grounded in
love'. At Col. 1.25 οἰκονομία is a responsibility given by God to
Paul, whereas in Eph. 1.10; 3.2, 9 it refers to the dispensation of the
grace of God, the 'hidden mystery'. As Kiley notes (40f.), 'the
grammar of Col 2.19 is somewhat awkward: οὐ κράτων τὴν κεφαλήν,
ἐξ οὗ πᾶν τὸ σῶμα … It seems more appropriate to say that Eph has
straightened out that grammar in Eph 4.15-16 ἡ κεφαλὴ Χριστός, ἐξ
οὗ πᾶν τὸ σῶμα than to say that Col has obfuscated Eph. Similarly,
Eph 6.9 specifies that there is no partiality *with him* (the Lord in
heaven) which may be implied but is not explicit in Col 3.25. It seems
doubtful that Col has deliberately made the issue less clear'.

A further point relates to the use of the OT in the two letters. E.
Earle Ellis (*Paul's Use of the Old Testament*) lists four express
quotations for Ephesians (152; the texts are printed out in full on pp.
182ff.)[51] and a dozen allusions, some of them 'manifestly intentional'
(154), but not one quotation and only four allusions for Colossians:
Col. 2.3 (Isa. 45.3); 2.22 (Isa. 29.13); 3.1 (Ps. 109 (110).1) and 3.10
(Gen. 1.27). The UBS Greek New Testament (1975) prints three of
the Ephesians texts in bold type, to mark explicit quotations (Eph.
4.8; 5.31; 6.2–3), and adds two more at Eph. 4.25, 26; the fourth in
Ellis's list is not so distinguished, obviously because of the difficulty
of identifying its source (cf. Salmond, *EGT* 360). The apparatus of
cross-references adds a few more, but even so the disparity is
considerable: a total of seven for Colossians (adding 3.18; 3.25; 4.1)
and some 25 for Ephesians. Moreover, two of the latter have

---

[51] For Eph. see the detailed discussion in Moritz, *A Profound Mystery* (reference
supplied by Professor G. N. Stanton).

parallels in Colossians (Eph. 5.22 (Gen 3.16) and Col. 3.18; Eph. 6.9 (Deut. 10.17; 2 Chron. 19.7) and Col. 3.25).[52]

Another feature is that in Colossians πνεῦμα occurs only twice (1.8; 2.5), against 14 occurrences in Ephesians; moreover the second of these is probably 'purely anthropological' and the first may be intended only to distinguish a 'spiritual' life from one merely secular (Schweizer, 'Christus und Geist im Kolosserbrief', 308f.). Could the same author show such a disparity in two letters written about the same time; and could Paul give so small a place to the Spirit?

According to Grant (*Historical Introduction*, 200f.) the most significant difference lies in the doctrine of the Church:[53] in Colossians Christ is the head of the Church (1.18, 24), and 'churches' are mentioned (4.15–16). In Ephesians the Church is the bride of Christ (5.25–32) and the instrument of God's revelation to the heavenly powers (3.10); she holds within herself 'the fulness of him who himself receives the entire fulness of God' (1.23 NEB).[54] Thus there is in Ephesians an expression of the cosmic meaning of the Church which is not in the other Pauline epistles, although there are premonitions earlier: in 1 Cor. 6.17 the Christian is the bride of Christ; in 2 Cor. 11.2 (cf. Rom. 7.4) the Church is his bride. About three-fifths of Col. seems to be reflected in Eph., though the phrases often bear different meanings (Grant, 201). Summing up the views of other scholars, Grant writes that if Ephesians is by Paul, it must have been written immediately after Colossians because so much of it is like Colossians; on the other hand the changes in the meaning of words show that it was written considerably later; therefore it is not by Paul (200). But Grant assumes its authenticity: 'since the authenticity of the letter cannot be disproved it should be regarded as genuine' (202).

This, however, is probably a minority opinion; on the view here taken, Ephesians is post-Pauline and in some degree dependent on

[52] NA[27] has no OT reference at Eph. 5.22, and Col. 3.18 is in any case differently worded. At Eph. 6.9 the marginal note refers back to Acts 10.34, where Deut. 10.17; Sir. 35.12f.; Rom. 2.11 are adduced; the note at Rom. 2.11 adds 2 Chron. 19.7 among other references. In all the OT cases the LXX formula is πρόσωπον λαμβάνειν (or in Deut. πρόσωπον θαυμάζειν); according to BAGD 720b, the compounds προσωπολημπτέω, προσωπολήμπτης and προσωπολημψία have so far been found only in Christian writers. For discussion of the quotations in Eph. see Best, *Ephesians*, 76–79.

[53] Cf. H. Chadwick, *Peake's Commentary* (revd edn 1962), §856e: 'This high ecclesiology and the revolutionary interpretation of history which it implies differentiate Eph. more deeply from Col. (with which its kinship is otherwise obvious) than any other single factor. In Col. the fundamental question at issue is the dignity of the person of Christ and his lordship in the cosmic hierarchy. In Eph. the question is the catholicity and divine origin of the Church. The glory of the Head is now transferred to his Body.' C. E. Arnold, however, (*Ephesians: Power and Magic*, 158–66) argues that 'ecclesiology is a function of Christology in Ephesians' and takes issue with the 'advocates of an early catholicism'.

[54] NRSV's 'the fullness of him who fills all in all' reverts to the rendering of AV. Cf. the contrasting interpretations of, for example, S. D. F. Salmond, *The Expositor's Greek Testament*, iii (1903), 281; J. Armitage Robinson, *The Epistle to the Ephesians* (1909), 152; Chadwick, *Peake's Commentary*, §859b. For full discussion cf. Best *Ephesians* (1998), 183–89.

Colossians. According to Vielhauer (209f.) there is a very close relationship, but one so complicated as to make the assumption that both are by the same author improbable. For him the decisive factor is the similarity in terminology with at the same time a difference in ideas. Comparing Col. 2.19 and Eph. 4.15f. he notes a transmutation of the cosmological into the ecclesiological; the 'mystery' in Col. 1.26f. is the eschatological salvation in Christ, in Eph. 3.3f. the acceptance of the Gentiles into the Church.[55] There is a similar transmutation with οἰκονομία from Col. 1.25 to Eph. 3.2. Also there are theological differences which cannot be reconciled either with Colossians or with Paul (210).

D   Colossians and other Pauline letters[56]

Reference has already been made to eleven words which appear in the New Testament only in Colossians and in other Pauline letters. The verb ἄπειμι ('to be absent'; not the ἄπειμι employed in Acts 17.10) is used in 1 Cor. and Phil., and four times in 2 Cor., but in every case in a participle whereas Col. 2.5 has the first person singular present indicative; εἰκῇ appears in Rom., 1 Cor. and Gal., and in a variant reading at Matt. 5.22; πάθος occurs in Rom. and 1 Thess. Most of these words, however, appear only in one other letter, and therefore do not provide much in the way of evidence: ἑδραῖος twice in 1 Corinthians, ἐρεθίζειν, θριαμβεύειν, ἱκανοῦν and ἰσότης (twice) all in 2 Corinthians, συναιχμάλωτος in Romans and Philemon, συνθάπτεσθαι again in Romans, φυσιοῦσθαι no fewer than six times in 1 Corinthians. The last case obviously has to do with one of the characteristics of Paul's Corinthian opponents, their tendency to 'think more highly of themselves than they ought to

---

[55] But cf. Arnold (*Ephesians*, 127f.): 'It is too restrictive to hold that the content of the mystery in Ephesians is defined solely as God's acceptance of the Gentiles and the unification of the Jews and Gentiles in Christ (Eph 3:3, 4). If we seek a precise definition of "mystery", it is best found in the proposition found in Colossians: "the mystery of God is Christ" (cf. Col. 2:2)'; 'In Ephesians, Christ is the content of the gospel message, termed a "mystery" (6:19) ... the starting-point for an accurate understanding of the concept of "mystery".'

[56] According to Koester (ii. 267) 'the author seems to depend more upon his familiarity with the Pauline proclamation and mission than upon knowledge of Paul's letters. In fact, of all the Pauline letters known to us, the author of Colossians seems to have known only Philemon.' Others, however, have pointed to similarities which in their view provide evidence for knowledge of one or another of the major letters. Thus E. P. Sanders, for example, argues for literary dependence in Colossians (*JBL* 85 (1966), 28–45); but this dependence includes quotation from memory, and does not necessarily imply the copying of a written document (30 n. 9). Hoppe (*Triumph*, 36–39) notes certain points of contact between Col. and 1 Cor. 1–4, particularly the use of the terms σοφία and μυστήριον. See also Standhartinger (*Studien*, 61–89), who observes that the usual approach reckons only with dependence on Paul's letters, and goes on to argue for influence from an oral tradition of Pauline theology (91–152). Cf. further Schenk, *ANRW* II.25.4, 3338ff., who also notes links with the Gospel of Mark.

think',[57] but the use of this term in Col. 2.18 does not necessarily mean that the opponents in Colossae were of the same kind; it would certainly be a mistake to assume a special link with 2 Corinthians on the strength of four words. All we can say is that these are words which Paul could have used, since he used them in other letters.

There are also some phrases which recall other letters, but here we must pay heed to the context: thus 1.26, τὸ μυστήριον τὸ ἀποκεκρυμμένον ἀπὸ τῶν αἰώνων (cf. Eph. 3.9), is reminiscent of 1 Cor. 2.7, but there the reference is to θεοῦ σοφίαν ἐν μυστηρίῳ τὴν ἀποκεκρυμμένην; it is the wisdom that is hidden. Col. 3.5 πορνείαν, ἀκαθαρσίαν, πάθος, contains two of the three vices listed in Gal. 5.19, where πορνεία, ἀκαθαρσία and ἀσελγεία are the first three in a much longer list; 2.12, τοῦ θεοῦ τοῦ ἐγείραντος αὐτὸν ἐκ νεκρῶν, can be paralleled in Rom. 4.24; 8.11; 2 Cor. 4.14; Gal. 1.1; 1 Pet. 1.21; but only Galatians and 1 Peter have specific reference to God, and in any case this is probably an early formula from pre-Pauline Christianity (cf. Hunter, *Paul and his Predecessors*, 28–30 on Rom. 10.8–9). Col. 1.25, κατὰ τὴν οἰκονομίαν τοῦ θεοῦ τὴν δοθεῖσάν μοι, is distinctly closer to the οἰκονομίαν πεπίστευμαι of 1 Cor. 9.17 than to the use of οἰκονομία in Ephesians for the purpose and plan of God. At most these references show that Paul could have used these terms; they do not prove that he wrote Colossians. On the other hand there is no very obvious reason why they should have been fastened upon by an imitator; but on the view taken here this is not a patchwork pieced together, like the apocryphal letter to the Laodiceans: it is an independent creation by a disciple of Paul, familiar with Paul's writings but perfectly capable of making up his own mind.

Another point which calls for consideration is that on occasion, as already noted, the author takes up 'Pauline' terms and concepts, and uses them in a subtly different way, sometimes carrying them further than Paul himself had done, or shifting the emphasis to some extent.[58] The most obvious example is perhaps the idea of the resurrection of believers: at Rom. 6.5 they 'have been united with him in a death like his' and 'will certainly be united with him in a resurrection like his' (NRSV)—here the resurrection is clearly something yet to come; but Col. 3.1 says explicitly, 'So if you *have been raised* with Christ', making it a past event. This of course leads one to think of the 'heresy' of Hymenaeus and Philetus (2 Tim. 2.18),

---

[57] This admonition actually occurs at Rom. 12.3, and a different word is used, involving a play on compounds of the verb φρονεῖν (cf. Cranfield, *Romans*, 612f.); but Barrett in his commentary (*Romans*, 235) has the significant note 'cf. 1 Corinthians *passim*'.

[58] Schweizer ('Christus und Geist', 297ff.) notes a string of passages in which Col. is subtly different from the other Pauline letters—but such differences are not in themselves enough to disprove Pauline authorship. In his opinion the facts displayed in his essay confirm his view that, while nothing clearly tells against authenticity, the assumption that Col. was written by a disciple is substantially more probable (297 n. 2).

which some scholars would trace back as far as the Corinthian situation. Is Paul coming round late in life to acceptance of a view which he had earlier rejected, or does he in Romans deny what he had previously affirmed in Colossians? At any rate there would appear to be something of a contradiction here, which has in itself been enough to convince some scholars that the same author could not have written both letters.[59] On the other hand Paul does speak of walking 'in newness of life' (Rom. 6.5; cf. 7.6) and affirms that 'if anyone is in Christ, there is a new creation' (2 Cor. 5.17); a change has already taken place, in the sacrament of baptism (Rom. 6.3–4; 7.4–6; cf. Col. 2.12f.), but the final consummation has yet to come (cf. Phil. 3.12ff.). It is not difficult to see how some converts, stressing the 'already' and neglecting the 'not yet', could draw a false conclusion from Paul's own words.

E. P. Sanders (*JBL* 85 (1966), 28–45) argues that in a number of cases (Col. 1.15–16; 1.20–22a; 1.26–27; 2.12–13; 3.5–11) the author has conflated material from the major Pauline letters. Of these, he says, the first two provide no clear evidence, but only a possibility (39); the clearest evidence is at 2.12–13 (40–42). Since it is unlikely that Paul would collate material from his own letters, this would point to another hand. He notes that this evidence is drawn almost exclusively from the first two chapters, and suggests that it might be worthwhile to reconsider Holtzmann's theory, in principle at least (45). Kiley finds his argument unconvincing, and prefers to stress an affinity with Philippians (cf. also Wedderburn, *Baptism and Resurrection*, 73f.).

Colossians shares with Philippians an emphasis on the exaltation and the sovereignty of Christ, and in both epistles Timothy is associated with Paul as sender in the opening words (cf. Pokorný 6, but see also 17f.), but the stylistic differences make it difficult to think of these two letters as sent by the same author at the same time (ibid. 4). As noted above (n. 41), Lightfoot already wrote that Philippians 'stands alone' among the Captivity Epistles. One possibility might be to place Philippians as written from Ephesus and Colossians (and Philemon) from Rome, but this too has its problems: the differences, already mentioned, as compared with Romans; perhaps the absence of any reference to the earthquake; the question whether Paul in Rome would have asked Philemon to have a room prepared for him in anticipation of a visit (Philem. 22), when in Romans he writes as if his work in the East was at an end and his eyes were turned to regions

---

[59] On the whole question see now Wedderburn, *Baptism and Resurrection*; also 'The Theology of Colossians'. Pokorný (3; cf. also §13, pp. 126ff.) remarks that the difference between 2.12f. and the analogous statements in Rom. 6.5f. excludes the possibility of dating Colossians in the vicinity of Romans. Cranfield ('Romans 6.1-14 Revisited') argues that 'for Paul, there are four different senses in which we may speak of our dying with Christ and (corresponding to them) four different senses in which we may speak of our being raised with him', and that these need to be carefully distinguished. On this showing the difference between Col. 3 and Rom. 6 is not so great as has sometimes been thought (see Commentary below on Col. 3).

further west (Rom. 15.22–24, 28); moreover some have regarded Philippians as the last of Paul's letters.

With somewhat greater plausibility Pokorný (12) suggests that in view of the common elements, which are also present in addition to the differences, Philippians might be considered as 'a theological link' between the major Pauline epistles and Colossians. That would appear to tell against placing Philippians in Ephesus, since it would have to follow at some distance after the major letters; if Philippians was written from Rome, this in turn would make it more difficult to find a place for Colossians within the context of what we know of Paul's life, and would hence provide a further indication of its pseudonymous character.[60]

Thus far, the relation between Colossians and the other Pauline letters has been considered mainly from the point of view of the question of authenticity: do the similarities noted point to Pauline authorship, or do the differences preclude it? There is, however, another aspect: these similarities could be evidence of dependence on the part of Colossians, particularly on Romans and Philippians (cf. Lohse, 182, emphasizing the Pauline school tradition, rather than strictly literary dependence; Schenk (*ANRW* II.25.4, 3342 and n. 51) regards the eleven words shared with the Pauline 'homologoumena' as reminiscences derived from the major letters). Collins (*Letters*, 184f.) notes that modern scholars 'are inclined to the view that any suggestion of the dependence of Colossians upon earlier Pauline texts should be taken as an indication of its inauthenticity'. If there are grounds for suspicion that the letter is pseudonymous, the similarities which have been noted could be interpreted as indications of the author's familiarity with Paul's language and ideas, while the differences point to his own independence of thought. The disciple has carried his master's teaching further, in the face of a new situation. This reasoning is not so circular as might appear: the conclusion that Colossians is not an authentic Pauline letter does not depend on any one argument, for none in itself is conclusive; it rests upon the cumulative effect of a whole series of arguments taken together.

---

[60] Posing the question whether Paul himself could have developed his theology into that of Colossians, Wendland already makes three points (*Die hellenistisch-romische Kultur*, 364): (1) there is not sufficient time for the bridging of the gulf which separates Col. from Rom. and Phil.; (2) Col. and Eph. are intended to be taken as written at the same time in prison, i.e. in Rome; but (3) Phil. certainly belongs to the Roman imprisonment, and therefore stands so close in time to Col. that the difference in theological views, in tone and style, is difficult to understand. This makes the authenticity of Col. doubtful. A footnote adds that to place Col., Eph. and Philem. in an imprisonment in Caesarea produces a sequence which gives rise to even greater difficulties: Rom., Col., (Eph.), Phil.

E Conclusions

It is now time to draw the threads together, and attempt to formulate, at least provisionally, such conclusions as may seem to emerge from the discussion; provisionally, because we have still to consider the nature of the Colossian 'heresy', which may have a bearing on the questions raised above. In the first place, we should probably dispose of the 'amanuensis theory' once and for all. As indicated above, there is no doubt that Paul did on occasion avail himself of the services of a secretary, but that does not mean that he always did so. Moreover, to invoke this theory in the effort to preserve some measure of authenticity is a desperate expedient, which does not in fact succeed: it only pushes the problem a stage further back. If the secretary copied down what Paul dictated, then it is truly Paul's letter, but we are still faced with the problem of accounting for those peculiarities of style and language which have led scholars to question the authenticity of Colossians. On the other hand, if Paul merely indicated in general terms what he wished to say, and left the precise formulation to the secretary, then it is open to question how far we can really call it a Pauline letter. The greater the part played by the amanuensis, the less ground we have for accepting the letter as authentic. Indeed there comes a point where one must ask if it would not be simpler to assume a letter written in Paul's name by some disciple, whether during the apostle's lifetime, when Paul for some reason was not able to attend to the matter himself, or in a new situation after Paul's death, when a disciple sought to apply his master's teaching to meet new problems. The weakness of the amanuensis theory is quite simply that it does not fulfil the function for which it is advanced.

We are therefore left with the choice between three alternatives: to accept the letter as authentically Pauline, to assume composition in Paul's name by some disciple during Paul's lifetime, or to consider it as a piece of pseudepigraphy. It should be emphasized once again that the last option does not necessarily carry with it the stigma of fraud or forgery. That might apply in the case of a work written to propound some heretical doctrine, and as noted above many such works were later to be stigmatized as apocryphal or heretical, and therefore rejected. In the case of New Testament pseudepigrapha, however, the situation is somewhat different: these works came to be recognized by the Church as valid and authentic witnesses to the genuine Christian faith. The judgement as to their authenticity may have been mistaken, but it may have been their orthodoxy that carried the day, their conformity with the Church's rule of faith. They witness to what the Church believed. It should also perhaps be emphasized that the arguments advanced against authenticity by responsible modern scholars are not arbitrary or destructive; they arise from real problems encountered in the effort to achieve a historical reconstruction of the situation in which the letter in question was composed, to fit it into what we know of the context of Paul's life and ministry.

In a survey published in 1989, Victor Furnish writes that 'one cannot speak of even an embryonic consensus about Colossians' ('Pauline Studies', 326).[61] The authenticity of the letter is still maintained by some scholars, and is a perfectly reputable position; but there are factors which for others weigh in the balance against it.

W. Schmithals (*Neues Testament und Gnosis*, 67) lists as supporting Pauline authorship: Lohmeyer; Lähnemann, *Der Kolosserbrief*, 1971, 177ff. (but at p. 181 Lähnemann appears to leave the question open, and much of his argument in these pages seems to point to a deutero-Pauline author); Kümmel, 1973 edn, 298ff. (ET 1975, 340ff.). To these we may add Guthrie, Moule and others mentioned above. (Stephen Neill, in *Interpretation of the New Testament*, 59, writes, 'British scholarship is almost unanimous in accepting the authenticity of Colossians' (cf. also 343). C. K. Barrett however (*Adam*, 83 n. 3) observes that 'the case for non-Pauline authorship is stronger than it is often felt in England to be'. Moreover, things may have changed in the past thirty years).

As supporting indirect Pauline authorship Schmithals lists Suhl, *Paulus*, 168 n. 93 (through Epaphras; but cf. Lähnemann 181f. n. 82); Schweizer (through Timothy); Ollrog, *Paulus*, 236ff. (through some fellow-worker—cf. Wedderburn—but there is much to be said for Timothy). Mention of Timothy in the superscription does not, however, mean that he was the secretary responsible (cf. 2 Cor. 1.1; Phil. 1.1; 1 Thess. 1.1; 2 Thess. 1.1: these letters do not show the stylistic peculiarities of Colossians, although the samples must be considered rather small for any comparison leading to a final judgement). The suggestion of Epaphras must be considered speculative; for one thing, could he have written of himself in such laudatory terms? It would seem rather that part of the purpose of the letter is to strengthen the authority of Epaphras (Lähnemann, *Der Kolosserbrief*, 181; cf. already Marxsen, *Introduction*, 178, 181, 184).

In a survey of research in the past twenty years, Hoppe (*Triumph*, 1) sees only Blanke among German-speaking scholars (*Eine Auslegung von Kol 1 und 2* (1987)) as attempting to trace back Colossians to Paul himself, but notes Melick (*Philippians, Colossians, Philemon* (1991)) and O'Brien (*Colossians and Philemon*) as taking the same view; to these we may further add Wright and Barth (114–26; he advocates the maxim 'innocent until proved guilty' (125)). More recently Aletti (280) concludes: 'on peut non seulement déclarer que l'épître est paulinienne, mais qu'elle est très probablement de Paul'. Cf. also the list in Arnold, *Syncretism*, 7 n. 10.

Schmithals' own view is a variation of the theory advanced by Holtzmann and others (cf. for example Moffatt, *Introduction*, 156ff., who speaks disparagingly of 'such filigree criticism' ; Guthrie, *NT*, 168 n. 3; Kümmel, 1975 edn, 340; Schenke and Fischer, 169; Lohse, 90–91; Schenk, *ANRW* II.25.4, 3341 and n. 46; for some criticisms cf. Wedderburn, *Baptism and Resurrection*, 77 n. 4): an original authentic Colossians was edited by a later hand to introduce the anti-Gnostic polemic as an interpolation. This is not of course impossible, but we have no evidence of any such earlier form of Colossians and it is difficult to imagine the whole process being completed at so early a stage. Moreover if the original 'authentic' letter was directed at a Jewish-Christian group the absence of the *Rechtfertigungsterminologie* is difficult to explain: as Lohse writes (87), 'the epistle to the Colossians is engaged in a controversy with a legalistic doctrine, and it is quite peculiar that the very terms which actually could be expected to occur in such a confrontation are exactly the ones which are missing'. This of course refers to Colossians as we now know it, but Schmithals (76) thinks of the original letter as warning against a Judaizing legalism. It is, however, significant that Schmithals

---

[61] In a later paper (*JBL* 113 (1994), 5), Furnish describes Col. as 'perhaps the earliest of the pseudo-Paulines', and notes that 'At the same time a certain *Paulusbild* emerges from Colossians, which likely reflects the place that this author himself assumes the apostle to have in the church'. See also his article on Colossians in *ABD* i. 1090–96. Dunn's suggestion (see n. 63) that Col. is a bridge between the major letters and the pseudo-Paulines is in some respects not so widely different.

(72ff.) tends to play down the 'Gnostic' element in the Colossian heresy. In his *Die Briefe des Paulus* (165ff.) he sets out both his reconstructed 'original' letter and the interpolations (1.9–23; 2.2–4, 6–15; 2.18–19; 3.15b-4.1, with 3.25 and 4.1 interchanged; cf. Eph. 6.9).

Kümmel (1975 edn, 337) thinks that the community 'consisted predominantly of Gentile Christians (2:13; 1:21, 27)', and finds 'no sign of a Jewish-Christian element in the church there' ; but this must be considered doubtful: observance of new moons and sabbaths surely points to Judaism in some form.

There are the questions of style and language, the questions of content, the problem of fitting the letter into what we know of Paul's career and of finding a place for it in the sequence of Paul's accepted letters. None of these in itself is reason enough for doubting the authenticity of Colossians; it is the cumulative result of all these factors taken together that gives rise to suspicion. The problem of the place of writing also comes in here, since the letter is written from prison and it is by no means clear where that prison was. Ephesus, Rome and Caesarea have all been suggested, but there is another aspect to be considered: in 2 Corinthians, Paul—speaking 'as a fool'—is driven to boasting, of 'far greater labours, far more imprisonments, with countless floggings, and often near death'. Then he specifies that 'Five times I have received from the Jews the forty lashes minus one. Three times I was beaten with rods. Once I received a stoning' (2 Cor. 11.23–25 NRSV). Acts 14.19 documents the stoning (at Lystra), Acts 16.22f. one of the Roman beatings, but of the rest we know nothing. Presumably such punishments were associated with periods of imprisonment, but we cannot say when or where, and to suggest an answer is to venture into the realm of conjecture. A further point is that these beatings are not likely to have been merely token punishments. The Roman beatings were probably administered by some lictor who relished the task, and as for the Jewish 'forty lashes minus one' we need only recall the Jewish hostility to Paul that is recorded in Acts. Such punishment would probably entail a prolonged period of recuperation, when Paul might well have had to delegate the writing of letters to some of his associates.[62] Here again, however, we are reduced to speculation. It may, however, be observed that such a conjecture would fit in very well with the suggestion made by Wedderburn and others (above, p. 18 and n. 35) of a letter written by one of Paul's associates during the apostle's lifetime, at a time when Paul was not in a position to do the writing himself.

If Colossians is not authentic, there are two alternatives: A. J. M. Wedderburn's suggestion, just mentioned, and the view of Lohse, Schenke and others that it was written by some disciple after the apostle's death. Here much depends on our assessment of the nature

---

[62] On the severity of such punishments cf. Deissmann, *Paul*, 61–62. L. W. Hurtado writes, 'The "forty lashes minus one" represents a serious punishment for serious religious crimes' (*JTS* 50 (1999), 55; the whole article (35–58) is concerned with 'Pre-70 CE Jewish opposition to Christ-devotion'). But according to Acts (16.35ff.), despite his mishandling in Philippi and a night in prison, Paul was perfectly capable of setting out for Amphipolis the following day.

of the 'Colossian problem', whether it was a purely local matter or more concretely a form of incipient gnosis or Gnosticism. One possible objection to Wedderburn's suggestion might be that it savours of an attempt to bring in the amanuensis theory by another door,[63] and on that score it may be preferable to think of composition by some later disciple seeking to meet a new situation. The date would then have to be some years after the earthquake, to allow for the recovery of the local community, but not too near to the end of the century, since the 'heresy', if such it was, does not as yet appear to be very far advanced; moreover we have to allow for the writing of Ephesians, if it is in some way dependent on Colossians. On the alternative possibility outlined above, that the author deliberately avoided mention of the earthquake in order to convey the impression of a letter written within Paul's lifetime, the lapse of time need not have been so great; but in that case the 'heresy' was probably not specifically 'Colossian', but possibly more widespread. At all events, Ephesus might well be the place of writing, as the probable location of the 'Pauline school' [64] and also as being fairly close to Colossae itself.

On the assumption that Colossians is pseudonymous, one possible reconstruction of events might be that Philemon is a genuine letter, written perhaps from Rome about the same time as Philippians, or possibly, in view of the visit anticipated in Philem. 22, at an earlier date from Ephesus. As a private letter, it was not generally circulated, but it was preserved. Later it served as the basis and framework upon which some disciple constructed Colossians, using for example some of the names which are mentioned in Philemon to give a measure of verisimilitude to his own work. Ephesians, which is in turn based on Colossians, would be somewhat later, but still well within the first century.[65] Time would have to be allowed for this, so that Colossians

---

[63] This is not intended as an accusation, rather as a warning of a possible danger. The strongest candidate is undoubtedly Timothy, one of Paul's closest associates (suggested e.g. by Schweizer and more recently by Dunn), and in his case the objection probably would not apply. Placing the letter late in the Roman imprisonment, Dunn (35–41) sees 'a strong likelihood' that it was written by a hand other than Paul's, and suggests that it forms a bridge between the major Paulines and the post-Pauline letters (including Eph.); for him the question of authenticity is not so significant as has sometimes been thought.

[64] So for example Lohse, 181; Gnilka, 22; Schenke and Fischer, 168, 244; Pokorný, 18, among others.

[65] According to Moffatt (*Introduction*, 154), 'The traces of Colossians in the earlier half of the second century literature are both dim and dubious' (see his survey). Guthrie, however, notes (100) that there are reminiscences of Eph. in Clement of Rome, Ignatius, Polycarp, Hermas and possibly the *Didache*, and that most scholars are agreed that it must be earlier than *1 Clement* (AD 95). W. Bauer on the other hand claims that 'we are unable to detect even the faintest trace prior to Marcion', and suggests that it was Marcion who brought Colossians (and Philemon) to the West (*Orthodoxy and Heresy* (ET 1971), 222). Later (235) he raises the possibility that Epaphras was 'not entirely blameless' with regard to the introduction of syncretistic ideas at Colossae, or at any rate failed to eliminate such ideas which were already present; here Bauer seems to regard Col. as authentic. Cf. E. Best's discussion of the early evidence for knowledge of Eph. in *ANRW* II.25.4, 3257–63.

cannot be dated very far into the second half of the century; this might suggest a date somewhere between AD 70 and 75.[66]

Such tentative and hesitant conclusions will not, of course, satisfy those who must at all costs have a definite and clear-cut answer to every question, but there are times when it is important to recognize the limitations of our knowledge. We do not always have the evidence upon which to base a firm judgement. In such cases we may review the various possibilities suggested, the arguments advanced in favour of this alternative or that, and form a judgement as to which is the most likely solution; but it is only by identifying the problems, and determining the strengths and the weaknesses of the suggestions offered, that we can hope to make any real progress—and sometimes the only hope of progress lies in some completely new discovery. On many issues there is at present only too much justification for Furnish's judgement, noted above, that 'one cannot speak of even an embryonic consensus about Colossians'.[67]

IV. THE COLOSSIAN HERESY[68]

There has been vigorous discussion of the Colossian 'heresy' for more than a hundred years, and various theories have been propounded. Broadly speaking, the main positions are already exemplified in the older commentaries; other theories are to a large

---

[66] Gnilka (27f.) and Pokorný (18), for example, suggest about AD 70 or later; Lindemann ('Gemeinde', 134) thinks of a period between about AD 65/70 and 80, but that a more exact dating is not possible. Schenk (*ANRW* II.25.4, 3344, (n. 54) thinks that, on the basis of the author's use of a collection of Paul's letters and of Marcan redaction, a date around AD 80 is more likely than around 70. Hübner (10) puts the *terminus a quo* after Paul's death, the *terminus ad quem* scarcely after 70. Goulder (*NTS* 41 (1995), 602 n. 9) thinks of the 60s.

[67] M. Hengel (*NTS* 40 (1994), 333 n. 39) writes that Col. is perhaps to be reckoned genuine—but only perhaps: 'Das historische Rätsel dieses Briefes läßt sich mit unserem Wissenstand m.E. nicht lösen'.

[68] Cf. Yamauchi, *Pre-Christian Gnosticism*, 44–47, 197. At p. 162 he writes, 'The Colossian heresy clearly betrays Jewish elements, but it cannot be shown to be Gnostic beyond dispute. This does not, of course, deny the possibility or even the probability that such a Jewish-tinged Gnosticism may have existed.' For a brief survey illustrating 'the tremendous diversity of opinion' on the subject, see Sappington, *Revelation and Redemption*, 15–17; he concludes, 'There is at present simply no consensus on this question', an opinion echoed by DeMaris (*Controversy*, 12). Cf. Hoppe, *Triumph*, 125: 'Die Bandbreite der Ergebnisse—von der Annahme judaistischer Frömmigkeitspraxis bis zu gnostisierenden Mysterien-kreisen ist fast alles vertreten—zeigt, auf welch unsicherem Boden man sich bei dieser (allerdings nicht zu umgehenden) Aufgabe befindet, die sicher auch nicht ganz ohne Hypothesen auskommt.' On pp. 125–37 he gives a succinct critical survey of the views advanced by various modern scholars: Dibelius, Lohmeyer, Percy, Bornkamm, Schenke, Lohse, Lähnemann and Schweizer. Cf. also Aletti, 13–20; Barth, 28–39; Hübner, 94–97. In his history of scholarship on the Colossian philosophy (*Controversy*, 18–40) DeMaris identifies five distinct schools of interpretation (38), all of which have their shortcomings (96). His own view (summarized at 17) sees the Colossian 'philosophy' as 'a distinctive blend of popular Middle Platonic, Jewish, and Christian elements that cohere around the pursuit of wisdom'. For a recent survey, with abundant references, see Standhartinger, *Studien*, 16–27.

extent variations upon these themes. It must, however, be noted that the discoveries at Qumran and Nag Hammadi, together with intensive investigations into the background of the New Testament, Jewish and Hellenistic, have in some respects materially altered the whole situation; we are now able to draw upon resources unknown to earlier generations. In more recent studies, the tendency has been more and more to 'specialize' and claim one particular factor as the dominant element; but the very range and variety of the suggestions offered prompts to caution. As will be seen, there is even yet no real consensus, except in very general terms, as to the precise nature of this 'heresy'.

Lightfoot notes two errors, one theological, the other practical, but both springing from the same source: the conception of matter as the origin and abode of evil. He also detected two distinct elements—one Judaic and one Gnostic—although he observes that it does not follow that they represent the teaching of two distinct parties. He traced the heresy back to the Essenes, on whom he has a long discussion of some 65 pages.[69] In his view Essene Judaism was Gnostic in character, and had established itself in Asia Minor in the apostolic age. The link between the incipient *gnosis* of the Colossian heretics and the mature *gnosis* of the second century he finds in Cerinthus, the traditional opponent of St John. It should however be added that he expressly says (94–95), 'when I speak of the Judaism in the Colossian Church as Essene, I do not assume a precise identity of origin, but only an essential affinity of type'.

Peake on the other hand says that it is difficult to find full-blown Gnosticism mirrored in the letter, and that it is improbable that we

---

[69] Moffatt (153) already writes: 'The affinities with Essenism ... do not amount to much; the parallel on angel-worship breaks down, the practice of asceticism differs, and other traits of the Colossian errorists do not correspond exactly to those of the Essenes'. On the other hand P. Benoit, after the Qumran discovery, says 'As J.B. Lightfoot suspected, and recent discoveries have confirmed, the error combated by the epistle to the Colossians appears to be tainted with Essenism. A return to the Mosaic Law by circumcision, rigid observance concerning diet and the calendar, speculations about the angelic powers; all this is part and parcel of the doctrines of Qumran. Paul himself can hardly have been unaware of the writings of the sect when writing Col 1:12-13' ('Qumrân et le Nouveau Testament', ET 16f.; cf. also his ''Αγιοι en Colossiens 1.12'). W. D. Davies had already noted that the Scrolls 'present what seem to be specific points of contact with the Colossian heresy' (*Christian Origins and Judaism*, 157). Kümmel, 1975, however, writes (339), 'it is scarcely a matter of Jewish nomism related to Qumran'. On the parallels which have been detected see Braun, *Qumran und das Neue Testament*, ii. 228–33. Lincoln (*Paradise*, 117) observes, 'there is no reference to the Mosaic law as such in Colossians and the use to which strict observance of ascetic and cultic regulations and interest in angelic worship were put is markedly different in the two cases, providing no warrant for too close an identification'. It is perhaps significant that Benoit (ibid.) adds, 'Literary influence of Qumran is still more striking in Ephesians', which for him was written at the same time and to churches in the same region. The evidence relating to Ephesians is set out in two articles in the same volume, by K. G. Kuhn (115ff.) and F. Mussner (159ff.); there is no article relating specifically to Colossians. Cf. also Saunders, 'The Colossian Heresy and Qumran Theology', and Murphy-O'Connor, 'Qumran and the New Testament', 60–61. Aletti (15 n. 12) observes that while there is evidence for Essenes at various places in Judaea, there is none for their possible migration to Asia Minor.

have Gnosticism here even in a rudimentary form. The Jewish nature of the false teaching is, however, evident from the references to observance of rules as to meats and drinks, festivals, new moons and sabbaths, and from the value apparently attached to circumcision and the Law. Lightfoot's theory he sets aside on the ground that some of the most striking features of Gnosticism are absent, and he tries to explain the doctrine of angels envisaged in Colossians from developments in late Judaism: 'A worship of angels, such as was inculcated by the false teachers, was quite a natural application of the Jewish doctrine' (482). On the other hand he notes that we have evidence that the Phrygian Jews 'compromised with heathenism to an extent possible only to those who held their ancestral faith most loosely' (478),[70] and he remarks that Paul does not, as in Galatians, attack with arguments drawn from the OT, probably because his opponents might have evaded their force by allegorical interpretation (487).

Scott refers to Lightfoot as tracing the heresy to the Essenes, and to others as finding affinities with the ideas of Cerinthus, but adds, 'these efforts to attach a particular label to the heresy may all be regarded as futile'.[71] His own view is that the heresy was one of many attempts to make Christianity an element in some form of composite religion, that 'teachers at Colossae were beginning to do what the Gnostics sought to do later on a more ambitious scale', namely to fit fragments of the Christian message into a framework mainly composed of pagan mythology and metaphysics. He notes as exceptional the place given to Jewish contributions, but explains this from the special conditions of the Lycus valley. The teachers may have been of Jewish birth, but apparently claimed to be Christians

---

[70] W. L. Knox, however, (*PCG*, 146f.) says, 'The Talmud records the fact that the luxuries of Phrygia separated the Jews of that region from their brethren, a statement which suggests rather a worldly wisdom, avoiding too much stiffness in refusing to share the public life of the Gentiles, than a serious adoption of heathen religion'. Trebilco (*Jewish Communities*, 142) finds no evidence that Judaism in Asia Minor was syncretistic or had been compromised by paganism. He speaks of a 'strong retention of Jewish identity', despite close relations with the pagan environment (187). Dunn (31) writes, 'the evidence of Jewish syncretism in these diaspora communities is lacking, despite older claims to the contrary'.

[71] Cf. Moffatt, 152: 'It is improbable that any definite system was being propagated. The likelihood is rather that the local Christians were being affected by a syncretistic, eclectic movement of thought, fostered by esoteric tendencies in the local Judaism'. This to some extent anticipates the view advanced by M. D. Hooker (see n. 72 below). More recently Schenke (162) suggests, on the basis of some Nag Hammadi texts, that in Colossians we have to do with the same branch of the Gnostic movement that later found expression in the classic Cerinthianism. He regards the heresy as 'die Gnosis' in a relatively early and Jewish-Christian form, but differs from the majority view in regard to its character and content. In contrast, Schenk (*ANRW* II.25.4, 3349–54, esp. 3350) argues that it is not a question of polemic against a heresy, but of immunizing the readers against a secession to Judaism. On the other hand Dunn (*Biblica* 76 (1995), 159) argues that the opponents' response to the Pauline gospel was not that of the Galatian Judaizers: it was not an attempt to convert Gentiles to full Judaism, but a supercilious dismissal of Paul's claim that Gentiles could be incorporated into the chosen race.

and professed to offer an improved Christianity, adding to the gospel all that was best in Judaism and paganism.

At first sight these three views seem quite distinct, and almost bewilderingly different; but to some extent it is a question of different shades of emphasis. Lightfoot, for example, speaks of an incipient *gnosis*, not a full-blown Gnosticism, and gives a place to the Judaic element; Peake lays a stronger emphasis on the Jewish element, and in consequence plays down the 'Gnostic' aspect. Scott is probably right in rejecting efforts to identify the heresy too closely,[72] but when Peake claims that we have no proof that the Essenes worshipped angels (486) he overlooks a passage in Josephus, where the names of the angels are among the things the initiate vowed to keep secret; this of course does not expressly indicate that the Essenes worshipped angels, but it surely means that they attached some significance and importance to them, and presumably they were just as likely to be tempted to worship angels as were other Jews.[73] However, some

---

[72] Cf. M. D. Hooker, who questions whether there was any explicit 'false teaching' at Colossae at all; she suggests that Paul's teaching in the letter is 'quite as appropriate to a situation in which young Christians are under pressure to conform to the beliefs and practices of their pagan and Jewish neighbours, as to a situation in which their faith is endangered by the deliberate attacks of false teachers' (329). Similarly Wright argues that 'the writer is not opposing an actual heresy in the church, but is writing to warn a young church against the blandishments of the synagogue which had proved so devastating to the young church in Galatia . . . a claim is being made for Christ (and his people) which has a double cutting edge'—first against Judaism and second against paganism—'a community that believed these things would be distinct from neighbours both Jewish and pagan' (463f.); but cf. Aletti 18 n. 35. Cf. also Koester, *Trajectories*, 144 n. 86.

[73] On Jewish angelolatry cf. Simon, *Le christianisme antique*, 450–64 (for Colossians see esp. 456ff.). Lightfoot (90) already quotes Josephus (*B.J.* ii.8.7 (ii.139–42)), italicizing 'the names of the angels' and adding 'It may be reasonably supposed that more lurks under this last expression than meets the ear. . . . At all events we seem to be justified in connecting it with the self-imposed service and worshipping of angels at Colossae.' In his note on 2.18 he cites the *Preaching of Peter*, quoted in Clement of Alexandria, *Strom.* vi.5, which speaks of the Jews λατρεύοντες ἀγγέλοις καὶ ἀρχαγγέλοις. A. L. Williams (*Colossians*, pp. xxiiff.) devotes a whole chapter to 'The Doctrine and Worship of Angels', and concludes that the Jews did not worship angels, but that under certain conditions they might be tempted to do so, especially in attempts to ward off disease by the use of magical practices: there is no question of worship, but only of invoking their names as a means of gaining power against the attacks of evil spirits. (See also Arnold, who seeks to build on the foundation laid by Williams, but apparently knows only the latter's *JTS* article, not his commentary. For Jewish veneration of angels see esp. Arnold, *Syncretism*, 32–60.) L. W. Hurtado (*One God, One Lord*, 24ff., esp. 28–35) argues against Jewish worship of angels, and regards the accusations in certain Christian writings as 'theologically motivated interpretations of Jewish ritual observances' in the interest of polemic against Judaism. He stresses the idea of divine agency, 'in which God is understood as having given a unique place and role to this or that heavenly figure who becomes something like a grand vizier of the imperial court' (39). Such figures—an angel, a personified divine attribute, a patriarch—did not in any way detract from the unique status and sovereignty of God, and certainly were not objects of worship. In some texts the 'chief angel', although accorded the highest rank and honour, specifically refuses worship which is due to God alone. In particular the Qumran texts 'give no indication that any of

recent studies have questioned whether what is in view in Colossians is a worship of angels, and not rather a worship offered by them (see below); this would make the question whether the Essenes worshipped angels largely irrelevant. At any rate, the general picture is the same in all three views: the heresy was a combination of alien elements with Christian belief which threatened to submerge the Christian in the pagan (or rather: non-Christian) and so destroy the very essence of the faith. A general indication is not too difficult to come by—it is when we try to be more specific that the problems arise. Moffatt (153) lists a string of suggestions, remarking that 'the compass has been pretty well boxed in the endeavour to ascertain the direction of Paul's refutation in Colossians', and the list has been expanded and elaborated by Gunther and Kiley.[74]

The difficulty arises from our lack of detailed knowledge on which to build our understanding of the period as a whole, and the background of this letter in particular. On the one hand, scholars in the past tended to look at Judaism too much from the point of view of the Rabbinic type, but it is now clear that in the New Testament period Judaism was much more varied than once was thought. E. R. Goodenough, for example, has collected archaeological evidence which in his opinion proves that some Jews employed pagan symbols as means for the expression of their own religious hopes and aspirations, and that even in Palestine.[75] Again, in the writings of Philo of Alexandria we have an attempt to interpret the OT in terms of Greek philosophy, and it is fairly probable that Philo was not an isolated figure.[76] And again, Lightfoot, Peake and Scott all wrote

---

God's angels were to receive worship', even principal angel figures such as Michael or Melchizedek (82–85). Other scholars simply reject worship of angels as quite un-Jewish. According to Baur (*Paul*, ii. 29), the Ebionites placed the angels 'in a co-ordinate relation to Christ', ascribing to them a redeeming function and regarding Christ as only ἕνα τῶν ἀρχαγγέλων. This does not appear to be altogether justified by the passage which he cites (Epiphanius, *Panarion* xxx.16.2), which does speak of Christ as 'created as one of the archangels' and as ruler 'both of angels and of all creatures' (16.4, tr. Williams), but does not mention any redeeming function of the angels; but shortly thereafter (17.4) Epiphanius speaks of Ebionites invoking 'heaven and earth, salt and water, winds and "angels of righteousness"' in cases of illness. The point of this reference is that the elements here invoked along with the angels are not too far removed from the Empedoclean στοιχεῖα; the 'elemental spirits of the universe' of Col. 2.8, 20 might conceivably be not the Gnostic archons but just these elements (see Commentary *ad loc.*).

[74] J. J. Gunther, *St Paul's Opponents and their Background* (1973); Kiley, *Colossians as Pseudepigraphy*. Aletti (13) remarks that Gunther 'en relève une bonne cinquantaine d'hypothèses'.
[75] *Jewish Symbols in the Greco-Roman Period* (1953–68). Trebilco (*Jewish Communities*, 44–45, 49–50, 57, 143–44, 176; cf. also 53–54) speaks of Jews and pagans sharing terms and images, but without prejudice to Jewish identity. Indeed he sees the conversion of a pagan building in Sardis into a synagogue as an indication of 'the boldness and strength of the community's Judaism' (54).
[76] On Philo and Gnosticism cf. Simon, 'Eléments gnostiques chez Philon'; Pearson, 'Philo, Gnosis and the New Testament' and 'Philo and Gnosticism'; Wilson, 'Philo and Gnosticism'. Cf. also P. Borgen, *Philo of Alexandria, An Exegete for his Time* (1997), 5–7.

before the discovery of the Dead Sea Scrolls, which have opened up fresh aspects for the study of primitive Christianity and its Jewish background. When these texts were first discovered, they were claimed to provide the missing evidence for a pre-Christian Jewish Gnosticism, but it was in fact quite remarkable how quickly these claims subsided.[77] The Scrolls are certainly important for the antecedents of Gnosticism, as they are for the background of the New Testament generally; but they are not yet 'Gnostic' in the sense in which that term is used with reference to the 'classic' systems of the second Christian century. Moreover, so far as Colossians itself is concerned, we have further problems: for one thing that of dating the spread of ideas from Qumran to Asia Minor.

The most obvious suggestion would link this with refugees from Qumran after the destruction of the settlement there; but that probably took place well after Paul's death.[78] Parallels are undoubtedly present, and some are noted in the Commentary below;[79] but we must also ask what these parallels signify. Are they merely chance verbal agreements, of no material significance? Or perhaps agreements due to a common Jewish background, in the Old Testament for example? Or are they such as to suggest a direct borrowing? Even in this last case we must also ask whether the elements taken over are used in the same way and with the same meaning.[80] Finally, we have

---

[77] Cf. W. D. Davies, *Christian Origins and Judaism*, 119ff., 136ff.; B. Reicke, *NTS* 1 (1954/55), 137–41; H. Ringgren in Bianchi (ed.), *Le Origini dello Gnosticismo*, 379–84; M. Mansoor in Bianchi (ed.), *Le Origini dello Gnosticismo*, 389–400; M. Wilcox in *The Scrolls and Christianity*, ed. M. Black (1969), 88–93; I. Gruenwald, *Israel Oriental Studies*, iii (1973), 63–107; Yamauchi, *Pre-Christian Gnosticism*, 151–56; Huppenbauer, *Der Mensch zwischen zwei Welten*, 12. Davies (157ff.) observes that the Scrolls 'present what seem to be specific points of contact with the Colossian heresy', but he also notes certain differences.

[78] Murphy-O'Connor (*RB* 81 (1974), 225) suggests that Essenes were among the Jews transported by Antiochus III (223–187 BC) from Babylon (cf. his 'Qumran and the New Testament', 61, where he refers (without reference to Lightfoot!) to the 'plausible hypothesis' that the Colossian heresy had its roots in an Essene-type theology). But the origin of the Essene movement is dated to the early part of the second century BC (Schürer, ii. 560, 586), which may raise questions of chronology; and were there Essenes in Babylon? Cf. Schürer, ii. 586 n. 51. Alternatively, 'serious attention will have to be given to the proposal that, after the destruction of Qumran, some members of the community fled to Asia Minor' (Murphy-O'Connor, 'Qumran and the New Testament', 61, referring to F. M. Braun, *RB* 62 (1955), 35). As noted above, that takes us into a period after Paul's death.

[79] Lohse in his commentary provides extensive references to the Qumran literature, which need not be repeated here.

[80] H. Braun (233) quotes K. G. Kuhn's judgement that in its special terminology and way of thinking Colossians stands particularly close to the Qumran texts; he adds that his own analysis has confirmed but also delimited this judgement. He also notes Graystone's comment that the Qumran influence ensued not in the beginnings of Christianity but in the course of the apostolic period, which might have some significance for the dating of the letter. For Lohse on the other hand (129) the adherents of the Colossian 'philosophy' cannot be considered Essenes or members of the Qumran community: 'the elements of the "philosophy" taken from Jewish tradition are not impregnated with the idea of radical legalism as is the case at Qumran' (n. 118).

evidence in this very region of Phrygia of some curious amalgamations of Jewish and pagan thought in the cults of Sabazius and of Zeus Hypsistos.[81] The problem is to reach a clear and balanced judgement.

On the other hand there have been developments also in the study of Gnosticism, which first attracted the attention of scholars as a heresy of the second Christian century.[82] It was long regarded as the result of the contamination of Christianity by Greek philosophy—in Harnack's phrase, the acute Hellenization of Christianity—but in the last century or so increasing stress has been laid on the 'oriental' element. The origins of the movement are not yet clear, but there is no question that we can trace particular elements far back to their sources in primitive religion. The danger here has been aptly summed up as that of 'motif methodology'.[83] It is easy enough to identify terms and concepts which appear in the developed systems of the second Christian century, and may therefore legitimately be described as 'Gnostic'. Sometimes, however, scholars have traced such motifs back to pre-Christian times, assumed that they are 'Gnostic' there also, and so produced divergent and conflicting claims to have discovered the 'origins' of Gnosticism. But were these terms and concepts already Gnostic at such earlier stages? The problem is to find the point at which these elements are combined

[81] On Sabazius cf. Trebilco (*Jewish Communities*, 140ff.), who finds no evidence that Jews identified Yahweh with Sabazius: 'Popular etymology is the most likely explanation for the very limited and solely pagan identification of the two gods'; see also Hengel, *Judaism and Hellenism*, i. 263f. For Hypsistos cf. Roberts, Skeat and Nock, 'The Gild of Zeus Hypsistos', *HTR* 29 (1936), 39–88, partly repr. in Nock, *Essays on Religion and the Ancient World*, 414–43; for Theos Hypsistos in the Bible see Simon, *Le Christianisme*, 495–508; Simon notes (499) the apologetic intention underlying the use of the designation, but also the danger of syncretism latent in that use—of which the Jews were fully aware. Cf. Trebilco, 127ff.; Hengel, index *s.v.* 'Highest'; Schürer, index *s.v.* 'Theos Hypsistos'; Arnold, *Syncretism*, 370, index *s.v.* 'Gods'. For Bornkamm ('Die Häresie des Kolosserbriefs', ET 135–37) it is 'indubitable' that the Hypsistos cult is the root of the fourth-century sect of the Hypsistarians, but he notes that 'The paucity of extant witnesses prevents our ascertaining whether specific speculations about stars and elements were already connected with the faith in Hypsistos in earlier times' (136). See also Bertram, *TWNT*, viii. 613–19.

[82] Cf. Bultmann, *Primitive Christianity*, 162ff. The best and most comprehensive modern study of Gnosticism is Rudolph, *Gnosis*. For bibliography, particularly in regard to the Nag Hammadi Gnostic library, see Scholer, *Nag Hammadi Bibliography 1948–1969* and annual supplements in *Novum Testamentum*; the supplements for 1970–94 are now incorporated into a second volume (NHMS 32, 1997). Among older works, reference may be made to Jonas, *Gnosis und spätantiker Geist* and *The Gnostic Religion*; R. M. Grant, *Gnosticism and Early Christianity* (2nd edn 1966); Wilson, *The Gnostic Problem, Gnosis and the New Testament* and 'Gnosis/Gnostizismus II' (with bibliography). See also G. Filoramo, *A History of Gnosticism* (ET 1990); Tröger, *Die Gnosis*. For Egypt, cf. B. A. Pearson, *Gnosticism and Christianity in Roman and Coptic Egypt* (2004).

[83] Cf. R. Haardt in Tröger (ed.), *Gnosis und Neues Testament*, 183–202; H. A. Green, *Numen* 24 (1977), 95–134.

into a system which can truly be called Gnostic in the second-century sense of the term.

Many scholars, particularly in Germany, claim that the movement, for which they prefer to use the term 'Gnosis', is pre-Christian, and some indeed regard Christianity itself as only part of a wider movement—but here there is room for further consideration, and for a much more accurate definition of terms. Alan Richardson, for example, objects that those scholars who speak of Gnosticism in the first century draw their evidence from the New Testament itself, which he calls 'a question-begging proceeding';[84] but we may ask whether he could have written thus if translators had retained the term 'Gnosis', which German scholars used, instead of substituting the English term 'Gnosticism', which is often employed in a somewhat narrower sense. Richardson himself in the context admits 'that certain notions were "in the air" in the later part of the first century, such as subsequently crystallized into the doctrines of the Gnostic sects about which we learn from such writers as Irenaeus in the second century'. In point of fact the false teaching refuted in the NT often has distinct affinities with the second-century heresy commonly described as Gnosticism. On the other hand, some modern authors use the term so loosely that it becomes simply a general label for the kind of syncretistic thought that was current in the background of the NT period.[85]

One thing has, however, become increasingly clear in recent years: if the Gnostics of the second century were in many ways anti-Jewish[86] there was nonetheless a considerable Jewish element in their systems, and some would claim that there was a Jewish Gnosticism

[84] *Introduction to New Testament Theology* (1958), 41f.

[85] H. J. Schoeps for example (*Urgemeinde, Judenchristentum, Gnosis,* 30) writes that most authors operate with concepts so ill-defined that the polemics in which they engage become sham fights, because each evidently understands something different by 'gnosis'. The problem is further complicated when translators render the German *Die Gnosis* by 'Gnosticism', which often has somewhat narrower connotations, referring more specifically to the developed second-century systems.

[86] Hans Jonas (in *The Bible in Modern Scholarship* (1965), 288) speaks of 'the anti-Jewish animus' with which Gnosticism is saturated, but at the same time notes (286) that the Gnostics 'made liberal use of Jewish material'. In *The Gnostic Religion* (33) he writes of 'the violently anti-Jewish bias of the more prominent gnostic systems', which, however, 'is by itself not incompatible with Jewish heretical origin at some distance'. The most obvious feature is of course the downgrading of the God of the Old Testament into a hostile Demiurge, but it is by no means clear that the Gnostics were uniformly hostile to Jews as such. Certainly they made quite extensive use of the Old Testament. In some of the Nag Hammadi texts, charges originally directed against the Jews are now levelled against the 'archons', which would seem to suggest that controversy with Jewish opponents was by this stage largely a thing of the past. Cf. Wilson, 'Anti-Semitism in Gnostic Writings'. See also Pearson's chapter 'Old Testament Interpretation in Gnostic Literature' in *Emergence of the Christian Religion*, 99–121.

before there was a Christian one.[87] In the most general terms, it is this kind of thinking—perhaps, as Moule puts it, a 'Gnostic' type of Judaism or a Jewish type of 'Gnosticism'—that is in the background of Colossians. According to Goppelt (*Apostolic and Post-Apostolic Times*, 101), 'Pre-Gnostic Judaism rather than legalistic Judaism, so Baur and his followers thought, was the dangerous trend with which Paul had to contend in his churches.' He thinks this 'clearly the case with the polemic of Colossians'. In his view the aberration in Philippi was brought into that church, as in Corinth, by Palestinian Jewish Christians who came as 'workers', whereas in Colossae the movement appears to have developed from within the church itself, possibly under the influence of a syncretistic Diaspora Judaism in her surroundings. However, when he goes on to claim that the character of this movement in Colossae and as depicted in the Pastorals is still the same as in Corinth, we must demur: as Goppelt himself notes, the ordinances which the community in Colossae was called upon to observe were Mosaic, but 'they had taken on a dualistic and ascetic significance (Col. ii.21)'.[88] It is quite frankly doubtful whether Paul's opponents were always uniformly of one and the same stamp, whether we identify them as Judaizers or as Gnostics or as Judaizing Gnostics. The evidence rather seems to suggest that Paul had to contend with different groups at different times and in different areas: Judaizers in Galatia, enthusiastic pneumatics in Corinth (who were not necessarily Gnostic in the full sense; and the opponents in 2 Corinthians may be a different group), and opponents of another sort in Colossae.

According to Grant (*Historical Introduction*, 206), 'All we can say about the Colossians situation is that there is nothing which seems to be specifically related to any form of Gnosticism which we know. Some of the terminology was employed by later Gnostics, but this fact proves nothing.' Vielhauer (192ff.) thinks of Gnosis in the form

[87] On the whole question cf. Yamauchi, *Pre-Christian Gnosticism*, 143–62, 233–43 and 'Jewish Gnosticism?'; Tröger, 'Gnosis und Judentum' and 'The Attitude of the Gnostic Religion towards Judaism'; also numerous articles by G. Quispel, collected in his *Gnostic Studies*, (cf. his 'Gnosticism and the New Testament'). An early advocate of the Jewish origins of the Gnostic religion was M. Friedländer, *Der vorchristliche jüdische Gnosticismus*; cf. Pearson, 'Friedländer Revisited', and most recently 'The Problem of "Jewish Gnostic" Literature' (other studies in the two volumes in which these articles appear are also relevant). Reservations are, however, expressed by Jonas (*The Bible in Modern Scholarship*, 286ff.), and van Unnik, ('Die jüdische Komponente in der Entstehung der Gnosis' and 'Gnosis und Judentum'). Cf. also Gruenwald, 'Knowledge and Vision' and 'Jewish Sources for the Gnostic Texts from Nag Hammadi'; Maier, 'Jüdische Faktoren bei der Entstehung der Gnosis?'

[88] Koester, on the other hand, after referring to the threat to Paul's missionary work from the Judaizers in Galatia, goes on to say, 'Soon after Paul's death (or departure from this area) a student of Paul tries to refute the same Judaizing antagonists in the Letter to the Colossians' (*Trajectories*, 144). In a footnote he adds that 'the heresy of Colossae was perhaps a more limited local phenomenon than is generally assumed' (cf. the view of M. D. Hooker mentioned at n. 72 above). Goppelt, however, (*Christentum und Judentum*, 138) notes differences between Gal. and Col. which suggest that the threat in Colossae was not the Judaizing tendency countered in Galatians.

of a mystery cult, and suggests that the author shares certain
presuppositions with his Gnostic opponents—more so than was the
case with Paul and the Corinthian pneumatics (201f.). He speaks of
'an important witness for the theological struggle within the church
against Christian Gnosis'. Koester on the other hand, although he
observes that the author of Colossians himself 'shows some affinity
to Gnosticism' (ii. 265), thinks the opponents were claiming to
present a 'philosophy' based on traditions which 'must have had a
Jewish origin', and that they probably practised rites of a mystery
character; but he adds 'It is doubtful, however, that this justifies their
characterization as Jewish-Christian gnostics'. That there are cosmic
powers who must be reckoned with was a widespread view at this
time. 'The opponents therefore were Jewish-Christian syncretists who
wanted to achieve a fresh interpretation of Jewish rites and rules of
cultic purity in accord with the religious thinking of their time, thus
adapting the worship of Christ to the general world-view of
Hellenism' (ii. 264f.).

From this survey it will be clear that there is still no consensus on
this question, beyond the general recognition mentioned at the
beginning, that there are both Jewish and 'Gnostic' elements present
in the 'philosophy'.[89] Reference should also perhaps be made to the
remarkable fact that Schmithals in his *Paulus und die Gnostiker*[90] has
no chapter devoted to Colossians—something particularly remarkable for one who has been accused of *Pangnostizismus*.

Our one source of information about the false teaching opposed in
Colossians is the letter itself, but before we turn to examine it some
words of warning are in order.[91] It might appear that all we have to

[89] Dunn (31) writes, 'The easy both–and solution to the dispute about the Colossian
"heresy"—viz. neither Jewish nor Hellenistic syncretism, but Jewish/Hellenistic
syncretism—is not supported by the evidence regarding the Jewish communities in
Asia Minor.' In his view, 'we need look no further than one or more of the Jewish
synagogues in Colossae for the source of whatever influences were thought to threaten
the young church there' (34). See his discussion (33–35) of 'The Trouble at Colossae',
also his 'The Colossian Philosophy'.

[90] ET *Paul and the Gnostics* (1972). Cf. also his *Neues Testament und Gnosis* (1984),
67–80, where he argues (76ff.) that the deutero-Pauline author of our canonical
Colossians has applied Paul's original polemic to the false teachers of his own time
(thus, like others (see his p. 68), following Holtzmann; see also his 'The Corpus
Paulinum', 117–21). One difficulty with this view is that we have no evidence for the
existence of any such earlier 'authentic' version of the letter; it has to be deduced by
removing the 'anti-gnostic' polemic. As noted above (p. 32), Moffatt already dismissed
such theories as 'filigree criticism'. With regard to the charge of *Pangnostizismus*, it
may be noted that in *Neues Testament und Gnosis* (153f.) Schmithals writes that it is
striking that some parts of the NT writings show no influence worthy of mention of
Gnostic concepts or a Gnostic world of ideas (in particular the Synoptic tradition, but
also 1 Peter, Revelation, and in varying degree the Pastorals, Hebrews and James).

[91] Some points made by Frederik Wisse are relevant here; see his paper 'The Use of
Early Christian Literature as Evidence for Inner Diversity and Conflict'. Hengel
('Aufgaben', 334) remarks that because of the nature of our sources 'we are constantly
in danger of over-interpretation, i.e. of reading more out of (or should one say: into?)
the texts than they actually yield'. Aletti in his Avant-Propos (p. 7) speaks of 'les pièges
dans lesquels une lecture en miroir ["mirror reading"] est souvent tombée'.

do is, as it were, to hold up a mirror to the letter: what the author condemns represents the opinions of his opponents, what he commends hints at their shortcomings. This, however, may be an over-simplification: is every part of the letter to be regarded as polemical? Such an approach might lead, for example, to the conclusion that the ethical admonitions are evidence of shortcomings in this respect on the part of the false teachers; but it is one of Paul's well-known and well-attested characteristics that he is always concerned to draw out the ethical implications of the Gospel. A failure to recognize this might lead to conclusions about libertine tendencies in the 'heretics', which would in fact conflict with the evidence which the letter itself provides for a legalistic and ascetic position (cf. e.g. 2.16, 20f.).[92]

A further danger lies in the assumption, sometimes made, that the author has not fully understood the position of his opponents, or has misinterpreted it, and that we know better; this may in fact lead to the reading in of ideas for which there is simply no evidence, to a conjectural reconstruction of the false teaching in terms of what we think it must have been, with no real basis in what is actually said in the letter. And finally, we need to be aware of the author's approach: does he deal in detail *et seriatim* with the false teaching, so that we really can hold up a mirror and determine what that false teaching was, or does he refer to it only in more general terms? It is all too easy to expand and elaborate the meagre hints at our disposal, and in the end produce an imposing edifice which is in fact no more substantial than a house of cards. The only proper course is to read the letter as it stands, without importing ideas from a later age, but at the same time recognizing throughout the possibility that there may be elements which suggest a development in the direction of the later Gnosticism.

Much of the first chapter of this letter is in fact cordial and friendly, and complimentary to the Colossians. The first note of warning comes at v. 23—'provided that you continue securely established and steadfast in the faith, without shifting from the hope promised by the gospel that you heard' (this and the following quotations are from the NRSV; for discussion, see Commentary). The element of polemic, such as it is, begins at 2.8: 'See to it that no one takes you captive through philosophy and empty deceit, according to human tradition, according to the elemental spirits of the universe, and not according to Christ', and is continued at 2.16, 'do not let anyone condemn you in matters of food and drink or of observing festivals, new moons or sabbaths'. This leads to the further warning (2.18), 'Do not let anyone disqualify you, insisting on self-

---

[92] Reference has often been made to the curious phenomenon that in Gnosticism asceticism and lubricity could both spring from the selfsame root, the Gnostic denigration of this world and its creator. The evidence of the Nag Hammadi library, however, tends to show that the emphasis was more towards asceticism than to libertinism. See Wisse, 'Die Sextus-Sprüche und das Problem der gnostischen Ethik'; Wilson, 'Ethics and the Gnostics'.

abasement and worship of angels, dwelling on visions, puffed up without cause by a human way of thinking'. Finally there is reference to regulations (2.20ff.), 'Do not handle, Do not taste, Do not touch', which 'have indeed an appearance of wisdom in promoting self-imposed piety, humility and severe treatment of the body, but they are of no value in checking self-indulgence'.[93]

This is frankly not much of a foundation on which to reconstruct the ideas of the opponents in view, although more might be added if the prominence given to the 'Christological hymn' at 1.15ff. and similar Christological and soteriological statements elsewhere may be taken to reflect a failure on their part to give to Christ the place which is his by right. As already indicated, Gnosticism was long regarded as the result of a fusion of Christianity and Greek philosophy, and it may have been the reference to 'philosophy' at 2.8 which led scholars in former years to think of some early form of the Gnostic heresy.[94] In that case the 'elemental spirits of the universe' would presumably be the Gnostic archons, although this is not the only possible interpretation of these words. At any rate there is no sign of any developed Gnosticism in the second-century sense—no primal deity distinct from the creator, producing a pleroma of aeons, no pre-mundane fall of one of these aeons which leads to the creation of this world, no hostile Demiurge. There is no suggestion that this world is a place of captivity, the body a tomb in which the soul is imprisoned, or that the way to deliverance is through some saving *gnosis*—the Colossians have indeed been delivered 'from the power of darkness' and transferred 'into the kingdom of his beloved Son' (1.13), but the passage goes on to refer to redemption (ἀπολύτρωσις, later a Gnostic

---

[93] Schenke ('Der Widerstreit', 392) lists the characteristics in the 'heretics', which, he says, are not given directly but have to be laboriously deduced from the polemic against these heretics and from allusions in the text. DeMaris (*Controversy*, 45ff.) identifies the polemical core in Colossians as 2.8, 16–23, and discusses it in detail.

[94] Thus Bornkamm writes, 'The gnostic character of the false teaching can be perceived already from its designation as φιλοσοφία (2:8)' ('Die Häresie des Kolosserbriefs', 126); but O. Michel (*TWNT*, ix. 185) notes that this word-group plays no role in Gnostic thought later; see his whole discussion (169–85). Greek philosophy was, however, in various ways and in varying degree, a factor in the development of 'Gnosticism proper'; where, when and by whom this element was introduced is another of our problems. It should also be noted that Josephus can speak of the Pharisees, Sadducees and Essenes as so many philosophical schools, while both for him and for Philo Judaism is clearly the true 'philosophy' (for the Jews as 'philosophers' cf. Hengel, *Judaism*, i. 255–61; see also Wilson, *The Hope of Glory*, 7ff.). Arnold (*Syncretism*, e.g. 98–100) is critical of attempts to explain Col. in terms of Gnosticism, but does not seem to allow for the possibility that the magical element which he emphasizes was a contributory factor in the later development of Gnostic ideas. What is envisaged here is not a developed Gnosticism, but (to use the terms of Robinson and Koester) a point somewhere on a trajectory that ends in Gnosticism. Φιλόσοφος occurs sporadically as a loan-word in the Nag Hammadi texts: NHC I 46.9–10 (*Rheginus*); *Gos. Thom.* log 13; III 70.15 (*Eug.*)//III 92.20, BG 81.3 (*SJC*); XII 34.16, 18 (*Sentences of Sextus*); the compound at I 110.14 = φιλοσοφία. For a study of Col. in the light of Hellenistic philosophy cf. Wilson, *The Hope of Glory* (cf. the review by C. F. D. Moule, *JTS* 49 (1998), 777–80); he lists the major points of comparison on p. 181.

technical term) as 'the forgiveness of sins'. The emphasis is on reconciliation to God, not on any Gnostic deliverance.

Many years ago Hans Jonas wrote: 'A Gnosticism without a fallen god, without benighted creator and sinister creation, without alien soul, cosmic captivity and acosmic salvation, without the self-redeeming of the Deity—in short: a Gnosis without divine tragedy will not meet specifications. For those are the things we have to account for when truly asking for the origins of "Gnosticism".'[95] In its original context, this statement was directed against a quite specific target, but it is capable of a wider application, and is certainly relevant to the false teaching in view in Colossians. This is in fact a case in which a distinction between the terms 'Gnosis' and 'Gnosticism' may be useful, the latter to be reserved for its traditional use with reference to the 'classic' systems of the second century, the former to be used as a broader term for earlier and more nebulous 'pre-Gnostic' or 'proto-Gnostic' ways of thinking,[96] in fact what Jonas calls 'a Gnosis without divine tragedy'.

In *St Paul and the Church of the Gentiles* (154), W. L. Knox presents an interesting reconstruction of the report of the false teaching which reached Paul from his friends in Colossae:

[95] Jonas in Hyatt (ed.), *The Bible in Modern Scholarship*, 293. This was originally directed against Gershom Scholem's description of Jewish Hekhaloth mysticism as a 'Gnosis': Jonas continues, 'A Gnosis merely of the heavenly palaces, of the mystical ascent, the ecstatic vision of the throne, of the awesome secrets of the divine majesty—in short: a *monotheistic* Gnosis of the *mysterium numinosum et tremendum*, important as it is in its own right, is a different matter altogether'. Cf. also Gruenwald, 'Knowledge and Vision'. Pearson (*Emergence of the Christian Religion*, 123) suggests that Scholem's 'Jewish Gnosticism' is more appropriately designated Jewish mysticism.

[96] Despite what has sometimes been written, this is not the definition adopted at the Messina colloquium in 1967, against which Kurt Rudolph protested as a rending apart of two terms which fundamentally belong together. The Messina definition (see Bianchi (ed.), *Le Origini dello Gnosticismo*, (p. xxvif.) began by defining 'Gnosticism' in terms of 'a certain group of systems of the Second Century AD which everyone agrees are to be designated with this term'; 'gnosis' in contrast is defined as 'knowledge of the divine mysteries reserved for an élite' (further refinement in para. B II of the document). In other words, 'Gnosticism' is the term for the movement, while 'gnosis' is the Gnostic knowledge. To deal with possible anticipations of the 'classical' Gnosticism, two other terms are introduced (B III), with a certain nuance of meaning: 'pre-Gnosticism' and 'proto-Gnosticism'. Rudolph himself (*Gnosis*, 56f.) adheres to 'the practice usual particularly in the German-speaking area' and understands by Gnosis and Gnosticism 'the same thing; the first as the self-designation of a religion of redemption in late antiquity, the latter as a newer form of it'. The point of making the distinction here proposed is precisely to give due recognition to the validity of the use of the term 'Gnosis' by German scholars, but at the same time to recognize that this gnosis may not yet be the fully developed Gnosticism of the second-century systems. Pearson suggests that we speak of 'the Gnostic religion' rather than Gnosticism or Gnosis (*Nag Hammadi, Gnosticism and Early Christianity*, 17 = *Emergence of the Christian Religion*, 123) and 'speculative wisdom' for the 'Gnosis' which is present in 1 Corinthians, Philo and Wisdom, and *The Teachings of Silvanus* (*Gnosticism, Judaism and Egyptian Christianity*, 181). Cf. also A. Khosroyev's discussion of the terms in *Die Bibliothek von Nag Hammadi* (1995), 143–57, esp. 150–51; C. Markschies, *Gnosis: An Introduction* (2003). For Silvanus, cf. Zandee, *The Teachings of Sylvanus*.

They tell us that we must learn to grow in 'wisdom and knowledge', thus 'increasing and bearing fruit'. Only so shall we gain the power and strength we need to attain to our full portion in the light. In Jesus we have forgiveness, but not full redemption, which is reserved for those who know how to triumph over the rulers of the higher spheres of the cosmos; Jesus was inferior to them, as is shown by the fact that they were able to cause Him to be crucified and are able to persecute Paul now. To attain to 'the fullness of wisdom' we must know the 'hidden mysteries' revealed by 'philosophy', which bring us to that 'completion' to which baptism is a preliminary stage, as circumcision was under the old covenant (and perhaps still is). It confers the first measure of the new life; but we must attain to its fullness by a complete putting off of the material. This can only be achieved by the observance of those sacred seasons and those ritual abstinences from food and material pleasures which will enable us to be initiated successfully into the higher orders of truth, where angels will reveal to us the secrets by which we can pass safely from the material world to the heights of heaven. When we have done this, we shall be fully equipped with the fivefold spiritual equipment, which must replace the five senses through which we live in the material world.

Knox adds: 'The whole system is a relatively simple type of Gnosis of the earlier type before Valentinus had introduced the complication which was bound to result from the attempt at a complete duplication of things celestial and things terrestrial.' Earlier (151) he had noted that the 'heretics' in Colossae 'do not appear to have allowed to Jesus that prominence in the scheme of redemption by which the Gnostics from the time of Cerinthus and Satornilus endeavoured to preserve, at least in theory, the position held by Jesus in the teaching of the Church'. [97] Knox himself regarded Colossians as an authentic letter of Paul, but it may be felt that this reconstruction belongs more to a period later than Paul's own time. At any rate his reference to Cerinthus and Satornilus serves to bring down the *terminus ante quem* for the letter: it certainly belongs in an early period, before the full development of the 'classic' Gnostic systems. It may be open to question whether the development shown here could have taken place as early as Paul's own lifetime, but certainly the letter would seem to belong in that rather shadowy area

---

[97] Writing of one of the earlier Nag Hammadi texts to be published, A. Böhlig notes that elsewhere too the NT presents analogies, yet in some trains of thought a Christian form is indeed known, but the world of ideas from which Christianity drew was more influential than Christianity itself. For our Gnostics, he says, the Christian form was a form without content; 'denn sie war entleert, nachdem Jesus Christus nicht mehr ihr Zentrum bildete' (*Die koptisch-gnostische Schrift ohne Titel aus Codex II von Nag Hammadi* (1962), 34). For Jesus in the Nag Hammadi texts, see Majella Franzmann, *Jesus in the Nag Hammadi Writings* (1996).

of Gnostic origins which German scholars often describe in terms of Gnosis, but which is not yet to be described as Gnosticism in the narrower sense commonly used by their British colleagues. It may be that we must reconcile ourselves to speaking in general terms of some form of incipient Gnosis, and abandon any attempt to be more specific in our description; but efforts have none the less been made (see below).

One point which calls for further mention in this connection is the worship of angels—the Gnostics did not advocate anything of the sort![98] For them the powers who control the heavens, and the destinies of men, are hostile archons; they are the keepers of the gates through the seven heavens, by which the soul must pass on its final journey to its true abode, and their challenge is to be countered by the use of the appropriate passwords.[99] This reference to worship of angels in Colossians can, broadly speaking, be interpreted in two main ways. On the one hand many scholars have understood the angels to be intermediaries between God and man, whose assistance must be enlisted for the heavenly journey.[100] Some even think of an angelic hierarchy of several different orders: angels, archangels, principalities, powers, dominions, thrones, authorities (cf. Lightfoot, 219 on Col. 1.16). This involves a positive assessment of the 'worship' as a means toward ensuring that necessary assistance. On such a view, the 'heresy' need not have been Gnostic, although it is often so taken by those who adopt this interpretation.

On the other hand H. M. Schenke (Schenke and Fischer, 159ff.; see also 'Der Widerstreit') takes a negative view: for him the *Engellehre* is a key point in the identification of the 'heresy' as a real Gnosis ('Der

---

[98] Foerster, 'Abfassungszeit', 138 says that to serve angelic powers would for Paul be a reversion to unadulterated heathenism; Gnosis did not serve such powers or worship them, but despised them. Moreover there is no evidence from the NT period that the expression στοιχεῖα τοῦ κόσμου designated angelic beings or astral powers. *Nor to his knowledge does this expression occur in Gnosis* (italics mine). This relates to the use of the phrase in Galatians; for Colossians, see 'Die Irrelehrer'. Cf. also S. Pétrement in Bianchi (ed.), *Le Origini*, 472.

[99] Cf. W. P. Funk in Schneemelcher, *New Testament Apocrypha*, i. 318, and the directions given in the *First Apocalypse of James* from Nag Hammadi, pp. 33–35 (ibid. 323). In the light of the material adduced by Arnold (see below), this might be regarded as an element taken over by the Gnostics from the realm of magic; but reference should also be made to some aspects of Jewish and early Christian apocalyptic.

[100] Koester, ii. 264: 'In order to be united with Christ, the mediation of angelic powers was needed so that the believer could be in accord with the cosmic reality of the true body of Christ ("humility" and service of the angels, 2:18).' Lightfoot (103) had already written, 'The successive grades of intermediate beings were as successive steps, by which man might mount the ladder leading up to the throne of God. This carefully woven web of sophistry the Apostle tears to shreds.' According to G. H. C. Macgregor (*NTS* 1 (1954/55), 22), 'The very crux of the Colossian heresy is that these folk are giving to the στοιχεῖα, as mediators between God and man, the place which can belong only to Christ'; this is correct as regards the crux of the 'heresy', but involves an interpretation of the στοιχεῖα which is by no means universally accepted (see Commentary below on 2.8). For further examples, and criticism, cf. Schenke, 'Der Widerstreit', 394–95.

Widerstreit', 393). The angels are to be identified with the στοιχεῖα τοῦ κόσμου and are in fact the Gnostic archons. They have indeed been vanquished through the ascent of the Saviour into the world of light, but are still exercising their power in human life, and even the Gnostic, although in principle delivered from their sway, is still subject to their authority so long as he lives in this present world. They bar the way to Christ, to the realm of light, which can be travelled only amid great danger.[101] They demand veneration from all men and women, including the Gnostics.[102] The worship which they demand is, however, for the Gnostic a matter of indifference, as something belonging to this world: he may refuse or conform as he will. But due respect, humility (ταπεινοφροσύνη, 2.18, 23), is appropriate in dealing with these powers, both in the heavenly ascent and also during life on this earth.

The merit of this suggestion is that it seeks to interpret the Colossian 'heresy' in terms of actual Gnosis, but it is perhaps open to question whether this Gnosis had developed so far by about AD 70, the date which Schenke would assign to the letter ('Der Widerstreit', 399). Also there are some points of detail which would seem to be open to criticism. It could, for example, be argued that this interpretation is simply a transposition into Gnostic terms of Paul's teaching, e.g. in Romans 6, on the situation of the Christian in his ongoing life in this world: 'we have been buried with him by baptism into death, so that, just as Christ was raised from the dead by the glory of the Father, so we too might walk in newness of life. . . . So you also must consider yourselves dead to sin and alive to God in Christ Jesus' (Rom. 6.4, 11). The Christian has been delivered from the power of sin, but must still strive for a life of righteousness. He has not yet finally and fully entered into eternal life. In the words of Ephesians (6.12), 'our struggle is not against enemies of blood and flesh, but against the rulers, against the authorities, against the cosmic powers of this present darkness, against the spiritual forces of evil in the heavenly places'.

It may be added that F. Siegert in his *Nag-Hammadi Register* (342f.) lists a whole string of allusions to Colossians in the Nag

---

[101] Cf. for example the Nag Hammadi *Acts of Peter and the Twelve* (NHC VI 1), 5.8—6.12.

[102] Contrast the view of Foerster (see n. 98 above). On the question of the στοιχεῖα see Commentary below on 2.8; a majority of scholars would regard them as cosmic powers, 'elemental spirits of the universe' (NRSV; NEB; but see also the translators' footnote in each). Barrett (*From First Adam to Last*) writes: 'i.20 and ii.15 make no sense unless we may suppose that powers that were created for subordination to the heavenly Man have rebelled, and deserted their appointed rank. As rebels, they have been overcome and reconciled in the cross; overcome and reconciled, yet not finally destroyed or appeased, since it is evident that they continue to be inimical to man and his interests' (86; cf. also 10f., 115f.). This does not go quite so far as Schenke's 'really Gnostic' position, but leaves the question: Why should the Colossians be called upon to worship such beings? For an English translation, by James M. Robinson, of the relevant parts of Schenke's argument, see the quotations in Logan and Wedderburn (eds), *The New Testament and Gnosis*, 11ff.

Hammadi texts—to 1.13, 14, 15, 16, 18; 2.9, 14; 3.1, 11. This might appear to indicate some link with Gnosticism, but the vital question is the nature of that link; the significance of these references has still to be examined. To take but one example, right at the beginning of the *Hypostasis of the Archons* (NHC II 4) we find the words 'the great apostle—referring to "the authorities of the darkness" (Col 1:13)—told us that "our contest is not against flesh and [blood]; rather, the authorities of the universe and the spirits of wickedness" (Eph 6:12)' (*NHLE* 1988, 162). This is not an exact quotation either of Colossians or of Ephesians, and without the opening words it might well be that some would claim that here we have 'Gnostic' influence on the New Testament; but the reference to 'the great apostle' is decisive. In this case, as in some other passages, we have clear evidence not of 'Gnostic' influence on Colossians, or on the teaching it opposes, but of the use of Colossians (and here of Ephesians also) by later Gnostics. All such parallels require to be carefully evaluated, to determine just what they signify. The Gnostics were not averse to the use of New Testament material for their own purposes.

A new line of approach was initiated by F. O. Francis, who has been followed by among others W. Carr, A. T. Lincoln and T. J. Sappington.[103] This places the emphasis on a Jewish ascetic-mystical piety: 'It was no cult of angels that threatened the faith and life of the congregation. Rather, Christians at Colossae were attempting to gain a visionary experience of heaven and to participate in the heavenly worship that the angels offer to God' (Sappington, *Revelation and Redemption*, 18). In the phrase θρησκεία τῶν ἀγγέλων (Col. 2.18) the genitive is not objective but subjective: the angels are not the object of the worship. On the contrary, one of the common themes of apocalyptic is the heavenly ascent, in which the visionary is privileged to behold the heavenly throne and hear the worship offered by the heavenly host surrounding it (see Sappington, 90–94); 'when a seer ascends to receive a vision of the Merkabah, he also receives a vision

---

[103] Francis, 'Humility and Angelic Worship in Col 2:18'; Francis and Meeks (eds), *Conflict at Colossae*, in which this essay is reprinted, also includes Lightfoot's essay on the Colossian heresy, from his commentary (13–59), and translations of Dibelius's study 'Die Isisweihe bei Apulejus' (61–121), Bornkamm's 'Die Häresie des Kolosserbriefes' (123–45), and Lyonnet's 'Les adversaires de Paul à Colosses' (147–61), with a further essay by Francis on the background of ἐμβατεύειν (197–207) and an epilogue (209–18). Followers of Francis' position include Carr, *Principalities and Powers*; Lincoln, *Paradise Now and Not Yet*; and Sappington, *Revelation and Redemption at Colossae*. The theory is not entirely new, since A. L. Williams (*Colossians*, p. xxv) mentions it as advanced by earlier scholars. For a critique of Francis cf. DeMaris, *Controversy*, 74–77; Arnold, *Syncretism*, esp. 90–98. According to Lincoln (*JTS* 48 (1997), 206) followers of Francis 'will be hard pressed to maintain their case in the light of Arnold's arguments'; L. W. Hurtado (*JBL* 117 (1998), 156–58) is less certain.

of the angelic hosts and their worship—and in certain cases he is
constrained to join them in giving praise to the Most High' (94).[104]
So in the *Ascension of Isaiah* (8.16; 9.33; 10.19) Isaiah even joins in
the praises offered in the sixth and seventh heavens; according to
J. M. Scott (*NTS* 42 (1996), 267; cf. 272), 'The Songs of the
Sabbath Sacrifice, which stand in continuity with later Hekhalot
literature, show that participation in the heavenly angelic liturgy
and contemplation of the Merkabah were practised in Qumran.' It
is participation in this worship that is the goal of the Colossian
sectarians.

Now this would seem at first glance to be entirely possible (for the
subjective use of the genitive BAGD 363b notes 4 Macc. 5.7 and
Josephus, *Ant.* xii.253; cf. τῇ θρησκείᾳ ἡμῶν in *1 Clem.* 62.1; Arnold,
Syncretism, 91 n. 5 adds some more), but doubts remain. According
to Arnold (91), 'A survey of the usage of θρησκεία fails to turn up
one example of a divine being, or a typical object of worship (e.g. an
"idol"), related to θρησκεία in the genitive case that should be taken
as a subjective genitive'. In all the cases mentioned where the
genitive is subjective, θρησκεία is the religion or worship of some
people, the Jews, the barbarians, humankind. In contrast, 'numerous
examples can be cited of a divine object given in the genitive case'
(92). Moreover, BAGD (363b) notes evidence for the worship of
angels in Phrygia (cf. also *TWNT* iii. 157f.), including Canon 35 of
the Council of Laodicea and Theodoret's comment on Col. 2.18,
that 'this disease long remained in Phrygia and Pisidia' (cf.
Lightfoot, 68 n. 1). The text in itself may offer no means of
deciding whether the genitive is objective or subjective, and we may
therefore have to make the choice on other grounds, but the
evidence of usage elsewhere seems to tell in favour of seeing the
genitive as objective.

From another angle, a point touched on by Sappington may be of
some significance in relation to Gnostic origins. He refers (21) to
Ithamar Gruenwald as stressing the mystical character of Jewish
apocalypticism, and at a later point observes (82): 'most are prepared
to acknowledge that there are significant points of contact between
Jewish apocalypticism and Merkabah mysticism, and that the latter

---

[104] Cf. Bockmuehl (*Revelation and Mystery*, 169): 'Part and parcel of the ascent
through the heavens was the visionary's observation of and sometimes *participation in*
the angelic hymns before the throne of God, the praises of the heavenly beings being
viewed as the model and example for earthly worship.' For April De Conick (in Turner
and McGuire (eds), *The Nag Hammadi Library after Fifty Years*, 397), 'There is
evidence that the Thomasine Christians were mystics seeking visions of God for the
purpose of immortalization', referring to her *Seek to See Him: Ascent and Vision
Mysticism in the Gospel of Thomas*, (1996). The article cited provides references for the
theme of the heavenly ascent in Jewish mysticism. On 'The Heavenly Ascent in
Hellenistic Judaism, Early Christianity and their Environment' cf. A. F. Segal, *ANRW*
II.23.2 (1980), 1333–94.

movement issued from the former'.[105] In a footnote he cites P. S.
Alexander (*JJS* 35 (1984), 10–12) as suggesting that Jewish
apocalypticism is a common ancestor for both Merkabah mysticism
and Gnosticism, which would to some extent serve to explain the
similarities which led Scholem to describe Merkabah mysticism as a
Jewish Gnosticism. But we should still have to remember that we
have here two divergent lines of development; the fact that they
spring from the same root and show certain similarities should not be
allowed to mislead us into thinking of them as the same. The
criticism voiced by Jonas still holds good. As Lincoln puts it
(*Paradise Now*, 117), 'What we have [sc. in Colossians] is rather a
syncretism of nonconformist Jewish elements and speculative
Hellenistic ideas and this could perhaps be seen as one stage in a
trajectory which leads from the interests of late Judaism via contact
with Christianity to the later Gnosticism we have attested in the Nag
Hammadi documents'.

Eduard Schweizer struck out in a new direction in his commentary
(ET 1982) and in various articles (listed in DeMaris, *Controversy*, 88
n. 2, 158), and sought to find a background in Greek philosophy,
specifically in Pythagoreanism (for a summary, see DeMaris, 37–38;
for criticism, ibid. 88–97). In particular he quotes a text preserved by
Diogenes Laertius (viii.25–33), an epitome of Pythagorean doctrine
composed by Alexander Polyhistor and allegedly drawn from
Pythagorean *Hypomnemata*. DeMaris (88) notes as a major
deficiency in Schweizer's theory his underestimation of Jewish
influence on the Colossian philosophy, and also raises questions
about the Pythagorean character of the *Hypomnemata* : 'An intense
demand for information about the shadowy Pythagoras coupled
with a paucity of knowledge about him and his teachings generated
a host of Pythagorean pseudepigrapha in the Hellenistic period.
These writings freely combined Platonic, Academic, Stoic,
Peripatetic and old Pythagorean ideas under the name of
Pythagoras or some early Pythagorean worthy' (102). It is therefore
at least open to question how far the text should be claimed as
Pythagorean.[106] Moreover, 'the portions of the *Hypomnemata* most

---

[105] For further references, including literature on the heavenly ascent, cf. A. F. Segal,
NTS 44 (1998), 405 n. 10; also 'The Heavenly Ascent'.

[106] Wedderburn ('Theology', 7) notes that most of the parallels betweeen
Pythagoreanism and the background of Col. could equally well be found in
Hippolytus' account of Elchasaite teaching, and that in some respects the latter
shows even closer parallels. Since Elchasaism originated in the second century, we
cannot assume that the opponents of Colossians were Elchasaite, but such traditions
show 'the sort of blend of idea and practice that could conceivably have arisen
anywhere where there were Jews or Jewish Christians living in a pagan environment
and seeking to blend their traditions with those around them' (cf. also Wilson, *The
Hope of Glory*, 35–38). For the Elchasaites cf. K. Rudolph in *The Cambridge History of
Judaism*, iii (1999), 483–92.

pertinent to the Colossian philosophy are those least likely to be Pythagorean' (103, 104).

DeMaris himself (100ff.) looks to the Middle Platonism of the first and second centuries as the appropriate philosophical milieu for Colossians, although he notes (118) that 'the Jewish practices of the Colossian philosophy distinguish it from all other known types of Middle Platonism'. (For criticism cf. Arnold, *Syncretism*, 206–07. At the outset (5) he asks, 'Is it really plausible that this kind of school philosophy would reach the rural sections of Asia Minor and have the kind of appeal and impact that is presupposed in Colossians?')[107]

Another new approach has been initiated by C. E. Arnold, taking up a suggestion made long ago by A. Lukyn Williams (*JTS* 10 (1909), 432): 'there is almost no evidence for the worship of them [angels] being recognised in early times by thoughtful Jews, save indeed in connexion with exorcism and magic'. 'The "worship of angels" in Colossians 2:18 refers essentially to a magical invocation of angels, especially for apotropaic purposes'—but 'surprisingly, Williams reached this conclusion without ever referring to the magical papyri, the amulets, and the lead curse tablets' (Arnold, *Syncretism*, 10; in fairness, we need to ask how far these resources were accessible when Williams was writing). Reviewing this evidence, Arnold argues that the invocation of angels, for apotropaic purposes, for incantations and love spells or in cursing, and for revelatory magic, was widespread in popular circles in the ancient world, even in Judaism. People had a sense of being a prey to hostile forces, against whom mere human power could not prevail (cf. Knox's reference to triumphing over the hostile powers in the quotation above). On this view, the Colossian error lay in the invocation of angels, and possibly local pagan deities, to assist them in the face of the problems of their daily living. Over against this, the author asserts emphatically the complete sufficiency of Christ. The case has only just been presented in detail, but together with Arnold's study of Ephesians along these lines there is enough to

---

[107] Still more recently T. W. Martin (*By Philosophy and Empty Deceit*) has sought to interpret the letter as a reply to criticism by Cynics who have penetrated into the Colossian community. Cf. the review by F. G. Downing in *JBL* 117 (1998), 542ff., a critique the more telling in that it comes from the author of *Cynics, Paul and the Pauline Churches* (1998). For criticism of theories linking the Cynics with Christian origins, cf. Betz, 'Jesus and the Cynics: Survey and Analysis of a Hypothesis', *JR* 74 (1994), 453–75; also Pearson, *Emergence*, 30–31, and references there to P. R. Eddy, *JBL* 115 (1996) 449–69 (31 n. 28) and J. M. Robinson in *Gnosisforschung und Religionsgeschichte* (1994), 247–65 (39 n. 46). For van Kooten (*Cosmic Christology*, 144), his own reconstruction of the Colossian 'philosophy' as an instance of Middle Platonism basically confirms the conclusions of Schweizer and DeMaris, but he differs from them in that his discussion of the author's cosmology shows it too to consist largely of Middle Platonist conceptions: '*Col.* is almost a modification of Middle Platonist doctrine from within.'

suggest that it merits consideration.[108] Reference has often been made in studies of Colossians to the overcoming of hostile powers, and certainly the Jews had a reputation for magic in the ancient world—even though the use of Hebrew names in magical literature may at times indicate no more than superficial pagan borrowing (for Jewish influence on magical literature cf. Knox, *PCG*, 208ff., also his index; on incantations and books of magic see P. S. Alexander in Schürer, iii.1, 342–79). Nock (i. 501f.) wrote, 'we must not forget the connotations of the term "philosopher" in our astrological Hermetica; it involves indeed an element of asceticism, but more commonly its associations are with the occult. Astrology, magic and the expression of devotion to the Emperor were the universal phenomena of paganism in Roman times.'[109]

One further aspect may be mentioned, to complete the picture: in *The New Testament Christological Hymns*, J. T. Sanders draws attention to the *Odes of Solomon*, although it must be added that direct references are lacking in the section of his book relating to the Colossian 'hymn':[110] 'If the redeemer concept and the stage of

---

[108] In his study of Ephesians, Arnold writes: 'A single common feature may be discerned among all the religious diversity in western Asia Minor: people had an extraordinary fear of the hostile spiritual "powers". Through their practices and rituals (some of which the various local cults shared), local religion and magic claimed to offer relief from this oppressive fear, and even promised means of control over the dreaded demonic realm. Although many of the new Christians in this area forsook their magical practices and burned their magical papyri, as Luke records, a good number would have been tempted to conflate their magical beliefs with Christianity' (*Ephesians: Power and Magic*, 167). It is not difficult to see how relevant this could be for the background to Colossians, and his *The Colossian Syncretism* seeks to present the case in detail (cf. the reviews by A. T. Lincoln in *JTS* 48 (1997), 205–09 and L. W. Hurtado in *JBL* 117 (1998), 156–58). On the relation between religion and magic in the ancient world, cf. A. F. Segal, 'Hellenistic Magic'. As to Gnosticism, Nock puts the matter very succinctly: 'while the two spheres have much in common, and while elements from the Gnostic writings have reached magic and elements from magic have reached this sort of Gnosticism, there is an essential difference of tone. The authors and readers of the *Pistis Sophia* (like Neoplatonist students of theurgy) were passionately eager to know how the wheels went round, the authors and readers of the magic papyri desired simply to be able to make them turn' (*Essays on Religion*, i. 193). Arnold (*Syncretism*, 31) observes that 'Apotropaic magic, in particular, is concerned to thwart the influence of evil forces for the present', whereas Gnosis 'is chiefly concerned about the dangers of the heavenly ascent after death'.

[109] In this connection, Canon 36 of the Council of Laodicea may perhaps take on a new significance: 'It is not right for priests or clergy to be magicians or enchanters or mathematicians or astrologers, or to make safeguards [φυλακτήρια] as they are called, for such things are prisons [δεσμωτήρια] of their souls' (Lightfoot, 69). Lightfoot comments, 'It is strange, at this late date, to find still lingering in these churches the same readiness to be "judged in respect of an holiday or a new moon or a sabbath", with the same tendency to relinquish the hold on the Head and to substitute "a voluntary humility and worshipping of angels", which three centuries before had called forth the Apostle's rebuke and warning in the Epistle to the Colossians.' He notes that while there is no direct mention of 'magic' in the letter, 'yet it was a characteristic tendency of this part of Asia'.

[110] Deichgräber (*Gotteshymnus*, 21) excludes the *Odes* from his detailed treatment on grounds of date, placing them between AD 125 and 175.

hypostatization evidenced in the *Odes of Solomon* are not to be explained as the result of influence from the New Testament, neither, however, would the reverse be correct. That would give too simple an answer, and would be historically unjustifiable. The relevance of the *Odes of Solomon* for understanding the historical religious background of the New Testament Christological hymns is rather that they reveal that motifs highly similar to those of the New Testament Christological hymns could, at a period not far from the first use of these hymns by Christianity, be utilized by one segment of Judaism' (119f.). He argues that some of these odes 'belong within the corpus of thanksgiving hymns of the Wisdom school' (136), and that it was the Wisdom circles of Judaism which 'seem to have provided the most convenient point of entry for redeemer motifs from other religions into Judaism' (139). The NT Christological hymns reflect one stage in a process of syncretism, the Coptic Gnostic materials from Nag Hammadi a considerably more advanced stage, 'at which time the connection with Wisdom groups has been entirely left behind'.[111] The *Odes* 'belong to some stage of the syncretistic process intermediate to the New Testament and the Nag Hammadi materials, but independent of the New Testament and showing in several respects a less advanced stage of the developing redeemer myth' (ibid.).

In the face of such a bewildering variety of opinion and divergent theories, one is reminded of some words of Reitzenstein quoted by C. H. Dodd (*The Bible and the Greeks*, p. xv): 'It is hardly to be avoided that according to inclination and the direction his studies have taken, one writer claims too much as Egyptian, another too much as Babylonian, a third all as Persian, and that the individual worker contracts a kind of colour-blindness, which makes him insensitive to important distinctions. Only the combined work of many can bring us nearer the goal of an understanding of Hellenistic mysticism.' Much of course has changed, and we are now perhaps more aware of the dangers of over-emphasis on one aspect at the expense of others of possibly equal moment, but the main point holds good. It may be that the proper path to a true understanding is not by way of trying to identify the one significant influence, but by building up as complete a picture as possible of the whole background of the New Testament period. Moreover, we need to remember that it is not merely a question of ideas and influences floating in some kind of vacuum: we have to think of people who

[111] In 'Nag Hammadi', 62f., Sanders notes that Gesine Robinson has pointed out some parallels to Col. 1.15–17 in the Nag Hammadi Trimorphic Protennoia (see her edition (G. Schenke, *Die Dreigestaltige Protennoia*, 90–91; further references to Colossians in the index, 167). Dr Robinson argues that Jewish Wisdom speculation is the background to both Colossians and the Nag Hammadi text, referring for discussion of the whole theme of 'Wisdom' and 'Gnosis' to H. M. Schenke, 'Die Tendenz der Weisheit zur Gnosis'.

were subject to these manifold influences, shared these ideas, and built them together into syntheses of their own. It may indeed be open to question whether these syntheses were always so coherent and consistent as the reconstructions of modern scholars would make them.

In particular, the old debate as to whether the Colossian 'heresy' should be thought of as 'Gnostic' or 'Jewish' is now a thing of the past. We can certainly see here pointers in the direction of the later Gnosticism, but the Colossian 'heresy' is beyond question not yet a developed Gnosticism such as we find in the 'classic' systems of the second century. On the other hand it is significant that the most recent proposals all in some way look back to Judaism in some form, to apocalyptic, to Merkabah mysticism, to Jewish magic, to Jewish Wisdom circles.[112] Here, however, it is well to remember a point made long ago by Alexander Böhlig, regarding the *Umdeutung* to which Jewish materials were subjected when they were used in a Gnostic context.[113] Further, we must make due allowance for the presence of other possible influences. G. Quispel once wrote that practically the entire Near East has made its contribution to the origins of Gnosticism (*Gnosis als Weltreligion*, 9), and there have been those who have sought to identify a more Hellenistic background to Colossians. The Colossian 'heresy' belongs somewhere at an early stage in the development, at some point, which we still cannot define more precisely, on a trajectory which leads from Qumran and Jewish apocalyptic on the one hand to the developed Gnostic systems of the second century on the other. Our problem, and the point at which the 'trajectory' analogy breaks down, is that we must also allow for other possible influences, from mysticism or

---

[112] It should perhaps be noted that Lightfoot had already written, 'All or nearly all the early Gnostic heresies were Judaic; and for a time a compromise was effected which involved more or less concession on either side. But the ultimate incompatibility of the two at length became evident, and a precarious alliance was exchanged for an open antagonism. This final result however was not reached till the middle of the second century' (108). He places the Colossian heretics between the Essenes and Cerinthus (109), and sees in Cerinthus 'the proper link between the incipient gnosis of the Colossian heretics and the mature gnosis of the second century' (110). Towards the end of his essay (113) he writes that in speaking of these ideas as Gnostic 'we here employ the term to express the simplest and most elementary conceptions of this tendency of thought, and ... do not postulate its use as a distinct designation of any sect or sects at this early date'.

[113] Böhlig writes that even though pieces of tradition from Judaism and also from Jewish Christianity may have penetrated into *die Gnosis* in ever so large numbers, it creates something entirely new; to speak of Jewish Gnosis can only mean that the material here disseminated is Jewish, but not that these circles still either could or wished to claim to be Jews. The transmutation of Jewish traditional material into Gnostic trains of thought becomes especially clear in the reinterpretation of biblical passages and of *heilsgeschichtliche* figures (see Bianchi (ed.), *Le Origini*, 112–13 = Böhlig, *Mysterion und Wahrheit*, (1968), 83). Cf. also the articles of I. Gruenwald listed at n. 87 above, Pearson, *The Emergence of the Christian Religion*, chs 6 and 7.

magic or from Wisdom circles, or from quite non-Jewish sources, impinging upon the development. Here the analogy of tributaries to a river might be more appropriate; but we cannot yet be sure which was the main stream and which the secondary tributaries. It may be that the hypotheses reviewed above are not altogether mutually exclusive, and that eventually more than one of these influences contributed to the final result.[114]

V. RECAPITULATION

The authenticity of Colossians is still maintained by quite a number of scholars, particularly in the English-speaking world. On this view, Paul is in prison, probably in Rome near the end of his career, but possibly in Ephesus at a rather earlier date. He is there visited by Epaphras, who brings the greetings of the congregation in Colossae but also reports on some disturbing tendencies which appear to be threatening the local church. This letter is Paul's response, to deal with the situation.

Against this view there are differences of language, style and content as compared with the 'accepted' Pauline letters, and a more advanced development in some aspects of Pauline theology. These factors are not in themselves enough to prove that the letter is not from Paul's own hand, but there are other points to be added: the uncertainty as to where and when Paul was in prison when he wrote, the difficulty of locating Colossians, and the Colossian 'heresy', within what we know of Paul's life and activity, the nature of that 'heresy', and the question whether it could conceivably have arisen within Paul's lifetime. The cumulative effect of all these factors is such as to give rise to discussion and debate, and present problems in the acceptance of this traditional view.

One alternative sometimes suggested is that Paul availed himself of the services of an amanuensis in the composition of the letter. It is known that he sometimes did employ a secretary, but that does not mean that he always followed this course. To speak of 'his usual practice' is to generalize without warrant. Moreover we have to consider what exactly the contribution of the secretary was: if he wrote to dictation, the problems of language and style remain, but the greater the freedom allowed to the secretary the less justification there is for claiming the letter as authentically Paul's. When the

---

[114] Another new approach is taken by M. Y. MacDonald (*The Pauline Churches*) who discusses Colossians and Ephesians at pp. 85–158. Her concern is with 'community-stabilizing institutionalization' and with the continuing existence of the Pauline churches in the absence of the apostle, or after his death. Here questions of authenticity and Pauline or sub-Pauline authorship are no longer directly relevant: the interest lies in the ways in which the churches learned to cope with the ongoing problems of living when Paul was no longer present in person to exercise control. The *Haustafeln*, for example, are seen as intended primarily to arrange internal communal relations, but also possibly to stabilize relations with outsiders (121). H. Van Broekhoven (*JSNT* 66 (1997), 73–90) seeks to delineate the 'social profiles' of author, readers and opponents.

'secretary' hypothesis is invoked purely in the effort to preserve the authenticity of the letter, it is a counsel of despair.

A second alternative is the suggestion that the letter was written in Paul's name and with his authority by some disciple, at a time and in circumstances when Paul was not able to write himself. Reference has been made above to the description in 2 Corinthians of the hardships Paul had suffered, and the necessary period of recuperation after one of the scourgings mentioned might indeed provide an appropriate context. This would serve to account for the differences in language and style, but the problems with regard to content would still remain. The disciple would be carrying Paul's ideas further than Paul himself did, and that within Paul's own lifetime.[115] This suggestion certainly merits consideration, but if it is put forward in a desperate attempt to preserve some shred of authenticity it must be regarded as little better than the secretary hypothesis.[116]

On the view adopted here, the letter was written not so very long after Paul's death, by some disciple who sought to apply his master's teaching to meet a new and dangerous situation which he saw developing. He was familiar with Paul's theology, and possibly knew some of Paul's letters,[117] but he was no slavish copyist; he was a man of independent mind and some considerable ability, perfectly able to adapt and develop Paul's ideas to meet the new situation with which he found himself confronted. The authentic letter to Philemon provided him with something of a frame within which to work, a cluster of names that could be mentioned to give some measure of verisimilitude, and he was able to draw upon earlier tradition to some extent, but the result is not a pastiche of Pauline phrases like the apocryphal letter to the Laodiceans; it is an independent contribution in its own right, which was in its turn to provide the basis for further development in Ephesians.

The weakness of this view is of course summed up in a simple question: why should anyone have thought it necessary, or desirable,

[115] Hübner (10) notes against Schweizer's version of this theory the arguments advanced by Lindemann ('Gemeinde', 115f.), that if Col. was written during Paul's imprisonment in Ephesus it must be older than Romans; but the assumption that the statements in Col. 2.12ff. were written before Rom. 6.4ff. and those in Col. 1.18 and 2.19 before Rom. 12.3ff. is 'extremely problematic'.

[116] As indicated above (n. 63), this criticism does not apply to Wedderburn's suggestion mentioned there, or to Dunn's hypothesis of a letter written by Timothy late in the Roman imprisonment and approved by Paul, who added the final greetings in his own hand. At the end of his discussion Dunn himself writes (41), 'In the end the choice probably has to be made between two sets of plausibilities, each linked with sets of implausibilities. And to choose between them is a matter of fine judgement.'

[117] Lars Hartman (HTR 79 (1986), 137–46) suggests that copies of Paul's letters were kept by Paul or at his 'school', and read and reread by his disciples (140); they were not merely 'occasional' letters, but intended to be read and reread, in the communities to which they were addressed and in others as well (139). Such rereading could lead to the application to a new situation of basic principles contained in the apparently 'occasional' letter (142). Colossians lends support to his argument (139f.).

to forge a letter in the name of an elderly itinerant missionary,[118] to concoct a situation of imprisonment in some unknown location, and embellish it with a cluster of names from a genuine letter to give it some vague appearance of authenticity? Furthermore, how on this view are we to account for the 'personal' touches which appear in the letter? What, for example, was the service which Archippus is charged to fulfil? Were it merely a fiction, such criticism would be valid; but this is not merely a fiction. It is an attempt to meet a new and possibly dangerous outbreak of false teaching, and the author is consciously trying to meet that situation as he thinks Paul would have done. To speak of fraud and forgery is anachronistic, since the standards of the ancient world were not those of today. It was not uncommon for the developed teachings of a school to be attributed to its founder, even though there might have been considerable development. Moreover, there is force in the claim of K. M. Fischer already quoted (n. 23), that there was at this time no person or institution possessed of general authority within the Church. Anyone who sought to speak to the Church at large could not do so in his own person, but only in the name of those who possessed an authority rooted in the past. Only as 'Paul' or 'Peter' could one hope to find a hearing.[119]

The various problems considered in this introduction are to some extent interrelated, so that decisions regarding one may have an effect on our judgement with regard to another. If the letter is authentic and from Rome, it must be among the latest of Paul's letters. If from Ephesus, it would be quite considerably earlier; but this would raise complications in regard to other matters, such as the place of Colossians in the development of Paul's thought. In this connection Ernst Käsemann's oft-quoted dictum (*RGG* iii. 1728) puts much into small compass: 'Wenn echt, um des Inhalts and des Stiles willen so spät wie möglich, wenn unecht, so früh wie denkbar' (If

[118] The use of 'elderly' in this context may be open to question. There is ground for accepting the tradition that Paul was executed in Rome about the time of the Neronian persecution, but we do not know the date of his birth, and therefore cannot deduce his age at any given point. According to Acts (7.58), he was a νεανίας at the time of Stephen's martyrdom, but this is not really helpful, since this term could describe any man aged between 24 and 40 (Knowling, *EGT*, ii. 201; so also BAGD). At the beginning of the next chapter (8.3) he is prominent among the persecutors of the Church (Haenchen, (*Acts*, 294) remarks, 'The transformation in the picture of Saul is breathtaking, to say the least'), and in ch. 9 he obtains authority from the high priest to pursue adherents of 'the Way' in the synagogues of Damascus. If Acts is historically reliable on this point (*Beg.* iv. 85 says, 'this surely must be a genuine Pauline reminiscence'), the explanation is presumably that Paul was somewhere in the upper levels of this age-group. Stalker (*DAC* ii. 139f.) suggests that he was about 35 at the time of his conversion—but goes on to note, 'In the last Epistle which proceeded from his pen he called himself "Paul the aged"', and deduces that Paul was then not far from the Psalmist's appointed span. The reading πρεσβύτης in Philem. 9 has, however, been questioned (see Commentary *ad loc.*); and was Philemon Paul's last letter?

[119] We must also consider the position of a disciple trying to deal with a problematic situation after Paul's death. Cf. Standhartinger, *NTS* 50 (2004), 588.

genuine, as late as possible, because of the content and the style; if not genuine, as early as conceivable).

The three main possibilities which appear to be open for consideration have their implications also for the nature of the 'false teaching' that is in view. If the letter is early and from Ephesus, then it is probable that we should not think of a 'heresy' in the full sense; it is perhaps more likely that the trouble was some local problem confined to the area of Colossae, as suggested by M. D. Hooker, Helmut Koester and others. If the letter is from Rome, then it is possible that we have here the beginnings of what later developed into the Gnostic movement of the second century. If the letter was written by a later disciple, the development in the direction of the later Gnosticism would be further advanced, perhaps even as far as the stage envisaged by H. M. Schenke. The fact that so wide a range of opinion is possible only serves to show the limitations of our knowledge. On many questions there is no firm consensus.

As to the background of the letter, and the nature of the Colossian 'heresy', several different views have been advanced. At the one extreme it has been regarded as a purely local phenomenon, confined to Colossae itself; at the other it has been seen as a more or less developed form of incipient Gnosticism. What is clear is that there are Jewish as well as 'Gnostic' elements in the false teaching, so that it could be described in general terms as a Judaizing Gnosticism or Gnosticizing Judaism. Attempts have been made to define it more precisely, by reference to Essenism for example, or to Pythagoreanism, to Jewish apocalyptic, to esoteric mysticism such as later developed into Merkabah mysticism, or to magic and the occult; but none of these has yet commanded the general consent of scholars. There has also been reference to the mystery religions, some of which had their origins in Asia Minor or the surrounding areas, but here again the evidence adduced falls short of complete conviction; to say the least, we cannot be sure of the precise state of development reached by these religions at any given point in the first century.[120] The very variety of these proposals prompts to caution: we are not yet in a position to affirm with confidence that we have finally identified the nature and origins of the Colossian 'heresy'.

---

[120] Some pertinent questions of methodology are raised by Metzger, 'Methodology'. The classic statement of the case for an association with the mystery religions is that of Dibelius, 'Die Isisweihe'; see also his commentary. He reconstructs the initiation rite described by Apuleius, noting the role played by the elements and 'the importance accorded the entry into the sacred room in the initiation ceremony' ('Die Isisweihe', 82), and then turns to Colossians. The στοιχεῖα worship was not an existing cult, but first appeared after the Christian congregation was already in existence. The problem was that 'some members of the Christian group entered the cultic fellowship of the στοιχεῖα without renouncing their Christianity' (83). A key point is the enigmatic phrase ἃ ἑόρακεν ἐμβατεύων in 2.18, which he interprets on the basis of inscriptions from the sanctuary of Apollo at Claros, which speak of the 'accomplishing' of mysteries and use the term ἐμβατεύων of some kind of 'entering' (texts on p. 86). The word is thus a technical term of the mysteries. Both Apuleius and the Claros

Ultimately it may be that our choice lies between two alternatives, each, as Dunn notes (41), with its plausibilities and its implausibilities: Dunn's view that both Colossians and Philemon belong to the Roman imprisonment, Colossians being written by Timothy and approved by Paul at a late stage, when Paul was not in a position to write himself; or the view taken here, which would place the letter to Philemon earlier, as written from Ephesus, and assign Colossians to some disciple (possibly Timothy) writing shortly after Paul's death. Here the absence of any reference to the earthquake might perhaps be significant; our author had no need to mention it, for the Colossians were only too well aware of it. Indeed, it might have contributed to the problem in Colossae: it had destroyed their faith, and left them a prey to magic and superstition, seeking comfort in the invocation of angels in the midst of the tragedy that had struck them. In that case our author is trying to convey the impression that Paul had some years before sought to deal with just such a situation. But this again is still no more than a conjecture.

What may be more significant is that in dealing with these problems we are confronted by many of the issues which arise in connection with the origins of the Gnostic movement: it is quite conceivable that the Colossian 'heresy' is in fact an early form of incipient Gnosticism, but there is a long road to travel before we reach the developed systems of the second century. It may indeed be important to distinguish as best we can the various stages of the development. The point of these varied proposals is that they bring before us several different aspects that contributed to the intellectual life of the period, elements which entered into the intellectual 'atmosphere' of the time. The whole range of these ideas would probably not be entertained by any individual person; most people would probably be influenced by those ideas which were most familiar, or most congenial to them: the old dictum *quot homines, tot sententiae* could be very apposite, even if not in its original sense.[121]

---

inscriptions, however, belong to the second century (for Claros, see p. 87 and nn. 69, 70), and the Claros sanctuary was an oracle, not the centre of a mystery cult in the usual sense (for an assessment, cf. Francis and Meeks (eds), *Conflict at Colossae*, 210f.). See also Lyonnet, 'L'Epître aux Colossiens (Col 2:18) et les mystères d'Apollon Clarien', (a modified version of the article translated in *Conflict at Colossae*, 141–61); F. O. Francis, 'The Background of EMBATEUEIN'.

[121] Arnold (*Syncretism*, 5; cf. his index *s.v.* 'Folk belief') suggests that 'the best explanation for the Colossian "philosophy" lies in the quite general classification of folk religion'. A modern example may be pertinent. Many years ago, on a first visit to the United States, a Church of Scotland minister, born, brought up and trained in the Presbyterian tradition, attended a service in a church which had 'Presbyterian' on the board outside. The service began with a small boy, wearing a surplice, proceeding up the aisle with a lighted taper to light the candles upon what the officiating clergyman, also in a surplice, twice in the service referred to as the altar. None of this bore any resemblance to the Presbyterianism with which the Scot was familiar! Somewhere along the line elements from a different tradition had been grafted into this particular branch of Presbyterianism. Such syncretism may be perfectly legitimate, and on occasion helpful, and up to a point certainly quite harmless; but at what point does it begin to endanger the authenticity of a tradition?

More particularly, our author, whether Paul or some other, also lived in this intellectual 'atmosphere', and was subject to these same influences. This suggestion is sometimes indignantly rejected by those who think it implies that he was tainted with heresy, which is not necessarily the case.[122] In point of fact, it is now realized that the lines of division between 'orthodoxy' and 'heresy' were by no means so clear-cut in the early period as they were later to become.[123] What the suggestion means is that our author was a man of his own age, influenced as others were by the ideas of his time; but where his opponents laid their emphasis on certain things, he is concerned to bring out the supreme significance of Christ as Lord of all, and as the one in whom God has reconciled all things to himself.

[122] Regarding *The Teachings of Silvanus*, which is not Gnostic, J. Zandee remarks: 'In explaining the Christian message for men of their time, our author and Gnostic writers often used the same terminology and the same imagery, both being influenced by Hellenistic thought and contemporary philosophy' (*The Teachings of Sylvanus*, 539). Weiss, 'Gnostische Motive' argues that it is not enough to concentrate on anti-Gnostic polemic in Colossians and Ephesians and seeks to identify Gnostic motifs which have influenced the writer(s)—but without any thought of making these letters mere 'products of the gnostic schools' (312). Cf. Böhlig's comment about Gnostic *Umdeutung* of Jewish traditional material (n. 113). Pearson writes that the relationship between Gnostic myth and Judaism 'is parasitical in that the essential building blocks of the basic Gnostic myth constitute a revolutionary borrowing and reinterpretation of Jewish scriptures and traditions. But the resulting religious system is anything but Jewish!' (*Gnosticism, Judaism and Egyptian Christianity*, 9; he offers supporting evidence in chs 2–9 of this volume). Friedländer long ago spoke of 'mancherlei Umgestaltungen' (quoted ibid. 19). The point is that the occurrence of concepts and terminology within a Gnostic system does not necessarily mean that they are Gnostic outside of that system. As Lindemann neatly puts it: 'not everything that also occurs in Gnosis is gnostic' ('Gemeinde', 121 n. 42). C. H. Turner ('Greek Patristic Commentaries', 488) notes that Cyril of Alexandria 'could lay down the rule that not all the writings of heretics are heretical: οὐ πάντα ὅσα λέγουσιν οἱ αἱρετικοὶ φεύγειν καὶ παραιτεῖσθαι χρή, πολλὰ γὰρ ὁμολογοῦσιν ὧν καὶ ἡμεῖς ὁμολογοῦμεν'.

[123] Dunn (24) remarks that it is now much harder to speak of 'orthodoxy and heresy' as well-defined and uniform categories in the second century, let alone the first: 'if one persists with the idea of "orthodoxy", it would be hard to deny that some of the forms of earliest "Christianity" would be better designated as "heresy", at least as judged by the subsequent course of theology'.

COMMENTARY

I
OPENING SALUTATION
(1.1–2)

[1.1]Paul, apostle of Christ Jesus by the will of God, and Timothy our brother, [2]to the saints and faithful brethren in Christ at Colossae; grace to you and peace from God our Father.

Letters in the ancient world normally began with a more or less conventional formula, containing the name of the sender, that of the intended recipient, and a word of salutation, commonly translated in the form: A to B, greeting.[1] This can be seen from numerous examples, in the letters of Cicero for instance, or in the papyri, as well as in the New Testament. The formula may, however, take one or other of two different forms: the 'Greek' type is normally a single unit (although it may be expanded), and uses the verb χαίρειν in the infinitive as the salutation;[2] the 'oriental' type on the other hand is in two distinct parts: first the names of sender and recipient, and then the salutation in the form of a direct address, 'peace be with you'. Paul's letters, with their salutation as a separate unit, conform to the 'oriental' pattern, although he always expands it, first by adding some statement of his credentials, as servant of Jesus Christ or more commonly as apostle (but not in 1 and 2 Thess.), and secondly by transforming the χαίρειν used in the conventional Greek formula into a specifically Christian greeting: 'grace to you and peace from God the Father and our Lord Jesus Christ'.[3] In Romans, indeed, the expansion is such that the salutation takes up the whole of the first

[1] On the form of ancient letters, and particularly those of Paul, cf. Wendland, *Die hellenistisch-romische Kultur*, 411–17; Lohmeyer, 'Probleme paulinischer Theologie. I. Briefliche Grundüberschriften', *ZNW* 26 (1927), 158–73 (repr. in *Probleme paulinischer Theologie* (1954), 9–29); Roller, *Das Formular der paulinischen Briefe*; Friedrich, 'Lohmeyers These über das paulinische Briefpräskript kritisch beleuchtet', *TLZ* 81 (1956), 343–46; Lohse, 5. On Christian greetings in letters, cf. Moule, 153ff. The most recent discussion is that of M. Luther Stirewalt, *Paul the Letter Writer* (2003; reviewed *JBL* 123 (2004), 573ff.).

[2] Cf. Jas. 1.1 in the NT; also Acts 15.23; 23.26. The first of the letters in Acts has at the end the normal Greek 'farewell' ("Ερρωσθε, 15.29), which is added in some manuscripts at 23.30 also.

[3] Against the view of many scholars that Paul follows the 'oriental' model, Cranfield (*Romans*, 45f.) argues that the Pauline formula is based not on Jewish convention but on the normal Greek prescript. The use of χάρις certainly seems to derive from the Greek χαίρειν, but the two-part pattern suggests the 'oriental' model (cf. Thrall, *2 Corinthians*, 94f., who writes (95) of 'a harmonious combination of Greek and Jewish epistolary forms'). Lohse (5 n. 7) and Conzelmann (*TWNT* ix. 384 n. 175) draw attention to *2 Bar.* 78.2, 'Mercy and peace be with you', which recalls the form in Jude 2 (see below), and may provide a pointer to the way in which the formula was developed.

seven verses. Where there is a shorter text, as in Col. (omitting 'and our Lord Jesus Christ') or in 1 Thess. (which has only 'grace to you and peace'), the variant readings show that scribes were not slow to assimilate the text to normal Pauline usage (cf. Metzger, *Textual Commentary*, 619, 629).

Comparison of the opening formulae in Paul's letters is not without interest: in 1 and 2 Thess. he associates Silvanus and Timothy with himself, with no statement of credentials, while Phil. begins with the names of Paul and Timothy, described as 'servants of Christ Jesus'. Philemon is unique in describing Paul as δέσμιος Χριστοῦ Ἰησοῦ (cf. Eph. 3.1; 4.1), and in its lengthy list of addressees. The most emphatic assertion of apostleship is in Galatians, not surprisingly in that it was an attack upon Paul's claims to independence and on his very gospel that provoked that letter. 1 Corinthians has the longer form Παῦλος κλητὸς ἀπόστολος Χριστοῦ Ἰησοῦ διὰ θελήματος θεοῦ καὶ Σωσθένης ὁ ἀδελφός. 2 Cor. and Col. have the identical formula Παῦλος ἀπόστολος Χριστοῦ Ἰησοῦ διὰ θελήματος θεοῦ καὶ Τιμόθεος ὁ ἀδελφός, which is shared, but without the reference to Timothy, by Eph. and 2 Tim. (1 Tim. has the slight variation κατ' ἐπιταγὴν θεοῦ). Romans combines the formulae of Phil. and 1 Cor. into a more ceremonial form of statement, Παῦλος δοῦλος Ἰησοῦ Χριστοῦ, κλητὸς ἀπόστολος, and finally Titus has a variation entirely of its own, δοῦλος θεοῦ, ἀπόστολος δὲ Ἰησοῦ Χριστοῦ. What is striking here is that if we take the major letters which are generally recognized as authentic (Rom., 1 and 2 Cor., Gal., 1 Thess. and Phil.), then all the formulae are subtly different: Paul does not repeat the same form mechanically every time. Moreover, in the two cases in which identical formulae occur (1 and 2 Thess., and 2 Cor., Col., Eph., 2 Tim., with a possible variation in 1 Tim.), the authenticity of one letter in the first group and at least one in the second has been called in question: whatever may be said of the authenticity of 2 Thess., the Pastorals are generally regarded today as deutero-Pauline, while Eph. may be dependent on Col. itself (see Introduction; Lohse, 4 observes that in certain passages it 'reads like the first commentary on Colossians'). Now if a disciple wished to place his work under the aegis of Paul's authority, the obvious thing to do was to give it a 'Pauline' opening chosen from one of the letters with which he was familiar (the Epistle to the Laodiceans does exactly that, choosing the opening of Gal., but as noted in the Introduction that 'letter' is a mere pastiche of Pauline phrases and quite different from something produced in a Pauline 'school' at a date much nearer to, if not actually within, Paul's lifetime). There is a similar situation at Col. 4.18, where the words ὁ ἀσπασμὸς τῇ ἐμῇ χειρὶ Παύλου are identical with the form in 1 Cor. 16.21 (the only other occurrence, perhaps significantly, is in 2 Thess. 3.17). Such points are not in themselves proof that Col. is not authentic, but may serve as confirmatory evidence if on other grounds we have reason to doubt its authenticity.

1. Παῦλος is the name used by the apostle in all his letters, and by which he is known in the history of the Church. It was common for Jews in the ancient world to bear a Greek or Latin name as well as a Jewish one;[4] often the 'Gentile' name resembled the Hebrew or Aramaic name (e.g. the Silas of Acts is usually identified with the Silvanus of Paul's letters; Jesus or Joshua becomes Jason, and Saul Paul). At Acts 13.9 the formula Σαῦλος ὁ καί Παῦλος marks a transition: up to this point Luke has been striving to present Paul as a strict Jew, but now 'at the point where Paul is donning the mantle of the great missionary well known to every Christian, Luke has to switch over to the Roman *cognomen* which alone Paul employed in his epistles and which alone is familiar to later Christendom' (Haenchen, *Acts* (ET 1971), 399 n. 1). Since the time of Jerome (*De*

[4]See Deissmann, *Bible Studies*, 313ff.; *EncBib* 3306, *s.v.* 'Names', §86; *Beg.* iv. 14, 144–46.

vir. ill. 5, PL 23, 646) it has often been suggested that Paul derived the name from the governor Sergius Paulus, mentioned two verses earlier at Acts 13.7, but for several reasons this is unlikely. Origen (*Comm. in Rom.*, PG 14, 836–38) already mentions this opinion, but prefers the simpler solution that Paul always had two names, the one for use in ministering to his own people, the other when he was engaged in the Gentile mission. According to Acts 22.28, Paul was a Roman citizen by birth, and a Roman citizen commonly had three names, the *praenomen* or personal name, the *nomen* or clan name, and the *cognomen* or family name (e.g. Marcus Tullius Cicero, Gaius Julius Caesar). In addition he might have an informal name, the *signum* or *supernomen*, used by his intimate friends, which in Greek was usually indicated by the ὁ καί formula used in Acts. The *signum* could either precede or follow the other name, separated by the ὁ καί, and in Paul's case it is probable that Paulus was the *cognomen* and Saul the *signum* (the family belonged to the tribe of Benjamin (Phil. 3.5), the tribe of King Saul).[5]

As indicated in the Introduction, the authenticity of Colossians is still in dispute. It therefore seems advisable to use neutral terms such as 'the author' or 'the writer' in referring to the person who actually wrote Colossians, and to reserve the name Paul for the Paul of the generally recognized major letters. Sometimes the two correspond very closely, but at other points a contrast has to be drawn. Those who are not convinced that the letter is pseudonymous are of course at liberty to substitute the name for the more neutral term. It would also appear desirable not to prejudge the issue in regard to date, or presuppose one or other of various possible scenarios for the letter. We have to determine the situation as it emerges from the evidence of Colossians itself.

ἀπόστολος in the New Testament is a rather fluid term, which does not always carry the connotations of rank and status commonly associated with the word (see Moule, 155ff.).[6] Sometimes the use is entirely general, with reference simply to a messenger (e.g. Phil. 2.25, where Epaphroditus is the Philippians' 'apostle' (NEB, 'whom you commissioned to minister to my needs'); cf. also John 13.16, where NEB translates with 'messenger', and 2 Cor. 8.23 ('delegates of our congregations')). In other passages it is clearly restricted to the Twelve: if the text is doubtful at Mark 3.14, there is no question about Luke 6.13, and the term is applied to them at Mark 6.30 as well as in Matt. 10.2 and in several passages in Luke, to say nothing

[5] See G. A. Harrer, 'Saul Who Also is Called Paul', *HTR* 33 (1940), 19–34; Haenchen, *Acts* 399 n.1; *Beg.* iv. 145–46; Knowling, *EGT* ii. 287; Barrett, *Acts*, i. 616; Cranfield, *Romans*, 48–50.
[6] See Kirsopp Lake, 'The Twelve and the Apostles', *Beg.* v. 37–59; K. H. Rengstorf, *TWNT* i. 406–46; Schnackenburg, 'Apostles Before and During Paul's Time'; J. A. Kirk, 'Apostleship since Rengstorf', *NTS* 21 (1975), 249–64; Barrett, 'Shaliach and Apostle'; J. Roloff, *TRE* 3 (1978), 430–45; Thrall, *2 Corinthians*, 946–55; Best, 'Paul's Apostolic Authority—?'; W. A. Bienert in Schneemelcher (ed.), *Neutestamentliche Apokryphen*, ii, 5th edn (1989), 6–28 (ET 1993, 5–27). Further references in Moule, 155; Lohse, 6 n. 12; Dunn, 44 n. 8. See also E. Earle Ellis's table ('Paul and his Co-workers', (438) listing the passages where the term is applied to one or another of Paul's co-workers. J. P. Meier (*JBL* 116 (1997), 636–42) discusses the 'three distinct but partially overlapping' terms—disciples, apostles and the Twelve—in an effort to clear up the confusion often encountered.

of numerous references in Acts (at Acts 1.26 Matthias is 'numbered with the eleven apostles' on his election to replace Judas). In still other cases the usage appears to be technical, but somewhat broader: thus Paul and Barnabas are called apostles at Acts 14.14; Andronicus and Junia(s) are ἐπίσημοι ἐν τοῖς ἀποστόλοις at Rom. 16.7;[7] James the Lord's brother seems to be counted an apostle at Gal. 1.19. Paul's claim to be an apostle is weak if we take Acts 1.21–22 as the standard, but this is the outlook of a later age than Paul's own time (cf., however, 1 Cor. 15.9, where he describes himself as 'unfit to be called an apostle, because I persecuted the church of God'; regarding Eph. 3.8, Scott (120) asks, 'Would [Paul] have overdone his humility by alluding to himself as less than the least of the saints?'). It is worthy of note that whereas in the NT we frequently find Paul fighting to establish his claim, in the second century he has become *the* Apostle (e.g. the Nag Hammadi *Hypostasis of the Archons* (NHC II 86.21ff.) begins with a reference to 'the great apostle' and an allusion to Col. 1.13, followed immediately by a quotation of Eph. 6.12; the *Treatise on the Resurrection* (NHC I 45.24) has 'as the Apostle said', followed by 'a non-literal mélange of Rom. 8.17 and Eph. 2: 5–6'; see M. L. Peel in Attridge (ed.), *Nag Hammadi Codex I: Notes*, (NHS 23 (Leiden, 1985), 162)). Lohse (6) notes that in Colossians there is no reference to any other apostle: 'as the apostle to the Gentiles who holds the commission to proclaim the Good News to the heathen, he is *the* Apostle'.[8] If the letter was written by a later disciple, this might suggest that it marks a stage on the way to the second-century situation; but too much should not be built on this.

Χριστοῦ Ἰησοῦ For the order, cf. for example Rom. 1.1; 2.16; 3.24; 1 Cor. 1.1, 2, 4; 4.15; Phil. 2.5. Elsewhere we find the order Ἰησοῦς Χριστός, without any difference of meaning (Rom 1.4, 6–8; 3.22 etc.; in 1 Cor. 1.1–4 Paul switches easily from the one order to the other, but the change in vv. 2–3 may be due to the prefixing of the title κύριος—cf. vv. 7, 8 and 10; in v. 9, εἰς κοινωνίαν τοῦ υἱοῦ Ἰησοῦ Χριστοῦ τοῦ κυρίου ἡμῶν, the κύριος title is naturally

---

[7] For the view that the latter name should be taken as feminine, Junia, see Cranfield, *Romans*, 788f.; Cervin, *NTS* 40 (1994), 464–70; Thorley, *NovTest* 38 (1996), 18–29; Plisch, *NTS* 42 (1996), 477–78; Schreiber, *NTS* 46 (2000), 212–14. Also Burer and Wallace, *NTS* 47 (2001), 76–91, who argue that the phrase *'almost certainly* means "well known *to* the apostles" '; but against this see L. Belleville, *NTS* 51 (2005), 231–49.

[8] Cf. J. Jervell, *NTS* 32 (1986), 389: 'In Colossians Paul is quite simply the Apostle. It is no longer a question of "Jews and heathen", but of the Creation, the whole world, 1:23; 3:11; cf. 1:20—for which Paul alone is now competent, 1:23b, 25, 28. Other Apostles are not mentioned, but also there is no place for them. Judaistic Christianity is still there as a problem, for there is polemic against observance of the law, 2:11, and the polemic is directed against members of the congregation, not against outsiders; the author also knows of Paul's last Jewish Christian co-workers, 4:11, who are recognisable as a group. Circumcision is now an expression for Baptism, 2:11–12, although the Jewish conception of uncircumcision, *akrobystia*, is used as a characteristic of heathen life, 2:13.' On Paul in the early Church, see Lindemann, *Paulus im ältesten Christentum* (for Col., regarded as 'the earliest of the post-Paulines', see 38–40, 114–22).

68   COMMENTARY ON COLOSSIANS

transposed to the end). According to M. E. Thrall (2 Corinthians, i. 80f.) 'Jesus Christ' is the normal form in the NT as a whole, and also in the Pauline epistles: there are 48 examples in the generally accepted letters as against 37 of 'Christ Jesus' (in each case excluding variants).[9] Dunn (46) notes this as 'one of the small stylistic features that suggest a different hand than Paul's'.

Χριστός[10] is properly a title, and translates the Hebrew (or Aramaic) Messiah (= the Anointed One), which was current among the Jews of the NT period as a designation for the long-awaited redeemer, usually regarded as of the lineage of David, who would deliver Israel from her enemies and restore her former glories. Here, as often in Paul's letters, it has become almost a second name for Jesus. The point in this verse is that Paul is Christ's apostle, his emissary, and speaks in his name.

διὰ θελήματος θεοῦ As in 1 Cor. 1.1 and 2 Cor. 1.1 (cf. also Eph. 1.1; 2 Tim. 1.1) these words state the basis of Paul's claim to apostleship: it is by the will of God, who 'had set me apart before I was born and called me through his grace' (Gal. 1.15). In Galatians Paul is emphatic that he does not owe his apostleship to any human agency ('not from men nor through man, but through Jesus Christ and God the Father' (RSV)), but here there is no such element of polemic. Whatever concern the 'false teaching' may have aroused, there is no need for defence against attacks such as were made in Galatia and in Corinth (Lohse refers to Gal. 1.1, 10–12; 1 Cor. 9.1, 3; 2 Cor. 10–13, and adds that there is no need as in Romans to win the approval of the community or canvass their support for his further mission; Lightfoot notes that the phrase is used also at Rom. 15.32, 2 Cor. 8.5, 'where no polemical reference is possible'[11]).

καὶ Τιμόθεος Cf. Ollrog, Mitarbeiter, 20–23. Timothy, one of Paul's most trusted co-workers, is named along with Paul in 2 Cor. 1.1; Phil. 1.1; 1 Thess. 1.1; 2 Thess. 1.1 (in these two cases together with Silvanus) and Philem. 1, as well as in Colossians, but this does not mean that he had a share in the writing of these letters, or acted

[9] Accepting the longer reading at the end of the salutation (see below), Drake, 'The Riddle of Colossians' argues for a deliberate purpose on the part of the author in his choice of word order: 'By enclosing the phrase, "in Christ", between "Christ Jesus" and the juxtaposed, "Jesus Christ", the author announces his theme (1.2) and declares the chiastic "Christ"-form of the letter itself' (129). It is, however, doubtful if Col. is really to be regarded as an elaborate piece of ironic word-play. Despite numerous acute observations the article does not really seem to solve the 'riddle' of which its title speaks. Moreover, the Χριστοῦ of v. 3 is omitted by B1739 1881; if this were the true text, it would spoil the symmetry of Drake's pattern.
[10] See BAGD 887; TWNT ix. 532ff. (Χριστός in Paul's letters), 550ff. (Χριστός in Col. and Eph.); cf. also Hengel, 'Erwägungen'; de Jonge, 'The Earliest Christian Use of Christos'.
[11] Lightfoot's commentary on Colossians and Philemon has the Greek text at the top of the page, with his notes beneath (so also Peake). This means that comments quoted are normally to be found on the page carrying the verse under discussion. It is therefore not so necessary to supply specific page references as in the case of running commentaries, where discussion of a passage may extend over several pages. References to Lightfoot are to the 1875 edition.

as Paul's secretary; the stylistic differences between the letters would rule that out. In any case, after using first person plurals at 1.3, 7 and 9 (disregarding those cases where the plural may be comprehensive, embracing all Christians, e.g. 1.13, 14), the writer switches at 1.23 to the singular, here as at 1.25 quite emphatically, and uses it throughout to the end of the letter (except at 4.8, where the text is in some doubt; Lightfoot notes (197) that the exceptions at 1.28 and 4.3 'are rather apparent than real'). The point of the reference to Timothy here, as in the other letters, is to indicate that Paul (if he is the author) is not writing merely on his own account; his fellow-workers also share his concern for the well-being of the addressees. It may be added that there is a subtle distinction in the appended titles: Timothy is not an apostle, but ὁ ἀδελφός, a fellow-member of the larger Christian community. Those who think of Colossians as written by a disciple during Paul's lifetime sometimes suggest the name of Timothy, which is certainly a possibility to be considered. It might also perhaps be suggested that he was the disciple who wrote the letter under Paul's name after the apostle's death: what would he have done, what could he have done, had he learned of an outbreak of false teaching in Asia Minor somewhere around AD 70? Even as Paul's co-worker he might not possess, or feel he possessed, the authority to write in his own name (cf. Cothenet, Fischer); but from long years of association he knew Paul's theology, and he probably also knew something of Paul's letters (he is after all named along with Paul in the superscription of at least four authentic letters). At any rate it is a Pauline answer to the situation that he is trying to present, so naturally he placed Paul's name before his own. Both these suggestions as to authorship, however, lead us into the realm of speculation.

2. τοῖς ἐν Κολοσσαῖς ἁγίοις καὶ πιστοῖς ἀδελφοῖς ἐν Χριστῷ The letter is clearly addressed to the Christian community in Colossae, but the term ἐκκλησία is not used in the opening salutation (contrast the letters to Corinth and Thessalonica; Galatians has ταῖς ἐκκλησίαις, implying not the local congregation in a city but several communities spread over a wider area). Abbott explains the absence of the term here on the assumption that Paul, writing to a church not known to him, wished to avoid an official-sounding expression,[12] but while this might apply in the case of Romans (1.7: πᾶσιν τοῖς οὖσιν ἐν Ῥώμῃ ἀγαπητοῖς, κλητοῖς ἁγίοις) it certainly would not hold for Philippians (1.1: πᾶσιν τοῖς ἁγίοις ἐν Χριστῷ Ἰησοῦ τοῖς οὖσιν ἐν Φιλίπποις), a church with which Paul clearly had the most friendly and cordial relations. Lightfoot sees here a chronological indicator: the earlier letters all use ἐκκλησία in some form, but beginning with

[12] Cf. G. C. Martin (130): 'In other Epistles the word "church" or (as in Philippians) a form that implies it, is employed. It may be that this more personal form is used expressly to denote his kindly feeling of Christian love towards churches in which he is not personally known.' The kindly feeling is beyond doubt, but whether this is the explanation is quite another matter.

Romans 'the Apostle always uses ἁγίοις in various combinations in addressing Churches (Rom, Phil, Col, Eph)'. This, however, raises questions of Pauline chronology and of authenticity, which cannot be entered into here; if Rom. and Phil. are commonly regarded as genuinely Pauline, Eph. is widely considered to be pseudepigraphic, and the authenticity of Col., as indicated in the Introduction, is the subject of debate. Those who hold to the traditional chronology, with Romans written before Paul came to Rome and the three 'Captivity Epistles' sent during his imprisonment there, will find no difficulty with Lightfoot's suggestion; but the numerous critical problems that have been raised make it doubtful if that traditional chronology is tenable any longer.

The formulation is unusual, and presents certain problems: ἅγιος is properly an adjective, meaning 'dedicated to God, holy, sacred' (cf. BAGD 9f.; TWNT i. 87–112) and could be so used here, in which case ἁγίοις καὶ πιστοῖς must be taken together as qualifying ἀδελφοῖς (so Moule, who argues that to treat τοῖς ἁγίοις as a noun and the rest as descriptive 'would probably require the repetition of the article: τοῖς καὶ πιστοῖς'.). Greek adjectives, however, can also be used substantivally, and Paul's use of the word in other letters suggests that for him ἅγιοι (in the plural)[13] was almost a technical term (cf. Rom. 1.7 and Phil. 1.1, quoted above, and εἰς πάντας τοὺς ἁγίους in v. 4 below). Lightfoot and others take the word as a noun in accordance with usage elsewhere ('in the salutations of 2 Cor, Eph. and Phil. it is certainly a substantive': Peake, 495. Bengel already wrote, 'This has the force of a substantive', taking it as describing their relationship to God, and the following πιστοῖς ἀδελφοῖς as descriptive of their relation to other Christians). A possible alternative is that our author, misunderstanding the Pauline usage, has written ἁγίοις as an adjective and then added καὶ πιστοῖς as a further qualification: 'to the holy and faithful brothers'; this would make it another point against authenticity.

More important is the significance of this term as a common designation for Christians (cf. BAGD, s.v. 2dβ), not in terms of any 'saintliness' of their own[14] but as 'elect of God, holy and beloved' (3.12). The background here lies in the OT: 'Israel is God's holy people (Exod 19: 6), who shall be holy because he is holy (Lev 11.44; 19.2; etc). His community is not holy by reason of its own power, but by reason of God's election' (Lohse, 7, who adds that the Qumran community understood themselves as 'the people of the saints of the

[13] Denney (EGT ii. 587) notes that 'as a synonym for Christian, it is never applied in the NT to an individual: no person is called ἅγιος'. Jesus is addressed as ὁ ἅγιος τοῦ θεοῦ at Mark 1.24; Luke 4.34 (cf. John 6.69). The singular is frequently used of God in LXX, in the phrase ὁ ἅγιος τοῦ Ἰσραήλ (Ps. 71 (70). 22; Ezek. 39.7 and often in Isaiah). 'Thine Holy One' (AV Ps. 16.10, quoted in Acts 2.27; 13.35) is ὅσιος.

[14] Cf. Moule (45): ' "Saint" is, to modern ears, misleading, for the Hebrew and Greek words are concerned less with any excellence of character (however much that may be implied as a result) than with the commitments and loyalties of the Church to the God who has made her his own.' Christians are 'a brotherhood dedicated and loyal to God'.

Covenant', citing 1QM X.10 and other passages). In the LXX version of the OT verses cited, ἅγιος is an adjective, but it is used substantivally in Pss. 15 (16).3; 33.10 (34.9); 88.6, 8 (89.5, 7); 105 (106).16 and in several verses of the seventh chapter of Daniel; in all these passages NRSV translates 'holy ones', although it regularly has 'saints' in NT passages. At Pss. 30.4; 37.28; 50.5; 79.2 and other verses AV uses 'saints' to translate a different Hebrew word, which LXX renders by ὅσιος, a word employed only eight times in the NT (BAGD 855b; *TWNT* v. 488–91); NRSV here has 'faithful' or 'faithful ones'; but at Ps. 31.23 it follows AV. In Ps. 89.5–7 the context suggests that the 'holy ones' are heavenly beings, which will be of relevance for the understanding of v. 12 below (for the use of the word of angels, cf. BAGD *s.v.* 1bβ, 2dα), but in the other cases mentioned they are quite certainly an earthly community.

If Col. is pseudepigraphic, and dated to about AD 70, this address presents a further problem, in that Colossae at that time was probably in ruins (see Introduction). The letter, however, gives the impression of being addressed to an actual situation, intended to deal with a real danger threatening a specific community. The implication is that the address is a fiction, and that the real destination is some other community: Lindemann for example suggests Laodicea, while Pokorný (21) thinks of 'the broader region of the province of Asia', but takes 4.16 as possibly conveying a hint of the actual destination. It is easy enough to speculate, to think of possible explanations, but this is an area where it is dangerous to pile one hypothesis upon another; any attempt to reconstruct the situation in detail must be considered speculative.

πιστοῖς This term presents something of a problem for the translator, since it can be used both actively and passively (see BAGD 664b–65a), i.e. as meaning either 'believing' or 'trustworthy'. It is used in the latter sense of God (πιστὸς δὲ ὁ θεός, 1 Cor. 1.9; 10.13; 2 Cor. 1.18; cf. Heb. 10.23) or of Christ (2 Thess. 3.3; 2 Tim. 2.13; Rev. 1.5; 3.14; 19.11), and in other passages of people counted as reliable (e.g. Matt. 25.21, 23; Luke 16.10–12; Heb. 3.2, 5); Paul uses it of Timothy at 1 Cor. 4.17, and it is used in this sense at Col. 1.7 (Epaphras); 4.7 (Tychicus; cf. Eph. 6.21) and 4.9 (Onesimus). In the present case however it is often taken to mean rather 'believing' (cf. John 20.27; so e.g. Peake, Lohse): the phrase as a whole would then mean 'the "saints" and brothers who believe' (i.e. in Christ). Lightfoot, however, objects that on this view πιστοῖς 'would add nothing which is not already contained in ἁγίοις and ἀδελφοῖς' and argues that the passive sense must be prominent here: 'when he speaks of the saints, he means the true and steadfast members' of the community. Certainly, even if the word is taken in the active sense, the element of trustworthiness is not entirely absent: those who are faithful and believing should also be trustworthy and reliable. Fortunately the English 'faithful' can also be used in both senses (cf. Scott, 14). It should perhaps be added that we cannot construe πιστοῖς with ἐν Χριστῷ and translate 'believing in Christ': πιστοῖς is separated from ἐν Χριστῷ by ἀδελφοῖς, and 'πιστός ἐν as = "trusting in" cannot be paralleled in the N. T. except (at most, and doubtfully) by Eph. i. 1' (Moule, 46).

ἀδελφοῖς This word, already applied above to Timothy, was a common term for Christians, and the plural here would include the female members of the community; the masculine form could be taken to include women, and repetition of the word with only minor changes in termination was felt unnecessary, unless there were special reasons. NRSV translates 'brothers and sisters', with the footnote 'Gk brothers', but it is questionable whether 'politically correct' turns of phrase should be imported into the translation of an ancient text (cf. J. Barton's review of the REB and NRSV in JTS 43 (1992), 548f.; also Dunn, 43 n. 4); the ancient world was in any case notoriously male-dominated. The word is often used in Paul's major letters as a vocative, in addressing the readers (e.g. Rom. 1.13; 7.1, 4; 1 Cor. 1.10, 11, 26 etc.), but as Schweizer notes, not in Colossians (cf. Schenk, ANRW II.25.4, 3333). In 4.7 it is used of Tychicus, in 4.9 of Onesimus, while at 4.15 the readers are enjoined to greet 'the brethren in Laodicea'. Ellis ('Paul and his Co-Workers', 445ff.) argues that in some passages the word may carry a more restricted meaning, referring specifically to Paul's co-workers, which may well be true but should not be generalized;[15] it may be relevant for Timothy and Tychicus in other letters, possibly also for Onesimus, but it seems more natural to take 'the brethren in Laodicea' at 4.15 as referring to the Christian community there.

ἐν Χριστῷ This phrase and its equivalents were popular with Paul to describe the relation of the believer to Christ (cf. BAGD 259 s.v. ἐν 5d and references there; TWNT ii. 537f.; Best, One Body in Christ, index.). The pioneer study of this formula was Deissmann's Die neutestamentliche Formel 'in Christo Jesu' (1892), but much has been written on the subject in the past century, and few would fully subscribe to Deissmann's view today (bibliography of older works in Deissmann, Paul, 140 n. 1). Duncan (Galatians, 103) observes that 'we find over 160 instances' of this and correlative expressions, 'the more remarkable in view of their absence from the Synoptic Gospels, Hebrews and James'. It is not enough, however, merely to count occurrences of the formula; we need also to distinguish the nuances in the use of the terms. To speak of a redemption which is ἐν Χριστῷ Ἰησοῦ (Rom. 3.24), or of ζωὴ αἰώνιος ἐν Χριστῷ Ἰησοῦ (Rom. 6.23), is not quite the same as to refer to people as ἐν Χριστῷ, although there is indeed a connection in that in each case there is a focus upon Christ. It has been remarked that at times the phrase is almost equivalent to 'Christian' (cf. Lohse, 9 n. 30; Moule, Origin of Christology, 54), but this cannot be said of each and every occurrence. These phrases have been interpreted in terms of

[15] Against this suggestion Dunn (48) writes, 'the term indicates a warmth of fraternal feeling and common (spiritual) kinship rather than a title or office restricted to a few special individuals'.

mysticism, but in so far as there is mysticism here it is a peculiarly Pauline 'Christ-mysticism', which centres in the thought of union with Christ; it is not a question of absorption into Christ, but of fellowship with him.[16] The background is rather the Hebrew concept of corporate personality or solidarity (cf. Best, *One Body in Christ*, 203–07): Adam and Christ are representatives of the old and the new humanity (1 Cor. 15.22; Rom. 5.12–21), so that the unredeemed are 'in Adam' and the redeemed 'in Christ'. We may recall also Paul's frequent use of the imagery of the body: as members of the Body of Christ, Christians may be said to be 'in Christ'. Again, those who are redeemed 'in Christ', i.e. by his death upon the cross, are delivered from bondage to sin and the law, set free to live a new life 'in Christ', i.e. in a new sphere of existence in which Christ alone holds sovereign sway. In short, the phrase is more wide-ranging than is sometimes realized, and not readily to be subsumed under a single definition. In Col. it occurs three times in this first chapter, but not thereafter (but we should add the pronominal phrases ἐν ᾧ, 1.14; 2.3, 11, and ἐν αὐτῷ 1.16, 17, 19; 2.9); later in the letter it is replaced by its equivalent ἐν κυρίῳ (3.18, 20; 4.7), probably because the readers are enjoined at 3.18 to do everything ἐν ὀνόματι κυρίου Ἰησοῦ. The phrase and its equivalents are much more frequent in Eph., where (including cases of ἐν with a pronoun replacing the name) there are a dozen occurrences in the first chapter alone. The phrase here in Col. is probably 'incorporative', but is not necessarily always so.[17]

The occurrence here of this familiar Pauline formula might be thought to tell in favour of the authenticity of Colossians, and against any theory of pseudepigraphy, but this is not necessarily the case. If a disciple writing in Paul's name could use a 'Pauline' opening (see above), he might equally have chosen on occasion to use a familiar Pauline formula. Its occurrence here cannot be used either in support of or against the authenticity of Col. Moreover, the phrase or something similar also occurs in several other, non-Pauline letters: 1 Tim. 1.14; 3.13; 2 Tim. 1.1, 9, 13; 2.1, 10; 3.12, 15; 1 Pet. 3.16; 5.10; cf. also 1 John 5.20; Jude 1. At one time the Pastorals would have been regarded as Pauline, and the other occurrences would all have been ascribed without more ado to Pauline influence, but the days of

[16] On mysticism in Paul cf. Schweitzer, *The Mysticism of Paul the Apostle*; Kennedy, *St Paul and the Mystery Religions*, 284–94; J. S. Stewart, *A Man in Christ* (1941), 147ff.; Best, *One Body*, 12ff., 23f.; T. W. Manson, *On Paul and John*, ed. M. Black (1963), 67ff.

[17] Cf. Kennedy, *Theology of the Epistles*, 119–25; Dodd, *Gospel and Law*, 36f.; C. A. A. Scott, *Christianity According to St Paul* (1939), 150ff.; Taylor, *Forgiveness and Reconciliation* (1941), 135ff.; Bultmann, *Theologie*, 307, 323f., and for Colossians, 520; Conzelmann, *Outline*, 199ff., esp. 208–11; Moule, *Origin*, 7ff., esp. 54ff.; Barrett, *Adam*, esp. 95f.; Thrall, *2 Corinthians*, 425–29; Best, *Ephesians*, 153–54. Also Neugebauer, 'Das Paulinische "In Christo"' and *In Christus*; Bouttier, *En Christ*; Wedderburn, 'Some Observations'. In 'Das Paulinische "In Christo"' (136) Neugebauer notes that in the first two chapters of Col. we find only the 'Christ' formula, in the last two only the 'kurios' formula, and adds that Col. is almost more Pauline than Paul himself. Cf. also Dunn, 'Transformation', 49–50; U. Schnelle, 68–69.

an 'all-pervasive Paulinism' are now long gone (cf. Hunter, *Paul and his Predecessors*; for 1 Peter, cf. Selwyn, *The First Epistle of Peter* (1955), 20f.). The Pastorals are now generally regarded as deutero-Pauline, i.e. the products of a Pauline school; and this is precisely the view here advocated for Col. and Eph. They are probably not by Paul himself, but the work of later disciples. If we may fairly speak of Pauline influence here in Col., the other references suggest that use of the formula was more widely spread.

χάρις καὶ εἰρήνη The distinctively Christian formula combines a variation of the Greek (χαίρειν) and the Jewish (εἰρήνη = *shalom*) forms of salutation into an expression of the Christian experience of God's grace and the peace which results.[18] The full formula χάρις ὑμῖν καὶ εἰρήνη ἀπὸ θεοῦ πατρός ἡμῶν appears in Rom., 1 and 2 Cor., Eph., Phil., Col., and Philem., while Gal. and 2 Thess. omit ἡμῶν; 1 Thess. has simply χάρις ὑμῖν καὶ εἰρήνη. Of the Pastorals, Titus has χάρις καὶ εἰρήνη ἀπὸ θεοῦ πατρός; 1 and 2 Tim. read χάρις, ἔλεος, εἰρήνη. That the formula is not merely Pauline is shown by the variation in 1 and 2 Peter, χάρις ὑμῖν καὶ εἰρήνη πληθυνθείη, and the χάρις ὑμῖν καὶ εἰρήνη ἀπὸ ὁ ὢν καὶ ὁ ἦν καὶ ὁ ἐρχομένος of Rev. 1.4.[19] Jude 2 has ἔλεος ὑμῖν καὶ εἰρήνη πληθυνθείη.

'In Paul χάρις is the central concept which gives the clearest expression to his understanding of the salvation event' (cf. Conzelmann, *TWNT* ix. 383–87).[20] The word means basically something that gives pleasure, a gift or favour, a gracious attitude, or thanks and gratitude on the part of the recipient. Paul uses it over and over again for the undeserved grace of God revealed in Christ. His gospel is neatly summed up in a verse in Ephesians (2.8) which Conzelmann (387) describes as 'formulated in consciously Pauline terms': 'by grace you have been saved through faith, and this is not your own doing; it is the gift of God—not the result of works, so that no one may boast'. In Rom. 1.5 and other passages (Rom. 12.3; 15.15; cf. 1 Cor. 3.10; Eph. 3.2, 7) Paul's own apostleship and authority are described as gifts of God's grace. This apparently simple greeting formula is thus full of significance.

As noted above, εἰρήνη (for the NT cf. Foerster, *TWNT* ii. 398–418; BAGD 227–28) is the equivalent of the Jewish greeting *shalom*, 'peace', but this also is a term too often passed over lightly. 'Since, according to the prophets, peace will be an essential characteristic of the messianic kingdom, Christian thought also frequently regards εἰρήνη as nearly synonymous with messianic salvation' (BAGD 227a, *s.v.* 3). This peace is not just a matter of the absence of war and

[18] See Moule, 153ff.; also Robinson, *Ephesians*, 221–26; Cranfield, *Romans*, 71f.; Thrall, *2 Corinthians*, 94–97.

[19] For Dunn (51) these 'probably reflect the influence of Paul's formulation'.

[20] Cf. also BAGD 877–78 (for use at the beginning and end of letters see 2c); Moffatt, *Grace in the New Testament*, (1931); Doughty, 'The Priority of ΧΑΡΙΞ'. Also the article 'Gnade', *TRE* 13 (1984), 459–511, esp. III, 'Neues Testament' (467–76, by E. Ruckstuhl).

strife; there are also more positive aspects. The philosopher Epictetus (iii.13.9ff.) wrote to the effect that 'Caesar can give peace from war, but he cannot give peace from sorrow': there are other cares and anxieties from which people may seek release; 'but the doctrine of the philosophers promises to give us peace from these troubles too' (Loeb translation). Later (iii.13.12) he speaks of 'peace proclaimed by God through the word' (i.e. philosophy). At Rom. 5.1 Paul writes, 'since we are justified by faith, we have peace with God through our Lord Jesus Christ'; justification, reconciliation and the peace with God that results are all God's gift, as the following ἀπὸ θεοῦ πατρός ἡμῶν here shows. 'Grace and peace come from God, upon whom as their Father the faithful call with complete confidence' (Lohse, 10).

ἀπὸ θεοῦ πατρὸς ἡμῶν This is the only letter in which Christ is not coupled with God in the greetings formula and, as noted above, scribes were not slow to supply the deficiency.

The textual evidence (see UBS text and Metzger, *Textual Commentary*, 619) is: ἡμῶν: BDKΨ 33 81 1739 it[d, 61, 86] vg syr[p, h] cop[sa] arm eth[ro]// ἡμῶν καὶ κυρίου Ἰησοῦ Χριστοῦ ℵACGI 88 614 Byz Lect al// The same addition appears also in other witnesses, in one case with a second ἡμῶν after κυρίου, in another with τοῦ κυρίου ἡμῶν transposed to follow Ἰησοῦ Χριστοῦ (the apparatus in NA[27] shows some differences in the citation of witnesses). There is no very obvious reason for omission, and such variations are often an indication of an insertion, different scribes making the addition at a different point or in a different order. Lightfoot remarks that both Origen and Chrysostom noticed the omission, so that the expansion would be after their time.
As already noted, Drake ('Riddle', 130f.) accepts the longer reading, but his dependence on such variant readings may in itself be a weakness in his theory.

The salutation is conventional, but not merely formal and remote. There is as yet nothing to indicate that the addressees are unknown to the author. They are addressed as brothers and sisters in Christ, fellow-members of the Christian society, although Lightfoot detects in the καὶ πιστοῖς ἀδελφοῖς an oblique hint at the defection in the community: 'the Apostle wishes it to be understood that, when he speaks of the saints, he means the true and stedfast members of the brotherhood'. This, however, is perhaps to read in more than is really there: has defection already taken place, or is it a danger the author seeks to warn against? Is there division within the community, or is there a threat from outside? Such questions will require our attention as we proceed. Whatever the situation, we may note a significant difference from Galatians, where the greeting in v. 3 is sandwiched between an emphatic assertion of Paul's commission to apostleship in v. 1 and a succinct summary of his gospel in v. 4 ('who gave himself for our sins to set us free from the present evil age'). There Paul moves immediately to the attack, whereas here the first note is one of thanksgiving; but in both cases the greeting wishes for the addressees that grace and peace which only God can give.

II
THANKSGIVING FOR THE FAITH OF THE COLOSSIANS
(1.3–8)

[3]We give thanks to God the Father of our Lord Jesus Christ at all times when we pray concerning you, [4]since we have heard of your faith in Christ Jesus and the love which you have towards all the saints [5]because of the hope that is laid up for you in heaven. Of this [hope] you heard before in the word of the truth of the gospel [6]that came to you. Just as it is bearing fruit and increasing in all the world, so it is also among you from the day you heard it and came to know the grace of God in truth; [7]even as you learned from Epaphras our beloved fellow-servant, who is a faithful minister of Christ on our behalf [8]and has also made known to us your love in the Spirit.

Paul regularly begins his letters with an expression of thanksgiving (see Rom. 1.8; 1 Cor. 1.4; Phil. 1.3; 1 Thess. 1.2; 2 Thess. 1.3; Philem. 4), normally using εὐχαριστῶ in the singular (Rom., 1 Cor., Phil., Philem).[1] The plural εὐχαριστοῦμεν appears here and in 1 Thess., while 2 Thess. reads εὐχαριστεῖν ὀφείλομεν. The benedictions beginning εὐλογητὸς ὁ θεός in 2 Cor. 1.3 and Eph. 1.3 serve much the same purpose (but cf. Eph. 1.16; the real parallel to Col. 1.3–4 is in Eph. 1.15–17). According to Schubert (*Form and Function*, 183f.), the 'less intimate εὐλογητός-proemium of II Cor' characterizes a letter 'directed to a church with which Paul is in open battle';[2] that letter certainly bears witness to the heat of the conflict, but it may be questioned whether the εὐλογητός form in itself is indeed 'less intimate'; Moule (47) would seem to be more accurate in speaking of 'the fervent εὐλογητὸς ὁ θεός'—these passages, like 1 Pet. 1.3ff., are more an exclamation of triumphant rejoicing. The one letter without

---

[1] The pioneer study is Schubert, *Form and Function of the Pauline Thanksgivings*. See also O'Brien, 'Thanksgiving and the Gospel in Paul', and his *Introductory Thanksgivings in the Letters of Paul* (for Col. see 62–104); cf. also his 'Thanksgiving within the Structure of Pauline Theology'. On the thanksgivings in Colossians and Philemon cf. Mullins, 'Thanksgiving'.

[2] Thrall (*2 Corinthians*, 99) remarks, 'It can hardly be that Paul felt the situation in Corinth did not allow for thankfulness' and adds in a footnote that Schubert's suggestion 'would be appropriate only if the letter were a unity'. O'Brien (*Introductory Thanksgivings*, 233; see the whole discussion, 233–58) calls 2 Cor. 1.3ff. 'the most personal of Paul's introductory paragraphs', and offers some explanations for his substitution of a *berakah* for the normal thanksgiving (239, 257): he had already given thanks for the Corinthian community's graces (1 Cor. 1.4–9), and apparently considered it more fitting to use the term with a Greek background when referring to graces given to others and employ the formula with a Jewish background where he himself was involved. As noted above, in Gal. Paul is too heated to include any thanksgiving at all.

a thanksgiving period is Galatians, where Paul is so heated that he launches immediately into attack (but cf. Schubert, 162f.). It may be noted that of the three cases which diverge from the pattern using εὐχαριστῶ or εὐχαριστοῦμεν (2 Cor., Eph., 2 Thess.) two relate to letters which have been regarded as post-Pauline.

According to Deissmann (*Light*, 181 n. 5), Paul was 'adhering to a beautiful secular custom when he so frequently began his letters with thanks to God'. Similarly Schubert writes that in this Paul follows 'a typical and general Hellenistic usage, adapting it, of course, in form and content to the particular epistolary situation' obtaining between him and his congregations (*Form and Function*, 168); the formula is, however, 'not by any means an empty convention', but 'used with propriety only where genuine feeling (personal as well as religious) is involved' (ibid. 172f.). These statements require a measure of qualification, in that the form found in extant ancient letters is not always precisely parallel to the Pauline εὐχαριστῶ formula. In some cases we find an expression of pious concern for the well-being of the addressee, and the thanksgiving is incorporated into that: 'If you are well and other things are going right, it would accord with the prayer which I make continually to the gods ... for the news that you are well I straightway thanked the gods' (quoted in Lohse, 12). The note of thanksgiving is indeed present, but it does not have the same prominence as in Pauline usage. Again, where the 'secular' letters are concerned with the material and physical well-being of the address-ees, Paul's concern is with the religious welfare of his readers, their salvation, their incorporation into the body of Christ. It is this that is the theme of his thanksgiving and intercession; here in Col. it is because the writer has heard of the Colossians' faith in Christ and their love towards all the saints that he gives thanks. Perhaps the closest formal parallel to the Pauline usage is a letter of one Apion, in the second century AD, who writes, 'I thank the Lord Serapis [Εὐχαριστῶ τῷ κυρίῳ Σεράπιδι] that he saved me so quickly when I was in danger at sea' (quoted by Lohse, 12 from Deissmann; other examples in Schubert, 158ff.). Lohse also draws attention to a letter in 2 Macc. 1.11ff., which reads: 'We have been saved by God from great dangers, and give him all thanks' (NEB). Regarding this passage Schubert writes: 'The importance of this example of a thanksgiving at the beginning of a letter for the understanding of the genesis of the Pauline epistolary thanksgivings can hardly be overestimated' (117); but this is 'not so much a structural and functional parallel to, but rather a prototype of, the Pauline epistolary thanksgiving' (119). He concludes that the immediate antecedents of the Pauline thanksgivings, and probably other features, are to be found in the Jewish Hellenistic epistolographic patterns. But Paul is no slavish imitator (ibid.).

For an assessment of Schubert, see O'Brien, *Introductory Thanksgivings*, 10ff.; J. M. Robinson ('Die Hodajot-Formel') sees both thanksgiving and *berakah* as develop-ments from the same older Jewish form, the *berakah* becoming so dominant in Jewish prayer that the tractate on prayer-praxis could be called simply Berachoth, while

Christian usage concentrated so much on thanksgiving that the Lord's Supper came to
be called the Eucharist after such prayers (210).

One question which calls for some consideration is that of the limits
of the 'thanksgiving period' (cf. O'Brien, 71–75). At first sight the
thanksgiving, with the following reference to intercession for the
readers, appears to consist of v. 3 only; it is interrupted in v. 4 by an
explanation of the reasons for giving thanks, and only resumed in v.
9, where ὑπὲρ ὑμῶν προσευχόμενοι picks up the περὶ ὑμῶν
προσευχόμενοι of v. 3. This explanation is not, however, an
intrusion, but a natural and integral part of the thanksgiving, so
that the 'thanksgiving period' extends at least to v. 8, if not beyond.
Schubert (6) already noted the difficulty of marking off the
thanksgiving in Col., and argued from the occurrence of the term
εὐχαριστοῦντες and for other reasons that 'at all events v.12 must be
included'.[3] An eschatological climax is reached with vv. 13f., and the
exposition of Christ's cosmic significance in vv. 15–20 is closely and
smoothly linked to the preceding vv. 12–14: 'Syntactically these
verses constitute an inseparable unit.' So he concludes: 'The question,
then, is whether we have in Col the anomalous case of a thanksgiving
without a well-rounded and clear-cut climax, passing imperceptibly
from the form of the thanksgiving to the form of the creed'. The
alternative is that the thanksgiving extends through v. 23;[4] in his view
the language and thought remind us of the conclusions of other
thanksgivings. It may be added that the UBS Greek New Testament
prints the whole of vv. 9–23 as a single paragraph (NA[27] marks a new
paragraph at v. 12, and indents the 'hymn' of vv. 15–20). Other
scholars, as O'Brien notes, have taken a different view: 'There seems
to be no lack of climaxes to the period—v. 14; v. 20; v. 23 and chap.
2: 3' (71). He himself concludes (75) that the period extends over vv.
3–14; but against this it has to be noted that the ὅς in vv. 15 and 18
links naturally with the ἐν ᾧ of v. 14, all three referring back to τοῦ
υἱοῦ in v. 13. At an earlier point (63) O'Brien observes that,
unusually, the passage moves 'from thanksgiving (v. 3) to intercession (v. 9) and back to thanksgiving again'.

Whatever view may be taken of the limits of the thanksgiving
period, it is for practical purposes convenient to divide the material
into shorter sections for examination. There is a natural division at v.
8, another at v. 20, and a third at v. 23, although there may be room
for some difference of opinion as to whether vv. 13–14 belong with v.
12 or with the 'hymn' which follows. Due attention should, however,

[3] But it should be noted, as Lightfoot long ago observed, that the εὐχαριστοῦντες of
v. 12 is 'most naturally coordinated with the preceding participles and referred to the
Colossians'. After three successive participles explanatory of περιπατῆσαι ἀξίως in v.
10 and dependent on ἵνα πληρωθῆτε in v. 9, it would be grammatically very awkward
to make the fourth dependent on οὐ παυόμεθα even further back. In this verse it is the
Colossians who are to give thanks. Cf. O'Brien, *Introductory Thanksgivings*, 88f.: the
participles 'define more precisely what it means to "walk worthily of the Lord"'.
[4] Dunn (53) treats vv. 3–23 as an extended thanksgiving, but in his commentary
breaks the passage into smaller units, as here: 3–8; 9–14; 15–20; 21–23.

be paid to the continuity of the whole: this is not a collection of disjointed aphorisms, but a well-worked and close-knit passage which flows steadily from one point to the next.

As with the opening salutation and the ἐν Χριστῷ formula (see above), it might be thought that the occurrence here of a 'Pauline' thanksgiving period lends support to the authenticity of Col. against any theory of pseudonymity, but once again this is not necessarily the case. The forms and the language are Pauline, but when the question of authenticity has been raised we must take all the possibilities into account. As already noted, if a disciple wished to place his work under the aegis of Paul's authority the obvious thing for him to do would be to give it a 'Pauline' opening, and the thanksgiving period is a regular part of the opening of a Pauline letter. These three elements in fact do not provide us with any conclusive argument either way. The problem with Colossians is that it is at once so close to Paul and yet in many respects so different; we must pay due attention to the differences as well as to the similarities. Schubert (15) and others have noted that the thanksgiving in Colossians falls into the same pattern as those of Philippians and Philemon, and there are in fact some parallels with the Philemon period (see below) which might suggest that this period provided the model for the one in Colossians.

In modern editions of the original Greek the whole of the present passage (vv. 3–8) is a single sentence, punctuated only by commas and by a colon after ἀληθείας at the end of v. 6. Modern translations generally break it up into shorter sentences for the sake of clarity and ease of reading. Lohse, following the lead of Dibelius, sets out the structure thus:

εὐχαριστοῦμεν (3a)
  προσευχόμενοι (3b)
    ἀκούσαντες τὴν πίστιν ... καὶ τὴν ἀγάπην (4)
    διὰ τὴν ἐλπίδα (5a)
      ἣν προηκούσατε (5b)
        καθὼς καὶ ἐν παντὶ τῷ κόσμῳ (6a)
      καθὼς καὶ ἐν ὑμῖν (6b)
    καθὼς ἐμάθετε ἀπὸ Ἐπαφρᾶ(7)
  ὁ καὶ δηλώσας ἡμῖν (8)

The author begins in v. 3a with thanksgiving, to which he adds in 3b a reference to his prayers for the community; this is followed in v. 4 by a statement of the reasons for the thanksgiving, the faith and love of the Colossians, and in 5a by the motive which has inspired that faith and love, the hope of which they have heard before 'in the word of the truth of the gospel'. This gospel is universal in its scope, bearing fruit in all the world, as it is among the Colossians. They have heard it from Epaphras, who has also informed the author of their love in the Spirit. The thought thus moves from the local community to the worldwide proclamation of the gospel, and back again to the community. Verses 7–8 lead directly into the intercession which begins at v. 9.

With the opening verse, 'We give thanks to God the Father of our Lord Jesus Christ at all times when we pray concerning you, since we have heard of your faith in Christ Jesus and the love which you have towards all the saints because of the hope that is laid up for you in heaven', we may compare Philem. 4–5: Εὐχαριστῶ τῷ θεῷ μου πάντοτε μνείαν σου ποιούμενος ἐπὶ τῶν προσευχῶν μου, ἀκούων σου τὴν ἀγάπην καὶ τὴν πίστιν ἥν ἔχεις πρὸς τὸν κύριον Ἰησοῦν καὶ εἰς πάντας τοὺς ἁγίους. The verbs here are in the singular and a different phrase is used in referring to Paul's prayers, but the content is the same, with its reference to hearing of Philemon's faith and love (Philem. does not mention hope; its addition here brings the three Christian virtues of 1 Cor. 13.13 together in the same sentence). It is at least possible that these verses provided the inspiration for the form in Col., although clearly it is not a question of a simple copying; indeed the author of Col. has expressed more clearly what in Philem. is rather condensed (see Commentary on Philem. *ad loc.*). Eph. 1.15–17 (i.e. at a later point in the letter) reads: Διὰ τοῦτο κἀγώ, ἀκούσας τὴν καθ᾽ ὑμᾶς πίστιν ἐν τῷ κυρίῳ Ἰησοῦ καὶ τὴν ἀγάπην τὴν εἰς πάντας τοὺς ἁγίους, οὐ παύομαι εὐχαριστῶν ὑπὲρ ὑμῶν μνείαν ποιούμενος ἐπὶ τῶν προσευχῶν μου (cf. Col. 1.9, οὐ παυόμεθα ὑπὲρ ὑμῶν προσευχόμενοι). Again the content is the same, but there are several minor differences in the formulation. Here the reference to hope is delayed to v. 18: εἰς τὸ εἰδέναι ὑμᾶς τίς ἐστιν ἡ ἐλπὶς τῆς κλήσεως αὐτοῦ. 1 Thess. 1.2–3 has the verbs in the plural and like Eph. and Philem. reads μνείαν ποιούμενοι ἐπὶ τῶν προσευχῶν ἡμῶν instead of προσευχόμενοι; it includes reference to the Christian triad of faith, hope and love, but in a different form, introduced by μνημονεύοντες. The most obvious and natural explanation is, of course, that all these letters are the work of the same author, who has merely exercised a certain freedom of choice in his formulation; but this is to ignore the factors which have led to reservations in regard to the authenticity of Colossians. The least likely solution is that some imitator has combined elements from Philem. and 1 Thess. to produce the form of thanksgiving which appears in Col.; it simply does not read like the product of a process of cutting and pasting. On the view taken here, a disciple familiar with Paul's usage has followed his master's example, but exercised a freedom of his own.

3. Εὐχαριστοῦμεν τῷ θεῷ πατρὶ τοῦ κυρίου ἡμῶν Ἰησοῦ Χριστοῦ πάντοτε περὶ ὑμῶν προσευχόμενοι This verse presents a number of points which call for some consideration: the plural εὐχαριστοῦ–μεν, the phrase τῷ θεῷ πατρί, the grammatical connection of the πάντοτε.

(1) Is the εὐχαριστοῦμεν a real or an 'epistolary' plural? That is, does it mean 'we thank' (i.e. including Timothy), or is the author using an editorial 'we' referring to himself alone? Moule (48) speaks of 'a nicely balanced issue'. In Rom. and other letters Paul uses the

singular form εὐχαριστῶ, even where he includes Timothy or another co-worker in the opening salutation (1 Cor., Phil., Philem.). The plural εὐχαριστοῦμεν in 1 Thess. (cf. εὐχαριστεῖν ὀφείλομεν, 2 Thess. 1.3) is commonly taken to indicate that the colleagues there mentioned share in the thanksgiving (cf. Moffatt, *EGT* iv. 23; E. Best, *1 & 2 Thessalonians* (1972), 26). O'Brien (*Introductory Thanksgivings*, 50, 76) thinks that the plural in Col. links Timothy with Paul; but if that is so, why does Paul use the singular in comparable cases elsewhere? At the very least, the usage is strictly not consistent, although Lohse (14) sees no difference between the singular and the plural forms: 'it is still the apostle as an individual who speaks'. Lightfoot (297, on Col. 4.3) writes, 'Indeed there is no reason to think that St Paul ever uses an "epistolary" plural, referring to himself solely', but Lohse (14 n. 13) points to Rom. 1.5 and 1 Thess. 3.1f. (cf. 3.5) as examples of plurals which clearly refer to Paul alone. O'Brien (ibid. 76 n. 57) adduces the ἡμᾶς of 2 Cor. 1.4, but Thrall (*2 Corinthians*, i. 103) thinks it not impossible that Paul may have had some of his collaborators in mind there. In an excursus on 'literary plurals' (105–07; cf. also Barth, 166–68), Thrall concludes that Paul does use 'the convention of the literary plural', but that some of his first plurals are real plurals 'or may be at least implicitly inclusive', i.e. referring to a wider group. This raises a broader issue, that of the use of the first person plural generally: in some cases it may be used in an 'editorial' fashion, but in others it refers to the author and a wider group to which he belongs; in others again, ἡμεῖς may be so wide that it can be translated 'We Christians' (e.g. v. 13 below). In Col., as already noted, after using plurals at vv. 3, 7 and 9 the author switches to the singular at 1.23 and uses it consistently to the end of the letter. This suggests that the plural here should be taken as a real plural. In any case it must be observed that the use of the plural in Col. and the two Thessalonian letters differs from the usage of the other letters.[5]

On the use of εὐχαριστῶ and cognate forms in the Hellenistic world see Schubert, 39ff. He counts 37 occurrences in the Pauline letters, including five in the pseudo-Pauline writings ('indisputably composed under Pauline influence'), against only 13 in the rest of the NT (83). Further on (91) he notes that G. H. Boobyer 'has convincingly shown that εὐχαριστία and εὐχαριστεῖν play a large and important role in many strata of religious life in the Hellenistic world' (*'Thanksgiving' and the 'Glory of God' in Paul*). In later Christian usage the terms are less frequent, since they came to be used almost exclusively with reference to the Eucharist. Cf. BAGD 328f.; *TWNT* ix. 397–405, esp. 402–04.

(2) Moule observes that τῷ θεῷ πατρὶ τοῦ κυρίου ἡμῶν 'is by no means certainly the correct reading', but that 'it is so unusual that it is arguable that it is the original'. Schubert (53 n. 1) speaks of 'a singular apposition'. Philem., Phil. and Rom. add μου to τῷ θεῷ in the thanksgiving formula, but no other letter has πατρὶ τοῦ κυρίου κτλ. The reading adopted for the UBS text has comparatively light

[5] For further references on the first plurals in Paul, see H. M. Jackson, *JTS* 50 (1999), 11 n. 19.

support (BC* 1739 Augustine), but is the reading which best explains the origin of the others: it contains 'a very unusual collocation of words' (Lightfoot, 316), and in order to avoid this some copyists inserted τῷ after θεῷ (D* G 2005 Chrysostom), others καί (אAC² Dᶜ I K P Ψ 33 81 614 Byz Lect). See Lightfoot, 315f.; Metzger, *Textual Commentary*, 619; and cf. 1.12; 2.2; 3.17. At each of these points there is a whole cluster of variant readings.

The greetings formula in all the letters of the Pauline corpus (except 1 Thess.) wishes the readers 'grace and peace from God our Father', with all except Col. adding 'and the Lord Jesus Christ'. As already noted, the variant readings in the manuscripts show that both in Col. and in 1 Thess. scribes were not slow to add the missing words. What is distinctive in the present verse is the reference to God as 'the Father of our Lord Jesus Christ', although there are some parallels, notably the three occurrences of the formula εὐλογητὸς ὁ θεὸς καὶ πατὴρ τοῦ κυρίου ἡμῶν Ἰησοῦ Χριστοῦ (2 Cor. 1.3; Eph. 1.3; 1 Pet. 1.3) and the ἵνα ... δοξάζητε τὸν θεὸν καὶ πατέρα τοῦ κυρίου ἡμῶν Ἰησοῦ Χριστοῦ of Rom. 15.6 (cf. also 2 Cor. 11.31 and perhaps 1 Cor. 15.24). These cases of course suggest that the scribal insertion of καί in some manuscripts (see above) may be due to assimilation to a familiar form of words. Equally, the insertion of τῷ in other mss may be due to scribal concern to clarify the meaning. For Moule (49), 'the translation "God, who is the Father ..." seems best' (cf. already Calvin, *Epistles of Paul*, 301).

More important is the significance of the description of God as Father: 'In the OT God is called "Father" in the first place to indicate his relationship to the Israelite nation as a whole, or to the king as the embodiment of the nation. Only in late writers is God called the Father of the pious Jew as an individual' (BAGD 635b). The Gospels present Jesus as regularly speaking of God as Father, thus showing his consciousness of a special relationship, and in particular using the familiar Aramaic form of address, *abba* (Mark 14.36), which was not so employed in Judaism (cf. *TWNT* i. 4–5; ix. 984–85) but was taken over by Greek-speaking Christians (cf. Rom. 8.15; Gal. 4.6) and translated by πατήρ (further references in Aletti, 48 n. 18). By teaching his disciples the Lord's Prayer, Jesus authorized them too to address God as Father (he speaks in the Gospels not only of 'my Father' but of 'your Father'). The Christian description of God as Father is new and distinctive, deriving not from precedents in other circles[6] but from the revelation given in Jesus Christ: God is Father in the first place as Father of our Lord

---

[6] For God as Father in Greek philosophy, in Philo and in the Hermetica see *TWNT* v. 954–59; according to G. Löhr (*Verherrlichung Gottes durch Philosophie* (1997), 178) the description of God as Father is firmly rooted in the Platonic tradition, but also traditional, as well as linked with the Stoic philosophy. Here the reference is rather cosmological: God is Father as αἴτιος πάντων.

Jesus Christ. (Cf. *TWNT* v. 946–1016, esp. 977–81 (God as Father in Judaism); 981ff. (Jesus); 1007–13 (Pauline usage).[7]

Exception is sometimes taken in modern times to the description of God as Father, but when seen in its historical context it is a very natural one and has stood the test of centuries. Moreover, it is difficult to see how it could be replaced. The mother goddesses of the ancient world would scarcely meet requirements! On the other hand, it is quite simply inadequate to think of God in terms of mere masculinity, and it should not be overlooked that the Bible sometimes makes reference to motherly aspects in God: cf. for example Isa. 66.13, to which we may perhaps add Jesus' lament over Jerusalem, Matt. 23.37 = Luke 13.34.[8] Again, as T. W. Manson noted long ago (*The Teaching of Jesus* (1939), 89–115), there are two distinct ways of understanding the word 'Father' used as a name for God, the one typical of Greek thought, namely that God 'is the *fons et origo* of human life, the Father of our spirits', and the other characteristic of Hebrew, Jewish and Christian utterances: 'that he watches over and cares for men and women in a manner analogous to the parental care of a good earthly father' (90). What is central to talk of God as Father is not any mere masculinity but the kindness, graciousness, tolerance and mercy, and other attributes which characterize the ideal father (firmness and judgement, of course, also have their place: he is not one to look kindly upon wrongdoing). Manson later speaks (91) of 'a moral tie, a fatherly love and care on the one side and a filial devotion and obedience on the other'.[9]

Dunn (55–56) suggests that there may be here 'a deliberate attempt to stress the sole sovereignty of God at the beginning of a letter that focuses so much on the divine status of Christ'; 'the high christology to be enunciated shortly is kept within the constraints of Jewish monotheism. God the Father is the one to whom prayer should properly be offered.'

(3) In Philem. the πάντοτε stands between εὐχαριστῶ τῷ θεῷ μου and μνείαν ποιούμενος and, as here, might well go with either. However, where a πάντοτε occurs in the formula in other letters (1 Cor., 1 Thess., 2 Thess.; the structure in Phil. is different), it clearly belongs with εὐχαριστῶ (cf. also Eph. 5.20), which suggests that here too it should be taken with εὐχαριστοῦμεν and not with προσευχόμενοι. Schubert however (65 n. 1) calls this a correct conclusion for the wrong reason. He identifies a structural pattern for

[7] On the author's theology 'in the strict sense of the word, his presentation of θεός', cf. Wilson, *The Hope of Glory*, 142–43, and for 'God the Father', Barth, *Colossians*, 168–70.

[8] It may perhaps be added that for Gregory of Nyssa later God is beyond gender; there is neither male nor female in the divine nature (see V. E. F. Harrison, *JTS* 47 (1996), 40). This of course belongs to the theological reflection of a later age, but it does suggest that talk of God as Father could arouse misgiving and misunderstanding even in the early Christian centuries.

[9] Cf. also Dodd, *Romans*, 128–31; H. F. D. Sparks, 'The Doctrine of the Divine Fatherhood in the Gospels', in D. E. Nineham (ed.), *Studies in the Gospels* (1955), 241–61.

the type of letter to which Col. belongs, consisting of (i) the principal verb εὐχαριστῶ; (ii) a participial construction referring to the author's intercessory prayer on behalf of his readers (here προσευχόμενοι); (iii) a second participial construction supplying a reason, in what the author has heard (here ἀκούσαντες); and (iv) 'a final clause reporting the content of the intercessory prayer'. In some cases the fourth element is delayed or suppressed—in Col. it does not appear until 1.9. 'In terms of syntactical theory, it is clear that the first participle clause has temporal force and that it defines τῷ θεῷ πάντοτε as a whole, and that in so doing it also defines πάντοτε, namely as: always = when I think of you (μνείαν ποιούμενος) in my prayers' (Schubert, 66). Bengel construes πάντοτε with προσευχό-μενοι, quoting Rom. 1.10, where, however, there is a question of punctuation, and Phil. 1.4, where as noted above the structure is different; but Calvin already notes that some interpreters take the adverb with εὐχαριστῶ, others with προσευχόμενοι, and then continues, 'It can also be expounded in this way, "Whenever we pray for you, we at the same time give thanks to God." And this is the more simple meaning' (*Epistles of Paul*, 301).[10]

The problem arises from the insertion of the words πατρὶ τοῦ κυρίου ἡμῶν Ἰησοῦ Χριστοῦ, which has the effect of separating the adverb rather widely from the verb and makes it at first sight seem natural to link it with the προσευχόμενοι. Once we recognize the structure identified by Schubert, however, and the usage in other letters, then all falls into place. Schubert (58) notes that πάντοτε occurs nine times in the thanksgivings of the seven Pauline letters which have a εὐχαριστῶ thanksgiving: once each in Philem., Rom., 1 Thess., Col., Phil., 1 Cor., and three times in 2 Thess., and calls it 'an important and regular syntactical unit in the structure of the Pauline εὐχαριστῶ thanksgiving period'. He also refers (130) to the idea of a continuous thanksgiving advanced by Philo (e.g. *De spec. leg.* i.297), which he describes as 'an explicit theological statement of what is implied in such formulas as πάντοτε and ἀδιαλείπτως εὐχαριστεῖν, which are so frequent in Paul and in other documents of Hellenistic piety'. 'The Pauline thanksgiving periods are unmistakable examples of a well-established Hellenistic epistolary convention' (148; as noted above, more recent studies would give a larger place to the OT Jewish background).

κύριος 'The profession "Jesus is Lord" is undoubtedly one of the oldest expressions of Christian belief' (Barrett, *Romans*, 200; cf. Rom. 10.9; 1 Cor. 12.3; Phil. 2.11), and probably goes back to primitive Aramaic-speaking Christianity (cf. the formula μαράνα θα

---

[10] O'Brien ('Thanksgiving within the Structure of Pauline Theology', 56) observes that the expressions used 'do not refer to continual prayer, but to the apostle's remembrance of them in his regular times of prayer', adding (n. 37) that this 'was part and parcel of the style of ancient letters, being a Jewish practice as well as a pagan one'.

in 1 Cor. 16.22). The title is very frequently applied to Jesus in Paul's letters,[11] but as Pokorný (*Christology*, 75) and others have noted there is no question of a simple identification of Jesus with God, who is always sovereign.

The Greek word itself (see BAGD 459–60; *TWNT* iii. 1038–94) means 'owner' (of a vineyard, Mark 12.9) or 'master' (of a slave, e.g. Luke 12.42–47); Mark 11.3 admits of at least two other translations apart from the AV 'the Lord hath need of him' (Mark does not use κύριος as a title for Jesus; contrast Luke). In the Greek world the word was used as a title for various Hellenistic rulers and also for certain deities (it is used of Serapis in the letter quoted at p. 77 above); later it appears as a title of several Roman emperors. In LXX it renders the Hebrew *adonai*, used as a substitute for the tetragrammaton, which made it easier for Greek-speaking Christians to apply to Jesus some OT texts which properly refer to God; but Moule remarks (*Origin*, 42), 'it is noteworthy that, at least in some of the instances of the transfer to Christ of passages originally relating to God, special care seems to be taken to safeguard, as it were, the supremacy of God'.

προσευχόμενοι This word is picked up in v. 9 below, when the theme of intercession is resumed. The verb in itself (BAGD 713b–14a; *TWNT* ii. 774–808, esp. 806–07) refers to prayer in general (cf. e.g. Matt. 6.5–9; 1 Cor. 11.4–5), but with περί or ὑπέρ relates particularly to prayers of intercession (cf. 4.3, where the author asks for the Colossians' prayers on his own behalf). The variant ὑπέρ read here by B D* F G and other mss means 'for, on behalf of' after a verb expressing request or prayer (BAGD 838b, 1a); περί, read by ℵ A C D² 1739 1881 and the Majority text and adopted by NA²⁷ and the UBS Greek Testament (also by e.g. Lightfoot, Peake, Lohse), 'introduces the person or thing in whose interest the petition is made', and takes the place of ὑπέρ (BAGD 644b, 1f). This is a case in which there is not much difference in meaning between the two variants, but they do make use of different words and leave the critic with the problem of the choice between them (Peake, 496 suggests that the ὑπέρ probably comes from v. 9; certainly it is probably the word that scribes would expect. Dunn (57 n. 2) claims that περί is Paul's more regular usage, citing Rom. 1.8; 1 Cor. 1.4; 1 Thess. 1.2; 2 Thess. 1.3; ὑπέρ occurs at Phil. 1.4; cf. 2 Cor. 1.11, Eph. 1.16).

The present verse, like vv. 9–14 below, belongs to the class of prayer passages described by G. P. Wiles as 'prayer-reports': 'At the beginning of most of his letters, in the formal thanksgiving period, the apostle assures his readers not only of his continual thanksgivings

[11] Cf. BAGD 458b–60; *TWNT* iii. 1038–94, for the NT esp. 1085ff. Further references in Lohse, 15 n. 21; cf. also Fuller, *Foundations*, 67f., 119, 184–86; Moule, *Origin*, 35ff.; Pokorný, *The Genesis of Christology*, 75–88 and index.

for them, but also of his constant intercessions on their behalf, and he indicates briefly some of the contents of his prayers'.[12]

4. ἀκουσάντες τὴν πίστιν ὑμῶν ἐν Χριστῷ Ἰησοῦ καὶ τὴν ἀγάπην ἣν ἔχετε εἰς πάντας τοὺς ἁγίους This verse provides the reason for the thanksgiving, in that the writer has heard of their faith in Christ and their love toward all the saints. This information is presumably to be understood as having come from Epaphras, cf. v. 8; but that verse does not mention their faith. Cf. Philem. 5, quoted above, which is best treated as a case of chiasmus (see Commentary *ad loc.*); as already noted, if the two are related, the author of Col. has clarified and simplified a somewhat obscure verse in Philem. Eph. 1.15 like Col. puts πίστις first and ἀγάπη second (against Philem.), but introduces other changes: ἀκούσας τὴν καθ᾽ ὑμᾶς πίστιν ἐν τῷ κυρίῳ Ἰησοῦ καὶ τὴν ἀγάπην τὴν εἰς πάντας τοὺς ἁγίους.

πίστις is one of the cardinal words in the New Testament (see BAGD 662a–64a and for this and cognate words *TWNT* vi. 174–230; for the NT, 203ff.; for Paul, 218ff.; cf. also Bultmann, *Theologie*, 310–26 (ET i. 314–30)). We have already met the adjective πιστός in the opening salutation (v. 2), where it was noted that this term may mean either 'believing' or 'trustworthy'. The noun has an even wider range of significance: that which inspires trust or confidence, i.e. faithfulness and reliability (e.g. of God's faithfulness, Rom. 3.3); or actively faith, trust and confidence, particularly of faith in God or in Christ; again, it may refer to true religion as opposed to unbelief (ἀπιστία; cf. 1.23; 2.7 below), or to that which is believed, i.e. the body of faith or doctrine. It is, however, important to recognize that in the New Testament faith is not merely a matter of the acceptance of a set of propositions. It is fundamentally a believing and trusting response to the revelation of God in Christ, with the obedience which such a response entails. This faith is the basis of the Christian life, the source and inspiration of Christian love and charity. It is therefore not surprising that in several letters Paul should commend his readers and give thanks for their faith and love (cf. Philem. 5; Rom. 1.8 mentions only their faith, but it 'is proclaimed throughout the world'; 1 Thess. 1.3, 'your work of faith and labour of love and steadfastness of hope', brings together the three cardinal Christian virtues of 1 Cor. 13.13).

Reading an English version, one is tempted to take the words 'in Christ Jesus' as indicating the object of their faith, but Lightfoot already notes that 'the preposition ἐν here and in the parallel passage, Ephes. i.15, denotes the sphere in which their faith moves, rather than the object to which it is directed', citing 2 Tim. 1.13, ἐν

---

[12] *Paul's Intercessory Prayers*, 156. This study is based on the major epistles and Philemon, but includes frequent reference to the deutero-Paulines, and provides ample evidence for the place of prayer and intercession in the context of Paul's mission (for references in the Pauline epistles to 'unceasing' or constantly practised prayer see 181 n. 3). Wiles speaks (229) of Paul's 'urgent desire to remind the churches of his prayers for them, and enlist them with himself in the same cultic service. All believers must be drawn into the one great underlying fellowship of loving concern "in Christ"'.

πίστει καὶ ἀγάπῃ τῇ ἐν Χριστῷ Ἰησου, 'where the meaning is unambiguous'. To express faith in Christ, i.e. faith directed towards him, Philem. 5 uses the preposition πρός (see above), as Col. 2.5 below uses εἰς.[13]

ἀγάπη (BAGD 5a–6a; for this and cognate terms cf. *TWNT* i. 20–55. See also C. Spicq, *Agapé dans le Nouveau Testament*, (1958–59); ET *Agape in the New Testament* (1963–66)): Greek has several words for 'love', with varying nuances, such as ἔρως (passionate love) or φιλία (friendship), but while the verb ἀγαπάω does appear in pagan sources the noun ἀγάπη is rare;[14] indeed it was long thought that the early Christians had coined the word for their own purposes. It does however occur in LXX (e.g. Cant. 2.4, 6, 7; 3.10; 7.6; 8.6, 7; Wisd. 3.9) and in Philo and other Jewish writers, and there is now evidence for its use in secular sources also, so that it is not of purely Christian origin. Rather the Christians chose a word that was not widely used, and gave to it a new depth of meaning. In Gal. 5.22 ἀγάπη is the first of the fruits of the Spirit, while in 1 Cor. 13.13 it is the chief among the three cardinal Christian virtues. This love is a human response to the love of God revealed in Christ, and knows no bounds; Jesus bade his disciples even to love their enemies (Matt. 5.44; Luke 6.35; cf. J. Piper, *'Love Your Enemies'* (1979)). If the present verse appears to restrict that love to fellow Christians (εἰς πάντας τοὺς ἁγίους), that is not really the case: as Aletti puts it (58), 'it is by faith and the love which they have for one another that Christians bear witness to the word of truth, the gospel' (cf. John 13.34–35). The love that reigns within the community should then extend outwards: the word of the truth of the gospel is bearing fruit not only among the Colossians, but in all the world (v. 6).

ἣν ἔχετε These words are omitted by B and replaced by the article τήν in D² Ψ1739 1881 and the Majority text; the strongest support (ℵ A C D and other mss and versions) is for inclusion of the words. Lightfoot (316) notes that this longer reading conforms to the parallel passage in Philem. 5, that of D² and the Majority text to the parallel in Eph. 1.15 (Lohse, 16 n. 34 speaks of assimilation to Eph.). ἣν ἔχετε is therefore open to suspicion, but as Lightfoot notes, the omission in B 'may be an instance of that impatience of apparently superfluous words, which sometimes appears in this ms'.

5. διὰ τὴν ἐλπίδα As already noted, v. 4 mentions two of the three Christian graces of 1 Cor. 13.13; this phrase adds the third (for ἐλπίς cf. BAGD 252b–53b; Bultmann, *TWNT* ii. 527–30; Bornkamm, 'Die Hoffnung im Kolosserbrief', 56–64. For the triad, see also Lohse, 16–18). It has sometimes been thought inappropriate that a future hope

---

[13] Dunn (57 n. 9) thinks it unlikely that the phrase ἐν Χριστῷ Ἰησου should be taken as referring to the sphere rather than the object of 'your faith'. In his main text he notes this phrase as 'one of the most interesting divergences from normal Pauline usage'.

[14] Cf. Wischmeyer, 'Agape': the word is first attested in literature in LXX, then sporadically in Greek-speaking Jewish literature and frequently in the NT and the Church Fathers; it is not certainly attested in profane Greek literature. At p. 222 it is documented from two pagan texts, both from the third or fourth century AD; at p. 227 reference is made to its use as a female name in inscriptions of 500 or 600 BC. Note the initial paragraph in BAGD 5a.

should be seen as the motive for Christian action—Christians should act without thought of reward—and it has therefore been suggested that the words belong with εὐχαριστοῦμεν, thus supplying a further reason for thanksgiving (Lohse, 16 n. 36 refers to Bengel, Masson and others), but probably the phrase should be taken with τὴν πίστιν κτλ. Peake comments: 'It is urged that a love of this calculating kind is foreign to Paul, but cf. 2 Cor. ix. 6, Gal. vi. 9'; at 3.23–24 below, slaves are urged to put their hearts into whatever they do, 'as for the Lord and not for men, knowing that you will receive from the Lord the reward of the inheritance'. The hope looks to the fulfilment of God's promise; it is not something to be earned by human achievement,

Lightfoot already notes against a connection with εὐχαριστοῦμεν (1) the distance between the two words is considerable; (2) the following clause suggests that the phrase describes the Colossians' motive, not Paul's reason for thanksgiving; (3) it would break up the triad of Christian graces (cf. 1 Thess. 1.3). The order of the 'graces', as he remarks, 'is the natural sequence. Faith rests on the past; love works in the present; hope looks to the future'.[15] Moule (49) aptly notes that hope in the distinctively Christian sense, as 'confidence that, in Christ, God's way of love "has the last word"' is 'anything but a mere opiate of the people'. 'Precisely because it is stored in heaven (ἀποκειμένην ... ἐν τοῖς οὐρανοῖς), it is a potent incentive for action here and now'. Part of the prayer in Eph. 1.18f. is that the readers may know 'what is the hope to which he has called you, what are the riches of his glorious inheritance among the saints (cf. Col 1:12), and what is the immeasurable greatness of his power for us who believe'. On the content of this hope, Lohse (18) writes, 'The hope of the Christian community is indeed directed toward nothing other than its Lord, who is enthroned at God's right hand (3: 1) and is himself the "hope of glory" (ἐλπὶς τῆς δόξης 1.27)', but Aletti (60) demurs: if the object of the Colossian hope cannot be separated from Christ, neither can it be directly identified with him; it is the glory that constitutes the ultimate hope of believers, a glory of which Christ represents the first-fruits; in 1.27 Christ is not the object of the hope, but rather the one who lays its foundation and gives it its *raison d'être*. He finds confirmation for this interpretation in 3.1–4, where Christians are already in the heavens with Christ, waiting to appear with him in full glory. The hope of reward, moreover, is not the only incentive: Christian love is above all a response to the love of God revealed in Jesus Christ. Patrick Walker, in his Life of the Covenanter Alexander Peden (1728), writes, 'I am perswaded that whoever gets right views, conceptions and apprehensions of the incomprehensible love of God, manifested in the sending of Jesus Christ into the world, it will have more weight and influence upon an

---

[15] Cf. Aletti, 60: 'La triade foi–charité–espérance épouse ainsi la totalité du temps chrétien, qui va de l'adhésion de foi en l'Évangile, dans le passé, à l'attente de la rédemption finale, en passant par l'amour fraternel au quotidien.'

inlightned, believing soul, to the sincere, serious, frequent perform-
ance of all commanded duties, than the threatening of ten thousand
hells for not doing' (*Six Saints of the Covenant*, ed. D. H. Fleming
(1901), 16).

ἀποκειμένην ἐν τοῖς οὐρανοῖς The verb (cf. BAGD 92b) is used
of something put away or stored up, whether literally (e.g. Luke
19.20) or metaphorically as here. Another compound (πρόκειμαι,
BAGD 707) is used in Hebrews (6.18; 12.1, 2) of something set before
someone, ready to be grasped. Cf. 2 Tim. 4.8: λοιπὸν ἀπόκειταί μοι ὁ
τῆς δικαιοσύνης στέφανος. Lohse (18) quotes several examples from
various sources: an inscription of Antiochus I of Commagene (the
favour of the gods laid up as a reward for piety), Iamblichus, *De
Mysteriis* 8.7 (τὰ ἀπὸ τῆς εἱμαρμένης ἀποκείμενα κακά: the evils
destined by fate), 2 Macc. 12.45 (the reward laid up for those who fall
asleep in godliness), Heb. 9.27 (ἀπόκειται τοῖς ἀνθρώποις ἅπαξ
ἀποθανεῖν); these show the general sense of something stored in
readiness, or something appointed to happen. For the idea, Peake
(497) refers to the reward or treasure in heaven (Matt. 5.12; 6.20;
19.21), the citizenship in heaven (Phil. 3.20), the inheritance reserved
in heaven (1 Pet. 1.4). In several of these verses the noun, as here, is in
the plural, reflecting the Jewish conception of a plurality of heavens,
although English versions normally translate it as singular (for
οὐρανός see BAGD 593–95; *TWNT* v. 496–536; for the plural, see
497 n. 2, 510f., 530f.).

ἣν προηκούσατε ἐν τῷ λόγῳ τῆς ἀληθείας τοῦ εὐαγγελίου
Lightfoot takes the compound verb (which occurs only here in the
NT) as 'intended to contrast their earlier with their later lessons', and
defines 'the truth of the Gospel' as 'the true and genuine Gospel as
taught by Epaphras, and not the spurious substitute of these later
pretenders'. So too Moule (50), who construes it as 'probably, "heard
before the false teaching", rather than "before the time of writing" or
"before a future fulfilment"' (Peake notes that the first of the two
latter interpretations was suggested by Bengel and Klöpper, the
second by Meyer, Hofmann and Haupt). It is, however, open to
question whether we should seek to define the 'before' more precisely:
the reference is surely just to some earlier date, unspecified. Moule
also suggests that 'the phrases which follow, in vv. 6f., may well be
chosen by way of contrast with the false teaching: the Gospel is true,
universal, and concerned not with decrees of men's devising but with
the graciousness of God'.

The complete phrase ἐν τῷ λόγῳ τῆς ἀληθείας τοῦ εὐαγγελίου
occurs only here in the NT, and some of the passages in which similar
phrases occur are not really parallel: the clearest is 2 Tim. 2.15,
ὀρθοτομοῦντα τὸν λόγον τῆς ἀληθείας, where the phrase obviously
refers to the gospel message; at 2 Cor. 6.7 NRSV translates ἐν λόγῳ
ἀληθείας as '[by] truthful speech' (among the characteristics of the
servants of God), at Jas. 1.18 it renders ἀπεκύησεν ἡμᾶς λόγῳ
ἀληθείας as 'he gave us birth by the word of truth' (Dibelius and
Greeven, *Der Brief des Jakobus* (1964), 134–37 relates this to rebirth

through the gospel); none of these has the additional genitive τοῦ εὐαγγελίου (but for ἀληθεία τοῦ εὐαγγελίου cf. Gal. 2.5, 14).[16] Peake (497) cites in comparison Eph. 1.13, ἀκούσαντες τὸν λόγον τῆς ἀληθείας, τὸ εὐαγγέλιον τῆς σωτηρίας ὑμῶν, 'according to which τ. εὐαγγ. should be taken as in apposition to λογ. τ. ἀλ., "the word of truth, even the Gospel"' (so too Masson; cf. NRSV: 'in the word of the truth, the gospel that has come to you'). This is certainly appropriate in terms of meaning, but the construction in Eph. is different: there τὸ εὐαγγέλιον stands in apposition to τὸν λόγον, whereas Col. has τοῦ εὐαγγελίου as a further genitive attached to τῆς ἀληθείας, or in apposition to it (not to τὸν λόγον).

ἀλήθεια is of very common occurrence in the NT, particularly in the Johannine literature (cf. Dodd, *The Interpretation of the Fourth Gospel*, 170–78; on the word generally, see Bultmann, *TWNT* i. 242–48). BAGD (35a–36b) subdivides its meanings under the headings (1) *truthfulness, dependability, uprightness*; (2) *truth* as opposed to falsehood, and especially of the content of Christianity as the absolute truth; (3) *reality* as opposed to mere appearance. Here the reference is clearly to the truth of the gospel. It may be added that one of the Nag Hammadi documents has come to be known, from its opening words, as *The Gospel of Truth*; that this is the *Veritatis Evangelium* mentioned by Irenaeus (*Adv. haer.* iii.11.9; ed. Harvey ii.52) has been disputed, but remains a possibility (see *Nag Hammadi Codex I*, ed. H. W. Attridge, (1985), 65f.). Col. is among the NT books identified as known to the author by van Unnik (*The Jung Codex*, 115ff.; cf. also the commentary in *Nag Hammadi Codex I: Notes* (1985)). As compared with Col., however, the two words appear in this *incipit* in inverse order, so that we should not be too hasty in claiming any influence from Col. where this title is concerned; if there is such influence, there is also adaptation.

εὐαγγέλιον (BAGD 317a–18; *TWNT* ii. 718–34) meant originally the reward given to the bringer of good tidings, but later came to signify the good news itself, and this is its primary meaning in the New Testament, with, of course, particular reference to the message of salvation through Jesus Christ. Its use for a book about the life and ministry of Jesus is a later development, although the transition can already be seen in the writings of the Apostolic Fathers (e.g. *2 Clem.* 8.5; *Didache* 8.2; 11.3; 15.3–4). Justin Martyr (*1 Apol.* 66.3) speaks of the memoirs of the apostles 'which are called "gospels"', thus clearly referring to written books. Some later texts which bear this title, such as the *Gospel of Thomas*, the *Gospel of Philip* and the *Gospel of Truth* from the Nag Hammadi library, are not 'gospels' in the proper sense.[17]

---

[16] The phrase 'the word of truth' occurs in the Nag Hammadi *Treatise on the Resurrection* (*NHTB* 42–43) and *Testimony of Truth* (*NHTB* 362), but since there are other NT occurrences these are not necessarily allusions to Col.

[17] Cf. Koester, *Ancient Christian Gospels*, 1–48. For information about these other documents see Schneemelcher, *New Testament Apocrypha*, i; Elliott, *The Apocryphal New Testament*, 3–204.

6. τοῦ παρόντος εἰς ὑμᾶς Despite the verse division, these words belong with what precedes them, the genitive agreeing with τοῦ εὐαγγελίου. The verb means 'to be present' (BAGD 624ab), which implies that the gospel not only came but has remained with them; cf. 2 Cor. 11.9; Gal. 4.18, 20 (here with πρός; for the use with εἰς BAGD 624a, *s.v.* 1b refers to Xenophon and Josephus). Cf. also 2 Pet. 1.12, ἐστηριγμένους ἐν τῇ παρούσῃ ἀληθείᾳ. Lohse (19) aptly cites the explanation of John Chrysostom, οὐ παρεγένετο, φησί, καὶ ἀπέστη, ἀλλ᾽ ἔμεινε καὶ ἔστιν ἐκεῖ.

καθώς Schubert (31) notes the regular occurrence of a clause introduced by καθώς in the Pauline thanksgivings (1 Cor. 1.6; 2 Cor. 1.5; Rom. 1.13; Phil. 1.7; 1 Thess. 1.5, 2.13; 2 Thess. 1.3; Col. 1.6 (*bis*), 7; Eph. 1.4): 'Even a cursory glance at these passages and their preceding contexts convinces us that this regular occurrence of the καθώς-clauses in the Pauline thanksgivings is not accidental, but that a very definite formal and functional significance within the thanksgiving pattern attaches to it.' This confident assertion is, however, weakened by his admission that the clauses 'to some extent differ among themselves in formal as well as functional detail'. The word occurs, but the usage varies. BAGD 391ab classes 2 Cor. 1.5 (with οὕτως following; cf. Col. 3.13 and other cases) as indicating comparison (cf. Rom. 1.13; 1 Thess. 1.5; 2 Thess. 1.3 without a corresponding οὕτως); 1 Cor. 1.6, Eph. 1.4 and Phil. 1.7 are identified as causal. In Col. καθώς occurs twice in v. 6, first with ἐν παντὶ τῷ κόσμῳ and then with ἐν ὑμῖν, the second evidently replacing the οὕτως which might have been expected: 'just as it is spreading in all the world, so it is among you'. The second καθώς would seem to have been deliberately chosen to provide two matching clauses at the pivotal point of the section (cf. the structure set out above). The third καθώς clause in v. 7 is quite normal, and presents no difficulties: 'even as you learned from Epaphras'.

καθὼς καὶ ἐν παντὶ τῷ κόσμῳ ἐστίν καρποφορούμενον καὶ αὐξανόμενον Some scribes evidently took καθὼς καὶ ἐν παντὶ τῷ κόσμῳ with what precedes it (this also serves to explain the verse division), and therefore inserted a καὶ before ἐστίν καρποφορούμενον (so the Textus Receptus; cf. AV: 'Which is come unto you, as it is in all the world; and bringeth forth fruit, as it doth also in you'). It would seem that they found the construction difficult (Metzger, like some commentators, speaks of 'a certain awkwardness of expression' (*Textual Commentary*, 619)). The weight of ms evidence, however, strongly supports omission of the καὶ (P[46] ℵABCD* etc.). Lightfoot takes ἐστίν καρποφορούμενον together, as a periphrasis for the simple verb, but Peake objects that this construction is very rare in Paul (a point already recognized by Lightfoot, but irrelevant if Col. is pseudonymous); like others before him he inserts a comma between these words: 'We thus get the same double comparison as with the TR., Paul passing from the special to the general, and from the general back to the special' (497). The translation would then have to run: '[the gospel] which came to you, even as it is also in all the world,

bearing fruit and increasing even as among you' (cf. the AV
rendering above; the TR, with D¹ and other mss, omits καὶ
αὐξανόμενον, but for Lightfoot the authority in favour of these
words is 'overwhelming'). It is, however, open to question whether
this really removes the 'awkwardness of expression'. The simplest
solution is to break up the sentence into smaller units and make these
καθώς clauses into a new sentence (cf. NRSV).

ἐν παντὶ τῷ κόσμῳ Lightfoot and Peake both detect hyperbole
here (cf. Rom. 1.8, ἐν ὅλῳ τῷ κόσμῳ; 1 Thess. 1.8 and 2 Cor. 2.14, ἐν
παντὶ τόπῳ), but both see more in these words than appears on the
surface: the gospel which the Colossians have received is 'not the
local perversion of it that has recently been urged on their notice, but
that which is spreading in the whole world, its truth authenticated by
its ever-widening area and deepening influence on its adherents'
(Peake, 497). 'The true Gospel ... proclaims its truth by its
universality' (Lightfoot). On this interpretation the author is already
sounding a note of warning here, but it is possible to press this too
far: it is open to question whether the original readers would have
detected such a warning at this point in the first reading. Lohse (19)
notes that reference to the catholic character of the message is also
found in the introductory thanksgivings of other Pauline letters (cf.
Aletti. 62 and n. 1), so that it is not specific to Col. and therefore does
not necessarily carry a special significance in relation to the situation
in the local community.

καρποφορούμενον καὶ αὐξανόμενον¹⁸ the compound verb
καρποφορέω occurs only eight times in the NT (Matt. 13.23; Mark
4.20, 28; Luke 8.15; Romans 7.4, 5; Col. 1.6, 10), and the middle
voice only here (Lightfoot notes that 'no other instance has been
found', but BAGD 405a lists an inscription, Brit. Mus. 918, with the
meaning 'bear fruit of itself'). The Gospels generally use the noun
καρπός in the accusative following either φέρειν or ποιεῖν, or in a
couple of cases διδόναι (Matt. 13.8; Mark 4.8); such phrases do not
occur in Paul's letters. In this verse these words are applied to the
gospel as a message of salvation: as it is bearing fruit and growing
throughout the world, so it is among the Colossians (the 'so it has
been bearing fruit among yourselves' of NRSV is an explanatory
expansion to bring out the meaning; the Greek has simply καθὼς καὶ
ἐν ὑμῖν). In v. 10 below the phrase is applied to the Colossians
themselves: they are to 'lead lives worthy of the Lord ... as you bear
fruit in every good work and as you grow in the knowledge of God'
(NRSV). The recurrence of the full phrase in v. 10 may perhaps tell in
favour of including καὶ αὐξανόμενον here, were further support
necessary; possibly some scribe thought that a plant must grow

---

¹⁸ Several commentators quote the comment of Chrysostom on this phrase:
καρποφορούμενον διὰ τὰ ἔργα, αὐξανόμενον τῷ πολλοὺς παραλαμβάνειν, τῷ μᾶλλον
στηρίζεσθαι, καὶ γὰρ ἐν τοῖς φυτοῖς τότε πυκνὰ γίνεται, ὅταν στηριχθῇ τὸ φυτόν
('Bearing fruit' through the works, 'increasing' by receiving many, by becoming the
more firmly established; for indeed in plants the plant becomes dense when it is
established).

before it can produce fruit, and having already written καρποφορούμενον simply omitted the following words.

Lightfoot claims that the middle is *intensive*, the active *extensive*:
'The middle denotes the inherent energy, the active the external
diffusion'; but Moule (50) finds it difficult to believe that any
difference in sense is intended. Perhaps more important is Moule's
reference to the Parable of the Sower, where the seed sown in good
soil ἐδίδου καρπὸν ἀναβαίνοντα καὶ αὐξανόμενα (Mark 4.8; Moule
notes that αὐξάνεσθαι is absent from the parallels in Matt. and
Luke); more particularly, three of the four occurrences of καρποφορέω in the Gospels are in the interpretation of the parable, and the
fourth (Mark 4.28) follows just a few verses later. Moreover, both in
Mark and in Col. the fruit-bearing is mentioned before the growth.
Moule, however, judiciously avoids any hasty conclusions: 'how far
St Paul's words are actually derived from the Gospel traditions it is
impossible to say'. After all, the Gospels on the usual dating were not
written until after Paul's death, and attempts to reconstruct the
traditions behind them inevitably involve an element of speculation.
A disciple writing about AD 70 might conceivably have had access to
the Gospel of Mark, but that is no more than a possibility, and
scarcely a firm foundation on which to build.

ἀφ' ἧς ἡμέρας ἠκούσατε καὶ ἐπέγνωτε τὴν χάριν τοῦ θεοῦ ἐν
ἀληθείᾳ 'From the day when you heard and came to know the grace
of God in truth'. These words carry the growth and spread of the
gospel among the readers back to the time when they first heard it.
Here rather than earlier we may perhaps detect a note of warning: it
is the true Pauline gospel that is meant, καθὼς ἐμάθετε ἀπὸ Ἐπαφρᾶ,
and not any newfangled doctrine, as yet unspecified; but there is as
yet no direct polemic. ἐπιγινώσκω is frequently employed instead of
the simple verb, without any difference of meaning (Bultmann,
TWNT i. 703; but BAGD (291, *s.v.* 1a) lists Col. 1.6 under cases 'with
the preposition making its influence felt', as meaning *to know exactly,
completely*, noting that ἐπιγινώσκειν is a second stage after ἀκούειν.
Other meanings noted are 1b *recognize, know again*, and 1c
acknowledge, give recognition. Uses with no emphasis on the
preposition are classed under 2, as 'essentially = γινώσκειν'). Peake
here comments that ἐπέγνωτε 'should strictly imply full knowledge,
but as the reference is to the time of their conversion it seems
doubtful whether this shade of meaning should be pressed'. The
prayer in v. 9 below is that the readers may be filled with the
ἐπίγνωσις of God's will 'in all spiritual wisdom and understanding',
and there a full knowledge would certainly appear to be intended.
Lohse (21) takes ἐπιγινώσκειν here to mean 'understanding' (cf. his
translation (12), 'from the day you heard and understood ...'.

As already noted (p. 74 above), χάρις is among the central
concepts of the New Testament. Lightfoot (212) calls it 'St Paul's
synonyme for the Gospel', quoting Acts 20.24, where Paul describes it
as his mission to testify to τὸ εὐαγγέλιον τῆς χάριτος τοῦ θεοῦ. Here
it sums up the content of the gospel. Lohse (20) cites 2 Cor. 8.9, and

the warning in 2 Cor. 6.1 against taking the grace of God in vain (cf. also Gal. 5.4). The readers have received the good news of the grace of God in Christ, and must not abandon it for some new doctrine.

ἐν ἀληθείᾳ These words are readily translated literally (as above) 'in truth', but it is open to question whether they should be treated as an adverb, meaning 'truly' (so NRSV: 'from the day you heard it and truly comprehended the grace of God'). Lohse (20) detects a connection to the reference to the content of the gospel in v. 5: 'Thus "in truth" (ἐν ἀληθείᾳ) corresponds to "in the word of truth" (ἐν τῷ λόγῳ τῆς ἀληθείας v. 5), and signifies that the community understood the word presented to them as the truth'.[19] Similarly Moule (51) comments, 'I.e. the grace of God "as it truly is", "untravestied"', and Lightfoot long before them 'i.e. "in its genuine simplicity, without adulteration"', again referring back to v. 5. Basically it is a question whether the phrase is to be regarded as modifying the verbs ἠκούσατε καὶ ἐπέγνωτε or as qualifying τὴν χάριν τοῦ θεοῦ; but the main point is that reliance on an English version without regard for the possible nuances and associations of the Greek may be misleading.

7. καθὼς ἐμάθετε ἀπὸ Ἐπαφρᾶ τοῦ ἀγαπητοῦ συνδούλου ἡμῶν This verse would seem to settle any question as to who was responsible for the evangelizing of Colossae and the surrounding area. The readers have received 'the word of the truth of the gospel' from Epaphras, from the time of the first missionary effort down to the present, and these words provide assurance that what he has taught them is the authentic Pauline gospel. He is described as σύνδουλος, a fellow-servant (BAGD 785b), which inevitably recalls Paul's designation of himself as δοῦλος Χριστοῦ Ἰησοῦ (Rom 1.1; Phil. 1.1; cf. Gal. 1.10). The title is accorded to Tychicus at 4.7 below, but does not occur in any of Paul's major letters. The word is used in its literal sense in the parable of Matt. 18.23–35 (cf. also Matt. 24.49); in Rev. 19.10; 22.9 the angel dissuades John from doing him reverence by saying σύνδουλός σου εἰμι καὶ τῶν ἀδελφῶν σου (cf. also Rev. 6.11). There are no other NT occurrences.

The name Epaphras is a shortened form of Epaphroditus, but this Epaphras is probably not to be identified with the Epaphroditus of Phil. 2.25; 4.18; both forms are common, and the Epaphroditus of Phil. appears to have belonged to Philippi, while Epaphras is described at 4.12 below as ὁ ἐξ ὑμῶν, which implies that he belonged

---

[19] In a footnote Lohse (21 n. 71) compares the language of the Qumran writings: 'The community had withdrawn from the world of falsehood and committed itself to undivided obedience to the law of God. The doers of the law are "Men of Truth" (1 QpHab VII 10; cf. also 1 QH XI 11; XIV 2) who have willingly shown that they will stand for God's truth (1 QS I 11; V 10). They have gained knowledge of the truth (1 QS IX 17; 1 QH VI 12; IX 10; X 29; XI 7; 1 QHf I 9) and demonstrate this by loyal observance of the Torah'. These similarities, however, are not necessarily proof of some relationship, for there are also differences to be considered. Cf. Lohse 128f.: 'the adherents of the "philosophy" cannot be considered Essenes, members of the Qumran community, or proponents of heretical Jewish propaganda'.

to Colossae. Epaphroditus is mentioned only in Phil., Epaphras only in Col. and at Philem. 23, where he is called ὁ συναιχμάλωτός μου ἐν Χριστῷ Ἰησοῦ. This phrase is often taken literally, as implying that Epaphras had voluntarily shared Paul's imprisonment (so e.g. Kümmel (1966 edn), 238; Lohse, 172 and n. 20), but Moule (136f., on Col. 4.10; cf. also G. Kittel in *TWNT* i. 196f.) urges that there are reasons for taking the noun in a metaphorical sense (a possibility already discussed by Lightfoot, 302): (1) αἰχμάλωτος properly means 'a prisoner of war', which Paul was not; for ordinary prisoners other terms were used, e.g. δέσμιος (Matt. 27.15, 16; Acts 16.25, 27 etc.) or δεσμώτης (Acts 27.1, 42); (2) συναιχμάλωτος occurs three times in the New Testament: at Philem. 23, referring to Epaphras; at Col. 4.10, referring to Aristarchus (who at Acts 27.2 is one of Paul's companions on the voyage to Rome); and at Rom. 16.7, referring to Andronicus and Junia(s). 'It is hard to believe that both Aristarchus and Epaphras were, or had been, literally fellow-prisoners with St Paul, not to mention Andronicus and Junias.' On the other hand, if Paul in Rome was under some kind of house arrest, and able to welcome 'all who came to him' (Acts 28.16, 30), he might well have had a number of his colleagues sharing his captivity for some part of the time (Kümmel (1966 edn), 245 can speak of 'an imposing staff of co-workers'). This is another of those cases of a nicely balanced issue, where we simply do not have the evidence on which to base a firm judgement. If Col. is the work of a later disciple, of course, the question is irrelevant, although in that case we should have to reverse Lightfoot's comment (302): the 'honourable title', given at Philem. 23 to Epaphras, is in Col. withheld from Epaphras and given to Aristarchus.

At any rate the reference to Epaphras is warm in its commendation, and this is continued in the following words, ὅς ἐστιν πιστὸς ὑπὲρ ἡμῶν διάκονος τοῦ Χριστοῦ: Epaphras is 'a faithful minister of Christ on our behalf'. This assumes the reading ἡμῶν (P46 ℵ*A B D* etc.), favoured by Lightfoot (202, 316f.), Moule, Lohse and others, against the ὑμῶν read by ℵ2 C D1 Ψ and other mss, which is preferred by NA27 and the UBS text (the 1966 edition read ἡμῶν). As noted below in the comment on Philem. 6, confusion of these pronouns is a very common cause of manuscript variation (Moule, 27 n. 1 observes that throughout Col. 'there is constant doubt about the correct reading as between first and second person'), and the problem is not always to be solved on purely textual grounds: there may be other factors which have to be taken into account. Metzger (*Textual Commentary*, 619f.) notes 'superior Greek evidence' for ἡμῶν, but 'a majority of the Committee … considered it probable that copyists introduced the first person pronoun under the influence of the preceding ἡμῶν and the following ἡμῖν'. Ollrog (*Mitarbeiter*, 101) thinks the ὑμῶν here confirmed by 4.12, where Epaphras is said to be 'always wrestling in his prayers on your behalf' (cf. Barth, 17 n. 15, 164–66 for arguments supporting this reading). On the other hand Lohse (23 n. 90) suggests that the change from the first person to the second 'is perhaps due to the influence of 4.12'. This, however, would seem to be less likely: why should a scribe be influenced by a passage three chapters ahead? It is not as if these were words readily held in the memory, so that a scribe with 4.12 in mind would insert them here. Lightfoot already noted that the phrase ὑπὲρ ὑμῶν occurs twice in the near context, in vv. 3 and 9, and one or other of these would appear to be a more probable influence. Moreover the first person would seem to provide a better sense: Epaphras in his ministry has been acting on Paul's behalf, as his representative. These words thus add a further touch to the commendation of Epaphras, who is, moreover, called ἀγαπητός (BAGD 6), a term indicating close relationship often used by Paul in addressing his readers (1 Cor. 10.14; 15.58; 2 Cor. 7.1; 12.19; Phil. 2.12; 4.1; cf. the greetings in Rom. 16.5, 8, 9, 12). In some of these cases (1 Cor. 15.58; Phil. 4. 1) it is combined with ἀδελφός (in the plural), but only in Eph. and Col. do we find the phrase ὁ ἀγαπητὸς ἀδελφός applied to an individual (Tychicus: Eph. 6.21; Col. 4.7; Onesimus: Col. 4.9; cf. Luke, ὁ ἰατρὸς ὁ ἀγαπητός, Col. 4.14; the salutation in Philem. 1 is Φιλήμονι τῷ ἀγαπητῷ καὶ συνεργῷ ἡμῶν); this is one of a number of factors which set these two letters apart from the main body of the generally accepted letters. If we accept the variant ὑπὲρ ὑμῶν the sense is more difficult: presumably the reference would be to services rendered to Paul by Epaphras, acting on behalf of the Colossians, but then it is hard to see why he should be called διάκονος τοῦ Χριστοῦ. These words surely imply a ministry in the service of the gospel.

διάκονος (BAGD 184; TWNT ii. 88–93) means basically 'a servant' (e.g. Matt. 20.26; 23.11; Mark 9.35; 10.43; in the first of these cases it is paralleled in v. 27 by δοῦλος); Paul, if he is the author, uses it of himself at 1.23, 25 below, in the first case as servant of the gospel, in the second as servant of the Church. In the Pastorals it becomes the title of a church official (1 Tim. 3.8, 12 and in a variant in a thirteenth-century ms at Tit. 1.9; on the reference to 'bishops and deacons' in Phil. 1.1 cf. for example F. W. Beare, *The Epistle to the Philippians*, (1959), 48–50; E. Best, 'Bishops and Deacons: Philippians 1, 1', in F. L. Cross (ed.), *Studia Evangelica IV* (1968), 371–76). The word has passed into English as an official title, but not all deacons (or deaconesses) fulfil the same function.

8. ὁ καὶ δηλώσας ἡμῖν τὴν ὑμῶν ἀγάπην ἐν πνεύματι δηλόω (BAGD 178b) is literally 'to reveal, make clear, show', but also 'to give information' (cf. 1 Cor. 1.11 NRSV: 'it has been reported to me by Chloe's people'). Here Epaphras has informed Paul of the community's love 'in the Spirit'. Since he sends his greetings at 4.12, he is with Paul, but there is no indication of when or why he came. Presumably he also brought news of the 'false teaching' which was threatening the community, but would he have travelled all the way to Rome to consult with Paul on this matter, and who was responsible for the guidance of the community in his absence? We are not told, but certainly a visit to Paul in Ephesus would be much easier and less time-consuming. This, however, takes us into the realm of speculation. If Col. is pseudonymous, the author was presumably not concerned with such details.

On the phrase ἐν πνεύματι, Lightfoot refers to Gal. 5.22: 'the fruit of the Spirit is love, joy, peace ...' (cf. also Rom. 14.17; 15.30); in this case the reference is to a love inspired by the Spirit. Moule, however, (52) suggests that the sense may well be more general—'your more than merely human love', 'your spiritual, supernaturally derived love',—noting that there is practically nothing in this letter about the Holy Spirit (cf. Schweizer, 'Christus und Geist im Kolosserbrief', who observes that 'there is a clear shift of emphasis in Colossians from pneumatology to christology'). πνεῦμα does occur again at 2.5, but there it appears in a contrast ('though I am absent in body, yet I am with you in spirit'; Schweizer, 308 compares 1 Cor. 5.3; 7.34; 2 Cor. 7.1, and says that 'spirit' here in Col. 2.5 is probably to be taken in a purely anthropological sense). The adjective πνευματικός appears at 1.9 ('in all spiritual wisdom and understanding') and 3.16 (referring to 'psalms, hymns and spiritual songs'), but that is all. The two occurrences of the noun in Col., only one of which may conceivably refer to the Holy Spirit, stand in marked contrast to the abundance of references in the major Pauline letters.

In this connection, however, it is not enough simply to count occurrences of the word πνεῦμα; we must pay due attention to the range of meanings which this word can bear (see BAGD 674b–78b; TWNT vi. 330–450, partial translation by A. E. Harvey, in E. Schweizer et al., The Spirit of God (1960)). It occurs, for example, fourteen times in Eph. compared with the two in Col., but Eph. 2.2 refers to 'the spirit that is now at work among those who are disobedient'. Here we may recall the 'unclean spirits' who are mentioned in the Gospels (e.g. Mark 1.23, 26, 27; 3.11; 5.2, 8, 13). Again, πνεῦμα may be used with reference to part of the human personality: spirit (or soul) and flesh together make up the whole person (cf. Col. 2.5 noted above). Not every occurrence of the word refers to the Holy Spirit, but even when allowance is made for these other shades of meaning there remains a disparity between Col. and the major Pauline letters.

The salutation and thanksgiving period present a problem for those who deny the authenticity of Col.: they correspond so well with Paul's normal practice. The factors adduced as arguments against authenticity all occur later in the letter. Even in these opening verses, however, there are some small variations from his usage in the generally recognized letters: the absence of any reference to Jesus in the salutation, for example; the use of the plural εὐχαριστοῦμεν instead of the singular; the elimination in v. 4 of the chiasmus which appears in Philem. 5. Again, the very similarity of some verses to parallels in other letters is enough to suggest to some scholars that these were derived from those other letters. None of these factors is in itself enough to suggest pseudepigraphy, but when the question has been raised they may serve as confirmatory evidence. A disciple

consciously trying to meet the situation as he thought Paul would
have done might well have decided to follow Paul's example by
choosing some verses from letters known to him, but introducing
minor modifications of his own.

Whether the author is Paul or a later disciple, the opening of the
letter is cordial and friendly, displaying the writer's concern for the
Colossians and giving thanks for their progress in the faith thus far.
The 'word of the truth of the gospel', which they first learned from
Epaphras, is producing its fruit among them, as in the wider world.
What is needful now is to ensure its progress, to guard against any
insidious infiltration of false ideas. There is as yet no direct reference
to such false teaching, but there are some phrases which in the light
of the letter as a whole may be taken as an initial warning. The tone,
however, is friendly and cordial, and there is no indignant rebuttal of
opponents such as we find in other letters.

III
INTERCESSION FOR THE COLOSSIANS
(1.9–14)

[9]For this reason we for our part, since the day we heard, do not
cease praying on your behalf, and entreating that you may be filled
with the knowledge of his will in all spiritual wisdom and
understanding, [10]that you may walk worthily of the Lord, fully
pleasing to him, bearing fruit in every good work and increasing in
the knowledge of God; [11]that you may be strengthened with all
power according to the might of his glory for all endurance and
forbearance. [12]Give thanks with joy to the Father who made you
fit for the lot of the inheritance of the saints in light, [13]who
delivered us from the power of darkness and translated us into the
kingdom of his beloved Son, [14]in whom we have redemption, the
forgiveness of sins.

Following the statement of the grounds for thanksgiving in vv. 4–8,
v. 9 picks up the theme of intercession from v. 3; as Lohse (24) notes,
the close connection of these sections is indicated by the repetition in
the intercession of several words and phrases (or their cognates) from
the earlier section: ἀφ' ἧς ἡμέρας (vv. 6, 9); the verb ἀκούω (vv. 4, 9);
ἐπίγνωσις (vv. 9, 10; cf. ἐπέγνωτε in v. 6); καρποφοροῦντες καὶ
αὐξανόμενοι (v. 10; in v. 6 this phrase is used of the gospel, here it is
the goal which the Colossians are exhorted to achieve). In Eph. 1.15–
16 there is a similar resumption following the εὐλογητός period
which replaces the thanksgiving period in Col.: διὰ τοῦτο κἀγὼ
ἀκούσας τὴν καθ' ὑμᾶς πίστιν ἐν τῷ κυρίῳ Ἰησοῦ καὶ τὴν ἀγάπην
τὴν εἰς πάντας τοὺς ἁγίους (cf. 1.3–4 above; Philem. 5) οὐ παύομαι
εὐχαριστῶν ὑπὲρ ὑμῶν μνείαν ποιούμενος ἐπὶ τῶν προσευχῶν μου
(cf. Philem. 4; Rom. 1.9–10). The content of the prayer is that the

Colossians may be filled with the knowledge of God's will (v. 9), so that they may lead lives worthy of the Lord, bearing fruit in all good works (v. 10) and in their turn giving thanks to the Father, who has enabled them to share in the inheritance of the saints in light (v. 12). Verses 13 and 14 are both relative clauses, the first relating to the Father, the second to the Son, which lead naturally into the 'hymn' of vv. 15–20, itself introduced by the relative pronoun ὅς.

9. διὰ τοῦτο καὶ ἡμεῖς According to Lightfoot, who cites 1 Thess. 2.13 (cf. Eph. 1.15), the καί 'denotes the *response* of the Apostle's personal feeling to the favourable character of the news', and he translates 'we on our part'. Moule, however, (52, adding 1 Thess. 3. 5; Rom. 3.7) thinks that it is 'to be regarded as belonging to the διὰ τοῦτο rather than to the ἡμεῖς: "that is *precisely* why"', while Lohse (24) claims that it belongs with the verb—three different interpretations for one small word, all of them citing more or less the same passages in support! Aletti in a rather more nuanced discussion (68f.) notes that the author can attach the καί to the verb, as is shown by v. 8 above (ὁ καὶ δηλώσας), but there are other possibilities in Pauline usage. Lohse, he says, is correct in not translating 'we also', for that would presuppose mention of the prayers of others; but we cannot separate the καί from the ἡμεῖς. The text in fact marks a change of subject, from Epaphras in v. 8 to Paul and Timothy, hence his rendering 'quant à nous'—which is in effect a return to the view of Lightfoot.

οὐ παυόμεθα ὑπὲρ ὑμῶν προσευχόμενοι As the parallels adduced above show, both Eph. and Philem. have the singular instead of the plural, and use μνείαν ποιούμενος ἐπὶ τῶν προσευχῶν μου in place of the προσευχόμενοι, which of course prompts speculation about the relationship of these passages. On the traditional view, Paul is merely exercising a certain freedom in his use of the words, rearranging them to suit the needs of the moment; but when the question of authenticity has been raised consideration must be given to other possibilities. If Col. is dependent on, or inspired by, Philem. then the author has introduced his own modifications; if Eph. is dependent on Col., then the writer of that letter has gone right back to the source and followed Philem. more closely, although still with his own modifications. It may be that the real solution is that both Col. and Eph. are inspired by Philem. independently, each making his own alterations. On the positive side, these words provide confirmation of the interpretation of the πάντοτε in v. 3 as indicating constant and unceasing prayer for the addressees.

καὶ αἰτούμενοι This phrase is omitted in B K and some mss of the Vulgate, which would attach the ἵνα clause directly to the preceding προσευχόμενοι. The addition is not, however, tautologous: as Peake notes, προσευχόμενοι is more general, αἰτούμενοι more specific, referring to the content of the petition. The latter verb is used in the middle only here and at Eph. 3.13, 20 in the Pauline corpus, although the active appears at 1 Cor. 1.22 (of the Jews' demand for signs; citation of Eph. 3.13 here is an error). Lightfoot notes as an exact parallel Mark 11.24: πάντα ὅσα προσεύχεσθε καὶ αἰτεῖσθε.

ἵνα πληρωθῆτε τὴν ἐπίγνωσιν τοῦ θελήματος αὐτοῦ Cf. Eph. 3.19, ἵνα πληρωθῆτε εἰς πᾶν τὸ πλήρωμα τοῦ θεοῦ. In regard to the construction, Aletti (70 n. 77) observes that πληρόω in the passive may be followed by the genitive (Rom. 15.14; but 15.13, which he also lists, has the verb in the active), the dative (Rom. 1.29; 2 Cor. 7.4) or the accusative (cf. Phil. 1.11, πεπληρωμένοι καρπὸν δικαιοσύνης; but some mss here read καρπῶν) of the content that is put in; cf. also BAGD 671 *s.v.* 1b.[1] Masson, like Peake before him, wished to claim this as an accusative of respect, but Moule (52) notes that while the construction with the accusative is rare it is not unknown; as he says, the general sense is not affected by the choice between the alternatives: the prayer is that the Colossians may be filled with the knowledge of God's will.

According to Lightfoot, the compound **ἐπίγνωσις** 'is an advance upon γνῶσις, denoting a larger and more thorough knowledge'. He notes that Paul himself contrasts γινώσκειν and γνῶσις with ἐπιγινώσκειν and ἐπίγνωσις 'as the partial with the complete' (cf. Rom. 1.21, 28; 1 Cor. 13.12). J. A. Robinson (*Ephesians*, 248–54) argued that ἐπίγνωσις is not a fuller knowledge but knowledge directed towards a particular object; but H. A. A. Kennedy (*St Paul and the Mystery Religions*, 172 n. 2) finds his arguments unconvincing. Bultmann (*Gnosis* (1952), 37) claims that 'the compound ἐπίγνωσις, like the compound verb, is almost a technical term for the decisive knowledge of God which is involved in conversion to the Christian faith', and adds, 'it is always presupposed that Christian knowledge includes a corresponding attitude in life'. We have already met with the verb ἐπιγινώσκειν (see p. 93 above), and it was noted that in some cases the preposition makes its influence felt, whereas in others the compound is practically equivalent to the simple verb. In other words, we must pay due attention to the context in which the word is used, and the same may apply to the noun. According to BAGD (291) it is in the NT and related literature limited to religious and moral things—consciousness of sin in Rom. 3.20, knowledge of God's mystery in Col. 2.2 , or knowledge of his will here in 1.9; in particular it refers to knowledge of God, or in Rom. 1.28 to acknowledgment of him. Moule in a note on the knowledge of God (159–64; cf. also his comment on 1.9, p. 53) remarks that the vast preponderance of these words in the NT 'is concerned with the perception of God's will or the recognition of him in his self-revelation in Jesus Christ'. Two points in his comment deserve special attention: (1) that this and kindred phrases do not mean 'merely a mental grasp of abstract propositions', but rather ' "the perception of God's will as seen in Christ, and the response to it (or rather, to

---

[1] Aletti adds: 'La souplesse avec laquelle le passif est utilisé interdit qu'on parle trop vite pour Col 1,9 de construction non paulinienne'.

him)" …, carrying all the implications of a changed life and conduct',
for which Moule refers especially to the context of the present
passage; and (2) that 'our "knowledge of God" in this sense is
dependent upon our *being known by God*—I Cor. xiii. 12, Gal. iv. 9—
and is in sharp contrast to the ψευδώνυμος γνῶσις, the "knowledge
falsely so called", of I Tim. vi. 20' (cf. Bultmann, 43).

The distribution of these terms is not without interest: γνῶσις
occurs twenty times in the major Pauline letters (Rom. 2.20; 11.33;
15.14; 1 Cor. 1.5; 8.1 (*bis*), 7, 10, 11; 12.8; 13.2, 8; 14.6; 2 Cor. 2.14;
4.6; 6.6; 8.7; 10.5; 11.6 and Phil. 3.8) and once each in Col. (2. 3)
and Eph. (3.19), while ἐπίγνωσις appears four times in the major
letters (Rom. 1.28; 3.20; 10.2; Phil. 1.9), four times in Col. (1.9, 10;
2.2; 3.10) and twice in Eph. (1.17; 4.13). The frequency of γνῶσις in
the Corinthian letters is of course in some measure due to Paul's
strictures, particularly in the eighth chapter, on the 'knowledge' on
which some Corinthians prided themselves, the knowledge which
'puffs up' (1 Cor. 8.1); but a careful examination of these passages
will serve to show that he can also use the word in a positive sense,
notably at several points in 2 Cor. What is clear is that he does not
employ ἐπίγνωσις in order to avoid the use of γνῶσις, as if the
latter were already a catchword of the heretics and therefore
unsuited to 'orthodox' use. The very form of the phrase in 1 Tim.
6.20 implies that there is a true γνῶσις, which is not merely a
knowledge about God but a relationship with God which entails
obedience to his will. The phrase itself may occur only in 1 Tim.,
but the distinction implied goes back a great deal further. γνῶσις,
in brief, can have quite a range of meaning. In secular usage it may
refer simply to knowledge, and is often so used in the Wisdom
literature (Bultmann, *Gnosis*, 23; cf. also his list of Christian uses of
γινώσκειν 'in the everyday sense of knowing', 30–31). LXX,
however, 'shows a clear leaning towards a religious reference'
(ibid. 23), i.e. it relates to knowledge of God (for the OT see ibid.
14–18), and it is this OT background that is the primary influence in
the NT usage of the term. Finally there is the specifically 'gnostic'
γνῶσις, which has been described as 'knowledge of the divine
mysteries reserved for an élite' (Bianchi (ed.), *Le Origini*, p. xxvi).[2]
Some, like Bultmann, would see in the NT an influence from and
reaction against this 'gnostic' γνῶσις, but the early history of the
Gnostic movement is still an obscure area about which it may be
dangerous to make confident statements. We do not know what
stage of development this movement might have reached at any
given point in the first century. γνῶσις in LXX renders the Hebrew
da'ath, and it was in part the occurrence of the latter word and its

---

[2] This 'gnostic' γνῶσις is further delimited in para. B II on the following page: 'Not
every *gnosis* is Gnosticism'. 1 Tim. 6.20 refers to a ψευδώνυμος γνῶσις, 'a passage that
can safely be regarded as directed against an incipient Gnosticism' (Pearson,
Emergence, 154), but a gnosis falsely so-called implies the existence of a true gnosis.
Cf. Pearson's discussion of the use of the phrase in Eusebius (153–67).

cognates in the Dead Sea Scrolls which led to the suggestion that these texts represent a form of Jewish Gnosticism; but as noted in the Introduction (p. 40 above and n. 77) these claims soon subsided.

ἐν πάσῃ σοφίᾳ καὶ συνέσει πνευματικῇ The two adjectives should probably be taken as qualifying both nouns—the wisdom as well as the understanding is wrought by the Spirit, and the author's prayer is that his readers may be endowed with both in full measure (cf. 1.28; 3.16, where the reference is to instruction 'in all wisdom', but without the qualification 'spiritual'). As Moule (53) notes, these words seem to define the preceding phrase: 'perception of God's will consists in wisdom and understanding of every sort, on the spiritual level'. σοφία and σύνεσις are frequently found together, not only in the OT but also in Graeco-Roman philosophy (for references cf. Lightfoot, 204): Aletti (71 n.) observes that exegetes quote above all Aristotle, *Eth. Nic.* i.13, according to which σοφία, σύνεσις and φρόνησις are the highest intellectual virtues, but adds that the most direct model for Col. 1.9 is biblical and Jewish (cf. Lohse, 26, with references to the relevant Qumran texts on the preceding page). The third of these terms, φρόνησις, appears in a partial parallel at Eph. 1.8: ἐν πάσῃ σοφίᾳ καὶ φρονήσει.

σοφία (BAGD 759f.; *TWNT* vii. 465–526—for Eph. and Col. see 524f.) is for Aristotle the highest of the virtues, but the NT references show a number of gradations: in contrast to the wisdom which God imparts there is a merely human wisdom (ἀνθρωπίνη σοφία, 1 Cor. 2.13, cf. σοφία ἀνθρώπων, 1 Cor. 2.5), a wisdom of the wise, of this world, of the present age (1 Cor. 1.19, 20; 2.6); 2 Cor. 1.12 can speak of a σοφία σαρκική, and Jas. 3.15 of a σοφία ἐπίγειος, ψυχική, δαιμονιώδης. σοφία λόγου at 1 Cor. 1.17 is neatly defined by BAGD as 'cleverness in speaking'. Koester (*Ancient Christian Gospels* (1990), 56) notes that the word occurs sixteen times in the first four chapters of 1 Cor., but only three times elsewhere in Paul's letters (Rom. 11.23; 1 Cor. 12.8; 2 Cor. 1.12); he finds 'quite striking' the frequent references in Eph. (1.8, 17; 3.10) and Col. (1.9, 28; 2.3, 23; 3.16; 4.5). The frequency of occurrence in the early chapters of 1 Cor. is, of course, due to the fact that Paul is there contrasting the wisdom of this world with the wisdom of God, once hidden in mystery (1 Cor. 2.7) but now revealed in Christ, the power of God and the wisdom of God (1 Cor. 1.24). Of the occurrences in Col., 2.23 relates to human ordinances which have indeed an appearance of wisdom, but are of no real value; of the rest, 2.3 speaks of Christ in whom all the treasures of wisdom and knowledge are hidden away, while the others refer to that 'spiritual' wisdom which is the gift of God.

Wisdom, of course, figures prominently in the Wisdom literature, where some interesting development can be traced. In Job 28.23–28, according to R. H. Fuller (*Foundations*, 73), it is 'a pre-existent entity, independent of God, but scarcely as yet a hypostatized figure'. In Proverbs, particularly at 8.22–31, she is a creation of God (note the change in the pronoun), 'present when God created the world, though as yet she played no active role in creation'.[3] Here Wisdom is 'figuratively personified', but 'hardly as yet a hypostatization'. In the book of Wisdom she is 'now fully hypostatized' (but for Schürer (iii. 570) 'it almost, but not entirely, becomes an independent hypostasis side by side with God'). Wisdom then 'plays a prominent part in the thinking of Philo' (Fuller, 74); for Schürer (iii. 571) 'we already have here (i.e. in Soph. Sol.) in an unworked form the same elements from which Philo formed his doctrine of the *logos* (= reason and word of God) as a hypostasis mediating between God and the world'. This 'wisdom tradition' was later to become a factor in the development of Christology, notably in the Logos doctrine of the Fourth Gospel, but not only there.[4]

J. M. Robinson (*Trajectories*, 43) speaks of 'a trajectory that led from wisdom literature to Gnosticism', with Q as 'one of the connecting links between the hypostasizing of Sophia in Jewish wisdom literature and the gnostic redeemer myth attested in the second century systems'.[5] It would, however, be a mistake to think of a single trajectory, as if the whole process moved smoothly and without a break from beginning to end. Kurt Rudolph ('Sophia und Gnosis', 224) notes that some features are gnostic *Eigengut*, peculiar to the gnostic systems; this would suggest that they were introduced at a later stage. A. H. B. Logan (*Gnostic Truth*, 32) would see the Sophia myth 'as *the* contribution of the Gnostics of Irenaeus 1.29 and 30 to Valentinus and Christian theology': 'It was the Gnostics who created it'. In Gnosticism Sophia (i.e. Wisdom) is one of the aeons, who is ultimately responsible for the creation of the world, and hence for the human predicament, the unhappy fate of immortal souls imprisoned in mortal bodies in a world that is alien to their true nature.[6] This Gnostic Sophia myth cannot simply be traced back without more ado to Jewish sources: there is Jewish influence, beyond doubt, Jewish material, but this material has been changed and adapted to suit the needs of Gnostic theory, and we need if possible to trace when and where these changes were made.

The later development of the Gnostic Sophia myth is not directly relevant to the study of Colossians, but it is sometimes important to be aware of the final outcome. It is also important to beware of reading back such later developments into earlier texts for which they may have no real relevance.[7] The developed myth of the second-century systems serves to show how far we have to travel from the 'incipient Gnosticism', if such it is, which we find in this letter. Here we are dealing not with a personified divine Wisdom, nor with the

[3] 'The picture painted is that of a child in his father's workshop (vv. 30f.)'.

[4] For later Christian use of the book of Wisdom, cf. Schürer, iii. 573–75; see also e.g. M. J. Suggs, *Wisdom, Christology and Law in Matthew's Gospel* (1970); R. G. Hamerton-Kelly, *Pre-existence, Wisdom and the Son of Man* (1973); R. A. Piper, *Wisdom in the Q Tradition* (1989); Pokorný, *The Genesis of Christology*.

[5] Cf. also the references in the index to the volume, *s.v.* 'Wisdom'.

[6] It is not possible to discuss this theme in detail here. See further Zandee, 'Die Person der Sophia'; Stead, 'The Valentinian Myth of Sophia'; MacRae, 'The Jewish Background of the Gnostic Sophia Myth', 86–101; Schenke, 'Die Tendenz der Weisheit zur Gnosis'; Rudolph, *Gnosis*, 76–86 (and index); D. J. Good, *Reconstructing the Tradition of Sophia in Gnostic Literature* (1987). For the *Gospel of Philip* see G. S. Gasparro, 'Il personaggio di Sophia nel Vangelo secondo Filippo', *VigChr* 31 (1977), 244–81.

[7] Cf. Rudolph ('Sophia und Gnosis', 223f.) on attempts to read back complexes of ideas to Jewish 'models'. U. Wilckens, whose *Weisheit und Torheit* is mentioned in this connection, later changed his opinion (see 'Zu 1 Kor 2.1–16', in Andresen and Klein (eds), *Theologia Crucis - Signum Crucis*, 501–37). E. H. Pagels (in Hedrick and Hodgson (eds), *Nag Hammadi, Gnosticism, and Early Christianity*, 278) notes that the exegesis of Gen. 2 in the *Hypostasis of the Archons* 'reflects the influence of Paul's own exegesis of the same chapter (and of other passages in which the apostle refers to spiritual conflict with hostile cosmic powers: cf. 1 Corinthians 2; Colossians 1; Ephesians 5–6).' Cf. her appendix (279–85) discussing passages parallel to the *Hypostasis* in the Pauline corpus and Proverbs.

Gnostic aeon Sophia, but with that quality of wisdom which is the gift of God.

σύνεσις, the second in the Aristotelian triad, is (1) '*the faculty of comprehension, intelligence, acuteness, shrewdness*' or (2) '*insight, understanding* in the religio-ethical realm ... such as God grants to his own' (BAGD 788b; cf. also *TWNT* vii. 886–94); here it is obviously the latter sense that is required. For Aristotle, incidentally, σύνεσις is subordinate to φρόνησις, because it can only judge, but not command (*Eth. Nic.* vi.11; cf. Conzelmann, *TWNT* vii. 887); 'while σύνεσις apprehends the bearings of things, φρόνησις suggests lines of action' (Lightfoot). Where the two words are found together, σοφία normally precedes σύνεσις, but not in Josephus, *Ant.* viii.24, where in response to Solomon's prayer (cf. 2 Chron. 1.7–12) God gives to him 'understanding and wisdom such as no other man ever had, whether of kings or of private individuals' (cf. also Wisd. 7.7).

πνευματικός, as Lightfoot notes, is emphatic because of its position; this is no ordinary human wisdom or understanding, but wrought by the Spirit (cf. BAGD 679, *s.v.* 2aβ). It should perhaps be emphasized that the reference is not to something otherworldly, ethereal, holy, 'religious' and remote from reality: according to Gal. 5.22 the fruit of the Spirit is 'love, joy, peace, kindness, generosity, faithfulness, gentleness and self-control' (NRSV)—all eminently practical virtues for the conduct of human relationships. There is of course, as already noted, a difference between merely human wisdom, a 'fleshly' wisdom, and the wisdom that is the gift of God, a difference between the sacred and the secular, between the spiritual and the merely material, but sometimes the search for a 'spiritual' significance must be bluntly considered misguided. Schweizer notes ('Christus und Geist', 301) that Col. no longer shows Paul's reserve about wisdom and knowledge, and Paul does not speak of 'spiritual wisdom' as here. There is a similar phrase, ἐν πάσῃ εὐλογίᾳ πνευματικῇ, at Eph. 1.3; the other occurrence of the word in Col. (3.16, ψαλμοῖς ὕμνοις ᾠδαῖς πνευματικαῖς) is paralleled in Eph. 5.19, while Eph. 6.12 (πρὸς τὰ πνευματικὰ τῆς πονηρίας) is a reminder that spiritual forces are not necessarily always good (cf. the 'unclean spirits' in the Gospels). As with σοφία, the majority of the occurrences of πνευματικός in Paul's major letters are in 1 Cor., but not all of them are due to the Corinthian situation.

The Valentinians later were to develop a threefold classification of humanity: the πνευματικοί, who alone were assured of full salvation, the ψυχικοί, who might if they made the proper choices attain to a kind of secondary salvation, and the ὑλικοί, χοϊκοί or σαρκικοί, for whom there was no hope whatever; they were doomed to perish. This belongs to a later age. There have been attempts to find such distinctions in Paul's use of the terms in 1 Cor., or in Gal. 6.1, but here there is a danger of reading back second-century ideas into first-century documents (cf. B. A. Pearson, *The Pneumatikos–Psychikos Terminology* (1973); R. A. Horsley, 'Pneumatikos vs. Psychikos: Distinctions of Spiritual Status among the Corinthians', *HTR* 69 (1976), 269ff.). At any rate there is no such distinction here in Col.

10. περιπατῆσαι ἀξίως τοῦ κυρίου εἰς πᾶσαν ἀρεσκείαν Cf. 1 Thess. 2.12; Eph. 4.1 (ἀξίως περιπατῆσαι τῆς κλήσεως); Phil. 1.27.

περιπατεῖν (BAGD 649, esp. 2a; *TWNT* v. 944–45: for LXX see 942–43) means literally 'to walk' (e.g. Mark 2.9 par; 5.42; John 5.8–12), but is also used, and particularly in Paul (e.g. Rom. 6.4; 8.4; 1 Cor. 3.3; 7.17; 2 Cor. 4.2, 5.7; Gal. 5.16), in a figurative sense of the conduct of life (Phil 1.27 uses πολιτεύεσθαι); in both these senses it corresponds to the use of the Hebrew *halak* (Dunn, 71 notes that this verb 'gives rise to the technical term "halakha" to denote rabbinic rulings on how the law should be interpreted in daily life'). The aorist infinitive here has been interpreted in various ways: as an infinitive of purpose (Lohse, 27; Aletti, 72), or as denoting 'the consequence (not necessarily the purpose) of the spiritual enlightenment' just described (Lightfoot), or as an imperatival infinitive (O'Neill, 'Source', 90), but whatever the precise grammatical usage the meaning is not in doubt: the wisdom and understanding just mentioned are not merely theoretical—they are to lead to right conduct. The readers are to 'walk worthily of the Lord', to whom they owe allegiance.

κύριος in this context would seem to refer most naturally to Christ, but 1 Thess. 2.12 reads εἰς τὸ περιπατεῖν ὑμᾶς ἀξίως τοῦ θεοῦ, and 4.1 πῶς δεῖ ὑμᾶς περιπατεῖν καὶ ἀρέσκειν θεῷ (cf. 2.15 of those who 'displease God', also Rom. 8.8). These might seem to suggest that the reference is to God, but Lightfoot already notes that 'St Paul's common, and apparently universal, usage requires us to understand ὁ Κύριος of Christ'. Aletti (73) observes that if we take Col. as a whole, the title κύριος is given to Christ (1.3; 2.6; 3.17; 3.24b), but never to God, which prompts to caution in those cases where κύριος stands by itself (1.10; 3.13, where, however, some mss read Χριστός, others θεός; 3.16, again with variants; 3.18, 20, 22, 23, 24a; 4.1b, 7, 17); the use of κύριος here, with τοῦ θεοῦ at the end of the verse, suggests two different referents, the former relating to Christ, the latter to God the Father. This yields a perfectly natural sense.

These parallels in 1 Thess. show certain minor differences, which should be noted as well as the similarities: the present infinitive in both cases, where Col. has the aorist; the articular infinitive in 2.12, where Col. has the simple infinitive; and the insertion of καὶ ἀρέσκειν at 4.1, whereas Col. has the noun ἀρεσκεία. Once again we may ask: are these due to the same author varying his form of expression, or do they suggest different writers, one of whom may have had some knowledge of the other's work?

εἰς πᾶσαν ἀρεσκείαν is literally 'to all pleasing', with no indication as to who is to be pleased with this conduct[8] (O'Neill, 91 translates 'to be entirely pleasing'); 'pleasing to him' in the translation above (so also NEB, RSV, NRSV) links it with the nearest person mentioned, but see below. The noun, which occurs only here in the NT, is used 'mostly in a bad sense' (BAGD 105, citing Aristotle and Theophrastus, both already quoted by Lightfoot), of obsequiousness or cringing, 'ingratiating oneself with

[8] 'wem gegenüber, ist nicht sicher auszumachen' (Foerster, *TWNT* i. 456).

a sovereign or potentate' (Lightfoot; cf. ἀνθρωπάρεσκοι at 3.22 below, also Gal. 1.10; 1 Thess. 2.4). It can also be used, however, in a positive sense, of what is pleasing to God, as in several passages in Philo (*Fug.* 88; *Spec. Leg.* i.176, 317; *Op.M.* 144 etc.). Lightfoot remarks, 'As this word was commonly used to describe the proper attitude of men towards God, the addition of τοῦ Θεοῦ would not be necessary' (quoting other passages from Philo). It is probably this that has led some to think that the κύριος earlier in the verse must refer to God, but in view of the usage of Col., already mentioned, it is better to take it as referring to Christ.

ἐν παντὶ ἔργῳ ἀγαθῷ καρποφοροῦντες καὶ αὐξανόμενοι τῇ ἐπιγνώσει τοῦ θεοῦ Cf. v. 6 above, where these two verbs are used of the gospel (with καρποφορέω in the middle voice); here they are applied to the readers: they are to bring forth fruit in every good work and increase in the knowledge of God. Moule (54) notes that this phrase 'provides a striking instance of the verbal arrangement (*a b b a*) called "chiasmus"':

(*a*) noun: ἐν παντὶ ἔργῳ ἀγαθῷ   (*b*) verb: καρποφοροῦντες

(*b*) verb: αὐξανόμενοι   (*a*) noun: τῇ ἐπιγνώσει τοῦ θεοῦ.

The alternative is to take the dative τῇ ἐπιγνώσει as instrumental (so Lightfoot: 'The simple instrumental dative represents the knowledge of God as the dew or the rain which nurtures the growth of the plant: Deut. xxxii. 2, Hos. xiv. 5'; cf. also his paraphrase of the passage, p. 203). In this case the verbs must be taken together, and link 'through the knowledge of God' with 'in every good work' (so e.g. Peake, 499, who translates: 'bearing fruit and increasing in every good work by the knowledge of God'; cf. Lohse, 29 n. 48: 'The growth comes about through the understanding, and produces good works'). The interpretation in terms of chiasmus, however, would seem to be more natural and straightforward (so also Aletti, 72–75). The passage evidently caused difficulty to scribes, for some mss read ἐν τῇ ἐπιγνώσει, others εἰς τὴν ἐπίγνωσιν (Lightfoot in his comment speaks of 'unsuccessful attempts to define the construction'). Strictly speaking, the two participles should be in the accusative, agreeing with the implied subject of περιπατῆσαι above, but according to Peake, 'the continuation of an infinitive by a nominative participle is frequent in classical Greek, and occurs several times in Paul'; his four examples, however, are all from Eph. (4.2, 3) and Col. (2.2; 3.16), both of which are often considered post-Pauline; moreover the two cases in Col. are not infinitive constructions and only Eph. presents a real parallel (ἀξίως περιπατῆσαι ... ἀνεχόμενοι ἀλλήλων ... σπουδάζοντες).

The reference to good works may appear strange in view of Paul's regular condemnation of 'the works of the law', i.e. of any attempt to achieve salvation by righteous conduct, but as Aletti (74) notes the 'good works' here in view are 'only the first sign of a believing life that is worthy of the Gospel', the fruit of divine grace and not the result of human effort. The difference is quite simply that between works done in order to achieve salvation, which are condemned, and those which are the fruit of salvation and expected of those who have experienced the grace of God in Christ. Paul constantly enjoins his readers to conduct themselves in a manner worthy of their calling.[9] They are still subject to the strains and stresses of this earthly life, but 'in Christ' they have already been introduced into a new order of being, and must conduct themselves accordingly.

11. ἐν πάσῃ δυνάμει δυναμούμενοι κατὰ τὸ κράτος τῆς δόξης αὐτοῦ εἰς πᾶσαν ὑπομονὴν καὶ μακροθυμίαν 'The universal scope of the apostolic gospel appears ... in the letter's extensive use of formulations with πᾶς, πᾶσα, πᾶν—over thirty of them' (Wilson, *The Hope of Glory*, 73). This is a perfectly valid statement in terms of its immediate context: 'The gospel bears fruits and grows in "all" the world (1.6), having been preached to "all" creation under heaven (1.23). Paul admonishes "all" people and teaches "all" people so as to present "all" people before God as perfect'[10]—but not every formulation with πᾶς, πᾶσα, πᾶν belongs in this context. We have already encountered the phrases ἐν πάσῃ σοφίᾳ καὶ συνέσει πνευματικῇ (v. 9) and εἰς πᾶσαν ἀρεσκείαν, ἐν παντὶ ἔργῳ ἀγαθῷ (v. 10), where the reference is not to universality but rather to fullness and completeness (for the range of meaning cf. BAGD 631a–33a). The prayer is that the Colossians may be filled with all wisdom, that they may conduct themselves in a manner fully pleasing to the Lord, bearing fruit in every good work. Here in v. 11 the prayer continues with a reference to equipment[11] with all the power that is necessary for full endurance and forbearance (on the terms ὑπομονή and μακροθυμία see below).

[9] 'The expression "in every good work" is certainly Pauline, as witnessed by the presence of the same vocabulary in Rom. 2.7, 10; 13.3; 2 Cor. 9.8; Gal. 6.10; Phil. 1.6' (Aletti, 74 n. 95). He refers also to Eph. 2.10 and the 'almost identical syntagma' in 2 Thess. 2.17, ἐν παντὶ ἔργῳ καὶ λόγῳ ἀγαθῷ, and to the 'massive presence' of the combination in the Pastorals (even more notable when we include cases with καλός). But his remark that we find analogous expressions in the Judaism of the time (e.g. 1QS 1.4–5) shows, together with the Pastorals, that the usage is not purely Pauline.

[10] The reference (not supplied) is to Col. 1.28. A footnote refers back to p. 54 n. 14, where it is noted in the text that 'the teaching of sages like Socrates, owing to the nature of their vocation, takes on universal dimensions; these venerable figures become, in effect, the tutors of all humankind'. The philosophical paraenesis, as Wilson shows, certainly provides interesting parallels which are important for the background of Col., but it is not necessarily to be inferred that our author was influenced by these writings. It is well to recall E. Earle Ellis's remark about the danger of converting parallels into influences, and influences into sources (*St Paul's Use of the Old Testament*, 82). Authors writing independently, in the same period and in similar circumstances, might well show a measure of agreement which might deceive the modern reader into thinking the relationship between them closer than it actually was.

[11] The verb δυναμόω occurs several times in LXX, but not elsewhere in the NT apart from Heb. 11.34 and as a variant reading at Eph. 6.10. The form normally used is the compound ἐνδυναμόω (Acts 9.22; Rom. 4.20; Eph. 6.10; Phil. 4.13; 1 Tim. 1.12; 2 Tim. 2.1, 4.17), which is read by some mss at Heb. 11.34 also.

Greek has several words commonly rendered by 'power', 'strength' or 'might' in English (e.g. ἐξουσία, δύναμις, κράτος, ἰσχύς), and failure to recognize nuances of meaning (or reliance upon an English translation) may lead to misleading conclusions. At Acts 1.7–8, for example, AV reads, 'It is not for you to know the times or the seasons which the Father hath put in his own power. But ye shall receive power, after that the Holy Ghost is come upon you'; but what the disciples are promised is not that they will receive the power which belongs to the Father alone (ἐξουσία), it is that they will be given a dynamic force (δύναμις) to sustain them amid the trials that lie ahead. At John 1.12 those who receive the Logos are given the right (ἐξουσία) to become the children of God, but they still have to exercise that right, and fulfil the obligations which it entails, if they are truly to be God's children. A subscription to a sports club conveys the right to make use of its facilities, but not the ability to excel in the sport—which has to be gained by practice and training. The problems for the interpreter are complicated by the fact that some of these words have a range of meanings which sometimes overlap.

Here the word is **δύναμις** (BAGD 207a; *TWNT* ii. 286–318), which in this context implies all the spiritual resources necessary to their Christian life. Peake (499) comments, 'This equipment with Divine power is not, as we might have expected, said to be given with a view to deeds of great spiritual heroism, but for the practice of passive virtues, since this often puts the greater strain on the Christian's strength'. **ὑπομονή** he defines as 'endurance, steadfastness in face of trials, temptations and persecutions' (cf. BAGD 846a; *TWNT* iv. 589–93), and **μακροθυμία** as 'forbearance, the patience of spirit that will not retaliate' (cf. BAGD 488a; *TWNT* iv. 377–93). It has to be remembered that for the first three centuries of the Church's life Christians were a minority group, exposed to hostility and even to outright persecution, with all the temptation to conform to the habits of their neighbours which that involved. There was a real need for steadfastness and endurance, and it is not surprising that these terms, especially ὑπομονή, feature regularly in the New Testament. Aletti (76) notes that there is nothing triumphalist in the existence of believers; the power received from God does not act as a talisman to ward off tribulation, but it does enable the believer to remain unshakeable amid all trials. To speak of 'passive' virtues may, however, be somewhat misleading; what is called for is rather fortitude, an attitude summed up in a classic passage in Ephesians (6.10–17) with its reference to putting on the whole armour of God 'that you may be able to withstand in that evil day, and having done everything, to stand firm' (NRSV). As Scott (18) puts it, the patience of the Christian 'is not a dull Stoical endurance, but is accompanied with joy, since the believer can be confident that all his trials are leading to some great end'. Superficially the Stoic αὐταρκεία, the Epicurean ἀταραξία and the Christian ὑπομονή may appear to be very similar, but a closer inspection reveals that there are very real differences.[12]

κατὰ τὸ κράτος τῆς δόξης αὐτοῦ Moffatt translates 'his glorious might', taking τῆς δόξης in Hebrew fashion as adjectival (BAGD 203b offers 'majestic power', and at 449a 'his glorious [divine] might'; cf. Aletti, 75 n. 100: 'il s'agit d'un sémitisme à traduire "selon sa puissante gloire" ', which, however, takes τὸ κράτος as adjectival, rather than τῆς δόξης). On the other hand Moule (*Idiom Book*, 175) observes that 'it is a mistake to claim a Semitic Genitive where a good Greek Genitive makes better sense', and this may be a case in point: a simple literal translation makes perfectly good sense. As Lightfoot puts it, δόξα stands 'for the majesty or the power or the goodness of God, as *manifested* to men' (he refers to Eph. 1.6, 12, 17; 3.16 and compares v. 27 below). Originally the word meant (1) opinion (hence *orthodox*, i.e. holding 'right opinions') or (2) reputation, but in LXX it was used as the equivalent for the Hebrew *kabod*, 'the usual word for the splendour or glory of God' (Moule, *Colossians*, 83; cf. Brockington in *Studies in the Gospels*, 1–8; *TWNT* ii. 236–56).[13] NT usage corresponds not to that of classical Greek but to that of LXX (*TWNT* ii. 250), so much so that BAGD 203b gives as the primary meaning 'brightness, splendour, radiance' (although Moule, 84 detects the 'secular' meaning in John 5.44, where the 'glory' received from others is dramatically contrasted with that bestowed by God; cf. John 7.18; 8.50; 1 Thess. 2.6; BAGD 204, *s.v.* 3. This is reputation or fame in contrast with true glory). It is in the first place the glory of God, 'in light inaccessible hid from our eyes', but by his grace may be shared by others: 'the "wealth of glory" represented by the Incarnation, and, since then, by the presence of God in his Church through the Holy Spirit, is the ground for the Christians' "confidence" (ἐλπίς) "in a glorious destiny to come" '(Moule, 84).

As already noted, **κράτος** (BAGD 449a; *TWNT* iii. 905–08) is one of several Greek words for 'power' or 'strength', but it is not used in any of the major Pauline letters; moreover there is no passage in the New Testament where it is said that man can either possess or obtain this power (*TWNT* iii. 907). At Heb. 2.14 the reference is to 'the one who has the power of death, that is, the devil', but elsewhere κράτος is always the power of God or of Christ. Ephesians (1.19; 6.10, ἐν τῷ κράτει τῆς ἰσχύος αὐτοῦ, cf. Isa. 40.26 LXX) twice links it with ἰσχύς, in the first case referring to God, in the second to Christ (apart

[12] For a comparison of Paul and Stoicism, taking due note of the differences, see Esler, 'Paul and Stoicism': 'Throughout the course of Rom. 12 Paul works closely with ideas and language that have parallels in Stoicism and yet thoroughly subverts them as he paints his own very distinctive picture' (124).
[13] In the Nag Hammadi *Tractatus Tripartitus* (110.17–18) a literal translation of the Coptic does not make sense: 'these are glories and theories'. The meaning required is 'opinions and theories'. The error is, however, easily explained on the basis of a Greek *Vorlage*: the translator, more familiar with the biblical than the classical sense of δόξα, did not realize that in this case the biblical sense did not fit (see Thomassen, *Le Traité Tripartite* (1989), 10–11). The mistake is the more understandable in that there are numerous cases of the biblical sense in this text.

from 1 Tim. 6.16, these two verses with Col. 1.11 are the only occurrences in the Pauline corpus). Like δόξα, and sometimes associated with it (1 Pet. 4.11; Rev 1.6; 5.13), it frequently occurs in doxologies (1 Pet. 5.11; 1 Tim. 6.16; Jude 25).

μετὰ χαρᾶς In the translation above these words are taken with what follows, in agreement with the text of NA²⁷ (cf. NRSV, and NEB translators' note); the text in UBS, 3rd edn takes them with what precedes (so AV, RSV, NEB; cf. also the punctuation apparatus in UBS, 3rd edn). Ancient manuscripts had no punctuation, and the verse division is a comparatively modern invention (devised by Stephanus for the NT in 1551); it is therefore sometimes difficult to determine whether a word or phrase belongs with what precedes or with what follows, and a decision has to be made on the basis of the content of the passage. In the view of some scholars, the εὐχαριστοῦντες clause introduces a new thought: 'The subject is no longer the conduct of life of the believers; rather the community is now urged to praise God with thanksgiving, as they are reminded of the saving action of God extolled in the confession' (Lohse, 32; the confession follows in vv. 12–14). Thanksgiving for deliverance is then naturally associated with joy. Peake, however, long ago objected that this 'would be tautological and throw a false emphasis on these words' (500). Taken with the preceding ὑπομονὴ καὶ μακροθυμία, the phrase 'forms a very necessary addition, for the peculiar danger of the exercise of these qualities is that it tends to produce a certain gloominess or sourness of disposition. The remedy is that the Christian should be so filled with joy that he is able to meet all his trials with a buoyant sense of mastery.' More recently Barth (183) says the words are 'most likely part of the *preceding* statement, for Paul speaks of joyful suffering or joyful endurance in the face of suffering also elsewhere' (referring to Rom. 5.3; 12.12; 1 Thess. 5.16; 1 Pet. 1.6; 4.13; compare Acts 5.41; Jas. 1.2ff.). Only three of Barth's references are, however, actually Pauline; the occurrence of the theme in the other passages suggests that this was a common motif in early Christian teaching: the writers knew that they and their readers were exposed to hostility, even to actual persecution, but their attitude was not one of despair; it was to focus on the joy that was set before them, the hope of the life everlasting, in this following the example of their Lord and Master (cf. Heb. 12.2).

In favour of the reading adopted here, it may be noted that each of the two preceding participles is preceded by a prepositional phrase (ἐν παντὶ ἔργῳ ἀγάθῳ καρποφοροῦντες, ἐν πάσῃ δυνάμει δυναμού-μενοι), which suggests that the third also should have such a phrase before it (cf. also Phil. 1.4: μετὰ χαρᾶς τὴν δέησιν ποιούμενος; on the other side, cf. already Lightfoot, 206, who rejects these arguments). The three participles are certainly closely linked, although it is convenient in translation to make a break at v. 11 and begin a new sentence at μετὰ χαρᾶς εὐχαριστοῦντες. What is important here is the note of joy, even in the face of suffering and hardship: too often Christianity appears to be stern and sombre,

puritanical in its attitude to even harmless pleasures. The true note is
that of Phil. 4.4: 'Rejoice in the Lord always; again I will say,
Rejoice.' The word χαρά itself occurs quite frequently in the NT.

12. εὐχαριστοῦντες τῷ πατρὶ τῷ ἱκανώσαντι ὑμᾶς εἰς τὴν
μερίδα τοῦ κλήρου τῶν ἁγίων ἐν τῷ φωτί[14] Lohse (32 n. 1) writes,
'In Jewish texts the participle often appears with an imperatival
meaning' (referring *inter alia* to D. Daube, 'Participle and Imperative
in I Peter', in E. G. Selwyn (ed.), *The First Epistle of St Peter* (1949),
467–88), and later adds, 'Since the participle εὐχαριστοῦντες is only
loosely attached to the preceding verses, the translation as an
imperative is completely justified.' Aletti, however, demurs (76f.),
urging that we consider the use made of participles in Col. and
setting out half a dozen passages (Col. 2.6–7; 3.9–10; 3.12; 3.16; 4.2;
4.5), in each of which an imperative is followed by one or more
participles in a structure similar to that of our passage. A participle
may have imperatival force, but that does not mean that it always
does; moreover in the present case it would seem rather awkward to
have two participles normally used, followed by a third with
imperatival meaning. In a sense all three could be taken as
imperatival, since they spell out what is meant by the περιπατῆσαι
of v. 10, but it would seem better to regard all three as participles,
rather than take two as participles and the third as an imperative; the
participles would appear to be more closely linked than Lohse
allows. As already noted, the translation above makes a break and
begins a new sentence, with an imperative, but that is simply because
this is a convenient point, and does not imply that the third participle
is to be taken as gramatically an imperative.

This verse shows a string of variants, some of which, however, do not really affect the
sense: a καί before εὐχαριστοῦντες in P[46] and 1175 suggests that some scribes thought
the μετὰ χαρᾶς should go with what precedes; but the support is not really very strong,
nor is that for ἅμα after εὐχαριστοῦντες (P[46] B). The insertion of θεῷ before πατρί in ℵ
and other mss indicates that some devout scribe felt the simple τῷ πατρί to be deficient
in reverence; but the variant θεῷ καί in C[3] etc. suggests that we have here a growing
text. Moule (55) notes that 'Except in the Fourth Gospel and the Johannine epistles,
"(the) Father" (without the addition of "God" or of a qualifying genitive or
possessive) is not common in the N.T.'; so scribes may have written what they
expected. More important is the variant καλέσαντι (D* F G etc.) for ἱκανώσαντι (P[46] ℵ
A C D[2] etc.): scribes evidently found the latter word difficult, since it is used in an
unusual sense (see below). This is a case where the more difficult reading should be
preferred. The καλέσαντι καὶ ἱκανώσαντι of B is an obvious conflation. Finally the
ὑμᾶς (ℵ B etc.) presents another case of the common variation between the first person
plural and the second (see p. 95 above): A C D F G with other mss and the Majority
text read ἡμᾶς, possibly influenced by the first person pronoun in the following verse.

This verse calls upon the readers to give thanks to the Father, 'who
has enabled you to share in the inheritance of the saints in the Light'
(NRSV), and thus provides part of the motivation for the thanksgiving to which they are called. The participial phrase in this verse is
followed by a relative clause in v. 13, which provides a further

[14] On this verse cf. Benoit, 'Ἅγιοι en Colossiens 1.12'.

motivation (see below). The only other occurrence in the NT of the verb ἱκανόω is at 2 Cor. 3.6: ὃς καὶ ἱκάνωσεν ἡμᾶς διακόνους καινῆς διαθήκης, but as noted in the Introduction (p. 28) it would be a mistake to assume a special link between these letters on the strength of just a few words. It means to make sufficient, to qualify, 'perhaps shading into the sense *empower, authorize*' (BAGD 374b): by the grace of God the readers have been qualified to take their place in the inheritance of the saints in light.[15] Lightfoot (317) already notes that confusion between ΤΩΙΙΚΑΝΩΣΑΝΤΙ and ΤΩΙΚΑΛΕΣΑΝΤΙ would be easy in a period when the iota was written adscript and not subscript, 'while at the same time καλέσαντι would suggest itself to scribes as the obvious word in such a connexion' (cf. 1 Pet. 2.9 τοῦ ἐκ σκότους ὑμᾶς καλέσαντος).[16] If we read ἡμᾶς here, the author is including himself, and other Christians, but since this may be the result of assimilation to the first person pronoun in the following verse it is probably better to read ὑμᾶς.

μερίς (BAGD 505) means '*part* of a whole that has been divided', and hence a share or portion; at Acts 16.12 it appears to refer to one of the four districts into which the province of Macedonia was divided (see most recently R. S. Ascough, *NTS* 44 (1998), 93–103). In the Pauline corpus the word occurs only here and in 2 Cor. 6.15, where it is differently used. κλῆρος (BAGD 435a; *TWNT* iii. 757–63, esp. 762–63) means 'lot', with reference to the casting of lots (cf. Mark 15.24 and parallels; Acts 1.26), and hence something apportioned by lot, a share or portion. It occurs only here in the Pauline corpus. The two words are close to one another in meaning (Lohse, 35), but not quite synonymous: μερίς is primarily a part, κλῆρος a portion appointed for someone; it often comes close in meaning to κληρονομία (see Foerster, *TWNT* iii. 758–60 on the relation of these terms in LXX: the Promised Land is the lot appointed for Israel, the inheritance into which by the grace of God they are destined to enter. In Deut. 10.9 the Levites are given neither part nor portion among their brothers when the land is distributed, because the Lord himself is their portion; at Num. 18.20 he is their κληρονομία). In Acts 26.18 there is an interesting parallel to the present verse: τοῦ λαβεῖν αὐτοὺς ... κλῆρον ἐν τοῖς ἡγιασμένοις (this participle is equivalent to a substantival ἁγίοις; cf. also Acts 20.32, δοῦναι τὴν κληρονομίαν ἐν τοῖς ἡγιασμένοις πᾶσιν). The words μερίς and κλῆρος appear together in Acts 8.21 (in Peter's rejection of Simon Magus), which itself echoes passages in LXX such as Deut. 10.9; 12.12. Lohse (35) notes that the Hebrew equivalents are often used in the writings of the Qumran community; particular interest attaches to 1QS XI.7f.: 'God has given them [the blessings listed in the preceding lines] to His chosen ones as an everlasting possession, and

---

[15] Benoit (83) notes that the sense is '"rendre capable de, apte à", mais non pas "rendre digne": *dignos* de la Vulgate est inexact, mieux *idoneos*'.

[16] As already noted, the καλέσαντι καὶ ἱκανώσαντι of B is a fairly obvious conflate reading.

has caused them to inherit the lot of the Holy Ones. He has joined
their assembly to the Sons of Heaven' (tr. Vermes, *Dead Sea Scrolls
in English* (1962)).
  As noted above (p. 71), the context of Ps. 89.5–7 suggests that the
'holy ones' there are heavenly beings:

> Let the heavens praise your wonders, O LORD,
> your faithfulness in the assembly of the holy ones.
> For who in the skies can be compared to the LORD?
> Who among the heavenly beings is like the LORD,
> a God feared in the council of the holy ones,
> great and awesome above all that are around him? (NRSV)

The imagery here is that of God seated in a heavenly council,
surrounded by the angels and other heavenly beings who minister in
his service. In the light of these and similar passages, particularly
from Qumran, it has been argued that the 'saints' of Col. 1.12 should
be understood as referring to the angels: 'The "holy ones" (ἅγιοι)
are the angels, and the Christian community has been authorized to
participate in their "portion of the lot" (μερὶς τοῦ κλήρου)—this is
unmistakably clear from the parallel statements from the Qumran
community' (Lohse 36, cf. Best, *Ephesians*, 167–68 on Eph. 1.18). To
this Barth (186) objects (1) that in Col. 'saints' is never used to
designate angels, 'but rather always human persons chosen by God'
(referring to 1.2, 4, 22, 26; 3.12); (2) account must be taken of Acts
26.18, where οἱ ἁγιάσμενοι 'are unequivocally the believers in
Christ'; (3) in the further course of the letter, the angels are not given
such significance, and the salvation of God is not presented in such a
way as to suggest that the hope of the readers should be seen as
participation in 'the lot of the angels' (but what of the theory that the
θρησκεία τῶν ἀγγέλων in 2.18 is the worship offered by the angels, in
which they hope to share?). Barth also notes that in this context
'saints' has 'a more circumscribed meaning' than in earlier occurrences: 'As in the OT, the word is used to designate the covenant
people Israel, in whose inheritance the "former outsiders" are now
entitled participants'. Something similar to this nuance had already
been noted by Benoit (87): 'Il s'agirait plus précisément des chrétiens
d'origine juive, ceux de Jérusalem, les premiers appelés au salut du
Christ': the 'saints' are the Jewish Christians in contrast to Gentiles.
It appears notably where Paul is concerned with his great collection
for the poor in Judaea (cf. also Eph. 2.19, where the former
'strangers and aliens' have become fellow-citizens with the saints, i.e.
Christians originating from the 'city of Israel'; but cf. Best,
Ephesians, 277–78).
  Benoit notes that the view which sees the ἅγιοι here as angels has
good support in the texts, but that in the NT the use of the
substantive in the sense of 'angels' is much more rare, and even
doubtful. He lists just three Pauline texts, apart from our present
verse: in 2 Thess. 1.10 he suggests an antithetic parallelism, in which
the Lord is glorified in his saints, the angels, and admired in those

who believe in him, i.e. human beings; at 1 Thess. 3.13 'it seems preferable to recognise angels in the "saints" of this passage'—unless we extend the term to include both angels and people who have become their companions; as for Eph. 1.18, the ἅγιοι here could represent angels just as much as beatified people. But why not both? Exegetes, he says (95), too often proceed on the basis of an 'either/or', when the author may have wished to embrace complementary aspects which are not mutually exclusive. It may be added that Lohse continues (36): 'The host of those chosen by God is joined to the angels and they are likewise called "Holy Ones". As God's possession, they are holy ones (cf. 1: 2 "saints") who will receive the heavenly inheritance'. The heavenly host includes not only angels but the elect who have kept the faith and finished their course.

ἐν τῷ φωτί Cf. with this and the next verse Acts 26.18, τοῦ ἐπιστρέψαι ἀπὸ σκότους εἰς φῶς καὶ τῆς ἐξουσίας τοῦ σατανᾶ ἐπὶ τὸν θεόν; also 1 Pet. 2.9, τοῦ ἐκ σκότους ὑμᾶς καλέσαντος εἰς τὸ θαυμαστὸν αὐτοῦ φῶς. The contrast of light and darkness is common in the Bible: at the very beginning, in the creation story, we are told that 'God separated the light from the darkness' (Gen. 1.4). Echoing that, 2 Cor. 4.6 says, 'it is the God who said, "Let light shine out of darkness," who has shone in our hearts to give the light of the knowledge of the glory of God in the face of Jesus Christ'. In Isa. 9.2: 'the people who walked in darkness have seen a great light'. According to 1 John 1.5, 'God is light and in him is no darkness at all', and in the next verse the conclusion is drawn that those who would be in fellowship with God must 'walk' in the light (cf. Eph. 5.8).[17] The *War Scroll* from Qumran (1QM) is 'not a military manual, but a theological consideration of a perpetual struggle between good and evil', the war of the Sons of Light against the Sons of Darkness (G. Vermes, *The Dead Sea Scrolls*) (1978), 51; for a translation see Vermes, *Dead Sea Scrolls in English*, 122–48). The terms are thus used both naturally, for light and darkness in the ordinary sense, and also metaphorically, light representing the good and darkness evil.

This contrast is not confined to the Bible: Lightfoot already notes, 'As a classical parallel, Plato *Resp.* vii. p.518A, ἔκ τε φωτὸς εἰς σκότος καὶ ἐκ σκότους εἰς φῶς, is quoted' (cf. *TWNT* vii. 424–46 on σκότος; ix. 302–49 on φῶς; also Hübner's excursus, 'Licht und Finsternis', 228–32). The most obvious reference is, of course, to Zoroastrianism, but the motif appears in other religions also; indeed, Moule (57) says, 'it would be surprising to find any religion in which this obvious but telling metaphor was ignored'. This 'dualism' is sometimes claimed as evidence of Gnostic influence, but we must consider in such cases how far the idea in question is specifically Gnostic, and how much may be due to common dependence on the

---

[17] For 'light' in the Gospel of John cf. Dodd, *The Interpretation of the Fourth Gospel*, 201ff.

same background of thought and ideas. Cf. Lightfoot's comment (210) on terms used in connection with the idea of the λόγος: 'their use in Alexandrian writers, such as Philo, cannot be taken to *define*, though it may be brought to *illustrate*, their meaning in St Paul and St John'. Some terms are definitely 'Gnostic' within the context of a Gnostic system, but are they 'Gnostic' outside of that system? It may be dangerous to draw conclusions from a superficial similarity in language and terminology: both Gnostics and orthodox were using the language and ideas of their time. In the present case we need to remember that there are several different kinds of dualism (cf. U. Bianchi, *Encyc. Britannica* (1974 edn) 1066–70 and 'Il dualismo come categoria storico-religiosa', *R. storia e lett. religiosa* ix (1973), 2ff.; Huppenbauer, *Der Mensch zwischen zwei Welten*), and not all of them are strictly Gnostic.

13. ὃς ἐρρύσατο ἡμᾶς ἐκ τῆς ἐξουσίας τοῦ σκότους καὶ μετέστησεν εἰς τὴν βασιλείαν τοῦ υἱοῦ τῆς ἀγάπης αὐτοῦ As already noted, this verse provides a further motivation for the thanksgiving to which the community is summoned: God 'has rescued us from the power of darkness and transferred us into the kingdom of his beloved son' (NRSV; the relative pronoun refers back to τῷ πατρί in v. 12). The verb ῥύομαι (BAGD 737b) means 'rescue, save, deliver, preserve'; it occurs for example in a petition of the Lord's Prayer (Matt. 6.13, ῥῦσαι ἡμᾶς ἀπὸ τοῦ πονηροῦ), while the present participle is used of Jesus in 1 Thess. 1.10 (τὸν ῥυόμενον ἡμᾶς ἐκ τῆς ὀργῆς τῆς ἐρχομένης; cf. the quotation of Isa. 59.20 at Rom. 11.26). The aorist here would seem to indicate that the author thinks of this deliverance not as something now in process, but as an accomplished fact: by virtue of their conversion and their baptism into Christ, Christians have already been delivered from the power of darkness and belong to the realm of light. It is therefore incumbent upon them to live as children of the light and of the day, not of the night (1 Thess. 5.4–8; cf. Eph. 5.8). This is one of the points at which our author seems to some scholars to go further than Paul himself does: for Paul there is always a certain tension between the 'already' and the 'not yet'—a decisive change has indeed taken place, but the full consummation is yet to come (cf. Rom. 6.5, 'if we have been united with him in a death like his, we will certainly be united with him in a resurrection like his'; note the future in the second clause); for our author, Christians are not only buried with Christ in baptism (Rom. 6.4–5) but already raised with him (Col 2.12; 3.1). It is, however, possible, as will be seen, to interpret such statements in Col. in thoroughly Pauline terms, so that it is by no means certain that there is such a difference.[18]

The change to the first person plural is perfectly natural: in v. 12 the reference is to the readers, predominately Gentiles, who have been accorded the privilege of admission into God's holy people; here the author includes himself, and indeed all Christians, among those

[18] For the theme in Pauline theology cf. Schnelle, 'Transformation'.

who have been delivered. As Paul puts it (Rom 3.23–24): 'all have sinned and fall short of the glory of God [Gentile and Jew alike, cf. v. 9]; they are now justified by his grace as a gift, through the redemption that is in Christ Jesus'.

ἐξουσία (BAGD 277a–79a; *TWNT* ii. 557–72) This word has a fairly wide range of meaning. Initially, it means 'freedom of choice' (cf. ἔξεστιν), i.e. the right to do something (cf. for example 1 Cor. 9: 4–6); secondly it may mean the ability to do something, capability, might or power. In BAGD (278a) it is noted that it is not always possible to draw a hard and fast line between this meaning and a third: authority, absolute power, warrant. A fourth meaning relates to the power exercised by rulers or others in high office, (1) of the ruling power itself (e.g. Luke 19.17; 20.20), (2) of the domain in which that power is exercised (e.g. Luke 23.7; the phrase ἐξουσία τοῦ σκότους occurs also in Luke 22.53), and (3) of the bearers of this authority, whether human officials or rulers and functionaries in the spiritual world (cf. Col. 1.16; 2.10, 15 below).[19] Here it refers to the realm of darkness, the sphere in which Satan holds sway (cf. Acts 26.18, quoted above). Lightfoot (207) suggests that the idea is that of a transference 'from an arbitrary tyranny, an ἐξουσία, to a well-ordered sovereignty, a βασιλεία'. Scott (19) wrote some seventy years ago: 'Perhaps we can best understand Paul's meaning when we translate his idea out of the terms of ancient mythology into those of modern thinking. We speak now, not of angelic powers throned in the planets, but of a world of mechanical law, in the clutches of which we are helpless ... To such a philosophy Paul would answer, as he answered the teachers at Colossae, that we have access to a world of freedom. God has delivered us out of the lower, mechanical sphere and placed us in the Kingdom of His Son.' As Paul wrote in Rom. 8.38–39, there is nothing in all creation that can separate us from the love of God in Christ Jesus our Lord. W. L. Knox (*PCG* 156ff.) observes that Paul's answer to the report of the new teaching (quoted in the Introduction above, p. 48) was 'a direct and emphatic negative', and adds, 'The initial thanksgiving and prayer contained potentially the whole of his answer.' There can be no question of belittling the place of Jesus in the scheme of redemption, as if the redemption obtained in him had to be completed by full knowledge

---

[19] As noted in the Introduction (p. 51 above), the *Hypostasis of the Archons* from the Nag Hammadi library appears to echo this verse (and Eph. 6.12); but where Col. has the singular ἐξουσία the Coptic has the plural, suggesting a number of hostile 'powers'. Regarding the terms used for the forces of evil (here and at 1.16; 2.14, 15, 20), W. D. Davies observes that the correspondence in terminology with Qumran is not very exact, and could not by itself be taken to point to influences of the Qumran type; nevertheless, when other factors are taken into account, 'it would seem that the forces of evil in Colossians may be the same as those referred to in the scrolls' (*Christian Origins and Judaism*, 159). The *Dialogue of the Saviour* (NHC III. 122.4) speaks of 'the power of darkness' which will come upon the disciples 'when the time of dissolution arrives' (ed. Emmel, (1984), 45; cf. the introduction by Koester and Pagels, p. 10). Cf. also *NHTB* index, p. 527.

of other powers through whose realms the soul had to pass (*PCG* 158).

σκότος (BAGD 757b–58a; *TWNT* vii. 424–46—for Eph. and Col. see 443) can be used either literally or figuratively. The metaphorical use of the contrast between light and darkness was common in the ancient world (see above, p. 114; and cf. Conzelmann in *TWNT*, also his article φῶς, *TWNT* ix. 302–49); as Moule (57) puts it, in words already quoted, 'it would be surprising to find any religion in which this obvious but telling metaphor was ignored'. This makes it dangerous to draw far-reaching conclusions on the basis of surface similarity: the theme is common in Gnostic texts, but not all cases in which it occurs are Gnostic.[20]

μετέστησεν (BAGD 498b–499a) Lightfoot remarks, 'The image of μετέστησεν is supplied by the wholesale transportation of peoples (ἀναστάτους or ἀνασπάστους ποιεῖν), of which the history of oriental monarchies supplied so many examples.' He cites Josephus *Ant.* ix.11.1 (ix.235 Niese), which tells of Tiglath-pileser transporting to his own kingdom the inhabitants of Israelite territories he had overrun. As noted in the Introduction (p. 5), Antiochus the Great settled considerable numbers of Jews in Phrygia, but Josephus (*Ant.* xii.149) does not use this verb there; it is unlikely that our author intended any allusion (the majority of the Colossian community would in any case be Gentiles). For other occurrences of the word cf. Acts 19.26 (of leading people astray); 1 Cor. 13.2.

εἰς τὴν βασιλείαν τοῦ υἱοῦ τῆς ἀγάπης αὐτοῦ For βασιλεία see BAGD 134b–35, where it is defined as: '1. *kingship, royal power, royal rule, kingdom*; 2. *kingdom*, i.e. the territory ruled over by a king; and 3. esp. *the royal rule or kingdom of God*, a chiefly eschatological concept'; also *TWNT* i. 579–92. The idea of the kingdom of God is a prominent feature of the teaching of Jesus in the Synoptics, but less so in John;[21] in the Pauline corpus (excluding the Pastorals) there are just a dozen occurrences. In five of these (1 Cor. 6.9, 10; 15.50; Gal. 5.21; Eph. 5.5) the reference is to inheriting the kingdom, which would seem to provide some justification for thinking of it as a realm to be entered, at a time still to come. Two others (1 Thess. 2.12; 2 Thess. 1.5) also seem to refer to the future (so too perhaps Col. 4.11). At Rom. 14.17 and 1 Cor. 4.20, however, the kingdom is referred to in the present tense (cf. also Eph. 5.5: οὐκ ἔχει κληρονομίαν). It is therefore in some sense a present reality. C. K. Barrett (*From First Adam to Last*, 100) finds an explanation in the thought of the partial anticipation in the present of the future kingdom, which he says is common in the New Testament: 'Where the Spirit is truly at work, anticipating the reign of God in Christian life and the work of

[20] Conzelmann (*TWNT* vii. 435) notes in some passages of Philo 'eine Vorstufe der Gnosis', but adds in a footnote 'Nicht mehr!'
[21] The literature is of course extensive. See for example Manson, *The Teaching of Jesus*, 116–284; N. Perrin, *The Kingdom of God in the Teaching of Jesus*, (1963). For the theme in the Bible as a whole, cf. *HDB* ii. 844–56.

evangelism, there righteousness, peace, joy and power are to be seen. In the work of the Spirit, the kingdom of God may be said to be proleptically present though it remains essentially future.'

The reference in the above quotation to the 'reign' of God recalls a debate of long standing, as to the meaning of the phrase 'the kingdom of God'. It has been argued that the primary significance is that of sovereignty, the rule of God in the hearts and lives of men and women, rather than that of a realm or kingdom.[22] This, however, may be to introduce a false contrast: sovereignty implies a territory within which that sovereignty is exercised, a community over which the sovereign rules, people who accept that rule. In his discussion of the concept in the teaching of Jesus, T. W. Manson (136) notes, 'three interdependent conceptions of the Kingdom as an eternal fact, as a manifestation in the present life of men, and as a consummation still to come': at least from the time of the Old Testament prophets, God is king in an absolute sense. His sovereignty becomes manifest in the lives and conduct of people who accept his rule, who in the rabbinic phrase take upon themselves 'the yoke of the kingdom'. But the full manifestation of that rule has still to come, when the last enemy is destroyed and all things are put in subjection to Christ: 'When all things are subjected to him, then the Son himself will also be subjected to the one who put all things in subjection under him, so that God may be all in all' (1 Cor. 15.24–28).

What is unusual in the present verse is that the reference is not to the kingdom of God, but to the kingdom of his beloved Son. The phrase ὁ υἱὸς τῆς ἀγάπης αὐτοῦ is generally recognized to be a Semitism, recalling the voice from heaven at the baptism and transfiguration of Jesus (Mark 1.11 par.; 9.7 par.; so e.g. Moule, 58), but this does not mean that it derives from the Gospels. A later disciple might conceivably have known the Gospel of Mark, but Paul could not; at most he could have known the traditions on which Mark draws. In any case Paul in his major letters uses ἀγαπητός either in addressing his readers or as a description of close colleagues and friends like Epaphras (v. 7 above) and Philemon (Philem. 1), but not with reference to Jesus (but cf. ἐν τῷ ἠγαπημένῳ in Eph. 1.6). Lightfoot (208) objects that 'the loose interpretation, which makes τοῦ υἱοῦ τῆς ἀγάπης equivalent to τοῦ υἱοῦ τοῦ ἀγαπημένου, destroys the whole force of the expression'. In his view the words are intimately connected with the expressions which follow in vv. 15 and 19 (εἰκὼν τοῦ θεοῦ τοῦ ἀοράτου and ἐν αὐτῷ εὐδόκησεν πᾶν τὸ πλήρωμα κατοικῆσαι): 'As love is the essence of the Father (1 Joh. iv. 8, 16), so is it also of the Son. The mission of the Son is the revelation of the Father's love.' He cites Augustine as offering the correct interpretation: 'The son of his love is no other than the one born of his substance.'

The idea of Christ as king appears of course in the Gospels, but there are very few references to the kingdom or kingship of Christ in

the Pauline corpus (for later writings cf. 2 Tim. 4.1, 18; 2 Pet. 1.11.
Eph. 5.5 refers to the kingdom of Christ and God).[23] The one clear
case in the major Pauline letters is in 1 Cor. 15.24–28, already cited,
where the kingdom of Christ is of limited duration; he is to reign
until the last enemy is conquered, and then hand over the kingdom
to God the Father. As Moule (57) notes, it is open to question
whether our author here intends the phrase to mean 'the "interim"
period between the resurrection and the final manifestation of the
kingdom of God'.

14. ἐν ᾧ ἔχομεν τὴν ἀπολύτρωσιν, τὴν ἄφεσιν τῶν ἁμαρτιῶν
Cf. Eph. 1.7, ἐν ᾧ ἔχομεν τὴν ἀπολύτρωσιν διὰ τοῦ αἵματος αὐτοῦ,
τὴν ἄφεσιν τῶν παραπτωμάτων. In both cases some witnesses (only
B here among mss, ℵ* D* and a few others in Eph.) read ἔσχομεν,
which Lightfoot (317) thinks possibly the correct reading here; but it
could be due to assimilation to the aorists in the preceding verse. The
first person plural is not 'editorial' but inclusive, i.e. it 'embraces not
only Paul and Timothy and those prayed for (1: 9) but all who are
"in Christ"' (Dunn, 80). The addition of 'in his blood' after τὴν
ἀπολύτρωσιν in some mss of Col. is an expansion under the influence
of the parallel passage in Eph.[24] This is one of the cases in which
Eph., while closely similar, substitutes a different word, παραπτωμάτων for ἁμαρτιῶν. The relative pronoun at the beginning of
the verse refers back to 'the son of his love' in the preceding verse, as
does the relative ὅς at the beginning of v. 15. As already noted, the
whole passage in the Greek continues smoothly without interruption,
and a break is made here purely for convenience, and to allow the
'hymn' to be treated as a separate unit.[25] NA[27] begins a new
paragraph at v. 12, which is another possibility; but that would
separate vv. 11 and 12, which surely belong together.

ἀπολύτρωσις originally meant buying back a slave or captive,
making him free by payment of a ransom; the word is comparatively
rare, and usage often diverges freely from the original meaning
(BAGD 96a; cf. also *TWNT* iv. 329–59 on the λύω word group, and
for ἀπολύτρωσις in particular, 354–59). In the New Testament it is
used figuratively, as here, of the deliverance wrought in Christ (Rom.
3.24; 8.23; 1 Cor. 1.30; Eph. 1.7, 14; 4.30; Heb 9.15; 11.35; cf. λύτρον

---

[23] Hübner (53) notes that the distinction between the kingdom of God and that of
Christ should not be overstressed: 'Wenn Christus herrscht, herrscht Gott'. In 1.15
Christ is the image of the invisible God. He sees here the messianic fulfilment of 2 Sam.
7.16. Moule (58) observes, 'There is no trace of a nationalistic Messianism in the N.T.
conception; nor yet of fancies about "escape" into immortality without a corresponding change of character (the kind of escape which may have been promised by the false
teachers at Colossae).' The Christian fulfilment of the messianic hope is not a merely
nationalistic one.

[24] On Paul's use of the term 'blood' see Davies, *Paul and Rabbinic Judaism*, 232ff.

[25] Cf. O'Neill, 'Source', 89, who writes of vv. 9–20, 'To translate all this as one
sentence is impossible, and no modern translator would even consider making the
attempt.' He challenges the common view which sees vv. 15–20 as a hymn.

in Mark 10.45 par.).[26] Reference to a ransom, of course, inevitably raises for some the question what that ransom was, to whom it was paid, and by whom; but recognition that this is metaphor would have saved much misunderstanding regarding the doctrine of the Atonement. Büchsel (*TWNT* iv. 357) observes that in the eschatological passages (Luke 21.28; Rom. 8.23; Eph. 1.14; 4.30) the idea of a λύτρον paid for the ἀπολύτρωσις simply does not lie within their horizon, and that the other Pauline passages also (Rom. 3.24; 1 Cor. 1.30; Col. 1.14; Eph. 1.7) do not reflect upon a transaction by virtue of which the deliverance ensued, but solely upon the fact of the deliverance as such. Hill (*Greek Words*, 81) sums up his discussion by saying: 'This approach to the λύτρον-words suggests that their interpretation should be in terms of "deliverance" or "emancipation", except when the context expresses or implies a payment made to gain freedom. By applying the words to the death of Christ, the New Testament writers emphasise the idea of freedom (after the pattern of the great deliverances of Israel) and do not intend to convey, by means of the word-group, a particular theory (the ransom theory) about the method by which this freedom was achieved on behalf of men. The field of meaning to which the words point is that of God's delivering his people.' Passages which speak of being 'bought with a price' (1 Cor. 6.20; 7.23) or 'ransomed not with perishable things but with the precious blood of Christ' (1 Pet. 1.18) are paraenetic, intended to encourage the readers to live in a manner befitting the new service into which they have been brought, no longer as slaves to human masters or in the futile ways inherited from their ancestors, but as liberated for the service of Christ.

The word and its cognates appear several times in Irenaeus' account of the Gnostics (cf. Sagnard, *La gnose valentinienne et le témoignage de Saint Irénée* (1947), index *s.v.* ἀπολύτρωσις (632) and λύτρωσις (646)); at *Adv. haer.* i.21.1 Irenaeus remarks 'there are as many systems of redemption as there are mystical teachers of this doctrine'(tr. D. Hill, in Foerster, *Gnosis*, i (1972), 218). Harvey at one point (*Adv. haer.* i.124; n. to p. 123) observes, 'The Marcosians ... were not content with baptizing their converts once; they repeated the rite, and the second lustration was their ἀπολύτρωσις that removed them from the cognizance of the Demiurge' (see *Adv. haer.* i.21. 2; Foerster, 218: the baptism of the visible Jesus was merely psychic, for the remission of sins; the redemption by the Christ who descended upon him was spiritual, for perfection). Elsewhere we read, 'The perfect redemption is said to be the very knowledge [ἐπίγνωσις] of the ineffable "Greatness"' (*Adv. haer.* i.21.4, Foerster, i.220). At an earlier point Irenaeus says, 'by reason of the "redemption" they claim that they are unassailable by and invisible to the judge' (i.e. the Demiurge or his archons). Should they be apprehended, they have their answer (*Adv. haer.* i.13. 6; Foerster, i.202).
   In the Nag Hammadi *Gospel of Philip* (NHC II 51.29–86.19; tr. W. W. Isenberg in B. Layton (ed.), *Nag Hammadi Codices II 2–7* (1989), 142–215; *NHLE* 139–60) the Coptic equivalent occurs some five times. In this text 'Redemption' appears among the sacraments, along with Baptism, Chrism, the Eucharist and the Bridal Chamber (cf. H. G. Gaffron, *Studien zum koptischen Philippusevangelium unter besonderer Berücksichtigung der Sakramente* (1969), 185ff.). The exact nature of this sacrament

---

[26] For the background and usage of λύτρον and cognate words in biblical Greek see Hill, *Greek Words and Hebrew Meanings*, 49–81; cf. also, among other works, Denney, *The Death of Christ*; Taylor, *The Atonement in New Testament Teaching*; Morris, *The Apostolic Preaching of the Cross*.

is by no means clear, but Gaffron (191) suggests that it may have been a sacrament for the dying; Lightfoot long ago (209), discussing earlier Gnostic texts, thought it referred to 'formularies of initiation'. All this is still in the remote future so far as the author of Colossians is concerned; there is no sign that the 'false teachers' had gone to such lengths as later Gnostics were to do. Sometimes, however, it is useful to see where one line of development or interpretation might eventually end. If there was any incipient Gnosticism at Colossae, our author provides an effective counter by placing in apposition to ἀπολύτρωσις his own definition of what redemption is, the remission of sins.

F. Siegert in his *Nag Hammadi Register* (88) compares this verse (wrongly listed as Col. 1.4) with the *Teachings of Silvanus* (NHC VII 104.13; for text and translation, by Malcolm Peel and Jan Zandee, see B. A. Pearson (ed.), *Nag Hammadi Codex VII* (1996), 328–31). The whole passage (103.34–104.14) has numerous NT echoes, although it would be difficult to identify any direct quotation: 'Although he (Christ) was God he [was found] among men as a man. He descended to the Underworld. He released the children of death. They were in travail, as the Scripture of God has said, and he sealed up the very heart of it (i.e. the Underworld). He broke its strong bows completely. And when all the powers had seen him, they fled so that he might bring you, wretched one, up from the Abyss and might die for you as a ransom for your sin. He saved you from the strong hand of the Underworld.' This 'descensus ad inferos' is interpreted by Peel (in Pearson (ed.), 257) as the Incarnation. There are other passages also in which the descent appears to be not into Hades but into this world (notably Eph. 4.9–10; cf. Best, *Ephesians*, 383–87). Cf. the *Second Treatise of the Great Seth* 51.20ff. (*Nag Hammadi Codex VII*, 153–55): 'I visited a bodily dwelling. I cast out the one who was in it previously, and I went in. And the whole multitude of the archons was disturbed. And all the physical matter of the archons along with the powers born of the earth began to tremble when it saw the likeness of the image (εἰκών), since it was mixed.'

Zandee, who worked for many years on the *Teachings of Silvanus*, provides abundant illustrative material in his commentary (Leiden, 1991). Although it was found in a mainly Gnostic collection, he regards this document as 'definitely anti-gnostic' (p. 9); Peel (in Pearson (ed.), 267) observes: 'With one notable exception, virtually all modern interpreters of our tractate have concluded that it is not Gnostic.'

Elaine Pagels finds several echoes of Col. and other Pauline letters in the *Hypostasis of the Archons*, and concludes that the author's exegesis of Gen. 2 'reflects the influence of Paul's own exegesis of the same chapter' (in Hedrick and Hodgson (eds), *Nag Hammadi, Gnosticism and Early Christianity*, 278; cf. her appendix of parallel passages in the Pauline corpus and Proverbs, 279–85). 'The *Hypostasis of the Archons*, far from being superficially "Christianized", draws its specific structure and much of its terminology from the only authority the author actually cites—the "spirit-inspired apostle", Paul' (258).

One point to be noted is that here ἀπολύτρωσις is immediately defined by the following words, which stand in apposition, as ἄφεσις τῶν ἁμαρτιῶν, the forgiveness of sins. This at once sets the passage in contrast to such Gnostic texts as those mentioned above: redemption does not consist in some particular kind of *gnosis*, as for example with the Marcosians, for whom the perfect redemption was ἡ ἐπίγνωσις τοῦ ἀρρήτου μεγέθους (Irenaeus, *Adv. haer.* i.21.4). Lightfoot (209) suggests that the 'studied precision' here may 'point to some false conception of ἀπολύτρωσις put forward by the heretical teachers', although he considers any direct historical connection between the Colossian heretics and later Valentinian Gnostics 'very improbable'. What is clear is that here again the Gnostics have taken up something from another tradition, and used it for their own purposes. Curiously, the noun ἄφεσις (BAGD 125a; *TWNT* i. 506–09), although common enough in the Gospels and

Acts,[27] does not appear at all in the major Pauline letters: the only occurrences elsewhere in the NT are at Eph. 1.7; Col. 1.14 and Heb 9.22; 10.18.[28] The Marcosians rightly say that Paul 'often clearly set forth the "redemption" in Christ Jesus' (*Adv. haer.* i.21.2), but he speaks in terms of righteousness and justification, the *Rechtfertigungsterminologie* which as Vielhauer (197) notes is absent from Colossians.

As already noted, there is no interruption to the flow of the Greek text. A pause here is simply a matter of convenience, to break up the passage into units of a manageable size. The following verse, like vv. 13 and 14, begins with a relative pronoun, which like the ἐν ᾧ of v. 14 refers back to τοῦ υἱοῦ in v. 13. It is, however, appropriate to have a break at this point, since v. 14 reaches something of a climax with its reference to the redemption. The readers are thus reminded of what has already been accomplished: they have been delivered from the power of darkness, out of bondage to Satan, sin and death, and translated into the kingdom of God's Son. Verse 4 above commends them for their faith and love: the gospel that is bearing fruit throughout the world has borne fruit among them also; but the following intercession indicates that they have still some way to travel. It is not enough merely to have heard the word of truth; they must grow in the knowledge of God's will, and be strengthened by his power, so as to live lives pleasing to him.

To use the athletic imagery sometimes employed in the New Testament,[29] it is not enough for an athlete to reach a pinnacle of fitness and then relax his efforts; he or she must maintain the training, or lose what has been gained. Similarly a musician must maintain constant practice, or lose mastery of the instrument. The Larger Catechism approved by the Assembly of Divines at Westminster in 1648 refers (qu. 167) to 'the needful but much neglected duty of improving our baptism', which 'is to be performed by us all our life long'. Our author's intercession for his readers, and the admonition there implied, is relevant not only for them but for Christians in all ages.

---

[27] The phrase ἄφεσις ἁμαρτιῶν appears in Matt. 26.28 (over the cup at the Last Supper); Mark 1.4 (with reference to the baptism of John; cf. Luke 3.3); Luke 1.77; 24.47 (in farewell instructions to the disciples); Acts 2.38 (in Peter's call to repentance at Pentecost); 5.31; 10.43; 13.38; 26.18, ἄφεσις alone in Mark 3.29; Luke 4.18.

[28] The cognate verb appears in Rom. 4.7, in a quotation of Ps. 32.1. At Rom. 1.27 it has the sense of 'abandon', while in the three occurrences at 1 Cor. 7.11, 12, 13 it relates to divorce.

[29] For Paul, see Metzner, 'Paulus und der Wettkampf: die Rolle des Sports in Leben und Verkündigung des Apostels (1 Kor 9:24–7; Phil. 3:12–16)', *NTS* 46 (2000), 565–83.

IV
THE COLOSSIAN 'HYMN'
(1.15–20)

[15]He is the image of the invisible God,
the first-born of all creation,
[16]for in him all things were created
in heaven and on earth,
things visible and invisible,
whether thrones or dominions
or rulers or powers—
all things have been created through him and for him.

[17]He himself is before all things,
and in him all things hold together.

[18]He is the head of the body, the Church.
He is the beginning,
the first-born from the dead,
so that he might come to have the first place in everything.
[19]For in him all the fullness (of God) was pleased to dwell,
[20]and through him to reconcile all things to himself,
by making peace through the blood of his cross,
whether the things on earth or the things in heaven.

Lähnemann describes Colossians as among the most debated of Paul's letters—and this section as the most debated passage of the book. The literature devoted to it is quite simply enormous.[1] This is not surprising, since the passage represents one of the high points in New

---

[1] See most recently Stettler, *Der Kolosserhymnus*. Of the older literature only a random selection can be presented here. Deichgräber (*Gotteshymnus*, 143–55, on 1.15–20) refers to H. J. Gabathuler, *Jesus Christus, Haupt der Kirche—Haupt der Welt* (1965) for a survey of the *Forschungsgeschichte*. Wedderburn, who writes, 'The wealth of literature on the Christological hymn (Col 1.15–20) is almost infinite' ('Theology', 168), adds J.-N. Aletti, *Colossiens 1,15–20; genre et exégèse du texte; fonction de la thématique sapientielle* (1981); P. Benoit, 'L'hymne christologique de Col 1,15–20; jugement critique sur l'état de recherches', in *Christianity, Judaism and other Greco-Roman Cults* (1975), i. 226–63; C. Burger, *Schöpfung und Versöhnung: Studien zum liturgischen Gut im Kolosser- und Epheserbrief* (1975). Cf. also Hegermann, *Die Vorstellung vom Schöpfungsmittler*, esp. 88–159; Barrett, *From First Adam to Last*, 83–88; Hoppe, *Triumph*, 146–223; O'Neill, 'The Source of the Christology in Colossians'; Beasley-Murray, 'Colossians 1.15–20'; Fossum, 'Colossians 1.15–18a in the Light of Jewish Mysticism and Gnosticism'; Pollard, 'Colossians 1.12–20: A Reconsideration'; Wright, 'Poetry and Theology in Colossians 1.15–20' (with bibliog.); Wedderburn, 'Theology', 23–34 (and index); Arnold, *Syncretism*, 246–70 (and index); Barclay, *Colossians*, 56–8. Testa ('Gesù pacificatore universale') adds Eph. 2.14–15 as a third strophe, and claims that on putting the Greek text back into late Hebrew we have 'excellent rhythmic poesy'; he provides a long and detailed commentary. See further the lists of references provided by Lohse (41 n. 64) and Hübner (55).

Testament Christology;[2] indeed, this may well have been a factor in the preservation of the book as a whole, just as much as the alleged Pauline authorship (on the continuing influence of Col. see Wedderburn, 'Theology', 64–71). In fact, we may wonder whether questions of authenticity are any longer really relevant: it was ultimately the quality of the text, not the name of its author, that was decisive.[3] Whether the author was Paul or another, the book itself deserves respect as one of the foundation documents of the Christian faith; our approach today must be critical, but it should be a reverent criticism.[4]

The passage has given rise to so much discussion, and so many issues have been raised, that the problem is to know where to begin. It is commonly regarded as a hymn, or part of a hymn,[5] but this only

[2] 'The passage represents a loftier conception of Christ's Person than is found anywhere else in the writings of Paul, and comes very near to the view set forth in the prologue to the Fourth Gospel. For this reason some critics have questioned its authenticity' (Scott, 20). Scott notes that Paul here 'appears to construe the Person of Christ by the Alexandrian doctrine of the Logos'—and it is argued that this identification was not made until after Paul's time. But as he rightly says, we do not know when the Logos doctrine was adopted. Paul could have learned something of Alexandrian ideas from such as Apollos. Others, however, would stress the associations with Wisdom, e.g. Dunn (89): 'the writer here is taking over language used of divine Wisdom and reusing it to express the significance of Christ'.

[3] A modern editor might receive an article from an unknown author, of a quality matching that of established scholars, and accept it on the grounds of that quality. For that matter, recognized scholars themselves have all had to establish their reputations. The situation was somewhat different in the ancient world (cf. Cothenet and Fischer, in the Introduction above).

[4] I. H. Marshall, in the editor's foreword to a volume of essays, *New Testament Interpretation* (1977), writes: 'We have written as conservative evangelicals who combine a high regard for the authority of Holy Scripture with the belief that we are called to study it with the full use of our minds.' Some today would question the use of the word 'authority', or at least seek to define it more exactly, but this raises problems which cannot be entered into here. Cf., for example, D. E. Nineham, *The Use and Abuse of the Bible* (1976). The main point is that a blind uncritical acceptance is no longer possible, but criticism should be constructive and not merely destructive. Cf. recently M. F. Lowe, *Gregorianum* 81 (2000), 693–721.

[5] Cf. Hunter, *Paul and His Predecessors*, 123–26, who suggests (125) that it betrays 'the hand of an exacting composer' whose hymnodal style was Semitic rather than Greek; J. M. Robinson, 'A Formal Analysis of Colossians 1:15–20', *JBL* 76 (1957), 270–87; Deichgräber, *Gotteshymnus*; Sanders, *New Testament Christological Hymns*, esp. 12–14, 75–87 (see also index); as Hunter and others note, the beginnings of this view go back at least to Eduard Norden (*Agnostos Theos*, 250–54). O'Neill ('Source') challenges the theory that the author has made use of a hymn; rather he was 'deliberately citing traditional literature of the community to which he belonged': 'The Christology was something that had grown up in Judaism long before' (99). Lohse, however, (42) notes 'an impressive number of terms which either do not appear at all elsewhere in the Pauline corpus, or are used otherwise with a different meaning', and claims that 'these observations exclude the possibility that the author of this letter could have composed these verses himself by using traditional phrases'. Hübner (55) like some other scholars regards the view that there is a hymn behind our present text as 'heute nahezu unbestritten'. Dahl (*Background*, 434) writes, 'Parallels to the christological hymn in Col. i can be found in Gnosticism and in Hellenism in general, but it can hardly be denied that the Jewish ideas of the Law, Israel, the Temple, etc., must also be taken into account', adding in a footnote, 'In such cases we should not assume that either the Jewish or the "Hellenistic" parallels are alone relevant.' For reviews of the debate see the references in Dunn, 83 n. 5.

leads to further questions. Did our author, whether Paul or some disciple, compose the hymn as he wrote, or did he take over an existing hymn? In the latter case, what changes has he introduced? Can we get back to the original? Various attempts have been made by scholars over the years to remove later accretions and recover the 'original' form, but as Schweizer observes (*NTS* 8 (1961/62), 6), 'commentators are far from reaching any agreement about the original extent of this hymn'. There is hardly a line the originality of which has not been called in question.[6] Gnilka (54) produced an effective *reductio ad absurdum* of all such efforts by removing every phrase about which doubt has been expressed, remarking that no interpreter would consider the resulting 'rump text' to be the original hymn. Speculation as to the original form is both natural and legitimate, but the very variety of the solutions offered prompts to caution; we do not have the original to verify our conjectures.[7] Sometimes, indeed, one has the impression that scholars have set out with certain presuppositions as to what the author might have written, and then have tailored the material to suit. There are, for example, correspondences between the strophes; anything that disrupts the correspondence is therefore suspect. For that matter, there has been difference of opinion in regard to the number of strophes; some have argued for two strophes, others for three, four or five.[8] Those seeking a pre-Christian Jewish hymn naturally eliminate any Christian element; but what grounds are there for assuming an underlying *Jewish* hymn?[9] Again, there are those who would excise any specifically Pauline material, in the attempt to

[6] In v. 16, for example, scholars have suggested the following excisions (see the Greek text at p. 126 below): (1) the four εἴτε phrases in l. 4–5; (2) from τὰ ὁρατά in l. 3 to ἐξουσίαι in l. 5; (3) from ἐν τοῖς οὐρανοῖς in l. 2 to ἐξουσίαι; (4) from ἐν τοῖς οὐρανοῖς to πρὸ πάντων in v. 17. A case can be stated for each suggestion, but which (if any) is correct?

[7] Hunter (*Paul*, 126 n. 1) acknowledges his indebtedness to J. M. Robinson's article (see p. 124 n. 5 above), but with regard to the removal of 'insertions' comments, 'His attempt is ingenious but, of necessity, rather speculative'. In the Gospels, assuming the Two-Document Hypothesis, we can identify the changes made by Matt. and Luke to their Marcan material, and may assume that they treated Q in much the same way. But we do not have Q, nor can we be confident as to Mark's treatment of his sources. Reading E. J. Pryke's *Redactional Style in the Marcan Gospel* (1978), one may have the impression that this Gospel is almost entirely redactional; but if Mark was writing the tradition he had received in his own words, the style and language would be Marcan, but the content still tradition.

[8] 'The most common division is of two strophes (1:15–18a and 1:18b–20), as suggested originally by Norden, *Agnostos Theos*, 252, or of two main strophes (1:15–16c, 1:18b–20) with transitional lines in 1:17–18a (marked by paralleling of "and he is" in 17a and 18a) or in 1:16d–18a (marked also by paralleling of "all things" in 16d and 17b), as suggested first by Schweizer, "Kirche" 295' (Dunn, 83 n. 5). For the range of possibilities suggested cf. Aletti, 90 (with references).

[9] 'Ernst Käsemann's theory that the Christ hymn in Col 1.15–20 is an adapted pre-Christian hymn about the Gnostic *Urmensch-Erlöser*, who had both a cosmological and a soteriological significance, has not fared well' (Fossum, 'Colossians 1.15–18a', 183). Cf. also Arnold (*Syncretism*, 248): 'a consensus has been achieved in rejecting E. Käsemann's suggestion'; but he also criticizes Fossum's argument for an Anthropos rather than a Wisdom Christology (n. 4).

recover the pre-Pauline form; but how far are we justified in assuming that the original was pre-Pauline?[10] Here as often our judgements on other questions may affect our decision: those who think Col. authentic will already rule out one set of conclusions, those who do not will rule out others.

Our primary concern must be with the text in its present form, with what our author sought to convey to his readers. The first point to note is that there are several other passages in the New Testament, all beginning with the relative pronoun ὅς, which contain material of a poetic or confessional nature: Phil. 2.6–11; 1 Tim. 3.16; Heb. 1.3–4; 1 Pet. 2.22. This does not, of course, mean that all the passages which begin with a ὅς are to be regarded as fragments of hymns, creeds or confessions; there is a ὅς at the beginning of v. 13, for example, not to mention numerous other cases where this pronoun simply introduces a normal relative clause. It is the combination of the initial relative pronoun with poetic or confessional material that is significant.

The first step must be to set out the passage as a whole for consideration (following the arrangement of sense-lines in NA[27]):

[15] ὅς ἐστιν εἰκὼν τοῦ θεοῦ τοῦ ἀοράτου,
πρωτότοκος πάσης κτίσεως,
[16]ὅτι ἐν αὐτῷ ἐκτίσθη τὰ πάντα
ἐν τοῖς οὐρανοῖς καὶ ἐπὶ τῆς γῆς,
τὰ ὁρατὰ καὶ τὰ ἀόρατα,
εἴτε θρόνοι εἴτε κυριότητες,
εἴτε ἀρχαὶ εἴτε ἐξουσίαι·
τὰ πάντα δι' αὐτοῦ καὶ εἰς αὐτὸν ἔκτισται·

[17]καὶ αὐτός ἐστιν πρὸ πάντων
καὶ τὰ πάντα ἐν αὐτῷ συνέστηκεν,
[18]καὶ αὐτός ἐστιν ἡ κεφαλὴ τοῦ σώματος τῆς ἐκκλησίας·

ὅς ἐστιν ἀρχή,
πρωτότοκος ἐκ τῶν νεκρῶν,
ἵνα γένηται ἐν πᾶσιν αὐτὸς πρωτεύων,
[19]ὅτι ἐν αὐτῷ εὐδόκησεν πᾶν τὸ πλήρωμα κατοικῆσαι
[20]καὶ δι' αὐτοῦ ἀποκαταλλάξαι τὰ πάντα εἰς αὐτόν,
εἰρηνοποιήσας διὰ τοῦ αἵματος τοῦ σταυροῦ αὐτοῦ,
εἴτε τὰ ἐπὶ τῆς γῆς
εἴτε τὰ ἐν τοῖς οὐρανοῖς

It is clear from the outset that we have here two main divisions, the first relating to creation (vv. 15–17) and the second to redemption (18–20). ὅς ἐστιν εἰκών in v. 15, followed by πρωτότοκος πάσης κτίσεως, is balanced by the ὅς ἐστιν ἀρχή followed by πρωτότοκος ἐκ τῶν νεκρῶν

---

[10] 'A persistent minority continue to deny the presence of pre-Pauline material here and thus to affirm that the "hymn" was composed by Paul himself (Dunn 84 n. 6; see his references). If Paul did compose it, he could have used pre-Pauline material!

in v. 18. In both divisions there is a ὅτι clause (vv. 16 and 19), and in both there is reference to things in heaven and on earth (vv. 16 and 20). It is not, however, possible to move directly to the conclusion that we have two strophes, vv. 15–17 and 18–20: the correspondences are not exact, and there is additional material which seems to interrupt the flow. Verse 18a for example appears to form the climax of the first division, not to belong to the second; if with its reference to the Church it is taken to be a rubric introducing the second section, it destroys the parallelism of ὅς ἐστιν εἰκών in v. 15 and ὅς ἐστιν ἀρχή in v. 18. It was such points as this that led scholars in search of an underlying hymn to assume various modifications and interpolations from the hand of the final author; but, as already indicated, there is little agreement as to the extent of these modifications. There is something to be said for J. C. O'Neill's suggestion (see n. 5 above) of composition by an author drawing on older traditions available to him, rather than using and adapting an existing hymn (but the traditions he used might have included hymnic or confessional material). The whole passage reads smoothly and consistently from beginning to end, and if the author did adapt an existing hymn he has done so very skilfully.

One possibility (see Hoppe, 130) would be to see the hymn as consisting of two strophes of eight lines each, the first beginning with ὅς ἐστιν εἰκών in v. 15 and the second with ὅς ἐστιν ἀρχή in v. 18. Verses 17–18a would then form an intermediate strophe, which might not have been part of the original hymn (Hoppe, 178) but serves to link the two main strophes together.[11] It must be remembered that, as noted earlier, the verse division is a comparatively modern innovation, introduced by Stephanus in 1551 (F. G. Kenyon, *Our Bible and the Ancient Manuscripts*, 4th edn (1939), 226; Metzger, *The Text of the New Testament,* 104; as Metzger notes, some of the divisions were 'infelicitous'). Certainly it should not be allowed to control our exegesis and interpretation of the passage.

The advantage of this alternative is that it would provide two stanzas whose opening words are parallel, while both vv. 17 and 18a in between begin with the same phrase, καὶ αὐτός ἐστιν. Other reconstructions, however, have been offered, and this would seem to be a case in which there is no room for dogmatism.[12]

15. ὅς ἐστιν εἰκὼν τοῦ θεοῦ τοῦ ἀοράτου The last four words in this line present a problem for those who seek to recover an

[11] This suggestion has been adopted in the arrangement of the Greek text above (cf. also Arnold, *Syncretism*, 250). Hoppe in his discussion offers his own suggestions as to the redactional insertions made by our author.
[12] To offer just one further alternative by way of example, Hegermann (*Schöpfungsmittler*, 92–93) presents a hymn of two five-line strophes by removing the last five lines of v. 16 and the first of v. 17. The first line of v. 18 completes the first strophe, with the omission of τῆς ἐκκλησίας. In the second strophe πρωτότοκος ἐκ τῶν νεκρῶν is taken into the same line as ὅς ἐστιν ἀρχή, and the last two lines of v. 20 are excised, together with the reference to 'the blood of his cross'. The hymn ends εἰρηνοποιήσας δι'αὐτοῦ. Hegermann admits that this can only rank as a hypothesis.

underlying hymn, for there is nothing to match them after ὅς ἐστιν ἀρχή in v. 18. Has something been omitted there, or are these words an insertion here?[13] This is, however, a case that calls for caution: what grounds have we for assuming that the 'original' hymn had a fixed and rigid structure like the hymns in a modern hymnbook? Lohse (44) writes: 'It is hardly probable that a primitive Christian hymn would have consisted of regularly constructed verses and strophes; rather the individual strophes probably differed in structure and were composed in the free rhythm of hymnic prose.'[14] This makes the original form rather difficult to visualize: ancient literature presents numerous examples of poems composed in carefully structured strophes, often with parallelism between one strophe and the next—why should this one be different? Are we justified in seeking for an 'original' hymn? Once again, there is reason to bear in mind J. C. O'Neill's suggestion (n. 5 above).[15]

In any case, our primary concern is with the text as we now have it, and here the last four words are essential to the meaning: a bare 'He is the image' would convey but little to the reader, and immediately prompt the question 'The image of what?' The text provides the answer: 'The image of the invisible God, the first-born of all creation'.[16] This at once recalls the Genesis creation story, according to which God created man in his own image (Gen. 1.27), but as Lohse notes we cannot interpret this verse in Col. as a direct reference to the biblical account;[17] there are other associations which have to be taken into the reckoning. For one thing, there is the Wisdom-Logos tradition, beginning with the book of Wisdom and continuing through the works of Philo of Alexandria to the Christian Fathers who were influenced by him.[18] For another, there is a whole

---

[13] Hoppe, 155f. sees these words as a redactional insertion.

[14] Cf. Lohse ('Christologie', 161): 'Schwerlich wird ein urchristlicher Hymnus aus regelmäßig gebauten Versen bestanden haben, sondern wahrscheinlich waren die Strophen im einzelnen verschieden durchgeführt und in freien Rhythmen hymnischer Prosa gehalten.' The difficulty mentioned above may arise from a translation which does not quite get the point: we are not to think of a hymn with regular verses, like our modern hymns, but of something composed in strophes with a free rhythm.

[15] Moule (61) asks, 'Is it so clear that this was a separate hymn—not to mention the question whether the "head of the church" clause is a further addition?' The 'hymn' theory may today, as Hübner and others suggest (see n. 5 above), be well-nigh undisputed, but that does not mean that it should not be questioned and scrutinized.

[16] Cf. NHTB 28, 75, 223 and references there.

[17] Cf. Aletti, 96, who notes that we must distinguish those texts which reflect an Adam/Christ typology (Rom. 8.29; 1 Cor. 15.49; 2 Cor. 3.18) from those like 2 Cor. 4.4 and Col. 1.15, in which Christ is presented as the image of God.

[18] C. A. A. Scott (Christianity according to St Paul, 264ff.) already emphasizes the Wisdom associations. S. Schulz (in Aland et al. (eds), Studia Evangelica (1959), 356f.) sets the Prologue to John, the Colossian 'hymn' and Heb. 1.2f. in the same religionsgeschichtliche context. For Col. and Heb. cf. Hurst, Epistle to the Hebrews, 177 n. 67, who lists both similarities and differences: 'while the hymn of Colossians is closer to Hebrews than is Paul in Philippians, Colossians and Hebrews cannot be placed into any relation of dependence at this point'. It is not a question of dependence, but of a common background.

tradition in Greek philosophy which has to some extent interacted with the Wisdom tradition, particularly in Philo and the Corpus Hermeticum.[19] Also there is the Adam/Christ typology.[20] All of these require to be taken into account, and given due consideration. This is one of those cases in which the 'simple' answer may be erroneous and misleading.

εἰκών This word means 'image' or 'likeness', as in a photograph or painting, and has come down into modern English as 'icon', used particularly of paintings or mosaics of sacred personages in the Orthodox Church.[21] In the Synoptic Gospels (Mark 12.16 par.) it is used of the emperor's image on a coin[22] (see BAGD 222a; *TWNT* ii. 378–96; for Col. 1.15 see 386f., 394f.),[23] while in the book of Revelation (13.14, 15; 14.9, 11; 15.2; 16.2; 19.20; 20.4) it is employed several times over with reference to 'the image of the beast'.[24] These references are, however, not directly relevant to our present purpose, for which the starting point must be the creation story in Gen. 1.26–27, where man is created κατ'εἰκόνα θεοῦ. In the New Testament, apart from the present passage, the word is directly applied to Christ only at 2 Cor. 4.4 (on which cf. Thrall, *2 Corinthians*, i. 309–11: 'it is very probable that in describing Christ as the image of God Paul thinks of him both as the embodiment of the figure of Wisdom and as

[19] Cf. Lohse, 47f. In the *Apocryphon of John*, NHC II 14.15—15.4 (synopsis in Waldstein and Wisse (eds), *Apocryphon of John*, 37–38, at pp. 85–87) the image of God appears in the waters of chaos, but the powers of darkness are unable to lay hold of it. The First Archon (i.e. the Demiurge) commands them to create a man according to this image, in the words of Gen 1.26. In the *Hypostasis of the Archons* (NHC II 4, 87.11–33; Layton (ed.), *Nag Hammadi Codex II 2–7*, 230) it is the image of Incorruptibility which appears. This in some respects recalls the myth of the fall of Man in Poimandres 14 (Foerster, *Gnosis*, i. 331; cf. Dodd, *The Bible and the Greeks*, 157–60). On Gnostic anthropology cf. Logan, *Gnostic Truth*, 167–210.

[20] Cf. for example Davies, *Paul and Rabbinic Judaism*, 36–51; Barrett, *From First Adam to Last*. Adam Christology is prominent elsewhere in Paul, but Adam is not here seen as an agent in creation, as was Wisdom. In Col. it is only in connection with redemption that the Adam Christology would seem to exercise an influence (cf. Dunn, 88, 99, 221–23). Fossum ('Colossians 1.15–18a') argues for an Anthropos-Christology rather than a Sophia-Christology, but still one rooted in Jewish tradition; but cf. Arnold, *Syncretism*, 248 n. 4; Aletti, 116 n. 98.

[21] Its use in the realm of computing is recent, derivative and secondary!

[22] Cf. *The Teachings of Silvanus* (NHC VII. 100.23–31; Pearson (ed.), 321): 'You cannot know God through anyone except Christ, who has the image (εἰκών) of the Father, for this image (εἰκών) reveals the true likeness in correspondence to that which is revealed. A king is not usually known apart from an image (εἰκών).' Lohse (48) observes: 'The Christian community applied the concept "image" to Christ so as to praise him as the one in whom God reveals himself.'

[23] Cf. also Hübner's excursus, 'εἰκών in philosophie- und religionsgeschichtlicher Sicht' (57–58); R. McL. Wilson, 'The Early History of the Exegesis of Gen. 1.26', in K. Aland and F. L. Cross (eds), *Studia Patristica*, pt 1, (1957), 420–37; F. W. Eltester, *Eikon im Neuen Testament* (1958); J. Jervell, *Imago Dei* (1960); Hegermann, *Schöpfungsmittler*, 96–98; Larsson, *Christus als Vorbild*, esp. 188–96; P. Schwanz, *Imago Dei als christologisch-anthropologisches Problem* (1970).

[24] For interpretation cf. for example G. B. Caird, *The Revelation of St John the Divine* (1966).

the prototype of the new humanity' (310). For Wisdom, see below; 'prototype of the new humanity', of course, reflects the Adam/Christ typology; cf. Rom. 5.12ff.). 1 Cor. 11.7 is closer to the Genesis narrative in describing man as 'the image and glory of God',[25] but other passages in Paul's letters suggest that he thought of Christ as the image *par excellence* (cf. Moule, 62): at Rom. 8.29 we read, 'those whom he foreknew he also predestined to be conformed to the image of his Son, in order that he might be the firstborn [πρωτότοκος] within a large family' (NRSV); at 1 Cor. 15.49, 'just as we have borne the image of the man of dust [i.e. Adam], we will also bear the image of the man of heaven'; at 2 Cor. 3.18, 'all of us, with unveiled faces, seeing the glory of the Lord as though reflected in a mirror, are being transformed into the same image from one degree of glory to another' (cf. Thrall, 282ff.; also A. F. Segal, 'Paul's Thinking', 407–09). On 1 Cor. 11.7 C. K. Barrett writes, 'Man exists to give glory to God, and in fact does give glory to God by being what he truly is, God's obedient and believing creature. This, however, he truly is only in Christ' (*1 Corinthians*, 252). As another early Christian writer puts it, 'What we do know is this: when he is revealed, we will be like him, for we will see him as he is. And all who have this hope in him purify themselves, just as he is pure' (1 John 3.2b–3 NRSV). Col. 3.10 speaks of 'the new self, which is being renewed in knowledge according to the image of its creator'. The object of Christian hope, the goal of Christian living, is likeness to Christ, who is himself the true image of God, the fulfilment of what the first man was intended to be.

There are other terms which suggest similar associations, and require to be considered in any full discussion of this theme:[26] the hymn of Phil. 2.6–11 describes Christ as ἐν μορφῇ θεοῦ ὑπάρχων; at Heb. 1.3 the Son is described as ἀπαύγασμα τῆς δόξης καὶ χαρακτὴρ τῆς ὑποστάσεως αὐτοῦ (sc. τοῦ θεοῦ).[27] In Wisd. 7.26 Wisdom is described as 'a reflection [ἀπαύγασμα] of eternal light, an unspotted mirror of the working of God and an image of his goodness [εἰκὼν τῆς ἀγαθότητος αὐτοῦ]'. A connection of Wisdom with creation is already to be found in Prov. 8.22–29: 'The Lord created me the beginning of his works, before all else that he made, long ago. ... When he set the heavens in their place I was there.' At Ps. 103.24 LXX we find πάντα ἐν σοφίᾳ ἐποίησας, while in Wisd. 9.1–2 Wisdom and Logos are associated with creation (see p. 131f. below). In Philo (*Leg. All.* i.43) Wisdom is ἀρχὴν καὶ εἰκόνα καὶ ὅρασιν θεοῦ. The Logos too can be described in similar terms: ἀρχὴ καὶ ὄνομα θεοῦ καὶ λόγος καὶ ὁ κατ᾽ εἰκόνα ἄνθρωπος προσαγορεύεται (*Conf. Ling.* 146; see also below). The early Christians took over these

[25] Cf. Wisd. 2.23 (NEB): 'God created man for immortality, and made him the image of his own eternal self.'

[26] Cf. R. McL. Wilson, 'Genesis 1.26 and the New Testament', *Bijdragen* 20 (1959), 117–25.

[27] ἀπαύγασμα and χαρακτήρ occur only here in the New Testament.

epithets of Wisdom and the Logos, and applied them to Christ. At 1
Cor. 1.23–24 Paul writes, 'we proclaim Christ crucified, a stumbling
block to Jews and foolishness to Gentiles, but to those who are the
called, both Jews and Greeks, Christ the power of God and the
wisdom of God.'[28]

In his interpretation of Gen. 1.27 Philo of Alexandria identifies the εἰκών as the mind
in man, his guiding principle (ἡ δὲ εἰκών λελέκται κατὰ τὸν τῆς ψυχῆς ἡγεμόνα νοῦν,
Op. M. 69). Later in the same treatise, however, when he comes to discuss Gen. 2.7, he
makes a distinction (*Op. M.* 134): the man moulded from the dust of the earth is not
himself the εἰκών, but only moulded κατὰ τὴν εἰκόνα; as is shown by other passages,
the true εἰκών is the Logos (e.g. *Spec. Leg.* iii.207: θεοειδὴς ὁ ἀνθρώπινος νοῦς πρὸς
ἀρχέτυπον ἰδέαν, τὸν ἀνωτάτω λόγον, τυπωθείς; *Som.* i.239: τὴν τοῦ θεοῦ εἰκόνα, τὸν
ἄγγελον αὐτοῦ λόγον; cf. also *Som.* ii.45). Philo's statements, at first glance, may
sometimes appear confusing and inconsistent, but they can be reduced to a coherent
pattern: Adam the first man is of the earth, earthy, but the πνεῦμα breathed into him
by God is not just ἀήρ κινούμενος; it is τύπον τινὰ καὶ χαρακτῆρα θείας δυνάμεως,
ἣν ὀνόματι κυρίῳ Μωυσῆς εἰκόνα καλεῖ (*Quod Det. Pot.* 83). Adam represents the
earthly and perishable mind, whereas the man after the image is heavenly (ὅταν
ἀκούῃς 'Αδάμ, γήϊνον καὶ φθαρτὸν νοῦν νόμιζε· ὁ γὰρ κατ' εἰκόνα οὐ γήϊνος, ἀλλ'
οὐράνιος, *Leg. All.* i.90). The Logos, in contrast, is described as τὸν πρωτόγονον
αὐτοῦ λόγον, the first-born of all creation, the model which one should seek to imitate
(*Conf. Ling.* 146).

It is not necessary to assume that our author is indebted to Philo, as
was Clement of Alexandria later (cf. Lilla, *Clement of Alexandria*, 5
n. 1: 'the fact is beyond any doubt that Clement knew Philo virtually
by heart'; this claim is amply borne out by the numerous parallels
cited). One problem here is that we have so much of Philo, and so
little of any other Jewish thinker; the danger is that we may tend to
make him more representative, and more influential, than he actually
was at the time of the composition of the New Testament writings.
We cannot just assume that he was typical of Alexandrian Judaism,
still less of the Diaspora as a whole. On the other hand it is probable
that he is representative of a fairly widespread tradition of Jewish
interpretation of the scriptures; he refers to his predecessors, and on
occasion criticizes their opinions. The point is that at least from the
Wisdom of Solomon onwards there was a long tradition of Jewish
interpretation of the Genesis creation story, which comes to a climax
in the works of Philo. This is the justification for Lohse's comment
(quoted above, p. 128) that we cannot interpret this verse as a direct
reference to the biblical account: it is not the creation story in
Genesis itself that lies behind it, but the creation story as understood
and interpreted in the tradition. In particular the substitution of the
masculine Logos for the feminine Sophia facilitated application to
the person of Jesus (in Wisd. 9.1–2 we find ὁ ποιήσας τὰ πάντα ἐν

---

[28] On Christ as the Wisdom of God cf. Davies, *Paul and Rabbinic Judaism*, 150–76.
On the development of the Wisdom tradition see pp. 102f. above. Cf. also, more
generally, R. G. Hamerton-Kelly, *Pre-existence, Wisdom and the Son of Man* (1973);
(for Col. 1.15–20 see 168–82).

λόγῳ σου, καὶ τῇ σοφίᾳ σου κατεσκεύασας ἄνθρωπον: Word and Wisdom are already closely related here).[29]

The idea of man as created in the image of God is not exclusively biblical (see the references in BAGD 222, *s.v.* εἰκών), and indeed it can be claimed that it does not play a large part in New Testament thought: the references for Gen. 1.26–27 in the table of *loci citati vel allegati* in NA[27] are Eph. 4.24; Col. 3.10; Jas. 3.9; Matt. 19.4; Mark 10.6; Acts 17.29; Rom. 8.29; 1 Cor. 11.7; 1 Tim. 2.13—and some of these have nothing to do with the εἰκών motif. The later Fathers, especially under the influence of Philo, make frequent reference to Gen. 1.26f., but in the New Testament clear allusions are comparatively rare, and not all of them are relevant for our present purpose.[30]

The use of the εἰκών motif in the Nag Hammadi texts has not yet been examined in detail, but a few further examples may be of interest (for a complete list cf. Siegert, *Nag Hammadi Register*, 238; account must also be taken of cases with the Coptic equivalent, although these are inevitably more conjectural):

Apocryphon of John (Codex II), 4.5ff. (and parallels; see Waldstein and Wisse (eds), *Apocryphon of John*): It is he who contemplates himself in his light which surrounds him … and in every direction he perceives his image (εἰκών) by seeing it in the spring of the Spirit'

4.34–35: Pronoia (= Barbelo) is described as 'the image of the invisible, virginal Spirit who is perfect'

5.5: Barbelo is 'the first thought, his image (εἰκών)'

6.2: the aeons produced at Barbelo's request are identified as 'the pentad of aeons of the Father, which is the first Man, the image of the invisible Spirit'

14.19ff.: 'And he taught them, namely the holy and perfect Metropator, the perfect Pronoia, the image (εἰκών) of the invisible One, who is the Father of the all, through whom everything came into being, the first Man' (*ad* 14.21 Siegert refers to Col. 1.15)

15.2ff.: 'Come, let us create a man according to the image (εἰκών) of God and according to our likeness, that his image (εἰκών) may become a light for us' (after the archons see the form of the image in the water; cf. above, n. 19).

The Second Treatise of the Great Seth (Codex VII), 51.20ff. (ed. Pearson, 153–55): 'I visited a bodily dwelling. I cast out the one who was in it previously, and I went in. And the whole multitude of the archons was disturbed. And all the physical matter of the archons along with the powers born of the earth began to tremble when it saw the likeness of the image (εἰκών), since it was mixed'

The Teachings of Silvanus (VII), 92.15ff. (ed. Pearson, 301): 'Understand that you have come into being from three races: from the earth, from the formed, and from the created. The body has come into being from the earth with an earthly substance, but the formed, for the sake of the soul, has come into being from the thought of the Divine. The created, however, is the mind which has come into being in conformity with the image (εἰκών) of God'.

100.22ff.: quoted above, n. 22

112.37–113.7: M. L. Peel (ap. Pearson, 354 n.) identifies this passage as a hymn about personified Wisdom from Wisd. 7.25–26, here transformed into a hymn about Christ: 'He is light from the power of God, and he is an emanation of the pure glory of

---

[29] J. Ashton (*NTS* 32 (1986), 161–86) discusses the Wisdom background of the prologue to John. At p. 172 he notes that the role of Sophia is taken over by the Logos in Wisd. 18: 'λόγος in the Prologue is more than utterance (λόγος προφορικός) and more than thought (λόγος ἐνδιάθετος): it is the plan of God, in a meaning closely related to, if not identical with Col 1:25, where τὸν λόγον τοῦ θεοῦ stands in apposition to τὸ μυστήριον τὸ ἀποκεκρυμμένον ἀπὸ τῶν αἰώνων καὶ ἀπὸ τῶν γενεῶν.' Cf. also Zandee, 'Die Person der Sophia'.

[30] Special studies have been devoted to the concept of the image of God in the works of various Fathers, e.g. Origen, Basil, Cyril of Alexandria.

the Almighty. He is the spotless mirror of the working of God, and he is the image (εἰκών) of his goodness.'

At 112.35 it is said of the Logos (= Christ), 'it is he who has come from your mouth and has risen from your heart, the Firstborn, the Wisdom (σοφία)'—cf. Rom. 8.29; Col. 1.15; Heb. 1.6. Peel (353 n.) observes that 'first-born' is used of personified Wisdom as the first created being in Sir. 1.4; 24.9. At 106.21–24 we find, 'For the Tree of Life is Christ. He is Wisdom (σοφία). For he is Wisdom (σοφία), he is also the Word (λόγος).'

115.16–19 (Pearson, 361): 'For all dwell in God, that is, the things which have come into being through the Word (λόγος), who is the Son as the image [εἰκών] of the Father. *Ad* 115.19 Siegert refers to Col. 1.15.

Trimorphic Protennoia (XIII), 35.3: Protennoia is 'the first-born among those who came to be'. At 38.11–12 she says, 'I am the image of the Invisible Spirit and it is through me that the All took shape.' At both points J. D. Turner compares Col. 1.15 (*Nag Hammadi Codices XI, XII and XIII*, ed. C. W. Hedrick, (1990), 435, 439); cf. also Y. Jannsens, *La Protennoia Trimorphe* (1984); G. Schenke, *Die Dreigestaltige Protennoia*, who identifies Protennoia as a 'gnosticised Wisdom' (91). Cf. also the references listed for the Colossian 'hymn' in *NHTB* 527–28.

No more than a provisional assessment is possible at this stage, since a full discussion would entail consideration of other possible contributory sources, for example by comparison with the works of Philo. When the archons see the image reflected in the waters of the primeval chaos, there may be some association with the myth of the Poimandres, and other possibilities remain to be explored. A few points may, however, be noted. It is likely that this kind of speculation goes back ultimately to the creation story in Genesis, and this speculation seems to have taken place particularly in Jewish Wisdom circles, but the Gnostics have given it a twist of their own, e.g. in identifying the image as Barbelo, Pronoia or Protennoia. At some points scholars have referred to Col. for comparison, and in these cases that letter may have contributed to the development; but due note must be taken of the differences. It is dangerous to speak of Gnostic influence on a New Testament text without clear definition of what is meant: there can be no thought of influence from second-century Gnosticism! Moreover several of the references listed above are to *Silvanus*, which is not a Gnostic text.

τοῦ θεοῦ τοῦ ἀοράτου 'No one has ever seen God' (John 1.18 NRSV). There are passages in the Old Testament in which some person is said to have seen God (e.g. Abraham, Gen. 12.7; 18.1 (cf. also Exod. 6.2); Jacob, Gen. 32.30; and especially Moses, Exod. 33.11; Num. 12.8; Deut. 34.10; cf. also Isaiah, Isa. 6.1, 5. In Exod. 24.9–10 Moses and Aaron, Nadab and Abihu, and seventy of the elders of Israel 'saw the God of Israel', but only Moses was allowed to 'come near the Lord' (v. 2)); but even where the possibility is admitted, it is clear that it was thought to be fraught with danger: at Exod. 33.20 even Moses is told, 'You cannot see my face; for no one shall see me and live.' In other passages the text is modified, so that it is not God himself who is seen, but an angel (in Exod. 24.10 LXX has 'they saw the place where the God of Israel stood').

On the other hand, the vision of God came to be regarded as the goal of human aspiration: 'Blessed are the pure in heart, for they shall see God' (Matt. 5.8). This was not something to be taken lightly, but a privilege reserved for a few, like the vision of Isaiah already mentioned. Jewish apocalyptic literature contains several accounts of a heavenly journey (e.g. *Ascension of Isaiah* 7ff.;[31] cf. also

---

[31] Text in Schneemelcher, *NT Apocrypha*, ii. 611ff.; H. F. D. Sparks (ed.), *The Apocryphal Old Testament* (1984), 775–812.

2 Cor. 12.2–4) in which some visionary ascends through the heavens, often under the guidance of an *angelus interpres*. These provide some basis for the view advanced by F. O. Francis and others (cf. Introduction, pp. 51–52 and Commentary below on 2.18) that visionaries in Colossae aspired to participate in the worship offered by the angels; but they do not establish that view as correct. There are also pagan anticipations (on the whole subject cf. K. E. Kirk, *The Vision of God* (1931), 10–54). As with so much else, the theme was later taken over by the Gnostics, as is shown by such texts from Nag Hammadi as the *Apocalypse of Paul* (V 2), the *Paraphrase of Shem* (VII 1) and *Zostrianus* (VIII 1); but some of the texts which carry 'apocalypse' in their titles are not apocalypses in this sense; they are revelation gospels, better classed as 'dialogues of the Redeemer' (cf. BAGD 92 for the various senses in which ἀποκάλυψις is employed; for these texts see Schneemelcher, *New Testament Apocrypha*, i. 228–341).

ἀόρατος (BAGD 79a; *TWNT* v. 369–71) appears only five times in the New Testament (compared with over a hundred occurrences in Philo: *TWNT* v. 369). Of these, one is in the immediately following verse, where it relates to the invisible things of creation—thrones, dominions, rulers or powers. A second, in Rom. 1.20, refers to the invisible attributes of God, his eternal power and divine nature. The other three (Col 1.15; 1 Tim. 1.17; Heb. 11.27) all refer to God himself.[32]

It should be added that John 1.18 does not end with the statement that no one has ever seen God—it continues, 'It is God the only Son, who is close to the Father, who has made him known' (NRSV). Later debates (see below) as to whether such passages refer to the pre-existent eternal Christ or to the Christ incarnate in Jesus only introduce confusion: the Christ of faith is both. Moule (62) writes on the present passage: 'It is worth the effort to recall that these stupendous words apply (if they are indeed Paul's own) to one who, only some thirty years before (and possibly less), had been crucified. The identification of that historical person—the Nazarene who had been ignominiously executed—with the subject of this description is staggering, and fairly cries out for some explanation' (cf. also his introduction, pp. 3–6). Dunn (89) writes, 'It is Christ in his revelatory and redemptive significance who is the subject of praise here . . . . And the praise is that his redemptive work . . . is entirely continuous and of a piece with God's work in creation. It is the same God who comes to expression in creation and definitively in Christ.' The 'hymn' centres on the figure of Christ, but vv. 19–20 make it clear that the initiative is of God; both in creation and in redemption Christ is his agent.

πρωτότοκος πάσης κτίσεως The word πρωτότοκος (BAGD 726; *TWNT* vi. 872–82; for the NT see 877ff., for this passage 879–

---

[32] εἰκών and ἀόρατος appear together, as loan-words, in the *Apocryphon of John* (II. 6.4; Waldstein and Wisse (eds), *Synopsis* 14, at p. 39; codices II, III and IV have ἀόρατος, BG the Coptic equivalent).

81) means quite simply 'first-born', and is used literally at Luke 2.7 and in the Textus Receptus at Matt. 1.25.[33] It is used figuratively of Christ at Rom. 8.29, already quoted above: 'those whom he foreknew he also predestined to be conformed to the image of his Son, in order that he might be the first-born within a large family'. This links very well with πρωτότοκος ἐκ τῶν νεκρῶν in v. 18 below: by virtue of his resurrection, he is the 'first-born from the dead', and therefore the inaugurator of a new 'family' of those who are raised 'in him'. The present verse, however, is more problematic: what exactly is meant by 'first-born of all creation'?

Lightfoot (214) observes: 'The history of the patristic exegesis of this expression is not without a painful interest'. To summarize his discussion, the earliest Fathers all refer it to the eternal Word, not to the incarnate Christ, but later the Arians argued from it that Christ was part of the creation. Some of their opponents sought to defeat them by maintaining that the words refer to the incarnate Christ, and consequently were obliged to understand κτίσις of the new creation. But this had other consequences—as Lightfoot says, 'A false exegesis is sure to bring a nemesis on itself' (215; see his whole discussion, 214–16). For one thing, it destroys the balance and contrast between the two strophes, the first relating to creation and the second to the new order.

The true meaning is that the place of Christ is outside of creation; he was 'born before it', as the link between the created world and the invisible God (Scott 21).[34] As noted above (p. 130) such terms are used of Wisdom in the Jewish Wisdom tradition, from the book of Proverbs on (cf. also Sir. 1.4; 24.9; but the term πρωτότοκος itself is not there used; in both cases we have a phrase with κτίζω: 1.4, προτέρα πάντων ἔκτισται σοφία; 24.9, πρὸ τοῦ αἰῶνος ἀπ᾿ ἀρχῆς ἔκτισέν με.[35] Moule (64) poses two alternatives: (1) to take 'first-born' as alluding to Christ's priority to the created world ('he was born (or, as more considered theology would say, begotten, not born) before any created thing'); or (2) to take it not so much as temporal but in the sense of *supreme* ('the one who is supreme over all creation'; note πρωτεύων in v. 18 below. In Heb. 1.6 the first-born is clearly superior to the angels.). For Lightfoot both ideas are present (so too Moule, 65), the first connected with the Alexandrian

[33] According to Exod. 13.2; 22.29, all the first-born, whether of human beings or of animals, are to be consecrated to the Lord. The first-born enjoyed a special birthright, but this was not just a matter of priority of birth; it might be sold, as by Esau to Jacob, or given to a younger son (Deut. 21.15–17 expressly forbids this, but there are several cases in which a younger son is accorded special favour).

[34] Dunn notes that 'Wisdom (and Logos) should not be understood in simplistic or mechanical terms as "intermediaries" between God and his world' (88). Christ is a climactic manifestation of the divine wisdom, by which the world was created (89).

[35] C. F. Burney (*JTS* 27 (1926), 160f.) saw here a direct reference to Prov. 8.22 (cf. Davies, *Paul and Rabbinic Judaism*, 150–52; Larsson, *Christus als Vorbild*, 190–94). Feuillet (*NTS* 12 (1965/66), 5) notes that a similar exegesis was already proposed by Epiphanius. Lohse (46 n. 101) is rather cool and sceptical in his appraisal. Further references in Dunn, 88 n. 12.

conception of the Logos, the second with the Palestinian idea of the Messiah.³⁶ We should note, however, that Philo's word is πρωτό-γονος, a word which does not appear in the New Testament—not πρωτότοκος (cf. for example *Conf. Ling.* 63, 146; *Agr.* 51; *Somn.* i.215).

As already noted (p. 133), the Coptic equivalent is applied to the Logos (= Christ) in *Silvanus* 112.35. The term used at *Tri.Prot.* 35. 4 is different, but Schenke (91) sees the underlying Greek word as a synonym of πρωτότοκος (she translates the passage as '[das Ers]tlingsgeschöpf unter den Gew[ord]enen' (73). The passage is indeed a *Sachparallele* to the Colossian hymn, although she sees no justification for assuming literary dependence; Jewish Wisdom speculation is the background to both. It may be noted that all the verses of Col. listed in her index are from 1.15–17; but at 44.33 Turner (in *Nag Hammadi Codices XI, XII, XIII,* 447) refers to Col. 1.26 (see below).

16. ὅτι ἐν αὐτῷ ἐκτίσθη τὰ πάντα ἐν τοῖς οὐρανοῖς καὶ ἐπὶ τῆς γῆς, τὰ ὁρατὰ καὶ τὰ ἀόρατα, εἴτε θρόνοι εἴτε κυριότητες, εἴτε ἀρχαὶ εἴτε ἐξουσίαι· τὰ πάντα δι᾽ αὐτοῦ καὶ εἰς αὐτὸν ἔκτισται³⁷ This verse provides the explanation, and the justification, for the preceding statement: he is the first-born of creation, *because* in him all things were created. The verb κτίζω and its cognates (BAGD 455f.; *TWNT* iii. 999–1034) are used in the NT only of God's creation (Foerster, *TWNT* iii. 1027); the noun may be used (1) of the act of creating; or (2) of the thing created, whether an individual creature or creation as a whole. The aorist ἐκτίσθη 'describes the definite historical act of creation', the perfect ἔκτισται below 'the continuous and present relations of creation to the Creator' (Lightfoot, 217); the former simply states something that has taken place in the past, while the latter indicates the abiding significance of that past event: it was created and remains in existence. Lohse (49) sees in the ἐκτίσθη a 'divine passive', signifying that God is the creator.

We have already had several occurrences of the adjective πᾶς in the common sense of 'all' (for the range of meaning cf. BAGD 631a–33a). Here we have the neuter plural, with the article, in what was in New Testament times the regular expression for the created universe (cf. J. Ashton, *NTS* 32 (1986), 171, with n. 37 on p. 184; Ellis, ib., 501 n. 105; BAGD, *s.v.* §2bβ).³⁸ Lightfoot already comments 'not πάντα "all things severally", but τὰ πάντα "all things collectively"'.

³⁶ Lohse (49 n. 116) cites Justin (*Dial.* 100.2) and Theodoret (*ad loc.*) for the rendering 'before all creatures', and Theodore of Mopsuestia (*ad loc.*) for the comment 'not concerning time alone, but concerning first honour also ... honoured above every creature'. Chrysostom on the other hand writes τὸ γὰρ Πρωτότοκος οὐχὶ ἀξίας καὶ τιμῆς ἀλλὰ χρόνου μόνον ἐστὶ σημαντικόν (cf. Swete's edn of Theodore, 264). Isidore of Pelusium (*Ep.* iii.31) took an independent line by reading the active πρωτοτόκος (with a change of accent), which makes our author say Christ πρῶτον τετοκέναι, τουτέστι πεποιηκέναι τὴν κτίσιν (Lightfoot, 216).

³⁷ Cf. Irenaeus *Adv. haer.* i.4.5 (Harvey, i. 38): ὅπως ἐν αὐτῷ τὰ πάντα κτισθῇ τὰ ὁρατὰ καὶ τὰ ἀόρατα, θρόνοι, θεότητες, κυριότητες (in the system of Ptolemy). Also the *Gospel of Truth* (19.7–10): 'It is he who set the all in order, and the all is within him, and the all had need of him'; but the reference here is to the Father, although a few lines further on it is Christ who reveals the Father who is in view.

³⁸ Cf. A. H. B. Logan, 'The Meaning of the Term, "the All", in Gnostic Thought', *Studia Patristica* XIV (1976), 203–08.

The prepositions in the phrases ἐν αὐτῷ, δι' αὐτοῦ and εἰς αὐτὸν are widely used in discussions of the relation of God and the cosmos.[39] The significance of these prepositions is neatly set out by Seneca (*Ep.* 65.8): 'Quinque ergo causae sunt, ut Plato dicit: id ex quo, id a quo, id in quod, id ad quod, id propter quod.' He uses the example of a bronze statue to make things clear: 'There are five causes, as Plato says: that from which (*the material cause, the bronze from which the statue is made*), that by which (*the agent, the sculptor*), that in which (*the formal cause, the form which is appropriate*), that according to which (*the exemplar which is imitated by the sculptor*), that for which (*the goal or purpose intended*).'[40] This, however, requires qualification, in that ἐκ in such discussions frequently denotes not just the material from which something is made, but God as the ultimate *fons et origo* of all things: cf. pseudo-Aristotle, *De mundo* 6: ἐκ θεοῦ πάντα καὶ διὰ θεοῦ συνέστηκεν (this last word occurs in v. 17 below); Marcus Aurelius, *Meditations* iv.3.2 (of Nature): ἐκ σοῦ πάντα, ἐν σοὶ πάντα, εἰς σὲ πάντα; Rom. 11.36: ἐξ αὐτοῦ καὶ δι' αὐτοῦ καὶ εἰς αὐτὸν τὰ πάντα; 1 Cor. 8.6: εἰς ὁ θεὸς ὁ πατήρ, ἐξ οὗ τὰ πάντα καὶ ἡμεῖς εἰς αὐτὸν, καὶ εἰς κύριος Ἰησοῦς Χριστός, δι' οὗ τὰ πάντα καὶ ἡμεῖς δι' αὐτοῦ; Heb. 2.10 (with reference to God), 'for whom and through whom all things exist'.[41]

The first of the phrases here presents a problem, in that the preposition ἐν can be used in such a variety of different ways (see BAGD 258a–61b). Is it to be understood here as local, or as instrumental? Lightfoot (217) writes that the Alexandrian teachers 'represented the Logos, which in their view was nothing more than the Divine mind energizing, as the τόπος where the eternal ideas, the νοητὸς κόσμος, had their abode', quoting Philo (*Op. M.* 20): οὐδὲ ὁ ἐκ τῶν ἰδεῶν κόσμος ἄλλον ἂν ἔχοι τόπον ἢ τὸν θεῖον λόγον τὸν ταῦτα διακοσμήσαντα. As an architect first forms in his own mind a conception of the building, and the actual building is 'only a projection in stone and lime of this ideal plan' (Scott, 21), so God first created the world in the Logos, and all things visible are modelled on this archetype. Percy, however, objects (*Probleme*, 69) that it is at most the world of ideas that is formed 'in' the Logos, and that this way of thinking is strange to Col. Peake (504) bluntly says

[39] Cf. Feuillet (*NTS* 12 (1965/66), 1–9), who postulates Paul's dependence upon popular philosophy in his use of these prepositions, but also notes that the value which he gives to them does not correspond to the use which philosophy made of the same prepositions; cf. the qualification in the main text above. On this 'prepositional metaphysics' cf. also van Kooten, *Cosmic Christology*, 122–25.

[40] Lohse, from whom this and other references are taken (49 n. 121), also cites Philo, *Cher.* 125 (n. 122): ἔστι τὸ μὲν ὑφ' οὗ τὸ αἴτιον, ἐξ οὗ δὲ ἡ ὕλη, δι' οὗ δὲ τὸ ἐργαλεῖον, δι' ὃ δὲ ἡ αἰτία—that by which is the cause, that from which the material, that through which the instrument, that for the sake of which the reason (or purpose).

[41] Dunn (91 n. 19) observes that the parallels were already noted by Eduard Norden, and also that they make it clear that the reference is to the old creation, not to 'the eschatological new creation'.

'that the ideal universe was at one time created in the Son is a highly improbable, if it is even an intelligible, idea'. ἐκτίσθη in his opinion must refer to the actual creation of the universe, and it is probably safest to say that the act of creation depended causally on the Son.

For Lohse (50 n. 129) the ἐν αὐτῷ is to be understood in an instrumental sense, as is shown by the religious background, Jewish speculations about Wisdom: 'To understand the phrase as referring to location is only possible on the basis of quite different history of religions backgrounds: in the Platonic understanding the Ideas have their "place" in the Logos or in Sophia' (he quotes Philo, *Op. M.* 20, already cited above). This understanding is not appropriate here because τὰ πάντα cannot be interpreted as the world of ideas: τὰ ὁρατά in v. 18 are part of τὰ πάντα. For Wedderburn ('Theology', 26) the phrase 'should perhaps not be taken locally or spatially, but rather in an instrumental sense or, possibly better, since it avoids making the following "through him" redundant, as a phrase expressing the manner, the pattern of, or model for, the creation of all things: all things were created according to him, with reference to him'.[42] Dunn, however, (91 n. 20) thinks that the phrase 'probably reflects the Hellenistic Jewish idea of the Logos as the "place" in which the world exists', and objects that to take the ἐν in an instrumental sense 'would cause confusion with an ἐκ reserved for God'.[43]

Both sides are agreed in stressing the influence of the Wisdom tradition. The problem is to know how strongly that tradition was affected by Platonic (or Stoic) ideas, and whether we should think of our author as influenced by the Philonic conception of the Logos as the 'place' of the ideal cosmos. We cannot assume without more ado that Philo's works were known to the author, or that such ideas were widely current in Asia Minor—although they may have been; our sources in that respect are quite simply inadequate. What is more important is that the creation here is quite certainly that of the visible world, not the ideal world, and this would seem to tell in favour of the instrumental rather than the local sense. A further point is that the preposition ἐν might conceivably have some connection with the Hebrew בְּ, which is also capable of a variety of interpretations (see below on ἀρχή). According to Acts (22.3) Paul claimed to have been 'brought up in this city [i.e. Jerusalem] at the feet of Gamaliel, educated strictly according to our ancestral law' (cf. his own words in

---

[42] Ashton (*NTS* 32 (1986) 176) sees the contrast between δι' αὐτοῦ and ἐν αὐτῷ in the Johannine prologue explained in a comment by P. Lamarche: 'All that took place "through him" (διά) contributed to the realisation of the divine plan, but it was only by the events which came about directly by and in him (ἐν αὐτῷ), that is in Jesus Christ, that the plan of salvation was accomplished.'

[43] Similarly BAGD (*s.v.* §5a) note, 'probably to be understood as local, not instrumental, since ἐν αὐτῷ would otherwise be identical with δι' αὐτοῦ in the same verse' (a statement which may be open to question). Two verses already noted, however, may perhaps be cited in favour of an instrumental sense: Ps. 103.24 LXX, πάντα ἐν σοφίᾳ ἐποίησας and Wisd. 9.1–2, ὁ ποιήσας τὰ πάντα ἐν λόγῳ σου, καὶ τῇ σοφίᾳ σου κατεσκεύασας ἄνθρωπον. In the latter case we have to consider whether any difference is intended between the ἐν λόγῳ with the preposition and the simple dative τῇ σοφίᾳ.

Phil. 3.4–6). At Acts 21.40 he addresses the people τῇ Ἑβραΐδι
διαλέκτῳ. Even if the author was one of Paul's disciples, some at
least of them were Jews, and may be assumed to have been familiar
with Hebrew or Aramaic; but here we are moving into the realms of
conjecture.

ἐν τοῖς οὐρανοῖς καὶ ἐπὶ τῆς γῆς, τὰ ὁρατὰ καὶ τὰ ἀόρατα,
εἴτε θρόνοι εἴτε κυριότητες, εἴτε ἀρχαὶ εἴτε ἐξουσίαι These
words emphasize the absolute completeness of τὰ πάντα: all things in
heaven and on earth, visible and invisible, thrones, dominions, rulers
or powers—all were created 'in him', and owe to him their very
existence. The thought is developed in the following words, τὰ πάντα
δι' αὐτοῦ καὶ εἰς αὐτὸν ἔκτισται: Christ is not only the mediator or
agent of creation, but also its goal (cf. the use of the prepositions in
Rom. 11.36; 1 Cor. 8.6; Heb. 2.10, cited at p. 137 above).[44] The
reference to heaven and earth is picked up again in v. 20: εἴτε τὰ ἐπὶ
τῆς γῆς εἴτε τὰ ἐν τοῖς οὐρανοῖς (cf. also Eph. 1.10: τὰ ἐπὶ τοῖς
οὐρανοῖς καὶ τὰ ἐπὶ τῆς γῆς).

The reference to heaven and earth recalls the opening words of
Genesis, 'In the beginning God created the heaven and the earth', but
here serves to emphasize that it is the whole of creation that is in
view, things invisible as well as those that can be seen. This includes
the thrones, dominions, rulers and powers: they are part of the
creation, and therefore subordinate to the one 'in whom' all things
were created.[45]

The list has given rise to discussion as to whether these are to be
regarded as hostile powers. Those who think of the 'heresy' as an
incipient Gnosticism naturally think of the Gnostic archons
(Lightfoot, 218 already writes, 'there can be little doubt that their
chief and primary reference is to the orders of the celestial hierarchy,
as conceived by these Gnostic Judaizers'; but that was in opposition
to commentators who referred the terms to earthly potentates and
dignities); but we must beware of reading back from the second
century into the first. The later systems show how such ideas could
develop, but the terminology used here does not necessarily indicate
that such developed systems were already present in the first century.
Indeed, the parallels that can be adduced from later Gnostic texts
may not be indicative of possible influences or sources, but serve to

[44] This finds an echo in the Nag Hammadi *Gospel of the Egyptians* (NHC III 49.8–12;
IV 61.8–14, ed. Böhlig and Wisse, NHS 4, (1975): 'This Adamas, the shining light, is
the one who is from Man, the first Man, he through whom and to whom everything
came into being, and without whom nothing came into being.'
The Codex IV version differs slightly. Böhlig and Wisse note (177), 'The quotation
from the New Testament (Col 1:16; John 1:3) and the identification of the Father with
the first man in IV make it clear that the "Man" from whom Adamas originates is
God.' For 'Man' as the supreme God in Gnosticism cf. H. M. Schenke, *Der Gott
'Mensch' in der Gnosis* (1962). But see also *NHTB* p. xxi n. 16.
[45] On the 'principalities and powers' cf. Macgregor, 'Principalities'; Carr, *Angels and
Principalities*; Best, *Ephesians*, 174–80 and index. Cf. also the list of allusions to Jewish
and other sources, adduced by various commentators (and repeated by their
successors) in Moule, 65.

show how the same terms and concepts may be employed with different shades of meaning in differing contexts.

It should be noted here that the sequence appears to be carefully structured, in a kind of double chiasmus: τὰ ὁρατά must surely be the things on earth, τὰ ἀόρατα the things in heaven. On this assumption, the thrones and dominions would belong to the heavenly realm, the rulers and powers to the earthly. The structure would then be:

A ἐν τοῖς οὐρανοῖς
B καὶ ἐπὶ τῆς γῆς
B τὰ ὁρατά
A καὶ τὰ ἀόρατα
A′ εἴτε θρόνοι εἴτε κυριότητες
B′ εἴτε ἀρχαὶ εἴτε ἐξουσίαι

Carr (48) notes but rejects the chiastic structure suggested by E. Bammel (*ZNW* 52 (1961), 88ff.), particularly on the ground that 'it seems perverse to split the one phrase that is found complete elsewhere—ἀρχαὶ καὶ ἐξουσίαι'. That criticism would not apply to the structure suggested here, but it should probably be regarded as no more than a possibility, since other suggestions have been made. Dunn (92) also rejects Bammel's theory, preferring to see here a hierarchy of heavenly powers (cf. Lightfoot, 218–20 for various classifications of the heavenly orders): for him ἀρχαί and ἐξουσίαι must be taken as referring to heavenly powers, in the light of 2.10, 15 and the other New Testament parallels (1 Cor. 15.24; Eph. 1.21; 3.10; 6.12); 'all four terms refer only to the invisible, heavenly realm'. For Arnold (*Syncretism*, 253), the use of these terms in this and certain other contexts 'is best explained by the Jewish usage of the terms to denote angelic powers' (see his references). The adjective ὁρατός occurs only here in the New Testament.

According to Carr (49), **θρόνος** in the New Testament 'refers exclusively to the throne of God or of Christ. Whenever it refers to some other throne it is qualified and the reference is explained. ... The only evil throne is that of Satan in Rev. 13.2 and 16.10. ... It would therefore appear impossible for the term θρόνοι, when used absolutely, to refer to anything other than the heavenly court, which sits with God and worships him' (49).[46] These then are not evil powers or angels, or even civil governments. Dunn, however, observes (93) that 'the most obvious inference of 1:20 taken in conjunction with 1:13 and 2:15 is that these powers are understood as somehow threatening to God's cosmos' (so too Arnold, *Syncretism*, 255). Against this we should note that there is as yet no clear indication that these are hostile powers; this must be inferred from v. 13, where ἐξουσία is expressly defined as τοῦ σκότους, but there we have the singular and not the plural as here. Indeed the present passage would seem to carry more force if the term was taken more

[46] The word is found in Matt., Luke, Acts, Heb. and frequently in Rev., but not elsewhere in the Pauline corpus.

generally—all the powers of heaven, both good and evil, owe their existence to the first-born of all creation. In the beginning there was no distinction between good and evil powers; but in time there came a revolt, so that for the readers now at least some of these powers are hostile and inimical (cf. Barrett, *Adam*, 86).

It is perhaps significant that this verse is the one New Testament reference in BAGD (364b, §2b) for θρόνος used figuratively as 'the name of a class of supernatural beings', although allusion is made to *Test. Levi* 3.8. Arnold (*Syncretism*, 254) notes that it is known in Jewish apocalyptic literature as a title for a class of angelic 'powers' (*2 En.* 20.1), while in *Test. Abr.* 13.10 it appears in conjunction with ἄγγελοι, ἀρχαί and ἐξουσίαι. It also occurs in a few magical texts. According to Schmitz (*TWNT* iii. 167) it is a question of one of the highest angel classes (see the whole discussion, pp. 160–67).[47]

κυριότης (BAGD 461, §3; *TWNT* iii. 1096) refers here and in Eph. 1.21 (ὑπεράνω πάσης ἀρχῆς καὶ ἐξουσίας καὶ δυνάμεως καὶ κυριότητος καὶ παντὸς ὀνόματος ὀνομαζομένου) to a special class of angelic powers, the other terms is known from Jewish apocalyptic (*1 En.* 61.10; *2 En.* 20.1) and Jewish magic (*Test. Sol.* 8.6). At Jude 8 and 2 Pet. 2.10, however, the usage is different: for one thing the word is in the singular (as a designation of angelic powers it is always in the plural). In these two verses it stands for God's majesty, and hence for God himself (Foerster, *TWNT* loc. cit.). There are no other occurrences of the word in the New Testament.

ἀρχαί and **ἐξουσίαι**, in the plural, frequently appear together (Luke 12.11; Eph. 3.10; 6.12; Col. 1.16; 2.15; Tit. 3.1). According to Carr (49ff.), ἀρχαί appears only twice without ἐξουσίαι (Acts 10.11; 11.5, in the same context, with the meaning 'corners'; Rom. 8.38), ἐξουσίαι only twice without ἀρχαί (Rom 13.1 of earthly authorities; 1 Pet. 3.22).[48] At Eph. 1.21; Col. 2.10 the singular is used (cf. also 1 Cor. 15.24, but in all three cases the reference is to 'every ruler and authority'; in Eph. the context suggests heavenly powers, but in the other two cases the reference might be more general). One point to be noted is that except for 1 Cor. 15.24 the combination does not appear in the major Pauline letters, another point of detail to be added to the dossier against authenticity.

We have already met with ἐξουσία at 1.13, where it refers to the realm of darkness from which the author and his readers have been delivered (BAGD, *s.v.* §4b). Here it is used with a different reference,

---

[47] In a footnote he refers to some passages in the *Ascension of Isaiah*: e.g. at 7.21 Isaiah is warned by his guardian angel: 'Worship neither angel nor throne which belongs to the six heavens—for this reason was I sent to conduct thee—till I tell thee in the seventh heaven. For above all the heavens and their angels is thy throne set, and thy garments and thy crown which thou shalt see' (Schneemelcher, *NT Apocrypha*, ii. 613). Wilson (*The Hope of Glory*, 29 n. 51) notes that if a vision of the Merkabah was a prominent element of the errorists' mystical episodes, then the author's reference to θρόνοι in Col. 1.16 might take on special emphasis.

[48] At 1 Pet. 3.22 ἀρχαί is replaced by ἄγγελοι, which lends support to the view that heavenly powers are in view in the present passage. But at Luke 12.11 the reference is quite clearly to earthly authorities.

of rulers and functionaries of the spiritual world (BAGD, *s.v.* §4cβ), as in the other passages listed above. ἀρχή also has a range of meaning (BAGD 111b–12b; *TWNT* i. 477–83, esp. 481–83): first of all 'beginning' (as at Heb. 1.10) or 'origin', but also 'ruler' or 'authority' (BAGD §3), used in particular of angelic and demonic powers as in the passages quoted. Here, however, it is important to pay due attention to the context: the word in itself does not signify that such powers are evil.[49] As Carr observes (52), the four terms used in this sequence, 'far from conveying to the Colossians the idea of hostile forces of the universe or malevolent spirits, would have at most described beings whose status was neutral, requiring definite signs from the context to be interpreted in an evil sense'. Dunn's objection, as already noted (p. 140 above), depends upon a conjunction of 1.20, 1.13 and 2.15, but it is by no means certain that the readers would have made this connection on a first reading, or even that it was intended by our author. The essential point of this passage is that all things in heaven and on earth owe their existence to the first-born of creation.

As already noted (n. 6), these lines have been subjected to more or less extensive excisions by scholars seeking to recover the original 'hymn'. This procedure could be justified on the ground that the words excised are insertions by the author intended to enhance the superiority of Christ over all things, in heaven and on earth (cf. Dunn, 92f.). The very variety of the suggestions offered, however, gives rise to doubt. We have no firm basis for the assumption that these are in fact interpolations, and in any case our primary concern must be with what our author intended to say to his readers. That is the letter as we now have it.

τὰ πάντα δι' αὐτοῦ καὶ εἰς αὐτὸν ἔκτισται These words round off the whole section: all things have been created through him and for him. As Moule puts it (66), 'the cumulative effect of this catalogue of powers is to emphasize the immeasurable superiority of Christ over whatever rivals might, by the false teachers, be suggested: he is himself the agent and the place of their creation, and their very *raison d'être*'.

This verse is quoted along with Isa. 9.6; Phil. 2.9–11; Eph. 4.9f. in the *Excerpta ex Theodoto* of Clement of Alexandria (43.2–5): 'when the Spirit gave all power, and the Pleroma united in praise, he is sent forth, "as the angel of the counsel", and becomes the head of the whole after the Father. "For all things were created by him, things visible and invisible, thrones, dominions, kingdoms, divinities, services." "So God also exalted him and gave him a name which is above every name that every knee should bow and every tongue confess that Jesus Christ, the Saviour, is the Lord of Glory". "He who ascended also descended. That he ascended, what does it imply but that he descended? He it is who descended into the lower parts of the earth and ascended above the heavens." ' (*The Excerpta ex Theodoto of Clement of Alexandria*, ed. and tr. R. P. Casey (1934) 69–71). Cf. Irenaeus, *Adv. haer.* i.4.5 (Harvey i. 38, quoted above, n. 37).

[49] The ἀρχαί and ἐξουσίαι are definitely hostile powers in *Melch.* 2.8–11 (Codex IX), where they are associated with the Cosmocrator and the archons; but this belongs to a later date. In Col. they appear as hostile only at 2.15, where Christ triumphs over them.

At 33.2 Clement criticizes Theodotus' interpretation of πρωτότοκος in Col. 1.15 as
a misunderstanding of the Christian teaching. Cf. the index of scriptural passages in
Casey's edition. There is perhaps a distant echo of v. 16 in the *Teachings of Silvanus*
(NHC VII 116.30—117.3): 'No one will be able to know God as he actually is, nor
Christ, nor the Spirit, nor the choir of the angels, nor the archangels, with the
thrones of the spirits and the exalted lordships and the Great Mind'. Comparing
96.9–10, Peel (*NH Codex VII*, ed. Pearson, 365 n.) suggests that the Great Mind is
probably Satan.

**17. καὶ αὐτός ἐστιν πρὸ πάντων καὶ τὰ πάντα ἐν αὐτῷ
συνέστηκεν**[50] On the surface these words would seem to be quite
simple and straightforward, but there has been debate regarding their
translation. αὐτός is clearly emphatic, as in v. 18 below, but is ἐστιν
merely a copula, or should the phrase be accented καὶ αὐτὸς ἔστιν?
As Moule (66) notes, 'the virtual absence of accentuation in the most
ancient MSS. leaves one free to choose'. Lightfoot, comparing the
ἐγώ εἰμι of John 8.58, confidently affirms that the verb is not enclitic,
and should be accented ἔστιν: it declares Christ's absolute pre-
existence.[51] Peake, however, (505) objects (1) that in John ἐγώ εἰμι
stands alone, whereas here αὐτός ἐστιν is completed by πρὸ πάντων,
and (2) that there is no object in the assertion of the existence of the
Son here (the latter point may be open to question; see below).

A further question relates to the πρό: does it signify temporal
priority (BAGD 701, §2) or precedence in rank (§3)? It can also be
used of location (§1), but that does not come into the reckoning here.
The only New Testament references for the sense of precedence are
the occurrences of the phrase πρὸ πάντων in Jas. 5.12 and 1 Pet. 4.8,
where the meaning is quite certainly 'above all'. All the other cases of
πρό in the Pauline corpus are clearly temporal, and given the present
context this must surely be decisive: the word is used here in a
temporal sense. Now as Peake observes, 'the sense of ἐστιν depends
to some extent on that of πρὸ πάντων'; the meaning must be 'he is
before all things'.[52]

Lohse (52) takes this to mean that 'as the pre-existent one he is
Lord over the universe', and sees here a reference back to the
πρωτότοκος πάσης κτίσεως of v. 15, emphasizing once again the
unique position of Christ as Lord over the cosmos. This would seem
to answer the second of Peake's objections to the view advanced by

[50] W. C. van Unnik (in F. L. Cross (ed.), *The Jung Codex* (1955), 116) finds an echo
of this verse in the *Gospel of Truth* (18.34): 'that perfect Father who produced the All,
in whom the All is and whom the All needs', noting that in Col. this is said of Christ
and not of the Father.
[51] Lightfoot, like Lohse after him, quotes Basil, *Adv. Eunom.* 4 (PG 29, 701): 'When
the apostle said "all things have been created through him and for him", he ought to
have said Καὶ αὐτὸς ἐγένετο πρὸ πάντων, but when he said Καὶ αὐτὸς ἔστι πρὸ
πάντων he showed that he exists eternally, but the creation came into being.'
[52] The Coptic equivalent appears in *TriProt* 35.5–6, where Protennoia proclaims
herself '[the first-]born among those who [came to be, she who exists] before the All'
(*Nag Hammadi Codices XI, XII, XIII*, ed. C. W. Hedrick (1990), 402–03; G. Schenke in
her edition (1984), 91 expressly refers to Col. 1.17. Cf. also p. 133 above).

Lightfoot: the fact that he is temporally 'before all things' gives him a unique status as Lord of all.[53]

συνέστηκεν For the sense Moule cites Wisd. 1. 7, where the Spirit is described as τὸ συνέχον τὰ πάντα; Ecclus. 43.26, ἐν λόγῳ αὐτοῦ σύγκειται τὰ πάντα; Heb. 1.3, φέρων τε τὰ πάντα, while Lightfoot adds references to Philo for descriptions of the Logos as the δεσμός of the universe, that which holds it together. The word itself (BAGD 791, §3) belongs to the Greek philosophical tradition as far back as Plato (*Rep.* 530a: οὕτω ξυνεστάναι τῷ τοῦ οὐρανοῦ δημιουργῷ αὐτόν τε καὶ τὰ ἐν αὐτῷ); reference has already been made above to pseudo-Aristotle, *De mundo* 6: ἐκ θεοῦ πάντα καὶ διὰ θεοῦ συνέστηκεν, while in POx 11. 1380, 183–85 a prayer to Isis addresses her as the mistress πάντων ὑγρῶν καὶ ξηρῶν καὶ ψυχρῶν ἐξ ὧν ἅπαντα συνέστηκεν. Philo speaks of the four ἀρχαί and δυνάμεις, ἐξ ὧν συνέστηκεν ὁ κόσμος (QRDH 281), and of the opposites in the structure of the world, ἐξ ὧν ἅπας ὁ κόσμος συνέστηκε (QRDH 311).[54]

In this passage there are points of contact with Alexandrian Judaism as represented by Philo, and beyond that with Stoic ideas about the Logos (although Peake, in another context, says (504) 'it is by no means clear that Alexandrian influence can be traced in the Epistle'); also with the Wisdom literature (cf. Lilla, 208ff. for agreements between Jewish-Alexandrian philosophy and the two Christian Platonists Clement and Justin). It is, however, difficult to be certain that our author is *directly* dependent on any one set of ideas, or that for example he was familiar with the works of Philo. It may rather be a question of ideas which were 'in the air', in more or less general circulation, which could be drawn upon by an author to suit his own ends. In any case, if our author has adopted any concepts, from whatever source, he has also adapted them to give expression to his faith in the supremacy and sufficiency of Christ.

18. καὶ αὐτός ἐστιν ἡ κεφαλὴ τοῦ σώματος τῆς ἐκκλησίας Lightfoot notes that the αὐτός here is 'repeated from the preceding verse, to emphasize the identity of the Person who unites in Himself these prerogatives', but prints the following ἐστιν without an accent (contrast v. 17). Here the verb is clearly a copula ('he is the head of the body'), which leaves one wondering whether it should not be so treated in the preceding verse. Would our author have used the verb in two different ways in successive verses, the more particularly when

---

[53] This may also explain the curious fact that Dunn (93 n. 24) includes Lohse among those who take the πρό as referring to superiority in status. It is by no means difficult to pass from the one sense to the other. Dibelius in the 1927 edn of his commentary writes: 'Bei πρό ist der Rang mindestens mit eingeschlossen; als nur zeitliche Aussage wäre der Satz allzu selbstverständlich'.

[54] On this cf. Hegermann, *Schöpfungsmittler*, 94–5, who quotes a document Περὶ κόσμου:
ἀρχαῖος μὲν οὖν τις λόγος
καὶ πάτριός ἐστι πᾶσιν ἀνθρώποις
ὅτι ἐκ θεοῦ πάντα
καὶ διὰ θεοῦ συνέστηκεν

they are clearly intended to be parallel? Moreover, since the original text was probably written without accents, we may also wonder whether the earliest readers would have noticed any difference. Christ is described as **κεφαλή** (BAGD 430; *TWNT* iii. 672–82, esp. 679–81) at Eph. 1.22 (καὶ αὐτὸν ἔδωκεν κεφαλὴν ὑπὲρ πάντα τῇ ἐκκλησίᾳ), 4.15 (ὅς ἐστιν ἡ κεφαλή, Χριστός), 5.23 (ἀνήρ ἐστιν κεφαλὴ τῆς γυναικὸς ὡς καὶ ὁ Χριστὸς κεφαλὴ τῆς ἐκκλησίας); also at Col. 2.10 (ὅς ἐστιν ἡ κεφαλὴ πάσης ἀρχῆς καὶ ἐξουσίας) and by implication at 2.19 (οὐ κρατῶν τὴν κεφαλήν), but in the major epistles he is not the head but the body itself (the classic passage is 1 Cor. 12.12ff., culminating in v. 27: ὑμεῖς δέ ἐστε σῶμα Χριστοῦ; cf. also 1 Cor. 10.16–17; Rom. 12.5: οὕτως οἱ πολλοὶ ἓν σῶμά ἐσμεν ἐν Χριστῷ; and v. 24 below: ὑπὲρ τοῦ σώματος αὐτοῦ ὅ ἐστιν ἡ ἐκκλησία). Reference should also be made, however, to the notoriously difficult passage at 1 Cor. 11.2–16, where v. 3 reads: παντὸς ἀνδρὸς ἡ κεφαλὴ ὁ Χριστός ἐστιν, κεφαλὴ δὲ γυναικὸς ὁ ἀνήρ, κεφαλὴ δὲ τοῦ Χριστοῦ ὁ θεός (cf. Eph. 5.23 above and Best, *Ephesians*, 535). This has no mention of the Church, but places man (described in v. 7 as εἰκὼν καὶ δόξα θεοῦ ὑπάρχων) as clearly subordinate to Christ. Two points emerge from these references. First, we can see from this how the association of words in new contexts may lead to quite new ideas. Even if Paul did not write Col., he prepared the way for our present passage. And second, it is dangerous to assume that the same word always means the same thing: the context and associations may be different, and give a new connotation to the word.

κεφαλὴ means in the first place the actual head of a person, but can also be used metaphorically of a leader or ruler, the head of a tribe; from this it is not a long step to the idea of superiority, as in several of the passages cited. In Col. as in the major Pauline letters **σῶμα** (i.e. τοῦ Χριστοῦ) is the regular term for the Church as the body of Christ, as may be seen from five of the eight occurrences of the word in this letter (1.18, 24; 2.17, 19; 3.15); τὸ σῶμα τῆς σαρκός αὐτοῦ at 1.22 refers clearly to the crucified body of Christ, and so too probably does τὸ σῶμα τῆς σαρκός at 2.11, although there the readers too are involved (see Commentary *ad loc.*). This leaves but one case (ἀφειδία σώματος, 'harsh treatment of the body', 2.23) in which it has its ordinary sense of 'body' (cf. BAGD 800, §5; for normal usage see 799, §§1–4; *TWNT* vii. 1024–91; for the body of Christ see 1064ff., for Col. 1072–75. Cf. also Best, *Ephesians*, 189–96 and literature cited there.) In its present context the genitive τῆς ἐκκλησίας should be taken as epexegetic of τοῦ σώματος, to which it stands in apposition: he is the head of the body, the Church.

The last two words of this verse have often been regarded as an obvious Christian insertion, and no part of the original 'hymn'. If they are deleted, the reference to a 'body' can be interpreted in cosmological terms: 'the likening of the cosmos to a body is very ancient in Greek thought, the cosmos understood as an ensouled and rationally controlled entity' (Dunn, 94; cf. Best, *Ephesians*, 193–96;

against this view of the passage see Arnold, *Syncretism*, 259f.). Lohse (53) notes that 'Plato conceives of the cosmos as a living being with a soul and pervaded with reason (*Tim.* 31b; 32a,c; 39e; passim). The cosmos as a body is directed by the divine soul which it follows as it is led (*Tim.* 47c–48b).' An Orphic fragment (no. 168) names Zeus as the head of the cosmos, the one who with his power pervades the universe. This way of thinking also passed into Hellenistic Judaism, at least as represented by the works of Philo (cf. Schweizer, *TWNT* vii. 1051f.; Hegermann, *Schöpfungsmittler*, 65f.): the Logos is δεσμὸς τῶν ἀπάντων, who holds all things together (*De fug.* 108ff.); in *De Somn.* i.128 the world of the heavens is a uniform body over which the Logos is set as the head. 'Just as the body of man needs the direction and guidance given by the head (*Spec. Leg.* 3.184), so also the "body" (σῶμα) of the cosmos needs the eternal Logos of the eternal God, which is the head of the universe (*Quaest. in Exod.* 2.117) and directs the whole body' (Lohse, 54).[55]

This discussion presupposes (1) that there was an original hymn behind the form which we now have in Col., and (2) that we are justified in recovering the original by deleting τῆς ἐκκλησίας. This is a possibility which must be seriously considered, but our primary concern is with what our author sought to convey to his readers, and that is the letter as we now have it. Here the body is not the cosmos but, as the text says, the Church. If our author has in fact made use of the concept of the cosmos as a body, he has subjected it to a radical reinterpretation.

It might seem that the author is now passing to the second part of the 'hymn': 'As Christ is the source of universal life so he is the source of that new life which is operative in the Church .... Through him not only the race of men but all created beings have entered on a new phase of existence. The Church in which he reigns is the beginning of a new world-wide process of reconciliation' (Scott, 23–24). This is certainly a valid statement, but it is open to question whether we have reached that stage in our author's argument; there are other points which call for some consideration.

For one thing, the second main strophe only begins at v. 18b (ὅς ἐστιν ἀρχή, πρωτότοκος ἐκ τῶν νεκρῶν, in parallel with v. 15). The theme of redemption and reconciliation is not yet taken up. For another, vv. 17 and 18b surely belong together, as the parallelism shows. They serve to mark the transition between the first strophe and the second. The first of these verses clearly accords to Christ a supremacy and authority over the creation; now the second proclaims his authority over the Church, and by the very juxtaposition of these verses this authority is linked with his authority over

---

[55] Lohse (54 n. 160) observes that Philo's statements about the cosmos as a body and the Logos as its head are not to be confused with the Gnostic myth of the primal man, citing Hegermann, Schweizer and Colpe ('Zur Leib-Christi Vorstellung', in Eltester (ed.), *Judentum, Urchristentum, Kirche*, 180f.) against Schlier, *TWNT* iii. 675–77. On the cosmological meaning of the concept 'body' in relation to Stoic and Middle Platonist physics, see van Kooten, *Cosmic Christology*, 17–58.

the creation. Dunn (96) aptly notes, 'to assert that Christ is head of the church does not narrow his cosmic mediatorial role; rather it expands the significance of the claims made for the church'. The head of the Church is no other than the first-born of all creation, to whom all things owe their very existence, even the principalities and powers enumerated in v. 16.

Aletti (105) notes the importance of this for the remainder of the letter, particularly for 2.6–23: it is Christ who is head of the Church, as he is lord of creation. None of the powers and authorities listed above can lay claim to such authority, for all owe their very existence to him. Indeed, we may go further: in so far as these powers and authorities are hostile to humanity, they have no place within the Church. They belong to the ἐξουσία τοῦ σκότους from which the author and his readers have been delivered (v. 13); as 2.15 later puts it, Christ has triumphed over them. The Church is a body of redeemed humanity, destined in due season to be raised to 'the inheritance of the saints in light' (v. 12). As noted above (pp. 113–14), the 'saints' there probably include the angels who form God's heavenly court. Those powers and authorities which are not hostile would also find their place there, but in obedient subordination to the Lord of all creation.

In Greek city-states with democratic constitutions, such as Athens, ἐκκλησία referred to the assembly of eligible citizens, the governing body of the city. In LXX, however, it is used of the congregation of the people of Israel, 'especially when gathered for religious purposes (Dt 31:30; Judg 20:2; 1 Km 17:47; 3 Km 8:14)' (BAGD 240, §3). In the New Testament it refers to the Christian community, but here there are nuances and shades of meaning which require to be noted: it can refer (1) to the totality of Christians living in one place (e.g. Jerusalem, Acts 8.1; 11.22; further references in BAGD §4b); or (2) to house churches such as those in the house of Philemon (Philem. 2) or Nymphas (Col. 4.15) or Aquila and Priscilla (Rom. 16. 5); or (3) to the Church universal as here (cf. also *TWNT* iii. 502–39; for Col. and Eph. see 512–16). Moule (154) notes that 'outside the greetings formulae ἐκκλησία is still applied in its local sense in Rom. xvi. 1, 4, 5, 16, I Cor. iv. 17, vii. 17, xi. 16, xiv. 33, xvi. 1, 19, II Cor. viii. 1, 18, 19, 23, 24, xi. 8, 28, xii. 13, and even Phil. iv. 15, Col. iv. 15, 16, Philem. 2. It seems, therefore, that, although a universal (catholic) *conception* of the Church underlies all the Epistles alike, the *word* ἐκκλησία is generally used (even in the later epistles) for a local congregation or embodiment of the Church universal: its "catholic" use in Eph. i. 22, iii. 10, 21, v. *passim* and in Col. i. 18, 24 is exceptional.'

ὅς ἐστιν ἀρχή, πρωτότοκος ἐκ τῶν νεκρῶν This is clearly intended to parallel the opening of the 'hymn' at v. 15, but as Dunn (97) observes, 'the possibility that this, too, in its original form, could be the work of a pre-Christian writer is simply not present: the πρωτότοκος ἐκ τῶν νεκρῶν ("firstborn from the dead") is both integral to the second strophe or echoing supplement and inescapably Christian'. If there is an underlying hymn here, then we must either restrict it to the first strophe or assume that it was the work of a Christian writer. In the latter case, the exclusion of some elements (such as τῆς ἐκκλησίας) on the ground of their Christian character becomes all the more problematic.

ἀρχή here, in the singular, clearly means 'beginning'.[56] The word is used of Wisdom at Prov. 8.22 LXX: Κύριος ἔκτισέν με ἀρχὴν ὁδῶν αὐτοῦ. This of course recalls the opening words of Genesis: 'In the beginning God created the heavens and the earth', a verse echoed also in the prologue to the Fourth Gospel.[57] C. F. Burney long ago saw in the Colossian hymn 'an elaborate exposition of *Bereshith* in Gen. 1. 1, in the Rabbinic manner' (*JTS* 27 (1926), 175ff., summarized by Davies, *PRJ* 151–52): three explanations are given of the preposition *be*, then four of the noun *reshith*.

Set out in tabular form, it appears as follows:
Prov. 8.22ff., where Wisdom (i.e. Christ) is called *reshith*, gives the key to Gen. 1. 1, 'Bereshith God created the heavens and the earth':

Bereshith	in *reshith*	ἐν αὐτῷ ἐκτίσθη τὰ πάντα
	by	πάντα δι' αὐτοῦ ἔκτισται
	into	πάντα εἰς αὐτὸν ἔκτισται
Reshith	Beginning	αὐτός ἐστι πρὸ πάντων
	Sum-total	τὰ πάντα ἐν αὐτῷ συνέστηκε
	Head	αὐτός ἐστιν ἡ κεφαλὴ τοῦ σώματος
	Firstfruits	ὅς ἐστιν ἀρχή, πρωτότοκος ἐκ τῶν νεκρῶν

Conclusion: Christ fulfils every meaning which may be extracted from *reshith*—ἵνα γένηται ἐν πᾶσιν αὐτὸς πρωτεύων.[58]

This is certainly an intriguing suggestion, and has been followed by some scholars (e.g. Davies, *PRJ* 151–52; Larsson, *Christus als Vorbild*, 190–96; Wright ('Poetry', 455–58) suggests some modifica-

---

[56] But cf. Rev. 3.14, ἡ ἀρχὴ τῆς κτίσεως τοῦ θεοῦ. C. R. Koester (*NTS* 49 (2003), 412) argues for the meaning 'ruler' both in Rev. and in Col. Whatever translation is adopted, the main point is as stated at the end of the verse, that in all things Christ is first in rank.

[57] The word occurs frequently in this sense, as a loan-word, in the Nag Hammadi texts; see Siegert, *Nag Hammadi Register*, 220. Siegert singles out *Gos. Eg.* IV 72.3 (= III 60.21–22) as referring to the first-born (of persons), comparing Gen. 49.3, Col. 1.18.

[58] Brownlee was reminded (especially by Christ as ἀρχή) of the constant repetition of *bereshith* in the acrostic at 1QS 10.1–4, which he thought bore a messianic sense; but the messianic interpretation of the acrostic *amen* is uncertain—and even if it is accepted, the messianic link in Col. hangs on the ἀρχή, whereas in 1QS it is supplied by the acrostic *amen*, while the *bereshith* looks to the beginning of the day and night festivals (Braun, *Qumran*, ii. 226f.). Referring to Burney's interpretation, Braun also notes (ii. 173) that even in Col. Paul 'does not make the expected declaration that Christ and Wisdom are one'. Cf. also Daniélou, *Théologie du judéo-christianisme*, 219–22, who writes (221): 'En tous cas cette interpretation d'ἀρχή comme désignant le Fils premier-né se trouve, en dépendance du judéo-christianisme, durant toute la patristique ultérieure.'

tions), but others have voiced criticism. Lohse (46 n. 101) for example writes, 'This thesis would presuppose that the passage was an exegesis of the Hebrew text, but the insight that 1.15–20 is a citation of a Hellenistic Christian hymn does away with this assumption'. But can we be certain that it was a hymn? Aletti (115) observes that this 'midrashic' reading of the text is 'more affirmed than demonstrated' (see also 98 n. 43), while Dunn confines his discussion to a brief footnote (88 n. 12).

The weakness is undoubtedly the fact that the theory presupposes that the passage is an exegesis of the Hebrew text:[59] our author might have been familiar with the language, but can we assume that he could expect a largely Gentile readership in Asia Minor to follow the argument? Even if there were Jews among them, did they still use Hebrew? In their dealings with Gentile neighbours they would naturally use the *lingua franca* of the time, which was Greek. According to Schürer (iii. 142), 'The normal language of the liturgy was probably Greek throughout the communities of the Graeco-Roman world' (see also the indexes, iii. 936: Greek language, and 938: Hebrew language).

In regard to πρωτότοκος ἐκ τῶν νεκρῶν,[60] Moiser (*IBS* 14 (1992), 20ff.) refers to 'Paul's clear distinction between anarthrous νεκροί and οἱ νεκροί, generally completely ignored by commentators, but even when adverted to, misunderstood': νεκροί in his view means 'the dead in general', οἱ νεκροί 'the Christian dead in particular'.[61] He continues, 'There are two apparent exceptions. Col. 1.18 reads at first sight as if νεκροί ought to be anarthrous, but whether we read πρωτότοκος ἐκ τῶν νεκρῶν or (with P46 and Sinaiticus) πρωτότοκος ἐκ νεκρῶν the sense of the phrase is that Christ is the first of those who are to rise (cf. Rom. 8.29, 'first-born among many brothers').'[62] In the other apparent exception (1 Thess. 1.10) some reputable mss omit the article, which prompts the question: could the text with the article point to some later scribe, unaware of Paul's distinction? As Moiser writes, 'The convention is not always observed in the deutero-Paulines: Eph 5:14 is a case in point' (22).[63]

This obviously gives rise to a number of questions. Did Paul in fact make such a distinction, and could he expect his readers to recognize it? Did the copyists who produced our manuscripts recognize it, and preserve the correct text? Or, as commentators have apparently assumed, are the two phrases more or less inter-

[59] 'Burney's thesis draws far too much out of a single Hebrew term' (Barclay, *Colossians*, 67).

[60] Cf. Rev. 1.5: ὁ πρωτότοκος τῶν νεκρῶν.

[61] This position appears to be anticipated by G. G. Findlay among others (*EGT*, 923, on 1 Cor. 15.13): some hold 'that P[aul] is making out the essential connexion between *Christ's* rising and that of *the Christian dead*—in which case he should have written ἡ ἀνάστασις τῶν νεκρῶν; he speaks of "the dead in Christ" first in ver. 18'.

[62] According to the apparatus in NA27, P46 and ℵ* omit ἐκ, not the article.

[63] Best (*Ephesians* 498, n. 26) writes: 'The article with νεκρῶν in this phrase is unusual (BDR §254 n. 8) but not impossible (Mt 14.2; 27.64; 28.7); no significance should be attached to its presence here.' In all three cases in Matt. the preposition is ἀπό, not ἐκ; this is also unusual.

changeable? In Romans there are a dozen relevant passages, beginning with ἐξ ἀναστάσεως νεκρῶν in 1.4. Eleven of them have the phrase ἐκ νεκρῶν (4.24; 6.4, 9, 13; 7.4; 8.11 (*bis*), 34; 10.7, 9; 11.15). At 8.11 there are variant readings that do not affect this phrase, while at 8.34 the phrase itself is omitted from the printed text, following ℵ² B D F G *et al.*, against ℵ* A C *et al.*, but not once does the NA²⁷ apparatus list a variant including the article. The one case in which νεκροί appears with the article is 4.17, τοῦ ζωοποιοῦντος τοὺς νεκρούς, which might well be understood as a reference to the dead in general. There is certainly nothing in the context to suggest a specific reference to *Christian* dead; but Sadducees, Greek philosophers and others who rejected resurrection could not envisage God giving life to the dead.

In 1 Cor. occurrences of the word are limited to ch. 15, in which Paul deals at length with the question of the resurrection of the dead. The phrase ἀνάστασις νεκρῶν occurs three times (vv. 12, 13, 21), but we should also note the climactic οὕτως καὶ ἡ ἀνάστασις τῶν νεκρῶν of v. 42. The first two cases may readily be understood of the dead in general, but v. 21 (καὶ δι᾽ ἀνθρώπου ἀνάστασις νεκρῶν) would seem to suggest the resurrection of Christians; but the resurrection of Christ inaugurates a new order in which resurrection is open to all 'in Christ'. It is by no means easy to draw lines of distinction here.

ἐγήγερται ἐκ νεκρῶν appears in v. 12 and with a difference in order in v. 20. In vv. 15 and 16, and again at vv. 29 and 32, the words νεκροὶ οὐκ ἐγείρονται quite clearly mean that dead persons do not rise again, the view Paul is disputing. In none of these cases is there any indication of a variant inserting the article. Verse 29, however, includes the somewhat enigmatic phrase οἱ βαπτιζόμενοι ὑπὲρ τῶν νεκρῶν: presumably the dead in this case are catechumens who have died before they could receive baptism; but if they were not baptized should they be regarded as Christians? Or did some Corinthian Christians undergo baptism on behalf of deceased relatives, to ensure that they too might have the benefit of resurrection, even if these relatives had never been Christian themselves?

From v. 35 on, all the occurrences of the noun have the article: v. 42 has already been mentioned above, while v. 35 raises the question πῶς ἐγείρονται οἱ νεκροί; and v. 52 leads into the triumphant conclusion, οἱ νεκροὶ ἐγερθήσονται ἄφθαρτοι καὶ ἡμεῖς ἀλλαγησόμεθα. The whole chapter presents Paul's refutation of the view, then widely held, that there is no such thing as a resurrection of dead persons. The resurrection of Christ negates that view, and carries with it the possibility that others too may be raised. There is some justification for Moiser's theory in the fact that the article is used with νεκροί in the closing verses of the chapter, but the logic of the argument surely does not require that *only* Christians may expect a resurrection.

2 Cor. 1.9 (τῷ ἐγείροντι τοὺς νεκρούς) corresponds closely to Rom. 4.17, and again there is nothing to suggest a specific reference to *Christian* dead. Gal. 1.1 conforms to Paul's usual practice (τοῦ ἐγείραντος αὐτὸν ἐκ νεκρῶν), as does Phil. 3.11 (εἰς τὴν ἐξανάστασιν τὴν ἐκ νεκρῶν), although here there are some variants (some mss replace τὴν ἐκ by τῶν, others by τῶν ἐκ). Eph. 5.14, as already noted, has the article, but if this is part of an early Christian hymn (see Best, *Ephesians*, 497ff.) then it would be due to the author cited, not to the author of Eph. In any case Eph. 1.20 (ἐγείρας αὐτὸν ἐκ νεκρῶν) corresponds to Paul's usual practice, as does Col. 2.12 (τοῦ ἐγείραντος αὐτὸν ἐκ νεκρῶν; here B D F G and other mss have the article, which is omitted by P⁴⁶ ℵ A C K *et al.*). At 1 Thess. 1.10 the article is present in ℵ B D F G and other mss, but omitted by P⁴⁶ᵛⁱᵈ A C K *et al.* At 1 Thess. 4.16 it is expressly said that 'the dead in Christ shall rise first', to be followed by those who are still alive at the Parousia. There is no indication of the fate of those who are not 'in Christ'.

It should be added that Col. 2.13 uses the word in a figurative sense: νεκρούς τοῖς παραπτώμασιν (cf. Eph. 2.1, 5). The reference here is not to a literal death, but to the alienation from God brought about by sin. This formulation is new to the Pauline corpus, but the way is already prepared by Rom. 8.10: τὸ μὲν σῶμα νεκρὸν διὰ ἁμαρτίαν.

According to BAGD (535, §2a), νεκροί without the article means 'all the dead, all those who are in the underworld', but sometimes the article is included in the prepositional combinations with which we are concerned 'without appreciable difference in meaning'. The normal usage in the New Testament is to omit the article, and its presence or absence is a slender basis on which to build a theory.

ἵνα γένηται ἐν πᾶσιν αὐτὸς πρωτεύων These words constitute a
climax in the steady building-up of our author's argument.⁶⁴ Christ is
the image of God, the first-born of all creation, and therefore may
claim the highest rank under God himself. He is also the first-born
from the dead, and therefore the beginning of a new creation, in
which also he must be accorded the highest place. The purpose of the
whole is that he should in all things have the supremacy (the αὐτὸς is
emphatic, and ἐν πᾶσιν should probably be taken as neuter rather
than masculine, in view of the context). The verb πρωτεύω (BAGD
725a; TWNT vi. 882–83) occurs only here in the New Testament. The
following two verses make it clear that all this is part of the divine
scheme of salvation.

19. ὅτι ἐν αὐτῷ εὐδόκησεν πᾶν τὸ πλήρωμα κατοικῆσαι⁶⁵ The
meaning here is clear enough, but there are problems in regard to
translation: what is the subject of εὐδόκησεν, and what does πᾶν τὸ
πλήρωμα mean?

In regard to the first question, three suggestions have been offered,
that the subject is (1) Christ; (2) God; or (3) πᾶν τὸ πλήρωμα. The
first of these is unlikely on various grounds (cf. Peake, 507), and the
choice really rests between (2) supplying ὁ θεός and taking πᾶν τὸ
πλήρωμα κτλ as an accusative and infinitive construction (for this
Peake lists 'Meyer, Alford, Lightfoot, Oltramare, Haupt and the
great majority of commentators'; cf. also TWNT ii. 739; vi. 302), or
(3) making πᾶν τὸ πλήρωμα the subject and taking the following
masculines (εἰς αὐτόν and εἰρηνοποίησας) as constructio ad sensum
(so for example Moule, 70; BAGD 319, s.v. §1; Dunn, 101). Peake
notes in favour of the latter view the fact that the subject of εὐδοκεῖν
is usually the subject of the following infinitive; moreover there is
then no need for a change of subject with ἀποκαταλλάξαι in the next
verse. Further, as Moule observes, in 2.9 πᾶν τὸ πλήρωμα τῆς
θεότητος is certainly the subject of κατοικεῖ.⁶⁶

Part of the problem lies in the fact that εὐδοκέω normally has a
personal subject, so that the neuter πλήρωμα appears somewhat
awkward, especially since there is nothing to define it, as the genitive

⁶⁴ 'Der Satz faßt zusammen, steigert und rundet ab, was von 1, 15 an ausgeführt war:
Christus ist πρωτότοκος πάσης κτίσεως, er ist πρὸ πάντων, er ist κεφαλὴ τοῦ σώματος,
τῆς ἐκκλησίας. Auch in allen diesen Beziehungen ist er πρωτεύων, aber er wäre es nicht
ἐν πᾶσιν, nicht im uneingeschränkten Sinn, wenn er nicht auch ἀρχή und πρωτότοκος
ἐκ τῶν νεκρῶν wäre' (Michaelis, TWNT vi. 883).
⁶⁵ This verse is fairly clearly echoed in Val.Exp. 33.30–32 (cf. NHTB 393) with its
reference to the Son 'whose alone is the fulness of divinity'; but here, in conformity
with Valentinian theory, the Saviour is the son of Sophia.
⁶⁶ Cf. Val.Exp. (NHC XI 2. 33.28–34): 'it pleased him to place in him the powers in
bodily form, and he descended'—'the verb "it pleased him" is a reflection of Col. 1.19'
(E. Thomassen, Muséon 102 (1989), 232 n. 28, referring to Irenaeus, Adv. haer. i.3.4
and ExcTheod 31.1). J. D. Turner's translation differs slightly (Nag Hammadi Codices
XI, XII and XIII, ed. C. W. Hedrick (1990), 129), and the notes (163) refer to Col. 2.9,
the text actually cited by Irenaeus (Foerster, Gnosis, 132); but the Coptic verb certainly
recalls Col. 1.19. Cf. also the account of the bringing forth of 'the most perfect beauty
and star of the Pleroma, its perfect fruit, Jesus' in Irenaeus, Adv. haer. i.2.6 (Foerster,
130).

τῆς θεότητος does in 2.9. Moreover, as Dunn observes (101), 'this verb is used regularly in the LXX and elsewhere in the New Testament with God as subject to describe his good pleasure' (he cites Ps. 68.16 (LXX 67.17); Mark 1.11; 1 Cor. 10.5, and refers for further examples to Schrenk, *TDNT* ii. 738). This regular use elsewhere points the way to a solution: as Moule suggests, πᾶν τὸ πλήρωμα is a periphrasis for 'God in all His fullness'. We may add that the absolute use of the phrase here, without an explanatory genitive, suggests that this is something which our author could assume to be familiar to his readers (BAGD 672, §3b cites 2.9 and adds 'without the genitive, but in the same sense 1.19').[67]

The word **πλήρωμα** (BAGD 672; *TWNT* vi. 297–304)[68] is a technical term, particularly in Valentinianism, for the totality of the intermediary powers or emanations produced by the supreme transcendent being, or for the region which they inhabit, but that does not mean that it has to be understood in a Gnostic sense here. It is often assumed that our author adopted the word from the false teachers,[69] but Percy (77) thinks it improbable that he would have borrowed a term to express something clearly so important from a system of thought so foreign to his own. Moreover, there is no suggestion of polemic in his use of the word, and as Moule says (166), 'evidence is lacking that the technical use of πλήρωμα was ever widespread—least of all as early as this'.

In classical Greek it can be used of the complement of a ship, its crew or its cargo, and its general sense may be defined as that of fullness or completion. In the New Testament it is used in a variety of ways, but apart from some verses in Col. and Eph. it would be difficult to find a 'Gnostic' meaning for any of them. In Gal. 4.4 ὅτε δὲ ἦλθεν τὸ πλήρωμα τοῦ χρόνου is quite simply the equivalent of ὅτε ἐπληρώθη ὁ χρόνος (cf. 'the fullness of time' in Eph. 1.10, although here we have τῶν καιρῶν). 1 Cor. 10.26 is a direct quotation of Ps. 24. 1: 'the earth is the Lord's and the fullness thereof' (cf. also Pss. 50.12;

[67] Cf. already Lightfoot, 327: 'It will be evident, I think, from the passages in St Paul, that the word πλήρωμα "fulness, plenitude", must have had a more or less definite theological value when he wrote.... The absolute use of the word, πᾶν τὸ πλήρωμα "all *the* fulness", would otherwise be unintelligible, for it does not explain itself.'
[68] See also Lightfoot's note on 'The meaning of πλήρωμα', 323–39; Moule, 164–69; Munderlein, 'Der Erwählung'; J. Ernst, *Pleroma und Pleroma Christi* (1970); R. Bultmann, *The Gospel of John* (ET 1971), 77 n. 1; P. D. Overfield, *NTS* 25 (1979), 384–96; Best, *Ephesians*, 183–89 and index, *s.v.* 'fullness'.
[69] Cf. for example C. A. A. Scott (*Christianity according to St Paul*, 266): 'The word Pleroma was probably employed by the Colossian syncretists, and suggested what it afterwards came to denote in developed Gnosticism, the totality of the divine emanation, "the spirit forces of the world", under whose government men were supposed to live. What St Paul asserts is that the true Pleroma, the Pleroma of the Godhead, the totality of the divine agencies, is found in Christ ... Moreover, Christ the true Pleroma had overcome the false one, when he stripped off from Himself the "principalities and powers" and "triumphed over them openly."' Nock (*Essays*, 88 n. 165) writes: 'It does not seem to me that πλήρωμα can be regarded as a technical term of religion till its use by Christian Gnostics.' In fact a passage in Irenaeus' account of the system of Ptolemy (see n. 66) seems to be an echo of Col., and it does not stand alone (cf. n. 37).

89.11; in all three psalms NRSV translates 'all that is in it'). In Mark 2.21 (Matt. 9.16) τὸ πλήρωμα is the new patch sewn on an old garment, while in Mark 6.43; 8.20 the plural πληρώματα refers to the fragments gathered up to fill the baskets after the feeding of the multitude. In John 1.16 the word 'looks back to v.14 where it is said that Christ was "full of grace and truth"; of this full complement of grace and truth "we" have all received' (C. K. Barrett, *The Gospel according to John* (1958), 140). Barrett notes that the word was 'taken over in something like its gnostic sense by some early Christian writers; see Col. 1.19; 2.9; Eph. 1.23; 3.19; 4.13. It is not used in this sense by John.' Dunn on the other hand writes (100): 'It would be quite unjustified on the basis of the evidence to conclude that the usage here is "Gnostic"; the line of influence and development most obviously runs from the undeveloped usage here to the much more developed language of the later Valentinian Gnosticism.'[70]

Of the passages in Eph. and Col., Eph. 1.10 presents no problem (see above). Eph. 3.19 is part of a prayer, that the readers may know the love of Christ which surpasses knowledge, so that they may be filled with all the fullness of God. Similarly Eph. 4.13 speaks of the building up of the body of Christ 'until all of us come to the unity of the faith and of the knowledge of the Son of God, to maturity, to the measure of the full stature of Christ'. In both these cases, as Moule notes (169), τὸ πλήρωμα (of God or of Christ) is the condition to which Christians are to be brought: 'it appears that Christ is thought of as containing, representing, all that God is; and that the destiny of Christians, as the Body of Christ, is to enter, in him, into that wealth and completeness'.

This leaves the notoriously difficult verse at Eph. 1.23, which Best translates 'and given him who is head over all to the church, which is his body, the fullness of him who is being totally filled' (*Ephesians*, 156; see his discussion, 183–89); NRSV renders it 'the fullness of him who fills all in all'. Whatever our interpretation in regard to detail, it is clear that this fullness or completeness is something that belongs to Christ or to God, as in Eph. 3.19 and 4.13, and this is confirmed by Col. 2.9, which speaks of the entire fullness of deity dwelling in Christ. The fact that it can be used here without a qualifying genitive indicates, as Lightfoot noted long ago (see above, n. 67), that it must have had a definite theological value that was familiar to the readers. Certainly there is no need to attempt to interpret it in terms of second-century Valentinianism: it was the Gnostics who took over the term, and adapted it to their own purposes. This is a cardinal example of the danger of what has been called 'motif methodology',[71] identifying a term or concept as 'Gnostic' because of its occurrence in the second-century systems, tracing it back to earlier occurrences, and assuming that it has consistently the same significance there.

[70] Cf. Aletti, 113–16 on the background of the passage, 116–18 on its Christology.
[71] Cf. R. Haardt in Tröger, *Gnosis und Neues Testament*, 183–202; H. A. Green, *Numen* 24 (1977), 95–134.

That is to read first-century documents with second-century spectacles.[72] There is a line of development, but we still have to trace in detail how that development took place.

Grammatically, then, πᾶν τὸ πλήρωμα is the subject of the sentence, but in terms of sense it is God in all his fullness who is pleased to dwell in Christ (cf. 2 Cor. 5.19: 'God was in Christ reconciling the world to himself';[73] but here the verb is καταλλάσσω and not the double compound used in Col.).

κατοικέω means basically to live, dwell or settle down, but can also be used 'in relation to the possession of human beings by God, Christ, the Holy Spirit, and other supernatural beings' (BAGD 424, §1b; see also *TWNT* v. 155–57). It is used of demon possession at Matt. 12.45; Luke 11.26, while in Rev. 2.13 the angel of the church in Pergamum is told, 'I know where you are living, where Satan's throne is.' Eph. 3.17 contains a prayer 'that Christ may dwell in your hearts through faith'. In the present verse as in 2.9 the whole fullness of deity dwells in Christ.

20. **καὶ δι᾽ αὐτοῦ ἀποκαταλλάξαι τὰ πάντα εἰς αὐτόν, εἰρηνοποιήσας διὰ τοῦ αἵματος τοῦ σταυροῦ αὐτοῦ, δι᾽ αὐτοῦ εἴτε τὰ ἐπὶ τῆς γῆς εἴτε τὰ ἐν τοῖς οὐρανοῖς** Two textual points are to be noted here. First, the sense seems to require the reading εἰς αὐτόν, with a rough breathing (2 Cor. 5.19, cited above, has the quite unambiguous ἑαυτῷ). The older mss were written without accents or breathings, and an editor is therefore free to choose, except when a preceding word such as οὐκ, οὐχ shows which is intended (Moule, 170; cf. *Idiom Book*, 119; Metzger, *Textual Commentary*, 621; for an opposing view see Lohse, 59 n. 201). Dunn (83 n. 1) objects that this 'would break the triple parallel of "in him", "through him", "to him" (1:16/1:19–20)'; but the sense still seems to require a reflexive. Whether we supply ὁ θεός as the subject of εὐδόκησεν or take πᾶν τὸ πλήρωμα in the sense of 'God in all his fullness', it is ultimately God who is at work in Christ, reconciling all things to himself.[74]

Secondly, there is quite impressive manuscript support for inclusion of the second δι᾽ αὐτοῦ (P[46] ℵ A C D[1] *et al.*), but equally impressive support for its omission (B D* F G I L *et al.*). Lightfoot

---

[72] Cf. Lohse, 57: 'Since, according to Valentinian teaching, the "pleroma" is indeed the heavenly fullness to which, however, God does not belong, this understanding of the word "pleroma" cannot contribute anything to the explanation of Col 1:19—for there can be no doubt that in the Christ-hymn God himself is called "pleroma".' In Valentinianism the Supreme Being is distinguished from the emanations that proceed from him.

[73] On the interpretation of this verse cf. Thrall, *2 Corinthians*, 431–34.

[74] For Aletti (111) the εἰς αὐτόν refers not to God but to the Son. He sees a parallel between 16f. and 20b: 'Just as Christ is the one for whom all things were created, so he is the one for whom all things are reconciled: *la réconciliation est ordonnée à la suprématie et à la seigneurie de Christ sur toutes choses.*' O'Neill ('Source', 92) takes δι᾽ αὐτοῦ to refer to the pleroma, and εἰς αὐτόν to the Son. This prepares for the transition to God as the subject of ἀποκαταλλάξαι: 'He [i.e. God] was pleased that all the Pleroma (of the Godhead, ii. 9) should dwell in the Son, and pleased through the Pleroma to reconcile all things to him, making peace through the blood of his cross.'

(226) already notes that there would obviously be a tendency for scribes to omit the words as superfluous; he takes them as resumptive of the preceding δι' αὐτοῦ 'for the sake of emphasis or distinctness'. Inclusion would give the more difficult reading, and it is hard to see scribes inserting the words, so the longer reading should be given the preference. NA²⁷ places these words within square brackets, indicating some uncertainty (cf. Metzger, *Textual Commentary*, 621; Dunn, 83 n. 4). It is not really necessary to include them in translation.

ἀποκαταλλάξαι F. Büchsel (*TWNT* i. 259) notes that there is no evidence for this word before Paul, and suggests that it may even have been coined by him. In the major letters, however, Paul consistently uses καταλλάσσω (Rom. 5.10 (*bis*); 1 Cor. 7.11; 2 Cor. 5.18, 19, 20), not the double compound, which may make it another item to be added to the dossier against authenticity. In the New Testament the word occurs only here, in v. 22 below and in Eph. 2.16 (see also BAGD 92). Büchsel observes that while ἀποκαταλλάσσω may have God or the pleroma (Col. 1.20) or Christ (Col. 1.22; Eph. 2.16) as subject, God alone is the subject of καταλλάσσω. On the other hand, with both verbs the object is never God, but always human beings, or them and the spirits. In Eph. (καὶ ἀποκαταλλάξῃ τοὺς ἀμφοτέρους ἐν ἑνὶ σώματι τῷ θεῷ διὰ τοῦ σταυροῦ) the reference is to the reconciliation of Jew and Gentile, which Moule (71) considers 'a more intelligible idea', taken up in our present passage in vv. 21ff., not as in Col. to the reconciliation of 'all things'.[75] This is a case where it may be felt that Col. is secondary to Eph. It may be added that in Eph. it is not just a question of the reconciliation of Jew and Gentile but of the reconciliation of both, now made one in Christ, to God.

Dunn (102) notes that this word 'presumes a state of estrangement or hostility. In other words, between the two strophes, and the two phases of divine activity in Christ, there is presupposed an unmentioned event or state, that is, presumably the falling of the cosmos under the domination of the heavenly powers created as part of τὰ πάντα (1:16), the state already spoken of in 1:13 ("the power of darkness").'[76] In regard to this 'cosmic' reconciliation, Moule observes, 'Perhaps the best comment on this inclusive hope is Rom. viii, with its promise of redemption for (apparently) Nature as well as Man.' The relevant passage is of course vv. 19–23:

For the creation waits with eager longing for the revealing of the children of God; for the creation was subjected to futility, not of its own will but by the will of the one who subjected it, in hope that the creation itself will be set free from its bondage to decay and will

[75] On reconciliation see the references supplied by Best, *Ephesians*, 264 n. 51.
[76] Cf. Barrett, *Adam*, 86: 'i.20 and ii.15 make no sense unless we may suppose that powers that were created for subordination to the heavenly Man have rebelled, and deserted their appointed rank. As rebels, they have been overcome and reconciled in the cross; overcome and reconciled, yet not finally destroyed or appeased, since it is evident that they continue to be inimical to man and his interests.'

obtain the freedom of the glory of the children of God. We know that the whole creation has been groaning in labor pains until now; and not only the creation, but we ourselves, who have the first fruits of the Spirit, groan inwardly while we wait for adoption, the redemption of our bodies. (NRSV)

εἰρηνοποιήσας This word (BAGD 228) occurs only here in the New Testament, but the elements of which it is composed appear at the end of Eph. 2.15, immediately before the passage quoted above (for discussion of these verses cf. Best, *Ephesians*, 259–66). In Eph. 2.16 the reconciliation is effected διὰ τοῦ σταυροῦ αὐτοῦ, but here we have διὰ τοῦ αἵματος τοῦ σταυροῦ αὐτοῦ, a phrase which does not appear elsewhere. Paul regularly speaks of the blood of Christ (Rom. 3.25; 5.9; 1 Cor. 10.16; 11.25, 27; cf. Eph. 1.7; 2.13) or of the cross of Christ (1 Cor. 1.17; Gal. 6.12, 14; Phil. 2.8; 3.18), but nowhere else do we find the two combined.

At vv. 13–14 above our author spoke of deliverance from the power of darkness, of redemption and the forgiveness of sins. Now he proclaims that it is not just a matter of the salvation of individuals: the whole cosmos somehow stands in need of redemption, and this has been effected through the cross of Christ. Scott (26) writes: 'For Paul the death of Christ is the divine act by which the whole work of salvation is accomplished. All the powers hostile to man—sin, death, the Law, the demonic agencies—were vanquished on the Cross, so that now there is peace .... The whole universe has been at war with itself, and Christ has brought peace into man's life because he has reconciled all (things), destroying those mysterious forces which have everywhere caused disunion.'

The δι' αὐτοῦ in this verse obviously looks back to v. 16, as do the final words, εἴτε τὰ ἐπὶ τῆς γῆς εἴτε τὰ ἐν τοῖς οὐρανοῖς: all things were created through him and for him, all things on earth and in the heavens, and through him all are reconciled. Dunn (104) observes: 'It says much for the faith of these first Christians that they should see in Christ's death and resurrection quite literally the key to resolving the disharmonies of nature and the inhumanities of mankind, that the character of God's creation and God's concern for the universe in its fullest expression could be so caught and encapsulated for them in the cross of Christ.'[77]

This passage is commonly considered to be an early Christian hymn, or based upon a hymn, which is certainly a possibility to be considered but should not be taken as firmly established. It is also possible that our author was himself responsible for its composition, drawing together elements from earlier tradition into an almost credal statement of the status and supremacy of Christ. The numerous suggestions that have been made with regard to the

---

[77] On notions of cosmic reconciliation and peace in contemporary philosophy cf. van Kooten, *Cosmic Christology*, 127–29.

excision of 'interpolations' only serve to show that we cannot with any confidence work back to an 'original' hymn.

Our primary concern, however, is with what the author wanted to say to his readers, and that is the text as we now have it. These opening sections of the letter provide us with some insights into the character and situation of the intended readers, and also into our author's strategy in dealing with the problems with which he is confronted.

The readers are quite clearly Christians, as is shown by the initial form of address, and probably not just recent converts. This is a pastoral letter, not a missionary address intended to win new adherents to the faith. The author has received good reports of their faith and love, and commends them accordingly. There is no hint of polemic in these opening sections, which contrasts with Galatians, where Paul goes immediately into attack. It would seem, therefore, that the opponents in view are not Judaizers, like those with whom Paul had to deal in Galatia. On the other hand the prayer in v. 9, that they may be filled with the knowledge of God's will, together with the reference in v. 10 to their growing in the knowledge of God, may suggest that in his eyes something is still lacking: they have not yet attained to the ἐπίγνωσις of which he speaks (the word occurs again at 2.2 and 3.10), although there is no clear indication of where the deficiency lies.

Our author begins where the readers are, reminding them of the gospel they have received: in Christ they have been delivered from the power of darkness, translated into the kingdom of the Son of God's love, in whom they have redemption, the forgiveness of sins (vv. 13–14). This leads directly into the 'hymn', which is quite casually introduced by a simple relative, ὅς. The implication may be that the deficiency lies, in the author's view, in a less than adequate appreciation of the significance of Christ, and he seeks to remedy it by his proclamation of the Son's absolute supremacy, in the cosmos and in the Church. As first-born of all creation he is superior to all the powers that may exist, in heaven and on earth.

Paul had already written to the Romans (8.38–39 NRSV), 'I am convinced that neither death, nor life, nor angels, nor rulers, nor things present, nor things to come, nor powers, nor height, nor depth, nor anything else in all creation will be able to separate us from the love of God in Christ Jesus our Lord.' In Phil. 2.6 he speaks of Christ being 'in the form of God', while in 2 Cor. 4.4 he expressly describes Christ as 'the image of God'. In 2 Cor. 5.19 he writes that 'God was in Christ reconciling the world to himself' (on this verse cf. Thrall, *2 Corinthians*, 431–36; also R. H. Bell, *JTS* 53 (2002), 8–16, esp. 10–11). There is a strong case for taking the ἦν καταλλάσσων in the latter verse as a periphrastic imperfect, but our author (if he knew the verse) would seem to have taken θεὸς ἦν ἐν Χριστῷ as a self-contained unit, and goes on to emphasize that this is no mere partial or token presence: the entire fullness of God is here at work. His readers have nothing to fear from hostile powers, and no need of assistance from other celestial beings.

As the references above show, Paul at times comes near to the ideas expressed in this passage, but nowhere in his major letters does he describe Christ as the first-born of all creation. If he wrote Col., then we must assume that towards the end of his life he developed his thoughts further into a majestic portrayal of Christ as sovereign in the Church and in the world; but acceptance of the authenticity of Col. raises other problems, such as the presence of Onesimus and Epaphras with Paul during his imprisonment in Rome. Would Epaphras have left the community in Colossae without a leader, in the face of false teaching serious enough to lead him to seek Paul's guidance? As for Onesimus, there is a case for the view that he sought refuge not in Rome but in Ephesus, and that the letter to Philemon was written from the latter city, at a much earlier date (see Introduction above and commentary on Philemon below).

A further point in regard to which our author seems to go further than Paul relates to the present state of the readers. Paul is in no doubt that in their baptism into Christ all Christians have undergone a radical change: they are buried with Christ in baptism, dead to the old life, and now live in a new order, no longer slaves to sin but servants of Christ. In this life, however, they have not yet attained to the final goal: they are still subject to trials and temptations. For Paul, the redemption in Christ and the hope of glory are incentives to a righteous and holy life, but he is always clear on the difference between the 'already' and the 'not yet'.[78] Our author would seem at times to cross the dividing line: he and his readers have been delivered from the realm of darkness and translated into the kingdom of God's Son. They have not only been buried with Christ (cf. 2.12; Rom. 6.4), but as he says at 2.12; 3.1–4 they have been raised with him. In the last passage he does in Pauline fashion urge them to set their minds on things above, not on things on earth, but at other points one sometimes has the feeling that for him the 'already' is more strongly present than the 'not yet' (cf. p. 115 above).

Reference has been made at various points to parallels in the Nag Hammadi and other Gnostic texts, which show that Col. was known to and used by the Gnostics. Indeed some of these allusions may be among the earliest pieces of evidence for knowledge and use of this letter. They do not show that Col. itself, or the teaching against which it is directed, is Gnostic. There was beyond question 'a kind of gnosis', or as A. D. Nock put it 'a gnostic way of thinking',[79] current

---

[78] Cf. Kennedy, *St Paul and the Mystery Religions*, 225–28, on Paul's statements regarding death and resurrection with Christ. 'It is exclusively a death to sin, and its correlative is a life to holiness in the most ethical sense conceivable' (228).

[79] Nock, *Essays*, 958. Cf. also E. Lupieri, *The Mandaeans* (ET 2002), 34: 'all cultured Christians at that time (according to the parameters of Hellenistic culture) were "Gnostics", the differences between them consisting in the content they each provided for the category "knowledge".' The 'orthodox' Church was the one which eventually succeeded in imposing its own ideas, rejecting other systems of belief as heretical.

in the world of the first century, but this is not yet the Gnosticism of the developed second-century systems. Colossians belongs somewhere along a 'trajectory' that culminates in Gnosticism,[80] but we have to recognize the changes and developments that take place along the way. Colossians shows none of the features singled out by Hans Jonas when he wrote, 'a Gnosis without divine tragedy will not meet specifications'.[81] One very clear point of difference emerges in v. 14, where ἀπολύτρωσις is immediately defined as the forgiveness of sins.

V
RELEVANCE FOR THE READERS
(1.21–23)

[21]And you, who once were alienated and hostile in mind through your evil works, [22]he has now reconciled in the body of his flesh through death, to present you holy and blameless and without reproach before him, [23]if indeed you remain firmly established and steadfast in the faith, without shifting from the hope of the gospel which you heard, which is proclaimed in all the creation that is under heaven, of which I, Paul, have become a servant.

Our author now turns back to the readers, to explain the significance for them of what he has just written: the reconciliation mentioned in v. 20 applies to them also. Once estranged from God, they have now been reconciled through the death of Christ. It is their hope, and indeed their destiny, to be presented before God blameless and without reproach; but there is a proviso: they must remain steadfast in the faith, without shifting from the gospel which they heard. At this point our author is clearly following in Paul's footsteps: there has certainly been a radical change in and for the readers; they have entered into a new order of life, but something still remains to be accomplished.

The text and punctuation of v. 21 are both uncertain: we may (1) place a stop at the end of v. 20 (οὐρανοῖς) and in v. 22 read ἀποκατήλλαξεν (ℵ A C D² and most other mss), taking παραστῆσαι in that verse as describing the purpose (or the result) of this reconciliation; or (2) take παραστῆσαι as yet another infinitive governed by εὐδόκησεν in v. 19 (the whole still forming a single sentence). The first of these would probably be accepted without question but for the textual variants ἀποκατηλλάγητε (P⁴⁶ B) and ἀποκαταλλαγέντες (D* F G et al.). To say the least, a main verb in v. 19 would be a long way back. The problem is that if we accept ἀποκατηλλάγητε we can explain the other two readings, but if we keep ἀποκατήλλαξεν we cannot explain ἀποκατηλλάγητε. Scribes would not deliberately alter a perfectly comprehensible text. Lightfoot

[80] Cf. Robinson and Koester, *Trajectories*; J. M. Robinson, 'From Q to the Gospel of Thomas', in Hedrick and Hodgson (eds), *Nag Hammadi, Gnosticism and Early Christianity*, 127–75.
[81] Jonas, in *The Bible in Modern Scholarship*, 293.

(318) thinks ἀποκαταλλαγέντες a careless emendation of ἀποκατηλλάγητε (to agree with the preceding participle, but it should be in the accusative), and ἀποκατήλλαξεν a grammatical correction to straighten the syntax. Accordingly he accepts ἀποκατηλ-λάγητε, which is certainly the *lectio difficilior*, in that it fits awkwardly after the accusatives at the beginning of the verse, and is the only reading which can explain the others. Moreover it appears to be the reading of P⁴⁶, our oldest extant witness. Other commentators however, with NA²⁷, prefer to read ἀποκατήλλαξεν, which gives a smooth text which presents no problem (e.g. Lohse, 64; Dunn, 105 n. 1: 'we may be justified in concluding that the early correction/improvement was wholly justified'). Cf. also Metzger, *Textual Commentary*, 621f.[1]

As to punctuation, Westcott and Hort make νυνὶ δὲ ... τοῦ θανατοῦ a parenthesis, while Peake and others put a stop at πονηροῖς, making νυνὶ δὲ κτλ a new sentence; but this leaves v. 21 as a rather clumsy anticlimax, whereas in fact it seems to mark the transition to a new line of thought. As noted above, the text printed in NA²⁷ would present no problem but for the variant readings.

21. καὶ ὑμᾶς ποτε ὄντας ἀπηλλοτριωμένους For the formulation cf. 2.13, καὶ ὑμᾶς νεκροὺς ὄντας, also Eph. 2.1, again applying what has just been said directly to the readers. For the content cf. Eph. 2.12, ἀπηλλοτριωμένοι τῆς πολιτείας τοῦ Ἰσραήλ; 4.18, ἀπηλλο-τριωμένοι τῆς ζωῆς τοῦ θεοῦ; also 2.13, ὑμᾶς οἵ ποτε ὄντας μακράν. These phrases present the pre-conversion status of the readers, and suggest a largely Gentile community. Eph. 2.12 refers to alienation from the commonwealth of Israel, and the reconciliation there is between Jew and Gentile, but Col. is not so specific. The alienation here is between humanity and God, who in Christ has reconciled all things to himself (v. 20).

The verb **ἀπαλλοτριόω** (BAGD 80; *TWNT* i. 265–66) occurs only in these three verses (Col. 1.21; Eph. 2.12; 4.18) in the New Testament. It is cognate with the adjective ἀλλότριος, that which belongs to another or, used substantivally, an alien, a stranger, even an enemy (Heb. 11.34). A related term is ἀλλογενής, which appears as the title of one of the Nag Hammadi texts (NHC XI, 3; see *Nag Hammadi Codices XI, XII, XIII*, ed. Hedrick, 1990, 173–267), but this represents a later development. 1 Pet. 2.11 can speak of Christians as aliens and exiles[2] in this world (πάροικοι καὶ παρεπίδημοι; cf. also Heb. 11.13), since their true home is in heaven, but the Gnostics were to carry this further: the soul does not belong to this world, but is a spark of divine fire imprisoned in the earthly body, from which it longs to escape. Here there is influence from the Hellenistic myth of the soul, itself influenced by Platonic ideas. Once again there are similarities, but we should not be too ready to assume identity: the fact that terms and concepts can be used in a Gnostic context does not necessarily mean that they already carry their Gnostic meaning

---

[1] C. Clare Oke (*ExpT* 63 (1951/52), 155f, following Driver, *Hebrew Tenses*, 163) observes that it was 'a common custom with Hebrew writers', after the use of a participle, to pass to the use of a finite verb. ἀποκαταλλαγέντες would then be a correction by scribes who did not recognize the Hebrew idiom.

[2] So RSV, NRSV; AV renders this 'strangers and pilgrims'. See BAGD 629, 625; *TWNT* v. 840–52; ii. 63–64.

when they are employed in earlier writings. We have to determine the significance given to these terms and concepts in each of the contexts, which may be very different.

καὶ ἐχθροὺς τῇ διανοίᾳ ἐν τοῖς ἔργοις τοῖς πονηροῖς The word ἐχθρός here means hostile, not necessarily 'hated' (cf. BAGD 331; TWNT ii. 810–14, esp. 814: in Col. it is to be taken in an active rather than a passive sense). Cf. Rom. 5.10: 'if while we were enemies, we were reconciled to God through the death of his Son, much more surely, having been reconciled, will we be saved by his life'; 1 Cor. 15.24–26: 'then comes the end, when he hands over the kingdom to God the Father, after he has destroyed every ruler and every authority and power. For he must reign until he has put all his enemies under his feet' (both NRSV). τῇ διανοίᾳ indicates that it is not a literal hostility that is in view: it is a question rather of attitude, of heart and mind. Lightfoot comments (227), 'It is the mind of man, not the mind of God, which must undergo a change.' The noun διάνοια (BAGD 187; TWNT iv. 961–65, esp. 964) occurs only three times in the Pauline corpus, here and in Eph. 2.3; 4.18 (the latter reads ἐσκοτωμένοι τῇ διανοίᾳ ὄντες). At Heb. 8.10; 10.16 it is used, along with καρδία, to translate two Hebrew words in the 'new covenant' passage from Jer. 31.33. In these two quotations the two Greek words are interchanged, a reminder that in the ancient world heart and mind were closely associated (cf. references in Lohse 63 n. 10).

The phrase ἐν τοῖς ἔργοις τοῖς πονηροῖς characterizes the former life of the readers from a Jewish or Christian point of view: since they were Gentiles outside the Law their works and deeds, to a Jew, were not done in accordance with the will of God, and hence were evil (Dunn offers an alternative translation, 'in works that are evil'); prior to their conversion, to a Christian, they were subject to the power of darkness, whereas now they belong to the kingdom of God's Son (cf. v. 13). Col. 2.13 speaks of the readers as once νέκρους ὄντας τοῖς παραπτώμασιν (cf. Eph. 2.1, 5), which expresses the same thought in terms of sin and death. Conversion from paganism, whether to Judaism or to Christianity, meant a radical break with the old way of life. This of course is bound to cause perplexity for people in the modern world who have grown up in a nominally Christian society, and have never experienced such a radical change.

Lohse (64 n. 14) observes that the phrase ἔργα πονηρά 'is otherwise not found in the Pauline letters', but in other notes compares Test. Asher 6.5; John 3.19; 7.7. Dunn (106 n. 4) writes: 'It is precisely in this context that we might have expected some use of the alternative metaphor of justification/making righteous, since that metaphor so dominates Paul's earlier presentation of a Jewish gospel for Gentiles (Romans 3–4; Galatians 3; Philippians 3; cf. even Eph 2:8; 4:24).' As noted in the Introduction (p.13 and n. 26), the absence of some of Paul's commonest concepts from Col. has often attracted attention; it must be given due weight when questions of authenticity are raised.

22. νυνὶ δὲ ἀποκατήλλαξεν ἐν τῷ σώματι τῆς σαρκὸς αὐτοῦ διὰ τοῦ θανάτου This verse affirms that the cosmic reconciliation of all things mentioned in v. 20 (cf. pp. 155–56 above) applies to the readers also (ὑμᾶς in v. 21 is the object of ἀποκατήλλαξεν here). The opening words, **νυνὶ δέ** (BAGD 546), mark a clear contrast: once they were estranged and hostile, but now they have been reconciled. Barrett (*Adam*, 87) writes: 'it is clear that if the powers and the rest of creation had remained in him in whom they were created there would have been no necessity to speak (in Col i. 20) of cosmic reconciliation .... As soon as Paul has said what needs to be said on cosmology in order to bring cosmology into the only setting in which it is intelligible, and to show that when he speaks of redemption and forgiveness he is not speaking of minor irrelevancies, he returns to the sphere in which the work of Christ can be seen and known.' That is in the life and experience of his readers, transported from the realm of darkness into the kingdom of God's Son (v. 13), granted forgiveness, and now reconciled to God, although for a season they are still subject to the trials and tribulations, and the temptations, of this earthly life.

This reconciliation is effected ἐν τῷ σώματι τῆς σαρκὸς αὐτοῦ διὰ τοῦ θανατοῦ, a clear reference to the crucifixion. The word σῶμα has already occurred in v. 18 above, where it is used with reference to the Church as the body of Christ (cf. v. 24, ὑπὲρ τοῦ σώματος αὐτοῦ, ὅ ἐστιν ἡ ἐκκλησία). Elsewhere it normally refers to the human body, but at Rom. 6.6 that body is characterized as τὸ σῶμα τῆς ἁμαρτίας, as the seat of sin (cf. Rom. 7.24: τὸ σῶμα τοῦ θανάτου). Here the word is defined by the addition of τῆς σαρκὸς αὐτοῦ, the body of his flesh, his fleshly body. This phrase appears again at 2.11, the only occurrences in the Pauline corpus.[3]

σάρξ (BAGD 743a–44b; *TWNT* vii. 98–161—for Col. see 136–37; cf. also Davies, *Christian Origins*, 145–77, esp. 157) refers literally to the material which covers the bones of a body, but can also, to some extent, overlap with σῶμα to mean the body itself. Thus at v. 24 'Paul' speaks of the sufferings he has endured in his flesh, i.e. his bodily sufferings, on behalf of the body of Christ, which is the Church. At 2.1 he refers to those who have not seen him in the flesh, at 2.5 he speaks of being absent in the flesh but present in spirit (NRSV here renders 'absent in body'; cf. 1 Cor. 5.3, ἀπὼν τῷ σώματι παρὼν δὲ τῷ πνεύματι). Of the two terms, σῶμα is the more neutral, and may require some qualification to define what kind of body is

---

[3] The phrase also occurs in Greek in Sir. 23.27; *1 En*. 102.4–5, and Davies (*Christian Origins*, 157) sees 'an exact parallel' in the Qumran *Habakkuk Commentary* on Hab. 2.7–8 (1QpHab 8.16—9.2). Braun (ii. 227) notes that Dupont-Sommer's 'Christological' exegesis of the Qumran text was emphatically contradicted by De Vaux and Elliger: the phrase in itself does not express incarnation; it refers simply to the natural body. Since the phrase occurs in Greek both in Sirach and in *1 Enoch*, it cannot be said to derive from Qumran. Cf. Lohse 64 n. 20.

meant: Dunn (108) notes the distinction made at 1 Cor. 15.44 between the natural body and the spiritual body as showing that 'different embodiments are necessary for different environments'. σάρξ on the other hand is, as Dunn puts it, 'rootedly of this world, inextricably part of it, so that "flesh and blood" cannot inherit the kingdom (1 Cor 15:50)'.

Scott (27) notes as one of the central ideas of Paul's theology 'that the sinful principle has its seat in the "flesh", by which he means not only the material of which man's body is composed but the lower nature as a whole'. 'By the destruction of his own flesh, Christ destroyed the principle of flesh which involves the whole race in sin.' This is another point that creates difficulty for people in the modern world who are not particularly concerned about sin, and almost certainly would not associate it in this way with the flesh, although they may be perfectly prepared to talk about 'carnal' appetites. The problem today, for both exegete and preacher, is to translate the valid insights of a bygone age into language that will speak home to people in our own time.[4]

παραστῆσαι ὑμᾶς ἁγίους καὶ ἀμώμους καὶ ἀνεγκλήτους κατενώπιον αὐτοῦ Cf. Eph. 1.4, εἶναι ἡμᾶς ἁγίους καὶ ἀμώμους. The verbs are different, and the pronouns, but this conjunction of the two adjectives occurs only in these two verses in the New Testament (but for παραστῆσαι cf. also v. 28; Eph. 5.27). Moreover the phrase κατενώπιον αὐτοῦ also appears only in these verses (cf. also Jude 24).

The positive side of the atonement is now set out. παρίστημι (BAGD 627b–28b; TWNT v. 835–40; cf. also Aletti, 125 with nn. 9 and 10) may be used as a technical term in the language of sacrifice (BAGD §1d; cf. Rom. 12.13, παραστῆσαι τὰ σώματα ὑμῶν θυσίαν ζῶσαν ἁγίαν εὐάρεστον τῷ θεῷ), which fits well with the following ἁγίους καὶ ἀμώμους. Both these terms are found in cultic use, the former (BAGD 9a–10a) of persons or things dedicated to God, the latter specifically (BAGD 47, §1; see also TWNT iv. 836) of unblemished animals offered in sacrifice (cf. Heb. 9.14; 1 Pet. 1.19). The third term, however, ἀνεγκλήτους (BAGD 64; TWNT i. 358–59) is not cultic, but means 'blameless, irreproachable' (cf. 1 Cor. 1.8; 1 Tim. 3.10; Tit. 1.6f; it does not appear in Eph. 1.4). This would seem to suggest that while a sacrificial element may certainly be present, the thought is not merely sacrificial. παρίστημι can also be used as a legal term for bringing before a judge (BAGD §1e), or more generally in the sense of 'presenting', as with the presentation of Jesus in the Temple by his parents (Luke 2.22; cf. BAGD §1b). Cf. also v. 28, ἵνα παραστήσωμεν πάντα ἄνθρωπον τέλειον ἐν Χριστῷ, and Eph. 5.27, ἵνα παραστήσῃ αὐτὸς ἑαυτῷ ἔνδοξον τὴν ἐκκλησίαν.

---

[4] Cf. Hübner, 64–65: 'Hermeneutische Überlegungen zur ersten Strophe des Hymnus'.

Moule (73) observes that it is an open question whether the infinitive here represents a final or a consecutive idea—'in order to present' or 'so as to present', but cuts the Gordian knot by adding, 'In any case, the presenting is in fact a consequence of Christ's death.' There are also questions (1) as to the subject of ἀποκατήλλαξεν, and also of παραστῆσαι; (2) as to the identity of the αὐτοῦ following κατενώπιον; and (3) as to whether we should think of the presentation as taking place at the final judgement or as relating to the present state of the readers.

As to (1), the flow of the Greek suggests the same subject for all the verbs from v. 19 to v. 22, i.e. πᾶν τὸ πλήρωμα (cf. pp. 151f., 154 above). NRSV translates v. 20 as 'and through him God was pleased to reconcile to himself all things', but on this line of interpretation v. 21 would have to mean that God has reconciled the readers 'in his fleshly body through death', whereas the reference is quite clearly to the crucifixion. Again, the most natural understanding is that it is Christ who presents the readers before God, but Aletti (124–25) argues that the logic of the passage requires that it is the Son to whom the faithful are presented holy and irreproachable by the Father. This also provides an answer to question (2): the αὐτοῦ following κατενώπιον must have the same referent as the first in the verse, ἐν τῷ σώματι τῆς σαρκὸς αὐτοῦ, and hence refer to the Son.

On the other hand it can be argued that there is a slight change of subject here, by a very natural transition. In point of fact, it is ultimately God himself who is at work in the whole process of reconciliation. In v. 19 it is his good pleasure that the entire fullness of deity should dwell 'in him', i.e. in Christ, and 'through him' (v. 20) to reconcile all things. The masculine participle εἰρηνοποιήσας is strange after the neuter πλήρωμα, but serves to show that our author is already thinking of the work of Christ, and this becomes clear beyond question in v. 22. On this interpretation, Christ himself must be the subject of ἀποκατήλλαξεν, and also of παραστῆσαι; certainly it is Christ who has reconciled the readers 'in the body of his flesh through death'. The meaning our author wishes to convey is plain enough, although his form of words may be somewhat ambiguous. It is God who has acted to bring about the reconciliation, and he has done so in Christ, who is after all the central figure in the preceding 'hymn'.

The third question has to do with the meaning of κατενώπιον, which is defined by BAGD (421) as 'before, in the presence of God', with two subheads: (1) with reference to Jude 24, actually *in the presence of God* on the day of judgement; and (2) with reference to Eph. 1.4; Col. 1.22, *in the sight of God* on his heavenly throne. Here it would probably be a mistake to give exclusive preference to one alternative and rule out the other: presentation without fault or blemish before God in the final judgement is of course the hope of any Christian, but for the readers that still lies in the future, as the following verse makes clear. On the other hand, they have been reconciled, delivered from the realm of darkness and translated into the kingdom of God's Son (v. 13); the more immediate danger is that they may lose that status.[5]

23. εἴ γε ἐπιμένετε τῇ πίστει τεθεμελιωμένοι καὶ ἑδραῖοι καὶ μὴ μετακινούμενοι ἀπὸ τῆς ἐλπίδος τοῦ εὐαγγελίου οὗ ἠκούσατε, τοῦ κηρυχθέντος ἐν πάσῃ κτίσει τῇ ὑπὸ τὸν οὐρανόν, οὗ ἐγενόμην ἐγὼ Παῦλος διάκονος Cf. Eph. 3.18 ἐρριζωμένοι καὶ τεθεμελιωμένοι ἵνα ἰσχύσητε καταλαβέσθαι, also Col. 2.7 below. Our author now approaches the definite aim of the letter: 'disloyalty to the true Christian message will entail the loss of that glorious inheritance which it promises' (Scott). Moule compares the parable of the two houses (Matt. 7.24–27; so also Lohse, 66), Lightfoot more specifically the foolish man who built χωρὶς θεμελίου (Luke 6.49). The Gospels are of course later than Paul, so that if he is the author he cannot be quoting them, although he might have known the traditions upon which they draw. A later disciple, writing about AD 70 or slightly later, might at most have known Mark.

The combination **εἴ γε** occurs only in Paul in the New Testament (cf. 2 Cor. 5.3; Gal. 3.4; Eph. 3.2; 4.21). It is defined by BAGD (152, §3a) as *if indeed, inasmuch as,* and thus does not necessarily carry a negative significance, although here it certainly introduces a word of warning. The readers must continue, persevere in the faith they have received (ἐπιμένειν, BAGD 296, §2). Dunn (110) comments, 'Such emphasis on the need for persistence in Christian belief and conduct is a regular feature in Paul (e.g. Rom 8:13, 17; 11:22; 1 Cor 9:27; 10:11-12; Gal 5:4) and should not be ignored.'

In Col. 1.4 (see p. 86), πίστις is quite clearly faith in Christ, the readers' response in trust and confidence to the gospel brought to them by Epaphras. Its occurrence here may echo that earlier use, as suggested in the paragraph above, but it is also possible that at this point it has a slightly different meaning, true religion (BAGD §2d), or even body of faith or belief (BAGD §3: it is noted that 'this objectivizing of the πίστις-concept is found as early as Paul: Ro 1:5; Gal 1:23 and perhaps Gal 3:23-25'). At any rate, what is in question is their continuing trust in Christ, their fidelity to the Gospel, their perseverance in Christian belief and conduct.

A further question relates to the structure of the passage: it is possible to take the words ἐπιμένετε τῇ πίστει τεθεμελιωμένοι καὶ ἑδραῖοι together, as in the translation above, or to separate

---

[5] Grundmann (*TWNT* i. 358) takes 1 Cor. 1.8 and Col. 1.22 together as both referring to the final judgement (against Haupt), and adduces the questions in Rom. 8.33f. as making clear how ἀνεγκλήτους is to be understood: no reproach can be raised against the Christians. In 1 Cor. the presupposition for this is the help of God, in Col. their perseverance: 'die Vorwurfsfreiheit beruht auf einem von Gott gewollten und gewirkten Glaubensleben'.

τεθεμελιωμένοι καὶ ἑδραῖοι and translate 'remain in the faith established and steadfast' (so e.g. Dunn, 105). The sense is not greatly affected: in either case the readers are to remain firm in their adhesion to the gospel.

θεμελιόω (BAGD 356; *TWNT* iii. 63–64) means to lay a foundation, and may be used literally as in Matt. 7.25; Luke 6.48 v.l., or figuratively as here (it is used in the passive only here and at Eph. 3.17 in the New Testament). It is natural to recall 1 Cor. 3.11: θεμέλιον γὰρ ἄλλον οὐδεὶς δύναται θεῖναι παρὰ τὸν κείμενον, ὅς ἐστιν Ἰησοῦς Χριστός, although Eph. 2.20 speaks of the readers being built on the foundation of the apostles and prophets, with Christ as ἀκρογωνιαῖος (on this verse cf. Best, *Ephesians*, 279–86). ἑδραῖος (BAGD 217; *TWNT* ii. 360–62) means firm or steadfast; interestingly, ἑδραῖοι τῇ πίστει is the reading of P⁷² at 1 Pet. 5.9. Elsewhere in the New Testament it occurs only in 1 Cor. 7.37; 15.58 (where it is used in conjunction with ἀμετακίνητοι).

μετακινεῖν (BAGD 511) is one of the 34 hapax legomena in Col., although as just noted a cognate word is used in 1 Cor. 15.58. Lightfoot notes the present tense: 'not constantly shifting'. For the idea in other words, cf. Eph. 4.14: περιφερόμενοι παντὶ ἀνέμῳ τῆς διδασκαλίας. The following phrases look back to v. 5, with its reference to the hope laid up in heaven, of which the readers heard 'in the word of the truth of the gospel'. It is this hope that they are in danger of forfeiting, if they do not remain steadfast. There is a similar warning, again stressing perseverance in faith, at 2.6–7: 'As then you have received Jesus Christ the Lord, conduct your lives in him, ἐρριζωμένοι καὶ ἐποικοδομούμενοι ἐν αὐτῷ καὶ βεβαιούμενοι τῇ πίστει.' Schweizer ('Christus und Geist', 301f.), citing Rom. 15.13; Gal. 5.5 and Gal. 3.1ff., notes a difference of emphasis as compared with Paul: the Spirit never appears in Col. as the power which continually brings about afresh all faith and hope and knowledge; faith and hope are spoken of as a possession given through the gospel teaching, and the call is for perseverance rather than for growth. Once again, this suggests a disciple familiar with Paul's teaching but not Paul himself as the author.

This recollection of the opening thanksgiving period continues in the following clause: the gospel which they heard 'is proclaimed in all the creation that is under heaven' (in v. 6 the gospel which 'came' to them is 'bearing fruit and increasing in all the world'). κηρύσσειν (BAGD 431; *TWNT* iii. 695–714; for the NT see 701–14) refers initially to proclamation, e.g. by a herald (κῆρυξ), but in the NT is regularly used for the preaching of the Christian message (cf. Rom. 10.8, 14–15; 1 Cor. 1.23; 15.11). A further small change is the substitution of ἐν πάσῃ κτίσει (cf. Mark 16.15) for ἐν παντὶ τῷ κόσμῳ. As noted above (p. 136), the noun κτίσις may be used (1) of the act of creating or (2) of the thing created, whether an individual creature or creation as a whole. Here as at v. 15 it is obviously the thing created, but there is difference of opinion as to whether we should translate 'to every creature' (so Lightfoot, 227, 229; Lohse,

62; Aletti, 125; NRSV) or 'in all creation' (so Dunn, 111). With
πρωτότοκος πάσης κτίσεως in v. 15 earlier, it would seem better to
choose the latter rendering.⁶

For ὑπὸ τὸν οὐρανόν cf. Luke 17.24; Acts 2.5; 4.12; this phrase
occurs only here in the Pauline corpus. For Lohse (67 n. 44) it
'accords with OT language': cf. LXX Gen. 1.9; 6.17; 7.19 (all
ὑποκάτω τοῦ οὐρανοῦ); Exod. 17.14; Deut. 2.25; 14.19 (both
ὑποκάτω); 9.14 (ὑποκάτωθεν); 25.19; etc. Aletti (127 n. 19) adds
Deut. 4.17; 29.19; 2 Macc. 2.18; Eccles. 1.13; 3.1 (all with the exact
phrase); and particularly Dan. 7.27; 9.12 (in both these cases
Theodotion has ὑποκάτω πάντος τοῦ οὐρανοῦ).

The closing words of this verse serve to mark the transition to a
new topic. For the first time, the author uses a first person singular
rather than the plural he has hitherto employed, and indeed with a
certain emphasis: ἐγὼ Παῦλος (cf. 2 Cor. 10.1; Gal. 5.2; Eph. 3.1; 1
Thess. 2.18; Philem. 19). Best (*Ephesians*, 295) notes that Paul uses
this form 'when he wishes to emphasise either an argument or his
own position', and that only in Eph. and Col. is it tied to his mission
to the Gentiles. What is striking here is that no claim is made for any
special status or authority: Paul has become a διάκονος of the gospel,
a word applied in v. 7 to Epaphras. This is another point to suggest
that the problem addressed in Colossians is not that of Galatians,
where Paul finds it necessary to make an emphatic defence of his
apostolic status. At v. 25 Paul is διάκονος of the Church, but neither
of these phrases appears in the major Pauline letters.

Some scribes evidently thought this description inappropriate for Paul, and either
added καὶ ἀπόστολος (81), substituted κῆρυξ καὶ ἀπόστολος (ℵ* P), or combined all
three readings to produce κῆρυξ καὶ ἀπόστολος καὶ διάκονος (A). This is quite clearly
a case of a growing text, and the shortest form should therefore be given the preference.

At this point it may be well to pause and take stock of what we have
seen thus far. There are numerous parallels with the major Pauline
letters, so that Col. is at least in some sense 'Pauline'. On the other
hand there are several words and phrases that do not occur in the
generally accepted letters, and these along with other factors suggest
composition by some member of a Pauline 'school', probably after
the apostle's death. Our author appears to be well enough informed
about the situation, and is complimentary to his readers, commend-
ing them at the outset for their faith and love. There is as yet no clue

⁶ Lightfoot (213f.) translates πάσης κτίσεως as ' "of all creation" rather than "of
every created thing" ', but later (229) renders ἐν πάσῃ κτίσει as 'among every
creature', without any explanation of the reasons for the difference. In his note he
adds, 'The expression πᾶσα κτίσις must not be limited to man. The statement is given
in the broadest form, all creation animate and inanimate being included.' Lohse (66–
67) sometimes has the one rendering, sometimes the other, and it is in fact quite easy to
pass from the one to the other. There is not much difference in meaning, but these
renderings are not quite the same thing: the one relates to individual creatures, the
other to creation as a whole. Aletti (127 n. 19) writes, 'Les commentateurs font
remarquer, sans aucun humour, que l'expression doit être restreinte aux humains. C'est
vrai, mais comment ne pas voir que le verset reprend expressément les termes des vv.
15–20?'

to the nature of the problems addressed, although the admonition in v. 23 to perseverance in the faith would suggest that there is some danger of their falling away. The 'hymn' in vv. 15–20 is clearly intended to establish the highest possible claims for Christ, in the Church and in the world. For various reasons it does not seem that the problem is that which Paul faced in Galatia, for in Gal. Paul goes at once on the attack, in defence at once of his gospel and of his own apostleship. Here the approach is much more cordial, and while there is warning against any falling away 'Paul' does not assert his authority in the same way. Indeed, in v. 23 he speaks of himself as a servant of the gospel.

VI
PAUL'S LABOURS FOR THE CHURCH
(1.24–2.5)

[24]Now I rejoice in my sufferings on your behalf, and fill up the deficiencies in the afflictions of Christ in my flesh for the sake of his body, which is the Church. [25]I became its servant according to God's commission that was given to me for you, to fulfil the word of God, [26]the mystery hidden from ages and generations—but now it has been revealed to his saints. [27]To them God willed to make known what is the richness of the glory of this mystery among the nations, which is Christ in you, the hope of glory. [28]Him we proclaim, admonishing everyone and teaching everyone in all wisdom, that we may present everyone perfect in Christ. [29]To this end also I labour, striving according to his working which is powerfully effective in me.

[2.1]For I wish you to know what a conflict I have concerning you and those in Laodicea, and all who have not seen my face in the flesh, [2]that their hearts may be encouraged, united in love and in all the wealth of assurance that understanding brings, that you may know the mystery of God, even Christ, [3]in whom all the treasures of wisdom and knowledge are hidden.

[4]This I say, that no one may deceive you by persuasive speech. [5]For even if I am absent from you in the flesh, yet in spirit I am with you, rejoicing to see your good order and the firmness of your faith towards Christ.

The whole of the first paragraph (1.24–29) is a single sentence in the Greek, with only colons at the end of vv. 27 and 28 to mark division. In the translation above the section has been divided into shorter sentences for ease of reading. Similarly vv. 1–3 of the second chapter form a single sentence (despite the chapter division, the first five verses clearly belong with what precedes; verse 6 begins a new section of a different character). NRSV makes v. 2 the beginning of a new sentence ('I want their hearts to be encouraged and united in love').

In the closing words of 1.23 'Paul' speaks of himself as a servant, a
minister of the gospel (cf. Eph. 3.7, οὗ ἐγενήθην διάκονος κατὰ τὴν
δωρεὰν τῆς χάριτος τοῦ θεοῦ). He now takes up and develops this
theme, dealing first with his commitment to the Gospel (1.24–29) and
then with his commitment to the Colossians (2.1–5; cf. Dunn's
division, 113ff., 128ff.). Scott (29f.), assuming Pauline authorship,
suggests that the motives for what he calls 'this digression about
himself' are (1) to justify his seeming presumption in writing to a
church he had never seen, and (2) to impress on his readers that he
can speak with authority, as gifted 'with a special insight which
enables him to penetrate into the deeper counsels of God'. Dibelius
(1927 edn, 16) saw here an attempt to establish closer relations with
readers who were not known to him.

Contrary to what is sometimes written, this description of himself
as a servant of the gospel does not in itself constitute a claim to
authority. At 1 Cor. 3.5 Paul applies the word to himself and
Apollos to set both in a proper position of subordination as
compared with Christ. At 2 Cor. 3.6 it is said that to be ministers of
a new covenant is a privilege bestowed by God, and what that
ministry may entail is set forth at 2 Cor. 6.4ff.; 11.23–28. It is only
through fidelity to that ministry, despite the hardships, that one may
lay claim to authority, and so it is here: he rejoices in his sufferings
on behalf of his readers.

**24. νῦν χαίρω ἐν τοῖς παθήμασιν ὑπὲρ ὑμῶν καὶ ἀνταναπληρῶ
τὰ ὑστερήματα τῶν θλίψεων τοῦ Χριστοῦ ἐν τῇ σαρκί μου ὑπὲρ
τοῦ σώματος αὐτοῦ, ὅ ἐστιν ἡ ἐκκλησία** Cf. Eph. 3.13, αἰτοῦμαι
μὴ ἐγκακεῖν ἐν ταῖς θλίψεσίν μου ὑπὲρ ὑμῶν. At 1.11–12 (see
p. 110) it was noted that the words μετὰ χαρᾶς could be taken
either with what precedes or with what follows. On the first
alternative, taking the words with ὑπομονὴν καὶ μακροθυμίαν, the
meaning would be that the Christian's response to suffering or
persecution should not be a matter of grim resolution but rather a
joyful acceptance (cf. Dunn's references (114) for 'a characteristic
Pauline theme, that of rejoicing in suffering'). Whatever view may
be taken of that passage, 'Paul' here sets an example in his own
person. Some mss insert a μου after παθήμασιν, but it is not really
necessary in Greek: one does not usually rejoice in the sufferings of
another.

πάθημα (BAGD 602; *TWNT* v. 927–34; for this verse see 932–33)
is normally used in the plural (except in Heb. 2.9). It may refer to the
suffering of Christians generally (1 Pet. 5.9; Heb. 10.32; cf. Rom.
8.18; 2 Cor. 1.6–7), or to the suffering endured by Paul himself, as
here, but only rarely in the major Pauline letters does it relate to the
sufferings of Christ (2 Cor. 1.5–7, cf. 4.10; Phil. 3.10; cf. Heb. 2.10; 1
Pet. 4.13; 5.1).[1] It is in the present context more or less synonymous

[1] It is used in a bad sense, meaning 'passion', only in Paul (Rom. 7.5; Gal. 5.24).

170   COMMENTARY ON COLOSSIANS

with θλῖψις (BAGD 362; *TWNT* iii. 139–48; see 143), which means
'distress, tribulation', and is used with the genitive τοῦ Χριστοῦ only
in this verse.[2] Elsewhere in the Pauline corpus it refers to the
tribulations suffered by Paul and his churches: Rom. 5.3; 8.35; 12.12;
2 Cor. 1.4, 8; 2.4; 4.17; 6.4; 7.4; 8.2; Phil. 1.17; 4.14; 1 Thess. 1.6; 3.3,
7; 2 Thess. 1.4, 6 (cf. also C. Wolff, *NTS* 34 (1988), 189f.).[3]
ἀνταναπληρῶ (BAGD 72; *TWNT* vi. 305) occurs only here in the
NT. It means to fill up or complete for someone else (ἀντί: in place
of, instead of).

The phrase ἀνταναπληρῶ τὰ ὑστερήματα τῶν θλίψεων τοῦ
Χριστοῦ has given rise to much discussion:[4] indeed this phrase has
been enough in itself to convince some commentators that Col. could
not have been written by Paul, who would never have dreamed of
suggesting that there was any deficiency in the sacrifice of Christ.
Vielhauer (199) bluntly says that this idea contradicts Paul's theology
of the cross, and cannot come from him. For that matter, it is
difficult to imagine a disciple familiar with Paul's teaching making
that suggestion. As Scott remarks (30f.), the whole argument of this
letter (we may add: whether it is by Paul or by a disciple) rests on the
belief that the work of Christ does not need to be supplemented by
other agencies.

The real problem lies in the word ὑστέρημα (BAGD 849; *TWNT*
viii. 596–98, esp. 598), which means 'want, deficiency', or a lack or
shortcoming. It is used for example in Luke's version of the story of
the widow's mite: 'she out of her *poverty* has put in all she had to live
on' (NRSV). At 2 Cor. 8.14; 9.12, in Paul's plea for his collection for
the saints in Jerusalem, it is used with reference to their need, their
lack of resources. Later in the same letter (11.9) he speaks of his own
needs being supplied by brethren from Macedonia (cf. Phil. 2.30, τὸ
ὑμῶν ὑστέρημα τῆς πρός με λειτουργίας, 'to make up for those
services that you could not give me'). At 1 Thess. 3.10 it refers to a
deficiency in the readers' faith. The conclusion is thus unavoidable: it

---

[2] Delling (*TWNT* vi. 305 n. 3) notes that θλῖψις in the NT never denotes the
sufferings of Jesus himself, but only tribulations which result from being united with
Christ. Schlier (*TWNT* iii. 143–45) writes (1) that in the NT θλῖψις is inseparable from
Christian existence in this world, (2) that these sufferings are understood as the
afflictions of Christ (because Christians are united with him), and (3) that there is an
eschatological element akin to the Jewish idea of the messianic woes, with the
difference that whereas for Jewish thought these woes lie still in the future, for the
Christian they have already begun (cf. also Moule, 75–79).
[3] It is worthy of note that there is nothing of this in Eph. The index to Best's
commentary has but one single reference to suffering (220), where he notes the absence
in the use of the σύν formula in Eph. of any connection with verbs of suffering and
dying with Christ. This leaves the impression that the author 'is concerned too much
with seeing Christians as in a position of glory without first passing through suffering
(Rom 8.17)'.
[4] Cf. Kremer, *Was an den Leiden Christi noch mangelt* (1956) and the literature cited
in the commentaries and in BAGD 73, 602.

signifies lack or deficiency—but how can that relate to the afflictions of Christ?

As noted above, it is only here that θλῖψις is followed by the genitive τοῦ Χριστοῦ. Elsewhere it refers to the sufferings endured by Paul and his churches. This suggests that the reference here is not to the sufferings of Christ himself, but to the tribulations which of necessity afflict the Church, as the body of Christ. We have to remember that Christians from the beginning were constantly liable to suspicion, hostility and even outright persecution, simply because of their faith. Discussing the theme of participation in Christ, M. D. Hooker (*NTS* 35 (1989), 339) writes: 'Christians must expect, not simply to die with Christ, but to *suffer* with him (Rom 8:17; 2 Cor 1:5; 4:10f.; Col 1:24),' and adds, 'it is a question of sharing in what Christ is, not a question of imitation'.

The simplest interpretation therefore seems to be in terms of union with Christ (cf. Dibelius; Best, *One Body in Christ*, 130ff.; Rowley, *Unity of the Bible*, 145; Thompson, *ExpT* 71 (1960), 187f. (cf. Eph. 3.18; 2 Tim. 2.10)), but there are other factors which require to be taken into account. For one thing, if the ordinary Christian could expect to undergo suffering, that was all the more true in the case of apostles and evangelists, as numerous references in Paul's letters show. For another, early Christians took over from Jewish apocalyptic the idea of the messianic woes, that there is an appointed measure of trials and tribulations, doom and catastrophe, which must be completed before the consummation of this present age (cf. Lohse, 70–71). Early Christians lived in expectation of an imminent *parousia* and the end of this world as we know it.

Aletti (135) urges that we should give due respect to the word order, and read together the sequence 'what is lacking in the afflictions of Christ in my flesh'. The reference then is to Paul's personal contribution (ἐν τῇ σαρκί μου),[5] made for the sake of Christ's body, which is the Church (cf. 1. 18; Eph. 1.22–23). What is lacking, still to be completed, is then not the atoning sacrifice of Christ but Paul's own share in the sufferings that must be faced in this present age, before the dawn of the new era.

Vincent Taylor (*The Atonement in NT Teaching*, 104) writes of this verse: 'In these words there is no suggestion that the work of Christ is incomplete, but it is distinctly suggested that the fidelity of a Christian minister and servant of Christ involves a real participation, within the limitations of his opportunities and powers, in the afflictions He endured in the fulfilment of His redemptive ministry for mankind.' So also Lightfoot earlier (232): 'it is a simple matter of fact that the afflictions of every saint and martyr do supplement the afflictions of Christ . . . . They continue the work which Christ began.

---

[5] Hübner (68) draws attention to 2 Cor. 4.10–11, where Paul speaks of 'always carrying in the body the death of Jesus ... so that the life of Jesus may be made visible in our mortal flesh' (ἐν τῇ θνητῇ σαρκὶ ἡμῶν).

They bear their part in the sufferings of Christ;[6] but St Paul would have been the last to say that they bear their part in the atoning sacrifice of Christ.' As Moule (76) puts it, the 'messianic woes' 'are themselves, in a sense, the sufferings of Jesus on the cross—of τοῦ Χριστοῦ in the sense of "Jesus Christ", since the Messianic community, incorporated in Christ, are one with him: their sufferings are his, his are theirs'.[7]

ὑστέρημα later became a technical term in second-century Gnosticism (cf. Sagnard, *La gnose valentinienne et le témoignage de saint Irénée,* (1947), index *s.v.*; U. Wilckens, *TWNT* viii. 599–600; Booth, '"Deficiency"'. For its use as a loan-word in Nag Hammadi texts see Siegert, *Nag Hammadi Register,* 318; for its Coptic equivalent ibid. 150). To assume that Paul here is picking up a word used by the false teachers is, as Moule says (79f.), 'only guess-work'. Dunn (115 n. 10) notes the danger of reading back the outlines of the 'Colossian heresy' from later sources. On Gnostic attitudes to suffering and martyrdom cf. C. Scholten, *Martyrium und Sophiamythos im Gnostizismus nach den Texten von Nag Hammadi* (1987).

The final words of this verse contrast the σάρξ of Paul, his fleshly body (cf. p. 162 above), and the σῶμα of Christ, which is immediately explained as the Church. The point of these words is that his sufferings are a blessing to the Church: 'To suffer in obedience to God's will is to contribute to the building up of a durable community which will transcend that realm of σάρξ' (Moule, 80).

25. ἧς ἐγενόμην ἐγὼ διάκονος κατὰ τὴν οἰκονομίαν τοῦ θεοῦ τὴν δοθεῖσάν μοι εἰς ὑμᾶς πληρῶσαι τὸν λόγον τοῦ θεοῦ As already noted, the opening words of this verse pick up the οὗ ἐγενόμην ἐγὼ Παῦλος διάκονος of v. 23, again with a certain emphasis marked by the ἐγώ. Cf. Eph. 3.7, οὗ ἐγενήθην διάκονος κατὰ τὴν δωρεὰν τῆς χάριτος τοῦ θεοῦ τῆς δοθείσης μοι, where the emphatic pronoun is missing, an aorist is substituted for the imperfect tense, and the commission given by God is replaced by the gift of God's grace (the commission is mentioned in Eph. 3.2, εἴ γε ἠκούσατε τὴν οἰκονομίαν τῆς χάριτος τοῦ θεοῦ τῆς δοθείσης μοι εἰς ὑμᾶς).[8] Here in Col. 'Paul' claims to be a servant of the Church, whereas above and in Eph. he is servant of the gospel. These similarities and differences of course prompt the question: are we to think of different authors using much the same terminology, but in different ways, or of a single author who is merely varying his phrasing to avoid monotony? It is by no means an easy question to answer.

[6] He cites κοινωνοὶ τῶν παθημάτων (2 Cor. 1.7) and κοινωνίαν τῶν παθημάτων (Phil. 3.10), which as noted above are the only passages in the Pauline corpus to use παθήματα of the sufferings of Christ. For I Peter cf. P. A. Holloway, *NTS* 48 (2002), 433–48.

[7] Standhartinger ('Colossians', 580) writes that Col. 'borrows the formula ἀναπληροῦν τὰ ὑστερήματα (sc. from 1 Cor 16:17; Phil 2:30; 2 Cor 11:9; cf. 2 Cor 9:12) and the shared suffering with Christ (παθήματα τοῦ Χριστοῦ; from Phil, 3:10; 2 Cor 1:5) that manifests itself bodily (ἐν τῇ σαρκί μου/ἐν τῷ σώματί μου from Gal 6:17; 2 Cor 4:10) but combines them in an entirely un-Pauline fashion'. She sees here an attempt by later writers to interpret Paul's death theologically.

[8] To be exact, the 'established formula' refers to the grace of God (Gal 2.9; 1 Cor. 3.10; Rom. 12.6); Col. replaces χάρις with οἰκονομία (cf. Standhartinger, 581).

οἰκονομία (BAGD 559; *TWNT* v. 154–55)[9] is one of the words
which are claimed to be used in Eph. and Col. with different
meanings. It refers initially to stewardship, the work of an οἰκονόμος
in a household (cf. Luke 16.1–4), but Paul uses it with reference to his
apostolic office, as a commission or assignment entrusted to him by
God (1 Cor. 9.17 οἰκονομίαν πεπίστευμαι), and this is the sense
required here (cf. Eph. 3.2, quoted above). In Eph. 1.10, however,
(εἰς οἰκονομίαν τοῦ πληρώματος τῶν καιρῶν), and also 3.9 (φωτίσαι
τίς ἡ οἰκονομία τοῦ μυστηρίου τοῦ ἀποκεκρυμμένου), it appears to
refer to God's dispensation or plan of salvation. Dunn (118,
following Reumann, 'OIKONOMIA-Terms', 162–63) suggests that
the thought here in Col. is already developing into the sense required
in these two passages in Eph. At any rate we should not make too
rigid a distinction, as if it could only have the one meaning or the
other. On the other hand, the variety of usage in later texts provides
ample warning of the dangers of assuming that a word always and
everywhere carries the same meaning.

This commission was entrusted to Paul εἰς ὑμᾶς (cf. Eph. 3.2), i.e.
for the sake of the readers (and of course other Gentiles reached
through his ministry). It is, to use a literal translation, to 'fulfil' the
word of God (for πληρόω see BAGD 670a–72a). Moffatt here
translates 'to make a full presentation of God's message'. The λόγος
is the gospel (cf. BAGD §1bβ),[10] not God's promise (Lightfoot, 233,
quoting Rom. 15.19, where Paul claims μεχρὶ τοῦ Ἰλλυρικοῦ
πεπληρωκέναι τὸ εὐαγγελίον); the verb is used at 4.17, where
Archippus is to fulfil the charge he has received.

**26. τὸ μυστήριον τὸ ἀποκεκρυμμένον ἀπὸ τῶν αἰώνων καὶ τῶν
γενεῶν – νῦν δὲ ἐφανερώθη τοῖς ἁγίοις αὐτοῦ** Cf. Eph. 3.9,
φωτίσαι τίς ἡ οἰκονομία τοῦ μυστηρίου τοῦ ἀποκεκρυμμένου ἀπὸ
τῶν αἰώνων; Rom. 16.25, κατὰ ἀποκάλυψιν μυστηρίου χρόνοις
αἰωνίοις σεσιγημένου; 1 Cor. 2.7, σοφίαν ἐν μυστηρίῳ τὴν
ἀποκεκρυμμένην. The thought is clearly the same in all these
passages, but the formulation in Rom. and 1 Cor. is different.[11] 'As
Christ is pre-existent and elected from eternity, and is revealed in the
last days, in him also the mystery of the whole divine plan of

---

[9] Cf. J. Reumann, *NovTest* 3 (1959), 282–99; 'OIKONOMIA-Terms in Paul'; further
references in Best, *Ephesians*, 138. For the use of the word in some later writings cf.
R. A. Markus, 'Trinitarian Theology and the Economy', *JTS* 9 (1958), 89–102; J.
Daniélou, *Message évangelique et culture hellénistique* (1961), 148ff. For its use as a
loan-word in the Nag Hammadi texts see Siegert, *Nag Hammadi Register*, 276; the
majority of the occurrences are in the *Tripartite Tractate* in Codex I, on which see
H. W. Attridge and E. Pagels in *Nag Hammadi Codex I*, ed. H. W. Attridge (1985), E.
Thomassen, *Le Traité Tripartite* (1989).

[10] In the prologue to John λόγος 'is more than utterance (λόγος προφορικός) and
more than thought (λόγος ἐνδιάθετος): it is the plan of God, in a meaning closely
related to, if not identical with Col 1:25, where τὸν λόγον τοῦ θεοῦ stands in apposition
to τὸ μυστήριον τὸ ἀποκεκρυμμένον ἀπὸ τῶν αἰώνων καὶ ἀπὸ τῶν γενεῶν' (Ashton,
NTS 32 (1986), 172–73).

[11] Doubts have been raised as to whether the doxology in Rom. is genuinely Pauline.
See for example the commentaries of Denney (*EGT*), Barrett, Käsemann and
Cranfield, and on the other side that of Sanday and Headlam.

salvation is revealed' (Dahl, 'Christ, Creation and the Church', in *The Background of the NT*, 432). This verse appears to be echoed in the *Trimorphic Protennoia* from Nag Hammadi (44.31–33: 'you have become worthy of the mystery hidden from the aeons').[12]

μυστήριον (BAGD 530; *TWNT* iv. 809–34)[13] has come down into modern English with a range of meanings, some (but not all) of which are already present in the Greek word. Basically it means a secret, something hidden or concealed: both here and in Eph. 3.9, it appears in close association with ἀποκεκρυμμένον.[14] It occurs six times in Eph. (1.9; 3.3, 4, 9; 5.32; 6.19) and four in Col. (1.26, 27; 2.2; 4.3), as compared with five occurrences in the singular in the major Pauline letters (Rom. 11.25; 16.25; 1 Cor. 2.1, 7; 15.57) and three in the plural (1 Cor. 4.1; but at 13.2 and 14.2 the meaning is somewhat different; 2 Thess. 2.7 with its reference to 'the mystery of lawlessness' stands apart). In the Gospels it occurs only in the one context, with reference to 'the mystery of the kingdom of God' (Mark 4.11; both Matt. 13.11 and Luke 8.10 have the plural against Mark's singular). G. W. H. Lampe neatly defines what he calls 'the normal New Testament sense of the word' as 'a secret in the counsel of God which is being made known in Christ; an element in the hidden purpose of God which has been made manifest in being fulfilled' (Lampe and Woollcombe, *Essays in Typology* (1957), 29).

In secular Greek μυστήριον is mostly applied to the mystery religions with their secret rites and teachings, first the Eleusinian mysteries and later the various cults which made their way into the Hellenistic world and the Roman Empire.[15] At one stage there was considerable debate as to the possible influence of these cults upon an emergent Christianity: some stressed the parallels and similarities

---

[12] See *Nag Hammadi Codices XI, XII, XIII*, 421. J. D. Turner, who notes the parallel (ibid. 447), translates 'hidden from (the beginning of) the Aeons', but G. Schenke in her edition (43) has 'das verborgen ist seit Ewigkeiten' (see below).

[13] Cf. also Kennedy, *St Paul and the Mystery Religions*, 123ff.; Robinson, *Ephesians*, 234–40; Böhlig, *Mysterion und Wahrheit*, 3–40; Nock, *Essays*, 791–820; Best, *Ephesians* (index, *s.v.*); Bockmuehl, *Revelation and Mystery*, and Hübner's excursus (191–93). On the reasons for the use of this word in Col. cf. Aletti, 153–57. For occurrences in the Nag Hammadi texts (with various meanings) cf. Siegert, *Nag Hammadi Register*, 273. For Gnostic use of the term see also H. G. Gaffron, *Studien zum koptischen Philippusevangelium* (1969), 101–16. Further literature in Lohse, 74 n. 44. The word also passed into rabbinic Hebrew as a loan-word: 'The Amoraic Rabbis claimed that the oral Torah was Israel's secret (מסטירין) which God wished to be revealed only to the righteous' (B. Gerhardsson, *Memory and Manuscript*, (1961), 158).

[14] The phrase occurs in the *Gospel of Truth* (NHC I 18.15), on which Attridge and MacRae comment, 'The language here is strongly reminiscent of Eph 3:3-4, 9; 6:19, Col 1:26; 2:2, as Ménard (*L'Evangile* 4, 87) notes' (*Nag Hammadi Codex I*, 49; punctuation corrected). Cf. already W. C. van Unnik in *The Jung Codex*, 116.

[15] For older literature see F. Cumont, *Les religions orientales dans le paganisme romain*, (4th edn 1929; ET 1911); R. Reitzenstein, *Die hellenistischen Mysterienreligionen*, (3rd edn 1927); Kennedy, *St Paul and the Mystery Religions*. Cf. also Nock, *Essays* (ed. Stewart) 49–133; 791–820; Metzger, 'Methodology'; Wedderburn, *Baptism and Resurrection*, 88–163 (and index). Cf. also W. G. Kümmel, *The New Testament: The History of the Investigation of its Problems* (ET 1973), 245–324.

and, since the mystery religions were for the most part already well established before the Christian era, concluded that the Christian religion was almost entirely derivative. Others reacted violently against any such suggestion. This is in fact a notable example of the danger, mentioned above in the Preface, of converting parallels into influences and influences into sources (cf. Ellis, *St Paul's Use of the OT*, 82). We must ask what the parallels really signify, take note of the differences as well as the similarities, and pay due attention to the relative chronology of our sources. Influences there certainly were, a salient example being the date of Christmas, which happens to be a significant date in the religion of Mithras; but that was adopted well after New Testament times, and not in the formative period of early Christianity.

As for μυστήριον itself, too much should not be read into the use of this word, in the sense of influence from the mystery religions on a nascent Christianity. Greek philosophers had long used 'mystery' terminology for their own purposes—at least as far back as Plato (*Phaedrus* 248c 2, 8; cf. Bornkamm, *TWNT* iv. 814–16)—and so can Philo (cf. the passages listed in Lilla, *Clement of Alexandria*, 148f. and his whole discussion of the esoteric character of *gnosis* in Clement and in Gnosticism, 144ff.), although otherwise he shows a strong aversion and a deep contempt for the mystery religions.[16] The author of Colossians has taken over a word from the pagan world, but gives to it a new range of meaning: the mystery is the hidden purpose of God, now revealed in Christ. Indeed, as he goes on to say in the next verse, it is Christ himself, the hope of glory, Christ in whom all the treasures of wisdom and knowledge are hidden (cf. 2.2–3).

One major difference deserves to be noted: the rites of the mystery cults were secret, and reserved to the initiate. Similarly, some Gnostic texts include a solemn warning against divulging the secrets of *gnosis* to all and sundry; they are a mystery reserved for an elite.[17] In the

---

[16] A few examples must suffice: in *Vit. Cont.* 25 he says that the Therapeutae τὰ τοῦ σεμνοῦ βίου μυστήρια τελοῦνται; at *Praem. et Poen.* 121 he speaks of the mind μύστην γεγονότα τῶν θείων τελετῶν; several times he refers to Moses as a hierophant, the guide who leads the initiates into the mysteries (e.g. *Virt.* 178, *Somn.* ii. 3); Moses does not haunt the outer court as one seeking initiation, but has always dwelt in the sanctuary (*Post. Caini* 173); he is the τελεώτερος καὶ μᾶλλον κεκαθαρμένος νοῦς τὰ μεγάλα μυστήρια μυηθείς in *Leg. All.* iii. 100 (see §101). For denunciation of the mysteries cf. for example *Spec. Leg.* i. 319ff.; iii. 40ff. See further Bockmuehl, *Revelation and Mystery* 69–81. Cf. also A. D. Nock's critique of E. R. Goodenough's *By Light, Light* in *Essays*, 459–68.

[17] Cf. for example the curse pronounced at the end of *Apoc. John* (Waldstein and Wisse (eds), *Apocryphon of John*, 82–83 (pp. 174–77)); also *Apoc. Jas* 1.8–25 (*NHLE* 30). Cf. also Lilla, *Clement of Alexandria*, 147f.: Clement (*Strom.* v.61.3) quotes the present passage, and distinguishes the μυστήριον τὸ ἀποκεκρυμμένον from the πλοῦτος τῆς δόξης τοῦ μυστηρίου: the former hints at the secret tradition of *gnosis*, which the Lord delivered to his disciples, and which they transmitted to their successors, whereas the latter represents the simple *pistis*. Later Lilla writes (148), 'Like Clement, Philo resorts to mystery terms extremely frequently in order to represent the secret character of his theological doctrines and stresses the necessity of keeping them hidden from the multitude.' In the NT, as noted above, the mystery is not an esoteric teaching to be concealed, but a gospel to be proclaimed.

New Testament, in contrast, the mystery, as just noted, is the hidden purpose of God, now revealed and to be proclaimed in all the world.

More recent research has tended to look for the background of this term not in the Hellenistic mystery religions but in the Jewish apocalyptic tradition.[18] The Greek word corresponds to the Hebrew *raz*, which is used to describe secrets of the divine purpose, formerly concealed but now made known to prophets and apocalyptic seers. The usage goes back to the book of Daniel (2.18–19 LXX), where the 'mystery' is Nebuchadnezzar's dream; the mystery is revealed to Daniel in a vision of the night. Later (2.27–30), before providing the king with the interpretation, Daniel speaks of God as ἀνακαλύπτων μυστηρία. The Hebrew word regularly recurs in this sense in later apocalypses (references in Lohse, 74; Dunn, 120); in the Qumran scrolls (1QpHab VII.4f.) a verse in Habakkuk is interpreted as referring to the Teacher of Righteousness, 'to whom God made known all the mysteries of his servants the prophets' (cf. also 1QH IV.27f.). In seeking to understand this term we therefore have to take account not only of the secular Greek and the philosophical use but also of the associations which came through the Jewish apocalyptic tradition.

In the major Pauline letters the verb **ἀποκρύπτω** occurs only at 1 Cor. 2.7, where as already noted the participle qualifies not μυστήριον but σοφίαν. The only other occurrence in the New Testament, apart from Eph. 3.9 (and a v.l. at Matt. 25.18), is at Luke 10.21, where Jesus speaks of things which God has hidden from the wise.

The phrase ἀποκεκρυμμένον ἀπὸ τῶν αἰώνων καὶ τῶν γενεῶν can be understood in two different ways: (1) with verbs of concealing, ἀπό may refer to the person from whom something is hidden (BAGD 86, §I.4), which would mean that the αἰῶνες and γενεαί would have to be understood as powers from whom the mystery was concealed. Thus some have compared 1 Cor. 2.6–16 with this passage, claiming that the αἰῶνες here are the ἄρχοντες τοῦ αἰῶνος τούτου of 1 Cor. 2.7f. It is then an easy step to the archons of the second-century Gnostic systems. Moule, however, (83) thinks that αἰών and γενεά are not likely to be personified. αἰών was later to become a technical term in Gnosticism,[19] where the ἄρχοντες are hostile powers or planetary spirits, but it is difficult to determine whether this usage was already current in Paul's time. Moreover it could be argued that

---

[18] Cf. Bornkamm in *TWNT* iv. 820–23; R. E. Brown, *The Semitic Background of the Term 'Mystery' in the NT* (1968); Moule, 81–83; Lohse, 74–75. Cf. also K. G. Kuhn, *NTS* 7 (1960/61), 336; J. Reumann, 'OIKONOMIA-Terms', 160f. and references there. Bockmuehl (*Revelation and Mystery*, 7–126) extends the range to cover apocalyptic, Qumran, the Wisdom literature, Philo, Josephus, the ancient versions and early rabbinic literature (cf. also his evaluation of previous research, 220ff.).

[19] Cf. Sagnard, *La gnose valentinienne,* index *s.v.* Cf. also Nock, *Essays*, 377–96, esp. 377f.: the term is used 'to indicate the several members in their chains of hypostases. But it should be noted that in the use of the term there is nothing that was thought to be specifically Gnostic; Irenaeus and Tertullian do not question its suitability.'

in 1 Cor. the reference is to earthly human rulers, as is certainly the case in Matt. 20.25; Luke 14.1; 23.13, 35; 24.20, although in these verses there is no reference to this present age, and admittedly these earthly rulers could be regarded as subject to the influence of supernatural powers. In any case it should not be simply assumed that the αἰῶνες here are Gnostic archons.

The alternative (2) is to take the ἀπό as temporal (BAGD 87, §II.2; cf. Luke 1.70; Acts 3.21; 15.18).[20] The mystery has then been hidden from past ages and generations ('throughout the ages and generations' NRSV), but is now revealed. Aletti, however, (139) makes the point that the phrase should not be regarded as merely temporal: as the formulation in the preceding sentence suggests, it includes reference to the people in past ages and generations from whom the mystery has been concealed (cf. Luke 10.21; Eph. 3.5).

αἰών (BAGD 27–28; TWNT i. 197–209) is another word which has come down into modern English, as 'aeon', with reference to a long period of time. The basic meaning of the Greek word is the same, but there are several shades of meaning: long time, eternity, a segment of time, even the world as a spacial concept. In a New Testament context a special interest attaches to the contrast between this age and the age to come (BAGD §2ab), which exactly corresponds to the Jewish contrast between this present age, dominated by Satan and his angels, and the longed-for messianic age. In our present context it is probably best to take it in a temporal sense, although as noted above the reference is not merely temporal.[21]

One would expect another participle here, to match ἀποκεκρυμ-μένον earlier (cf. Eph. 3.5, ὃ ἑτέραις γενεαῖς οὐκ ἐγνωρίσθη τοῖς υἱοῖς τῶν ἀνθρώπων ὡς νῦν ἀπεκαλύφθη τοῖς ἁγίοις ἀποστόλοις αὐτοῦ καὶ προφήταις ἐν πνεύματι, where both verbs are in the indicative), but the sentence breaks off and resumes with νῦν δὲ ἐφανερώθη τοῖς ἁγίοις αὐτοῦ, which has the effect of giving a greater emphasis to the contrast (cf. the use of νῦνι δέ in v. 21 above). This verse in Eph. provided Baur with an argument for a late date for Eph.: ἅγιοι is not used of the apostles in any apostolic letter, although it was 'a standing predicate of the apostles in a later age' (Paul, 32).[22] Unlike Ephesians, Colossians does not use ἀποκαλύπτω (BAGD 92; TWNT iii. 565–97), from which our modern English 'apocalypse' and 'apocalyptic' derive, but a near synonym, φανερόω (BAGD 852–53; TWNT ix. 4–6).

[20] Cf. e.g. Hübner's lapidary comment (70): 'Die Angabe ἀπὸ τῶν αἰώνων und ἀπὸ τῶν γενεῶν ist zeitlich zu verstehen: seit Äonen und Geschlechtern, also: von Urbeginn an.'

[21] Bornkamm (TWNT i. 208) notes that the idea of a personal Αἰών or αἰῶνες, important for Hellenistic syncretism, is alien to the NT. It may be added that the Gnostic aeons are either emanations from the Supreme Being (cf. Nock, Essays, 377) or the realms which they inhabit. The archons produced by the Demiurge do not appear to be described as aeons.

[22] On this verse cf. Best, Ephesians, 304–10. Some mss omit the reference to the apostles (B b; Ambst), but manuscript support is weak (ibid. 307).

In the light of normal Pauline usage, and the use of the word elsewhere in Col. (1.2, 4, 22; 3.12; 1.12 may be an exceptional case, see above), it is most natural to think of the 'saints' as ordinary believers, but some scholars (references in Lohse, 75 and notes; cf. also Aletti, 140) have made other suggestions: angels (cf. 1.12), a charismatic elite, and so on. Such suggestions are prompted by doubt as to whether ordinary Christians could be said to have received direct divine revelation—which may be the very reason for the choice of φανερόω here, rather than ἀποκαλύπτω. Aletti cogently refers to the book of Daniel for proof that God reveals his mysteries (ἀποκαλύπτειν) only to those whom he has chosen, that they may then make them known (γνωρίζειν, a word which appears in 1.27) to all the world (cf. Eph. 6.19, γνωρίσαι τὸ μυστήριον τοῦ εὐαγγελίου). Eph. 3.5 specifically speaks of the revelation being made to apostles and prophets, and vv. 8–10 use several different verbs (εὐαγγελίσασθαι, φωτίσαι, γνωρίζω) for Paul's own contribution in making the revelation known.[23]

27. οἷς ἠθέλησεν ὁ θεὸς γνωρίσαι τί τὸ πλοῦτος τῆς δόξης τοῦ μυστηρίου τούτου ἐν τοῖς ἔθνεσιν, ὅ ἐστιν Χριστὸς ἐν ὑμῖν, ἡ ἐλπὶς τῆς δόξης[24] Cf. Eph. 1.18, τίς ὁ πλοῦτος τῆς δόξης τῆς κληρονομίας αὐτοῦ. The relative at the beginning refers back to the saints of the previous verse, to whom God willed to make known the wealth of the glory of this mystery, now finally disclosed as 'Christ in you, the hope of glory'.

θέλω (BAGD 354–55; TWNT iii. 43–52) has several shades of meaning, of which the two main ones are (1) to wish in the sense of desire (§1) and (2) to wish or will in the sense of purpose or resolve (§2). As Dunn notes (121), 'the aorist tense indicates more of a decision made', so the latter sense is to be preferred.[25] The primary sense of γνωρίζω (BAGD 163, §1; TWNT i. 718) is to make known or reveal. There is thus a deliberate divine purpose to the disclosure of this mystery (but Eph. 6.19, 21 for example show that the verb itself does not necessarily signify *divine* revelation). πλοῦτος (BAGD 674; TWNT vi. 316–30, esp. 326–28) can be used either literally of the possession of many worldly goods, or figuratively, as here, of a wealth or abundance of something. The phrase πλοῦτος τῆς δόξης occurs not only in Eph. 1.18 (see above) and 3.16, but also in Rom. 9.23 (ἵνα γνωρίσῃ τὸν πλοῦτον τῆς δόξης αὐτοῦ). The noun is strictly masculine (as at Eph. 1.18), but BAGD notes that Paul on eight occasions has the neuter in the nominative and accusative cases:

[23] In a footnote (140 n. 28), Aletti observes, with a string of references, that the usage is already the same in the *Homologoumena*: φανερόω relates to universal manifestation, not to a personal divine revelation.

[24] P46 omits the words τῆς δόξης, while some witnesses read τοῦ θεοῦ for τούτου. Lohse (76 n. 64) prefers the reading ὅς ἐστιν (‍ℵ C D *et al.*), but the neuter pronoun ὅ (P46 A B F G *et al.*) refers back naturally to the preceding μυστήριον.

[25] *NHTB* 269 lists *Authoritative Teaching* (VI 3, 26.8–10): 'He, then, the Father, wishing to reveal his [wealth] and his glory', comparing Rom. 9.23; Eph. 1.17–18; Col. 1.27.

2 Cor. 8.2; Eph. 1.7; 2.7; 3.8, 16; Phil. 4.19; Col. 1.27; 2.2.[26] Six of thes, however, are in Eph. and Col., and only 2 Cor. and Phil. rank among the major Pauline epistles, so that it may be that this use should be ascribed to Paul's disciples rather than to Paul himself.

We have already encountered δόξα at v. 11 (see p. 109), where it was noted that NT usage corresponds with that of LXX rather than with that of classical Greek (cf. also Kennedy, *St Paul and the Mystery Religions*, 191–97 and the article on 'Glory' in *HDB* ii. 183–87). Here the word occurs twice in the same verse, first associating glory with the 'mystery' of God's purpose in Christ, and later referring to the hope of glory to which the readers may look forward. The word ἐλπίς has already occurred twice in this letter, at 1.5 where it is said to be laid up for them in the heavens, and at v. 23 with its warning against any deviation from the hope of the gospel which they heard. Since that hope is now defined as 'Christ in you', it may be assumed that the danger facing the community is some kind of loss of faith in Christ, but there is nothing as yet to specify precisely the nature of that lapse. Some have thought of relapse into Judaism, but our author's approach is not that taken by Paul in Galatians; others think of an attempt to supply alleged deficiencies by appeal to other agencies. The latter view is supported by the clear emphasis in this first chapter on the supremacy and sufficiency of Christ as first-born of all creation and head of the Church.

The words ἐν τοῖς ἔθνεσιν could be taken with the verb γνωρίσαι as meaning 'to proclaim among the nations', but to this Aletti (142) objects, first because of the distance between the words and more particularly because the verb already has a complement in the οἷς, referring back to the saints who are mentioned in v. 26. That the gospel was for the Gentiles as well as for the Jews was of course fundamental to Paul's whole missionary effort, but that is not the point here, or at least not the whole point. The phrase 'this mystery among the nations' is immediately defined by the following words, 'which is Christ in you, the hope of glory'. As Moule (82) observes, 'the μυστήριον is *both* Christ himself *and* the fact that he is among them' (cf. also Dunn, 121–22).

It should be noted at this point that in the translation above the word ἐν has been rendered in two different ways, first as '*among* the nations' and at the end of the verse as 'Christ *in* you'. The first is quite simply a matter of normal English style, but the second may call for some justification, since some commentators (e.g. Lohse, 76 and nn. 65, 66) prefer to read 'among' in both cases (further references for both sides in Dunn, 123 n. 25).

Paul's regular usage is to speak of the Christian as ἐν Χριστῷ (cf.

---

[26] At 2 Cor. 8.2 some mss read the masculine, but the neuter is read by P⁴⁶ ℵ B P *et al*. Similar textual variation occurs also at Eph. 2.7 and Col. 2.2. Lightfoot (235) writes, 'St Paul uses the neuter and the masculine forms indifferently in these epistles (e.g. τὸ πλοῦτος Ephes. i.7, ὁ πλοῦτος Ephes. i.18), as in his other letters (e.g. τὸ πλοῦτος 2 Cor. viii.2, ὁ πλοῦτος Rom. ix.23). In most passages, however, there are various readings.'

above, p. 72f.), but in several of the major letters he speaks of Christ as in the Christian (Gal. 2.20; 4.19; Rom. 8.10; 2 Cor. 13.5; cf. also Eph. 3.17. See *TWNT* ii. 538–39). The first case is his famous declaration 'I have been crucified with Christ, and it is no longer I who live, but Christ lives in me'; the second suggests that for the Galatians the 'formation' of Christ in them is not yet complete. Rom. 8.10 in its context may be significant for the interpretation of our present passage: 'You are not in the flesh; you are in the Spirit, since the Spirit of God dwells in you. Anyone who does not have the Spirit of Christ does not belong to him. But if Christ is in you, though the body is dead because of sin, the Spirit is life because of righteousness.' At 2 Cor. 13.5 Paul challenges his readers to test their own authenticity as Christians (cf. Thrall, *2 Corinthians*, 887–92).

In this life the Christian is still subject to all the trials and tribulations, and the temptations, which this life brings with it. In Paul's thinking he or she has not yet achieved the goal (cf. Phil. 3.12); that comes only with death and resurrection. Yet a decisive change has already taken place, which sets the Christian apart from his or her contemporaries who still hold to their old ways and customs. In a sense the Christian has already died and risen with Christ, and is therefore living a new life. It is the presence of Christ or his Spirit within them, as the guide and inspiration of their lives, that makes the difference (cf. Davies, *PRJ* 177f.).

28. ὃν ἡμεῖς καταγγέλλομεν νουθετοῦντες πάντα ἄνθρωπον καὶ διδάσκοντες πάντα ἄνθρωπον ἐν πάσῃ σοφίᾳ, ἵνα παραστήσωμεν πάντα ἄνθρωπον τέλειον ἐν Χριστῷ The initial relative pronoun refers back to Χριστός in the preceding verse; it is convenient in English to begin a new sentence here.

In the preceding verses our author has used the first person singular, sometimes with an emphatic pronoun; here he reverts to the plural. The 'we' is probably not an editorial 'we', but a recognition that others also have shared in the proclamation of the gospel; at least it includes the apostles and evangelists, and Paul's co-workers, but it could have an even wider reference, 'we Christians'. In v. 29 'Paul' returns again to the singular, emphasizing his own contribution according to the power that is operative in him. Lightfoot (236) notes parallels 'in St Paul's own language' at Thessalonica (Acts 17.3) and at Athens (Acts 17.23); the same verb is used, but there in both cases in the singular, since Paul alone is the preacher. (Modern scholars would be less confident that Paul's speeches in Acts were actually delivered by him: from Thucydides on, ancient historians regularly composed for the characters in their narratives speeches appropriate to the occasion. See for example Dibelius, 'The Speeches in Acts and Ancient Historiography', in *Studies in the Acts of the Apostles* (1956), 138–85.)

καταγγέλλω (BAGD 409; *TWNT* i. 68–71) is one of several words used of missionary preaching (e.g. εὐαγγελίζεσθαι, κηρύσσειν), and bears the sense of a solemn proclamation. νουθετέω (BAGD 544; *TWNT* iv. 1013–16) and διδάσκω (BAGD 192; *TWNT* ii. 138–50) present two aspects of the preacher's task, the first relating to admonition and warning, the second more directly to teaching and instruction. They occur again together at 3.16, where it is the readers who are to teach and admonish one another. The formal proclamation of the gospel may at times be reserved to those trained and qualified for this service, but all Christians have their part to play.

Lightfoot also notes the repetition of πάντα ἄνθρωπον, 'three times repeated for the sake of emphasizing the *universality* of the Gospel'.[27] This is not some esoteric *gnosis* reserved for an elite—it is for all, that all may be instructed in all wisdom (yet another occurrence of πᾶς), in order that all may be presented perfect in Christ. The Gnostics later laid claim to a secret *gnosis* which was the prerogative of the few (as was apparently the case in Corinth), so that these words could be regarded as 'a deliberate rejoinder to some exclusive aspect of the false teachers' "gospel"' (a view cited by Moule, 85); but while there was certainly a kind of *gnosis* current in the NT period there is no indication that it had yet developed into anything comparable to the systems of the second century. As Robert Law put it long ago, Paul's Corinthian correspondence shows 'into how congenial a soil the seeds of Gnosticism were about to fall' (*The Tests of Life* (1909), 28). This is the only hint as yet in Col. to suggest that the 'false teaching' might have been of a Gnostic character.

We have already encountered **παρίστημι** at v. 22 above (see pp. 163–64); here it is the apostle who seeks to present every man perfect in Christ. **τέλειος** (BAGD 809; *TWNT* viii. 74–79, esp. 76; cf. also P. J. du Plessis, *TELEIOS: The Idea of Perfection in the New Testament* (1959)) was a technical term in the mystery religions for an initiate (BAGD, *s.v.*, 2bβ), and Lightfoot (236) thinks that here and in 1 Cor. 2.6, 7 it is 'probably a metaphor borrowed from the ancient mysteries'.[28] Scott, however, (35) sees no ground for supposing that it has any but its general meaning of 'mature' or 'full-grown'. Here we may recall a remark of Polybius (v.29.2) that the Aetolians thought that in Philip of Macedon they had to do with a παιδίον νήπιον, but soon discovered that they were dealing with a τέλειος ἀνήρ. The fact that a word has a technical sense in certain contexts does not mean that it always necessarily carries that sense. Moule (85) judiciously comments, 'There is no need to see in τέλειον an allusion to the "initiation" (τελεόω) of mystery religions, though this is not impossible.'

29. εἰς ὃ καὶ κοπιῶ ἀγωνιζόμενος κατὰ τὴν ἐνέργειαν αὐτοῦ τὴν ἐνεργουμένην ἐν ἐμοὶ ἐν δυνάμει. Cf. Eph. 1.19–20, κατὰ τὴν ἐνέργειαν τοῦ κράτους τῆς ἰσχύος αὐτοῦ. ἣν ἐνήργησεν ἐν τῷ Χριστῷ; 3.7, κατὰ τὴν ἐνέργειαν τῆς δυναμέως αὐτοῦ; 3.20, κατὰ

---

[27] Some scribes evidently disapproved of the repetition: the words are omitted at the second occurrence in D* F G and other witnesses. Some mss also supply Ἰησου at the end.

[28] On τέλειοι in 1 Cor. 2.6 cf. Bockmuehl, *Revelation and Mystery*, 158–60.

τὴν δύναμιν τὴν ἐνεργουμένην ἐν ἡμῖν. Cf. also Phil. 3.21; 2 Thess. 2.9, 11. Apart from Phil., the noun ἐνέργεια occurs only in 'suspected' letters (the other occurrences are at Eph. 4.16 and at Col. 2.12 below), although the verb is of more common occurrence.

At 2 Cor. 11.28 Paul brings to a climax his catalogue of the experiences he has undergone, with the words 'And, besides other things, I am under daily pressure because of my anxiety for all the churches' (NRSV). In the present verse also our author stresses the arduous labour involved: κοπιῶ (BAGD 443; *TWNT* iii. 827–29) conveys the sense of strenuous effort, of toil amid trouble and difficulty (the cognate noun κόπος). The oversight of the communities he had founded was no simple matter. Paul uses the word frequently, both literally of his labours to support himself (1 Cor. 4.12) and metaphorically of his missionary effort (e.g. 1 Cor. 15.10; Phil. 2.16) as well as of the service rendered by others (e.g. Rom. 16.6, 12). Here it is reinforced by a metaphor from the athletic field, ἀγωνιζόμενος (BAGD 15; *TWNT* i.134–40; cf. 1 Tim. 4.10). As 1 Cor. 9.24–27 reminds us, the athlete must strain every effort, in training and in competition, if he is to achieve his goal (see also V. C. Pfitzner, *Paul and the Agon Motif* (1967)). The word is used again at 4.12, of Epaphras constantly agonizing in prayer for the Colossians.

The Christian, however, is not left to his own resources. At 1.11 (see p. 107) our author's prayer for his readers is that they may be 'strengthened with all power according to the might of his glory for all endurance and forbearance'. So here 'Paul' labours, but it is 'according to his working which is powerfully effective in me'. ἐνέργεια (BAGD 265; *TWNT* ii. 649–51), here reinforced by the present participle of the cognate verb, means 'working, operation, action', and normally refers to the working of supernatural powers. That this working was effective (cf. 1 Cor. 15.10, 58; Phil. 2.16) is emphasized by the climactic ἐν δυνάμει, 'with power', at the end of the verse. As Dunn puts it (127), 'no room for doubt is left as to Paul's own utter dependence on God's enabling for the exhausting schedule that he followed, or as to its effectiveness'.

2.1. Θέλω γὰρ ὑμᾶς εἰδέναι ἡλίκον ἀγῶνα ἔχω ὑπὲρ ὑμῶν καὶ τῶν ἐν Λαοδικείᾳ καὶ ὅσοι οὐχ ἑόρακαν τὸ προσωπόν μου ἐν σαρκί Despite the chapter division, the next five verses clearly belong with what goes before, and provide a glimpse of Paul's intense interest in and concern for the well-being of his converts (cf. Gal. 4.11, 19; 2 Cor. 11.28).[29] The metaphor from the arena is continued from the preceding verse in the use of ἀγῶν.[30]

The anxieties must have been considerable: how could a mission-

---

[29] A close disciple, such as postulated here, would be well aware of Paul's concern.

[30] Zandee (*The Teachings of Sylvanus*, 490) sees an allusion to this and other passages referring to the spiritual battle in *Silv.* 114.2: 'Fight the great fight as long as the fight lasts.' It is, however, difficult to see an allusion on the strength of one word. For other NT references cf. *NHTB* 332.

ary be confident that the community he had established would
remain faithful to the teaching he had given them, and not relapse
into their old ways and customs, whether in Judaism or in paganism?
Paul's letters give us some insights into the problems that could arise,
but they are far from giving us the complete picture. For that matter,
Paul himself would be suspect in the eyes of some: he had not himself
been a disciple of Jesus, and therefore could not bear witness to
Jesus' life and ministry, or to his teaching. Paul's gospel of Christ
crucified was something other than a gospel that had the teaching of
Jesus at its centre. There are problems and tensions here of which the
modern reader is simply not aware.

For **θέλω γὰρ ὑμᾶς εἰδέναι** cf. 1 Cor. 11: 3. As Lightfoot (238)
already noted, the corresponding negative form οὐ θέλω ὑμᾶς
ἀγνοεῖν is more common in Paul's letters (Rom. 1.13; 11.25; 1 Cor.
10.1; 12.1; 2 Cor. 1.8; 1 Thess. 4.13). The reference to Laodicea leads
Lightfoot to the conclusion that the Laodiceans 'were exposed to the
same doctrinal perils as the Colossians'; he explains the absence of
any mention of Hierapolis (cf. 4.13) on the assumption (1) that they
are included in the ὅσοι; (2) that they were less closely connected
with Colossae 'and perhaps also because the danger was less
threatening there', but some of this is no more than conjecture.
Dunn (129) suggests that the mission in the nearer and more
important Laodicea had been the more successful, and that there
were quite close relations between the two churches (we may note the
injunction to exchange letters at 4.16). On the assumption that the
author is a disciple writing under Paul's name, an alternative view
might be that this is a hint as to the real destination of the letter: with
Colossae still in ruins, it was actually meant for Laodicea; but this
leads into the realm of conjecture. Some late witnesses (104 424 *pc*
vg^ms sy^h**) add καὶ τῶν ἐν Ἱεραπόλει, but there is no early evidence
for this.

Lightfoot translates καὶ ὅσοι '*and all who*, like yourselves, *have not
seen*', commenting that the words introduce a whole class to which
those mentioned belong (cf. Acts 4.6; Rev. 18.17). It is, however,
open to question whether Paul had never met any of the Colossian
community: one thinks of Epaphras and Philemon, whom he
probably met during his stay in Ephesus, and there may have been
others. The alternative 'all who have not seen me' suggests that the
author has in mind two groups, the Colossians and the Laodiceans
on the one hand and a wider anonymous group for whom 'Paul' is
no less concerned. Lohse, however, (80 n. 95) rejects this rendering,
and suggests 'all who are among you and do not yet know me
personally'. At any rate the verse suggests a community which Paul
himself had not founded. Dunn (130) notes that this extension of his
concern 'confirms that in his city bases he was at the centre of a
network of expanding and successful mission undertaken by such as
Epaphras'.

πρόσωπον (BAGD 720–21) means quite simply 'face', but is used
'in all kinds of more or less symbolic expressions which, in large part,

represent OT usage' (§1b; cf. *TWNT* vi. 776–77). Here the meaning is clearly 'who have not seen me in person' (cf. Gal. 1.22, where Paul says that he was still ἀγνοούμενος τῷ προσώπῳ, unknown by sight, to the churches in Judaea). The ἐν σαρκί is strictly superfluous, since they could not have seen him in other than bodily form. W. D. Davies (*Origins*, 153) notes that here, as at 1.22, 24; 2.5, 23 and 3.22, the word σάρξ is used with a physical connotation, whereas at 2.11, 13, 18 it has a moral connotation

2. **ἵνα παρακληθῶσιν αἱ καρδίαι αὐτῶν συμβιβασθέντες ἐν ἀγάπῃ καὶ εἰς πᾶν πλοῦτος τῆς πληροφορίας τῆς συνέσεως, εἰς ἐπίγνωσιν τοῦ μυστηρίου τοῦ θεοῦ, Χριστοῦ** 'The end to which St Paul's labours are directed is described in terms reminiscent of the noble prayer of i. 9ff.: that these Christians' hearts (i.e. their wills, their spirits) may be encouraged or stiffened to boldness, that they may be welded together in love (συμβιβασθέντες being a nominative *ad sensum*, cf. iii.16, Eph. iii.17, iv.2), and in such a way as to attain to the full wealth of conviction which spiritual insight brings—that is, to the perception of God's "mystery", which is Christ' (Moule, 85–86).

The masculine participle is unusual, since we should expect a feminine to agree with αἱ καρδίαι, or a genitive in agreement with αὐτῶν (some witnesses actually read a genitive, but this is probably due to scribal pedantry; the masculine nominative has strong support in P46 ℵ*c A B C D* and other mss). The explanation is that the author is thinking not of strict grammatical agreement but of the people concerned: their hearts are to be encouraged, and they themselves united in love and assurance. The verb **συμβιβάζω** (BAGD 777; *TWNT* vii. 763–65) appears again at 2.19 and in Eph. 4.16 with the meaning 'unite', 'hold together', and most scholars opt for that meaning here (e.g. Lightfoot: 'united', 'compacted'; Moule: 'welded together'; others listed in BAGD §1b. So also Delling in *TWNT* vii. 764). Dibelius and Scott, however, prefer the other possible meaning, 'instructed': 'taught the meaning of love' or 'lovingly instructed' (BAGD §4 cites Acts 19.33; Delling, 765 identifies this as LXX usage, comparing 1 Cor. 2.16). A third sense appears in Acts 9.22 ('demonstrate' or 'prove'), which acording to Delling corresponds with Greek usage.

παρακαλέω (BAGD 617; *TWNT* v. 771–98; for the NT see 790–98) is another word with a considerable range of meaning. Basically it is to call to one's side, to summon, and hence to summon to one's aid (the cognate παράκλητος (BAGD 618) means one called in to help). Another group of meanings includes appeal, urge, exhort, encourage, and a third request, implore, entreat. Finally a fourth group of meanings includes comfort, encourage, cheer up. We have to select the meaning most appropriate to the context. With reference to the fourth group it should be added that the associations are not with soothing words addressed to a crying child, to take away the tears. This is something altogether more robust: the encouragement afforded by the presence of a staunch friend, upon whom one can rely. 'Comfort' in this context does not mean the cosiness of a feather bed. We may note the difference in the use of this word in Eph. 4.1 as compared with 6.22 and Col. 2.2; 4.8.

At 4.8 and also in Eph. 6.22; 2 Thess. 2.17 the verb has τὰς καρδίας as its object; here it appears in the passive, with αἱ καρδίαι as subject. Once again there is a piling up of words to bring out the full meaning, with yet another occurrence of a form of πᾶς: εἰς πᾶν πλοῦτος τῆς πληροφορίας τῆς συνέσεως (a cluster of variants here is due to scribal uncertainty as to whether πλοῦτος should be masculine or neuter (see p. 178f. above), and whether or not to include the article).

πληροφορία (BAGD 670; *TWNT* vi. 309) has two possible meanings, and the dictionaries are slightly at variance as to which should be given the priority: one is 'fullness', which as Delling (in *TWNT*) observes would be tautologous after πλοῦτος, the other 'full assurance' (so already Lightfoot) or 'conviction' (so Moule). BAGD note that the latter meaning is possible in all the occurrences in our literature: Col. 2.2; 1 Thess. 1.5; Heb. 6.11; 10.22; *1 Clem.* 42.3, but that in all except 1 Thess. 1. 5 the other meaning is also possible. Avoidance of tautology would seem to justify choice of the meaning 'assurance' or 'conviction', the more particularly since it makes excellent sense. Calvin (*Epistles of Paul*, 325) writes: 'That man truly knows God who does not vacillate or waver in doubt, but stands fast in a firm and constant persuasion. This constancy and stability Paul frequently calls πληροφορίαν (he uses it here also), and always connects it with faith, for undoubtedly it can no more be separated from faith than heat and light from the sun.' Those brought up in the classical tradition will recall Horace's *Justum et tenacem propositi virum ... si fractus illabatur orbis, impavidum ferient ruinae* (*Odes* iii.3.1–8). But that is Stoic, and not Christian.

We have already met with **σύνεσις** at 1.9 above (p. 104). Here as there it means 'insight' or 'understanding'. Moule (86) suggests that the genitive 'may be a genitive of origin: the conviction is the result of insight, of understanding'. Scott (36) writes, 'A mere intellectual assent is worth little. He wishes to produce a free and entire conviction which will change the whole life into something richer.' ἐπίγνωσις also appears at 1.9, 10 (see pp. 100f.) and again at 3.10. These two clauses are parallel, both introduced by an εἰς, but some recasting is necessary to convey the meaning in English. NRSV renders it, 'I want their hearts to be encouraged and united in love, so that they may have all the riches of assured understanding and have the knowledge of God's mystery, that is, Christ himself, in whom are hidden all the treasures of wisdom and knowledge.'

τοῦ μυστηρίου τοῦ θεοῦ, Χριστοῦ is a striking phrase, placing Christ in apposition to God's mystery (cf. 1.27). For Moule this is probably the true reading, and 'the spate of variants are either explanatory ... or are modifications of the sense'. Metzger in his *Textual Commentary* (622) writes, 'Among what at first sight seems to be a bewildering variety of variant readings, the one adopted for the text is plainly to be preferred (a) because of strong external testimony (P⁴⁶ B Hilary Pelagius Ps-Jerome) and (b) because it alone provides an adequate explanation of the other readings as various scribal attempts to ameliorate the syntactical ambiguity of τοῦ θεοῦ, Χριστοῦ' (cf. also his *Text of the NT*, 236–38, listing no fewer than fifteen variant readings). According to Bockmuehl (*Revelation and Mystery*, 188), 'the author's concern is not ontological but epistemological: ἐπίγνωσις of the mystery of God. We expect the term μυστήριον τοῦ θεοῦ to be synonymous with Paul's gospel message: and if this identification holds, the appositional Χριστοῦ comes as much less of an innovation. Paul can use the terms εὐαγγέλιον and Χριστός almost interchangeably ... .³¹ Paul is introducing no theological *res novae* by equating full knowledge of God's mystery with full knowledge of the Christ who has manifested it' (188).³²

3. ἐν ᾧ εἰσιν πάντες οἱ θησαυροὶ τῆς σοφίας καὶ γνώσεως ἀπόκρυφοι The relative pronoun here refers back most naturally to Christ, as the nearest antecedent, although the dative could be either masculine or neuter.³³ The situation is somewhat different with the similar phrase at 4.3 (τὸ μυστήριον τοῦ Χριστοῦ, δι' ὅ καὶ δέδεμαι), where some mss read the masculine.

We have already met the term σοφία in the 'prayer report' at 1. 9 (see p. 102), and also at 1.28; it appears again at 2.23; 3.16 and 4.5, not always with quite the same significance (we must pay attention to the context). That is six occurrences in a comparatively short letter. By way of contrast, Conzelmann ('Paulus', 235) remarks on its comparatively meagre distribution in the major Pauline letters: it does not appear before 1 Cor., and there only in the first two chapters, elsewhere only in the list of χαρίσματα at 12.8 (we should add ἡ σοφία τοῦ κόσμου τούτου at 3.19, but that is a different and inferior kind of wisdom), and then at 2 Cor. 1.12 and in the liturgical phrase of Rom. 11.33: ὦ βάθος πλούτου καὶ σοφίας καὶ γνώσεως θεοῦ. This last verse is significant, for it shows that Paul draws the word from tradition: the combination of σοφία and γνῶσις is

---

³¹ In a footnote he adduces 1 Cor. 1.23; 15.12; Gal. 2.2; Phil. 1.15; Col. 1.23; etc. '— and, not implausibly, 1:27'.

³² Lilla (148 n. 1) sees proof of Clement's 'inclination to give an esoteric interpretation of St Paul' in his particular predilection for 1 Cor. 8.7, which he quotes in *Strom.* v.61.3 (as well as in other passages) to explain his interpretation of Col. 2.2f. Cf. also Lilla's discussion (147) of Clement's interpretation of the term μυστήριον. *NHTB* 20 lists the *Gospel of Truth* (I 3, 18.11–19): 'Through this, the gospel of the one who is searched for, which [was] revealed to those who are perfect through the mercies of the Father, the hidden mystery, Jesus, the Christ, enlightened those who were in darkness through oblivion. He enlightened them', with references to Col. 1.25–27; 2. 2b–3; Eph. 3.2–5, 9–10 and other passages.

³³ Bockmuehl (*Revelation and Mystery*, 188) observes that to take the relative with the mystery 'would effect a malapropism: our earlier results suggest that the "treasures" [of wisdom and knowledge] can hardly be hidden in a "mystery", since the former are instances of the latter.'

already present in the Wisdom literature (Prov. 8.12; 21.11; Eccl. 1.16f. etc).[34]

These references to wisdom and knowledge and the warning in 2.8 recall the Dead Sea Scrolls: W. D. Davies writes, 'The claim of the sect to a special wisdom or knowledge needs no emphasis; it is writ large over the Scrolls' (*Origins*, 158, referring to his chapter on '"Knowledge" in the Dead Sea Scrolls and Matthew 11:25-30', pp. 119ff.). Several passages in these chapters draw attention to parallels with Col. (see also his index), but on a broader view it is open to question whether these parallels are enough to establish a direct connection between Col. and the Scrolls; consideration must also be given to the possibility of a common background in Jewish tradition.

In *Paul and Rabbinic Judaism* (173), Davies quotes W. F. Howard as saying, 'Even in Colossians, where his language is evidently chosen from the vocabulary of the Wisdom books, and he writes of Christ as the "image of the invisible God, the first born of all creation", he does not make the expected declaration that Christ and Wisdom are one. But with a side glance at the shibboleths of Gnosticism he does say that in Christ "all the treasures of knowledge and wisdom are hidden".' Since this quotation occurs in a chapter entitled 'Old and New Torah: Christ the Wisdom of God' (147–76), it is not surprising that Davies does not altogether agree. There are, however, a few further points to be taken into consideration. In the first place, Howard's book appeared in 1943, *Paul and Rabbinic Judaism* in 1948, and much has happened in the interval. Then, both authors treated Col. as an authentic letter by Paul, but on the view taken here it is open to question whether a disciple some years later would necessarily and specifically identify Christ and Wisdom as Paul sometimes does. Thirdly, when Howard speaks of 'the shibboleths of Gnosticism' he would appear to be thinking of the classic systems of the second century, and it is doubtful if many would make that link for Col. today. This letter may be a point on the 'trajectory' which leads from the rather nebulous *gnosis* of the first century to the developed systems of the second, but that does not mean that our author could have been influenced by the ideas of these later systems.

Moule once again seems to sum up the verse very aptly: 'That in Christ are hidden away all (God's) stores of wisdom and knowledge, is an overwhelmingly impressive way of saying once more what has already been noted as implied by other phrases—namely, that Christ has become to Christians all that the Wisdom of God was, according to the Wisdom Literature, and more still ... . There may also be a reference to secret, esoteric knowledge claimed by the false teachers: "if there *is* a secret, it is all in Christ" is the apostle's reply.'

---

[34] Conzelmann adds that this proves nothing for a 'Gnosis' (in the technical sense) in Corinth. As to Col., cf. Lyonnet ('St Paul', 541): 'S'il est certain que Col. accorde à la connaissance religieuse une place considérable, bien plus que les épîtres précédentes, il suffit sans doute de préciser de quel genre de connaissance il s'agit pour que disparaisse toute véritable ressemblance avec le gnosticisme.'

ἀπόκρυφος (BAGD 93; *TWNT* iii. 962) is one of the fifteen words in Col. which appear elsewhere in the New Testament (Mark 4.22; Luke 8.17, in opposition to φανερός) but not in Paul. It means quite simply 'hidden away', and here is emphatic from its position at the end. Lightfoot (240) observes that Paul here 'adopts a favourite term of the Gnostic teachers, only that he may refute a favourite doctrine'. For Dunn, however, (132) this hypothesis is unnecessary, 'given the play between hiddenness and revelation both in Jewish wisdom tradition (and already in the Jesus tradition: Matt 11:25 and Mark 4.22) and in Jewish apocalyptic tradition (already in Paul's use of μυστήριον)'.[35] However that may be, the Gnostics certainly appealed to secret books and esoteric teaching, and several of the Nag Hammadi texts have this word in their titles, e.g. the *Apocryphon of John*. We may note the change which took place in the use of the word as applied to books, from a term of honour to one of disparagement (cf. W. Schneemelcher in *NT Apocrypha*, i. 14): the books revered by the Gnostics were stigmatized as heretical by the orthodox, and therefore rejected. It should perhaps be added that there is a difference between the apocrypha and pseudepigrapha of the Old Testament (the texts included in the LXX but not in the Hebrew Bible) and the NT apocrypha: the former are recognized and used by some churches, whereas the latter are not.

4. τοῦτο λέγω, ἵνα μηδεὶς ὑμᾶς παραλογίζηται ἐν πιθανολογίᾳ Cf. the similar warnings at 2.8, βλέπετε μή τις ἔσται ὁ συλαγωγῶν διὰ ... κενῆς ἀπάτης; 2.18, μηδεὶς ὑμᾶς καταβραβευέτω; Eph. 5.6, μηδεὶς ὑμᾶς ἀπατάτω κενοῖς λόγοις. This verse marks the transition to the more polemical section of the letter.

παραλογίζομαι (BAGD 620) means to deceive or delude. It occurs only here and at Jas. 1.22, and nowhere else in the NT; it is, however, widely attested outside the NT (Lohse 83 n. 121). πιθανολογία, 'persuasive speech', is another of the 34 hapax legomena in this letter. Paul in the major letters at several points shows reservations about persuasive eloquence, 'words taught by human wisdom' (e.g. Rom. 16.18; 1 Cor. 1.17; 2.4, 13; cf. Eph. 5.6).[36]

Lightfoot takes **τοῦτο λέγω** as referring to what precedes – 'I say all this, that no-one lead you astray' (so too Lohse 83 n. 119). Moule, however, prefers to paraphrase – 'What I mean is—let no-one lead you astray', comparing 1 Cor. 1.12; Gal. 3.17 (passages cited by Lohse) and possibly Eph. 4.17, as well as the use of τοῦτο δέ φημι at 1 Cor. 7.29. In this case we have the so-called 'ecbatic' use of ἵνα in an imperatival sense (cf. *Idiom Book*, 145). Scott notes that Paul is intentionally vague—his warnings are not against personalities, but against the type of thought they stand for. Dunn (133f.) thinks of 'a more general marketplace apology', on the part of the local synagogue, 'which was proving quite appealing to God-worshipping

[35] For discussion of this theme cf. Bockmuehl, *Revelation and Mystery*.
[36] Dibelius quotes from a papyrus: διὰ πιθανολογίας τὰ ἁρπαγέντα ζητοῦσι κατέχειν.

Gentiles', and suggests that a critical situation would have called forth a less leisurely response. Against that it may be observed that Paul's reaction in Gal. is quite different, which makes it less likely that the problem here was the same, i.e. the danger of a relapse into Judaism. Moreover, on the traditional view the situation was serious enough for Epaphras to travel all the way from Colossae to Rome to seek Paul's guidance.

5. εἰ γὰρ καὶ τῇ σαρκὶ ἄπειμι, ἀλλὰ τῷ πνεύματι σὺν ὑμῖν εἰμι, χαίρων καὶ βλέπων ὑμῶν τὴν τάξιν καὶ τὸ στερέωμα τῆς εἰς Χριστὸν πίστεως ὑμῶν This verse should warn us against reading too much into Paul's frequent contrast of flesh and spirit (on which cf. B. A. Pearson, *The Pneumatikos–Psychikos Terminology* (1973)) – cf. 1 Cor. 5.3, ἀπὼν τῷ σώματι, παρὼν δὲ τῷ πνεύματι, where the same thought is expressed in terms of body rather than flesh. Schweizer ('Christus und Geist', 308) observes that 'spirit' here is 'probably purely anthropological': Paul may be absent in the body, but he is with them in spirit. That was already the view of Lightfoot (241: '*in my spirit*', not '*by the Spirit*'); but others like Lohse (83 and n. 126) and Dunn (134) see some connection with the Holy Spirit. What is not in question is Paul's vivid sense of a bond uniting him with his churches, even at a distance. The verb ἄπειμι here is a compound of εἰμί 'to be', and not of εἶμι (note the accent) used as the future of ἔρχομαι, which is rare in Hellenistic Greek (BAGD 83; 222b–26a).

The two participles χαίρων καὶ βλέπων are best taken together as a single expression, 'rejoicing to see' (Lohse 84 n. 127 refers to Blass-Debrunner, §471.5). The cordial note that was struck at the beginning sounds right through this section, in marked contrast to Gal. 1.6ff., where Paul goes at once on the offensive.

Both τάξις (Xenophon *Anab.* i.2.18; Plutarch, *Vit. Pyrrh.* xvi.7) and στερέωμα (1 Macc. 9.14) are found in military contexts, and Moule thinks it not unlikely that they are military metaphors here: 'your orderly formation and the firm front which your faith in Christ presents' (this view goes back at least as far as Lightfoot, (242)). For Lohse, however, (84) the context does not suggest the position of troops prepared for battle, and both concepts are employed in a more general sense: 'The well-ordered condition which, according to the apostle's exhortation, should characterize the community is what "order" (τάξις) means .... . The firm strength which supports the faith of the community is what "firmness" (στερέωμα) means .... . The faith of the community is firmly founded because it is oriented towards Christ alone.' For τάξις see BAGD 803f., for στερέωμα BAGD 766; *TWNT* vii. 614; in LXX the latter word may refer to the firmament of heaven (Gen 1.6–10; Ezek 1.22–26 etc.). The main point in any case is our author's confidence in the firmness and solidity of his readers' faith.

Paul in his major letters frequently shows his concern for the well-being of his churches, and also provides some insights into the toil and effort that was involved for him personally in their oversight and guidance. This very personal passage would therefore be entirely in keeping with authentic Pauline authorship. Indeed, it may be that this passage is one of the strongest arguments against any theory of pseudepigraphy. On the other hand, as already noted, any close associate of Paul (such as Timothy) would know very well both the apostle's concern for his churches and what it had cost him personally, so that this argument cannot be considered conclusive.

A notable feature of the whole letter thus far is the cordiality with which the author addresses his readers. He commends them for their faith, of which he has received favourable reports, and urges them to continue steadfast in their loyalty. This is completely different from Paul's reaction in Galatians to what he sees as the proclamation of 'another gospel'. As M. D. Hooker puts it, the strangest feature about the traditional reconstruction of the Colossian situation 'is the extraordinary calm with which Paul confronts it. If there were within the Colossian Christian community any kind of false teaching which questioned the uniqueness of Christ, which suggested, for example, that he was a member of some kind of gnostic series of spiritual powers, then Paul would surely have attacked such teaching openly and explicitly' ('Were There "False Teachers"', 316). Indeed, we may go further: if there was in Colossae an outbreak of false teaching serious enough to send Epaphras all the way to Rome to seek Paul's counsel as to how to deal with it, can we imagine that Paul would have treated the matter with such equanimity? Or are we to assume that in his later years Paul grew less combative, more tolerant, more ready to meet such threats by quiet and reasoned argument rather than indignant rebuttal?

Compared with Gal., the tone of Romans is much more tranquil, although here too Paul is dealing with several of the issues discussed in the earlier letter. Here, however, we have to consider the situation in each case: Rom. was written to prepare the way for a visit, to a church in a city with a large Jewish population, in hopes of a favourable reception and of support for the further mission which Paul planned. He therefore had to be diplomatic and tactful, and present a reasoned case. Gal. on the other hand is a response to a serious threat to all that Paul stood for. Had Epaphras reported a resurgence in Colossae of the Judaizing tendencies which prompted Paul to write Galatians, it is hard to think that the apostle would not have responded with equal vigour.

VII
THE SIGNIFICANCE OF CHRIST'S WORK
(2.6–15)

[6]As then you have received Christ Jesus the Lord, walk in him, [7]rooted and built up in him and confirmed in the faith, as you were taught, abounding in thanksgiving. [8]Beware lest there be anyone who leads you captive through philosophy and vain deceit, according to human tradition, according to the elements of the world and not according to Christ. [9]Because in him the whole fullness of deity dwells in bodily form, [10]and you are fulfilled in him, who is the head of all rule and dominion.

[11]In him also you were circumcised with a circumcision not wrought with hands, in the stripping off of the body of the flesh, in the circumcision of Christ; [12]you were buried together with him in baptism, in which also you were raised together with him through faith in the effective working of God who raised him from the dead.

[13]You who once were dead in your transgressions and the uncircumcision of your flesh God has made alive together with him, freely forgiving us all our transgressions. [14]He wiped out the bond that stood against us with its decrees, and set it aside, nailing it to the cross. [15]Having divested himself (in death), he put the rulers and authorities to open shame, triumphing over them in it.

Verses 6 and 7 form a transition to the more polemical part of the letter, urging the readers to hold fast to the tradition they have received. In vv. 8 and 9 there is an initial warning against false teaching, with a reference back to the 'hymn' of the first chapter. The following verses set out the present status of the readers, as a consequence of Christ's death and resurrection: this is what they are in danger of losing.

6. Ὡς οὖν παρελάβετε τὸν Χριστὸν Ἰησοῦν τὸν κύριον, ἐν αὐτῷ περιπατεῖτε παραλαμβάνω means generally to accept or receive (BAGD 619), but is also 'more or less a technical term for the receiving of a tradition' (Dunn, 138; E. E. Ellis, *NTS* 32 (1986), 486); cf. 1 Cor. 11.23; 15.1, 3; Gal. 1.9 etc.; cf. also BAGD §2bγ; *TWNT* iv. 14–15).[1] The tradition about Christ is virtually identified with Christ himself (see Moule's note, and his rendering: 'As, therefore, you received as tradition (the account of) Jesus as Christ and Lord, conduct your lives as incorporated in him'). **Χριστός** in Paul is

---

[1] On this terminology of tradition, cf. B. Gerhardsson, *Memory and Manuscript* (1961), 290f., 300f.

nearly a proper name, but here probably has the force of a title—'the Christ, even Jesus the Lord'.

Mere acceptance of the tradition is not enough, nor is any mere acknowledgement of Jesus as Lord: the confession must be translated into life and conduct. The verb περιπατεῖν recalls the prayer of 1.10, where the readers are to 'walk worthily of the Lord' (see p. 105 above). Here they are to walk 'in him'. Schweizer ('Christus und Geist', 302f.) compares and contrasts Gal. 5.25: εἰ ζῶμεν πνεύματι, πνεύματι καὶ στοιχῶμεν (cf. also Gal. 5.16 πνεύματι περιπατεῖτε). There is undoubtedly a similarity, but these phrases are not quite the same (although Dunn, 140 treats them as equivalent): NRSV translates the dative πνεύματι in Gal. 'by the Spirit'. Schweizer speaks of a shift of emphasis in Col., from pneumatology to Christology. As Moule remarks (52), 'There is practically nothing in this epistle about the Holy Spirit; although others (e.g. Romans) are rich in allusions.'

In v. 8, the teaching 'according to Christ' (κατὰ Χριστόν) is set in contrast to teachings 'according to the tradition of men' (κατὰ τὴν παράδοσιν τῶν ἀνθρώπων) and 'according to the elements of the world' (κατὰ τὰ στοιχεῖα τοῦ κόσμου). The latter teachings are clearly merely human and of this world, whereas the readers have received a new tradition 'in Christ', and are to live accordingly.

7. ἐρριζωμένοι καὶ ἐποικοδομούμενοι ἐν αὐτῷ καὶ βεβαιούμενοι τῇ πίστει καθὼς ἐδιδάχθητε, περισσεύοντες ἐν εὐχαριστίᾳ For καθὼς ἐδιδάχθητε cf. Eph 4.21, εἴ γε αὐτὸν ἠκούσατε καὶ ἐν αὐτῷ ἐδιδάχθητε; for ἐρριζωμένοι καὶ ἐποικοδομούμενοι ἐν αὐτῷ cf. Eph. 3.17, ἐν ἀγάπῃ ἐρριζωμένοι καὶ τεθεμελιωμένοι; Eph. 2.20, ἐποικοδομηθέντες ἐπὶ τῷ θεμελίῳ τῶν ἀποστόλων.

The verb ῥιζόω (BAGD 736; *TWNT* vi. 990–91) occurs in the NT only here and at Eph. 3.17, but the usage is slightly different: in Eph. the prayer is 'that Christ may dwell in your hearts through faith, as you are being rooted and grounded in love',[2] whereas here the readers are to be rooted and built up in Christ. ἐρριζωμένοι is a perfect participle, whereas ἐποικοδομούμενοι and βεβαιούμενοι are present participles (note the accents on these three words). Moule brings out the difference neatly: 'Their faith *has taken root* in Christ; they are therefore (with a change of metaphor and of tense) *being progressively built up* in union with him and are *progressively reinforced* in their Christian conviction.'

It is curious that in Eph. 3.17 ἐρριζωμένοι is combined with τεθεμελιωμένοι, a verb we have already met at 1.23 (p. 166), while the second verb used here, ἐποικοδομέω (BAGD 305), appears as an aorist passive participle at Eph. 2:20. Once again it is difficult to determine what conclusion, if any, should be drawn from the use of these words: is it the same author, merely varying his usage, or different authors using the same words and imagery? θεμελιόω relates to the laying of foundations, ἐποικοδομέω to the subsequent building upon them, whereas ῥιζόω has to do with the rooting of

---

[2] So NRSV, but this ignores the tenses: both participles are perfect participles.

plants; both images are in their several ways appropriate for the early development of a new community.³ At 1 Cor. 3.5–15 Paul passes readily from the one to the other, affirming in v. 11 that for the Church there is but one true foundation.

βεβαιόω (BAGD 138; *TWNT* i. 602) means to make firm or establish, and follows on naturally from the preceding words: a building requires to be consolidated if it is to stand firm and endure.⁴ τῇ πίστει may be taken either (1) as instrumental, 'by faith', or (2) as local, 'in the faith'. Here, in view of the following καθὼς ἐδιδάχθητε, it is most probably the latter meaning that is required. The teaching would in the first instance be what they learned from Epaphras (cf. 1.7), but it would also include all that they had learned later. Schweizer ('Christus und Geist', 301f.) notes that there is reference to faith and hope in 1.23, and to faith here, but that the emphasis in Col. is different from that in the major letters.

Finally, their life is to be marked by an abundance of thanksgiving: 'In this context firmness and strength of faith, coupled with thanksgiving, describe the Christian way of life' (O'Brien 'Thanksgiving within the Structure of Pauline Theology', 59).⁵ περισσεύω (BAGD 651f.; *TWNT* vi. 58–61) means to be more than enough, to overflow, or of persons to have an abundance. We have already seen two occurrences of the verb εὐχαριστέω (1. 3, 12; cf. also 3.17); now we have the cognate noun εὐχαριστία, which appears again at 4.2.

At this point there is another cluster of variant readings: several mss (B D² Hᶜ etc. sy sahᵐˢ boh) read ἐν αὐτῇ ἐν εὐχαριστίᾳ (the αὐτῇ referring back to τῇ πίστει), which agrees with the text of 4.2 and could be an assimilation to that verse; others (א² D* vgᶜˡ syʰ ᵐᵍ) have ἐν αὐτῷ ἐν εὐχαριστίᾳ, which may be a modification of that reading, due to the preceding ἐν αὐτῷ. The shortest reading, ἐν αὐτῇ (P Ψ 048ᵛⁱᵈ), is probably due to a simple oversight, in which ἐν εὐχαριστίᾳ was omitted. The original reading would seem to be ἐν εὐχαριστίᾳ, supported by א* A C H* Iᵛⁱᵈ 33 81 1739 *et al.* vg saᵐˢˢ (see Metzger, *Textual Commentary*, 622).

8. βλέπετε μή τις ὑμᾶς ἔσται ὁ συλαγωγῶν διὰ τῆς φιλοσοφίας καὶ κενῆς ἀπάτης κατὰ τὴν παράδοσιν τῶν ἀνθρώπων, κατὰ τὰ στοιχεῖα τοῦ κόσμου καὶ οὐ κατὰ Χριστόν At the outset we should note the indicative **μή τις ἔσται** (cf. other cases at Heb 3.12; Mark 14.2). The normal construction has the subjunctive (cf. Luke 21. 8); the indicative shows that the danger is real (Lightfoot, 244). βλέπω (BAGD 143) means to see or look at something, as in v. 5, but

³ Aletti (161 n. 4) notes that these two images 'sont devenues pratiquement inséparables depuis Jérémie', listing references to the OT, the apocrypha and pseudepigrapha, and Qumran.
⁴ Dunn (142), referring to Schlier in *TWNT*, sees here a metaphor from the marketplace, the verb and its cognates being used of 'the formal legal guarantee required in the transfer of property or goods'. This, however, would seem to be a secondary usage, and it is difficult to think of our author employing three different metaphors in the same sentence. The themes of planting and building occur together elsewhere, and it is perhaps more natural to see here a continuation of the building metaphor. Cf. also 1 Cor. 1.8; 2 Cor. 1.21.
⁵ Cf. also his 'Thanksgiving and the Gospel in Paul', and *Introductory Thanksgivings in the Letters of Paul.*

in certain contexts may have a more specialized meaning: take care
(§4a) or beware (§6). Here it introduces a warning against being led
astray by plausible argument.

τις 'This indefinite τις is frequently used by St Paul, when
speaking of opponents whom he knows well enough but does not
care to name' (Lightfoot, 244, who refers to his note on Gal. 1.7 and
cites Ignatius *Smyrn.* 5: ὅν τινες ἀγνοοῦντες ἀρνοῦνται ... τὰ δὲ
ὀνόματα αὐτῶν, ὄντα ἄπιστα, οὐκ ἔδοξέ μοι ἐγγράψαι). The plural
is used in Gal. 1.7; 2.12 (cf. Ign.), which prompts the question: does
the singular here indicate that the problem stemmed from only one
person? That is, was it perhaps not a regular 'heresy' to which the
Colossians had fallen victim, or were in danger of so doing, but a
single agitator threatening to cause trouble among them? The
possibility has to be reckoned with, but against it is the fact that on
the traditional view of the situation Epaphras felt the danger serious
enough to make him seek Paul's counsel. (We may recall, however,
the problems created for the church in Rome, according to the
apocryphal *Acts of Peter*, by Simon Magus: they were serious enough
to require the intervention of the apostle Peter, and were only
resolved when Peter defeated Simon in a contest in the forum. This
may be pious invention rather than history, but even a single person
may cause severe disruption within a community.)

συλαγωγέω (BAGD 776) is another of the hapax legomena in Col.
It means to carry off as booty or as a captive: 'make you his prey'
(Lightfoot), 'kidnap, carry off bodily', like a slave-raider (Moule).
For the construction cf. Gal. 1.7, εἰ μή τινές εἰσιν οἱ ταράσσοντες
ὑμᾶς, 3.21.

φιλοσοφία also occurs only here in the NT (see BAGD 861;
TWNT ix. 169–85, esp. 182–84), and here it is defined by the words
which follow: 'philosophy which is an empty deceit'. So Lightfoot,
who thinks that probably Paul is throwing back one of their own
favourite terms at the false teachers—'their vaunted philosophy,
which is hollow and misleading'.[6] Scott suggests putting 'philosophy'
in inverted commas. It should be observed that this is not a
condemnation of all philosophy—as Scott says, 'Philosophy in Paul's
day had run to strange extravagances'.[7]

[6] Cf. Wilson, *The Hope of Glory*, 7ff.: 'the lack of any pejorative connotation
attached to the term at 2. 8 suggests that it was in fact their (i.e. the opponents') own
manner of self-description' (8)—but is the association with 'vain deceit' not pejorative?
Cf. Dunn, 148: 'The language, of course, is pejorative and expresses the contempt
which Paul, confident in the rootedness and firmness of his own gospel, evidently felt
for the teachings masquerading as philosophies which competed for the ear of his own
audience when he spoke in the open.'

[7] Cf. Bultmann, *Theologie*, 479 n. 1: 'Naturlich ist nicht die griechische Philosophie
gemeint, sondern die gnostische Spekulation.' It should be noted that 'gnostische' here
relates to Gnosis as German scholars use the term, not to Gnosticism in the stricter
sense (see above, pp. 42, 47 and n. 96). Michel in *TWNT* ix. 185 notes that the word-
group plays no role in later Gnostic thinking. The traditional view of Gnosticism 'from
Irenaeus to Harnack' saw in it a fusion of Christianity and Greek philosophy; see
below. Moffatt speaks of a theosophy.

The word is used by Philo and other Greek-speaking Jews to describe Judaism (references in Gnilka 122; *TWNT* ix. 177–80). Here it is directed more particularly against the 'philosophy' falsely so-called (cf. 1 Tim. 6.20) of the false teachers, whatever its character may have been. Among the early Fathers two attitudes to philosophy are found: broadly speaking, the Alexandrians welcomed it, but others, and especially Tertullian, set their faces against it ('What has Athens to do with Jerusalem?'). It should be noted that Irenaeus, Hippolytus and others found the origins of heresy in the philosophical schools; Hippolytus indeed seeks to identify the specific school which in his view lies behind each of the Gnostic sects. But Dibelius notes that Justin uses the word in his Apologies eight times, never in a bad sense and three times in association with εὐσεβεία.[8] Could Christianity have made its way in the wider world without coming to terms with contemporary philosophy? And how far are the results still relevant in the very different world of today? At one time the two pillars of Western civilization were the classical heritage from Greece and Rome and the Christian tradition, but that is no longer the case. In a world where most people have 'little Latin and less Greek', and even knowledge of the Scriptures can no longer be taken for granted, the first task for the modern interpreter must be to understand his author and his work in their original context; only then can he try to see their relevance for our own world, and since that world is constantly changing no interpretation can ever be considered final and definitive.

The noun **ἀπάτη** (BAGD 82; *TWNT* i. 384) occurs only at Eph. 4.22, Col. 2.8 and 2 Thess. 2.10 among the Pauline epistles, although it also appears in three synoptic passages (ἡ ἀπάτη τοῦ πλούτου, the seduction which comes from riches, Matt. 13.22; Mark 4.19; cf. also Luke 8.14) and once in Hebrews (ἀπάτη τῆς ἁμαρτίας, the deceitfulness of sin, 3.13). Here it is described as κενός, empty, vain and worthless (BAGD 427). The author warns against the 'philosophy' because it is quite simply unprofitable.

The verb παραδίδωμι (BAGD 614–15) has the general meaning of 'hand over' or 'deliver', but was also used with particular reference to the handing on of traditions (§3). The cognate noun **παράδοσις** (BAGD 615; *TWNT* ii. 174–75) is primarily used in the latter context: thus at Gal. 1.14 Paul speaks of himself as formerly ζηλωτὴς τῶν πατρικῶν παραδόσεων. Here it is employed to describe the teachings which the readers are in danger of accepting as merely human traditions, in contrast to the authentic Christian teaching handed on by Paul and his co-workers.

στοιχεῖα This word occurs seven times in the NT, always as a

---

[8] Cf. H. A. Wolfson, *Philosophy of the Church Fathers* (1956); J. N. D. Kelly, *Early Christian Doctrines*, 5th edn (1985), 4f.

plural (BAGD 768–69; *TWNT* vii. 670–87, esp. 683–86).[9] Three of
the occurrences present no problem: at Heb. 5.12 ('you need someone
to teach you again the basic elements of the oracles of God') the
reference is clearly to elementary instruction. So far from being
themselves teachers, as they ought to be, these readers in the author's
eyes ought to be back in primary school, learning the letters of the
alphabet. At 2 Pet. 3.10, 12, where 'the elements' will be dissolved or
melt with fire, the reference is no less clearly to the basic elements of
which the world is composed. According to the theory developed by
Empedocles, these elements are earth, air, fire and water, and this
theory was widely influential (see Delling, *TWNT* vii. 672ff.). To take
but one example, Philo (*De Spec. Leg.* ii.255) condemns those who
worship the elements rather than the creator: πόσης ἄξιος τιμωρίας
ὁ τὸν ὄντως ὄντα θεὸν ἀρνούμενος καὶ τοὺς γεγονότας πρὸ τοῦ
πεποιηκότος τιμῶν καὶ μὴ μόνον γῆν ἢ ὕδωρ ἢ ἀέρα ἢ πῦρ, τὰ
στοιχεῖα τοῦ παντός, ἢ πάλιν ἥλιον καὶ σελήνην καὶ πλάνητάς καὶ
ἀπλανεῖς ἀστέρας ἢ τὸν σύμπαντα οὐρανόν τε καὶ κόσμον σεβεῖν
ἀξιῶν. Philo and other writers frequently list the four elements when
they use the term, and in these cases there is no doubt as to the
meaning of στοιχεῖα.[10]

In the other four cases the meaning has been disputed. At Gal. 4.3
NRSV translates 'we were enslaved to the elemental spirits of the
world', with a footnote 'Or *the rudiments*'. Similarly at 4.9 it has 'how
can you turn back again to the weak and beggarly elemental spirits?',
again with a footnote: 'Or *beggarly rudiments*'. Here and at v. 20
below it has 'the elemental spirits of the universe', with the
alternative 'Or *the rudiments of the world*'.[11] The form of words is

[9] 'Was mit "*Stoicheia* des Kosmos" gemeint ist, gehört zu den umstrittensten Fragen
der Kolosserforschung' (Standhartinger, *Studien*, 19; see her discussion and references
there). The older literature is listed in BAGD and *TWNT*. Cf. also W. Foerster, 'Die
Irrlehrer des Kolosserbriefes'; E. Schweizer, 'Slaves of the Elements'; Dunn, 'The
Colossian Philosophy'; Arnold, *Syncretism*, 158–94; and 'Returning to the Domain of
the Powers'; also Hübner's excursus, 76–79. For the elements of the cosmos in
contemporary philosophy cf. van Kooten, *Cosmic Christology*, index p. 338, and for
this section of the letter (2. 8—3: 4) pp. 129–35. Cf. p. 49 n. 98 above.

[10] It may be noted that Philo, as in the example quoted, and others frequently
associate sun, moon and the other planets with the 'elements', but these are not
themselves described as στοιχεῖα until a later period.

[11] Barclay (*Colossians and Philemon*, 51) writes: 'As the alternative translations
indicate, the Greek phrase used here, *ta stoicheia tou kosmou*, is open to a range of
interpretations, and has been the topic of scholarly debate for decades. But whose
terminology is this anyway? It is almost universally assumed by scholars that this
phrase takes us straight to the language of the "heresy", so that one may immediately
debate what kind of "elements" were meant and what sort of fear or veneration they
elicited in the "heresy". But the alternative should be seriously considered (it was once
argued very effectively by Ernst Percy): that *ta stoicheia tou kosmou* is a polemical
phrase coined by our author (or borrowed from Gal. 4: 3, 9), which *caricatures* the
"heresy" as enslavement to physical or cosmological "elements" (e.g. in rules
concerning things which may not be touched or eaten), but hardly reflects its own
view of the matter, let alone its precise terminology. This is a prime case where we have
to assess whether the clues we are following are those left by the "heresy" itself or by
the author's (polemical) representation of it.'

identical, but that does not signify that the meaning is the same or, as
Delling observes (685 n. 102), that the same false teaching is in view.

Gal 4.8 speaks of the readers being formerly enslaved 'to beings
that by nature are not gods', and it is then natural enough to identify
the 'elements' in 4.9 as elemental beings or heavenly bodies (cf.
BAGD §4),[12] but as Moule observes (91, commenting on Col.; cf. his
whole note, 90–93) the evidence for this sense of the word is 'in all
determinable cases' later than the NT. As for Col., Lightfoot already
notes that several early Fathers took it in this sense, but singles out
Clement of Alexandria and Tertullian as giving the correct interpretation (246; cf. also his commentary on Gal. (1890), 167): στοιχειω-
τικήν τινα οὖσαν [i.e. elementary] καὶ προπαιδείαν τῆς ἀληθείας
(Clement); *non secundum caelum et terram dicens, sed secundum literas
seculares* (Tertullian). 'In Col ii. 8 the στοιχεῖα τοῦ κόσμου are the
rudimentary religious ideas of philosophy and "vain deceit and the
tradition of men", the preceding language being sufficient to justify
the use of the word in its educational sense' (Knox, *PCJ* 114).[13]

It would not be difficult to go from the assumption that the reference
is to elemental *spirits* to the inference that they are hostile, and so on to
the further conclusion that here we have to deal with the Gnostic
Demiurge and his archons, but this is to make several deductions which
are not at all well based. It is by no means certain that the στοιχεῖα are
to be identified, without further ado, with hostile powers, and a direct
equation of the στοιχεῖα with archons (or angels) is too simplistic.[14]
We must beware of reading back ideas from a later period which may
not have been present to the mind of our author. The primary reference
of this term is either to elements of learning, the fundamental
principles, or to the elemental substances of Empedoclean theory.

This is not to deny that people in the ancient world believed in alien
forces, hostile powers who had to be propitiated. We need only think
of the classic passage in Eph. 6.12: 'our struggle is not against enemies

[12] Cf. K. L. Gaca (*JTS* 53 (2002), 42 n. 39): 'In Hellenistic philosophy, such as
Stoicism, the elemental principles (στοιχεῖα) are the divinely inspirited physical
elements that constitute the world, such as air and fire. In the broader religious thought
of this period, the elements as divine forces were also believed to be powers holding
sway over human lives, such as the zodiac forces. Paul (Gal 4:3, cf. Col 2:8, 20) harbors
a strong hostility to them. As H. D. Betz observes, Paul regards the στοιχεῖα as
"demonic forces which constitute and control 'this evil aeon'" and oppress human
beings unless Christ liberates and saves them.'

[13] But at *PCG* 108 Knox identifies the elements as 'the material world, which in
virtue of its material character was subject to the power of the stars under which it lay'.

[14] Cf. M. D. Goulder ('Colossians and Barbelo', 616): 'We must think it possible that
the Colossian opposition saw the heavenly powers as aeons who were symbolised by
the alphabet, and so could be spoken of as the Universal Letters; they may, of course,
also have been thought to have inhabited the stars.' This shows very neatly how the
later understanding could have developed, but it is by no means clear that this
development had already taken place in the time of Paul. Lohse (99) writes, 'the
context of Col 2 compellingly demands the identification "elements of the universe"
(στοιχεῖα τοῦ κόσμου) = "powers and principalities" (ἀρχαὶ καὶ ἐξουσίαι) = "angels"
(ἄγγελοι).' See his whole discussion, 96–99; but does our author necessarily use the
phrase he has borrowed from Gal. in the same sense as Paul originally used it?

of blood and flesh, but against the rulers [τὰς ἀρχάς], against the authorities [τὰς ἐξουσίας], against the cosmic powers of this present darkness, against the spiritual forces of evil in the heavenly places'. The terms used here are ἀρχαί and ἐξουσίαι, but not στοιχεία.[15]

καὶ οὐ κατὰ Χριστόν These words set out the final criterion by which, in Paul's eyes and those of his disciples, any philosophy or system of belief, or any code of conduct, must be judged: if it is not 'in accordance with Christ', he will have none of it. 'Over against the fear of the Colossian Christians that the *stoicheia* must be placated even by Christians, the author of the Epistle to the Colossians insists that there is no dimension of the human condition which has not already been dealt with decisively in the event of Christ. Consequently, he explicates a christological hymn in such a way as to show that believers do not live in a world whose hostility outruns Christ's capacity to deliver them' (L. E. Keck, *NTS* 32 (1986), 364f.).[16] The following verses present what J. C. O'Neill calls 'the second great Christological passage in Colossians' ('Source', 95–99).

9. ὅτι ἐν αὐτῷ κατοικεῖ πᾶν τὸ πλήρωμα τῆς θεότητος σωματικῶς This verse quite clearly refers back to the 'hymn' at 1.19 (ἐν αὐτῷ εὐδόκησεν πᾶν τὸ πλήρωμα κατοικῆσαι), with the addition of σωματικῶς, 'in bodily form', quite emphatic from its position.[17] As Lightfoot notes (247), the noun θεότης ('deity', BAGD 358) occurs only here in the NT, while the similar but quite distinct word θειότης ('divinity', BAGD 354) appears only at Rom. 1.20; to explain the difference, commentators frequently quote Bengel: *non modo divinae virtutes, sed ipsa divina natura*, 'not just the divine virtues, but the divine nature itself'.[18]

One possible objection is that the verb κατοικεῖ here is in the present tense, which as Moule (93) says 'is not easy to treat as a reference to a past event in history'. The thought that most obviously and naturally comes to mind is of the incarnation, but that belongs to the past; a present tense refers to what is happening now. Moule

---

[15] Aletti (167) sums up his discussion of the phrase in Col. (164–67) with the words: 'Le contexte interdit donc qu'on identifie les στοιχεία τοῦ κόσμου avec les ἀρχαὶ καὶ ἐξουσίαι.'

[16] Cf. Koester, *Trajectories*, 147: 'The Christian's task is not to revere powers beyond and above time and history through the observance of their rules' (citing Gal. 4.10, with reference to Col. 2.8, 16ff. in footnote).

[17] For other interpretations suggested for this word, cf. Moule, 92–94; Aletti, 168–69; Hübner, 79–80. It appears only here in the New Testament.

[18] 'Theodoret closes his comment on Col 2[19] lwith the words θεὸς γάρ ἐστι καὶ ἄνθρωπος, καὶ τὸ ὁρώμενον τοῦτο πᾶσαν ἔχει ἡνωμένην τοῦ μονογενοῦς τὴν θεότητα, and he would hardly have thus expressed himself, until the progress of the Nestorian controversy had led the more moderate Antiochenes about A.D. 432 to adopt the terminology of the ἕνωσις as a definite guarantee of their orthodoxy' (C. H. Turner, *HDB* v. 517: Theodoret's commentary on Paul was written between 429 and 438, but this point reduces the interval by some years). Cf. also *Rheginus* (NHC I 4, 44.21–33): 'The Son of God, Rheginus, was Son of Man. He embraced them both, possessing the humanity and the divinity, so that on the one hand he might vanquish death through his being the Son of God, and that on the other through the Son of Man the restoration to the Pleroma might occur' (see *NHTB* 42–43).

asks, 'Is it possible that it is used here as a Greek perfect tense is
normally used—to represent the continuance in the present of some
state begun in the past?' This may be difficult to accept from a
grammatical point of view, but there can surely be no doubt of the
validity of Moule's reconstruction: 'the totality of deity lives in him—
as it was embodied in him at the incarnation'. It is the same Jesus,
crucified and buried but risen again, and now alive for evermore as
Christ the Lord, in whom the totality resides.[19]

This verse is frequently echoed or alluded to in the Nag Hammadi texts: e.g. *Tract.
Trip.* (NHC I 5) 116.28–30: 'The saviour was an image of the unitary one, he who is the
Totality in bodily form'; *Apoc. John* (NHC II 1) 14.21–24: 'the image of the invisible
one who is the Father of the all, through whom everything came into being, the first
Man. For he revealed his likeness in a human form';[20] *Val. Exp.* (NHC XI 2) 33.30–32:
'her own Son, whose alone is the fullness of divinity'.[21] An echo of Col. 1.15 (image)
can also be seen in two of these passages.

**10. καὶ ἐστὲ ἐν αὐτῷ πεπληρωμένοι, ὅς[22] ἐστιν ἡ κεφαλὴ πάσης
ἀρχῆς καὶ ἐξουσίας** Cf. Eph. 1.21, ὑπεράνω πάσης ἀρχῆς καὶ
ἐξουσίας; 4.15 ὅς ἐστιν ἡ κεφαλή, Χριστός.[23] With its references to
Christ as ἡ κεφαλη (cf. 1.18) and to his supremacy over every ἀρχή
and ἐξουσία (cf. 1.16), this verse also clearly harks back to the
'hymn' in the first chapter. There are, however, differences, in that
here Christ is head not of the Church, as at 1.18, but of the cosmos:
κεφαλὴ πάσης ἀρχῆς καὶ ἐξουσίας.[24] These words serve to confirm

---

[19] For van Kooten (*Cosmic Christology*, 26) there is no reason to relate the
conception of the divine nature dwelling in Christ solely to the body of the incarnate
and/or resurrected Christ. He argues (23–27) for a cosmological interpretation of
σωματικῶς, as referring to 'the cosmic body which is constituted by the principles,
powers and other cosmic forces'.

[20] The other three versions omit some lines here (see Waldstein and Wisse (eds),
Apocryphon of John, 85).

[21] As noted above (p. 151 n. 65) this has been adapted to Valentinian theory. The
reference is to the restoration of Sophia in the Valentinian system, hence 'her own Son'
(see the note on this passage in Hedrick (ed.), *Nag Hammadi Codices XI, XII, XIII*,
163). The word σωμάτικως appears as a loan-word in line 33.

[22] P46 B D F G substitute the neuter ὅ for ὅς, taking the ἐν αὐτῷ to refer to τὸ
πλήρωμα in the preceding verse, but this according to Lightfoot (315) is 'plainly wrong'
(the result of 'a very common interchange', for which he lists five other instances in
Col. alone). The reference is quite clearly to Christ (ℵ A C and other mss read ὅς).

[23] For 'head' *NHTB* lists XI 1, 13.20–36; 16.28–31;17.30–31; 18.28–19.1; 21.33–34,
all from the same text, the *Interpretation of Knowledge*, which takes over just this word
and uses it in its own way. In view of the other references listed, it is by no means
certain that the word was taken from Col., but there are clear Pauline echoes (see the
notes by E. H. Pagels and J. D. Turner in Hedrick (ed.), *Nag Hammadi Codices XI,
XII, XIII*, 83, 86, 87). *Tri. Prot.* (XIII 1, 35.30–31) has Protennoia declare, 'I [am the
head of] the All. I exist before [the All, and] I am the All.' Unfortunately there is a
lacuna in the text, and the reading (adopted by both Schenke and Turner) cannot be
regarded as absolutely certain; and again other references are listed. The phrase 'the
head of every aeon' appears in all four versions of *Apoc. John* (see Waldstein and Wisse
(eds), *Apocryphon of John*, 28–29, line 16 = BG 26.9–10).

[24] We may compare other occurrences of these words: ἀρχή and ἐξουσία appear
together in the plural only in Eph. 3.10, 6.12 and Col. 1.16, 2.15 (but cf. Rom. 8.38); 1
Cor. 15.24 has the singular; at Luke 12.11 the reference is to human authorities. Cf.
pp. 141–42 above.

the view that the principalities and powers of the 'hymn' are not to be regarded as solely hostile powers: all things in heaven and on earth owe their existence to Christ, so that in all things he holds the first place. There has been disruption, and some of these powers have rebelled, but that does not detract from his supreme position: as v. 15 affirms, he has triumphed over all hostile powers.

Further, the perfect participle πεπληρωμένοι presents a clear play on words with πλήρωμα in 1.19 and 2.9 above. As Moule (94) notes, this phrase 'is clearly an attack on the mistake evidently current at Colossae, of supposing that "completeness" could not be found through Christ alone, but must be sought by additional religious rites and beliefs' (cf. W. L. Knox's reconstruction, quoted at p. 48 above; Moule cites Rom. 8.32 as saying much the same thing in different words). Lightfoot claims that ἐστέ should be separated from the following participle, comparing John 17.21; Acts 17.28, but most recent commentators take them together as a periphrastic perfect. This could be of some significance since, as Dunn observes (153), the tense 'indicates a state of fullness accomplished in the past and sustained since then'; he adds 'in receiving the tradition of Jesus as Christ and Lord and believing in him (2:5-7), the Colossian Christians already had all that is necessary for fullness of life, unrestricted access to the divine power that will shape them, too, into the divine image (3:10)'. It may be that our author here goes beyond Paul's teaching, in that he seems to think of his readers as already risen with Christ (cf. 3.1), whereas Paul always makes a distinction between the 'already' and the 'not yet' (cf. Phil. 3.12, οὐχ ὅτι ἤδη ἔλαβον ἢ ἤδη τετελείωμαι, διώκω δὲ εἰ καὶ καταλάβω, ἐφ'ᾧ καὶ κατελήμφθην ὑπὸ Χριστοῦ Ἰησοῦ).[25]

However, even if he does go beyond Paul, he is not far on the other side of the line: it would probably be wrong to accuse him of the fault of Hymenaeus and Philetus (2 Tim. 2.17–18). As to the 'fulfilment', Lightfoot aptly quotes John 1.16: ἐκ τοῦ πληρώματος αὐτοῦ ἡμεῖς πάντες ἐλάβομεν.

ἀρχή and ἐξουσία appear as loan-words in the Nag Hammadi *Melchizedek* (NHC IX 1, 2.5–11; Pearson (ed.), *Nag Hammadi Codices IX and X*, 45; BCNH edn (2001), 67): 'Death will [tremble] and be angry, not only he himself, but also his [fellow] world-rulers, and archons [and] the principalities (ἀρχή) and the authorities (ἐξουσία), the female gods and the male gods.' For another version of Christ's descent into hell, with no reference to Col. but aptly quoting Ps. 24, see the *Gospel of Nicodemus* (Schneemelcher, *NT Apocrypha*, i. 521ff.; Elliott, *The Apocryphal NT*, 185ff.).

11. ἐν ᾧ καὶ περιετμήθητε περιτομῇ ἀχειροποιήτῳ ἐν τῇ ἀπεκδύσει τοῦ σώματος τῆς σαρκός, ἐν τῇ περιτομῇ τοῦ Χριστοῦ Circumcision (περιτομή: BAGD 652; *TWNT* vi. 72–83) is

<hr />

[25] Cf. Cranfield, *Epistle to the Romans*, on Romans 6.1–14, also his articles 'Dying with Christ' and 'Romans 6.1-14 Revisited': Paul speaks of dying and rising with Christ in four different senses, and it is not by any means certain that even Col. 3.1 is un-Pauline.

often mentioned in Greek and especially Roman authors as one of the characteristic distinguishing marks of the Jews, although it was practised also by other peoples (cf. T. Reinach, *Textes d'auteurs grecs et romains relatifs au Judaïsme* (1895),[26] index, *s.v.* 'Circoncision'; Schürer, i. 537–40; iii. 615). It was the demand of the Judaizers in Galatia that Gentiles should accept the full rigour of the Law, including circumcision, that aroused Paul's wrath: 'I, Paul, am telling you that if you let yourselves be circumcised, Christ will be of no benefit to you. Once again I testify to every man who lets himself be circumcised that he is obliged to obey the entire law. You who want to be justified by the law have cut yourselves off from Christ; you have fallen away from grace' (Gal. 5.2–4 NRSV). At Gal. 5.12 he goes so far as to write, 'I wish those who unsettle you would castrate themselves!'

In the light of this and similar passages in which Paul flatly rejects any suggestion that his Gentile converts should undergo circumcision, it is at first sight surprising to find the rite introduced here as something that has been undergone by the Colossians;[27] but this is to overlook the word ἀχειροποιήτῳ, 'not made with hands'. This word with its opposite, χειροποίητος, appears in Mark 14.58, where the false witnesses claim to have heard Jesus say, 'I will destroy this temple made with hands, and in three days I will build another not made with hands'. Acts (7.48; 17.24) denies that God dwells in temples 'built with hands'; at Heb. 9.11, 24 the heavenly sanctuary is οὐ χειροποίητος; 2 Cor. 5.1 speaks of 'a house not made with hands, eternal in the heavens'. Such passages clearly show the contrast: χειροποίητος refers to what belongs to this world, the work of human hands and therefore transitory, even fleshly (cf. Eph. 2.11, ὑμεῖς τὰ ἔθνη ἐν σαρκί, οἱ λεγόμενοι ἀκροβυστία ὑπὸ τῆς λεγομένης περιτομῆς ἐν σαρκὶ χειροποιήτου[28]), whereas ἀχειροποιήτος refers to what is spiritual and heavenly.[29] In fact, Paul takes over the Jewish rite, and gives it a new interpretation: at Rom. 2.28–29 he says that true circumcision is not something external and

[26] This book is now somewhat dated. For a more modern collection see M. Stern, *Greek and Latin Authors on Jews and Judaism*, 3 vols (1974, 1980, 1984).

[27] This difference between Col. and Gal. must surely tell against any suggestion that the 'false teachers' in Colossae were Judaizers like those opposed in Gal. Discussing Col. in Evans and Hagner (eds), *Anti-Semitism and Early Christianity*, J. D. G. Dunn concludes (156) that 'the simple thesis of an anti-Jewish polemic is hardly adequate to reflect the complexity of the situation out of which and for which Colossians was written'. For 'Paul's Quarrel with Judaism' cf. D. A. Hagner in the same volume, 128–50.

[28] Cf. Jervell, *NTS* 32 (1986), 389 (writing of Col.): 'Die Beschneidung ist nunmehr ein Ausdruck für die Taufe, 2.11-12, obwohl der jüdische Begriff vom Unbeschnittensein, *akrobustia*, als Kennzeichen des heidnischen Lebens gebraucht wird, 2.13.'

[29] Lohse (102) notes that in LXX χειροποίητος is used for the graven images which pagans made for themselves, and therefore has 'fundamentally negative connotations'.

physical, but a matter of the heart, spiritual and not literal.[30] At Phil. 3.3 he writes ἡμεῖς γάρ ἐσμεν ἡ περιτομή, οἱ πνεύματι θεοῦ λατρεύοντες καὶ καυχώμενοι ἐν Χριστῷ Ἰησοῦ καὶ οὐκ ἐν σαρκὶ πεποιθότες. The fleshly rite is thus not ultimate, but only points to the true reality, circumcision of the heart (cf. Deut. 10.16; 30.6; Jer. 4.4; 9.23–26 etc.; see Barclay, 'Paul and Philo', 551ff.).[31]

The Colossians, then, have undergone the true circumcision, explained in the following verse as their baptism. In the present verse it is defined as ἐν τῇ ἀπεκδύσει τοῦ σώματος τῆς σαρκος, ἐν τῇ περιτομῇ τοῦ Χριστοῦ, phrases which have given rise to some perplexity (cf. Moule, 94–96 for a variety of possible interpretations). ἀπέκδυσις is yet another of the hapax legomena in Col., and indeed according to BAGD (83; cf. TWNT ii. 321) is 'found nowhere independent of Paul'. Like the cognate verb ἀπεκδύομαι, which appears at 2.15 and 3.9, it refers to the stripping off of clothes, and is here used metaphorically of stripping off the body of the flesh. This might seem at first sight to suggest the Gnostic idea of the ultimate deliverance of the soul from its prison in the body,[32] but for one thing that takes place only after death.[33] At v. 15, the verb is used of Christ 'divesting himself' of the rulers (see on that verse), while 3.9 refers to

[30] For this passage see J. M. G. Barclay, 'Paul and Philo on Circumcision: Romans 2.25-29 in Social and Cultural Context', NTS 44 (1998), 536–56. Cf. the Gospel of Thomas, logion 53 (NHC II 2, 42.18–23): 'His disciples said to him, "Is circumcision profitable or not?" He said to them, "If it were profitable, their father would beget them circumcised from their mother. But the true circumcision in spirit has become profitable in every way"' (tr. A. Guillaumont et al. (1959); cf. A. Marjanen in Uro (ed.), Thomas at the Crossroads, 178–80). For references to circumcision in the Nag Hammadi texts cf. Siegert, Nag Hammadi Register, 81, s.v. SBBE. On the renunciation of circumcision in early Christianity see F. W. Horn, NTS 42 (1996), 479–505.

[31] Cf. Epiphanius. Pan. viii. 6.7: ἐκεῖ γὰρ περιτομὴ σαρκική, ὑπηρετήσασα χρόνῳ ἕως τῆς μεγάλης περιτομῆς, τουτέστι τοῦ βαπτίσματος τοῦ περιτέμνοντος ἡμᾶς ἀπὸ ἁμαρτημάτων καὶ σφραγίσαντος ἡμᾶς εἰς ὄνομα θεοῦ ('The Law provides for physical circumcision. This did temporary duty until the great circumcision, baptism, which cuts us off from our sins and has marked us in the name of God'; tr. F. Williams (1987), 26); also Pan. xxx. 26.8–27.8; 34.1–2 (on the circumcision of Christ and its significance; Williams, 142–43; 150–52), xxx. 33.3 (other peoples too have circumcision; Williams, 150).

[32] Cf. the Gospel of Philip (NHC II 3) 82.26–29: 'When Abraham [. . .] that he was to see what he was to see, he circumcised the flesh of uncircumcision [ἀκροβυστία, the foreskin, here used as a loan-word], teaching us that it is fitting to destroy the flesh' (see Wilson, The Gospel of Philip, 184ff.; W. W. Isenberg, in Layton (ed.), Nag Hammadi Codex II 2–7 (1989), 207). On the circumcision of Abraham, cf. Epiphanius. Pan. iv. 1.1–3; viii. 4.1–2 and see the index to Williams' translation s.v. 'Abraham, circumcision'. Test. Truth (NHC IX 3, 36.29–37.5) reads: '[Do not] expect, therefore, [the] carnal resurrection, which [is] destruction, [and they are not] [stripped] of [it (the flesh) who] err in [expecting] a [resurrection] that is empty.' In a footnote Pearson comments, 'To be "stripped" of the flesh is the eschatological goal of the gnostic, and of Platonically-oriented religion in general' (Codices IX and X, 138; cf. further his references).

[33] Lohse (102) refers to the initiation rites of the mystery cults, e.g. as described by Apuleius, and adds that in Hellenistic circles 'it was a matter of course that the body, which had been formed from perishable material, must remain on earth when the soul rose to God', citing Philo, Leg. All. ii.55: ἡ φιλόθεος ψυχὴ ἐκδῦσα τὸ σῶμα καὶ τὰ τουτῷ φίλα καὶ μακρὰν ἔξω φυγοῦσα ἀπὸ τούτων πῆξιν καὶ βεβαίωσιν καὶ ἱδρυσιν ἐν τοῖς τελείοις ἀρετῆς δόγμασι λαμβάνει ('the soul that loves God, having stripped off

stripping off the old man with his practices and putting on the new; neither of which is particularly helpful here.[34] We must ask: whose body of the flesh? And what is the connection between these and the following words, with their reference to 'the circumcision of Christ'?

The phrase τὸ σῶμα τῆς σαρκός is comparatively rare, although it appears in Sir. 23.17; *1 En.* 102.4–5, and W. D. Davies notes an exact parallel in the Qumran Habakkuk commentary (*Christian Origins*, 157). It is the more striking that it occurs twice in Col. (cf. 1.22, ἐν τῷ σώματι τῆς σαρκὸς αὐτοῦ, on which see p. 162 above), and nowhere else in the Pauline corpus.[35] We have already seen several references back to the first chapter, and this might conceivably be another.

For Lightfoot (228, 250) the phrase is used at these two points with a different emphasis and meaning: at 1.22 the words τῆς σαρκὸς αὐτοῦ are added to distinguish the natural body of Christ from the mystical body mentioned just above in v. 18, whereas here the phrase means the fleshly body, 'the body with all its corrupt and carnal affections'. Similarly Davies (157) sees an exact parallel to the Habakkuk commentary phrase in 1.22, but says that here the phrase 'is made to refer to man's lower nature which the Christian has put off in Christian "circumcision"'. For Lohse (102), 'The phrase "body of flesh" (σῶμα τῆς σαρκός) characterizes the human body in its earthly frailty wherein it is subject to suffering, death and dissolution. It must be stripped off if the devotee wants to experience the divinizing vision and be filled with divine power' (this leads naturally to his comparison with the initiation rites of the mystery cults, but cf. Wedderburn, cited in n. 33 above).

This line of interpretation assumes that the phrase goes along with and explains the preceding περιετμήθητε περιτομῇ ἀχειροποιήτῳ: the Colossians have been 'circumcised' by the stripping off of their fleshly body; but as already noted this properly takes place only at death. The initiate in the mystery religions underwent a kind of symbolic anticipation in the initiation rites, but we cannot simply assume that our author is thinking in the same kind of way. Further, such an interpretation does not match very well with the following ἐν τῇ περιτομῇ τοῦ Χριστοῦ, which has to be taken to mean 'a

---

the body and the things dear to it and fled far away from these, receives a fixed and assured settlement in the perfect ordinances of virtue'). Despite certain affinities with Gnosticism, Philo is not to be considered a Gnostic in the strict sense (see above, p. 39 n. 76): the 'Gnostic thinking' current in the first century had not yet developed into the full-scale Gnosticism of the second. On Paul and the mysteries, cf. Wedderburn, *Baptism and Resurrection*; he concludes (396): 'we can no longer interpret either in the light of the other: the mysteries were not saying the same thing as Paul, nor was Paul borrowing his ideas from the mysteries'.

[34] Things become clearer later, when the pieces of the mosaic fall into place. See p. 250 below.

[35] Some scribes evidently felt difficulty with these words: ℵ² D¹ and other mss insert τῶν ἁμαρτίων (cf. Rom. 6.6; BAGD 43, §3 adds 'Col 2:11 t.r.' in brackets). Lightfoot (250) considers this 'clearly a gloss'. These two words are omitted by P⁴⁶ ℵ* A B C D* *et al.*

Christian circumcision'.[36] It is surely more natural to think of a circumcision undergone by Christ, and that in the light of 1.22 suggests that ἡ περιτομὴ τοῦ Χριστοῦ here is a metaphor for the death of Christ (cf. Dunn, 157: 'an adaptation of the description of physical circumcision ... applied to Jesus' death in deliberate echo of 1:22'). The chief objection to this interpretation is the absence of the αὐτοῦ which in 1.22 makes it clear that the reference is to the fleshly body of Christ, but Moule (95) says, 'conceivably the identification of the baptized with Christ is regarded as so close as to render a specifying pronoun out of place'.

As Moule (94) observes, the main sense of vv. 11–12 is clear: 'if it is asked *how* this "completeness", which has been brought within human range by the incarnation, is appropriated, the answer is that in Christian Baptism (a rite deeper and greater than Jewish circumcision, whatever parallels may exist between the two) the believer is identified, by faith, with Christ in his obedient death and his triumphant resurrection'. The difficulties emerge when we endeavour to translate what our author has written in terms of what he so clearly means.

On 2.11–3.4 cf. Larsson, *Christus als Vorbild*, 80–92. See further Davies, *Christian Origins and Judaism*, 156–62; G. Vermes, 'Baptism and Jewish Exegesis: New Light from Ancient Sources', *NTS* 4 (1957/58) 308–19; N. J. McEleney, 'Conversion, Circumcision and the Law', *NTS* 20 (1974), 319–41; Joel Marcus, 'The Circumcision and the Uncircumcision in Rome', *NTS* 35 (1989), 67–81; Yates, 'Colossians 2.15: Christ Triumphant', esp. 583ff.; F. W. Horn, 'Der Verzicht auf die Beschneidung im frühen Christentum', *NTS* 42 (1996), 479–505; J. D. G. Dunn, 'Who Did Paul Think He Was? A Study of Jewish-Christian Identity', *NTS* 45 (1999), 174–93, esp. 189f.

12. συνταφέντες αὐτῷ ἐν τῷ βαπτισμῷ, ἐν ᾧ καὶ συνηγέρθητε διὰ τῆς πίστεως τῆς ἐνεργείας τοῦ θεοῦ τοῦ ἐγείραντος αὐτὸν ἐκ νεκρῶν In the preceding verses we have seen a succession of occurrences of the phrase ἐν αὐτῷ (vv. 6, 7, 9, 10), followed in v. 11 by ἐν ᾧ, all clearly referring to Christ. It is very natural to take the latter phrase in our present verse as another in a sequence; so for example Dunn (145), who begins a new sentence here: 'having been buried with him in baptism. In whom also you were raised with him through faith in the effective working of God who raised him from the dead.'[37]

This, however, would leave συνταφέντες αὐτῷ ἐν τῷ βαπτισμῷ rather awkwardly tagged on to what precedes,[38] and moreover there is a certain incongruity in the thought of the readers being raised

[36] Lightfoot (249) writes: 'It is the circumcision not of Moses, or of the patriarchs, but of Christ', i.e. he is its author (cf. Aletti, 172: the phrase 'ne fait pas allusion à la mort du Christ, mais à la qualification christologique (et non patriarchale ou mosaïque) de la circoncision à laquelle le croyant a été soumis').

[37] Cf. Lohse, 104 n. 73 and Dunn's discussion (160: he notes that this view is the majority view in commentaries written in English, with a couple of exceptions, but that elsewhere opinion is strongly against it, again with exceptions).

[38] Dunn (159) rightly notes that the passage is not intended as an exposition of baptism: '"in baptism" is mentioned almost incidentally in a sequence of vigorous metaphors'.

both 'in him' (ἐν ᾧ) and 'with him' (σὺν αὐτῷ, implied by the συν- in the verb συνηγέρθητε). It is therefore better to take the relative here as referring back to the immediately preceding noun, βαπτισμῷ. More important is the fact that this linking of resurrection with baptism seems to many to run contrary to Paul's usage elsewhere. For the last five words cf. Rom. 4.24; 8.11; 10.9; 2 Cor. 4.14; Gal. 1.1; Eph. 1.20; 1 Pet. 1.21. The raising of believers is mentioned in only two of these verses, in both cases in the future: Rom. 8.11 (ζῳοποιήσει) and 2 Cor. 4.14 (ἐγερεῖ). Similarly, in the only other occurrence of the verb συνθάπτω the reference to the believers is in the future: Rom. 6.4, συνετάφημεν οὖν αὐτῷ διὰ τοῦ βαπτίσματος εἰς τὸν θάνατον, ἵνα ὥσπερ ἠγέρθη Χριστὸς ἐκ νεκρῶν διὰ τῆς δόξης τοῦ πατρός, οὕτως καὶ ἡμεῖς ἐν καινότητι ζωῆς περιπατήσωμεν.[39] Here in contrast we have the aorist passive συνηγέρθητε. Moule (97) notes (with Masson) that 'Colossians and Ephesians alone speak of the resurrection of believers as a *fait accompli*', and contrasts the future tense of Rom. 6.5 (εἰ γὰρ σύμφυτοι γεγόναμεν τῷ ὁμοιώματι τοῦ θάνατου αὐτοῦ, ἀλλὰ καὶ τῆς ἀναστάσεως ἐσόμεθα; cf. also Rom. 6.8). The verb συνεγείρω appears only in Eph. 2.6 (cf. Best, *Ephesians*, 217–23 and compare the usage); Col. 2.12, 3.1.

Cf. also *Rheginus* (NHC I 4, 45.24–46.2): 'Then indeed, as the apostle said, "We suffered with him, and we arose with him, and we went to heaven with him." Now if we are manifest in this world wearing him, we are that one's beams, and we are embraced by him until our setting, that is to say, our death in this life. We are drawn to heaven by him, like beams by the sun, not being restrained by anything. This is the spiritual resurrection which swallows up the psychic in the same way as the fleshly' (tr. M. L. Peel, in Attridge (ed.), *Nag Hammadi Codex I*, 151; notes in NHS 23, 162–67). Peel (NHS 23, 162) notes Col. 2.12–13 among the sources suggested for this passage,[40] but observes (163) that 'unlike many Gnostics who connected resurrection expectation with the present experience of baptism (e.g. Simon Magus in Irenaeus, *Haer.* 2.31.2; Ps.-Clem. *Hom.* 2.22.5; Menander in Irenaeus, *Haer.* 1.23.5; Justin, *1 Apol.* 1.26; Tertullian, *De res. mort.* 5; cf. *Gos.Phil.* 72.29–73.8), the author of *Treat. Res.* makes no mention of baptism whatsoever'. As noted above (p. 67), Peel considers this 'a non-literal mélange of Rom: 8.17 and Eph. 2.5–6.'

As Udo Schnelle observes, Paul takes a radical view of conversion.[41] The Christian has been delivered from the power of darkness (cf. 1.13), from thraldom to sin; he no longer belongs to the domain of sin. But Paul is realistic enough to be aware that this does not mean that a Christian can no longer sin: the temptations and the tribulations of this earthly life remain. Paul's constant challenge to

[39] Cf. Standhartinger, *Studien*, 138–40; she considers literary dependence of Col. 2.12f. on Rom. 6.4 unlikely (140).
[40] For the opening 'citation' Tröger (*Die Gnosis*, 107) compares Rom. 6.5 with Col. 2.12; 3.1; Eph. 2.6. Cf. also *NHTB* 44; the echo at *Gos. Phil.* 77.7–12 (ibid. 166) is more distant.
[41] 'Paulus denkt den Bruch mit der Vergangenheit radikal; die Glaubenden und Getauften sind dem Machbereich der Sünde entrissen und leben nun in der Gemeinde als einem sündenfreien Raum. ... Freiheit von der Sünde bedeutet bei Paulus nicht Abwesenheit von Fehlverhalten, sondern weitaus grundsätzlicher, daß Christen dem Bereich der Sünde nicht mehr gehören' ('Transformation', 66).

his readers is that they should live a life in conformity with the new order into which they have entered. The sixth chapter of Romans relentlessly drives home the message: those baptized into Christ were baptized into his death (v. 3), but if they have died with Christ they will also live with him (v. 8). 'So you also must consider yourselves dead to sin and alive to God in Christ Jesus. Therefore, do not let sin exercise dominion in your mortal bodies' (vv. 11–12). This theme of baptism into the death of Christ, with the hope and prospect of future resurrection with him, thus provides a powerful incentive for the conduct of life in the new order.

Attempts have been made to reconcile our author's treatment of this theme with what Paul says in his major letters, but the fact remains that he speaks of resurrection as well as of baptism as something in the past.[42] The best solution is probably that of Wedderburn (*Baptism and Resurrection*, 83), that a disciple of Paul, facing a different situation from that confronting Paul and seeking to emphasize the sufficiency and adequacy of the salvation brought by Christ over against tendencies to belittle his significance, sought to find an answer by stressing the completeness of what his readers had received in Christ: 'Drawing what so obviously seemed to be the corollary of Paul's statement that we died with Christ, namely that we also shared his resurrection, served a valuable purpose.'

This raising to new life is not the outcome of any mysterious rites or magical processes: it came about through faith in the effective working of God, who raised Christ from the dead (for ἐνέργεια see 1.29: the power of God that was at work in Paul's labours for the Church was also effective in the conversion and renewal of life for his readers).

The reading βαπτισμῷ is found in P[46] ℵ[2] B D* and other witnesses, the one occurrence of this word in the Pauline corpus. Elsewhere (Mark 7.4; Heb. 6.2; 9.10) this term is used of various kinds of washings, but not of baptism. The normal word for baptism is found in ℵ* A C D[2] and the Majority text (ἐν τῷ βαπτίσματι), but this may be influenced by scribal recollection of Rom. 6.4. Since βαπτισμῷ is not the normal word, it must rank as the *lectio difficilior* (cf. Aletti 172 n. 39) and hence have the preference, as more likely to have been changed (cf. Metzger, *Textual Commentary*, 623).

13. καὶ ὑμᾶς νεκροὺς ὄντας ἐν τοῖς παραπτώμασιν καὶ τῇ ἀκροβυστίᾳ τῆς σαρκὸς ὑμῶν, συνεζωοποίησεν ὑμᾶς σὺν αὐτῷ,

[42] 'The present nature of new life with Christ following on a past death with him is certainly indicated in the genuine Pauline letters (Rom 6.4, 10, 11, 13, 7.4; Gal 2.20; 2 Cor 4.10, 12; 5.17); there is no point in exhorting believers to live a new life if that life belongs only to the future. In Rom 6.1ff dying and rising with Christ is associated with baptism; baptism was a past fact for believers; it was inevitable that some who had been baptised should eventually come to think of their resurrection as past fact since they were already enjoying the new life that resurrection would bring; indeed we find that when the pastness of resurrection is first positively stated in Col 2.12 it is linked to baptism; A/Col may however have had some hesitation about this, since in 3.5 he writes of the new risen life as hidden with God. In Eph 2.6 there is no explicit reference to baptism and it is difficult to argue for an implicit one, since AE does not use the verbs denoting dying and being buried with Christ which are particularly linked with it in Rom 6' (Best, *Ephesians*, 218–19). Cf. *NTS* 9 (1962/63) 292 n. 1.

χαρισάμενος ἡμῖν πάντα τὰ παραπτώματα For the use of
ἀκροβυστία here cf. Eph. 2.11, οἱ λεγόμενοι ἀκροβυστία ὑπὸ τῆς
λεγομένης περιτομῆς; for the verse as a whole cf. Eph. 2.1, ὑμᾶς
ὄντας νεκρούς τοῖς παραπτώμασιν, followed by an anacoluthon (cf.
Best, *Ephesians*, 198f.) and resumed at v. 5, καὶ ὄντας ἡμᾶς νεκρούς
τοῖς παραπτώμασιν συνεζωοποίησεν τῷ Χριστῷ. Contrast Rom.
6.11, where the readers are enjoined to consider themselves νεκρούς
μὲν τῇ ἁμαρτίᾳ ζῶντας δὲ τῷ θεῷ ἐν Χριστῷ Ἰησοῦ. The word
νεκρός is used in its normal literal sense at 1.18; 2.12.

There are several minor variants in this verse, but only one that has any bearing on the
translation, the choice between first and second person pronouns after συνεζωοποίησεν: ἐν is omitted by ℵ* B L and several other mss, and this reading was adopted by
Nestle²⁵; NA²⁷, following P⁴⁶ ℵ¹ A C D *et al.*, reads ἐν, but in square brackets. A
second ἐν appears before τῇ ἀκροβυστίᾳ in D* F G vgᵐˢˢ, but is not strictly necessary.
P⁴⁶ B 33 and other witnesses read ἡμᾶς for ὑμᾶς after συνεζωοποίησεν, presumably to
agree with the following ἡμῖν. This pronoun is omitted by ℵ² D F G and other mss,
while the above text is found in ℵ* A C K L *et al.* Finally, ℵ² K* L P *et al.* read ὑμῖν for
ἡμῖν after χαρισάμενος, which brings all the pronouns into agreement, and may
therefore be a scribal correction. These pronouns are frequently interchanged by
scribes, but ἡμῶν appears to be firm at v. 14, which would seem to support the reading
ἡμῖν here. It is curious that in Eph. 2.5 the author resumes with a change from ὑμᾶς to
ἡμᾶς. If we read the first person plural, the author in each case is including himself and
other Christians along with the readers: all have received the benefit of God's
forgiveness.

This verse would seem to indicate that the community in Colossae
was mainly Gentile⁴³: it looks back to their pagan past, from a Jewish
point of view. ἀκροβυστία (BAGD 33; *TWNT* i. 226–27), which
occurs only in biblical and ecclesiastical Greek, means literally
'foreskin', but was also used figuratively for '*uncircumcision* as a state
of being' (BAGD §2, citing Rom. 2.25ff.; Gal. 5.6; 6.15), and as
abstract for concrete (§3) to mean 'heathenism, the Gentiles' (Rom.
3.30; 4.9; Col. 3.11, Eph. 2.11). In former days they had been dead,
νεκροί, not literally but figuratively, by reason of their transgressions
(ἐν τοῖς παραπτώμασιν: BAGD 621; *TWNT* vi. 170–73).⁴⁴ As
Gentiles who did not observe the Law they were, as Eph. 2.11–12
puts it, 'aliens from the commonwealth of Israel, and strangers to the
covenants of promise, having no hope and without God in the
world'. But now God has made them alive with Christ (συνεζωοποίησεν: BAGD 776; in the NT only here and at Eph. 2.5, and
elsewhere only in Christian writers); since σὺν αὐτῷ fairly obviously

⁴³ Davies (*Christian Origins*, 187) notes that Johannes Munck took 1.21, 24 and 2.13,
with other passages in the Pauline corpus, to show that Paul's letters point only to
Gentile readers. As noted in the Introduction (pp. 5–6, 8 above), there is little firm
evidence for Jews, or Jewish Christians, in Colossae itself, but it would seem unwise to
rule out entirely the possibility that there was a Jewish element in the Colossian church.
The congregation, however, was most probably predominantly Gentile.
⁴⁴ Wedderburn (*Baptism and Resurrection*, 63) notes that 'such a figurative use of
"death" and "dead" was found also in Greek (especially Stoic) philosophy and in
Hellenistic Judaism, where Philo speaks of the life of the wicked in estrangement from
God as true death, a death of the soul (as opposed to that of the body which is
liberation)' (references in his footnotes).

applies to Christ, it is necessary to supply a subject from τοῦ θεοῦ τοῦ ἐγείραντος αὐτόν in the preceding verse.

This raises questions with regard to the following verses: there is no problem about understanding God as the subject of συνεζωοποίησεν and the following participle χαρισάμενος, but in vv. 14 and 15 it would seem more natural to take Christ as the subject; yet there is no hint of a further change of subject. The alternatives are either to take God as the subject of the whole passage, as acting in and through Christ, or as Moule (100) puts it, to acknowledge 'an illogical transition from one to the other in the course of this section'. As he adds, 'This is in keeping with that identification between the activity of God and the activity of Christ which is a familiar feature of N.T. thought.'

χαρίζομαι (BAGD 876; *TWNT* ix. 388), a verb cognate with the noun χάρις (see p. 74 above), means basically to give freely or graciously, but here has the more specific meaning of forgiving: God has made the Colossians alive with Christ, forgiving them (and other Christians also: ἡμῖν; the change to the first person is perfectly natural) all their transgressions. Baptism means entrance into a new order, a new beginning and a fresh start: Paul's letters constantly bring out the ethical implications of the new life. By the grace of God the sins and transgressions of the past have been forgiven; it is for the Christian now to live accordingly, in a manner consistent with the new order into which he or she has entered, as the servant of Christ and no longer a slave to sin. At 3.13 this verb is used of Christians forgiving one another: καθὼς καὶ ὁ κύριος ἐχαρίσατο ὑμῖν, οὕτως καὶ ὑμεῖς (cf. Eph. 4.13; 2 Cor. 2.7).

14. ἐξαλείψας τὸ καθ' ἡμῶν χειρόγραφον τοῖς δόγμασιν ὃ ἦν ὑπεναντίον ἡμῖν, καὶ αὐτὸ ἦρκεν ἐκ τοῦ μέσου προσηλώσας αὐτὸ τῷ σταυρῷ[45] Cf. Eph. 2.15, τὸν νόμον τῶν ἐντολῶν ἐν δόγμασιν καταργήσας (the word δόγμα occurs in the Pauline corpus only in these two verses). This verse continues the theme of forgiveness: God has blotted out the bond that stood against us (cf. *Interp. Know.* (NHC XI 1, 14.31–33): 'And he removed the old bond of debt, the one of condemnation'). **ἐξαλείφω** means to wipe out or erase, or more generally to remove, destroy or obliterate 'in so far as the removal results from the *blotting out* of a written record' (BAGD 272). A **χειρόγραφον** (BAGD 880; *TWNT* ix. 424–25) is a written document, more specifically a bond of indebtedness; Moule (97) aptly cites Philem. 19 as an example of the form: ἐγὼ Παῦλος ἔγραψα τῇ ἐμῇ χειρί, ἐγὼ ἀποτίσω. M. R. James (*The Apocryphal NT*, 534 n. 1, on *Apoc. Paul* 17) quotes *Apoc. Zeph.*, where the same word is used for the document in the hands of the accusing angel when a soul is brought to judgement. That, however, may represent an adaptation to a different (and possibly later) set of associations;

---

[45] The history of the exegesis of this verse has been the subject of a dissertation: E. C. Best, 'An Historical Study of the Exegesis of Colossians 2, 14', (Rome, 1961; cited in Aletti, 176 n. 54; this is not the editor of the ICC volume on Ephesians).

the primary emphasis here is on the obligations which have been
incurred, and which have not been met. This word also is used only
here in the New Testament. Moule adds, 'This χειρόγραφον is
"against us" because we have manifestly failed to discharge its
obligations—no one felt this more keenly than Paul the Pharisee (cf.
Rom. vii. 16, 22, 23).'⁴⁶

The phrase τοῖς δόγμασιν is awkward and perplexing (cf. Moule,
98; Dunn, 165); it is omitted by one manuscript (1881, 14th c.), and
its omission is one of the rare conjectures noted (but not accepted) in
NA²⁷. Its occurrence in Eph. 2.15 presents no difficulty, since there
the reference is clearly to 'the law with its commandments and
ordinances' (NRSV; lit. 'the law of the commandments in ordinances'). Eph. also uses a different verb, καταργήσας, which further
complicates any question of relationships.

Lightfoot and others have explained the dative 'as governed by the
idea of γεγραμμένον involved in χειρόγραφον', but Moule (98)
observes, 'it has to be admitted that such a construction seems to be
unparalleled'. Nor is it any more satisfactory to explain it as an
instrumental or causal dative (for a range of suggestions cf. Aletti,
178f.). The simplest solution would seem to be to take it as qualifying
χειρόγραφον (Aletti, 178; cf. Dunn, 165): 'the bond with its decrees'.⁴⁷

The primary meaning of **δόγμα** in the New Testament (BAGD
201; *TWNT* ii. 233–35) is that of a decree or ordinance, e.g. of
imperial edicts in Luke 2.1; Acts 17.7; the other meaning, of a
religious or philosophical doctrine or dogma, does not appear. The
word is used in 3 Macc. 1.3 and in Philo (*Leg. All.* i.55; *Gig.* 52) and
Josephus (*C. Apion.* i.42) of the Law of Moses, and this with the
similar passage in Eph. suggests that the Law is somehow involved in
the background to this verse. This does not, however, justify our
assuming an explicit and direct reference to the Law here: the Greek
word νόμος never occurs in Col. It is different in Eph., where the use
of νόμος (even if only this once) and the context clearly point to the
Jewish Torah (Best, *Ephesians*, 259); but it is by no means certain
that we should interpret Col. in the light of Eph. when a closer
examination reveals differences as well as similarities. Here the
reference would appear to be somewhat wider: the cognate verb
δογματίζω appears in v. 20 in the sense of submitting to rules and
regulations (BAGD 201), and Aletti (179) plausibly suggests

⁴⁶ See further Lohse, 108; Aletti, 177–78; Dunn, 164; Arnold, *Syncretism*, 292–93.
⁴⁷ J. Luttenberger ('Der gekreuzigte Schuldschein') sees it as a *Schuldschein*, a
promissory note or IOU (with an example on p. 84 drawn from Deissmann), and
interprets the passage in the light of ancient practice regarding the discharge of debt. If
it was written on papyrus, the ink could be washed off (ἐξαλείφειν) when the debt was
discharged, leaving the former debtor with a clean sheet. On p. 95 Luttenberger refers
to the ὀφειλήματα of Matt. 6.12, immediately explained in the following verses as
παραπτώματα, the word used in Col. 2.13. Matthew here gives a literal rendering of an
Aramaic word, where Luke's ἁμαρτίας interprets for Gentile readers (cf. M. Black, *An
Aramaic Approach to the Gospels and Acts* (1967), 140).

submission to ascetic and cultic regulations (which might include prescriptions from the Mosaic law) intended to prepare those who wished to participate in the heavenly vision (cf. also Dunn, 165: 'although τὸ καθ᾽ἡμῶν χειρόγραφον itself cannot be identified with the law as such ... behind it lie the decrees of the law giving the χειρόγραφον its condemnatory force ... At all events, this probably alludes to the halakhic rulings about to be denounced in 2.16, 21-22, which includes talk of "judgement" (2.16) and uses the verbal equivalent (δογματίζω) in 2.20' (see further his references).

The χειρόγραφον was ὑπεναντίον ἡμῖν, opposed to us, hostile, another term not common in the New Testament (BAGD 838; the only other occurrence is at Heb. 10.27).[48] Now God has blotted it out (ἐξαλείψας), set it aside (ἦρκεν ἐκ τοῦ μέσου, lit. 'taken out of the midst'; αἴρω means to lift up, take away, remove; for this verse BAGD 24, §4 suggests *destroy*), indeed, in a daring metaphor, nailed it to the cross (Moule, 98 remarks, 'the metaphor is so violent as practically to rupture itself; but it opens a window into St Paul's thought about *how* Christ's death brings life to us').

Several of the Nag Hammadi parallels listed in *NHTB* focus on the word 'to nail', echoing προσηλώσας here (for which see BAGD 714). Thus *Gos. Eg.* (NHC III 64.3 = IV 75.18) speaks of the great Seth, through Jesus, nailing the powers of the thirteen aeons; later (III 65.18 = IV 77.15) it refers to Jesus 'who came and crucified that which is in [or: under] the law'. The closest echo (apart from *Interp. Know.*, already noted) is in *Gos. Truth* (NHC I 3, 20.23–27): 'For this reason Jesus appeared; he put on that book; he was nailed to a tree; he published the edict of the Father on the cross.'

K. Grobel (*The Gospel of Truth*, (1960), 67), writes 'There can be little doubt but that the Colossian passage inspired this one, but it did so in an author who dared to vary images.' Here indeed the images are reversed: 'In Colossians the writing is "*against* us" and is "expunged" by Christ, while here it is (implicitly) *for* us and is validated by being fastened to the cross.' Possibly the author was influenced by recollection of the indictment set over the head of the condemned man (Mark 15.26), a point which some have sought to use in the interpretation of the present verse. Cf. also the notes by H. W. Attridge and G. W. MacRae in NHS 23, 59–60.

One *NHTB* reference provides a cautionary tale of the danger of working on the basis of words in English: *NHTB* 405 adduces Col. 2.13–15 as a parallel for *Tri. Prot.* 41.4–11: 'Every bond I loosed from you, and the chains of the Demons of the underworld, I broke, these things which are bound on my members, restraining them. And the high walls of darkness I overthrew, and the secure gates of those pitiless ones I broke, and I smashed their bars.' Evidently the compilers were misled by the word 'bond', which in *Tri.Prot.* is not a χειρόγραφον but a chain or fetter, as the following clause makes clear. A better parallel for this would be the *Gospel of Nicodemus*, cited above, p. 200. J. D. Turner (in Hedrick (ed.), *Nag Hammadi Codices XI, XII, XIII*, 444) refers to 'the Nekyia literature from Homer onward', supplying references to Homer, Hesiod and Virgil among others.

---

[48] Aletti (176 and n. 55) remarks on the number of hapax legomena in vv. 14–15: (1) for the NT, χειρόγραφον and the verbs προσηλοῦν and ἀπεκδύεσθαὶ (2) for the Pauline corpus, ὑπεναντίος and the verbs ἐξαλείφειν and δειγματίζειν. To these we may add συλαγωγεῖν and φιλοσοφία in v. 8, σωματικῶς in v. 9, and ἀπέκδυσις in v. 11 (all for the NT); συνεγείρειν (v. 12) appears only in Eph. and Col., δόγμα only in Eph. and Col. in the Pauline corpus. There are still eight NT hapaxes to come before the end of the chapter, and six words which do not appear elsewhere in the Pauline corpus (excluding Hebrews).

15. ἀπεκδυσάμενος τὰς ἀρχὰς καὶ τὰς ἐξουσίας ἐδειγμάτισεν ἐν παρρησίᾳ, θριαμβεύσας αὐτοὺς ἐν αὐτῷ 'Colossians 2.15 is a notoriously difficult verse both to translate and to interpret' (Yates, 'Colossians 2.15', 573, who after detailed discussion offers his own translation (591): 'Having stripped himself in death, He boldly made an open display of the angelic powers, leading them in triumphal (festal) procession on the cross.' See further Lightfoot, 255–58; Moule, 99–102; Lohse, 111–13; Aletti, 181–90; Dunn, 166–70; Carr, *Angels and Principalities*, 58–66; Wedderburn, 'Theology', 42–48; Arnold, *Syncretism*, 277–87, esp. 282f.; Standhartinger, *Studien*, 212–18 and index).

We may begin with the last word in the verse, which could be either masculine or neuter, i.e. referring either to Christ or to τῷ σταυρῷ in v. 14. From a purely grammatical point of view, there is no nominative in these three verses to provide a subject for the various verbs and participles. We have no means of determining whether our author thought of God or of Christ as the agent, although of course it is ultimately God who is at work in the whole process. In the translation at the head of this section, as already noted (p. 208), 'God' has been supplied from τοῦ θεοῦ τοῦ ἐγείραντος αὐτόν as the subject of συνεζωοποίησεν and the following participle χαρισάμενος in v. 13, but while there is no indication of a change of subject, it does seem more natural to think of Christ as the subject in vv. 14 and 15.

There are, then, two alternatives. One is to think of God as the subject in all three verses, in which case the αὐτῷ should probably be taken as masculine, and translated 'in him'. In support of this view it may be added that this would make the phrase one more in a sequence of 'in him, in whom' phrases which recur throughout the passage. On the other hand, if Christ is the subject in vv. 14 and 15, it would seem more appropriate to take the αὐτῷ as neuter and refer it to Christ's triumph on the cross. Our author, of course, never imagined that centuries later his words would be subjected to detailed scrutiny by modern scholars intent on elucidating his grammar and reconciling what he actually writes with what he clearly means to say.

We have already met with the noun ἀπέκδυσις in v. 11. Now we have the cognate verb **ἀπεκδύεσθαι** (BAGD 83), another word which occurs only in Col. It appears at 3.9, with reference to stripping off the old man and putting on the new, but in our present verse this sense (BAGD §1) has presented problems to some commentators, particularly with the following accusatives **τὰς ἀρχὰς καὶ τὰς ἐξουσίας**. How could Christ 'strip off' these powers? How did he come to be clothed with them in the first place? To meet this problem, some (cf. the NRSV text; further references in Dunn, 167) have followed BAGD (§2) in rendering this verb as 'disarm'. Wedderburn, however, ('Theology', 45) notes that both verb and noun do not seem to appear in Greek literature before Col., and pertinently asks, 'how likely is it that the author would introduce a pair of seeming new coinages, but in two different senses?'

One possible solution might be to take ἀπεκδυσάμενος, with Yates (and the Latin fathers; cf. Lightfoot, 256), as an independent participle, harking back to ἀπέκδυσις above, and the two following accusatives as governed only by ἐδειγμάτισεν. That course has been followed in the translation above, although it has to be said that many commentators prefer to take the accusatives with ἀπεκδυσά-μενος, and wrestle with the problems that result (the word order certainly suggests that the accusatives are governed by both verbs).[49]

The *Gospel of Truth* (NHC I 3, 20.28–34, immediately following the lines quoted above) contains the words 'He draws himself down to death though life eternal clothes him. Having stripped himself of the perishable rags, he put on imperishability, which no one can possibly take away from him.' The echo here is not of Col. but of 1 Cor. 15.53–54; 2 Cor. 5.2–4 (see *NHTB* 28–29 for these and other NT references). The *Apocryphon of James* (NHC I 2, 14.35–36) has Jesus say, 'from this moment on I shall strip myself that I may clothe myself'.

These and similar passages show the Gnostic idea of the body as a garment of the soul, which must be stripped off before the soul is free to ascend to the heavenly spheres. There are similarities to what Paul has to say, and the Gnostics later were often to adapt his words for their own purposes; but we should not assume without more ado that the ideas are identical.[50] As Yates remarks (586), ' "Stripping off" was a concept conducive to gnostic development.'

δειγματίζω (BAGD 172; *TWNT* ii. 31–32), which occurs only twice in the NT, means to expose to public disgrace (cf. Matt. 1.19). **παρρησία** (BAGD 630; *TWNT* v. 869–84) has the general meaning of openness, frankness, plainness of speech, e.g. in contrast to speaking in parables (John 16.25, 29); sometimes this sense of openness develops, as here, into that of openness to the public, i.e. 'publicly' (cf. Eph. 6.19: ἵνα μοι δοθῇ λόγος ... ἐν παρρησίᾳ γνωρίσαι τὸ μυστήριον). A further sense is that of confidence or boldness in the presence of superiors, whether with reference to men or in one's approach to God (cf. Eph. 3.12: ἐν ᾧ ἔχομεν τὴν παρρησίαν καὶ προσαγωγὴν ἐν πεποιθήσει διὰ τῆς πίστεως αὐτοῦ). **θριαμβεύω** (BAGD 363; *TWNT* iii. 159–60) appears only in 2 Cor. 2.14 (on which see Thrall, *2 Corinthians*, 191–96) and here in the NT. The general sense of the word is clear: it is a metaphor from the Roman triumph, in which a victorious general led his troops through the city, with the spoils of war displayed for all to see and the

[49] For Christ's subjugation of the powers cf. 1 Cor. 15.24 ὅταν καταργήσῃ πᾶσαν ἀρχὴν καὶ πᾶσαν ἐξουσίαν καὶ δύναμιν, which is certainly clearer than the formulation in Col. For 1 Cor. 15.23–28 in relation to Col., cf. van Kooten, *Cosmic Christology*, 79ff. He sees Col. as a further Hellenization of Paul's cosmology and cosmic Christology (110–46).

[50] Cf. Moule, 'St Paul and Dualism'. He notes (116) that Paul makes considerable use of the metaphor of clothing, which in Gnostic and other literature is applied to a dualistic doctrine of the soul, and suggests that in 1 Cor. Paul is thinking in terms of addition, i.e. that the heavenly body is a kind of overcoat to be put on over existing garments, whereas in 2 Cor. he is 'more realistically reckoning with exchange' (123), i.e. the replacement of the earthly body by the heavenly. Paul's use of the metaphor is sometimes reminiscent of Gnostic usage, but use of the same terms and concepts does not necessarily indicate a relationship: we have to take note of the associations given to these terms and concepts in the different contexts in which they are employed. In taking over Pauline terms and phrases the Gnostics frequently reinterpreted them to suit their own purposes.

defeated enemy paraded before his chariot. In 2 Cor., however, the verb is followed by the accusative ἡμᾶς, which has led to debate: is Paul counting himself among the troops (cf. NRSV: 'always leads us in triumphal procession'), or as one of the defeated enemy? Some commentators opt for the meaning 'cause to triumph' (cf. 1 Cor. 15.57). In the present verse the problem lies in the accusative τὰς ἀρχὰς καὶ τὰς ἐξουσίας.

These words clearly refer back to the 'hymn' of the first chapter (1.16; cf. pp. 141f. above), where the ἀρχαί and ἐξουσίαι are among the things created by and for Christ, and to which he is therefore superior (cf. v. 10 above). It was noted there that there is nothing to indicate that these powers are to be regarded as hostile: all things in heaven and on earth, good or evil, are subject to Christ. Here, however, on the usual interpretation, these powers must be hostile, even though nothing has been said of any revolt on their part. Some accordingly (e.g. Carr, Yates) have argued that the true interpretation must see them as the angelic host accompanying Christ in his triumphal procession. It has to be said, however, that the traditional interpretation seems to give a more natural meaning to the verse, and this has therefore been adopted in the translation above. The fact that some powers had risen in revolt, for whatever reason, may have been something our author could assume as known to his readers, so that he felt it unnecessary to explain (cf. Eph. 6.12, quoted at pp. 197f. above).

As already noted (p. 200 above), the Nag Hammadi text *Melchizedek* (NHC IX 1, 2.5–11) contains the words, 'Death will tremble and be angry, not only he himself, but also his [fellow] world rulers (κοσμοκράτωρ), and archons (ἄρχων) [and] the principalities (ἀρχή) and the authorities (ἐξουσία), the female gods and the male gods together with the archangels (ἀρχάγγελος).' Pearson in his edition (NHS 15, (1981), 45) refers for such lists in the NT to 1 Cor. 15.24; Col. 1.16; 2.10, 15; Eph. 1.21; 3.10, adding 'but here these beings have become thoroughly demonized'. In his introduction, Pearson notes, 'it is precisely in his role as heavenly holy-warrior that Melchizedek seems, in our tractate, to be identified with Jesus Christ' (33), and further (34) that the career of the Saviour is clearly depicted 'as culminating in warfare with the archontic powers and in the final destruction of their chief, Death (13.9-14.9)'. The primary inspiration is of course from Hebrews, but there are other possible influences to be taken into account, including a Melchizedek text from Qumran.

Cf. also *Test. Truth* (NHC IX 3, 31.22–32.8): 'The foolish—thinking [in] their heart [that] if they confess "We are Christians", in word only (but) not with power, while giving themselves over to ignorance, to a human death, not knowing where they are going nor who Christ is, thinking that they will live when they are (really) in error—hasten towards the principalities (ἀρχή) and the authorities (ἐξουσία). They fall into their clutches because of the ignorance that is in them' (tr. Giversen and Pearson, *Nag Hammadi Codices IX and X* (1981), 127–29). For other occurrences of these terms cf. Siegert, *Nag Hammadi Register*, 220–21, 243.

The general argument of this section is clear enough; it is when we try to match what is meant with what is actually said, and determine the exact meaning of the passage, that the problems arise. We also have to reckon with the possibility that an ancient author did not write with the same regard for accuracy and observance of the rules of grammar as a modern scholar. In addition, our author may be incorporating material from older tradition, and not always with complete mastery.

Verses 6 and 7 present an admonition to steadfastness in the faith, all too often necessary for new converts who sooner or later found themselves wondering whether they had in fact made the right choice, and hankering after their old ways of life. Verse 8 then warns against the specious charms of the 'philosophy', which is denounced as deceptive and worthless, merely human and of this world; the only tradition of value is that 'according to Christ'. The following verses then present a vivid account, in a variety of metaphors, of what it all means for them: as circumcision was the rite of initiation for the Jews, so there is a new circumcision, 'not made with hands'. The circumcision of Christ is either the circumcision which he inaugurated (as Lightfoot and Aletti take it: see n. 36 above), or more daringly a circumcision which he himself has undergone 'in the stripping off of the body of flesh', i.e. in his death. The readers in their baptism have shared in that death, and in Christ they have been raised again to life through faith in the effective working of God who raised him from the dead. In former times they were 'dead' in their sins and transgressions, but now they have been raised to life again, freely forgiven all their transgressions. The 'bond' that stood aganst them has been cancelled, through the cross of Christ, who has triumphed over all the powers that once brought fear into their lives.

From this we may gain some insight into the nature of the 'philosophy', although much inevitably remains obscure. Evidently in some way it belittled the significance of Christ, suggesting that the salvation he had wrought was not enough, that more was required: for example in the worship of other powers, whether the στοιχεῖα or the gods of their old religion.[51] Our author hammers home his message, that in Christ they already have all that is required: they are fulfilled in him who is the head of all rule and dominion.

---

[51] For R. N. Longenecker (*NTS* 14 (1967/68), 540–41) 'it is plausible to view the basic problem in the Colossian church as that of the harmonization of a primarily religious conviction with an interest that is dominantly cosmological. It was the problem of reconciling the Christian conviction of the primacy and priority of Jesus ... with a Grecian understanding of gradations and relative orders of primacy in the universe'—indeed, a conflict of differing *Weltanschauungen*, rendered the more complex in that many of the same terms were used in the expression of these differing orientations. Paul's response was to insist that the primacy and priority of Jesus must be asserted in the cosmological sphere as well. 'That this extension from categories of religious and historical primacy to one of cosmic supremacy was considered legitimate within the cycle of Jewish Christianity is seen in the somewhat similar treatment of the opening sentences of Hebrews and the Prologue to the Fourth Gospel' (541).

VIII
FURTHER ADMONITIONS
(2.16–23)

[16]Do not, then, let anyone judge you in eating and in drinking, or in a matter of a festival or new moon or sabbath, [17]which are a shadow of the things to come, but the substance is of Christ. [18]Let no one disqualify you, taking pleasure in humility and worship of angels, entering into what he has seen, vainly puffed up by the mind of his flesh [19]and not holding fast the head, from whom the whole body, supported and held together by the joints and ligaments, grows with a growth from God.

[20]If you died with Christ to the elements of the world, why do you submit to regulations as if you were living in the world? [21]Do not handle, do not taste, do not touch— [22]all these are for destruction when they are consumed, according to the commandments and the teachings of men. [23]They have indeed an appearance of wisdom, in self-chosen worship and humility, unsparing treatment of the body, but are of no value where indulgence of the flesh is concerned.

The last section came to a climax in v. 15 with a declaration of the triumph of Christ over the 'rulers and authorities'. Who these authorities are is not stated, nor are we given any indication of their relation to the στοιχεῖα, mentioned again in v. 20, nor is there any explanation as to why the triumph should have been necessary; but the implication is that at some stage there has been a revolt, that some of these powers, created by and for Christ and therefore properly subject to him (cf. 1.16), have rebelled and sought to dominate the cosmos, and with it the lives of its inhabitants.[1] In 1.13 our author speaks of deliverance from the power of darkness, in the following verse of the redemption which is explained as the forgiveness of sins. Now (2.15) he proclaims Christ's final triumph on the cross.

The passage also deals with the significance of this for the readers: buried with Christ in their baptism and raised again through faith in God who raised him from the dead, they have entered into a new life; but they must continue to 'walk' in Christ, rooted and built up in

---

[1] Presumably the idea of a revolt by supernatural powers was so familiar to the author (and his readers) that he felt it unnecessary to go into detail. One starting point would seem to be the myth of the 'fallen angels' in Gen. 6.1–4, but there were also other myths which sought to explain the origins of evil. For a brief review of some Jewish and Christian sources, see G. A. G. Stroumsa, *Another Seed: Studies in Gnostic Mythology* (1984), 18–34. Cf. also the articles on Angels, Demons and Satan in *HDB* and *Enc. Bib.*

him, confirmed in the faith. Verse 8 contains an initial warning against a 'philosophy' which is in fact vain and deceptive, belonging to merely human tradition and to the 'elements' of this world and not 'according to Christ'. Now the author goes on to draw out further implications (οὖν is an inferential conjunction, 'denoting that what it introduces is the result of or an inference from what precedes'; BAGD, 593 §1b).

16. Μὴ οὖν τις ὑμᾶς κρινέτω ἐν βρώσει καὶ ἐν πόσει ἢ ἐν μέρει ἑορτῆς ἢ νεομηνίας ἢ σαββάτων This verse, particularly in its reference to the Sabbath, provides a clear indication that the 'false teaching' at least included a Jewish element, for the Sabbath was 'another Jewish tradition which marked out Jews as distinctive from Gentiles, another essential mark of Jewish identity and covenant belonging (Exod 31:16-17; Deut 5:15; Isa 56:6)' (Dunn, 174; see 171–75 for the Jewish background here).[2] Juvenal (*Sat.* xiv.96ff.) speaks of some who *sortiti metuentem sabbata patrem nil praeter nubes et caeli numen adorant, nec distare putant humana carne suillam qua pater abstinuit; mox et praeputia ponunt* (Reinach, *Textes*, 292f.; to paraphrase, the father was a σεβόμενος, a God-fearer observing the Sabbath; the son worshipped only the clouds and some heavenly deity, making no distinction between human flesh and pork, from which his father abstained; soon he submitted to circumcision. As Reinach observes, the son of a σεβόμενος frequently became a full Jew.).

In the light of this, it is very natural to relate the other items mentioned to Jewish practice: festivals, new moons and Sabbaths are mentioned together at Ezek. 45.17 and Hos. 2.11, and in a different order at 1 Chron. 23.31; 2 Chron. 2.4; 31.3; Neh. 10.33; Isa. 1.13–14 (for an extensive list cf. Aletti, 193 n. 112). This does not necessarily mean, however, that the opponents were Judaizers like those of Galatians: Aletti observes that the formulation in Gal. 4.10 is different (ἡμέρας παρατηρεῖσθε καὶ μῆνας καὶ καιροὺς καὶ ἐνιαυτούς), and does not necessarily relate to the same milieu.[3]

For Dunn (174) the Jewish associations are paramount: the first item, relating to eating and drinking, 'points fairly firmly to an essentially Jewish faction in Colossae who were deeply critical of Gentile Christian failure to observe the Jewish food laws', and the

---

[2] Lars Hartman, however, (*SEÅ* 49 (1995), 28) notes that, while the rules regarding food, the calendar and the Sabbath were important to the Jews, our author does not connect them with Judaism; otherwise these rules would probably have included circumcision, and as Gal. shows, Paul's reaction to any attempt to force circumcision on his Gentile converts was, to say the least, heated.

[3] Cf. also Thornton, 'Jewish New Moon Festivals'; Troy Martin, 'Pagan and Judeo-Christian Time-Keeping Schemes', A. Marjanen, '*Thomas* and Jewish Religious Practices', in Uro (ed.), *Thomas at the Crossroads*, 163–82. For van Kooten, however, (*Cosmic Christology*, 138) 'the combination of the three categories as such does not necessarily and exclusively point to a Jewish background of the philosophy at issue in *Col*'. There is ample evidence for pagan reverence for the Sabbath (Schürer, iii. 625 n. 183 refers to Tcherikover, *Corpus Papyrorum Judaicarum*, iii.43–56).

issue is put beyond doubt by the last in the sequence of three which follows, the reference to the Sabbath.⁴ He has to admit, however, that both ἑορτή and νεομηνία are somewhat less favourable to his position: festivals of various kinds, including that of the new moon, were observed by Gentiles as well as by Jews. When we recall that the evidence for the presence of Jews in Colossae is comparatively slight (cf. pp. 5–6, 8 above) it would seem advisable not to lay too much emphasis on the Jewish character of the false teaching, although there is undeniably a distinct Jewish element.⁵ If the real target was some other community, such as that of Laodicea (Lindemann; cf. Introduction, n. 35 above), there might have been a stronger Jewish presence, but this takes us into the realms of speculation. We should also make allowance for the earlier background of the readers, in the religious beliefs from which they were converted. Converts may grow disillusioned with their new faith, begin to doubt, and wonder if they have in fact made the right choice.

The verb **κρίνειν** (BAGD 451–52)⁶ has a range of meanings, of which the one required here is *criticise, find fault with, condemn* (§6b). The English derivative 'criticism' is unfortunately all too often associated only with this negative sense: the basic meaning is to distinguish or separate, for example distinguishing truth from error. Applied to the Scriptures, criticism should be objective, and reverent.⁷

The nouns **βρῶσις** (BAGD 148) and **πόσις** (BAGD 694) appear together three times in the same context (John 6.55; Rom. 14.17; and here), with reference either to eating and drinking or to food and drink,⁸ and πόσις nowhere else in the NT, although βρῶσις occurs more frequently. Lightfoot (259) compares also Heb. 9.10, μόνον ἐπὶ βρώμασιν καὶ πόμασιν καὶ διαφόροις βαπτισμοῖς, δικαιώματα σαρκὸς μέχρι καιροῦ διορθώσεως ἐπικείμενα: such rules and

---

⁴ W. D. Davies (*Origins*, 158) notes that the specific reference to the Sabbath here 'comports with the many regulations of the Sabbath in CDC x, 14—xi, 18; so too the distinctions between meats and drinks find an echo in CDC vi, 18. Thus the asceticism condemned in Col 2:20ff. could well be illustrated by the life of the sectarians.' At an earlier point (77) he observes that Paul is more tolerant in Rom. 14.5 than in Gal. 4.10–11, 'and the same tolerant attitude lies behind Col 2:16f.' This again must make it less likely that the situation in Colossae was the same as in Galatia.

⁵ Hübner (86) speaks of the undeniable fact that the Colossian 'philosophy' had taken over some Jewish ideas, and quotes Gnilka (146) as saying that the 'heretics' may have been inspired by Judaism, but the meaning associated with their seasons and festivals may have been quite different. The Gnostics later gave new meaning to the Jewish material they took over, but this does not mean that the opponents here are already 'Gnostic' in the second-century sense; at most it indicates that a kind of *gnosis*, a Gnostic way of thinking, was already current.

⁶ The article in *TWNT* iii. 920–42 concentrates mainly on the theme of divine judgement, which is not relevant here.

⁷ The proper approach is well expressed by I. H. Marshall, quoted at p. 124 n. 4 above.

⁸ Aletti (192 n. 108) observes that some commentators rightly see here a play on the difference between βρῶσις (eating) and βρῶμα (food), πόσις (drinking) and πόμα (drink), which puts the emphasis on the action rather than on the foodstuffs. Cf. his references.

regulations are merely fleshly, of this world, and of temporary
validity.

There is a fairly close parallel to this verse in Rom. 14.3 (ὁ δὲ μὴ
ἐσθίων τὸν ἐσθίοντα μὴ κρινέτω); indeed that whole chapter is
largely concerned to warn against criticism of one's fellow-
Christians. Here we may go right back to the teaching of Jesus as
recorded in the Gospels: 'Do not judge, so that you may not be
judged' (Matt. 7.1; cf. Luke 6.37).[9] There are few things more
disruptive of community life than a constant stream of criticism by
some member against another, and it is clear from the warnings given
that early Christians could all too easily be at fault in this respect.

In Col., however, it is a question of not submitting to such
criticism from others, and our author is quite firm in his injunction:
his readers are not to allow others to judge them, or to suggest that
they, the readers, are in any way inferior.[10] Paul's letter to the
Galatians is concerned to vindicate the freedom of Gentile Christians
from the requirements of the Jewish Law: 'For freedom Christ has set
us free. Stand firm, therefore, and do not submit again to a yoke of
slavery' (Gal. 5.1). In this respect Col. does stand close to Gal., but
that does not mean that the situation is the same in both cases. The
other side of the coin, of course, is that the Christian has a
responsibility, but to Christ and to him alone. What that responsibility may entail is clear from what Paul has to say in Rom. 14 and in
his discussion of food sacrificed to idols in 1 Cor. 8. The Christian is
no longer bound by the regulations of the law of Moses, or indeed of
any other legal system, but he must have due regard for the scruples
of his weaker brother: 'When you thus sin against members of your
family, and wound their conscience when it is weak, *you sin against
Christ*. Therefore, if food is a cause of their falling, I will never eat
meat, so that I may not cause one of them to fall' (1 Cor. 8.13; cf.
also Gal. 5.13).

μέρος (BAGD 505–06) means a part in contrast to the whole, but
here is used in the idiomatic phrase ἐν μέρει, 'in the matter of, in
regard to' (§1c).[11] This word is differently used in Eph. 4.9, 16. ἑορτή
(BAGD 280) in the Gospels refers normally to one of the Jewish
festivals, e.g. Passover or Tabernacles, but this is the one occurrence
in the Pauline corpus, and there is nothing to indicate what feast is
meant. As noted above, it is natural to think of a Jewish feast, but
that is not the only possibility. νεομηνία (BAGD 535) is another of
the hapax legomena in this letter, and once again, while it is natural
to think of Jewish celebration of the new moon, that is not the only
possibility, since it was observed also by Gentiles. In short, this verse

---

[9] 'To sit in judgment on others is to invite condemnation by God, and that
condemnation may operate through judgment by others. It is possible, but not
necessary, to understand the second clause as referring to God's final judgment' (D.
Hill, *Matthew* (NCB), 146).

[10] Cf. Sumney, 'Those Who "Pass Judgment"'.

[11] This neuter noun is distinct from the feminine μερίς, used at 1.12 (BAGD 505),
although there is some overlap in meaning.

offers proof that there was a Jewish element in the false teaching, but
it would be a mistake to conclude from this that it was purely Jewish,
and go on to assume that the situation in Colossae was the same as in
Galatia.

The plural τὰ σάββατα is quite often used, as well as the singular,
for a single Sabbath day (BAGD 739, §1bβ), and so probably here;
elsewhere it can mean a week (§2). Cf. also Lohse in *TWNT* vii. 1–35
(for this verse see esp. 31).

17. ἅ ἐστιν σκιὰ τῶν μελλόντων, τὸ δὲ σῶμα τοῦ Χριστοῦ Cf.
Heb. 10. 1, σκιὰν γὰρ ἔχων ὁ νόμος τῶν μελλόντων ἀγαθῶν, οὐκ
αὐτὴν τὴν εἰκόνα τῶν πραγμάτων. As Dunn puts it (176), 'The
response to such Jewish criticism is brief and to the point. Such
practices are but "a shadow of things to come, but the reality is with
Christ".' He goes on at once, however, to add: 'The language is
ultimately Platonic, but here is probably drawn from the Hellenistic
Judaism which we find most clearly expressed in Philo.'[12]

This introduces a new factor into the situation. The Judaizers in
Galatia are commonly associated with the party of James in
Jerusalem, and certainly it was 'certain people from James' (Gal.
2.12) who were responsible for the clash between Peter and Paul in
Antioch. There seems to be nothing to suggest that this group were in
any way influenced by the Philonic type of Judaism, which in turn
would suggest that the opponents in Colossae, if they could be
countered in Platonic or Philonic language, belonged to a different
group. Admittedly, according to Acts (21.27) it was 'the Jews from
Asia' who stirred up the riot which led to Paul's arrest in the Temple,
but that only serves to warn against the assumption that all Jews
everywhere shared the same beliefs, the same opinions, the same
prejudices. It is perfectly possible that some were more conservative,
even to narrowness of mind, whereas others were more tolerant,
more ready to adopt new ideas from the world around them, so long
as such ideas were compatible with their own Jewish faith. We have
to think of people as individuals, with minds of their own, in the first
century as much as in the twenty-first.

At first sight the phrase τῶν μελλόντων might seem to provide

---

[12] 'Philo makes a fair use of the term "shadow" (σκιά) in a number of variations of
this Platonic distinction (e.g. *Legum allegoriae* 3.100-103; *De plantatione* 27; *De
Abrahamo* 119-120). Most significant is the fact that he sets σκιά over against σῶμα as
the name over against that which it represents (πρᾶγμα) (*De decalogo* 82), or as copy to
archetype (ἀρχέτυπος, *De migratione Abrahami* 12), or again: "the letter is to the
oracle as the shadow to the substance (σκιάς τινας ὡσανεὶ σωμάτων) and the higher
values therein are what really and truly exist" (*De confusione linguarum* 190, LCL
translation; see also S. Schulz, *TDNT* 7.396; Lohse, *Colossians and Philemon* 116;
Gnilka, *Kolosserbrief* 147)' (Dunn, 176). Cf. also BAGD 755, esp. §2. For van Kooten
(*Cosmic Christology*, 27–30) 'the things destined, including all calendrical events, are
the reflection caused, the shadow cast, by Christ's cosmic body (2.16-17), and all
things, including the planetary "thrones" and "dominions", are located in him'. One
wonders if the readers would have picked that up quite so easily, without some advance
warning. The preparation may, however, have been provided in the σωματικῶς of 2.9,
which van Kooten takes to refer to 'the cosmic body which is constituted by the
principles, powers and other cosmic forces' (26).

further evidence of a Jewish element, for both Jews and early Christians made a distinction between this present evil age and the longed-for age to come. So Dunn, who writes, 'This no doubt is a reflection of Jewish eschatology', and sees here a transformation of 'an essentially static Platonic dualism' into an expression of Jewish eschatological hope. That may be so, but we should not place too great a weight on it: the participle is used absolutely with the meaning 'future, to come' as far back as Pindar (*Ol.* X.7), and there are references to secular as well as to Jewish and Christian sources (BAGD 501, §2). σκία here, as often in Philo (cf. n. 12 above), means a shadow in contrast to the reality (BAGD 755, §2), while σῶμα naturally refers to the body which casts the shadow, i.e. the reality (BAGD 799, §4). This word σῶμα, however, has already been used twice with reference to Christ's physical body, the body of his flesh (1.22; 2.11), and twice with reference to the Church (1.18, 24; cf. also 2.19). It is difficult to avoid the conclusion that these associations were somehow present to the mind of our author as he wrote.[13]

18. μηδεὶς ὑμᾶς καταβραβευέτω θέλων ἐν ταπεινοφροσύνῃ καὶ θρησκείᾳ τῶν ἀγγέλων, ἃ ἑόρακεν ἐμβατεύων, εἰκῇ φυσιούμενος ὑπὸ τοῦ νοὸς τῆς σαρκὸς αὐτοῦ According to Standhartinger (*Studien*, 22; see also her index) this is the most debated verse in attempts to reconstruct the Colossian 'heresy': almost every word has been variously interpreted. The simple verb βραβεύειν appears at 3.15 with the meaning 'rule, control', also as a hapax legomenon like the compound here. The prefixed κατά has as often a negative force, so that **καταβραβεύειν** (BAGD 409) means to decide against (as an umpire), to rob of a prize, or to condemn.[14] Evidently some in Colossae were giving themselves airs, and treating their fellow-Christians as somehow inferior. One is reminded of Paul's warnings to the Corinthians (the verb φυσιόω occurs quite frequently in 1 Cor.: see 4.6, 18f.; 5.2; 8.1; 13.4) but, as the following words here show, the situation is not the same: in Corinth the problem seems to arise from some claim to a superior knowledge (1 Cor. 8.1), or from rivalry between supporters of Paul and those of Apollos (1.11ff.; 4.6), whereas here it would appear to be due to a false humility and misguided asceticism.

The verb **θέλω** normally means to wish, will or desire, as in 2.1 above, but the sense required here is rather to take pleasure in

---

[13] Cf. Lohse, 117: 'Just as Adam was "a type of the one who was to come" (τύπος τοῦ μέλλοντος Rom 5:14) and just as the law had only the shadow "of the good things to come" (τῶν μελλόντων ἀγαθῶν Heb 10:1), so it becomes apparent under the sign of the fulfillment in Christ that the regulations are merely shadows of things to come, i.e. "the body that belongs to Christ" (τὸ δὲ σῶμα τοῦ Χριστοῦ). ... The reality which exists solely with Christ is shared only by those who, as members of the body of Christ, adhere to the head (2:19).' In a footnote he adds, 'The term "body" (σῶμα), therefore, refers to Christ as the Lord and to the Church as the domain of his lordship.'

[14] Moule (103f.) observes that, judging by its etymology, the verb might mean 'decide (as an umpire) against you', i.e. 'declare you disqualified', adding, 'this would apply remarkably well to a situation in which the theosophic ritualist declares the Pauline believer to be no genuine competitor at all'.

(BAGD 355, §4b). Its use here is commonly regarded as a Semitism, translating the Hebrew ⊐ ץ⊃ῌ (so Lightfoot, 261, referring to 1 Sam. 18.22; 2 Sam. 15.26; 1 Kgs. 10.9; 2 Chron. 9.8; Pss. 111.1; 146.10; cf. also Dunn, 178; Standhartinger, 188). The alternative, which is adopted by Dibelius-Greeven and others,[15] but was already criticized by Lightfoot, is to take the participle absolutely, with various meanings such as 'gladly' or 'wilfully', but for Lightfoot these senses 'are either unsupported by usage or inappropriate to the context'.

ταπεινοφροσύνη (BAGD 804: humility, modesty; *TWNT* viii. 23–24) is in the NT normally a Christian virtue, as at 3.12, where it appears in a list of virtues (cf. also Acts 20.19; Eph. 4.2; Phil. 2.3; 1 Pet. 5.5). Here, however, and at v. 23 it would appear to be either a false or a misguided humility, for the context at both points is distinctly disparaging (εἰκῇ φυσιούμενος κτλ here; at v. 23 λόγον μὲν ἔχοντα σοφίας stands in contrast to οὐκ ἐν τιμῇ τινι). Moule (104) notes, following Dibelius, that this word is a technical term for 'fasting' in Hermas (*Vis.* iii.10.6; *Sim.* v.3.7), and compares the use of the cognate verb for fasting in Lev. 23.29; Ezra (LXX 2 Esd.) 8.21. More recently this has been carried further: Dunn (178f.) and Aletti (195, citing F. O. Francis) note the use of ταπεινοῦν and ταπείνωσις in LXX, in the sense of self-discipline and fasting, even to humiliation and self-mortification (adding Ps. 35.13; Isa. 58.3, 5; Judith 4.9 (fasting); Lev. 16.29, 31; 23.27, 29, 32. Cf. also *TWNT* viii. 7, 27ff.). As Moule observes, 'This fits the present context well, and is supported by the addition, in v. 23, ἀφειδίᾳ σώματος.'[16] The natural inference is that the Colossian 'philosophy' included 'a fair degree of ascetic practice' (Dunn, 179): its adherents prided themselves on their rigorous observance, and disparaged those who did not conform to their standards.

The word θρησκεία (BAGD 363; *TWNT* iii. 1) appears in the NT only here and in Acts 16.5; Jas. 1.26, 27; it refers to the worship of God, or more generally religion, 'especially as it expresses itself in *religious service* or *cult*'. Since the normal usage was to name the deity worshipped in the genitive case (BAGD supplies references naming Serapis and Apollo, as well as for worship of God or of idols), it is natural to take the phrase θρησκεία τῶν ἀγγέλων as meaning 'worship of angels'. This, however, raises problems; as Dunn puts it (179f.), 'worship of angels is something one would not expect in any of the forms of Judaism known to us from this period. ... More characteristic of Judaism, however, was warning against worship of the host of heaven (Deut 4:19; 17:3; Jer 8:2; 19:13; Zeph

[15] Cf. Lohse, 118 n. 30; also Dunn, 178 n. 15. In his main text Dunn observes that θέλων 'cannot signify something imposed on the Colossian Christians or required of them' and that the NRSV translation 'insisting on' is therefore misleading.
[16] Lohse (118), while admitting that ταπεινοφροσύνη can mean fasting, insists that it 'must in no way be restricted to this meaning. It describes the eagerness and docility with which a person fulfils the cultic ordinances.' He translates it as 'readiness to serve'.

1:5), including the repeated warnings in first-century Judaism against worship of angels.'[17]

This brings us to the heart of the problem which we face in seeking to determine the nature of the Colossian 'philosophy'. Was it fundamentally Jewish, as Dunn would have it, or was it more syncretistic in character? Here we must recall once again the comparative lack of firm evidence for the presence of Jews in Colossae (cf. pp. 5–6 and 217).[18] If the community in Colossae was largely Gentile, its members might have taken over elements from Judaism without full understanding, putting their own interpretation on them and producing something that was quite un-Jewish.

As noted in the Introduction (pp. 51–52), F. O. Francis initiated a new line of approach, which has been followed by several others:[19] for these scholars, the genitive τῶν ἀγγέλων is not objective, but subjective; i.e. what is in view here is not a cult of angels, worship offered to them, but *the worship of the angels*, the worship offered by them to God. This is not to be dismissed lightly: there are numerous passages in the apocalyptic literature which speak of a visionary's ascent into the heavens, where he hears the praises sung by angelic choirs, and on occasion is even able to join in himself.[20] It is entirely possible that one aspect of the 'philosophy' was an aspiration to make this heavenly journey, which of course would entail due preparation by rigorous ascetic practices, as suggested by ἀφειδία σώματος in v. 23.

Nevertheless, doubts remain: Lightfoot long ago (68 and n. 2) cited Canon 35 of the Council of Laodicea (*c.* AD 363) against invocation of angels, and the comment of Theodoret that this disease 'long remained in Phrygia and Pisidia'. Arnold (*Syncretism*, 90–95) argues cogently that the genitive here is objective, not subjective; cases of a subjective genitive all relate to the worship of a people (e.g. Josephus, *Ant.* xii.253, τῇ Ἰουδαίων θρησκείᾳ; *1 Clem.* 62.1, τὰ ἀνήκοντα τῇ θρησκείᾳ ἡμῶν). Ideas of a heavenly ascent may indeed be somewhere in the background, but they are not the whole answer; we must also take account of the invocation of angels in magic and for apotropaic purposes, as argued by Arnold (*Syncretism*, 62–89),

[17] Cf. the references he supplies, also the Introduction, n. 73. As Dunn remarks, various second-century sources accuse Jews of worshipping angels, but none of them can be described as a friendly witness. For detailed discussion cf. Arnold, *Syncretism*, 8–102.
[18] Consideration must also be given to the point made by Moritz (*A Profound Mystery*, 220), that Eph., while drawing on material from Col, deliberately enriches it with OT traditions, and to his suggestion that Eph. is 'a re-written version of Colossians, but for a more Jewish-minded audience'.
[19] Cf. Aletti, 196f.; Dunn, 180ff., and references there.
[20] Cf. the references in Dunn, 180ff., including evidence that 'such worship was coveted at Qumran' (181), also Dunn, 'The Colossian Philosophy', 170–79 (for Qumran see 174–75); Bockmuehl, *Revelation and Mystery*, 169 n. 60. Cf. also Paul's account of a rapture into heaven in 2 Cor. 12.2–4. Lohse (120 n. 49) notes against Francis that ἐμβατεύειν (see below) occurs in none of the passages he lists, and that there is no indication in the present verse that we should imagine a soul being raptured up to heaven.

and much more. In short, there is beyond question a Jewish element in the 'philosophy', but it is not purely Jewish; we have to allow also for at least some degree of syncretism.²¹

The phrase ἃ ἑόρακεν ἐμβατεύων 'has proven to be the single most perplexing exegetical problem of the letter' (Arnold, *Syncretism*, 104).²² For one thing, there is the problem of translation, of finding a meaning which is appropriate to the context. ἃ ἑόρακεν obviously means 'what he has seen',²³ but ἐμβατεύων presents some difficulty. How does it relate to the preceding words? Does it govern them ('ἐμβατεύων on what he has seen'), or does it in some sense modify ἑόρακεν ('what he has seen while ἐμβατεύων')?

This verb is yet another NT hapax legomenon (BAGD 254; *TWNT* ii. 531–33),²⁴ with a range of meanings: (1) set foot upon, enter, visit; (2) come into possession of, even by force; (3) enter into a subject, go into detail.²⁵ The most widely accepted meaning is, however, perhaps a fourth, first suggested by Dibelius, which sees in it a technical term of the mystery religions for entrance into the sanctuary at the time of initiation.²⁶ BAGD §4 offers the renderings 'who enters (the sanctuary) which he saw (in ecstasy)' or 'taking his stand on what he has seen' in the mysteries (but Moule notes that there appears to be no evidence for the meaning 'taking his stand', which is that of RV margin. The NRSV 'dwelling on visions' must also be considered doubtful, though in fairness it should be added that the translators themselves are by no means confident: a footnote reads, 'Meaning of Gk uncertain'.).

This interpretation is, however, by no means universally accepted (cf. Moule, 105; Aletti, 197–99; Dunn, 182–83). Nock (*Essays*, 342) points out that the entrance was always the sequel to the initiation,

²¹ Reitzenstein long ago wrote to the effect that the occurrence of Jewish names in magic did not prove any familiarity with Judaism, 'sondern die Kenntnislösigkeit'. Böhlig, as noted above (Introduction, n. 113), refers to the *Umdeutung* to which Jewish materials were subjected when they were used in a Gnostic context, while Pearson (Introduction, n. 122) speaks of 'revolutionary borrowing and reinterpretation of Jewish scriptures and traditions', adding, 'But the resulting religious system is anything but Jewish!' We have to look beyond the superficial similarities to the use that is made of such materials in a new context.

²² The text evidently caused problems for some scribes: ℵ² C D¹ and other mss read ἃ μή, F G ἃ οὐκ (both rejected by Lightfoot, 320 as later corrections); P⁴⁶ ℵ* A B D* *et al.* omit the negative. There have also been attempts to emend the text, e.g. Lightfoot's suggestion, αἰώρᾳ κενεμβατεύων (cf. Moule, 104–06 for some other conjectures).

²³ Moule aptly cites John 3.11, ὃ ἑωράκαμεν μαρτυροῦμεν; 8.38, ἃ ἐγὼ ἑώρακα παρὰ τῷ Πατρὶ λαλῶ.

²⁴ Cf. also Dibelius, 'The Isis Initiation'; Francis, 'The Background of EMBATEUEIN'; Arnold, *Syncretism*, 104–57.

²⁵ Nock (*Essays*, 342) writes, 'the rhythm of the words suggests ... that ἐμβατεύων governs the implied antecedent of ἃ ἑόρακεν and the only translation which I can then offer is "entering at length upon the tale of what he has seen (in a vision)"' (citing 2 Macc. 2.80).

²⁶ Hübner (88), for example, writes, 'Nun hat Dibelius, Isisweihe [= 'The Isis Initiation'] 55ff, nachgewiesen (s. auch Dibelius/Greeven K 35, Exkurs EMBATEUEIN), dass ἐμβατεύειν in die Mysteriensprache gehört'. See the references in Arnold, *Syncretism*, 106 n. 9.

and not part of it (so too Preisker in *TWNT*, who adds that the entrance takes place in a sanctuary, of which there is no mention here). For Moule, 'the use of ἐμβατεύειν with the *visions*, not the *shrine*, as the object seems far-fetched and inappropriate, especially since the tense of ἑόρακεν would produce the meaning "penetrating into visions he has already seen"!' In contrast, the phrase would fit very neatly into a background of heavenly ascents and visions, as in the theory proposed by Francis and others; but the whole question has been reopened by C. E. Arnold's detailed discussion of the religious background in Phrygia, following which he reaffirms (*Syncretism*, 155) the conclusions reached by Dibelius (and independently by W. M. Ramsay), 'that a) a technical usage of the term for the second stage of mystery initiation is clearly attested in the inscriptions from the Apollo temple at Claros, and b) this technical usage of the term is the appropriate meaning for its use in Col 2:18' (see his conclusion, 155–57). 'Entering into the things he has seen' is then 'a technical way of summarizing the initiate's entry into the holy chamber of the temple, where the priest would have led the person through a whole series of ecstatic visionary experiences (perhaps including ascent to heaven and/or descent to the underworld).'

The implications of this for our understanding of the 'philosophy' are considerable: we have to think not of purely Jewish ideas, but of something rather more syncretistic, of people nurtured in some form of local cult who even after becoming Christians still retained some vestiges of their old beliefs, and thought it necessary to placate the powers they had formerly worshipped and the 'rulers' and 'authorities' of their old religion. Some of them might at some time have undergone initiation, and claimed that this set them apart from lesser beings without such experience. Our author's opinion emerges clearly in the following words.

εἰκῇ φυσιούμενος ὑπὸ τοῦ νοὸς τῆς σαρκὸς αὐτοῦ As noted above (p. 220), the verb φυσιόω (BAGD 869) occurs quite frequently in Paul's warnings to the Corinthians against arrogance, pride or conceit. εἰκῇ (BAGD 221) means 'without cause, in vain, to no purpose'. So here BAGD offers the rendering *groundlessly inflated by his fleshly mind*. The sting comes in the final words: such presumption does not betoken true religion. There is nothing 'spiritual' about it. It belongs in the realm of our lower nature, and the reason is given in the following verse: such a person does not hold fast to the head. Christ is supreme and all-sufficient.

19. καὶ οὐ κρατῶν τὴν κεφαλήν, ἐξ οὗ πᾶν τὸ σῶμα διὰ τῶν ἁφῶν καὶ συνδέσμων ἐπιχορηγούμενον καὶ συμβιβαζόμενον αὔξει τὴν αὔξησιν τοῦ θεοῦ Cf. Eph. 4.15–16, ὅς ἐστιν ἡ κεφαλή, Χριστός, ἐξ οὗ πᾶν τὸ σῶμα συναρμολογούμενον καὶ συμβιβαζόμενον διὰ πάσης ἁφῆς τῆς ἐπιχορηγίας ... τὴν αὔξησιν τοῦ σώματος ποιεῖται. Once again Eph. and Col. show striking similarities, but there are also differences. Some words in this verse occur only in these two letters, e.g. ἁφή (BAGD 125), a joint or ligament, or αὔξησις (BAGD 122), growth, but with the latter there is a different

nuance of meaning (the verb αὔξω is a shorter form of αὐξάνω,
BAGD 121). σύνδεσμος (BAGD 785) appears only in Acts 8.23;
Eph. 4.3; Col. 2.19; 3.14, but with three different shades of meaning:
here of the sinews of the body, at Eph. 4.3 and Col. 3.14 below of the
bond of peace or unity, in Acts of the bond or fetter of wickedness.[27]

Lohse (121) writes, 'Whoever espoused the "philosophy" cannot at
the same time adhere to Christ as the "head" (κεφαλή) over the
powers and principalities. And every Christian who is of the opinion
that he should become a devotee of that teaching must clearly realise
that at that very moment he severs his relationship with the head,
who is the Lord alone.' This is of course true enough, but seems to
imply a tacit change of subject, from the opponent who 'disqualifies'
the readers to any Christian who opts to espouse the 'philosophy';
but here we have a sequence of four present participles (θέλων,
ἐμβατεύων, φυσιούμενος, κρατῶν), all in the nominative and clearly
relating to μηδείς at the beginning of v. 18: it is the adverse critic
who does not adhere to the head, and that is his ultimate
condemnation. Incidentally, this could be another hint that the
whole trouble stemmed from one person.[28] Even if several people
were involved, dissident groups frequently have a single leader who is
largely responsible.

The verb **κρατεῖν** means to take hold of or grasp, but here more
particularly to hold fast (cf. Mark 7. 3, 4, 8; 2 Thess. 2.15; BAGD
448, §2eβ; *TWNT* iii. 910–11). κεφαλή in the light of 1.18 and 2.10
naturally refers to Christ, and indeed the name is added in some mss
(but probably through assimilation to Eph. 4.15). ἐξ οὗ is then a
natural *constructio ad sensum*, our author thinking not of the
grammatical antecedent but of Christ who is implied. The head is the
organ which controls all that happens in the body (Schweizer, *TWNT*
vii. 1074), and it is from it, from Christ, that the body which is the
Church derives its growth. ἐπιχορηγεῖν (BAGD 305) means to
furnish, provide or support (the cognate noun appears in Eph.),
συμβιβάζειν (cf. 2.2) to unite or knit together. Dunn here aptly
quotes Gnilka's comment: 'It should not be overlooked that God is
and has the last word in this section' (*Kolosserbrief*, 144).

[27] On the use of ἁφή and σύνδεσμος in ancient medical literature cf. Lightfoot, 264–
66. G. H. van Kooten, however, takes up an interpretation originally suggested by
Dibelius, and claims that 'a physical, cosmological understanding of the terms σῶμα
("body"), δεσμός ("bond") and ἁφή ("band") ... is to be preferred to a medical,
physiological one' (*Cosmic Christology*, 57; see his whole discussion, 30–58). He argues
for a background in Stoicism and Middle Platonism, presenting evidence that was not
available to Dibelius. 'With regard to Christ's body, the author of Col. seems to
distinguish between three different senses of body (σῶμα)' (26–27): (1) ecclesiastical
(1.18, 24); (2) physiological (1.21; 2.11, in both cases qualified as σῶμα τῆς σάρκος); (3)
cosmological (2.9, 17, 19).
[28] Cf. p. 194 above, also Dunn's comment (186): 'It was presumably the failure of the
individual who had let go of Christ that he had gone in for flights of mystical
experience, glorying in the company of angels, without regard to the other members of
the body. And his advocacy of such experiences, criticizing and disqualifying those
who saw their spirituality in more humdrum terms, must have been the very opposite
of supportive of the Christian community.'

20. Εἰ ἀπεθάνετε σὺν Χριστῷ ἀπὸ τῶν στοιχείων τοῦ κόσμου, τί ὡς ζῶντες ἐν κόσμῳ δογματίζεσθε The final verses of this chapter round off the argument, and lead into the 'ethical' section of the epistle. The readers have died with Christ, their old life is now behind them (cf. vv. 11–13); they have entered into a new life, no longer in the realm of darkness but in the kingdom of God's beloved Son (cf. 1.13). Why then should they submit to regulations (**δογματίζω** in the passive, BAGD 201; cf. the noun τοῖς δόγμασιν in v. 14) that belong only to the world of their old life?

The statement that the readers have died 'to [lit. 'from'] the elements of the world' is perhaps the strongest indication that the στοιχεῖα are in some sense to be regarded as hostile powers, but in the light of the evidence discussed above (pp. 195–98) it is scarcely sufficient to justify the conclusion that the word is always to be taken in this sense. Here and at Gal. 4.8–9 the context does suggest that the reference is to heavenly powers, but that meaning depends on the context, and does not justify a generalization from these particular cases. Lightfoot (268) translates 'from the rudimentary, disciplinary, ordinances, whose sphere is the mundane and sensuous', so that reference to hostile powers is not the only possible interpretation.

The question our author asks in this verse is slightly incongruous, since the readers are in fact still living in the world, and must continue to do so to the end of their mortal lives. What is meant is 'as if you still belonged to the world' (so NRSV), as if that were the only reality, the only existence. Having died to the στοιχεῖα the readers are no longer under their dominance and control, no longer subject to the rules and regulations they have imposed. Our author is following Paul's radical view of conversion, perhaps even extending it further: the old life was under the power of sin and darkness, but from that the readers have been delivered. They must now live accordingly, and the ethical section which follows provides guidelines for their future conduct as they seek to 'walk' with Christ: they are to lead lives worthy of the Lord (1.10), to remain firm in the faith (1.23; cf. 2.7); our author's hope is to 'present everyone mature in Christ' (1.28). They have been 'fulfilled' in Christ (2.10, another verse referring to Christ as κεφαλή); why should they now throw all this away?

21. μὴ ἅψῃ μηδὲ γεύσῃ μηδὲ θίγῃς This verse presents three examples of the rules and regulations referred to in the preceding verse. At first glance these may seem to be trivial, not worthy of further consideration, but closer investigation reveals a different picture. The first of the three, μὴ ἅψῃ, recalls the words of Jesus to Mary Magdalene at John 20.17: μή μου ἅπτου, where the present tense is used, not the aorist (Dodd, *Interpretation*, 443 n. 2, suggests that the words might mean 'Do not cling to me'), and Jesus at once explains why he has so spoken: he has not yet ascended to the Father; ten verses later Thomas is in contrast invited to touch Jesus' hands and side. As Dodd says, 'It seems difficult to avoid the position that

some change in reference to what is called ἀνάβασις is implied
between xx.17 and xx.27.'

The verb ἅπτω in the middle voice (BAGD 102, §2a) means
basically to touch or take hold of, but there are several nuances of
meaning: e.g. it can be used of intercourse with a woman (cf. 1 Cor.
7.1), or of contact with unclean things (2 Cor. 6.17, cf. Isa. 52.11);
Dunn (190) refers to 'fear of impurity being transferred by physical
contact (as regularly in Lev 5:2-3; 7:19, 21; 11:8, 24-28 etc.)'. The
priest and the Levite in the parable of the Good Samaritan had their
reasons for passing by on the other side: contact with a corpse would
have rendered them unclean for a week (cf. Num. 19.11–13), and
therefore unfit for service in the Temple. The point in all these cases is
that the 'touching' is for one reason or another inappropriate,
particularly where there are cultic associations. The word can also
mean to eat ('touch food'), but as BAGD (103) notes, 'We would
then have in this passage the anti-climax *eat, taste, touch.*'

γεύομαι (BAGD 157), which occurs only here in the Pauline
corpus, means to taste or partake of something, or figuratively to
come to know something. Used absolutely, it can also mean 'to eat'
(cf. Acts 10.10). The third verb, θιγγάνω (BAGD 361), which in the
NT appears only here and in Heb. 11.28; 12.20, also means to touch,
but according to Lightfoot (269) ἅπτεσθαι is the stronger word of
the two (Dunn, 191 thinks the meaning 'touch' more appropriate
here, 'as the Leviticus references make clear'. But can we assume that
a largely Gentile community in Asia Minor would be familiar with
that book?). BAGD 103 (*s.v.* ἅπτω) quotes from a papyrus the words
ὀψαρίου μὴ θιγγάνειν (POx 1185, 10f.), so that this verb too may
refer to eating. It is, however, unlikely that our author is merely
citing three possible ways of forbidding people to eat; more probably
each word should have a somewhat different meaning. Lightfoot
(270) sees here a gradation: 'Both ἅπτεσθαι and θιγγάνειν refer to
defilement incurred through the sense of touch, though in different
degrees; "Handle not, nor yet taste, nor even touch."'

The key to understanding these prohibitions lies in ancient ideas of
purity and defilement, as has long been recognized, and here the
Jewish rules and regulations readily come to mind (cf. Dunn, 190–
92). Lightfoot (85ff.) already referred to the extreme asceticism of the
Essenes, and as Dunn notes this has been confirmed by the Qumran
scrolls: 'With the Essenes the concern was accentuated to an extreme
degree, with strict regulations in place to ensure and safeguard "the
purity of the Many" (1QS 6-7).'[29] Dunn himself observes, however,
that Lohse (123 n. 77) cites Lucian, *De Syria dea* 54, evidencing the
same concern, while Arnold can quote similar regulations for the cult
of Isis, for example (*Syncretism*, 134), or the 'Mithras liturgy' (140).
A Jewish background must be relevant for the New Testament, but
we must also remember that this was not the only background: the

[29] In a footnote he cites M. Newton, *The Concept of Purity at Qumran and in the
Letters of Paul* (1985), particularly 10–26.

Jews shared many ideas with other peoples, even if sometimes they
held these ideas with a greater intensity, so that we cannot without
more ado label such ideas as exclusively Jewish.

At this point it may be appropriate to introduce a reflection on more modern times: it
has to be said that Christians have sometimes been accused of an unduly negative
attitude, as if the most important words in the Christian faith were 'Thou shalt not'!
What is the point, the purpose, of such a prohibition? The prohibitions enshrined in
the Ten Commandments are one thing, the banning of quite harmless pleasures on
allegedly religious grounds is quite another. Often enough a perfectly valid principle is
advanced, but when the legalists, and officialdom, seek to define precisely what that
principle implies, the rules and regulations are multiplied to cover the most remote and
unlikely possibilities. We do well to remember the AV of Deut. 26.11: 'And thou shalt
rejoice in every good thing which the Lord thy God hath given unto thee, and unto
thine house, thou, and the Levite, and the stranger that is among you'.[30] After all, the
'pale Galilean' of the poet Swinburne (echoing the emperor Julian the Apostate) could
cheerfully accept the reputation of being 'a glutton and a drunkard, a friend of tax
collectors and sinners' (Matt. 11.19, par. Luke 7.34), which Dorothy L. Sayers neatly
paraphrased as meaning that he ate too much and drank too freely, and kept rather
doubtful company. There are standards to be observed, but we are not meant to spend
our lives in unrelieved gloom.

**22. ἅ ἐστιν πάντα εἰς φθορὰν τῇ ἀποχρήσει, κατὰ τὰ ἐντάλματα
καὶ διδασκαλίας τῶν ἀνθρώπων** For the closing words of this verse
cf. Isa. 28.13 LXX, μάτην δὲ σέβονταί με διδάσκοντες ἐντάλματα
ἀνθρώπων καὶ διδασκαλίας. Lohse (124) observes that this OT
passage is also cited in Mark 7.7 (par. Matt. 15. 9) in the argument
against the legalism of the Pharisees 'and was obviously quoted often
in disputes with proponents of a legalistic type of piety'. It appears
again in Papyrus Egerton 2, in what according to Koester (*Gospels*,
214f.) 'looks like a quilt of pieces from at least four different New
Testament passages' (he adds a reference to *1 Clem.* 15.2, but that is
only the first part of the verse in Isaiah). It is just conceivable that our
author might have known Mark, but that would imply a fairly late
date for the letter, some years after Paul's death. In view of the
echoes in other texts it is more likely that he is echoing Isaiah direct.
Dunn notes that ἔνταλμα (BAGD 268) occurs only in these three
passages in the NT, and only in one other passage in LXX (Job
23.11–12), while outside the Pauline corpus διδασκαλία appears only
in these two Gospel verses, and again rarely in LXX.[31] Such
prohibitions and such teachings are not 'spiritual' (though our
author does not use that word here), not 'according to Christ'; they
are of this world only, and belong to the traditions of men (cf. 2.8).

The relative pronoun at the beginning of the verse refers back to
the implied objects of the three prohibitions, the things which must
not be handled, touched or tasted, and here these things are most
obviously 'unclean' foods. Dunn (193) sees an echo of Mark 7.19/

[30] This theme recurs regularly throughout the book: Deut. 12.7, 12, 18; 14.26; 16.11,
14; 27.7.
[31] Cf. the use of this word in Eph. 4.14: κλυδωνιζόμενοι καὶ περιφερόμενοι παντὶ
ἀνέμῳ τῆς διδασκαλίας ἐν τῇ κυβείᾳ τῶν ἀνθρώπων, ἐν πανουργίᾳ πρὸς τὴν
μεθοδείαν τῆς πλάνης ('tossed to and fro and blown about by every wind of doctrine,
by people's trickery, by their craftiness in deceitful scheming', NRSV).

Matt. 15.17, but as noted above our author might at most have known Mark, and Paul himself could not have known either Gospel. It is more likely that this is drawn from the tradition that lies behind the Gospels. (Lightfoot, 270 more circumspectly says that the expression ἐστιν εἰς φθοράν here 'corresponds to εἰς ἀφεδρῶνα ἐκβάλλεται' in Mark and Matthew.[32] For εἰμὶ εἰς as meaning 'destined for' or 'intended for' cf. BAGD 225, §III.2; 229, §4d; φθορά (BAGD 858) means ruin, destruction, corruption.) Paul himself writes, 'Food is meant for the stomach and the stomach for food, and God will destroy both one and the other' (1 Cor. 6.13).[33] These things belong in this world only, and are of no ultimate significance; they are intended to be consumed, used up (ἀπόχρησις, BAGD 102, is another word which occurs in the New Testament only here), and finally perish.

23. ἅτινά ἐστιν λόγον μὲν ἔχοντα σοφίας ἐν ἐθελοθρησκίᾳ καὶ ταπεινοφροσύνῃ [καὶ] ἀφειδίᾳ σώματος, οὐκ ἐν τιμῇ τινι πρὸς πλησμονὴν τῆς σαρκός 'This verse is by common consent regarded as hopelessly obscure[34]—either owing to corruption or because we have lost the clue. Perhaps the best that can be made of it is something like this: "which (rules about diet, etc.) have indeed a reputation for wisdom, with their voluntary delight in religiousness and self-mortification and severity to the body, but are of no value in combatting sensual indulgence"' (Moule, 108; see his discussion for some other suggestions—the rendering just presented was 'ably defended by Lightfoot' (110; see Lightfoot, 271–73). Cf. also Lohse, 124 and the references in his notes.).

To begin with, the καί in brackets above is omitted by P⁴⁶ B 1739 and some other witnesses, but included by ℵ A C D and the majority of the other mss. Lightfoot (272) thinks it should be omitted: 'While the insertion would naturally occur to scribes, the omission gives more point to the sentence. The ἐθελοθρησκία καὶ ταπεινοφροσύνη as the religious elements are thus separated from the ἀφείδεια σώματος as the practical rule.' Another way of looking at it would be to see the latter words as in apposition to and explanatory of the former: what the 'self-chosen worship' and 'humility' amount to is harsh treatment of the body. In any case, having written two datives linked by καί a scribe would almost inevitably think that a third should also be so linked.

The ἅτινα at the beginning obviously looks back to the relative at the beginning of the previous verse: all these things, the rules and regulations and the concerns about purity, are of no real significance.

---

[32] Lohse (124 n. 83) quotes Theodoret *ad loc.*: Εἰς κόπρον γὰρ ἄπαντα μεταβάλλεται.

[33] C. K. Barrett (*First Corinthians* (1968), 146) thinks this probably part of a quotation from Paul's opponents: 'Paul probably did not frame it, and does not note its relation with the teaching of Jesus (Mark vii.19), but he appears to accept it.'

[34] Schneider in *TWNT* viii. 133 n. 45 quotes Theodore of Mopsuestia: ἀσαφὲς μέν ἐστι—*obscurus quidem versus* (PG 66, 931a). It is not only modern commentators who have found it difficult!

For λόγον ἔχειν BAGD 477–78 offers two possible meanings: have the appearance of wisdom, pass for wisdom (§1aβ, citing Plato and Demosthenes), or have a concern for wisdom (§2f, comparing Plutarch. For other meanings cf. Lightfoot, 271). Of these the first appears the more suited to the context: these things have 'a reputation for wisdom', but not the reality (so Lightfoot).

The particle μέν normally comes second in its clause, so that the words λόγον μὲν ἔχοντα go together, leaving ἐστιν as a separate and independent unit (the participle is a neuter plural, agreeing with ἅτινα). One difficulty often seen here is that there is no following adversative particle to mark a contrast, but BAGD (503, §2) notes that μέν is frequently found in anacolutha, suggesting ὄντα δὲ ἄλογα or something similar. There is, however, a contrast of a sort in οὐκ ἐν τιμῇ τινι, and it may be that our author is merely expressing himself somewhat loosely. At any rate, λόγος here has a significance which depends on the context: either *have the appearance of wisdom, pass for wisdom* (BAGD 477b, §1aβ) or perhaps less probably *have a concern for wisdom* (§2f).

ἐθελοθρησκία (BAGD 218) 'is obviously a special coinage for the occasion (it is not found anywhere else)' (Dunn 195; but BAGD cites the definition of Suidas, ἐθελοθρησκεῖ: ἰδίῳ θελήματι σέβει τὸ δοκοῦν). It almost certainly echoes the θρησκεία of v. 18 above, with the prefixed ἐθελο- conveying the sense of deliberate choice: Lightfoot (272) renders '*in* volunteered, self-imposed, officious, supererogatory *service*'. This self-chosen worship, like the 'humility' mentioned above and the ἀφειδία σώματος which they involve, is of no value whatsoever. **ἀφειδία** (BAGD 124) is yet another word which occurs in the New Testament only here (it means literally 'unsparing treatment', and suggests a rigorous asceticism), while σῶμα here, in contrast to some of its earlier uses, clearly relates to the physical body.

In the phrase οὐκ ἐν τιμῇ τινι it is open to question whether the τινι should be taken as qualifying τιμή (not of any value) or in its own right (of no value to anyone), but this does not really affect the sense (for τιμή see BAGD 817, where it is suggested (§1) that the phrase may be a Latinism; *TWNT* viii. 170–80: for this verse see 178). In either case the point is that these things are of no value.

Finally there is the phrase πρὸς πλησμονὴν τῆς σαρκός, containing yet another word which appears only in Col.: **πλησμονή** (BAGD 673; *TWNT* vi. 133–34). It means satiety, satisfaction, gratification, and in itself could be used either in a good or in a bad sense (Dunn, 196 cites Exod. 16.3, 8; Lev. 25.19; Prov. 3.10; Lam 5.6 as examples of a neutral sense, satisfaction of hunger, but thinks that a negative note is present in Ezek. 16.49 and Hos. 13.6; for the usage in LXX cf. *TWNT* vi. 132). The Fathers almost universally equated σάρξ with σῶμα, and hence treated it positively, taking the phrase to mean the satisfaction of natural (not sinful) desires (see Delling in *TWNT*), but in the light of v. 18 above it is more likely that σάρξ should be given its normal physical sense, referring to the lower nature. The harsh treatment of the body is of no value when it comes to checking natural desires. Some patristic sources suggest that certain Gnostic leaders, while ostensibly austere, were in fact guilty of immoral conduct.

An alternative rendering is argued for by Hollenbach ('Col. II.23'), who notes that the main points were already proposed by Bengel and by B. Reicke (254 n. 1). This takes the main clause to be ἅτινα ἐστιν ... πρὸς πλησμονὴν τῆς σάρκος: 'which things lead to the fulfilment of the flesh' and 'The words λόγον μὲν ἔχοντα σοφίας ἐν ἐθελοθρησκίᾳ καὶ ταπεινοφροσύνῃ καὶ ἀφειδίᾳ σώματος form a subordinate concessive clause, with the clause οὐκ ἐν τιμῇ τινι subordinate to it.' The resultant translation is 'Which things (actually) lead, even though having a reputation for wisdom in the areas of self-made worship, humility and severity to the body, without any honour whatsoever, to the fulfilment of the flesh.' Such constructions are, however, rare, 'particularly those where the subordinate clause is embedded after the verb of the main clause, as the present proposal necessitates' (260),[35] and one may wonder what the original readers would have made of it. Dunn (196) comments: 'the lack of an adversative at the same point is still a problem and the whole remains awkward'. There is still something to be said for adhering in general to the interpretation advanced so long ago by Lightfoot.

The 'polemical' section of the letter is comparatively brief, and in some respects not altogether informative. Our author does not go into detail, or explain the nature of the 'philosophy'; but his readers would already know, so that it was not necessary. Not surprisingly, attempts to reconstruct the 'heresy' have varied widely: some have emphasized the Jewish element which is undoubtedly present, and thought of the Judaizers opposed in Gal.; others from the outset have seen links with Gnosticism; more recently it has been suggested that there is some kind of link with the Qumran sect, while Lightfoot already saw affinity both with Gnosticism and with the Essenes. Some again have seen links with the mystery religions or, yet again, there is the theory of F. O. Francis and others, affirming that what is in view in v. 18 is not a ('quite un-Jewish') worship of angels but the worship offered by them, so that what is envisaged is a heavenly journey like those in some apocalyptic texts, in which the visionary not only hears the worship offered in heaven by the angels, but is himself enabled to participate. At the other extreme, doubts have been raised as to whether there was anything that could really be called a heresy at all: the letter is directed 'to a situation in which young Christians are under pressure to conform to the beliefs and

---

[35] A footnote runs: 'It was because of his inability to accept such a possibility that H.A.W. Meyer, *Critical and Exegetical Handbook to the Epistles to the Philippians and Colossians and to Philemon* (New York 1885), p. 328, rejected the interpretation taken here, which he was aware had been proposed by Bengel.'

practices of their pagan and Jewish neighbours' (Hooker, False Teachers', 329). Most recently C. E. Arnold has urged the importance of magic and of popular folk belief, and for that matter of astrology (e.g. *Syncretism*, 166–73; cf. also his index) as part of the background to the letter.

It is not difficult to construct a theory; the problem is to make it carry conviction, to demonstrate that this is *the* explanation. For example, it has been noted above that there are indications in the letter that the disruption might have been caused by a single person. One might imagine a former Essene advocating the observance of Qumran rules as a preparation for the heavenly ascent; or a single Jew, priding himself on his knowledge of the Hebrew Bible, a closed book for many Gentiles, and strict in observance of the Law, despising 'the lesser breeds without the law'; or some native of the area, initiated into the cult of some local deity, who still clung to some remnants of his former faith and sought to combine them with his Christian belief. The possibilities are legion; but how to *prove* that any one of them, and only that one, is right? It is not surprising that Martin Hengel could write ('Aufgaben', 333 n. 39), 'Das historische Rätsel dieses Briefes läßt sich mit unserem Wissenstand m.E. nicht lösen' (in my opinion the historical riddle of this letter cannot be resolved in the present state of our knowledge).

Where so many theories have been advanced, but there has been no real consensus of scholarly opinion, it is rather pointless to seek to construct another. What we can do is to seek to illuminate the background of the letter, to form some impression of the ideas that were current, the kind of thinking that lies behind the 'philosophy', and so reach some insight into the nature of the problem facing our author. Here he provides us with a number of clues, not enough to enable us to make a firm identification but sufficient to provide some understanding.

In the first place, there is beyond question a Jewish element, as is clear from the reference to the Sabbath in v. 16. That being so, it is natural to think of the festivals and new moons referred to as Jewish festivals, and to relate judgement in matters of eating and drinking to the Jewish food laws. To this we may add the affinities noted with the Qumran sect, the LXX use of ταπεινοῦν and ταπείνωσις in the sense of self-discipline and fasting, and the descriptions of a heavenly journey which appear in Jewish apocalyptic texts. On the other hand, some of these features are not exclusively Jewish, but were shared by other peoples also; the evidence for the presence of Jews in Colossae itself is comparatively slight; and our author's approach is very different from that of Paul in Galatians. It is therefore probably not a matter of some person or persons seeking to compel Gentile converts to Judaize.

A further point is that Jewish material does not necessarily indicate that it was Jews who were using it. The Gnostics later took over much from both Jewish and Christian scriptures, but the use they made of this material produced something entirely different (cf. n. 21

above). The parallels adduced from Nag Hammadi texts show that Col. itself was known to and freely used by Gnostic writers. We have to consider the possibility that the opponents in Col. were using and adapting Jewish material for purposes of their own, reading their own interpretation into the text.

The warning against accepting judgement from others, coupled with the references to 'humility' and unsparing treatment of the body, and also the scathing 'vainly puffed up by the mind of his flesh', suggests that some in the community were subjecting themselves to ascetic practices, and given to disparaging those who were not so rigorous in their observance. One may recall here the Pharisaic attitude towards 'publicans and sinners', as seen in the Gospels, but once again that is not the only possibility: we need only to think of the Cynics. This does not mean that we must think of Cynic influence here, simply that the Cynic attitude illustrates the kind of thing of which we should be thinking.

The suggestion of a link with the mystery religions has taken on a fresh lease of life with Arnold's study, but here it is important to note his emphasis on folk religion: 'I am suggesting that the best explanation for the Colossian "philosophy" lies in the quite general classification of folk religion. This forces us to think more deeply about what is most likely from the standpoint of the belief structures of common people in Phrygia' (*Syncretism*, 5). All too often attention is focused on ideas, whereas we should be thinking of the people who held these ideas. Some things are widely believed, but people as individuals may vary quite widely in their beliefs.

As to Gnosticism, the Gnostics later used this letter, but that does not make it in itself a Gnostic document. There was certainly a good deal of Gnostic thinking current in this period, and it is reasonable enough to speak of 'a kind of *gnosis*', but in the words of Hans Jonas this is 'a Gnosis without divine tragedy'.[36] We have a long way to go to the developed Christian Gnosticism of the second century.

Such a presentation will not of course satisfy those who must at all costs have a simple, clear-cut answer to every question; but sometimes the simple, clear-cut answer is only found by reading more into the text than is actually there.[37] What is beyond dispute is our author's imperious and withering dismissal: these things have an appearance of wisdom, but are of no value where indulgence of the flesh is concerned.

[36] Jonas, in *The Bible in Modern Scholarship*, 293.
[37] Cf. Hengel, 'Aufgaben', 334: 'Wir stehen hier ständig in der Gefahr der Überinterpretation, daß wir mehr aus den Texten heraus- (oder muß man sagen: hinein-?) lesen als sie hergeben.'

IX
SEEK THINGS ABOVE
(3.1–4)

[3.1]If then you were raised up with Christ, seek the things above, where Christ is, seated at the right hand of God. [2]Think of the things above, not the things on earth. [3]For you died, and your life is hidden with Christ in God. [4]When Christ is revealed, who is our life, then you will be revealed with him in glory.

These four verses, as Moritz puts it (*A Profound Mystery*, 12, referring to O'Brien, commentary 168), 'clearly sum up the first half of the epistle while, at the same time, re-focusing on what is to come'. Lähnemann for example (31) notes that the συνηγέρθητε at the opening of the first verse picks up the συνηγέρθητε of 2.12 and the συνεζωοποίησεν of 2.13, preparing the way for the summons to 'put on the new man' in 3.10, 12; the ἀπεθάνετε γάρ in v. 3 picks up the συνταφέντες in 2.12, the νεκροὺς ὄντας in 2.13 and the ἀπεθάνετε in 2.20, and provides the basis for the imperative νεκρώσατε in 3.5. The τὰ ἄνω in 3.1 is a summary of what was said in the first two chapters about the lordship of Christ (to whom the cosmic powers are subject), and at the same time gives a point of orientation for the 'new man'. Finally the charge not to strive for the things on earth (τὰ ἐπὶ τῆς γῆς, 3.2) recalls the last section of ch. 2 (vv. 20–23), where the teaching and practice of the 'false teachers' are described as mere human invention, but also looks forward: the vices to be 'put to death' in v. 5 are described as τὰ μέλη τὰ ἐπὶ τῆς γῆς. Cf. also Dunn (199–201), who finds this section 'clearly of a piece with what has gone before', and sees in it confirmation of the essentially Jewish character of the Colossian opposition. It is, however, probably unwise to concentrate only on one aspect of the general background. On a broader view the evidence is not entirely conclusive.

At the end of the last section it was noted that while our author does provide some clues they are not sufficient to enable us to make any firm statement about the nature of the 'heresy'. Opinions have varied widely, and it has even been questioned whether there was anything that could really be called a heresy at all. Reference was made above (p. 231) to a comment by M. D. Hooker about 'a situation in which young Christians are under pressure to conform to the beliefs and practices of their pagan and Jewish neighbours', while N. T. Wright (see Introduction, n. 72) argues that in Col. 'a claim is being made for Christ (and his people) which has a double cutting edge'—first against Judaism and second against paganism: 'a community that believed these things would be distinct from neighbours both Jewish and pagan'. When we add to these the fact that people can sometimes be a

prey to doubts, wondering if they have made the right choice and
hankering after the securities of their former beliefs, and Arnold's
reference to folk religion, 'the belief structures of common people in
Phrygia' (above, p. 233), it may perhaps be appropriate to suggest
that a better approach might be to ask what were the concerns, the
anxieties, of the local community: what problems did they face, and
what answers does our author seek to give them?

From this angle, a few things are quite clear. For one, in our
author's view, there has been among some of his readers a quite
inadequate appreciation of the significance of Christ and his work.
He has been regarded as at best only one among many supernatural
powers—hence the emphasis in the first two chapters on his absolute
supremacy, in the Church and in the world. Again, some people have
not grasped the full significance of his death and resurrection: they
have been burdened with anxiety as to whether the work of Christ
was enough to deliver them from the cosmic powers, from the sway
of Fate, from the dangers of a hereafter that lies beyond death[1]—
hence the assurance (1.13) that they have been delivered from the
realm of darkness and translated into the kingdom of God's Son.
This also explains our author's insistence that they must continue to
walk with Christ, rooted and established in the faith (2.6–7). There is
much for which he can give thanks in his opening thanksgiving
period, but there is a danger that if they falter they may lose
everything. The purpose of the letter then is to give warning,
reassurance and encouragement in the face of this danger.[2] This
incidentally does not apply only to the first readers: there is a
message here for Christians in every age.

**3.1. Εἰ οὖν συνηγέρθητε τῷ Χριστῷ, τὰ ἄνω ζητεῖτε, οὗ ὁ
Χριστός ἐστιν ἐν δεξιᾷ τοῦ θεοῦ καθήμενος** Cf. Eph. 1.20,
καθίσας ἐν δεξίᾳ αὐτοῦ ἐν τοῖς ἐπουρανίοις. The last five words are
an echo of Ps. 110.1, which is widely quoted or echoed in the New
Testament (cf. the references in NA[27] 787; also C. H. Dodd,
According to the Scriptures (1952); Loader, 'Christ at the Right
Hand'. For Eph. see Moritz, 9–22, discussing the use of Pss. 110.1
and 8.7 in Eph. 1.20–23; Col. does not include Ps. 8 in this

---

[1] For just one example from a later date, cf. the 'hardships on the road' to the city of
Lithargoel in the *Acts of Peter and the Twelve* (NHC VI 1, 5.21–6.12; 7.23–8.3; D. M.
Parrott (ed.), *Nag Hammadi Codices V, 2–5 and VI*, (1979), 215–17, 219–21). The
Gnostic expected to be challenged by the keepers of the gates as he ascended through
the heavens, and so had to know the appropriate responses.

[2] Against this suggestion, there is the reference to a 'philosophy' (2.8) and to
persuasive speech (2.4), and there are the indications that some persons are going in for
ascetic practices (2.23), priding themselves on their achievement and on ostensibly
'spiritual' experiences, and disparaging those who have not enjoyed such experience
(2.8, 16). These must also be taken into account, but it is not impossible that several of
the factors mentioned might belong together: the problem might not lie in paganism *or*
Judaism *or* some kind of *gnosis*, but in some mysterious blend of all three. We simply
do not have enough information to be certain.

context).³ καθήμενος (BAGD 389, §1a; but note also §2) could be construed with the preceding ἐστιν, as forming a periphrastic tense (so AV), but most scholars appear to separate the words, inserting a comma (so NRSV): they are to seek the things above, where Christ is, seated at the right hand of God. There may not seem to be much difference between these renderings, but a difference is certainly present: this is not a single bland and rather colourless statement, 'where Christ is sitting at the right hand of God', but in fact two statements, (1) that Christ is above, i.e. in heaven, and (2) that he is seated at the right hand of God. As Dunn says (204), 'The image is one of power. The right (hand) of God (ἡ δεξιὰ τοῦ θεοῦ) was a way of expressing strength, powerful protection, and favor in Hebrew poetry, and to sit at the king's right hand was a sign of special recognition and authorization' (for both these points see the references he supplies).

Lightfoot (274) writes, 'The aorist συνηγέρθητε, like ἀπεθάνετε (ii.20), refers to their baptism; and the εἰ οὖν here is a resumption of the εἰ in ii.20.' He argues that baptism has a twofold symbolism, for death or burial and for resurrection, and that the negative side—the death and burial—implies the positive—the resurrection.⁴ 'Hence the form of the Apostle's resumption, εἰ ἀπεθάνετε, εἰ οὖν συνη-γέρθητε.' In Rom. 6.4, however, baptism is specifically related to the 'death' and 'burial' *of the believer* (συνετάφημεν οὖν αὐτῷ διὰ τοῦ βαπτίσματος εἰς τὸν θάνατον) and in v. 5 the resurrection of believers is seen as still future (εἰ γὰρ σύμφυτοι γεγόναμεν τῷ ὁμοιώματι τοῦ θανάτου αὐτοῦ, ἀλλὰ καὶ τῆς ἀναστάσεως ἐσόμεθα). In the view of many scholars, accordingly, our author here goes beyond Paul's own teaching and sees the resurrection of believers as already an accomplished fact. That this is not just a passing slip is shown by the fact that he has already used the same verb, συνηγέρθητε, at 2.12 (see pp. 204–06).

J. M. Robinson (*Trajectories*, 35) writes, 'The interpretation of baptism in Col. 2:12-13 has already brought the believer's rising into line with his dying by omitting the eschatological reservation ...⁵ That this is a growing edge in the Pauline school is indicated by Eph. 2.5-6, where even our enthronement in heaven is already accomplished .... In view of this direction of Pauline interpretation in the Deutero-Pauline period it is not too surprising when the same Paul who had opposed baptismal resurrection in Corinth came to be

³ In *Apoc. Jas.* (NHC I 2, 14.30–31) Jesus says, 'today I must take my place at the right hand of the Father' (*NHTB* 17), but in view of the other texts cited it cannot be claimed that this Gnostic text is necessarily quoting Col. Cf. Attridge (ed.), *Nag Hammadi Codex I*, 34.

⁴ As Dunn (203) rightly observes, 'a message of the cross without the resurrection would not be gospel'. But what is at issue here is the resurrection of *believers*.

⁵ Note 19 (on p. 36) cites our present verse as evidence that 'Colossians has indeed taken the first step in affirming that we have risen with Christ, as an indicative on which the imperative can be based .... Yet our relation to our resurrected selves is in Colossians still understood as paradoxical or indirect' (citing 3.3–4, with the insertion of 'then [and only then]'.

claimed as theirs by precisely those gnostic movements that held to this heresy, such as the Valentinians.' The Nag Hammadi treatise *On the Resurrection* (quoted at p. 205 above) 'quotes Paul (45:24-28) in support of precisely the same left-wing Deutero-Pauline development once opposed by Paul himself.'

The point of this is that it brings to our notice trends and tendencies in early Christian thinking which help towards the understanding of some later developments: Robinson (36) can speak of 'a clean split in the understanding of Paul' fairly early in the second century: 'gnostics appeal to him for support of baptismal resurrection, while the pastorals reject that view as heresy (2 Tim 2:18)'.[6] Similarly E. Cothenet, citing Eph. 2. 6 and 2 Tim. 2.18, refers to a conflict of interpretation within the Pauline school.[7] Others, however, from Lightfoot on, have seen no real contradiction here as compared with the major epistles: C. E. B. Cranfield for example can claim that Paul speaks of dying and rising with Christ in four different senses, which require to be carefully distinguished, and that therefore Col. 3.1 is not necessarily un-Pauline.[8] Bockmuehl (*Revelation and Mystery*, 190) writes: 'in baptism the believer has already died (ἀπεθάνετε) to the things of earth, and has been raised with Christ (v. 1). The new life is, however, still "hidden with Christ in God", and so the Christian's orientation must clearly be to the mode of life appropriate to the heavenly world (3:5-4:6 goes on to spell this out). ... We have in Col 3:3f., then, another clear confirmation of the idea of a continuing residual hiddenness of God's mysteries which was encountered in 1 Cor 2:6-10; Col 2:3.' If our author has indeed gone beyond Paul's own teaching, he has not gone very far: he bids his readers to seek 'the things above', to set their minds on heavenly things, not on things on earth, just as Paul regularly urges the readers in his major epistles to conduct themselves in a manner befitting the new life into which they have entered.

As noted above (p. 122), the Larger Catechism[9] refers to 'the needful but much neglected duty of improving our baptism', to be performed by us all our life long, and including 'by drawing strength from the death and resurrection of Christ, into whom

[6] For Gnostic views of the resurrection cf. Wedderburn, *Baptism*, 212–18.

[7] 'On pensera que les opposants poussent à l'extrême les affirmations d'Ephésiens sur le *Déja là* du salut: Ne sommes-nous pas déjà ressuscités et associés au règne du Christ dans les cieux (Ep 2. 6)? En de telles conditions il n'y a plus à attendre de résurrection, comme le disent les hérétiques dénoncés en 2 Tm 2.18. Le conflit d'interpretation a existé bel et bien à l'intérieur de ce qu'on peut appeler l'école "paulinienne"' ('La Tradition', 417). Cf. also Koester (*NTS* 8 (1961/1962), 329 n. 2): 'There is not a single instance in the genuine epistles of Paul in which the resurrection of the Christians in the past or present is referred to as the basis of the imperative. On the contrary, the resurrection of the believer remains a future expectation, or it is contained in the imperative itself, that is, it is only present in the dialectical demand to walk in newness of life.'

[8] Cf. Cranfield, *Romans* on Rom. 6.1–14, also 'Dying with Christ' and 'Romans 6:1-14 Revisited'.

[9] Appended to the Westminster Confession of Faith and agreed upon by the Westminster Assembly, and approved in 1648 by the General Assembly of the Church of Scotland.

we are baptized, for the mortifying of sin, and quickening of grace; and by endeavouring to live by faith, to have our conversation in holiness and righteousness, as those that have therein given up their names to Christ, and to walk in brotherly love, as being baptized by the same Spirit into one body' (answer to q. 167).

ἄνω (BAGD 76: 'above' or 'upwards') appears several times in the NT (John 2.7; 11. 41; Acts 2.19; Gal. 4.26; Phil. 3.14; Heb. 12.15), but the phrase τὰ ἄνω occurs only three times: in this and the following verse, and at John 8.23. Its significance is made clear by the contrast with τὰ ἐπὶ τῆς γῆς in verse 2, for which we may compare Phil. 3.19, οἱ τὰ ἐπίγεια φρονοῦντες. The verb ζητέω (BAGD 338) means basically to seek or look for something, while φρονέω in v. 2 (and in Phil.) has the somewhat stronger sense of 'set one's mind on, be intent on' (BAGD 866, §2; Lightfoot draws the distinction: 'You must not only *seek* heaven; you must also *think* heaven.').[10]

The striking thing is that as we proceed we shall find the implications of this worked out in thoroughly this-worldly, practical terms: it is easy enough to see the vices listed in vv. 5–9 as 'of the earth, earthy', but the virtues that are to be put on in the following verses belong equally to this life. The explanation is that what is called for is 'a complete reorientation of existence' (Dunn, 205, citing Wolter, *Der Brief an die Kolosser* (1993), 166). There is in fact a danger (both then and now!) of a false spirituality: it has been said of some people that they are so heavenly-minded that they are no earthly use! Setting one's mind on the things above does not mean concentration on something remote, ethereal, 'spiritual'—and divorced from the realities of everyday living. We may recall Phil. 2.1–13, where the verb φρονέω appears several times over, and particularly v. 5, the introduction to the Philippians hymn: τοῦτο φρονεῖτε ἐν ὑμῖν ὃ καὶ ἐν Χριστῷ Ἰησοῦ.[11] The new life is to be oriented towards Christ, inspired by him, no longer of this world only; but the virtues that characterize that new life are essentially practical, and such as to promote the betterment of human relationships. In his emphasis here, our author is at one with his teacher Paul.

3. ἀπεθάνετε γὰρ καὶ ἡ ζωὴ ὑμῶν κέκρυπται σὺν τῷ Χριστῷ ἐν τῷ θεῷ As the γάρ indicates, this verse is explanatory of what has just been said. As already noted above, the ἀπεθάνετε looks back to the earlier occurrence of this word at 2.20, and beyond it to the συνταφέντες of 2.12: in their baptism the readers died to their old life, whatever their former religious beliefs. In their previous

---

[10] Cf. the *Teachings of Silvanus* (NHC VII 4, 102.34–103.11): 'My son, do not allow your mind to stare downward, but rather let it look by means of the light at things above. For the light will always come from above. Even if it (the mind) is upon the earth, let it seek to pursue the things above. Enlighten your mind with the light of Heaven so that you may turn to the light of heaven' (*NHTB* 319f.; see also Zandee, *The Teachings of Sylvanus*, 288–91).

[11] For some other occurrences of this verb cf. Koester, *NTS* 8 (1961–62) 328f., who writes, 'The polemical reference in the usage of the verb in all these cases is obvious', adding in a footnote, 'The use of the word φρονεῖν indeed seems to be motivated primarily by such controversial concerns. This is particularly clear if we notice that out of twenty-five occurrences of the word in the Pauline epistles as many as nineteen are to be found in Rom. xii-xiv and Phil. i-iv.'

existence, in our author's view, they were not truly alive, but 'dead in your transgressions and the uncircumcision of your flesh' (2.13; see pp. 206–08 above).[12] Their true life is not yet manifest, but 'hidden with Christ in God' (the perfect κέκρυπται indicates that it has been hidden in the past, and remains hidden). Moule (112) suggests that there may be some connection with the ἀπόκρυφοι of 2.3: 'Christ is the storehouse of all God's secrets, including the Church's new life' (cf. also Dunn, 207).

ζωή (BAGD 340; *TWNT* ii. 833ff.) may refer to life in the physical sense, as opposed to death (BAGD §1), but in the New Testament is predominantly used 'of the supernatural life belonging to God and Christ, which the believers will receive in the future, but which they also enjoy here and now' (§2). In this sense it is especially common in the Fourth Gospel (cf. Dodd, *Interpretation*, 144–50, who notes 36 occurrences of the noun, with sixteen of the cognate verb ζῆν and three of ζωοποιεῖν). In that Gospel it is often qualified as αἰώνιος, eternal, which, however, does not mean merely everlasting, without end: it is the life of the aeon to come, a life of a new quality. As Dunn writes (207), 'it is a life lived from day to day within the world of every day, but lived out of a hidden resource (Rom 6:4; 2 Cor 4:10-11; 13:4) ... lived for God and his Christ (Rom 6:10-11; 14:8; 2 Cor 5:15), a life lived by faith in the Son of God (Gal 2:19-20)'. This is the life into which the readers have entered at their baptism, and which they are in danger of losing.

N. A. Dahl ('Christ, Creation and the Church', 441) makes an interesting link with Rom. 8.18–28 (cf. also pp. 155f. above):

The restoration of creation in Christ is not simply an empirical, visible fact; like the life of the Christians it can rather be said to be hidden with Christ in God (Col. iii. 3). Creation is in the present time not yet delivered from the futility to which it was subjected. It is still 'groaning', and even those who are in Christ and have received the Spirit as firstfruits, are groaning and waiting with patience. Until the day of redemption they have to endure sufferings; their relation to the course of events in the world is restored only in so far as they know that 'everything works for good with those who love God' (Rom. viii. 18-28).

Christians have to face sufferings, and they have also to face temptations. There exists a real danger, that the deception of Eve shall also find an analogy within the Church, a satanic travesty of the correspondence between the first and the last things (II Cor. xi. 3). But sufferings and temptations are not the only actual experience of Christians; the renewal of the 'new man' in a life of Christian virtues is also part of their experience (Col. iii.10f.).

---

[12] Lähnemann's suggested link between ἀπεθάνετε here and the νεκροὺς ὄντας in 2.13 is not entirely apposite, since the latter relates not to their baptism but to their pre-baptismal life.

If our author has gone beyond Paul's teaching in speaking of the readers as 'raised' with Christ, this verse restores the balance: their full and final resurrection has still to come, as the following verse makes plain.

4. ὅταν ὁ Χριστὸς φανερωθῇ, ἡ ζωὴ ὑμῶν, τότε καὶ ὑμεῖς σὺν αὐτῷ φανερωθήσεσθε ἐν δόξῃ The verb φανερόω has already appeared at 1.26 (p. 177 above), with reference to the revelation of the mystery 'hidden from ages and generations'. Here, however, the reference is clearly to the Parousia of Christ (the only explicit reference in this letter): when he appears, the faithful also will appear with him in glory (BAGD §2bβ compares 1 Pet. 5.4; 1 John 2.28; 3.2b; cf. also 1 Cor. 15.42–49, 51–54; 1 Thess. 4.13–18). This and nothing less is the hope to which they may look forward, and which they are in danger of jeopardizing.

The text printed above is that of NA²⁷, but this is another of the many cases in this letter (cf. Moule, 27 n. 1) where it is difficult to decide between a first and a second person pronoun. Metzger (*Textual Commentary*, 624) notes, 'the considerably stronger manuscript evidence which supports ὑμῶν, including P⁴⁶ and good representatives of both the Alexandrian and Western text-types (ℵ C D* F G P Ψ 33 81 88 104 1739 it vg copᵇᵒ goth arm eth al)', but on the other hand several commentators (e.g. Lightfoot, Moule, Lohse, Dunn) take the view that an original ἡμῶν (supported by B Dᶜ H K *et al.*) was altered by copyists to agree with the second person pronouns in the rest of the paragraph. Lohse (134) writes quite simply 'Christ is our life', and cites several further references: Phil. 1.21; 1 John 5.12; Ignatius, *Eph.* 3.2; 7.2; *Magn.* 1.2; *Smyrn* 4.1. Lightfoot (276) speaks of Paul's 'characteristic transition from the second person to the first': he is including himself among the recipients of this life. The first person has accordingly been adopted in the translation above.

Two points in this verse call for brief comment. The first is the phrase ἡ ζωὴ ἡμῶν placed in apposition to the name of Christ. This emphasizes once again his cardinal position (cf. the references above from Lohse in the previous paragraph). He is no mere subsidiary figure, but central to Christian faith and life, the source and inspiration for the life of faith, the supreme revelation of the grace and love of God. The second is the word δόξα, which has already been used three times in this letter (1.11, 27 (*bis*); see pp. 109, 179 above) but only now appears in its full significance. Scroggs (*The Last Adam*, 64; cf. also 95f., 103f.) writes, 'Glory belongs first and foremost to God. God manifests His divine nature and power through this glory. Yet it was intended by God for man in creation and will be restored to him in the world to come. ... It belongs essentially also to Christ, and what awaits man is precisely this very glory which Christ possesses. Christians are "heirs of God and fellow heirs with Christ, provided we suffer with him in order that we may also be glorified with him" (Rom 8:17).' This gives an added depth of meaning to the phrase in 1.27, Χριστὸς ἐν ὑμῖν, ἡ ἐλπὶς τῆς δόξης.¹³

¹³ On the following page Scroggs says, 'Despite Rom 8:30 this glory will not be manifest until the consummation': in that verse Paul lists in sequence election, calling, justification and glorification, all in the aorist (οὓς δὲ ἐδικαίωσεν, τούτους καὶ ἐδόξασεν). So Paul can himself omit 'the eschatological reservation'.

X
GUIDELINES FOR THE NEW LIFE
(3.5–17)

[5]Put to death, then, your earthly members, unchastity, impurity, passion, evil desire, and the covetousness which is idolatry, [6]on account of which the wrath of God is coming upon the sons of disobedience. [7]Among them you also once walked when you lived in these. [8]But now you too, put away all of them, wrath, anger, malice, slander, evil speaking from your mouth. [9]Do not lie to one another, since you have put off the old man with his practices, [10]and put on the new, who is being renewed unto knowledge according to the image of him who created him, [11]where there is no longer Greek and Jew, circumcision and uncircumcision, barbarian, Scythian, slave, free, but Christ is all and in all.

[12]Put on, then, as elect of God, holy and beloved, compassion, kindness, humility, gentleness, tolerance; [13]bear with one another and forgive one another, if anyone has a complaint against another; even as the Lord forgave you, so do you also. [14]And in addition to all these put on love, which is the bond of perfection. [15]And let the peace of Christ rule in your hearts, to which you were called in one body. And be thankful. [16]Let the word of Christ dwell in you richly, teaching and admonishing one another in all wisdom, singing with psalms and hymns and spiritual songs to God with thankfulness in your hearts. [17]And whatever you do in word or in deed, do all in the name of the Lord Jesus, giving thanks to God the Father through him.

W. D. Davies, in *Jewish and Pauline Studies* (115, 287),[1] observes, as others too have done, that most of the letters in the New Testament reveal a twofold structure: a first part dealing with doctrine is followed by a second, dealing with ethics. He takes Romans as his example, but Colossians would also serve his purpose. He goes on to say, 'The ethical sections of the various letters reveal a common tradition of catechesis, which may have been used in the instruction of converts, especially at baptism (cf. Rom 12:1; Eph 4:20-6:19; Col 3:8-4:12; Heb 12:1-2; Jas 1:1-4:10; 1 Pet 1:1-4:11; 4:12-5:14). This common tradition must not be regarded as having a fixed pattern, but the similarity in the order and contents of the material in the above sections is too marked to be accidental.'[2] Moule before him

---

[1] Chapter 15 (pp. 278–88) is devoted to 'The Moral Teaching of the Early Church', ch. 16 (289–302) to 'The Relevance of the Moral Teaching of the Early Church'.

[2] Cf. the tables setting out the relevant passages in Eph., Col., Jas. and 1 Pet., *PRJ*, 122–28.

(113) observes that recent research[3] 'has shown reason for believing that, before any of our known Christian writings took shape, there was already a recognized body of teaching delivered to enquirers who were seeking Baptism; and the various "headings", so to speak, of such teaching seem to appear (sometimes, significantly, in the same order and with the same catchwords) in independent writings.'

One problem here is that of determining how far such teaching is to be regarded as 'merely conventional', without any specific relation to a local situation, and how far we may assume a direct reference to shortcomings in the life and conduct of the readers addressed. This is a case in which 'mirror reading' may be quite misleading: warning against particular vices does not necessarily mean that these vices were prevalent. Moralists may be prone to painting a bleak picture, in the hope of effecting some reform.[4] Rather it is a question of setting out norms and standards of conduct, a pattern of life to be followed.

This is not the introduction of a new law, or a new legalism. We may recall the apparent clash between Paul's rejection of 'the works of the law' and the assertion in James (2.26) that 'faith without works is dead', on which Jülicher writes that the works which Paul rejects are those of the Law which was abrogated through Christ, while those for which James calls are fruits of faith, which even in Paul's view are not to be neglected: they are what in Rom. 12.1 is called 'our reasonable service'.[5] The desperate effort to gain salvation by scrupulous observance, the bland complacency generated by the knowledge that one has fulfilled one's obligations to the letter (but not necessarily in the spirit)—these are what Paul rejects. The glad service which is born of faith, of gratitude for forgiveness and for life and hope, is quite another matter. The old packman, Patrick Walker (quoted above, pp. 88f.), had it exactly right.

---

[3] He mentions in particular P. Carrington, *The Primitive Christian Catechism*, (1940) and E. G. Selwyn's commentary on 1 Peter (1946), Essay II (365–466). Moritz (*A Profound Mystery* 185 n. 21) notes among the key elements listed by Carrington the expressions *put off* (Col. 3.8f.; Eph. 4.25ff.; 1 Pet. 2.1 and Jas. 1.21); *new creation* (Col. 3.9–15; Eph. 4.22–23; 1 Pet. 2.22f.; Jas. 1.18); *watch and pray* (Col. 4.2–6; Eph. 6.18; 1 Pet. 4.7); and *stand and resist* (Col. 4.12; Eph. 6.10–17; 1 Pet. 5.8–12; Jas. 4.7b).

[4] Cf. Best, *Ephesians*, 423–25: 'Moralists tend to overstress the dark side of any society they attack. Small groups seeking to distinguish themselves from their prevailing culture do the same; this has been particularly true of small religious groups' (424). He notes that it is possible to find similar pessimistic descriptions of contemporary culture in non-Jewish and non-Christian sources (e.g. the satirists), but there were areas where there was much to commend in the ancient world.

[5] 'Die Werke, die P. zurückweist, sind Werke des durch Christus abrogierten Gesetzes, die Werke, die Jak fordert, sind Früchte des Glaubens, wie sie auch nach P. nicht ausbleiben dürfen und können: sie sind, was Rm 12 1 der *vernünftige Gottesdienst* heißt.' (in Jülicher and Fascher, *Einleitung*, 207). Davies (*PRJ*, 70) notes the dilemma: 'The Apostle who first turned to the Gentiles on the ground that salvation could be received apart from the Law, himself lived and died "a Pharisee".' Cf. his whole discussion, also Knox, *PCJ*, 122 n. 54. On the alleged clash between Paul and James cf. W. Pratscher, *Der Herrenbruder Jakobus* (1987), 213–16; J. Painter, *Just James* (1997), 265–69.

5. νεκρώσατε οὖν τὰ μέλη τὰ ἐπὶ τῆς γῆς, πορνείαν ἀκαθαρσίαν πάθος ἐπιθυμίαν κακήν, καὶ τὴν πλεονεξίαν, ἥτις ἐστὶν εἰδωλολατρία[6] Cf. Eph. 5.3, πορνεία δὲ καὶ ἀκαθαρσία πᾶσα ἢ πλεονεξία μηδὲ ὀνομαζέσθω ἐν ὑμῖν; also the 'works of the flesh' in Gal. 5.19–21: πορνεία, ἀκαθαρσία, ἀσέλγεια, εἰδωλολατρία κτλ. Dibelius (1927 edn, 31) argued for a five-point catalogue of vices,[7] which could have been merely a conventional listing of the sins of Gentiles, as is suggested by the appearance of some of these vices in other lists, and without specific reference to the local situation. R. M. Grant, however, (*HTR* 40 (1947), 6) asks, 'Is not this list based on a combination of the sixth (fornication, impurity, passion) and tenth (evil desire, covetousness) commandments interpreted in relation to the first table of the Law (idolatry)?' That would suggest that such lists were traditional summaries of the main points of the Decalogue, to serve as guidelines for life and conduct.

Dunn (213) notes that such catalogues were standard items in the ethical teaching of the time, particularly popular among the Stoics but also common in Judaism (he cites e.g. Wisd. 14.25–26; 4 Macc. 1.26–27; 2.15; 1QS 4.9–11; Philo, *Sacr.* 32; *2 En.* 10.4–5). He draws special attention to CD 4.17–19 (already noted by Lohse), which includes Hebrew equivalents of four of the vices listed above (πορνεία, ἀκαθαρσία, πλεονεξία and εἰδωλολατρία); but Lohse observes that this text does not correspond exactly with Col. 3.5 (πάθος is missing, and so, we may add, is ἐπιθυμία κακή, both included in Grant's decalogue list above). For Dunn, 'such lists are never merely formal and always contain distinctive elements, presumably judged appropriate for the particular occasion'.

On **νεκρώσατε** (BAGD 535; *TWNT* iv. 898–99) Moule compares Rom. 8.13, εἰ δὲ πνεύματι τὰς πράξεις τοῦ σώματος θανατοῦτε, ζήσεσθε, where the same thought is conveyed in different terms. The only other occurrences of this verb in the NT are at Rom. 4.19 and Heb. 11.12, both with reference to Abraham's aged body (BAGD cites passages for its use in the passive in the sense *worn out, impotent* 'of persons whose physical capabilities have failed in a certain respect'). There is a slight incongruity here, since the readers are said above (2.12, 20; 3.3) to have already died with Christ in their baptism, and now they are bidden to put to death their 'earthly members' (lit. 'the members which are on the earth'). As noted

---

[6] Davies (*PRJ*, 139), taking Col. as written by Paul himself, lists this verse among a number which reveal a knowledge of the words and spirit of Jesus. Cf. Matt. 5.29, 30; Mark 9.43, 47; Matt. 18.8, 9. On the beginnings of the Jesus tradition, comparing Paul and (the sources of) the Synoptics, cf. J. Schröter, *NTS* 50 (2004), 53–76. Col. is not there mentioned, but the references listed by Davies show the survival of that tradition in the Pauline school.

[7] On this subject see A. Vögtle, *Die Tugend- u. Lasterkataloge im NT* (1936). Further references in Lohse, 138 n. 8; Best, *Ephesians*, 474 n. 2; P. S. Zaas, 'Catalogues and Context: 1 Corinthians 5 and 6', *NTS* 34 (1988), 622 n. 4; cf. also Pokorný's excursus 'Lists of Virtues and Vices', 162–75. Zaas opposes the 'scholarly consensus' that these catalogues are traditional and not specifically related to the situation addressed in the letter.

above, however (p. 226, on 2.20), the explanation is very simple: they have died to the στοιχεῖα, to the old life which they lived before their conversion, but they are still living in this world and subject to all its dangers and its temptations. The brief catalogue of vices which follows indicates some of the things which must be 'put to death', as not compatible with a Christian life.

μέλος (BAGD 501; *TWNT* iv. 559, esp. 570) means literally a limb or member, part of the body. It is also used figuratively in speaking of the Christian community as a body with many members (BAGD §3), e.g. 1 Cor. 12.27 ὑμεῖς δέ ἐστε σῶμα Χριστοῦ καὶ μέλη ἐκ μέρους (cf. also Eph. 5.30, μέλη ἐσμὲν τοῦ σώματος αὐτοῦ); at Rom. 12.5 and Eph. 4.25 Christians are ἀλλήλων μέλη (cf. also the v.l. at Eph. 4.16). This is another case in which the same word is used in Eph. and Col. with different meanings. Here BAGD (§2) paraphrases: *put to death whatever in your nature belongs to the earth* (cf. NRSV, 'put to death, therefore, whatever in you is earthly'). The phrase τὰ ἐπὶ τῆς γῆς clearly looks back to v. 2: the vices listed belong to this world, not to the things above.[8] In the translation above a paraphrase has been used rather than a literal translation, to make the point more clearly and succinctly.

The vices themselves are not parts of the body, which presents a problem for the interpreter. Moule (115) writes, 'It seems best (although it is decidedly odd) to treat the phrase as meaning "your limbs as put to earthly purposes", the use of your limbs for sensuality—a meaning which provides a parallel to πορνείαν κ.τ.λ. which follows. ... It is possible, thus, that "to put to death the limbs which are on earth" means to be "dead" as regards their immoral use.' He adds that Lightfoot 'virtually takes τὰ μέλη τὰ ἐπὶ τῆς γῆς as = τὸν παλαιὸν ἄνθρωπον (v. 9): "the old man with all his members must be pitilessly slain."'

Théodore Reinach, in the preface to his *Textes d'auteurs grecs et romains relatifs au Judaïsme*,[9] writes to the effect that once hatred has taken root against a group or class of people, for whatever reason, then everything in the object of that hatred becomes deserving of hate, adding that the Jew in antiquity did not escape this fatal law.[10] This 'fatal law' was by no means confined to the ancient world: it can be seen right down through history into modern times, as groups or classes or even whole peoples form a judgement about some other group, class or nation.[11] Those on the one side are firmly convinced

---

[8] Several mss insert ὑμῶν after τὰ μέλη (cf. Rom. 6.13, 19), but the witnesses for omission include P⁴⁶ ℵ* B C* *et al.* and it is not really necessary.

[9] See p. 201 n. 26 above.

[10] 'Une fois l'aversion contre une classe d'hommes créée et enracinée par un motif quelconque, dans l'objet haï tout devient haïssable; l'opinion préconçue donne naissance ou crédit à des fables, à des calomnies, qui contribuent, à leur tour, à la généraliser et à la fortifier, quelquefois même survivent à ses véritables causes. Le Juif, dans l'antiquité, n'a pas échappé à cette loi fatale.'

[11] Lohse (138) at this point writes, 'Sexual sins, covetousness, and idolatry are cited, because these were vices for which the Jews especially reproached the pagans.'

that those on the other side are guilty of sundry faults and misdemeanours, and the catalogue may be passed down through generations. It is this that gives one pause about accepting such allegations at face value. We can see the same kind of prejudice and hostility in various areas of conflict in our modern world. The perennial problem in these areas is quite simply how to change that attitude.

The vices listed characterize pagan life as seen from a Christian point of view, and particularly as marked by sexual depravity. πορνεία (BAGD 693; *TWNT* vi. 579–95; for Paul see 592–94) means *prostitution, unchastity, fornication*, and is used of every kind of unlawful sexual intercourse (cf. 1 Cor. 5.1). It is one of the items listed in the apostolic decree of Acts 15.20. Paul warns his readers ἀπέχεσθαι ἀπὸ τῆς πορνείας in the earliest of his letters (1 Thess. 4.3; cf. 1 Cor. 6.18, φεύγετε τὴν πορνείαν), and the word and its cognates appear regularly in such lists as this. Several of the mother goddess cults in the Near East had temple prostitutes on a more or less permanent basis (*TWNT* vi. 581), although Herodotus (i.199) appears to be somewhat shocked to find this in Babylon; the Greeks generally rejected it, but the temple of Aphrodite in Corinth was notorious.[12]

ἀκαθαρσία (BAGD 28; *TWNT* iii. 430–32) refers originally to *impurity* or uncleanness, often with a cultic significance, since uncleanness rendered a person unfit to tread upon holy ground. In Hellenistic Judaism, however, there was a tendency towards an ethical emphasis, which predominates in Christian usage. In the Gospels this word appears only once, at Matt. 23.27 (the 'whited sepulchres'), where NRSV renders ἔσωθεν δὲ γέμουσιν ὀστέων νεκρῶν καὶ πάσης ἀκαθαρσίας by 'inside they are full of the bones of the dead and of all kinds of filth'. In Paul's letters (nine out of ten occurrences in the NT) it is used predominantly in the sense of *immorality,* and especially of sexual sins (Rom. 1.24; 6.19; 1 Thess. 2.3; 4.7). At Gal. 5.19; Eph. 5.3; Col. 3.5, as noted above, and also at 2 Cor. 12.21 (where it comes first), it is associated with πορνεία.

πάθος (BAGD 602; *TWNT* v. 926–29) occurs only three times in the NT, in the plural at Rom. 1.26 (πάθη ἀτιμίας, degrading passions), in the singular here and at 1 Thess. 4.5 (ἐν πάθει ἐπιθυμίας, lustful passion). It could mean suffering (BAGD §1; cf. *Barn.* 6.7 and frequently in Ignatius), but that is ruled out by the context, since the two preceding terms in the list both relate to sexual misconduct; we must therefore adopt the other meaning (BAGD §2), passion, especially of a sexual nature, as in Rom. and 1 Thess.

ἐπιθυμία (BAGD 293; *TWNT* iii. 168–72) can be used in a good sense (e.g. Phil. 1.23; 1 Thess. 2.17), but is frequently employed in a

---

[12] A German introduction to the NT refers to a great seaport, with temples for every kind of deity, *zum Teil mit Scharen von Hierodulen*. The English translation runs 'some of them thronged with worshippers'—a flagrant mistranslation: such hierodules were not worshippers in our sense!

bad sense, as a desire for something forbidden (e.g. Rom. 1.24; 6.12; 7.7–8; 13.14; Gal. 5.16, 24; Eph. 2.3; 4.22). Here any ambiguity is removed by the qualification κακή (BAGD 397f.; this phrase was already used by Plato, *Laws* 854a: *TWNT* iii. 168, 30). Best (*Ephesians*, 208, on Eph. 2.3) notes that the word 'regularly carries an evil connotation in the NT, probably under Jewish influence'. But it also has a bad sense in Stoic philosophy, as one of the passions which reason ought to control, if not eliminate. 'The desires of Jews and Christians however are evil because they are opposed to God's will, not because they disturb "calm reason".'

πλεονεξία (BAGD 667; *TWNT* vi. 266–74, esp. 271) means greediness, avarice, covetousness, literally 'a desire to have more'. It occurs twice in the Gospels (Mark 7.22, in a list of vices; Luke 12.15), eight times in the rest of the NT: Rom. 1.29; 2 Cor. 9.5; Eph. 4.19; 5.3; Col. 3.5; 1 Thess. 2.5; 2 Pet. 2.3, 14. This is not a sexual vice like those which precede, although we may note that the Decalogue includes the command 'You shall not covet your neighbour's wife' (Exod. 20.17). At 1 Tim. 6.10 the love of money (φιλαργυρία) is the root of all kinds of evil. According to Luke 12.15 Jesus already warned against this vice (φυλάσσεσθε ἀπὸ πάσης πλεονεξίας): a man's life does not consist in the abundance of his possessions. Here it is characterized as εἰδωλολατρία. Delling (*TWNT* vi. 271) finds the best explanation for this in another saying of Jesus, Matt. 6.24; par. Luke 16.13: 'You cannot serve God and Mammon'.[13] The preceding καὶ τήν serves to differentiate πλεονεξία from the vices mentioned before it, and points forward to the following ἥτις ἐστὶν εἰδωλολατρία. This identification with idolatry is not made in Eph. 5.3, but in Eph. 5.5 the πλεονέκτης is characterized as εἰδωλολάτρης.

6. δι' ἃ ἔρχεται ἡ ὀργὴ τοῦ θεοῦ ἐπὶ τοὺς υἱοὺς τῆς ἀπειθείας Cf. Eph. 5.6, διὰ ταῦτα γὰρ ἔρχεται ἡ ὀργὴ τοῦ θεοῦ ἐπὶ τοὺς υἱοὺς τῆς ἀπειθείας.

The text is firm at Eph. 5.6, and there is no indication of the words ἐπὶ τοὺς υἱοὺς τῆς ἀπειθείας being omitted in any ms. In Col., however, these words are missing in P⁴⁶ B copˢᵃ ethʳᵒ and several Fathers (Clement Cyprian Macrobius Ambrosiaster Ephraem Jerome), which prompts the question whether this is an interpolation influenced by the parallel in Eph. Moulton, for example, says bluntly, 'In Col. 3⁶ "sons of disobedience" is interpolated', arguing that this Semitism is almost completely confined to Eph. (*Grammar of NT Greek*, ii, (1929), 23). These words are omitted also by Lightfoot (279, 312), Lohse (136, 139 n. 30), Pokorný (158) and others (including Bultmann, *TWNT* vi. 12 n. 2).

On the other hand, the evidence supporting inclusion is very strong (ℵ A C D F G H K L P almost all minuscules it vg syrᵖˑʰ copᵇᵒ goth arm ethᵖᵖ Clement Chrysostom al); the following ἐν οἷς seems to require a reference to people (the ἐν τούτοις would appear to be redundant on the shorter reading); and the καὶ ὑμεῖς appears to suggest some previous reference to unbelieving Gentiles. The UBS committee retains the words, but in square brackets (so also NA²⁷) to indicate a measure of doubt (see Metzger, *Textual Commentary*, 624f; the attestation in NA²⁷ differs in some points). This reading is adopted by Lindemann (55), Wright (135 n. 1) and Dunn (210).

[13] Lohse (139 n. 24) observes that direct dependence on a saying of Jesus can hardly be assumed: 'The critique of "covetousness" is based on a value judgment common to Judaism and primitive Christianity.'

The relative ἅ at the beginning refers back to the vices listed in the preceding verse. ἔρχεται could be rendered as a simple present ('through which the wrath of God comes', i.e. this is the natural consequence), but as Dunn notes (216) the concept of the wrath of God as taken over by the first Christians 'is more typically future oriented; so predominantly in Paul (Rom 2:5, 8; 3:5; 5:9; 9:22; 1 Thess 5:9). And the closest parallel (1 Thess 1: 10 τῆς ὀργῆς τῆς ἐρχομένης; cf. Matt 3:7/ Luke 3:7: "the coming wrath"[14]) suggests that this is what is in view here.' Lightfoot long ago (279) observed that 'the present ἔρχεσθαι is frequently used to denote the *certainty* of a future event, e.g. Matt. xvii. 11, Joh. iv. 21, xiv. 3, whence ὁ ἐρχόμενος is a designation of the Messiah.'

ὀργή (BAGD 578–79; *TWNT* v. 382–448; for the NT see 419ff.) means anger, wrath or indignation, whether as a human emotion (e.g. Eph. 4.31; Jas. 1.19–20 and Col. 3.8 below) or (frequently) of the wrath of God as the divine reaction against evil (e.g. Rom. 1.18). Here as in Matt. 3.7; Luke 3.7; 1 Thess. 1.10 (see above) and several other passages it is used of God's future judgement, often simply as 'the wrath' without further qualification. C. H. Dodd in a lengthy note (*Romans*, 20–24) observes that Paul never uses the verb 'to be angry' with God as subject, and that there are only three places where he uses the expression 'the wrath of God' (Rom. 1.18; Eph. 5.6; Col. 3.6. If Eph. and Col. were written by later disciples, this might suggest that both are here drawing upon Rom.). 'On the other hand, he constantly uses "wrath", or "the Wrath", in a curiously impersonal way' (21, citing Eph. 2.3; Rom. 9.22; Rom. 2.5; 1 Thess. 1.10; Rom. 4.15). Paul in fact retains the concept 'not to describe the attitude of God to man, but to describe an inevitable process of cause and effect in a moral universe, as we shall find in the verses which now follow' (23). He concludes, 'In the long run we cannot think with full consistency of God in terms of the highest human ideals of personality and yet attribute to Him the irrational passion of anger' (24).[15]

According to 1 John (4.8, 16), God is love, and his love is revealed in the fact that he sent his Son into the world, that we might live through him (4.9–10; cf. also John 3.16). Some people find it difficult to reconcile this with any thought of the wrath of God, but that rests on a false conception of God. He is not a benign old gentleman over whose eyes the wool may be pulled with impunity, a God whose only function is to forgive. According to Hebrews (10.31), 'It is a fearful thing to fall into the hands of the living God.' He is holy, and expects holiness from his people (Lev. 11.44–45), not a sanctimonious piety but the resolute and steadfast observance of proper rules of life and conduct. A father has to discipline his children if they are to grow up responsible adults.

[14] Both Matt. and Luke read the unambiguous μελλούσης.
[15] Cf. also G. H. C. Macgregor, 'The Concept of the Wrath of God in the New Testament', *NTS* 7 (1960/61), 101–09; further references in Best, *Ephesians*, 210 n. 28.

It should be added that ὀργή and θυμός both appear in v. 8, in a
list of things to be 'set aside'.

As noted above, there is some doubt as to whether the words ἐπὶ
τοὺς υἱοὺς τῆς ἀπειθείας should be retained. This Semitism[16] occurs
twice in Eph. (2.2; 5.6), in both cases as firm text, whereas here it is
omitted in P[46] and B. As noted above, the phrase has been retained in
the translation because of the weight of evidence in its favour.
ἀπειθεία (BAGD 82; *TWNT* vi. 11–12) means disobedience toward
God (Rom. 11.30, 32; Heb. 4.6, 11). Under the cognate verb ἀπειθέω
BAGD (§3) note, 'since, in the view of the early Christians, the
supreme disobedience was a refusal to believe their gospel, ἀ. may be
restricted in some passages to the meaning *disbelieve, be an
unbeliever*'; but this meaning is disputed. K. G. Kuhn (*NTS* 7
(1960/61), 339) writes that there is no word in Hebrew which exactly
corresponds to ἀπειθεία; at Qumran sinners are called 'sons of
wickedness', 'sons of darkness', or 'sons of corruption', and
prohibition of any association with them is a regular feature of the
texts.

7. ἐν οἷς καὶ ὑμεῖς περιεπατήσατέ ποτε, ὅτε ἐζῆτε ἐν
τούτοις Cf. Eph. 2.2, ἐν αἷς ποτε περιεπατήσατε κατὰ τὸν αἰῶνα
τοῦ κόσμου τούτου. In Eph. the relative at the beginning refers back
to the nearer of the two antecedents, ἁμαρτίαις, and is consequently
feminine. Here the οἷς is either masculine or neuter, according to the
text adopted. If we omit ἐπὶ τοὺς υἱοὺς τῆς ἀπειθείας, the
antecedent is the ἅ in v. 6, referring back to the vices of v. 5, and
the final ἐν τούτοις is somewhat redundant. If on the other hand we
retain these words, then the antecedent is τοὺς υἱοὺς, and the final
phrase finds appropriate meaning: 'these' are the vices which marked
the lives of the readers before their conversion, when they lived
among the 'sons of disobedience'.[17] The aorist περιεπατήσατε
simply states the fact, whereas the imperfect ἐζῆτε is durative: when
you were living in them.

All that is now behind them, and our author continues with a
further list of vices which are to be 'set aside' (ἀποτίθημι in a
figurative sense (BAGD 101, §1b) means to lay aside something, or
rid oneself of it (cf. Rom. 13.12, ἀποθώμεθα οὖν τὰ ἔργα τοῦ
σκότους; Eph. 4.22 ἀπόθεσθαι ὑμᾶς ... τὸν παλαιὸν ἄνθρωπον; Eph.
4.25, ἀποθέμενοι τὸ ψεῦδος). The νυνὶ δέ of v. 8 marks a clear
contrast with the ποτε of v. 7.

---

[16] F. W. Danker (*NTS* 7 (1960/61), 94) writes: 'Evidently the idiom felt at home in
both Hebrew and Greek, and therefore the New Testament writers do not hesitate to
employ it along with their best literary phrasing.'
[17] NRSV offers an alternative: 'These are the ways you also once followed, when you
were living that life' (or: 'among such people'). This takes the relative to refer right
back, via the δι' ἅ in v. 6, to the vices listed in v. 5, and the final τούτοις (on the
alternative rendering) as referring to the sons of disobedience. However we construe
the verse, the meaning is clear: the readers once lived among the sons of disobedience,
and their 'walk', their way of life, was characterized by these vices.

8. νυνὶ δὲ ἀπόθεσθε καὶ ὑμεῖς τὰ πάντα, ὀργήν, θυμόν, κακίαν, βλασφημίαν, αἰσχρολογίαν ἐκ τοῦ στόματος ὑμῶν Cf. Eph. 4.31, πᾶσα πικρία καὶ θυμὸς καὶ ὀργὴ καὶ κραυγὴ καὶ βλασφημία ἀρθήτω ἀφ᾽ ὑμῶν σὺν πάσῃ κακίᾳ; also Eph. 4.29, πᾶς λόγος σαπρὸς ἐκ τοῦ στόματος ὑμῶν μὴ ἐκπορευέσθω.

θυμός (BAGD 365, §2; *TWNT* iii. 167–68: 'Ein sachlicher Unterschied zwischen ὀργή und θυμός besteht nicht'—there is no material difference between these two terms) is another word for anger (cf. Luke 4.28; Acts 19.28; Heb. 11.27), and frequently appears along with ὀργή (as often in LXX): Rom. 2.8 (of the wrath of God; cf. Rev. 16.19; 19.15); Eph. 4.31 and here. At 2 Cor. 12.20 and Gal. 5.20 it appears in the plural in another list of vices. It may be possible to justify the wrath of God as the divine reaction against evil, but there is no place in the Christian life for what Dodd (see p. 247) calls 'the irrational passion of anger'.[18] **κακία** (BAGD 397; *TWNT* iii. 483–85) means generally depravity or wickedness, but often seems to denote 'a special kind of moral inferiority' (BAGD), something like *malice* or *malignity* (cf. Rom. 1.29; Tit. 3.3; 1 Pet. 2.1, in addition to Col. and Eph.). **βλασφημία** (BAGD 143) is another word which has come down into modern English, but usually in the restricted sense of blasphemy against God (*TWNT* i. 621–23 stresses this aspect for the NT, but note §A*ab* on p. 620). In Greek it refers more generally to abusive speech or slander (e.g. Mark 7.22, in a list of vices; Matt. 12.31; in the plural, Matt. 15.19; 1 Tim. 6.4, also in lists of vices). We may recall the words of James (3.5–12) about the tongue: 'a restless evil, full of deadly poison'; an earlier verse (1.26) is critical of those who think they are religious, but do not bridle their tongues. Malicious gossip can be severely disruptive of good relations within any community. **αἰσχρολογία** (BAGD 25: *evil speech* in the sense of *obscene speech* or *abusive speech*), occurs only here in the New Testament. It is, to say the least, difficult to maintain friendly relations with people who are foul-mouthed and abusive.

9. μὴ ψεύδεσθε εἰς ἀλλήλους, ἀπεκδυσάμενοι τὸν παλαιὸν ἄνθρωπον σὺν ταῖς πράξεσιν αὐτοῦ Cf. Eph. 4.25, διὸ ἀποθέμενοι τὸ ψεῦδος λαλεῖτε ἀλήθειαν ἕκαστος μετὰ τοῦ πλησίον αὐτοῦ, ὅτι ἐσμὲν ἀλλήλων μέλη; also Eph. 4.22, ἀπόθεσθαι ὑμᾶς ... τὸν παλαιὸν ἄνθρωπον (for ἀπόθεσθαι cf. on v. 7 above).

In a small, close-knit community mutual trust and confidence are vital: if its members cannot trust one another to be truthful and honest in their dealings, the whole life of the community is based on very shaky foundations. This is brought out more clearly in Eph. 4.25, where it is said that Christians are 'members of one another' (cf. Rom. 12.5). The Decalogue already contains a commandment against bearing false witness (Exod. 20.16), and falsehood and lying are often condemned in the Old Testament.

---

[18] Best (*Ephesians*, 450) notes that the question whether righteous anger is possible goes back as far as Origen; but even a righteous anger must be controlled. Blind irrational rage is quite another matter.

For ψεύδομαι and its cognates see BAGD 891–92; *TWNT* ix. 590–99 (for the NT see 596–99). The verb occurs in the story of Ananias and Sapphira (Acts 5.3, 4), also in the Beatitudes (Matt. 5.11, ψευδόμενοι; cf. the false witnesses (ψευδεῖς) against Stephen at Acts 6.13), but apart from our present verse, Eph. 4.25 and Jas. 3.14 injunctions against falsehood are not common in the NT.[19] On several occasions, however, Paul is concerned to emphasize that he is speaking the truth and not lying (Rom 9.1; 2 Cor. 11.31; Gal. 1.20; cf. also 1 Tim. 2.7). The εἰς ἀλλήλους shows that our author is thinking primarily of relations within the Christian community, but Lohse (140–41) observes that this phrase 'should in no way be taken to mean that Christians could take the question of truth less seriously when speaking to non-Christians'.

The participles ἀπεκδυσάμενοι here and ἐνδυσάμενοι in v. 10 could be taken as imperatival (cf. p. 111 above), introducing further injunctions (so e.g. Lightfoot, 280f., Lohse, 141, Pokorný, 168f.; further references in Dunn, 210 n. 6), but it is more natural to take them as genuine participles (so Aletti, 229, Dunn, ibid.). They supply the reason for the injunctions just given; in their baptism the readers have stripped off the old man, and at least made a start on putting on the new; an imperative ἐνδύσασθε follows in v. 12, which indicates that the process is not yet complete.

The key to the understanding of what is at times rather confusing (cf. p. 203 above) lies in our author's interpretation of baptism. As the rite which marked the admission of a convert, it replaces circumcision, which was the initiation rite for a Gentile convert to Judaism (cf. 2.11). It signified the end of the old life and the beginning of a new one: the convert had in fact 'died' to that old life and entered into a new sphere of existence (cf. 2.20; 3.1). Our author interprets it as 'burial' with Christ, and resurrection through faith in the power of God (2.12). The 'circumcision' of Christ is interpreted as a stripping off of the body of flesh (cf. ἐν τῇ ἀπεκδύσει τοῦ σώματος τῆς σαρκός at 2.11), which is somehow associated with his death, and in his death he 'stripped off' the principalities and powers (2.15; we have already met the participle ἀπεκδυσάμενος in that verse, cf. pp. 211–12 above). Baptism by immersion lent itself to the development of an imagery of 'garment symbolism': the candidate left his garments behind as he entered the water, and put on a fresh set of clothing when he emerged.[20] Hence the talk of putting to death

---

[19] In *Gos. Thom.* log. 6 (NHC II 2, 33.15ff.) the disciples ask Jesus about fasting, prayer and almsgiving (matters in which this Gospel shows no interest; cf. log. 14, 104). In reply, Jesus says, 'Do not tell lies, and do not do what you hate, for all things are plain in the sight of heaven'. For the first four words J. E. Ménard in his commentary ((1975), 86) compares Eph. 4.25 and Col. 3.9. *NHTB* 92, however, compares Exod. 20.16; Lev. 19.11; Deut. 5.20; Eph. 4.25; Col. 3.9; Jas. 3.14. This logion could have been drawn from any of these, and not necessarily from Col. Cf. also R. Uro, *Thomas* (2003), 72 n. 92. For Eph. 4.25 cf. Best, *Ephesians*, 445f.

[20] Cf. the *Gospel of Philip* (NHC II 3, 75.22–24; ed. Layton, 193): 'It is necessary that we put on the living man. Therefore, when he is about to go down into the water, he unclothes himself, in order that he may put on the living man.'

the vices of the old life, of putting off the old man and (v. 10) putting on the new.[21]

The 'old man' is their former pre-conversion way of life, which they have now left behind. παλαιός (BAGD 605—cf. also ἄνθρωπος §2cβ, p. 68; *TWNT* v. 714–17, esp. 715f.) 'is used consistently by Paul to denote what belonged to life prior to faith in Christ (1 Cor 5:7-8), the "old covenant" (2 Cor 3:14), and in this phrase "the old self" (Rom 6:6; also Eph 4:22). The figure is clearly a way of indicating a whole way of life (more comprehensive than the τὰ μέλη of 3:5 and the ἐζῆτε ἐν τούτοις of 3:7), a way of life prior to and without Christ and characterized by the sort of vices listed in 3:5 and 8, here referred to as "its practices" (as in Rom 8:15)' (Dunn, 220).[22]

10. καὶ ἐνδυσάμενοι τὸν νέον τὸν ἀνακαινούμενον εἰς ἐπίγνωσιν κατ' εἰκόνα τοῦ κτίσαντος αὐτόν Cf. Eph. 4.24, ἐνδύσασθε τὸν καινὸν ἄνθρωπον, also Eph. 6.11, ἐνδύσασθε τὴν πανοπλίαν τοῦ θεοῦ; Rom. 13.14, ἐνδύσασθε τὸν κύριον Ἰησοῦν Χριστόν; Gal. 3.27, ὅσοι γὰρ εἰς Χριστὸν ἐβαπτίσθητε, Χριστὸν ἐνεδύσασθε.[23] That this imagery is not confined to associations with baptism is shown by Rom. 13.12: ἡ νὺξ προέκοψεν, ἡ δὲ ἡμέρα ἤγγικεν. ἀποθώμεθα οὖν τὰ ἔργα τοῦ σκότους, ἐνδυσώμεθα δὲ τὰ ὅπλα τοῦ φωτός.[24]

W. D. Davies (*PRJ* 37 n. 3) quotes A. Plummer (*2 Corinthians*, 85) as saying 'καινός always implies superiority to that which is not καινός, whereas what is νέος may be either inferior or better than what is not νέος.' If Plummer is correct, one may wonder what to make of νέος here, with ἀνακαινούμενον in apposition. It is better to follow Lightfoot's distinction (281): 'Of the two words νέος and καινός, the former refers solely to time, the other denotes quality also.'[25] He adds 'Here the idea which is wanting to νέος, and which καινός gives in the parallel passage [i.e. Eph. 4.24] is more than supplied by the addition τὸν ἀνακαινούμενον κ.τ.λ.'

The two participles ἀπεκδυσάμενοι and ἐνδυσάμενοι are both

[21] Cf. van der Horst, 'Observations on a Pauline Expression', who notes that 'clothing' metaphors were used rather frequently (184; cf. also Best, *Ephesians*, 431), and quotes a tale about the philosopher Pyrrho, founder of the Sceptic school, who when mocked for inconsistency excused himself by saying χαλεπόν ἐστιν τὸν ἄνθρωπον ἐκδῦναι (recorded by Eusebius, *PE* xiv.18.26 from Antigonus of Carystus, 3rd c. BC). The reference to the 'old' man must, however, be 'a specific Pauline addition' (184 n. 4). Cf. also Moule, 'St Paul and Dualism, discussed earlier (p. 212, n. 50). Philostratus, in his Life of Apollonius of Tyana (iv.20), tells of a young man who 'fell in love with the austerity of the philosophers, and donned their cloak, and stripping off his old self modelled his life in future upon that of Apollonius' (cited in C. K. Barrett, *The New Testament Background: Selected Documents* (1956), 78).
[22] For the language of παλαιὸς and καινὸς ἄνθρωπος H. D. Betz (*NTS* 46 (2000), 339 n. 100) lists Rom. 6.6; 7.6; also Col. 3.9–10; Eph. 2.15; 4.20–24; and for καινὴ κτίσις (see below) Gal. 6.15; 2 Cor. 5.17; cf. Rom. 6.4; 7.6. The theme of the article is ὁ ἔσω ἄνθρωπος in Pauline anthropology.
[23] On Col. 3.10ff.; Eph. 4.24 cf. Larsson, *Christus als Vorbild*, 188–230.
[24] For this imagery in the *Gospel of Thomas* and other texts cf. Uro, *Thomas*, 54–79.
[25] Cf. Larsson, 199, referring to Behm, *TWNT* iii. 450–56; iv. 899–904; also BAGD 394, 535–36.

aorist, relating to the past; ἀνακαινούμενον is a present participle, referring to what is in process: the new man is being renewed. The readers are still living in this world, and their renewal is not yet complete. Our author has not entirely abandoned Paul's 'eschatological reservation'. The verb **ἀνακαινόω** (BAGD 55) occurs only twice in the NT, in both cases in the passive and referring figuratively to the rebirth of the Christian (cf. 2 Cor. 4.16, εἰ καὶ ὁ ἔξω ἡμῶν ἄνθρωπος διαφθείρεται, ἀλλ' ὁ ἔσω ἡμῶν ἀνακαινοῦται ἡμέρᾳ καὶ ἡμέρᾳ).

This new man is being renewed according to the image of his creator (κατ' εἰκόνα τοῦ κτίσαντος αὐτόν), which of course recalls 1.15 with its description of Christ as εἰκὼν τοῦ θεοῦ τοῦ ἀοράτου. In the light of Rom. 13.14 and Gal. 3.27 it is very natural to think of the new man as Christ, but here care is necessary. The old would then be Adam, and we should have here an allusion to the Adam/Christ typology of Rom. 5 and 1 Cor. 15.45, 47 (cf. Moule, 119). This, however, is not explicitly stated, and while that typology is certainly somewhere in the background (τοῦ κτίσαντος αὐτόν suggests an allusion to the creation story in Genesis) there are differences which require to be observed. We may not simply assume that our author uses Pauline language in the same way as Paul himself (if Paul wrote this letter, that would be another matter, but the differences would remain).

Schweizer ('Christus und Geist', 307) remarks that the 'old man' in Paul is hardly thought of in purely individualistic terms, as is probably the case in Col.[26] The new quality for Paul is not located in the baptized person, but in the one into whom he is baptized. Hence the references in Rom. and Gal. to 'putting on Christ'. In the Colossian situation Schweizer sees a new legalism of an ascetic stamp, or in Pauline terms a contrast not between Adam and Christ but Moses and Christ. Barrett (*Adam*, 98f.) sets out two lists of passages, the first referring to the 'image' (Rom. 8.29; 1 Cor. 15.49; 2 Cor. 3.18; Col. 3.9ff.—Rom. 1.23; 1 Cor. 11.7 are excluded as not relevant, 2 Cor. 4.4 and Col. 1.15 as belonging to a different context), and the second to the old man and the new (Rom 6.6; Col. 3.9ff.—Rom. 7.22; 2 Cor. 4.16, which use the terms 'outward' and 'inward',[27] are also relevant), and writes, 'In these passages the "new" or "inward" man is not precisely Christ, as objectively distinct from the believer, nor, at the other extreme, is it a new nature, mystically or sacramentally bestowed upon and received by the believer, which he henceforth objectively and personally possesses. The terms, though applied primarily to the individual Christian, nevertheless (as Col. iii.

[26] But cf. already Moule: these phrases 'carry deeper, wider and more *corporate* associations, inasmuch as they are part of the presentation of the Gospel in terms of the two "Adams", the two creations' (119). He suggests (120) that κατ' εἰκόνα may refer specifically to Christ (cf. 1.15): 'As Adam was made "in the likeness of God", so the new Adam, Christ, "is", eternally, God's likeness". Accordingly, when God recreates Man, it is *in the pattern of Christ*, who is God's Likeness absolutely.'
[27] On this theme cf. H. D. Betz, *NTS* 46 (2000), 315–41.

11 shows) point also to the new community' (see the whole section, 97–99). For Paul, Jesus was the Man to come, but this word 'Man' also denotes 'the new humanity that is to be in Christ, and is already partially and inadequately adumbrated in Christians. The full conception of the Man to come can be disclosed only at the last day, when the heavenly man appears with the holy ones who are conformed to his image' (99; cf. v. 4).

Scroggs (*The Last Adam*, 69f.; cf. also 110) focuses on the phrase κατ' εἰκόνα τοῦ κτίσαντος αὐτόν, and sees in the αὐτόν 'the redeemed man of the new creation': 'Man does not become an image of Christ, but the image of God, conformable to Christ who now already exists in that image' (70). 'Although the Christian still lives in "this world" in his outer being, his inner life is made new by the Spirit, according to the nature of the resurrected Christ, who is the true image of God and thus the true reality of man' (110).[28]

This new man is being renewed εἰς ἐπίγνωσιν, literally 'into knowledge'. We have already met this noun twice in the intercessory prayer of 1.9–10, that the readers may be filled with the knowledge of God's will and again that they may increase in the knowledge of God; also at 2.2 with its reference to knowledge of the mystery of God, which is Christ. It is clear from the first of these references that such knowledge is not merely theoretical: knowledge of God's will is of no avail without obedience. In the same way, knowledge of the mystery which is Christ entails a recognition of his supreme place in the ordering of things, and again obedience. Lohse ('Christologie', 168) observes that the third and fourth chapters of this letter, in which paraenetic instructions are set out, are closely linked with the first two, in which the false 'philosophy' is rejected and the correct Christological doctrine developed.

Reference has already been made to a parallel to this verse in *Gos. Phil.* (see n. 20). In the *Gospel of Mary* (BG 8502, 1) Levi responds to criticism of Mary by Peter, saying that the Saviour knew her very well: 'That is why he loved her more than us. Rather let us be ashamed and put on the perfect man and acquire him for ourselves as he commanded us' (18.14–18; NHS 11, ed. D. M. Parrott, 469). The *Second Treatise of the Great Seth* (NHC VII 2, 59.4–7; NHMS 30, ed. B. A. Pearson, 173) develops Matthew's account of the dead who rose at the time of the crucifixion (Matt. 27.51–53): 'They walked about boldly, having laid aside jealousy of ignorance and unlearnedness beside the dead tombs, having put on the new man, having come to know that blessed and perfect one of the eternal and incomprehensible Father.' Other examples of this 'garment imagery' in the Nag Hammadi texts include the *Letter of Peter to Philip* (NHC VIII 2, 137.6–9; NHS 31, ed. J. H. Sieber, 243): 'When you strip off from yourselves what is corrupted, then you will become illuminators in the midst of mortal men' (137.21–22 speaks of the archons fighting against the inner man). The *Trimorphic Protennoia* (NHC XIII 1, 48.12–15; NHS 28, ed. C. W. Hedrick, 429) reads, 'All these I put on. And I stripped him of it and I put upon him a shining light, that is, the knowledge of the Thought of the Fatherhood. And I delivered him to those who give robes' ('All these' refers to the corporeal element which Protennoia/Logos strips from man and puts on himself, replacing it with a garment of light. See the note at p. 450). At 49.28–32 we find, 'He who possesses the Five Seals of these particular names has stripped off the garments of ignorance and put on a shining light'. Cf. also the

[28] Cf. also Dahl, 'Christ, Creation and the Church', 436.

farewell words of Jesus before his ascension in *Apoc. Jas.* (NHC I 2, 14.35–36; NHS 22, ed. H. W. Attridge, 51, with the note in NHS 23, 34): 'from this moment on I shall strip myself that I may clothe myself'.

Since 'clothing' metaphors were widely used (cf. n. 21 above), we may not assume influence from Col. at every turn: our author is using imagery that was current, and familiar to him. This imagery was congenial to the Gnostics, for whom the soul was imprisoned in the body as in a tomb; the flesh had to be stripped off to release the spirit. Such ideas are not present in Col.[29]

11. ὅπου οὐκ ἔνι Ἕλλην καὶ Ἰουδαῖος, περιτομὴ καὶ ἀκροβυστία, βάρβαρος, Σκύθης, δοῦλος, ἐλεύθερος, ἀλλὰ [τὰ] πάντα καὶ ἐν πᾶσιν Χριστός[30] Cf. 1 Cor. 12.13, ἡμεῖς πάντες εἰς ἓν σῶμα ἐβαπτίσθημεν, εἴτε Ἰουδαῖοι εἴτε Ἕλληνες, εἴτε δοῦλοι εἴτε ἐλεύθεροι; Gal. 3.28, οὐκ ἔνι Ἰουδαῖος οὐδὲ Ἕλλην, οὐκ ἔνι δοῦλος οὐδὲ ἐλεύθερος, οὐκ ἔνι ἄρσεν καὶ θῆλυ· πάντες γὰρ ὑμεῖς εἷς ἐστε ἐν Χριστῷ Ἰησοῦ.[31]

Wedderburn ('Theology', 13) sees here 'a more pronouncedly Greek point of view' as compared with 1 Cor. and Gal., with the addition of 'barbarians and Scythians' to the list of divisions transcended in Christ. The Greeks tended to classify people either as 'Greeks' (sophisticated, cultured, intellectual) or as 'barbarians' (all the rest, including the Jews; cf. BAGD 133, §2b; *TWNT* i. 544–51, esp. 550; also Lightfoot, 283–84). Josephus must have been quite delighted to be able to quote the tale told by Clearchus of Soli, who had it from his master Aristotle, of a Jew who was Ἑλληνικὸς οὐ τῇ διαλέκτῳ μόνον, ἀλλὰ καὶ τῇ ψυχῇ (*C. Apion.* i.180).[32] The Jews saw

[29] Echoes of and allusions to the second half of Col. are markedly less frequent in the Nag Hammadi texts (cf. the index to *NHTB*, 528–29: of 28 passages listed, only nine are printed in bold to indicate a probable relationship, while the rest indicate no more than a possible connection).

[30] This verse has attracted considerable attention in recent years: see Bouttier, 'Complexio Oppositorum'; Martin, 'The Scythian Perspective'; Campbell, 'Unravelling Colossians 3.11b', 'The Scythian Perspective' (a response to Martin); F. W. Horn, *NTS* 42 (1996), 486; F. G. Downing, 'A Cynic Preparation'. Cf. also Wendland, *Kultur*, 231f. and his cross-reference to 42f. (Stoic parallels). C. D. Stanley ('"Neither Jew nor Greek"'), discussing tensions between Jews and Greeks in Asia Minor, mentions Laodicea, but not Colossae. He argues that the reference here is specifically to Greeks, not to Gentiles generally.

[31] The *Tractatus Tripartitus* from Nag Hammadi (NHC I 5, 132.20–28) reads: 'The end will receive a unitary existence, just as the beginning was one, the place where there is no male nor female, nor slave and free, nor circumcision nor uncircumcision, neither angel nor man, but Christ is all in all' (translation based on those of Thomassen (BCNH 19, 247; cf. his note, 448f.) and Attridge and Pagels (NHS 22, 329; cf. their note, NHS 23, 447)). Here the words are applied to the future destiny of the psychics (described by Heracleon as 'female' and 'slaves'), who are generally granted a secondary kind of salvation, but outside the Pleroma. This text appears to envisage their eventual admission in full equality with the pneumatics.

Cf. also *Gos.Phil.* 62.26–32: 'If you [*sg.*] say "I am a Jew", no one will be moved. If you say "I am a Roman", no one will be disturbed. If you say "I am a Greek, a barbarian, a slave, a free man", no one will be troubled. [If] you [say] "I am a Christian", the [...] will tremble' (tr. W. W. Isenberg, NHS 20, 165; cf. Wilson, *The Gospel of Philip*, 110f.).

[32] On this cf. Lewy, 'Aristotle and the Jewish Sage', *HTR* 31 (1938), 205ff. The story was taken over from Josephus by Eusebius (*Praep. evang.* ix.5), who notes that Clement of Alexandria also mentions it (*Strom.* i.15).

themselves as the chosen people of God, and grouped other people under the heading of 'Greeks', a reminder as Dunn (224) notes 'of the pervasiveness of Hellenistic culture in the Mediterranean basin'. He adds that this was also Paul's normal way of expressing the contrast (Rom. 1.16; 2.9–10; 3.9; 10.12; 1 Cor. 1.22, 24; 10.32; 12.13; Gal. 3.28). The Jews responded to the aspersions cast upon them by pagan authors by producing a range of literary propaganda designed to stress the antiquity of their people and vindicate their claim to recognition (including the claim, *inter alia*, that the Greeks had borrowed everything from the inspired teachings of Moses).[33]

The ὅπου at the beginning of this verse is initially perplexing, since there is nothing about a place in what precedes (Dunn avoids the problem by translating 'the new nature, in which ...'). As already noted, however (see pp. 252f. above on v. 10), the terms here used point not only to the individual Christian but also to the new community: within that community there is no place for the old divisions, for all have been baptized into one body (1 Cor. 12.13), all are one in Christ (Gal. 3.28), and that same Christ is Lord of all (Rom. 10.12). On οὐκ ἔνι Lightfoot (*Galatians*, 150) writes, ' "*there is no room for, no place for*", negativing not the fact only, but the possibility, as James i.17 παρ᾽ ᾧ οὐκ ἔνι παραλλαγή.'

The first four items in the list form a chiasmus (ABBA), with 'Jew' corresponding to 'circumcision' and 'Greek' to 'uncircumcision', and D. A. Campbell ('Unravelling Colossians 3.11b', 128) argues that the second group of four should also be understood as a chiastic arrangement. 'Barbarian' would then correlate with 'free', and 'Scythian' with 'slave', a perfectly plausible interpretation given his subsequent discussion of references to 'Scythian' slaves. One problem is, however, that the lists in 1 Cor. and Gal. are not chiastic: in 1 Cor. there is neither Jew nor Greek, slave nor free, and in Gal. no male and female. Our author has introduced the chiastic arrangement by his insertion of circumcision and uncircumcision, and the four terms in the second group are simply set out one after another without any connective or sign of contrast. Moreover, one may wonder if people in Asia Minor would be aware of free barbarians dwelling beyond the frontier of the empire to the north, in contrast to Scythian slaves living in their own vicinity.

The alternative is to see the reference to Scythians in traditional terms, as the most barbaric of barbarians (cf. Lightfoot, 284–85). W. L. Knox, *PCG* 175, speaks of 'cultured barbarian or pure savage', suggesting that the distinction 'may allude to some claim on the part of Paul's opponents that their system contained the truth not only of Judaism but of the ancient wisdom of the barbarians'. (For the

---

[33] Cf. Wilson, 'Jewish Literary Propaganda', in *Paganisme, Judaïsme, Christianisme* (1978), 61–71 and the references in Schürer to the authors there mentioned. For the allegation of borrowing from Moses see Wilson, *The Gnostic Problem*, 28 n. 147, 149. This claim is taken over by Clement of Alexandria (see Lilla, *Clement of Alexandria*, 31–33), who quotes Numenius of Apamea as saying τί γάρ ἐστιν Πλάτων ἢ Μωυσῆς ἀττικίζων.

wisdom of the barbarians and for the Scythians as 'a type of the wildest savagery' see the references in his n. 4.[34]) For Σκύθης see also BAGD 758; *TWNT* vii. 448–51, esp. 450. It occurs only here in the NT. It should be added that these two words, 'barbarian', 'Scythian', are also an insertion into the shorter lists in 1 Cor. and Gal.

Whatever the problems presented by this verse in point of detail, the main thrust is clear: all such distinctions and differences are now irrelevant. The verse comes to yet another climax in the statement that Christ is all and in all.[35] Reference has been made above to some passages in Paul's major letters which relate to the same theme, to which we may add the somewhat enigmatic Eph. 1.23 (on which see Best, *Ephesians*, 183–89) and 1 Cor. 15.28, ἵνα ἦ ὁ θεὸς [τὰ] πάντα ἐν πᾶσιν.[36] The latter verse may serve as a reminder that, despite the exalted language which Paul so often uses in referring to Christ, he nowhere in his major letters describes him as θεός—apart from the much-debated text at Rom. 9.5 (on which see Metzger, in 'The Punctuation of Rom. 9.5', 95–112;[37] on the whole subject see R. E. Brown, *Jesus: God and Man* (1967)). He may accord to Christ 'the highest place that heaven affords', but God remains sovereign and supreme.

12. ἐνδύσασθε οὖν, ὡς ἐκλεκτοὶ τοῦ θεοῦ ἅγιοι καὶ ἠγαπημένοι, σπλάγχνα οἰκτιρμοῦ χρηστότητα ταπεινοφροσύνην πραΰτητα μακροθυμίαν Cf. Eph. 4.2, μετὰ πάσης ταπεινοφροσύνης καὶ πραΰτητος. The fruit of the Spirit in Gal. 5.22–23 includes χρηστότης and πραΰτης.

Our author now returns to the theme of the 'new man': he has already charged his readers to set aside certain vices (vv. 5 and 8), and here he bids them 'put on' a series of virtues. Moule (123) aptly remarks: 'What St Paul chooses for mention here might be called the "ordinary" virtues—precisely those which reduce or eliminate friction: ready sympathy, a generous spirit, a humble disposition, willingness to make concessions, patience, forbearance.' The next verse calls on them to bear with one another and forgive one another—all of which is calculated to promote a close-knit fellowship within the community, whereas the 'false teaching' would appear to have been disruptive.

On ἐκλεκτοὶ τοῦ θεοῦ ἅγιοι καὶ ἠγαπημένοι Lightfoot (287) notes

---

[34] Josephus (*C. Apion.* ii.269) describes them as βραχὺ τῶν θηρίων διαφέροντες.

[35] Cf. *Gos. Thom.* 77 (NHC II 2, 46.24–6): 'It is I who am the all. From me did the all come forth and unto me did the all extend' (on this *NHTB* 131 compares Eph. 1.23; Col. 3.11('I am the all'); 1 Cor. 8.6; Eph. 1.10; Col. 1.16–17 ('From me did the all come forth')).

[36] In some mss the τά is omitted both in 1 Cor. and in Col., but only A 33 81 1241 are listed for omission in both cases. Dunn (210 n. 8) thinks an allusion to the hymn of 1.15–20 is probably intended. In 1 Cor. the phrase τὰ πάντα occurs in v. 27 and earlier in v. 28, as well as in the words quoted.

[37] This text is also discussed in a rather unexpected place: in the letters of Isaac Newton. See H. W. Turnbull (ed.), *The Correspondence of Isaac Newton*, (1961), iii. 141, a letter (no. 359) discussing various corruptions of scripture. The preceding item (no. 358) is a lengthy discussion of 1 John 5.7–8 and 1 Tim. 3.16.

---

that all three terms 'are transferred from the Old Covenant to the New, from the Israel after the flesh to the Israel after the Spirit' (cf. also M. Black, *The Book of Enoch* (1985), 104; Dunn, 227–28). He adds that the καί is omitted 'in one or two excellent copies' (including B 33 1739 in the NA²⁷ apparatus), and that 'it is impossible not to feel how much the sentence gains in force by the omission', comparing 1 Pet. 2.6; accordingly he brackets the word, but most scholars appear to retain it.

We have already met ἅγιοι several times above, as one of the most common designations for Christians (1.2, 4, 26; cf. Rom. 1.7; 1 Cor. 1.2; 2 Cor. 1.1 etc.), or with reference to 'the inheritance of the saints in light' (1.12, where, as noted at pp. 113–14, it may include the heavenly host as well as the elect); at 1.22 it is part of the purpose of the reconciliation wrought in Christ to present the readers before God 'holy and blameless and without reproach'. Here it is used as an adjective, as in our present verse, where with the participle ἠγαπημένοι it qualifies ἐκλεκτοί.

ἐκλεκτός (BAGD 242, §1b; *TWNT* iv. 186–97; for Paul see 194– 95) is found only rarely in Paul's major letters (Rom. 8.33; 16.13), but as Moule notes the cognate noun ἐκλογή occurs several times (Rom. 9.11; 11.5, 7, 28; 1 Thess. 1.4). They are 'elect' or chosen not from any merit of their own but through the grace and love of God (hence the ἠγαπημένοι; cf. 1 Thess. 1.4, εἰδότες, ἀδελφοὶ ἠγαπημένοι ὑπὸ τοῦ θεοῦ, τὴν ἐκλογὴν ὑμῶν; 2 Thess. 2.13, ἀδελφοὶ ἠγαπημένοι ὑπὸ Κυρίου. The cognate verb ἐκλέγομαι appears at 1 Cor. 1.27, 28, of God choosing the foolish things of the world to shame the wise.). As Dunn notes (227f.), 'the idea of a people "chosen by God" was wholly and exclusively Jewish, a fundamental feature of Israel's self-perception' (cf. his references, 228 n. 35). He sees here a striking echo of 'the classic covenant text, Deut. 7:6-7', and goes on to add, 'More clearly than anywhere else in Colossians it is evident that the Gentile recipients of the letter were being invited to consider themselves full participants in the people and heritage of Israel.'[38] We may recall 1 Pet. 2.9, ὑμεῖς δὲ γένος ἐκλεκτόν, βασίλειον ἱεράτευμα, ἔθνος ἅγιον, λαὸς εἰς περιποίησιν; that letter is addressed ἐκλεκτοῖς παρεπιδήμοις διασπορᾶς (1.1).

The privilege of being 'elect' carried with it a responsibility, a point not always remembered by some people today, more concerned to assert their rights than to accept their obligations. As already noted, the virtues to be put on here are precisely those calculated to promote fellowship within the community. **σπλάγχνα** (BAGD 763; *TWNT*

[38] His further suggestion, that 'this assumption on the part of uncircumcised Gentiles (2:13) was a bone of contention with or provocation to the more traditional Jewish synagogues in Colossae', is at least open to question: as noted above, there is little evidence for the presence of Jews there, and even less for the existence of several synagogues. That there were Jews among the population is a possibility not to be ruled out, but even if there were we do not know how many, or whether there were enough to form a synagogue congregation. Even a single dissident Jew, however, might have caused considerable disruption within the local church.

vii. 548–59; for Paul see 555f., for this verse 556), almost always used in the plural, means literally the inward parts, the entrails (cf. Acts 1.18), but is employed figuratively (BAGD §b) of the seat of the emotions, in modern usage the heart (cf. 2 Cor. 6.12; 7.15; Phil. 1.8; Philem. 7, 12, 20). Here it is combined with οἰκτιρμός, mercy, compassion (BAGD 561; *TWNT* v. 161–63), which again is almost always used in the plural (Rom 12.1; 2 Cor. 1.3; Heb. 10.28). The two words occur together at Phil. 2.1 (εἴ τις σπλάγχνα καὶ οἰκτιρμοί), but in view of the difference in the construction (and the singular here) it is doubtful if we should assume any dependence of Col. on Phil. As Dunn remarks, the linking of the two words makes the emotional content even stronger: 'heartfelt compassion'.

χρηστότης (BAGD 886; *TWNT* ix. 478–81) appears with μακροθυμία and πραΰτης among the fruits of the Spirit at Gal. 5.22–23, also (again with μακροθυμία) at 2 Cor. 6.6. It means goodness, kindness, generosity, in these two cases and here with reference to people, but also at Rom. 2.4; 11.22 of the goodness of God ('the more typical thought (BAGD), and so characteristic of the new self being renewed in accordance with the image of its creator (3:10)': Dunn, 229). Its use in Eph. 2.7 (τὸ ὑπερβάλλον πλοῦτος τῆς χάριτος αὐτοῦ ἐν χρηστότητι ἐφ' ἡμᾶς) makes it another word used differently in Eph. and in Col.

The presence of ταπεινοφροσύνη in this list is at first sight surprising, in view of its occurrence in the polemical section above (2.18, 23; see p. 221). There, however, the context in both cases and the association of the word with 'self-chosen worship' and unsparing treatment of the body make it clear that this is not a true humility but a canting humbug. Here in contrast it stands in a sequence of virtues which all relate to dealings with other people (cf. Phil. 2.3, τῇ ταπεινοφροσύνῃ ἀλλήλους ἡγούμενοι ὑπερέχοντας ἑαυτῶν, which, as Grundmann (*TWNT* viii. 18) notes, links up with the ἐταπείνωσεν ἑαυτόν of the Carmen Christi at 2.6–11). There is to be no arrogance here, no contempt of others, no disparagement, but a true humility which regards others as better than one's self. At Eph. 4.2, ταπεινοφροσύνη is the first of the three virtues listed, linked as here with πραΰτης and μακροθυμία, and the whole rounded off by ἀνεχόμενοι ἀλλήλων ἐν ἀγάπῃ (cf. v. 13).

Grundmann (*TWNT* viii. 12) notes a difference in the use of the ταπεινός word group in Greek literature and in the biblical writings: the Greeks with their high regard for the free citizen over against 'the coward slave'[39] and others like him gave to these terms a negative value, whereas in Israel and in post-exilic Judaism the emphasis lay upon man's proper standing before God, which led to a positive assessment: before God one cannot be other than humble and obedient. In contrast, πραΰτης (BAGD 699; *TWNT* vi. 645–51) was

---

[39] Cf. the poem by Robert Burns, 'A Man's a Man for a' that'. 'For Greek thought generally ταπεινοφροσύνη was too closely related to servility for it to be able to serve as a positive virtue' (Dunn, 229).

sharply distinguished from ταπεινοφροσύνη by the Greeks and given a positive value (*TWNT* viii. 24 n. 72, referring to *TWNT* vi. 646, 18ff.). It means gentleness, courtesy, considerateness. As already noted, it appears among the fruits of the Spirit at Gal. 5.23, also at Eph. 4.2. At 1 Cor. 4.21 Paul asks ἐν ῥάβδῳ ἔλθω πρὸς ὑμᾶς ἢ ἐν ἀγάπῃ πνεύματί τε πραΰτητος; (cf. Gal. 6.1). At 2 Cor. 10.1 he entreats his readers διὰ τῆς πραΰτητος καὶ ἐπιεικίας τοῦ Χριστοῦ. Cf. also 2 Tim. 2.25; Tit. 3.2; Jas. 1.21; 3.13; 1 Pet. 3.15.

We have already met with **μακροθυμία** at 1.11 (see p. 108). In that verse it is coupled with ὑπομονή, and the sense required is that of forbearance or endurance, with a suggestion of the trials a Christian might be required to undergo, even to persecution, because of his faith. Here, however, the emphasis is rather on virtues calculated to promote the inner life of the Christian community, and while 'forbearance' might still be an adequate translation perhaps 'tolerance' or 'patience' (so NRSV) may be better. Lightfoot (287) suggests that πραΰτης and μακροθυμία 'are best distinguished by their opposites. πραΰτης is opposed to "rudeness, harshness", ἀγριότης, χαλεπότης; μακροθυμία to "resentment, revenge, wrath", ὀργή, ὀξυχολία.'[40]

Dunn (230) aptly observes: 'Such virtues (or graces), particularly as in the combination here, can appear to encourage a "milksop" weakness as in people whose calling in life is to be a doormat for others—at least as those caught up in the cut and thrust of the rat race count strength. But in fact to live out such a character calls for a strength which is rarely seen in the marketplace (as Jesus demonstrated). And without such an attitude toward others no group of individuals can become and grow as a community, with a proper care for others and willingness to submerge one's own personal interests.'

13. ἀνεχόμενοι ἀλλήλων καὶ χαριζόμενοι ἑαυτοῖς ἐάν τις πρός τινα ἔχῃ μομφήν· καθὼς καὶ ὁ κύριος ἐχαρίσατο ὑμῖν, οὕτως καὶ ὑμεῖς Cf. Eph. 4.2, ἀνεχόμενοι ἀλλήλων ἐν ἀγάπῃ; Eph. 4.32, χαριζόμενοι ἑαυτοῖς, καθὼς καὶ ὁ θεὸς ἐν Χριστῷ ἐχαρίσατο ὑμῖν; Eph. 5.2, καθὼς καὶ ὁ Χριστὸς ἠγάπησεν ἡμᾶς.

There is one textual point in this verse which calls for mention. P46 A B D* and other mss read ὁ κύριος, but there are three variants: two of them, ὁ θεός (ℵ* vgmss) and ὁ θεὸς ἐν Χριστῷ (33), may be due to assimilation to Eph. 4.32, while the third, ὁ Χριστός (ℵ2 C D1 *et al.*) might conceivably be influenced by Eph. 5.2. It would seem that scribes sought to clarify the rather indefinite κύριος; as Dunn puts it (210 n. 9), 'to whom does "the Lord" refer?', i.e. to God or to Christ? Cf. Metzger, *Textual Commentary*, 625. There is a cluster of similar variants in this context: cf. vv. 15–16 below. It may be added that there is a marked difference in the use of these titles from 3.11 on: Χριστός appears in the printed text at 3.15, 16; 4.3, 12, but in every case there

---

[40] Lohse (147) notes that all of these five terms are used elsewhere to designate acts of God or Christ: 'In Rom 12:1 and 2 Cor 1:3 "mercies" (οἰκτιρμοί) describes God's compassion. Rom. 2.4; 11.22; Eph. 2.7; Tit. 3.4 speak of God's kindness (χρηστότης). Phil 2.8 says: Christ "humbled himself" (ἐταπείνωσεν ἑαυτόν). In 2 Cor 10.1 the Apostle refers to the "meekness of Christ" (πραΰτης τοῦ Χριστοῦ). In his dealings with men God practises "patience" (μακροθυμία Rom 2.4; 9.22, etc.).' The following verse provides justification for Dunn's comment (230 n. 38) that there is no reason why an element of *imitatio Christi* should be excluded here.

are variant readings. The two appear together at 3.24, and in a v.l. at 3.17. κύριος appears with variants at 3.13, 17, 22, without variants at 3.18, 20, 23, 24; 4.1, 7, 17. Neugebauer ('Das Paulinische "In Christo"', 136) notes that in the first two chapters, essentially devoted to the unfolding of the salvation event, we meet only the Christ formula, but the last two chapters with their paraenetic content contain only the Kurios formula.

The verses listed from Ephesians (for which see Best, *Ephesians*, 361–64, 462–65) present both similarities and differences, which raise questions about a possible relationship between the two letters: the phrase ἀνεχόμενοι ἀλλήλων appears in both, but Eph. 4.2 adds ἐν ἀγάπῃ.[41] Is this an addition in Eph., or an omission in Col.? Eph. 4.32 omits ἐάν τις πρός τινα ἔχῃ μομφήν, running the rest together into a single sentence, and also substitutes ὁ θεὸς ἐν Χριστῷ for ὁ κύριος. In Col., as Lightfoot notes (287), the καθὼς καί is answered by the οὕτως καί, so these words must be treated as a separate sentence, or at least a separate clause.

As noted above, it is entirely possible that later scribes assimilated the text of Col. at some points to that of Eph., but did either of our authors know and use the work of the other? And if so, on which side does the dependence lie? Or have we to do with two members of the same school writing independently, but using material that was familiar within the school? Following his discussion of 4.32, Best (465) writes that the probable reason for the similarities and differences is the membership of both authors in the same Pauline school, rather than dependence of either on the other (cf. his article 'Who Used Whom?'). 'χαρίζετε ἑαυτοῖς καθὼς καὶ ὁ θεὸς (Χριστὸς) ὑμῖν may have been a saying of that school which each author has modified to suit his own requirements.'

This verse follows very naturally after the list of virtues, showing what it means to put them into effect. **ἀνέχομαι** (BAGD 65, §1a; *TWNT* i. 360–61; in the NT always in the middle) means to endure, bear or put up with someone or something. χαρίζομαι we have already met at 2.13 (see p. 208). Here again it is used in the sense of forgiving (BAGD 867, §2), and that twice over: Christians are to forgive one another, as the Lord has forgiven them. (Some have seen here a conscious echo of the Lord's Prayer.[42] Aletti, 238 n. 58, compares Rom. 15.7, 'Welcome one another, therefore, just as Christ has welcomed you', for the same type of argumentation.) These two participles are commonly translated as imperatives, as above, in part at least to simplify the style, but Aletti[43] objects that

[41] One is reminded of ἀληθεύοντες ἐν ἀγάπῃ a few verses later (Eph. 4.15). The classic passage is of course 1 Cor. 13. But it is notable that ἀγάπη occurs ten times in Eph. (1.4, 15; 2.4; 3.18, 19; 4.2, 15, 16; 5.2; 6.23) compared with five in Col. (1.4, 8, 13; 2.2; 3.14).
[42] Davies (*PRJ* 139) quotes E. F. Scott as writing: 'We can hardly doubt, with a verse like this before us, that it [the Lord's Prayer] was familiar to Paul'.
[43] 'Les participes ... expriment les modalités de l'impératif ... du verset précédent. On peut évidemment, avec la plupart des commentaires et des Bibles, les traduire par des impératifs qui s'ajoutent au premier, mais on perd alors la nuance que ces participes visent à exprimer' (237).

this entails the loss of a nuance which the participles are intended to express: they describe how the 'putting on' is brought into effect, 'put on these virtues, bearing with one another and forgiving one another'.

The noun **μομφή** (BAGD 527), which occurs in the NT only here, means blame or cause for complaint. This brings the whole discussion down to a very practical level: in 1 Cor. 1.10ff. Paul appeals to his readers 'that there be no divisions among you'; at 1 Cor. 6.1–8 he is clearly shocked to find that some have sought to resolve complaints and disputes in the public courts: 'In fact, to have lawsuits at all with one another is already a defeat for you' (v. 7). In any community, large or small, it is vital that members should not harbour grudges against one another, 'nursing their wrath to keep it warm'.[44] The old admonition of Eph. 4.26, 'let not the sun go down upon your wrath', is as valid today as when it was written.

The textual variants noted above are due to scribal uncertainty over the referent of κύριος (for which see pp. 84f., 105 above), and possibly also to some feeling that forgiveness was the prerogative of God alone. Dunn (231) observes that 'in the Paulines, apart from Old Testament quotations, κύριος always denotes Christ'; Aletti (238), after examining the use of κύριος in Col., concludes (1) that θεός appears alone or accompanied by πατήρ, but never by κύριος, while Χριστός is several times flanked by κύριος, and (2) that a verse like Col. 1.10 and the *Haustafel* of 3.18–4.1 also indicate that Col. reserves κύριος for Christ. These considerations provide further support for the choice of the reading adopted above.

As to the change from ἀλλήλων after the first participle to ἑαυτοῖς after the second (the same change occurs in Eph. 4.32, although the form of words in the first part of the verse is different), the former is the genitive of the reciprocal pronoun (BAGD 39), the latter the dative of the reflexive (BAGD 211–12). The reflexive can be used for the reciprocal pronoun, even in classical authors (§3, citing for the NT Eph. 4.32; Col. 3.13, 16; 1 Thess. 5.13; 1 Pet. 4.9). For Lightfoot (287) 'The reciprocal ἑαυτῶν differs from the reciprocal ἀλλήλων in emphasizing the idea of *corporate unity*: hence it is more appropriate here (comp. Ephes iv. 2, 32) with χαριζόμενοι than with ἀνεχόμενοι.'

14. ἐπὶ πᾶσιν δὲ τούτοις τὴν ἀγάπην, ὅ ἐστιν σύνδεσμος τῆς τελειότητος As already observed (n. 41 above), **ἀγάπη** occurs only five times in Col., compared with ten occurrences in Eph.: at 1.2, 8 of the love shown by the Colossians, at 1.13 in the phrase 'the son of his love', at 2.2 in the description of the end to which Paul's labours are directed, that his readers may be συμβιβασθέντες ἐν ἀγάπῃ. Here it appears as the climax and culmination of the whole series, the

---

[44] Robert Burns again, this time from 'Tam o' Shanter'.

supreme virtue of all (cf. 1 Cor. 13.13; also Rom. 13.8–10; Gal. 5.14). This love is not something that can be conjured up at will by human beings; it is primarily a response to and inspired by the love of God revealed in Christ (cf. 1 John 3.1, 11; 4.7–11. Dunn, (58) writes, 'it is clear that for Paul the self-sacrifice of Christ is the definitive expression of this "love" (Rom 5; 6-8; 8:31-35; 2 Cor 5:14-15; so also Col 1:13-14).' We might add the passage which inspired Patrick Walker (p. 88f. above): Rom. 8.38–39).

The natural understanding of ἐπὶ πᾶσιν δὲ τούτοις is to take it as meaning 'in addition to all these' (BAGD 287, §II 2bβ), although Moule (123) notes that it could be elative, 'above all'. In either case the accusative ἀγάπην here is still governed by the ἐνδύσασθε of v. 12, although it is open to question whether we should think of the clothing metaphor being carried on into this verse (cf. Lightfoot, 288: 'Love is the outer garment which holds the others in their places.'). The problem lies in the following words, which do not readily lend themselves to such an interpretation.

We have already met σύνδεσμος at 2.19 (cf. p. 225), where it is used of the sinews of the body. On the present verse Moule (123) writes: 'Commentators, at least from Wettstein onwards, quote Simplicius' saying (in *Epictet.* p. 208) that the Pythagoreans honoured φιλία more than any other virtue, and called it σύνδεσμον ... πασῶν τῶν ἀρετῶν.[45] ... If there were evidence that σύνδεσμος was an article of attire, the phrase would be easier to grasp, but "belt" or "girdle" is not attested among its meanings.' The senses listed in BAGD (785) are (1) a bond that holds something together; (2) the bond that hinders, a fetter (Acts 8.23); and (3) that which is held together by a bond.

This word, then, might conceivably be forced into a continuance of the clothing metaphor, but only against its use elsewhere. Even that cannot be said of τελειότης (BAGD 809), which is used in the NT only here and at Heb. 6.1, and means perfection, completeness, maturity. It is better therefore, with Dunn (232), to assume that 'the metaphor itself is not pursued further and it is the importance of love as such which determines the second clause'. 'Love is σύνδεσμος τῆς τελειότητος, the *bond that unites* all the virtues (which otherwise have no unity) *in perfect harmony* or *the bond of perfect unity* for the church' (BAGD 785). When we recall Eph. 4.3, τηρεῖν τὴν ἑνότητα τοῦ πνεύματος ἐν τῷ συνδέσμῳ τῆς εἰρήνης, it is not surprising that some scribes (D* F G *et al.*) substituted ἑνότητος for τελειότητος; but the thought of unity is here reserved for the next verse (ἐν ἑνὶ σώματι). The ὅ at the beginning refers back to τὴν ἀγάπην (see

---

[45] He adds a reference to Plato, *Polit.* 310a for σύνδεσμος ἀρετῆς in a different sense, and notes other references for the word in Chadwick, 'All Things to All Men', 273. B. A. Pearson's chapter, 'Philanthropy in the Greco-Roman World and in Early Christianity' (*Emergence*, 186–213) may also be relevant here.

Lightfoot, 288, who writes, 'The common reading ἥτις is obviously a scribe's correction'; ℵ² D¹ *et al.*; ℵ* D* 81 read ὅς).[46]

15. καὶ ἡ εἰρήνη τοῦ Χριστοῦ βραβευέτω ἐν ταῖς καρδίαις ὑμῶν, εἰς ἣν καὶ ἐκλήθητε ἐν ἑνὶ σώματι· καὶ εὐχάριστοι γίνεσθε Cf. Eph. 4.4, ἓν σῶμα καὶ ἓν πνεῦμα, καθὼς καὶ ἐκλήθητε ἐν μιᾷ ἐλπίδι τῆς κλήσεως ὑμῶν; Eph. 2.16, καὶ ἀποκαταλλάξῃ ἀμφοτέρους ἐν ἑνὶ σώματι τῷ θεῷ.

Here again there are variant readings.

1. For Χριστοῦ (ℵ* A B C* D* *et al.*) some mss (ℵ² C² D² *et al.*) read θεοῦ (cf. Phil. 4.7; also ὁ θεὸς τῆς εἰρήνης at Rom. 15.33; 16.20; 2 Cor. 13.11; Phil. 4.9; 1 Thess. 5.23; Heb. 13.20). As noted above (p. 75), Col. is the only letter in which Christ is not associated with God in the opening salutation, and scribes were not slow to supply the deficiency. This could be a similar case, the scribes associating peace with God rather than with Christ, as the more common usage, and hence making the substitution. But Lightfoot (289) comments, ' "*Christ's peace*", which He left as a legacy to His disciples', citing John 14.27 and comparing Eph. 2.14. Dunn (233) notes that some regard the phrase as a mark of post-Pauline authorship (cf. 2 Thess. 3.16; Eph. 2.14), but concludes, 'either way does not make much difference, since the Christ of 1:15-20 and 2:9 is so much the embodiment of God's wisdom and fullness that it comes to the same thing.'

2. Dunn (211 n. 12) remarks, 'For some reason P⁴⁶ and B omit "one" '. The word is, however, essential to the context, and was presumably omitted simply by haplography after the preceding ἐν. In copying a text without division of words, such errors could easily be committed.

εἰρήνη appears in the salutation of Col., as in all the letters of the Pauline corpus, but this is the only other occurrence of the word in this letter, a marked contrast to Eph., where it occurs eight times (1.2; 2.14, 15, 17 (*bis*); 4.3; 6.15, 23); but Col. alone has the verb εἰρηνοποιέω (1.20). The closing verses of the 'hymn' present problems for the translator (cf. pp. 151ff. above), but the author's meaning is not in doubt: to paraphrase, it was God's good pleasure that all the fulness of deity should dwell in Christ, and through him to reconcile all things to himself, making peace through the blood of his cross. This provides at least the start of an understanding of the unusual phrase here: ultimately it is God's peace, the gift of the God of peace, but it is mediated through Christ and may therefore be described as his peace. Eph. 2.13–14 goes even further: 'But now in Christ Jesus you who once were far off have been brought near by the blood of Christ. *For he is our peace*' (NRSV; italics added).

As noted in the discussion of the salutation (p. 74f. above), this peace is not simply the absence of war. Dunn (51) writes that the Jewish greeting 'peace' 'denotes not simply cessation of war but all that makes for well-being and prosperity in the absence of war, and not simply individual or inner peace, but also the social wholeness of harmonious relationships.' On the present verse he suggests (233)

[46] Lohse (89) calls ὅ ἐστιν a formulaic phrase, which is retained unaltered even when the gender of the word to be explained does not fit the ὅ. He cites 1.24, where the relative in fact agrees with the gender of τοῦ σώματος; also 2.10, 17, but at both these points he regards the neuter relative as 'an assimilation to the common expression ὅ ἐστιν' (101 n. 54; 116 n. 15). 'Other Pauline letters never employ this device for making connections.'

that we should recognize a more titular force in the name 'Christ': 'in prophetic perspective the peace promised to God's covenant people was a hope for the future new age (Isa 9:6-7; 54.10; Ezek 34:25-31; 37:26; Mic 5:4; Hag 2:9; Zech 8:12; *I Enoch* 5:7, 9; 10:17; 11:2; *Testament of Dan* 5:11). The peace the Colossian believers could experience in their hearts was further proof that they belonged to the people of the Messiah in the age of the Messiah already come (cf. Gnilka, *Kolosserbrief*, 198–99).'

We have already met the compound καταβραβεύειν at 2.18 (p. 220). Here we have the simple verb **βραβεύειν** (BAGD 146; *TWNT* i. 636), without the negative prefix; like the compound, it occurs only in Col. in the NT. It meant originally to award prizes (βραβεῖον; cf. 1 Cor. 9.24; Phil. 3.14) in contests, but came to be used more generally in the sense of 'be judge (Lightfoot renders it '*be umpire*'), decide, control, rule'; Dunn (211, 234) offers 'arbitrate, be arbiter'. Moule (124) writes, ' "The peace of Christ" seems to mean the peace which Christ brings (cf. John xiv. 27), that is the peace which is the result of obedience to him: obedience to the will of Christ is to be the "umpire" in their hearts, settling conflicts of will and bringing co-ordination and direction to life.' Lightfoot (289) supplies several references from various sources, and concludes, 'In all such cases it appears that the idea of a *decision* and an *award* is prominent in the word, and that it must not be taken to denote simply *rule* or *power*.'

Looking back over this passage, we may note that the five 'members' which are to be 'put to death' in v. 5 are the sins which characterized pagan life, as seen from a Christian point of view. The second group of vices listed in vv. 8 and 9, which are to be 'put away', are such as are likely to be disruptive of life in any small and close-knit community. The 'new man' of v. 10 is not merely a new nature for the individual Christian, for here, as Barrett notes (see pp. 252–53 above), there is a pointer to the new community: in Christ the old divisions of race and class are simply no longer relevant (v. 11). The virtues to be 'put on' in v. 12 are those likely to be conducive to harmonious relations within the community, as are the tolerance and readiness to forgive in v. 13. ἀγάπη in v. 14, 'the bond of perfection', forms the climax and culmination of the series, and the whole is rounded off by this reference to the peace of Christ, the peace which only he can give, but which others may so easily destroy.[47] As Dunn observes (234), 'this is something the Colossians have not to accomplish but to let happen—to let go any attempt to control and manipulate and to let the peace of Christ be the determiner—just as in the following clause peace is a call to which they can only respond.'

To this peace they were called: the εἰς ἥν refers back to ἡ εἰρήνη as its antecedent (Lightfoot, 289 compares 1 Cor. 7.15, ἐν δὲ εἰρήνῃ κέκληκεν ἡμᾶς ὁ θεός). Moreover they were called not just as

[47] Cf. Best, *Ephesians*, 366 on the author's stress on the unity of the Church in Eph. 4.3.

3.16 265

individuals, but ἐν ἑνὶ σώματι (Lightfoot compares Eph. 4.4, ἓν σῶμα καὶ ἓν πνεῦμα, and notes that this passage 'strikes the keynote of the companion Epistle to the Ephesians', citing 2.16ff., 4.3ff. Forms of εἰς occur no fewer than twelve times in Eph. Under 'unity' Best's index lists 356–413 *passim*, with a cross-reference to 'one body'. The imagery of one body with many members is already a prominent theme in Rom. 12.4–5; 1 Cor. 12.12–27 (cf. Schweizer, *TWNT* vii. 1066–69; for Col. see 1064; 1072–75)).[48]

The verb **καλέω** (BAGD 398f.; *TWNT* iii. 488–92) means to call, with a variety of nuances, in particular the figurative sense (BAGD §2) in which it is employed here, of God's calling of persons to be his chosen people (cf. the use of ἐκλεκτός in v. 12 above). Both here and in Eph. 4.4 we have an aorist passive, ἐκλήθητε, 'you were called', i.e. by God.

The final clause, **καὶ εὐχάριστοι γίνεσθε**, an independent unit, reads almost as an afterthought (Dunn, 235) but, for one thing, Lightfoot long ago wrote, 'In this epistle especially the duty of thanksgiving assumes a peculiar prominence by being made a refrain, as here [at 2.7] and in iii.15, 17, iv.2: see also i.12' (243). The life to which the readers are called is not one of dour, unremitting puritanical observance: whether we take μετὰ χαρᾶς at 1.11 with what precedes or with what follows, the words mean 'with joy', and would fit admirably with the following εὐχαριστοῦντες. Gratitude and thanksgiving are an appropriate response for people delivered from the realm of darkness, called into the fellowship of Christ's church, raised to new life and offered the hope of glory. εὐχάριστος (BAGD 329) appears only here in the NT.

16. ὁ λόγος τοῦ Χριστοῦ ἐνοικείτω ἐν ὑμῖν πλουσίως, ἐν πάσῃ σοφίᾳ διδάσκοντες καὶ νουθετοῦντες ἑαυτούς, ψαλμοῖς ὕμνοις ᾠδαῖς πνευματικαῖς ἐν τῇ χάριτι ᾄδοντες ἐν ταῖς καρδίαις τῷ θεῷ Cf. Eph. 5.19, λαλοῦντες ἑαυτοῖς ψαλμοῖς καὶ ὕμνοις καὶ ᾠδαῖς πνευματικαῖς, ᾄδοντες καὶ ψάλλοντες τῇ καρδίᾳ ὑμῶν τῷ κυρίῳ. Once again we have both similarities and differences, notably in the sequence 'psalms, hymns and spiritual songs'; but Col. reads νουθετοῦντες (cf. 1.28; this word does not occur in Eph.) whereas Eph. has λαλοῦντες, and Eph. also transfers the ᾄδοντες into the following clause. This combination of similarity and difference once again raises questions: has the one author borrowed from the other, or are they both drawing upon the same words independently? It is not surprising that the manuscripts show assimilation of one to the other.

The most important of the variant readings relate to τοῦ Χριστοῦ at the beginning and τῷ θεῷ at the end. On the first, Metzger (*Textual Commentary*, 625) writes: 'Instead of the unusual expression "the word of Christ", which occurs nowhere else in the New

[48] At p. 1037 Schweizer mentions the famous fable of Menenius Agrippa (Livy ii.32), often referred to in Stoic writings (cf. *TWNT* iv. 560, *s.v.* μέλος). This imagery was thus fairly widely current.

Testament, several witnesses substitute the more customary "the word of God" (A C*
33 451 1241 al) or "the word of the Lord" (א* I 2127 cop^{bo} Clement). Χριστοῦ is
strongly supported by P⁴⁶ א^c B C² D G K P Ψ 81 614 1739 Byz Lect it vg syr^{(p), h} cop^{sa,}
^{bo ms} goth arm al' (in both cases the NA²⁷ apparatus differs slightly).

On the second, he says: 'In place of θεῷ, which is strongly supported by early and
diversified testimony (P⁴⁶vid א A B C* D* G Ψ^c 33 81 1739 it^{d, g, 86} vg syr^{p, h} cop^{sa, bo} arm
Clement Speculum al), the Textus Receptus, influenced by the parallel in Eph 5.19
(where there is no variation), substitutes κυρίῳ, with C² D^c K Ψ* 614 Byz Lect it⁶¹ goth
al'. Some mss also insert καί after ψαλμοῖς and ὕμνοις (cf. Eph. above). The singular
τῇ καρδίᾳ is probably an assimilation to the parallel in Eph.

Deichgräber (*Gotteshymnus*, 33) notes that hymns directed to Christ are generally to
be placed late, and sees the development reflected especially clearly in the transition
from this verse (ᾄδοντες ... τῷ θεῷ) to Eph. 5.19 (ᾄδοντες καὶ ψάλλοντες ... τῷ
κυρίῳ). The latter reading in Col. (for which he lists P⁴⁶ Koiné pm) is a harmonization
with Eph. 5.19 (against L. Cerfaux, 'Hymnes', 4). Hurtado, however, (*One God, One
Lord*, 101ff.) traces the practice of singing hymns in Christ's honour to 'the earliest
stratum of the Christian movement' (102).

On ὁ λόγος τοῦ Χριστοῦ Moule (125) comments: 'i.e. the Gospel,
the "Word" uttered by Christ in his life and ministry and through his
person, and repeated by each Christian as he proclaims the Gospel by
life and witness'. As Lightfoot noted long ago (290), the genitive
marks Christ as the speaker of this word. The more common formula
ὁ λόγος τοῦ θεοῦ appears at 1.25 (cf. 1 John 2.14, ὁ λόγος τοῦ θεοῦ ἐν
ὑμῖν μένει), 'the word of the truth of the gospel' at 1.5,⁴⁹ but apart
from 4.3 (ἵνα ὁ θεὸς ἀνοίξῃ ἡμῖν θύραν τοῦ λόγου) the word λόγος
does not elsewhere carry this special sense in Col. (for 2.23, see p.230
above; at 3.17; 4.6 it refers rather to the ordinary spoken word). We
should however also recall, with Dunn (236), the formula ὁ λόγος τοῦ
κυρίου (1 Thess. 1.8; 2 Thess. 3.1; Acts 8.25; 12.24 etc., but not in
Col.), which as he says could denote the gospel of which Christ is the
content, as well as the word which he spoke: 'there is no reason why
the genitive form should be pressed to an either–or decision (either
objective or subjective)'. As with βραβευέτω in v. 15, ἐνοικείτω here
is a third person imperative, indicating that this is not something the
Colossians are to achieve, but something they are to allow to happen,
and not hinder. This word is used 'always with ἔν τινι and of God or
of other spiritual things that take up their abode in or among men'
(BAGD 267). The adverb πλουσίως, 'richly', occurs elsewhere only in
1 Tim. 6.17, Tit. 3.6 and 2 Pet. 1.11.

Moule also notes that there are problems of punctuation and of
interpretation.⁵⁰ Does ἐν πάσῃ σοφίᾳ go with ἐνοικείτω or with
διδάσκοντες? And does ψαλμοῖς κτλ go primarily with διδάσκοντες
καὶ νουθετοῦντες ἑαυτούς or with ᾄδοντες? The translation above
follows the punctuation of NA²⁷, which makes good sense and goes

⁴⁹ For ἡ ἀλήθεια τοῦ εὐαγγελίου cf. Gal. 2.5, 14.
⁵⁰ Lightfoot, for example, puts a colon after σοφίᾳ and a comma after χάριτι, and
takes the three participles as imperatives, which yields: 'Let the word of Christ dwell in
your hearts richly in all wisdom. Teach and admonish one another with psalms and
hymns of praise and spiritual songs in God's grace' (his own version is a paraphrase
rather than a translation).

readily into English, although the final words, ἐν τῇ χάριτι ᾄδοντες ἐν ταῖς καρδίαις τῷ θεῷ, require some rearrangement of order (cf. Dunn, 211 n. 14). At 1.28 the phrase ἐν πάσῃ σοφίᾳ certainly goes with νουθετοῦντες and διδάσκοντες (in that order),[51] while psalms and hymns are more naturally associated with singing than with teaching and admonition. The three nominative plural participles are strictly ungrammatical, but as Moule observes the sense is easily understandable: they refer back to ὑμῖν, and it is the readers who are to teach and admonish one another. For the reflexive used instead of the reciprocal pronoun see v. 13 above (p. 261 above).

Dunn rightly sees here a description of early Christian worship, 'the worship which the Colossian Christians should be enjoying and, by implication, should find sufficiently fulfilling'. The elements commended are, as he says, 'not altogether surprising: "the word of Christ", teaching and admonition, and singing and thanksgiving, elements which have been a feature of typical Christian worship from the beginning until now' (see his discussion, 235–40).

On the closing words of this verse Schubert compares Epictetus i.16.21: νῦν δὲ λογικός εἰμι θ᾽ ὑμνεῖν μὲ δεῖ τὸν θεόν. τοῦτο μου τὸ ἐργόν ἐστιν, ποιῶ αὐτὸ οὐδ᾽ ἐγκαταλείπω τὴν τάξιν ταύτην, ἐφ᾽ ὅσον ἂν δίδωται, καὶ ὑμᾶς ἐπὶ τὴν αὐτὴν ᾠδὴν παρακαλῶ ('I am a rational being, therefore I must be singing hymns of praise to God. This is my task; I do it, and will not desert this post, as long as it may be given me to fill it. I invite you also to sing the same song'; tr. W. A. Oldfather, Loeb Classical Library). 'It goes without saying that for Epictetus ὑμνεῖν τὸν θεόν is the same as εὐχαριστεῖν τῷ θεῷ. It is the business of the modest and the grateful and the rational person'; 'Thanksgiving and gratitude are the distinguishing marks in the behavior of his disciple, of man at his best.' (*Form and Function*, 133f.). Epictetus is 'expressing in his own way an idea and a type of religious experience which had become increasingly influential in the Hellenistic world' (135). This does not mean, of course, that our author was influenced by Epictetus, a slightly later contemporary (c. AD 60–140), or even by Hellenistic culture. The Jews already had the Psalms in their sacred scriptures, and singing is in any case a natural and spontaneous way of expressing gratitude and thanks to God.

The words **ψαλμοῖς ὕμνοις ᾠδαῖς πνευματικαῖς** appear both in Eph. and in Col., but in Eph. they are preceded by λαλοῦντες ἑαυτοῖς, and ᾄδοντες follows in the next clause with καὶ ψάλλοντες; Eph. also inserts καί after ψαλμοῖς and ὕμνοις. The text there is firm, whereas in Col. there are variant readings, so that these probably represent assimilation of Col. to Eph. Of the three terms, **ψαλμός**

[51] On these verses Dunn (237) writes, 'The most significant difference is that whereas 1:28 described the apostolic mission of proclaiming the gospel (though as a task shared by others, Timothy at least), here warning and teaching are seen as a corporate responsibility .... Indeed, it is a striking feature of the Pauline corpus how much Paul insisted that the members of the churches to which he wrote should recognize their mutual responsibility to instruct and admonish each other (Rom. 12:7; 15:14; 1 Cor. 14:26; 1 Thes. 5:14 ; 2 Thes. 3:15; note also Gal. 6:1–3).'

(BAGD 891; *TWNT* viii. 492ff., *s.v.* ὕμνος, esp. 501f.) is used several times with reference to the book of Psalms (Luke 20.42; 24.44; Acts 1.20; 13.33), but at 1 Cor. 14.26 (NRSV 'each one has a hymn [ψαλμόν], a lesson, a revelation, a tongue, or an interpretation') it may refer rather to a Christian hymn, and the same may apply here (cf. Delling, *TWNT* viii. 502; C. K. Barrett, *First Corinthians* (1968), 327 comments, 'a fresh, perhaps spontaneous, composition, not an Old Testament psalm, is intended; cf. Col. iii. 16; Eph. v. 19').

In the NT ὕμνος (BAGD 836) occurs only in Eph. 5.19 and here, but it is linked with ψαλμός in Josephus (*Ant.* xii.323), who elsewhere uses it in the same context with ᾠδή (*Ant.* vii.305). Association of these words is thus by no means unusual, and in fact it is very natural. ᾠδή (BAGD 895) occurs only in Eph. 5.19, Col. 3.16; and Rev. 5.9; 14.3 (*bis*); 15.3 in the New Testament; all four cases in Rev. are in the singular, whereas Eph. and Col. use the plural. The three words are very similar in meaning, but it is possible to make some distinction between them. Lightfoot (291) suggests that ᾠδή 'is the general word for a song, whether accompanied or unaccompanied, whether of praise or on any other subject'. For ψαλμός the reference is 'specially, though not exclusively (1 Cor. xiv. 26), to the Psalms of David, which would early form part of the religious worship of the Christian brotherhood', while ὕμνος 'would more appropriately designate those hymns of praise which were composed by the Christians themselves'. Among the several quotations he adduces, one from Philo deserves mention: ὁ ἀναστὰς ὕμνον ᾄδει πεποιημένον εἰς τὸν θεόν, ἢ καινὸν αὐτὸς πεποιηκὼς ἢ ἀρχαῖόν τινα τῶν πάλαι ποιητῶν (*Vit. Cont.* §10, p. 484); Dunn (239 n. 47) quotes from Tertullian (*Apol.* 39.18) a description of a Christian *agape*: 'Each is asked to stand forth and sing, as he can, a hymn to God, either one from the holy scriptures or one of his own composing/from his own heart.' The early Christians were just as capable of composing new hymns as Philo's Therapeutae: Dunn (238) refers to 'the more distinctively Christian compositions which have been widely recognized within the New Testament itself, particularly the Magnificat and the Benedictus in Luke 1, but also the more disputed items in the Pauline corpus (Eph. 5:14; Phil. 2:6–11; Col. 1:15–20; 1 Tim. 3:16).'[52]

According to Lightfoot, 'The third word ᾠδαῖς gathers up the other two, and extends the precept to all forms of song, with the limitation however that they must be πνευματικαί.' But what are 'spiritual' songs? The most obvious and natural reference would of course be to songs inspired by the Spirit, but Dunn (239) raises the question whether this might include glossolalic singing. As he says, this is difficult to determine, but the evidence of 1 Cor. 14 suggests a

---

[52] In a footnote he refers to R. P. Martin, *Worship in the Early Church* (1964), 39–52; Deichgräber, *Gotteshymnus*; Sanders, *The NT Christological Hymns*; K. Wengst, *Christologische Formeln und Lieder des Urchristentums* (1972), Teil III.

negative: 'those who speak in a tongue do not speak to other people but to God; for nobody understands them, since they are speaking mysteries in the Spirit' (v. 2 NRSV); 'in church I would rather speak five words with my mind, in order to instruct others also, than ten thousand words in a tongue' (v. 19; see the whole chapter). Glossolalia without an interpreter is of no value, because people cannot understand. Paul's concern is for what will edify and build up all members of a congregation.

As already noted (p. 267), the words ἐν τῇ χάριτι ᾄδοντες ἐν ταῖς καρδίαις τῷ θεῷ, with two phrases beginning with ἐν, require some rearrangement of order. The translation above (p. 241) takes these phrases together, 'singing with psalms and hymns and spiritual songs to God with thankfulness in your hearts', but in the Greek the phrases are separated by the verb ᾄδοντες, and it is by no means certain that they should be taken so closely together. The article before χάριτι is omitted by ℵ* A C D² and other mss, but is included by P⁴⁶ ℵ² B D* et al. Lightfoot (291) is quite firm in holding that the latter is the correct reading, and also in interpreting the noun as referring to God's grace: 'The definite article seems to exclude all lower senses of χάρις here, such as "acceptableness", "sweetness" (see iv. 6). The interpretation "with gratitude", if otherwise tenable (comp. 1 Cor. x. 30), seems inappropriate here, because the idea of thanksgiving is introduced in the following verse.' There is, however, no reason why our author should not have spoken of thankfulness in this verse and giving thanks in the next, and later commentators (and, according to Dunn, 239, 'all translations') take the word in the sense of gratitude. Moule (126) writes that the context favours 'gratefully', and on the textual point comments: 'It looks as though τῇ were the true reading, and subsequent scribes had encountered as much difficulty in interpreting it as we do.'

A further reason for not taking these phrases too closely together is that to do so does not quite do justice to ἐν ταῖς καρδίαις. 'With gratitude in your hearts' (so NRSV) is all too easily passed over without reflection. It is not just a matter of having gratitude in their hearts, but of having a heartfelt gratitude. For Dunn (240) the addition of this phrase 'underlines the importance of a worship rooted in the depths of personal experience and springing up from that source—heart worship and not merely lip worship' (he sees here perhaps one further allusion to Isa. 29.13: 'these people draw near with their mouths and honour me with their lips, while their hearts are far from me' (NRSV; cf. 2.22).

17. καὶ πᾶν ὅ τι ἐὰν ποιῆτε ἐν λόγῳ ἢ ἐν ἔργῳ, πάντα ἐν ὀνόματι κυρίου Ἰησοῦ, εὐχαριστοῦντες τῷ θεῷ πατρὶ δι᾽ αὐτοῦ

The final verse of this section condenses the whole range of Christian ethics into one single pointed and memorable aphorism: whatever you do, in word or in deed, do all in the name of the Lord Jesus, giving thanks to God the Father through him. Once again, everything is carried back to the love of God revealed in Jesus

Christ. Anyone acting 'in the name' of Jesus, or for his sake, could not possibly do harm to another.

On the phrase 'in the name of the Lord Jesus' Schweizer ('Christus und Geist', 304) compares 1 Cor. 10.31, which speaks of doing all 'for the glory of God' (just a few verses later, at 11.1, Paul writes 'Be imitators of me, as I am of Christ'); also Rom. 14.4ff., which includes v. 8, 'If we live, we live to the Lord, and if we die, we die to the Lord; so then, whether we live or whether we die, we are the Lord's.' At 1 Cor. 5.1–5 Paul speaks of having already passed judgement on the offender, and continues, ἐν τῷ ὀνόματι τοῦ κυρίου [ἡμῶν] Ἰησοῦ συναχθέντων ὑμῶν καὶ τοῦ ἐμοῦ πνεύματος σὺν τῇ δυνάμει τοῦ κυρίου ἡμῶν Ἰησοῦ, παραδοῦναι τὸν τοιοῦτον τῷ σατανᾷ (C. K. Barrett translates: 'When you have been gathered together, with my spirit, in the name of the Lord Jesus, we should, with the power of our Lord Jesus, hand over such a man as this to Satan' (*1 Corinthians*, 119, 124).[53] NRSV takes ἐν τῷ ὀνόματι τοῦ κυρίου Ἰησοῦ with what precedes, and renders it 'I have already pronounced judgement in the name of the Lord Jesus on the man who has done such a thing.')

Among other occurrences of the phrase 'in the name of the Lord' we may note two which remind us of its OT background: the quotation of Ps. 118.26 at the Triumphal Entry (Matt. 21.9, cf. also 23.39; Mark 11.9; Luke 19.38, cf. also 13.35; John 12.13) and the citation of Joel 2.32 at Acts 2.21. In the original context in each case 'the Lord' is clearly God himself, but in numerous other cases the title is applied to Jesus (cf. BAGD 459f., *s.v.* κύριος §2c; 460, §2d lists several passages where it is not clear whether God or Christ is meant: Acts 9.31; 1 Cor. 4.19; 7.17; 2 Cor. 8.21; Col. 3.22b; 1 Thess. 4.6; 2 Thess. 3.16 al; see also 571, *s.v.* ὄνομα §I 4).[54] One of them is in relation to baptism (Acts 8.16; 19.5; cf. also Matt. 28.19; Acts 2.38; 10.48, where baptism is 'in the name', but without the title κύριος). Another is in relation to healing (Acts 3.6, 16; 4.10, again simply 'in the name'). At Acts 19.13 some Jewish exorcists try to use the name of Jesus in exorcism (cf. the repudiation of some who claim to have prophesied, cast out demons, and worked wonders 'in your name' in Matt. 7.22–23; contrast Mark 9.38–41; Luke 9.49–50).

At Matt. 10.22 Jesus warns his disciples that 'you will be hated by all because of my name' (cf. 24.9; Mark 13.13), while at Acts 4.18 Peter and John are ordered by the Jerusalem authorities 'not to speak or teach at all in the name of Jesus' (cf. 5.28, 40). Acts 9.28 tells how Saul 'went in and out among them in Jerusalem, speaking boldly in the name of the Lord'. At Acts 21.13 Paul speaks of his readiness 'not only to be bound but even to die in Jerusalem for the name of the Lord Jesus'. These and many other passages illustrate the significance which the phrases 'in the name of Jesus' or 'in the name of the Lord' quite clearly had for early Christians.

The final words of this section make it clear that for all the high esteem in which our author holds the Lord Jesus he does not quite go so far as to identify him as God: do all in the name of the Lord Jesus,

---

[53] 'It goes without saying that the assembly, being a Christian body, will meet *in the name of the Lord Jesus*—under his authority, and with the intention of acting in obedience to him. Under these circumstances the act contemplated will be the act of the whole church, not of the apostle only' (124).

[54] Cf. p. 261 above, with Dunn's remark that 'in the Paulines, apart from Old Testament quotations, κύριος always denotes Christ', and Aletti's conclusion that Col. reserves κύριος for Christ.

giving thanks to God the Father through him.[55] As Paul writes to the
Philippians, God has highly exalted Jesus, given him the name that is
above every name, but he is still God's agent: God remains sovereign
and supreme (cf. above, pp. 225, 256).

On the phrase θεῷ πατρί Metzger (626) writes: 'The very unusual collocation τῷ θεῷ
πατρί, which is widely supported by P[46vid] ℵ A B C 81 442 1739 1985 it[86] syr[p] cop[sa, bo]
goth eth Ambrose Speculum, was emended by copyists who inserted και, thus
imitating Eph 5.20 and similar passages. (See also the comments on 1.3 and 12)'.

The first list of vices in this passage could be more or less
conventional, listing the faults which the Jews regarded as typical
of their Gentile neighbours 'without the law', and Christians as
characteristic of the life which some had lived before their conversion (cf. v. 7). The second list, in vv. 8 and 9, and more particularly
the virtues with which the readers are to 'clothe' themselves (NRSV)
in vv. 12 to 15, may perhaps have a more direct relevance to the local
situation. If this is the case, the problem may not have been a
doctrinal error (apart from a failure to give to Christ the place that is
due to him), but more of a quarrelsome and factious spirit within the
community: anger, malice, slander. Some difference of opinion has
been allowed to get out of hand, to mushroom into division and
hostility which threatens to rend the community apart. As already
noted, it might all have begun with a single individual, some Jewish
Christian with leanings towards apocalyptic and an austere attitude
in regard to preparation for approach to the heavenly ascent. But
here we are entering into the realms of conjecture and speculation.
The point is that we do not necessarily need to think of a formal
'heresy', of the spread of false teaching on a large scale, of large
numbers of Jewish Christians of strict observance condemning their
Gentile Christian fellow-members for alleged shortcomings in regard
to food laws or observance of festivals. What is of permanent
importance is our author's insistence on the kind of spirit that
should animate any Christian community: compassion, kindness,
humility, gentleness, tolerance, readiness to forgive, and above all
love.

[55] Cf. Barclay, *Colossians*, 81f.: 'it is clear that our author could not reflect on God
without also reflecting on Christ'. On 2.9 Barclay remarks, 'that gets about as near to
calling Christ "God" as it is possible to go without actually doing so'.

XI
The *Haustafel*: A Household Code
(3.18–4.1)

[18]Wives, be subject to your husbands, as is fitting in the Lord. [19]Husbands, love your wives, and do not become embittered towards them. [20]Children, obey your parents in all things, for this is pleasing in the Lord. [21]Fathers, do not provoke your children, that they may not be discouraged.

[22]Slaves, obey your masters according to the flesh in every respect, not with eye-service as men-pleasers, but in simplicity of heart, fearing the Lord. [23]Whatever you do, labour from the heart, as for the Lord and not for men, [24]knowing that it is from the Lord that you will receive the inheritance as a reward. It is the Lord Christ whom you serve. [25]For the wrongdoer shall be paid back for the wrong he has done, and there is no partiality.

[4.1]Masters, grant what is just and equitable to your slaves, knowing that you also have a Lord in heaven.

The last section was concerned with admonitions addressed to the community as a whole, with virtues which would be likely to promote good relationships among its members. Further admonitions follow in vv. 2–6 of the next chapter, again addressed to the whole community. The present section, in contrast, is more narrowly focused on relationships within a household, between husbands and wives, fathers and children, masters and slaves (hence the description *Haustafel* or household code).[1] Not unnaturally, it has sometimes been suggested that these verses are an intrusion into the text.[2] As

---

[1] Once again only a selection of the literature can be offered: Crouch, *The Origin and Intention of the Colossian Haustafel* (with earlier literature); Schrage, 'Zur Ethik der neutestamentlichen Haustafeln'; E. Schweizer, 'Traditional ethical patterns in the Pauline and post-Pauline Letters', in Best and Wilson (eds), *Text and Interpretation* (1979), esp. 201–10; Lührmann, 'Neutestamentliche Haustafeln'; G. E. Cannon, *The Use of Traditional Materials in Colossians* (1983); P. Fiedler, 'Haustafel', *RAC* xiii (1986), 1063–1073; D. L. Balch, 'Household Code', in D. E. Aune (ed.), *Greco-Roman Literature and the New Testament*, (1988), 25–50; G. Strecker, 'Die neutestamentliche Haustafeln', in Merklein (ed.), *Neues Testament und Ethik* (1989), 349–75; Moritz, *A Profound Mystery*, 165–68; Barclay, *Colossians*, 68–73, 90–92; Standhartinger, *Studien*, 247–76. For the similar passage in Eph. see Best, *Ephesians*, 519–27, 528–82 (literature at 519–20, 528–29, 562, 571) and 'The Haustafel in Ephesians'.
[2] Cf. for example W. Munro, 'Col. III.18-IV. 1 and Eph. V.21-VI. 9', *Authority in Paul and Peter*, 27–37, and *NTS* 36 (1990), 431–43, esp. 438; but see already Crouch, 10 n. 1, who argues for a pre-Colossian unit; also Best, *Ephesians*, 522–23. Moritz (153 n. 1) is unconvinced by Munro's theory: apart from 'the sheer intricacy' of the proposal,

Barclay puts it (68), 'Both in style and in content this passage seems like an island in its present context, not obviously connected to what goes before or what comes after; in fact, if you took it away, you could move easily from 3.17 to 4.2 without realizing anything was missing in between.' This is, however, one of those cases in which a simple and apparently obvious conclusion may be quite misleading. The fact that a passage could easily be omitted does not mean that it does not belong, or that it is an interpolation.[3]

There are two similar passages in the New Testament, Eph. 5.21–6.9 and 1 Pet. 2.13–3.7, both of which expand upon the relatively simple form that is found in Col.,[4] and several other passages both in the New Testament and in early Christian literature which seem to represent a tendency to form codes of Christian duties. Thus Barclay (68) lists passages urging an attitude of submission in relation to state authorities (Rom. 13.1–7; 1 Pet. 2.13–17; Tit. 3.1–2), or directed to slaves (1 Tim. 6.1–2), in male-female relationships (1 Tim. 2.8–15), or in general relationships within the community (e.g. Tit. 2.1–10; 1 Pet. 5.1–5). For subsequent Christian literature, where the material is less clearly organized, he lists *Did.* 4.9–11, *Barn.* 19.7, *1 Clem.* 1.3 and 21.6–8, Polycarp's letter to the Philippians 4–6 and Ignatius' letter to Polycarp 4–6 (cf. the similar lists in Pokorný (176), Dunn (242), etc.).[5] Crouch (34) observes that these later Christian codes 'stand closer to Hellenistic parallels than does the Colossian *Haustafel'*.

The parallels referred to are first of all in the 'unwritten laws' of Greek popular ethics (Crouch, 37–46), the generally valid norms and standards of conduct which people were expected to observe as a matter of course. These duties were taken over by the Stoics and

'Munro does not explain sufficiently how Col. 3.18–20 could have resulted on the basis of its Ephesian counterpart(s)', while Dunn (243 n. 8) finds 'little to be said, and no support' for Munro's arguments. It may be added that we need to be able to explain why our author (or a later interpolator) made the insertion just at this point, and not elsewhere, where it might have fitted in more easily. We must also ask if there are not other possible explanations, such as Crouch's suggestion noted above. Best (520ff.) argues for a pre-Christian form taken over by the Church and modified for Christian usage. W. D. Davies writes (*PRJ* 136), 'in Col. 3.18–4.1, as elsewhere, Paul has Christianized material of a "foreign" origin by the addition to it of a formula ἐν κυρίῳ, this being added to show that all the exhortations were regarded as inspired by the Spirit of the Lord.'
[3] Barclay does not make that deduction. At a later point (91) he writes, 'It is thus quite fitting that Colossians should be the occasion for the first occurrence of the "household code". Here we find the mundane relationships of daily life claimed for Christ and brought under the sway of his ultimate authority.'
[4] 'It is noteworthy that the expansions of both Col 3:18f in Eph 5:22–33 and Col 3:20f in Eph 6:1–4 incorporate explicit OT quotations. Whereas Col 3:18–4.1 is virtually devoid of OT material, the author of the Ephesian *Haustafel* was at pains to incorporate Pentateuchal material' (Moritz, 153). Moritz thinks (168) that our author had little interest in alluding to the OT because of the particular audience he envisaged. This would seem to tell against Dunn's view that the opposition in Colossae was largely Jewish. Long ago Wettstein wrote: 'Nulla ex V.T. attulit testimonia, quia haec Epistula scripta est ad Ecclesiam non ex Judaeis, sed ex gentibus collectam' (*Novum Testamentum Graecum* (1752; repr. 1962), ii. 281).
[5] On Ignatius, in comparison with Paul, cf. M. Y. MacDonald, 'The Ideal of a Christian Couple', *NTS* 40 (1994), 105–25.

incorporated into their own philosophy, although with certain modifications and changes of emphasis (47–56), and from Stoicism they passed into the popular philosophy of the early Roman Empire (57–73).[6] There was also a Jewish tradition, as far back as the Wisdom literature, but in Hellenistic Judaism, as represented by Philo and Josephus, we can detect not only the legacy of the Old Testament but also traces of a Greek and particularly Stoic influence (74–101).[7]

Dieter Lührmann (in n. 1, 85) sees the closest parallels in texts 'On the economy', writings which deal with the mutual relationships between husband and wife, parents and children, masters and slaves. In this context the 'household' might vary from a small group with perhaps one or two slaves to a major operation involving quite large numbers (one may recall the *latifundia* of the Roman period). An important point here is that we have to consider this passage in the light of the period in which it was written: we are not dealing with a modern 'nuclear' household, both parents working to pay off the mortgage, run a car, provide for their children's education, and generally maintain their lifestyle, commuting from the suburbs to work in shops or offices or factories. People in the first century did not live in an industrialized society. There were of course merchants and traders, and there were craftsmen who specialized in certain fields, like the carpenter or the silversmith; but to set things in true perspective we should be thinking of the estates and farms of a former generation, with a row of cottages in which the farmhands lived, where the family could be more or less self-sufficient, growing its own crops and only having to purchase occasional luxuries. In addition, conditions would be different for the family in the big house and for the families of those who lived in the cottages. In this area it is not possible to take the injunctions of a New Testament writer and apply them directly to modern conditions. Our author is not to be faulted for failing to comply with a 'political correctness' that was not to be promulgated for some two thousand years! We must interpret his work in the context of his own period before we

---

[6] One interesting passage appears in Tacitus' account of the Jews (*Hist.* v.5): 'apud eos fides obstinata, misericordia in promptu. Sed adversus omnes alios hostile odium. ... Transgressi in morem eorum idem usurpant; nec quidquam prius imbuuntur quam contemnere deos, exuere patriam, parentes, liberos, fratres vilia habere.' To paraphrase: 'among themselves there is a steadfast faith, and compassion ever ready, but towards all others an implacable hatred. Those who convert to their way of life adopt the same habits, and the first thing they learn is to despise the gods, renounce their native country, and consider parents, children and brethren of little worth.' Here elements of the traditional scheme are used in denunciation of the Jews.

[7] At one point (84) Crouch's formulation is at first sight startling: 'Adultery is enjoined [*sic!*] in all three codes (i.e. in Philo's *Hypothetica*, the *Contra Apionem* of Josephus, and ps.-Phocylides) as is homosexuality and the rape of a virgin.' According to the first two senses of 'enjoin' reported in the *Concise Oxford Dictionary*, the word means 'prescribe, impose, command', which is scarcely the sense required! But the entry continues: '(Law) prohibit by injunction (*from doing*).'

can think of applying the principles which he sets forth to our modern times.[8]

Some scholars, evidently thinking that early Christians would not have taken over anything from a pagan society, have sought to claim that these household codes were a specifically Christian creation, but that is ruled out by the parallels that have been identified. Nor would it be correct to say that they have merely been slightly Christianized by the addition of ἐν κυρίῳ, for these two words in fact give a new significance to the whole: as 3.17 puts it, they are to do everything in the name of the Lord Jesus. Early Christians, whether from a Jewish or a Gentile background, inevitably brought with them something of the standards and traditions of their earlier life. They also had to live their daily lives according to the standards of contemporary society. The household code calls upon them to live up to the highest standards, but *as Christians*, in the name of the Lord Jesus.

The admonition here consists of three pairs of exhortations, with each member of a pair balanced against the other (cf. Crouch's arrangement, 9); only the admonition to the slaves is given more extended treatment. In Eph. 5.21–33, in contrast, it is the admonition to husbands and wives that is most expanded. 'Here the value of Christian marriage is stated very strongly: it is an expression of the mysterious relationship between Christ and the church' (MacDonald, 'Ideal', 117). In each case it is the 'subordinate' member of the pair that is addressed first (Dunn, 243 notes that Dionysius of Halicarnassus praises Roman household relationships using the same three pairs, in the same order (*Roman Antiquities* ii.25.4–26.4); on the following page Dunn sees 'clearly Jewish features', for example in the concern for the weaker members of the three pairings, and finally 'distinctive Christian features', most notably the sevenfold reference to 'the Lord', which is not just a vague Christianization as some have suggested, but provides the orientation for the whole.)

18. αἱ γυναῖκες ὑποτάσσεσθε τοῖς ἀνδράσιν ὡς ἀνῆκεν ἐν κυρίῳ Cf. Eph. 5.21–22, ὑποτασσόμενοι ἀλλήλοις ἐν φόβῳ Χριστοῦ, αἱ γυναῖκες τοῖς ἰδίοις ἀνδράσιν ὡς τῷ κυρίῳ;[9] 5.24, ἀλλὰ ὡς ἡ

---

[8] We may recall the description of the 'capable' wife in Prov. 31.10–31, which might leave a modern reader wondering what is left for the husband to do: presumably the writing of a few more proverbs! But note v. 23: the wife's control of household affairs leaves her husband free for service in the wider community, even to affairs of state. J. C. Rylaarsdam writes: 'The good wife is here defined in terms of her role as "home-economist". Initiative, inventive ingenuity, and industry characterise her life as a far-sighted manager. In her function as householder she claims a degree of independence consonant with her capabilities (cf. v. **11**). It is to be noted that this sort of career is praised in the context of a society in which the *individual* legal rights of a wife were very slight; she is, therefore, presented as motivated by eagerness for the "name" and reputation of her husband and family (cf. vv. **12, 21, 23, 28, 31**) rather than by a desire for "personal self-realisation" ' (*Peake's Commentary on the Bible*, (revd edn (1962), 457).

[9] Some mss insert ὑποτάσσεσθε or ὑποτασσέσθωσαν after the word ἀνδράσιν, but this is probably an assimilation to Col. or, as Best (*Ephesians*, 531) suggests, was introduced when vv. 22–33 were used as a unit in worship.

ἐκκλησία ὑποτάσσεται τῷ Χριστῷ, οὕτως καὶ αἱ γυναῖκες τοῖς ἀνδράσιν ἐν παντί. This verse is inevitably the target for criticism in certain circles, but has to be seen in its proper context. Where the family depended for its sustenance on hunting or on the produce of its farm, the natural division of labour was for the husband, as physically the stronger, to undertake the heavier work, and for the wife to take charge of the running of the household and look after the children. In a male-dominated society it was natural for the husband to be master of the house, even when his sons had grown to manhood, but a wise man would always give due regard to the opinions of his wife.[10]

Here it is important to see things in perspective: male dominance does not necessarily mean that women were mere chattels, submissively enduring a life little better than that of their slaves, at the mercy of their husbands.[11] It might be so in some cases, but it is dangerous to generalize. Xanthippe, the wife of Socrates, had the reputation of a scold (*Oxford Companion to Classical Literature* (1940), 399), and there is evidence in classical literature of women's ability to cope with the situation, even to persuading their husbands to see another point of view. In the New Testament there are several cases in which women come to prominence, e.g. Lydia (Acts 16.14–15) or Priscilla (Acts 18.2, 18, 26; Rom. 16.3; 1 Cor. 16.19); the list of greetings in Rom. 16 suggests that there were several women in prominent positions in the leadership of the Church (cf. S. Schreiber, *NTS* 46 (2000), 204–26, who sees in the post-Pauline writings a change from the earlier situation visible in Romans and elsewhere; also M. Y. MacDonald, *NTS* 36 (1990), 181, who writes that the deutero-Pauline letters are 'far more determined to communicate the importance of a believing wife's subjection to her husband in the household than are Paul's writings').[12] In short, the ancient world

---

[10] 'In actual practice also the wife is often the wiser and more sensible person; should she, rather than the husband, not be the controlling person?' (Best, 561). We should remember also the 'capable wife' of Prov. 31.10–31, surely a supportive partner rather than meekly submissive.

[11] 'It is important to note that it is wives and not women generally who are in view (as also in 1 Cor 14:34). Women who were single, widowed, or divorced and of independent means could evidently function as heads of their own households, as in the case of Lydia (Acts 16:14–15), Phoebe, the first named "deacon" in Christian history and patron of the church at Cenchreae (Rom 16:1–2), Chloe (1 Cor 1:11), and presumably Nympha in Colossae itself (see on 4:14)' (Dunn, 246). On 'the lot of women in antiquity' cf. Crouch, 107–11, who notes (108) that attitudes in Greece and Rome were more liberal than in Judaism. Epiphanes, son of the early Gnostic Carpocrates, mocks at the commandment 'You shall not covet your neighbour's wife' (Exod. 20.17), advocating community of women; but this is the logic of a rather precocious teenager (he died at the age of 17). See Clement of Alexandria, *Strom.* iii.9.3, in Foerster, *Gnosis*, i. 40.

[12] Best (533) observes that the Pauline and deutero-Pauline letters contain contrasting attitudes to women and in particular to wives: in Gal. 3.28 women are regarded as equal members of the church with men, while in 1 Cor. 7.3ff. 'husbands and wives have equal sexual rights within marriage and the husband is not depicted as governing his

was indeed male-dominated, but the actual experience of women
might vary considerably from one case to another, and in different
periods.[13] We have to bear in mind possible nuances, and not
generalize without real grounds. In any case what matters here is the
mutual respect and obligation imposed, as the following verse shows,
on both husband and wife.[14] Early Christians could not have hoped
to change the existing order by direct challenge and confrontation,
but this mutual respect and obligation contained the seed of a
transformation from within.

ὑποτάσσω in the passive (BAGD 848; *TWNT* ix. 40–47) means to
become subject or be subordinate.[15] In its use here Delling (*TWNT*
ix. 44) sees the observance of an ordinance willed by God, comparing
1 Cor. 11.3; 14.34; Gen. 3.16 and 1 Pet. 3. 5–6: in the beginning the
woman was created after the man and for his sake. The verb ἀνήκω,
used impersonally (BAGD 66; *TWNT* i. 361), means 'to be fitting',
and appears in the NT only at this point in Col. and Eph. and in
Philem. 8. It almost inevitably recalls the very similar term used by
the Stoics, τὰ καθήκοντα, although it is not identical and probably
should not be claimed as evidence of Stoic influence. Crouch (53)
writes, 'On the basis of these considerations [i.e. his discussion of the
Stoic list of duties] we are justified in accepting as basically accurate
those reports which indicate the existence of καθήκοντα, including
the elements of our schema, in Stoicism from the very beginning'
(references for authors who wrote treatises on the subject in n. 38).

19. οἱ ἄνδρες ἀγαπᾶτε τὰς γυναῖκας καὶ μὴ πικραίνεσθε πρὸς
αὐτάς Cf. Eph. 5.25, οἱ ἄνδρες ἀγαπᾶτε τὰς γυναῖκας, καθὼς καὶ ὁ
Χριστὸς ἠγάπησεν τὴν ἐκκλησίαν. Col. does not have the comparison found in Eph., which leads into 'a lyrical account of the love of
Christ for his church' (Dunn, 249). There has been some difference of
opinion over the precise force of the verb ἀγαπάω here: on the one

wife in this respect'. In 1 Cor. 11.2ff. women are permitted to take part in public
worship but are subordinate to their husbands. In the Pastorals, on the other hand, 'the
less egalitarian attitude predominates'. Cf. also MacDonald, 'The Ideal of the
Christian Couple'.
[13] Cf. Crouch's discussion of this verse (107–10): 'The context of the codes in
Hellenism, viz., Stoic and popular philosophy, is precisely that area in which one finds
the most enlightened views toward women. In the corresponding area in Hellenistic
Judaism we find just the opposite, viz., a low view of women and the specific
instruction that the wife is to be submissive to her husband' (111).
[14] 'Whatever advance may have been made since New Testament times, under the
guidance of the Holy Spirit, towards a deeper understanding of personal relations, the
really remarkable thing is, not that the N.T. writers regarded women as essentially
subordinate—this was a legacy from Judaism itself, let alone any pagan influences,
which could not rapidly be lost—nor that slavery was accepted as inevitable for the
time being, but rather that household life was so transformed "in the Lord" that each
person was seen as precious to God, and that husbands and masters recognized that
they had duties no less than rights' (Moule, 128). No small part of the problems of
modern society is quite simply due to emphasis on rights to the neglect of
responsibilities.
[15] 'The exhortation should not be weakened in translation in deference to modern
sensibilities .... But neither should its significance be exaggerated; "subjection" means
"subordination", not "subjugation"' (Dunn, 247).

hand Crouch (111f.) claims that 'the opinion of the majority of commentators that we are dealing with specifically Christian material in the exhortation to the husbands is based merely on the rather superficial assumption that the term ἀγάπη bears a specifically Christian content whenever found in the New Testament' ... 'The simple, most natural sense of ἀγάπη in the *Haustafel* is the normal, human love of a husband for his wife.' On the other hand Dunn (248), although admitting that 'the ideal of a husband being tenderly solicitous for his wife was not distinctively Christian', is no less firm on the other side: 'But again a distinctive Christian note comes through in the use of the verb ἀγαπάω, which, as elsewhere in the Paulines (Rom 8:37; Gal 2:20; Eph 2:4; 5:2, 25), gains its character-istic emphasis from Christ's self-giving on the cross. Thus ἀγαπάω plays the role in 3:19 of "in the Lord" in 3:18 and 20 and is of itself sufficient to refer the reader back to the traditions of Jesus as the Christ and Lord (2:6-7).' The choice is difficult, but the prominence of ἀγάπη in the New Testament generally may perhaps be enough to tilt the balance: for Christian readers the verb would inevitably recall the noun, with all its associations.[16] Best (*Ephesians*, 540) remarks that ἀγάπη is not used in Hellenistic literature in relation to households.

The verb **πικραίνω** (BAGD 657; *TWNT* vi. 124–25) occurs elsewhere in the NT only at Rev. 8.11; 10.9, 10, where it is used in its normal sense of something being made bitter. Here it is used figuratively: husbands are not to allow anything to embitter their relations with their wives. For Moule (129) μὴ πικραίνεσθε here and μὴ ἐρεθίζετε in v. 21 'speak of friction caused by impatience and thoughtless "nagging", and remind us that the new life in Christ transforms relationship on the "ordinary" levels, as well as conquering the spectacular vices'. Dunn (249) notes that the word is often translated 'do not be harsh with them' (cf. NRSV 'never treat them harshly'), but that the passive voice 'presumably implies that the bitterness is experienced by the husbands'. He thinks what is in view 'is probably the feeling of the dominant partner who can legally enforce his will on his wife but who will not thereby win her love and respect and can thus feel cheated and embittered at not receiving what he regards as his due'. That may be, but it is perhaps better not to be too specific, and the general statement made above may suffice: a husband who harbours bitter feelings against his wife is not likely to be loving.[17]

---

[16] Crouch (112 n. 73) observes that Schroeder 'is correct in maintaining that a Stoic source would have used the term φιλεῖν in this context'. Stauffer (*TWNT* i. 651) writes: 'Nicht der ἔρως schafft die Ehegemeinschaft, sondern die ἀγάπη.'

[17] Pokorný 181 notes that bitterness (πικρία) appears as the first in a list of vices in Eph. 4.31.

20. τὰ τέκνα ὑπακούετε τοῖς γονεῦσιν ὑμῶν κατὰ πάντα, τοῦτο γάρ ἐστιν εὐάρεστον ἐν κυρίῳ Cf. Eph. 6.1, τὰ τέκνα ὑπακούετε τοῖς γονεῦσιν ὑμῶν [ἐν κυρίῳ]· τοῦτο γάρ ἐστιν δίκαιον.[18] Once again there are close similarities between Eph. and Col., but there are also differences. Best (565) observes that the author of Eph. has already used εὐάρεστον at 5.10: 'He had therefore no objection to this word and had he been copying Colossians, there would have been no reason for him to alter it.' In Best's view it is more likely that the two authors independently added to the tradition here.

Moritz (*A Profound Mystery*, 169) observes that when Paul wants to emphasize youth as symbolic of immaturity, he prefers παιδίον (1 Cor. 14.20), but when he wishes to stress 'the spiritual dimension of the nurturing relationship between himself and his converts' he uses τέκνον (1 Thess. 2.7).[19] παιδίον (BAGD 604; *TWNT* v. 636–53, esp. 637, §3) is a diminutive, frequently used of very young children (but cf. 1 John 2.18; at John 21.5 it is used by the risen Christ in addressing his disciples), whereas τέκνον would appear to be the term more frequently employed with reference to 'a spiritual child in relation to his master, apostle, or teacher' (BAGD 808, esp. §2b; see also *TWNT* v. 637–38, §5). Here it is used in its ordinary sense for the younger members of the household. Dunn (250), comparing Eph. 6.4, thinks they were 'presumably still minors', but that is not a necessary conclusion: a father retained authority over his family even when they had reached maturity. Sons when they married did not necessarily move to homes of their own, while daughters who married passed under the authority of their husbands, or it might be their husbands' parents (Dunn's reference to single women of independent means, quoted above in n. 11, would apply only to women of mature age, whose parents had died leaving them in control of their own fortunes.) In the Jewish tradition, respect for parents goes back at least as far as the Decalogue (Exod. 20.12, quoted at Eph. 6.2–3), but it was also part of the tradition in the wider world (cf. the references in Dunn, 250).

ὑπακούω (BAGD 837; *TWNT* i. 224–25) means to obey. It is significant for the authority of the head of a household that both children here and slaves in v. 22 are instructed to obey κατὰ πάντα, in all respects. Indeed, 1 Pet. 3.6 in its admonition to wives refers to the example of Sarah, who ὑπήκουσεν τῷ Ἀβραὰμ κύριον αὐτὸν καλοῦσα (BAGD pertinently cites the pre-Christian author Philemo: ἀγαθῆς γυναικός ἐστιν μὴ κρείττον᾿ εἶναι τ᾿ἀνδρος, ἀλλ᾿ ὑπήκοον. Cf. also Josephus, *C. Ap.* ii.201). If such dominance is no longer

---

[18] On the changes made by the author of Eph. see Moritz, 175f. – the Colossian *Vorlage* has been re-arranged to accommodate the fifth commandment. As noted above, Col. 3.18–4.3 is practically devoid of OT material.

[19] A later note (170 n. 38) claims that 'Every single reference to τέκνα in the Pauline corpus apart from the household codes denotes relationship' (see references supplied).

normal in the western world, it has to be remembered that it is still
prevalent in certain cultures.

εὐάρεστος is 'in our literature almost without exception of God,
to whom something is acceptable' (BAGD 318, §1; Foerster in
TWNT i. 456–57 notes only Tit. 2.9 for approval by men). This raises
questions about the construction of the following ἐν κυρίῳ. Moule
(130) notes three possibilities: (1) to take it as 'a sort of conditional
clause—"provided that the children's obedience is ἐν Κυρίῳ, on a
truly Christian level of motive"'; (2) to reckon it an unnecessary
addition; or (3) to take it as 'an odd expression for "to the Lord"',
as if it were a plain dative (cf. Eph. 5.10). Against (3) is the fact that in
LXX the word does not occur with such a construction, while the
cognate verb εὐαρεστεῖν, when used with ἐν, 'does not correspond to
a Hebrew verb of *pleasing* at all, but usually to a verb of *conduct* (to
"walk" before God)'. He therefore thinks the 'conditional' interpretation possibly the best. Dunn (250) takes εὐάρεστον as meaning
'pleasing to God', and observes that here 'a more conventional value
has been Christianized even before the next phrase is added'. The
phrase 'in the Lord' 'roots the justification thus claimed in the
tradition which formed the basis of Christian identity and conduct.
... In the face of the challenge from the Colossian Jews it was no
doubt important for the Christians to be able both to affirm their
heritage of Jewish parenesis and to affirm it as "well-pleasing (to
God) in the Lord (Jesus Christ)".' The verse reads well enough in a
literal English translation, but this is a case where accepting the
English version at face value could lead to neglect of nuances which
are present in the Greek.[20]

21. οἱ πατέρες μὴ ἐρεθίζετε τὰ τέκνα ὑμῶν, ἵνα μὴ ἀθυμῶσιν
Cf. Eph. 6.4, οἱ πατέρες μὴ παροργίζετε τὰ τέκνα ὑμῶν, ἀλλὰ
ἐκτρέφετε αὐτὰ ἐν παιδείᾳ καὶ νουθεσίᾳ κυρίου. Best (568) notes as
significant the change from 'parents' (in both letters) to 'fathers' here:
had the authors meant to include the mothers, they would have had
to make it explicit in view of contemporary thought. Eph. uses
παροργίζω where Col. has ἐρεθίζω, to express much the same idea,
and if one author was using the other it is difficult to see why he
should have made the change. The second part of the verse is totally
different in each case, Eph. instructing the fathers to see to the
Christian upbringing of their children whereas Col. warns against
anything that might discourage them. Best sees the difference in verb,
though expressing a similar thought, as 'a further indication that the

---

[20] The Westminster Confession (ch. 1, para. 8), specifically states that 'in all
controversies of religion, the Church is finally to appeal' to the Old Testament in
Hebrew and the New Testament in Greek. Vernacular translations are to be provided
for the benefit of people who do not know the original languages. This Confession was
'ratified and established by Acts of Parliament 1649 and 1690, as the publick and
avowed Confession of the Church of Scotland'.

writers were independent of one another and of their common membership of the same Pauline school'.

There is no indication of the age of the children here in view, but it would probably be unwise to think of them all as minors. Some might have been, but in an early Christian community several different age-groups might well have been represented, and each of these groups might have reacted in a different way to parental authority. Here we may recall the Parable of the Prodigal Son (Luke 15.11–32): the younger son is evidently not content with a life restricted to the narrow confines of the family circle, and wants to see the world. His father shows exceptional liberality in giving him his share of the inheritance—the young man is clearly of an age to be independent, but 'squandered his property in dissolute living'. On his return, his elder brother is not unnaturally angry (ὠργίσθη) at the reception extended to him, in contrast to his own experience. These are clearly grown men, but the father addresses the elder as τέκνον (v. 31).

ἐρεθίζω (BAGD 308) means to arouse or provoke, usually in a bad sense, but in its only other occurrence in the NT (2 Cor. 9.2) it is used in a good sense of an encouraging example. It was noted in the Introduction (p. 28) that it would be a mistake to assume a special link with 2 Corinthians on the strength of just four words, and this is all the more so when one of them is employed in a different sense. παροργίζω in Eph. means to make angry (cf. Rom. 10.19, quoting Deut. 32.21; it appears as a variant here in some mss, ℵ A C D* et al., but that may be due to influence from Eph.), and is perhaps a slightly stronger term. In the rest of the admonition Eph. and Col. diverge completely, Eph. giving positive advice where that in Col. is negative. ἀθυμέω (BAGD 21) is another of the hapax legomena in Col., and means to be discouraged or lose heart. There is no indication of what might cause such discouragement, but Dunn plausibly suggests that some of the younger members of Christian families might have been in a vulnerable position, simply because they were different. 'Peer pressure' is by no means a phenomenon of modern times, as the reaction of Greek and Roman authors to Jewish exclusivism shows. The father had to be tactful and understanding, and not provoke his children by laying down the law in an arbitrary fashion.

22. οἱ δοῦλοι, ὑπακούετε κατὰ πάντα τοῖς κατὰ σάρκα κυρίοις, μὴ ἐν ὀφθαλμοδουλίᾳ ὡς ἀνθρωπάρεσκοι, ἀλλ' ἐν ἁπλότητι καρδίας φοβούμενοι τὸν κύριον Cf. Eph. 6.5–6, οἱ δοῦλοι, ὑπακούετε τοῖς κατὰ σάρκα κυρίοις μετὰ φόβου καὶ τρόμου ἐν ἁπλότητι τῆς καρδίας ὑμῶν ὡς τῷ Χριστῷ, μὴ κατ' ὀφθαλμο-δουλίαν ὡς ἀνθρωπάρεσκοι, ἀλλ' ὡς δοῦλοι Χριστοῦ ποιοῦντες τὸ θέλημα τοῦ θεοῦ ἐκ ψυχῆς. The admonition to slaves is the longest in the Colossian *Haustafel*, extending to v. 25, and once again Col. and Eph. show both similarities and differences: the words κατὰ πάντα are omitted by P46 and other witnesses, which would bring the whole of the first part into line with Eph., but this may be due to assimilation to Eph. Both share the words ὀφθαλμοδουλία and ἀνθρωπάρεσκοι, two words which occur in the NT only in these two verses, and the phrase ἐν ἁπλότητι καρδίας, but Eph. inserts τῆς.[21] The phrase ἐκ ψυχῆς appears in the following verse in Col., and there is something of a parallel to the last part of Eph. 6.6 in the τῷ κυρίῳ Χριστῷ δουλεύετε of v. 24. But Eph. has κατ᾽ ὀφθαλμοδουλίαν instead of ἐν ὀφθαλμοδουλίᾳ,[22] and in several other respects they differ.

Reference to slavery inevitably conjures up the slave trade to America, but it has to be remembered that not every slave owner in the southern states was a Simon Legree (see further the Introduction to Philemon below). Slaves were valuable property, and would be more likely to perform their work well if they were properly treated. At the one extreme we may recall the oft-quoted notices regarding the treatment of captured runaway slaves, or the aftermath of the Spartacus revolt, when the Appian Way was lined with crosses. What could happen is rather grimly illustrated in the punishment meted out to the slave-girl Euclia, and the slaves who informed on her, in the apocryphal *Acts of Andrew* (22; Schneemelcher, *NT Apocrypha*, ii. 141; Elliott, *The Apocryphal NT*, 251), but we cannot assume that this was a common occurrence.[23] At the other extreme, a slave in the service of a good master might actually be better off than some of the poorer members of the free population: food and shelter were provided, and there were therefore no financial worries. He did not have his freedom, but he could work towards it if he chose. Moreover, the regulations varied in different areas and in different periods: Exod. 21.2–6 for example lays down that a Hebrew slave (evidently enslaved because of debt) should serve six years and become free in the seventh; but if his master provides him with a wife and he has a family, he would have to leave them when he became free—unless he was prepared to commit himself to lifelong servitude for their sakes. Once again, it is dangerous to generalize; we simply cannot assume that conditions were the same everywhere in the ancient world.

W. D. Davies writes, 'It is illegitimate to argue ...—as did the older exegetes—that the words in Col 3.22: "Servants, obey in all things your masters ..." are of necessity inserted because of a possible misunderstanding of Paul's intervention in the case of Onesimus; this

---

[21] The noun ἁπλότης itself occurs at Rom. 12.8 and four times in 2 Cor. (8.2; 9.11, 13; 11.3), but the phrase ἐν ἁπλότητι (τῆς) καρδίας appears only in Eph. and Col.

[22] ℵ C and other witnesses read the plural, the reading adopted in Nestle[25] and hence also in BAGD. If the text a scribe was copying read ΕΝ᾽ΟΦΘΑΛΜΟΔΟΥΛΙΑΙ, he might have assumed that a final sigma had been omitted. On the other hand, if our author wrote the plural (referring to repeated cases), the final sigma might have been accidentally dropped. The choice is difficult, but the weight of ms evidence (P[46] A B D F G *et al.*) may be enough to tilt the balance.

[23] Cf. also Barth's discussion (*Philemon*, 18–22) of changes in the legal position during the early Christian centuries, generally to the advantage of slaves. He devotes over 100 pages to the consideration of slavery in the social background of Paul's time. See further 151–70 (and index) on the section of the *Haustafel* relating to masters and slaves.

may or may not have been the case, but is not a foregone conclusion'
(*PRJ* 136). He sees here traditional material 'baptised into Christ'.
On the traditional view, with both Col. and Philem. written about the
same time from Rome, and to the same destination, it was very
natural to think that Paul here had the case of Onesimus in mind
when he wrote; but if Col. is by a later disciple and Philem. was
written from Ephesus some years earlier, the situation is completely
different. Moreover we have to take into account the fact that our
author appears to be incorporating a block of existing material: it
may not therefore be specifically directed to a situation in Colossae.

The words κατὰ σάρκα are inserted to distinguish these earthly
masters from the κύριος mentioned later in the verse; the difference is
clearly marked in this and the following verses: the slaves are to obey
'fearing the Lord', to work 'as for the Lord and not for men',
knowing that it is 'from the Lord' that they will receive their reward.
In 4.1 the masters themselves are firmly reminded that they have 'a
Lord in heaven'.

As already noted, both ὀφθαλμοδουλία and ἀνθρωπάρεσκος
appear only here and in Eph. 6.6. The former (BAGD 599) means
'service that is performed only to attract attention, not for its own
sake nor to please God or one's own conscience'; one may think of a
slave who is diligent and industrious so long as someone is watching,
but slacks off as soon as his master's back is turned.[24] The latter
(BAGD 67) is defined as 'one who tries to please men at the sacrifice
of principle'.[25] From a master's point of view, neither of these
attitudes is very laudable in a servant, of whatever grade and in any
age. In contrast, the Christian attitude is succinctly summed up in the
words ἐν ἁπλότητι καρδίας φοβούμενοι τὸν κύριον: ἁπλότης
(BAGD 85) means simplicity or sincerity, and the addition of
καρδίας (BAGD 403f.) suggests a frank and open disposition in
contrast to the duplicitous conduct of the 'men-pleasers'. Moule
(130) writes, 'lit. "in singleness of heart", i.e. "in honesty", "with no
ulterior motives"', comparing 1 Chron. 29.17 (LXX and Hebrew).
Dunn (254) sees here the influence of Jewish wisdom, aptly citing
Test. Reub. 4.1 ἐν ἁπλότητι καρδίας ἐν φόβῳ κυρίου. Eph. uses a
somewhat different formulation to much the same effect.

**23. ὃ ἐὰν ποιῆτε, ἐκ ψυχῆς ἐργάζεσθε ὡς τῷ κυρίῳ καὶ οὐκ
ἀνθρώποις** Cf. Eph. 6.6–7, ὡς δοῦλοι Χριστοῦ ποιοῦντες τὸ θέλημα
τοῦ θεοῦ ἐκ ψυχῆς, μετ' εὐνοίας δουλεύοντες ὡς τῷ κυρίῳ καὶ οὐκ
ἀνθρώποις. Here there are textual variations in both letters (in Eph.
ὡς τῷ κυρίῳ καὶ οὐκ ἀνθρώποις is omitted by D² K L and other
witnesses, while in Col. δουλεύοντες is inserted from Eph. by a few
witnesses and καὶ οὐκ ἀνθρώποις is omitted by P⁴⁶ B and 1739),

---

[24] Moule (130) notes that the word is not found before the Pauline writings, and
(assuming Pauline authorship) 'may be of the apostle's own coining'; so too Lightfoot
(294) before him.
[25] Dunn (254) aptly refers to Gal. 1.10, which deserves to be quoted: εἰ ἔτι
ἀνθρώποις ἤρεσκον, Χριστοῦ δοῦλος οὐκ ἂν ἤμην.

which raises questions about possible contamination one way or the other in the manuscript tradition. What is more important is that both urge the same wholehearted devotion to the service rendered, 'as for the Lord' and not just for human masters. ψυχή (BAGD 893) is commonly translated 'soul', but in fact has a range of meanings; the phrase used here means 'from the heart, gladly' (§1bγ).[26] The point is well caught in George Herbert's hymn:

> A servant with this clause
> Makes drudgerie divine:
> Who sweeps a room, as for thy laws,
> Makes that and th' action fine.

This is not a justification of slavery, or in a later age a glorification of domestic service, which could at times indeed be drudgery, to say the least. The principle applies to all work, and all kinds of service: if it is done ἐκ ψυχῆς, from the heart and willingly, it can be transformed.

24. εἰδότες ὅτι ἀπὸ κυρίου ἀπολήμψεσθε τὴν ἀνταπόδοσιν τῆς κληρονομίας. τῷ κυρίῳ Χριστῷ δουλεύετε Cf. Eph. 6.8, εἰδότες ὅτι ἕκαστος ἐάν τι ποιήσῃ ἀγαθόν, τοῦτο κομίσεται παρὰ κυρίου εἴτε δοῦλος εἴτε ἐλεύθερος. Some witnesses here, including P[46], read the simple verb λήμψεσθε, but ℵ* B D and others have the compound. Also it would seem that some scribes have attempted to improve the text by writing, after κληρονομίας, the words τοῦ κυρίου ἡμῶν Ἰησοῦ Χριστοῦ, ᾧ δουλεύετε (F G et al.; the text above is found in P[46] ℵ A B C D* and other witnesses).

'The answer to the suggestion that the N.T. sometimes speaks in apparently mercenary terms of reward and punishment is that the "reward" is always something to do with our relations with God, and the "punishment" is deprivation of his fellowship. The κληρονομία, the dwelling in the "promised land" or the possession of the Kingdom of God, is precisely that life in the presence of God which mercenary-mindedness would make impossible' (Moule, 131). We have already touched on this point at 1.5 (see pp. 87–89), where the hope laid up in heaven is the motive for the Colossians' love for all the saints. There is nothing of a mercenary quid pro quo here: it all begins with the love of God revealed in Jesus Christ his Son, and Christian faith is a response to that love, which as Patrick Walker wrote (see p. 88f. above) is the most powerful incentive of all to right living.

ἀνταπόδοσις (BAGD 73; TWNT ii. 171) means quite simply requital or recompense, and occurs in the New Testament only here. It is defined by the following genitive, τῆς κληρονομίας, the inheritance (BAGD 435; TWNT iii. 766–86, esp. 781ff.). In secular writings this word is 'almost always' used of a literal inheritance (§1; cf. Matt. 21.38; Mark 12.7; Luke 20.14; also Luke 12.13), but 'in

---

[26] For Dunn (256) this rendering 'does not seem sufficiently forceful'. In his own translation (242) he has 'put yourself wholly into it', but also commends the NEB 'put your whole heart into it'. What is in view is quite certainly a wholehearted and willing service.

specifically Christian usage (corresponding to the LXX)' it refers to salvation ('as the inheritance of God's children', §3): cf. Gal. 3.18; Heb. 9.15; 1 Pet. 1.4; Eph. 1.14, 18; 5.5.²⁷ As already indicated, the original reference was to the inheritance promised to Abraham, but as Dunn (257) observes 'the imagery lent itself to eschatological reference'. Since the verb ἀπολήμψεσθε is in the future, our author has not entirely abandoned Paul's distinction between the 'already' and the 'not yet': the inheritance still awaits them.²⁸

The final words of this verse, τῷ κυρίῳ Χριστῷ δουλεύετε, evidently presented a problem to some scribes, as the variant in F G shows: is the verb an indicative or an imperative? The variant was presumably intended to clear up the difficulty. Moule (137) thinks it an imperative (pace Lightfoot), on the grounds that (1) the following γάρ would lose point if the verb were an indicative, and (2) the ἐργάζεσθε in v. 23 is beyond doubt an imperative. But in the preceding note, on τῷ κυρίῳ Χριστῷ, he says, 'Only here and in Rom. xvi. 18 does St Paul speak of "the Lord Christ" (or "our Lord Christ" in Romans); and in both places (it is contended) he is contrasting Christ as Lord with other lords. (In this context it is the slave's master who provides the implied contrast: "It is Christ who must be your Master".)' That contrast may be enough to justify taking the verb as indicative: the words τῷ κυρίῳ Χριστῷ are brought forward into an emphatic position at the beginning. The imperative ἐργάζεσθε is some distance away, and there is an indicative verb between.

25. ὁ γὰρ ἀδικῶν κομίσεται ὃ ἠδίκησεν, καὶ οὐκ ἔστιν προσωπολημψία Cf. Eph. 6.8, εἰδότες ὅτι ἕκαστος ἐάν τι ποιήσῃ ἀγαθόν, τοῦτο κομίσεται παρὰ κυρίου εἴτε δοῦλος εἴτε ἐλεύθερος; Eph. 6.9, προσωπολημψία οὐκ ἔστιν παρ' αὐτῷ (cf. Rom. 2.11, οὐ γάρ ἐστιν προσωπολημψία παρὰ τῷ θεῷ). Once again the same words are employed in both letters, κομίσεται and προσωπολημψία, but they are used in different ways, Eph. speaking of recompense for a good deed while Col. singles out retribution for a wrong done. As for προσωπολημψία, Eph. uses it in a different context, addressed to the masters, not to the slaves. A few witnesses in Col. add παρὰ τῷ θεῷ at the end, but this is probably a contamination from Eph.

The verb **κομίζω** (BAGD 442) is used in the active in Luke 7.37 of a woman bringing an alabaster jar of ointment, but is most commonly employed in the NT in the middle, meaning to obtain or receive (§2: Heb. 10.36; 11.13, 39; 1 Pet. 1.9; 5.4) or to recover (§3: Matt. 25.27; Heb. 11.19). Its only other occurrence in the Pauline corpus, apart from Eph. and Col., is at 2 Cor. 5.10, again in a context of recompense for deeds done (ἵνα κομίσηται ἕκαστος τὰ διὰ τοῦ σώματος πρὸς ἃ ἔπραξεν, εἴτε ἀγαθὸν εἴτε φαῦλον; cf. also the variant at 2 Pet. 2.13, κομιούμενοι μισθὸν ἀδικίας). Dunn (258) notes that this 'measure for measure' retribution was 'a strong

---

²⁷ Foerster in *TWNT* (ii. 781 n. 27) remarks that in some passages the use of κληρονομία is close to that of κλῆρος, which we have met at 1.12 (see p. 112).

²⁸ T.D. Still's 'Eschatology in Colossians' appeared just after this was written.

instinct in Jewish tradition' from the *ius talionis* of Exod. 21.23–25 on (see his references), and adds, 'The force of this warning or reassurance was twofold: it encouraged harshly treated slaves that their masters could not escape due judgment, in the final judgment if not in this life, and it warned the slaves themselves to maintain their own high standards of integrity so far as possible.'

On προσωπολημψία (BAGD 720) Moule (132) notes that 'it seems not to appear before the N.T., and to have been coined in Christian circles, though from O.T. metal'.[29] The Hebrew idiom for 'to show partiality' is literally 'to accept the face', occasionally represented in LXX by πρόσωπον λαμβάνειν (he cites e.g. Lev. 19.15; Job 42.8; Mal. 2.9; Ecclus. 4.22, 27), and it was evidently from this that Christian writers formed the compound word and others like it. Gal. 2.6 actually has πρόσωπον ... οὐ λαμβάνει, 'just like the LXX'. The meaning is neatly illustrated by the 'acts of favouritism' condemned in Jas. 2.1–4, where the rich man is cordially welcomed but the poor man treated with contempt. The translation 'respect of persons' in AV requires some qualification: the whole of the *Haustafel* calls for a proper respect for other people, as persons. What is condemned is partiality, a favour shown to some at the expense of others, often on quite trivial and superficial grounds. Rom. 2.11 (οὐ γάρ ἐστιν προσωπολημψία παρὰ τῷ θεῷ) uses the word in expressing the thought of Gal. 2.6 (cf. also 1 Pet. 1.17, εἰ πατέρα ἐπικαλεῖσθε τὸν ἀπροσωπολήμπτως κρίνοντα κατὰ τὸ ἑκάστου ἔργον). God shows no partiality, nor should Christians. As Dunn (259) puts it, there is 'a God-given justice among peoples and individuals ... and those who ignore or flout it cannot expect to escape the consequences, whether slaves or masters'.

4.1 οἱ κύριοι, τὸ δίκαιον καὶ τὴν ἰσότητα τοῖς δούλοις παρέχετε, εἰδότες ὅτι καὶ ὑμεῖς ἔχετε κύριον ἐν οὐρανῷ Cf. Eph. 6.9, Καὶ οἱ κύριοι, τὰ αὐτὰ ποιεῖτε πρὸς αὐτούς, ἀνιέντες τὴν ἀπειλήν, εἰδότες ὅτι καὶ αὐτῶν καὶ ὑμῶν ὁ κύριός ἐστιν ἐν οὐρανοῖς καὶ προσωπολημψία οὐκ ἔστιν παρ' αὐτῷ. Here again the general thought is the same, but Eph. has formulated it differently, used the plural ἐν οὐρανοῖς instead of the singular,[30] and transferred the reference to προσωπολημψία to the end.

The admonition to the masters is surprisingly brief, consisting of a single verse only, but as Dunn points out the head of the household is here addressed for the third time (first as husband, then as father, now as master). In the conditions of the time, it could hardly have been otherwise: masters were concerned to get the best out of their slaves, and in any consideration for their welfare the primary thought was likely to be maintaining their fitness for work rather than the

[29] Cf. Aletti 255 n. 109: 'La motivation de l'impartialité divine est un topos qui vient de l'AT, parcourt la littérature intertestamentaire et même le NT' (see the references supplied).
[30] In Col. the plural is read by ℵ² D F G and the Majority text, the singular by ℵ*A B C *et al.*

well-being of the slaves themselves. A slave who did not meet the required standard would soon be got rid of. Here again we have to remember the circumstances in which these early Christians lived: it simply was not possible for them to advocate far-reaching measures of social reform.[31]

παρέχω, here used in the middle voice (BAGD 626, §2b), has a range of meanings, but at this point means to grant something to someone. Masters are to grant their slaves τὸ δίκαιον, what is just, fair and right (BAGD 196, §5)[32] and τὴν ἰσότητα (BAGD 381; TWNT iii. 355–56). The only other occurrence of the latter word in the NT is at 2 Cor. 8.13–14, where it means 'equality', but masters could scarcely be called upon to grant their slaves equality![33] The meaning required here is 'equity' or 'fairness'. This means, incidentally, that another of the four words which Col. shares only with 2 Cor. is used with a different meaning, which only reduces further the likelihood of any special link (cf. on ἐρεθίζω, p. 281 above).

The reason given for the admonition is quite simple: the masters may have absolute power and authority here on earth, but they know that they are themselves responsible to their Lord in heaven. We may recall, from another context, the centurion of Matt. 8.9 (par. Luke 7.8), who described himself as a man ὑπὸ ἐξουσίαν, ἔχων ὑπ'ἐμαυτὸν στρατιώτας. He had the authority, and could give orders, but he knew that he was responsible to a higher authority.

The first verse of this section, taken in isolation, is quite unacceptable by modern western standards. In its context, however, it was perfectly normal for the period in which it was written. It is only when we detect the principles which underlie the whole that we can see the relevance of this 'table of household virtues' for our own day, and indeed for any age: respect for other people, as persons, tolerance and understanding, avoidance of anything that could lead to bitter feeling, fair and equitable treatment of subordinates, recognition of one's responsibilities as well as one's rights, with due regard for the rights and interests of others—these are the only true

[31] B. D. Ehrman (*NTS* 34 (1988), 25) notes a citation of this verse in the biblical commentary of Didymus the Blind: 'Didymus quotes Paul as saying that masters must treat their slaves fairly (Col 4. 1), which he understands to mean that a master should regard only a slave's work, not his or her temperament. Didymus then finds further confirmation of his views in the story of Jesus and the adulteress (EcclT 223.6b–13a).' As Ehrman observes, if Didymus drew this story from mss of John, this would make it the earliest patristic witness to the *pericope adulterae* by several centuries.

[32] Schrenk in *TWNT* ii. 189 compares Matt. 20.4, where the owner of the vineyard promises the labourers ὃ ἐὰν ᾖ δίκαιον. On ἰσότης Stählin (*TWNT* iii. 356) quotes Abbott: 'what cannot be brought under positive rules, but is in accordance with the judgment of a fair mind'.

[33] 'While we can find humanitarian treatment urged for slaves, as in Seneca's well-known discourse on treating slaves as human beings (*Epistle* 47), and while Philo can speak of masters "showing the gentleness and kindness by which inequality is equalized (δι' ὧν ἐξιστοῦται τὸ ἄνισον," *De decalogo* 167), the idea of equality of treatment for slave and free *in law* was an impossible thought for the time' (Dunn, 260).

basis on which to build a successful marriage, a happy family, a strong community.

As already noted, it is dangerous to generalize from particular cases, or from the legal position. The actual situation could vary from one region to another, or from one period to another, from one household to another. Some husbands may have been tyrants, some fathers oppressive to their children, some masters cruel to their slaves—but this does not mean that all were. Nor were all children rebellious, all slaves untrustworthy.

As Best observes (e.g. *Ephesians*, 524), it would seem that in both Eph. and Col. the authors have wholly Christian households in mind. The problems might be very different in a mixed household, especially where the master was not Christian, a situation reflected in some of the apocryphal Acts; e.g. in *Act. And.* Maximilla is a Christian but her husband Aegeates is not. So too in *Act. Thom.* Mygdonia, wife of Charisius the kinsman of king Misdaeus, becomes a Christian, which leads eventually to the conversion of the king's wife Tertia and her son and daughter-in-law; but Charisius and Misdaeus are not converted until after the martyrdom of Thomas. These texts are of course pious fiction, but they do shed light on the attitude and outlook of people in that period.[34] Incidentally they also indicate that some women at least could enjoy a measure of independence: at one point in *Act. And.* Aegeates the governor is reduced to pleading with his wife, who happens to be of more noble birth than he is. Thecla in the *Acts of Paul* is both independent and a very determined young lady.

Best notes the problem for a Christian wife whose non-Christian husband commanded her to worship his pagan gods. There would also be problems for Christian slaves in non-Christian households. The slave-girl Euclia in *Act. And.* is presumably not a Christian, but it is rather startling that the author should so complacently have Maximilla arrange for Euclia to take her place in Aegeates' bed. Presumably he simply gave no thought to the ethics of the matter. All this only serves to show that the situation was much more complex than is sometimes imagined.

As to the relationship between the *Haustafeln* in Eph. and Col., there are a few points that call for attention. In writing about any subject, authors may have only a limited vocabulary on which to draw. It is therefore almost inevitable that two authors writing on the same subject may on occasion use the same words. The fact that they do so does not necessarily indicate any relationship. In assessing their work, we have to consider various possibilities. In the case of the *Haustafel* there is the further complication that some commentators consider Col. an authentic letter of Paul. We therefore have to ask: are we dealing with one author, Paul, who is using his words with a certain freedom, even to employing them in different contexts with a

---

[34] For English translations of these texts see Schneemelcher, *NT Apocrypha*; Elliott, *The Apocryphal NT*.

different meaning? Or have we to do with two authors other than
Paul, one of whom has known and drawn from the work of the
other? Or is it a question of two authors with a common background,
but working independently? It is at times by no means easy to reach a
decision. Indeed, there may be cases in which the evidence at some
points suggests one decision, whereas at others it might suggest a
different conclusion. The search for a 'simple', clear-cut answer may
sometimes be misguided. In the case of the *Haustafeln* in Col. and
Eph. we have the same injunctions in both cases, in the same order
(cf. Eph. 5.22, 25; 6.1, 4, 5 and Col. 3.18, 19, 20, 21, 22), and often the
use of the same words; but there are differences, as noted in the
discussion of the text above. Were they both written by the same
author, or has one author drawn upon the work of the other, or
again are two authors both drawing upon the same model but each
adapting it in his own way? All things considered, it would seem best
to think of two independent authors in a Pauline school, both
following a traditional form but each adapting it in his own way.

XII
FINAL ADMONITIONS
(4.2–6)

[2]Continue steadfast in prayer, being watchful in it with thanksgiving, [3]praying at the same time also on our behalf, that God
may open to us a door of the word, to speak the mystery of Christ.
Because of it indeed I am in bonds, [4]that I may show it forth as I
ought to speak. [5]Walk in wisdom with regard to those outside,
redeeming the time. [6]Let your word always be gracious, seasoned
with salt, that you may know how you must answer each one.

As already noted (p. 273 above), Barclay observes that the *Haustafel*
could quite easily be lifted out of its context, and we could move
from 3.17 to 4.2 without noticing that anything had been omitted.
This does not, however, mean that the passage is an interpolation. As
in most commentaries, the text has been broken up here into smaller
units for ease of handling, whereas in the original Greek the whole of
the paraenetic section is all of a piece. From another point of view it
could be argued that these verses are a natural application of the
principle laid down at 3.17: 'whatever you do in word or in deed, do
all in the name of the Lord Jesus'. In the *Haustafel*, that principle is
applied to the practical concerns of daily living within a household.
As the parallels in secular literature show, our author has taken up
an element of conventional wisdom, but in the process he has given it
a new orientation by his repeated reference to 'the Lord'. It would
probably be wrong to speak of a merely superficial Christianization,
but as Barclay remarks (71), 'apologetic attempts to find some special
Christian character in this code are largely unconvincing'. The fact

remains, however, that as it now stands it is a Christian code, and probably one taken over from a tradition of quite long standing.

2. τῇ προσευχῇ προσκαρτερεῖτε, γρηγοροῦντες ἐν αὐτῇ ἐν εὐχαριστίᾳ The paraenetic section is now rounded off by a few admonitions of a more general kind, once more addressed to the whole community. **προσκαρτερέω** (BAGD 715; *TWNT* iii. 620–22) carries the basic idea of persistence: with reference to people, it means to attach oneself to someone or remain faithful (Acts 8.13; 10.7; at Mark 3.9 Jesus tells the disciples to have a boat *wait in readiness* for him, because of the crowd); with reference to things, it means to busy oneself with something, to be devoted to it, or to continue or persevere in something. In four of the other NT occurrences it refers to prayer (Acts 1.14; 6.4; Rom. 12.12; Col. 4.2; cf. Acts 2.42, referring to the teaching of the apostles; in Acts 2.46 the believers continue daily in the Temple). Only Rom. 13.6 is somewhat different: 'For the same reason you also pay taxes, for the authorities are God's servants, busy with this very thing' (NRSV).

Here the members of the community are urged to devote themselves to prayer, γρηγοροῦντες ἐν αὐτῇ, lit. 'being watchful in it'. The verb **γρηγορέω** (BAGD 167) can be used both literally (of being awake: Matt. 24.43; 26.38, 40; Mark 13.34; 14.34, 37; Luke 12.37, 39 v.l.) and figuratively (of being alert or watchful: Matt. 24.42; 25.13; 26.41; Mark 13.35, 37; 14.38; Acts 20.31; 1 Cor. 16.13; 1 Thess. 5.6, 10; 1 Pet. 5.8; Rev. 3.2f.; 16.15).[1] At Matt. 26.41 and Mark 14.38 it appears in the phrase γρηγορεῖτε καὶ προσεύχεσθε, and in that context must be understood literally; but the transition to a figurative use was by no means difficult. The references above, together with our present verse, indicate the importance of prayer for the early Christians.[2] In the garden of Gethsemane, as his earthly ministry drew towards its close, Jesus had bidden his disciples to watch and pray, and the same attitude of vigilant and prayerful watchfulness is incumbent on his followers in every age. The last two words, ἐν εὐχαριστίᾳ, are omitted by D*, but that is probably due to a momentary lapse by the scribe: references to thanksgiving are frequent in this letter (εὐχαριστέω, 1.3, 12; 3.17; εὐχαριστία, 2.7; 4.2; εὐχάριστος, 3.15).[3]

3–4. προσευχόμενοι ἅμα περὶ ἡμῶν, ἵνα ὁ θεὸς ἀνοίξῃ ἡμῖν θύραν τοῦ λόγου λαλῆσαι τὸ μυστήριον τοῦ Χριστοῦ, δι᾽ ὃ καὶ δέδεμαι, ἵνα φανερώσω αὐτὸ ὡς δεῖ με λαλῆσαι Here 'Paul'

---

[1] Cf. E. Lövestam, *Spiritual Wakefulness in the New Testament* (1963).

[2] This is another verse at which W. D. Davies (*PRJ* 139) sees evidence of Paul's knowledge of the words and spirit of Jesus: cf. also Luke 22.40, 46.

[3] Cf. O'Brien, in 'Thanksgiving within the Structure of Pauline Theology', 58f.: 'The Colossian Christians (Col 4:2) who are exhorted to persevere in this latter activity (a point stressed by προσκαρτερεῖτε, "devote yourselves," on the one hand, and γρηγοροῦντες, "being watchful", on the other), are to match it with the giving of thanks (ἐν εὐχαριστίᾳ), i.e. their petitions will be accompanied by prayers of thanksgiving' (59).

particularly asks for the readers' prayers for himself and his mission. As noted above (p. 81) Lightfoot affirms that 'there is no reason to think that St Paul ever uses an "epistolary" plural, referring to himself solely', but as indicated there that may be open to question. In the present verse, however, we should note that περὶ ἡμῶν at the beginning is followed by ὡς δεῖ με λαλῆσαι at the end, which would suggest that in this case the plural is a real plural (Lightfoot thinks that Paul is referring especially to Timothy (1.1) and Epaphras (4.12, 13), but it might also include others among his co-workers).

The reference to a door recalls 1 Cor. 16.9, 'for a wide door for effective work has opened to me, and there are many adversaries'. At Acts 14.27, after the first missionary journey, Paul and Barnabas 'called the church [at Antioch] together and related all that God had done with them, and how he had opened a door of faith for the Gentiles'. θύρα (BAGD 365; *TWNT* iii. 173–80) is thus yet another word which can be used both literally and figuratively. Here it is 'a door of the word', i.e. a door for the word, immediately explained in the following words, 'to speak the mystery of Christ'.[4] B* and a few other witnesses read τὸ μυστήριον τοῦ θεοῦ, but that may be due to recollection of this phrase at 2.2 (where there is a whole cluster of variants (see p. 185f. above); cf. also 1 Cor. 2.1). At Col. 1.27 and 2.2 it is Christ himself who is the mystery.

The phrase δι' ὃ καὶ δέδεμαι is the first indication in this letter that 'Paul' is a prisoner (cf. vv. 10 and 18, and contrast Phil. 1.7, where Paul mentions his 'bonds' at the very outset). He has spoken earlier of his sufferings for the gospel (1.24; cf. also 2.1), but there is no mention there of imprisonment. A few mss read the masculine δι' ὅν, which would make Christ the antecedent, but as Lightfoot wrote long ago (297) this destroys the point of the sentence: it is because of the mystery, hidden from past ages and generations but now revealed (1.26), the mystery that is 'Christ in you, the hope of glory' (1.27; cf. 2.2), that he is a prisoner.[5] On the traditional view of Col., taking it as a 'captivity' epistle, one naturally thinks of the Jewish hostility to Paul's gospel for the Gentiles, which led to his arrest in the Temple and subsequent imprisonment. If the letter was written by some later disciple, that is the impression the author wished to convey.

At this point the accepted verse division splits a single sentence into two parts: the ἵνα φανερώσω κτλ in v. 4 belongs with what precedes. We have already met this verb at 1.26, of the public revelation of the 'mystery', and at 3.4, of the manifestation of Christ (and his followers) in glory. Moule (132) remarks, 'It is a particularly pointed paradox to speak of τὸ μυστήριον in connexion with φανεροῦν (v. 4), when that verb means (as it does here) a public

[4] Davies (*PRJ* 139) compares Luke 8.10; Mark 4.11; Matt. 13.11, where Jesus speaks of the mystery, or mysteries, of the kingdom of God.
[5] At 2.3 the relative, in the dative, could be either masculine or neuter, but is most naturally taken as referring to Christ, the nearest antecedent. Recollection of this phrase may have led scribes to write the masculine here.

manifestation. But in itself the verb is suitable enough (as Masson says) for the communication of a revelation privately.' Paradoxical it may be, but the whole point of this verse is a public proclamation of the mystery, proclaiming it indeed from the housetops.[6]

M. Bockmuehl (*JTS* 39 (1988), 489ff.; cf. also *Revelation and Mystery*, 191ff.) draws attention to a variant already noted by Wettstein, and suggests a slightly different layout from that printed in NA[27] and reproduced above:

λαλῆσαι τὸ μυστήριον τοῦ Χριστοῦ·
διὸ καὶ δέδεμαι,
ἵνα φανερώσω αὐτό,
ὡς δεῖ με λαλῆσαι

The difference lies first in placing a stop after τοῦ Χριστοῦ, and secondly in reading the conjunction διό rather than the relative δι' ὅ (the reading δι' ὅν in B F G would make the relative refer back to Christ rather than to the mystery; but it is the mystery that Paul is concerned to proclaim).[7] As it stands, the text is somewhat tortuous and overloaded (cf. Aletti, 259f. for three possible interpretations of the passage), but this reading makes what follows into an independent proposition.[8] Moreover, it establishes a connection between the apostle's physical bonds and his obligation to speak the word of Christ: the text asserts 'not simply that Paul is bound for the sake of the mystery of Christ; but that in fact his preaching and his very bonds together constitute his manifestation of the mystery' (Bockmuehl, 493). Bockmuehl therefore translates it: 'For it is to this end that I have been imprisoned, in order that I might manifest it, as indeed I am obliged to do' (492). If Col. is from Paul's own hand, the evidence of Pauline usage would be decisive; if, however, the letter is by a later disciple, the question must remain open. On the other, more usual, arrangement of the text vv. 3 and 4 form a single sentence: the Colossians are to pray that God may open a door for the word, so that 'Paul' may speak the mystery of Christ, because of which he is in bonds. The ἵνα φανερώσω αὐτὸ ὡς δεῖ με λαλῆσαι of v. 4 looks back to the λαλῆσαι of v. 3: 'that I may make it manifest as I ought to speak'.

Bockmuehl sees 'an apparent chiastic substructure of the verbs

[6] Aletti (260) observes that nowhere else does Paul say that he 'manifests' the mystery. The verbs used are λαλεῖν, εὐαγγελίζεσθαι, καταγγέλλειν or κηρύσσειν (see the references in his note). Cf. also 139f. on Col. 1.26. This may be another point to add to the dossier against authenticity.

[7] δι' ὅν occurs at 1 Cor. 8.11; Phil. 3.8; δι' οὗ at Rom. 1.5; 5.2, 11; 1 Cor. 1.9; 8.6; 15.2; Gal. 6.14. δι' ὅ on the other hand would be a Pauline (and New Testament) hapax legomenon. διὸ καί in contrast is a favourite Pauline turn of phrase (Rom 4.22; 15.22; 2 Cor. 1.20; 4.13 (*bis*); 5.9; Phil. 2.9). But conclusions here are bound to differ according to the presuppositions with which we begin; Bockmuehl is not convinced that Col. is not authentic.

[8] 'Given the rather inelegant and overloaded syntax of Col 4:2–3b, it seems reasonable to insert after Χριστοῦ [not a comma, but] a colon, thus enabling 4:3c–4 to stand on its own.'

λαλέω, δέω, δέω, λαλέω in these verses' (*Revelation and Mystery*, 192). 'The mystery of Christ is his work of redemption announced in the gospel. Paul's desire and intention to "manifest" and to "speak" this mystery is fully consistent with his understanding of the apostolic ministry elsewhere (e.g. 1:28; cf. Eph 3:5f.; Rom 16:25f.).' φανερόω, however, does not mean that Paul himself does the revealing—his ministry is an instrument of God's revelation (192). The verb is not synonymous with ἀποκαλύπτω, but means rather 'to demonstrate' or 'manifest'. So here 'Paul desires to make the gospel manifest, as indeed he is bound to. ... Full knowledge of "the mystery of God" ... is equivalent to full knowledge of Christ who resides in heaven and with whom the believer's future life of glory is already stored up. In his labour in the gospel Paul prays that he may demonstrate the "mystery of Christ" by the very fact that he is a prisoner on its behalf' (193).[9]

Of the verbs Bockmuehl mentions, λαλεῖν (BAGD 463) presents no problem, since in both cases we have the aorist infinitive λαλῆσαι. It means to speak, with in this case possibly the stronger meaning of 'assert, proclaim' (§2b; cf. 1 Cor. 2.6f.; 14.2). With the other verb, however, things are somewhat different: δέδεμαι is the perfect passive of δέω (BAGD 177; *TWNT* ii. 59–60), which means to bind, whether literally or figuratively, whereas the δεῖ denoting compulsion or necessity is a word of such common occurrence in the NT as to command a separate entry in the concordance and in BAGD (172; cf. *TWNT* ii. 21–25; E. Fascher, 'Theologische Beobachtungen zu δεῖ', FS Bultmann 1954 (BZNW 21), 228–54). It may perhaps be open to question whether the chiastic substructure is any more than 'apparent'.

5. ἐν σοφίᾳ περιπατεῖτε πρὸς τοὺς ἔξω τὸν καιρὸν ἐξαγορ-αζόμενοι Cf. 1 Thess. 4.12, ἵνα περιπατῆτε εὐσχημόνως πρὸς τοὺς ἔξω; Eph. 5.16 (i.e. in a different context), ἐξαγοραζόμενοι τὸν καιρόν, ὅτι αἱ ἡμέραι πονηραί εἰσιν. In his closing words our author looks to relations with the outside world: 'St Paul probably has in mind the difference between bold, uncompromising witness to the Christian allegiance when occasion offers, and a harsh, unloving, tactless obtruding of it at the wrong time' (Moule, 133). Early Christians were a minority group in a largely hostile world, and ill-judged attempts to assert their faith or impose it on others were not likely to be productive. In the words of Ecclesiastes (3.7) there is 'a time to keep silence and a time to speak'. That is an age-old lesson which some in our modern world have still to learn.[10] Ill-judged or

---

[9] Cf. Eph. 6.19f. (passages set out in parallel on p. 205), where 'the epexegetical genitive μυστήριον τοῦ εὐαγγελίου, albeit hitherto unparalleled, expresses the familiar notion of 1 Cor 2:1; Col 4:3'. ὡς δεῖ με λαλῆσαι is exactly paralleled in Eph. 6.20.

[10] Aletti (261) observes that this wisdom is not just a human ability to conduct relations with those who do not share our political and religious views; it is a grace received, an effect of our being with Christ, of the fullness received in him, 'in whom are all the treasures of wisdom' (2.3): a grace received that we may know how to bear witness to the fullness received.

294

badly timed efforts to promote some perfectly valid cause have sometimes only made things worse.

Where χρόνος (BAGD 887; *TWNT* ix. 576–89; for the NT see 587–89) refers mostly to a period of time, καιρός (BAGD 394–95; *TWNT* iii. 456–63, esp. 460–63) appears more commonly in the sense of a point of time, more particularly the right or favourable time, an opportunity. The problem in this verse lies with the verb ἐξαγοράζεσθαι, which 'cannot be interpreted with certainty' (BAGD 271, §2). The active means to buy or to redeem (cf. Gal. 3.13; 4.5), and is used both in LXX and in Theodotion at Dan. 2.8, καιρὸν ὑμεῖς ἐξαγοράζετε, but there the reference is to gaining time, which does not help us here. Moule (134) notes that two explanations have been offered, one from the market in general, the other from the slave market in particular, and remarks that it is 'slightly bizarre' to treat ὁ καιρός as a person needing help, a slave to be emancipated. He therefore chooses the other option, and takes it to be a commodity to be eagerly bought. Büchsel (*TWNT* i. 128) also speaks of the compound verb here as intensive (the usual force of ἐκ in such compounds), i.e. referring to a buying which exhausts the possibilities available: the opportunities are to be grasped, whatever the cost or effort (he notes that the use in Dan. 2.8 LXX and Θ is different from that of Paul).

6. ὁ λόγος ὑμῶν πάντοτε ἐν χάριτι, ἅλατι ἠρτυμένος, εἰδέναι πῶς δεῖ ὑμᾶς ἑνὶ ἑκάστῳ ἀποκρίνεσθαι We have already met with χάρις several times over: in the salutation at 1.2 (cf. also the final words of the letter at 4.18), of the grace of God at 1.6, and of 'singing to God with grace in your hearts' at 3.16, and these different occurrences illustrate the range of meaning which this word can have (cf. BAGD 877f.). Basically it means grace or favour, a gift bestowed, but it can also refer to gratitude on the part of the recipient; here it refers to graciousness or attractiveness in speech (BAGD §1 cites Plutarch, *Mor.* 514f, χάριν τινὰ παρασκευάζοντες ἀλληλοῖς, ὥσπερ ἁλσὶ τοῖς λόγοις ἐφηδύνουσι τὴν διατριβήν: 'they seek to ingratiate themselves with each other by seasoning with the salt of conversation the pastime or business in which they happen to be engaged' (tr. W. C. Helmbold, Loeb Classical Library)).[11] ἅλας (BAGD 35) can be used both literally of salt as a seasoning for food, and figuratively ('Attic salt' was a common term for wit. Cf. *HDB* iv. 355; *DAC* ii. 422; *EncBib* 4247–50, which observes (4250) that the term here is 'not to be understood of wit, the "Attic salt" of the ancients, but rather of sober, good sense, as contrasted with "profane and vain babblings" (1 Tim. 6:20; 2 Tim. 2:16)'.)[12] Lightfoot (298), who already has the

---

[11] Moule (135) observes that this reference is not really apposite: 'it is about seasoning *life* with *words* as one seasons food with salt; it says nothing about seasoning *words* with *wit*'.

[12] W. D. Davies (*PRJ* 139) compares Luke 14.34, 35; Mark 9.49, 50; Matt. 5.13. Sophia appears to be called 'salt' in an unfortunately damaged passage in the *Gospel of Philip*. See H. M. Schenke's reconstruction in Schneemelcher, *NT Apocrypha*, i. 192, with his notes.

reference to Plutarch, observes that the salt has a twofold purpose, first as giving flavour to the discourse and recommending it to the palate, and secondly as preserving from corruption; citing Eph. 4.29, πᾶς λόγος σαπρὸς ἐκ τοῦ στόματος ὑμῶν μὴ ἐκπορευέσθω (σαπρός = 'corrupt'), he suggests that 'this secondary application of the metaphor was present to the Apostle's mind here', but that of course assumes that both Eph. and Col. are Pauline. The infinitive εἰδέναι, like the λαλῆσαι in v. 3, is explained by Lightfoot as 'the infinitive of the consequence', meaning 'so as to know', i.e. that you may know. Christians must at all times have a ready answer for those outside, so that they may proclaim their faith as opportunity may afford; but it is to be done wisely, and not aggressively.[13]

This brings us to the conclusion of the main body of the letter. What remains is first a brief note (vv. 7–9) that Paul is sending Tychicus and Onesimus, who will bring to the Colossians all necessary information about his own affairs; then greetings from several people who are with Paul (vv. 10–14), followed by an injunction for the Colossians to greet the brethren and sisters in Laodicea, and to see to an exchange of certain letters (vv. 15–16), and instructions to tell Archippus to fulfil some service he has undertaken (v. 17). Finally (v. 18) there is Paul's own closing greeting: ὁ ἀσπασμὸς τῇ ἐμῇ χειρὶ Παύλου, a request that they remember his bonds, and a brief benediction.

XIII
THE CLOSE OF THE LETTER
(4.7–18)

[7]As for my own concerns, Tychicus will make everything known to you. He is a beloved brother and a faithful servant and fellow-slave in the Lord. [8]I am sending him to you for this very purpose, that you may know the things concerning us and that he may encourage your hearts, [9]along with Onesimus the faithful and beloved brother, who is one of you. They will make known to you everything that is happening here.
[10]Aristarchus my fellow-prisoner greets you, and Mark, the cousin of Barnabas (about whom you have received instructions: if he comes to you, welcome him), [11]and Jesus who is called Justus. They are of the circumcision, and these alone are fellow-workers for the kingdom of God, who have become a comfort to me. [12]Epaphras, who is one of you, a slave of Christ [Jesus], greets you, always wrestling on your behalf in his prayers, that you may stand perfect and fulfilled in all the will of God. [13]I testify for him that he has much labour on your behalf, and for those in Laodicea

[13] Davies (*PRJ* 139) cites Luke 12.12; Matt. 10.19; Mark 13.11; Luke 21.14.

and in Hierapolis. [14]Luke, the beloved physician, greets you, and Demas.

[15]Greet the brethren in Laodicea, and Nympha and the church at her house. [16]And when the letter is read among you, make sure that it is read also in the church of the Laodiceans, [17]and that you also read the letter from Laodicea. And say to Archippus, 'See to the ministry which you received in the Lord, that you fulfil it.' [18]The greeting of Paul in my own hand. Remember my bonds. Grace be with you.

In one of the apocryphal *Letters of Paul and Seneca*, Paul is made to write: 'I was happy to receive your letter yesterday. I could have answered it at once if I had had the young man at hand whom I intended to send to you.'[1] In the ancient world the sending of a letter was not simply a matter of putting a stamp on the envelope and popping it into a convenient letter-box, leaving the postal authorities to do the rest. One frequently had to find a messenger to carry the letter, and obviously it had to be someone whom one could trust, and who could if necessary expand upon the contents of the letter so that the author's meaning was entirely clear. In the present case, that task is assigned to Tychicus and Onesimus, both here mentioned for the first time.

It is very natural to identify Onesimus here as the slave mentioned in the letter to Philemon, but Tychicus is not there mentioned at all, which would be surprising if both these letters were sent at the same time and to the same area. Philem. 12 expressly states that Paul is sending Onesimus back, but there is no reference there to Tychicus, although here he would appear to be the senior member of the delegation. Again, it is only here in Col. that Onesimus is said to be ἐξ ὑμῶν, which has led to the inference that both he and Philemon belonged to Colossae, and hence that this was the intended destination for Philem. A critical assessment has to take all the relevant factors into account, and avoid forming judgements based on evidence that may prove to be inadequate. Similar problems arise, as will be seen, in the next paragraph (vv. 10–14), in regard to the persons who send their greetings.

7. τὰ κατ' ἐμὲ πάντα γνωρίσει ὑμῖν Τύχικος ὁ ἀγαπητὸς ἀδελφὸς καὶ πιστὸς διάκονος καὶ σύνδουλος ἐν κυρίῳ Tychicus appears first in Acts 20.4, where it is said that he was from Asia, i.e. Asia Minor,[2] and was one of a group who went ahead of Paul to Troas. From the other four references in the New Testament he would seem to have been one of Paul's regular emissaries: at 2 Tim.

[1] Schneemelcher, *NT Apocrypha*, ii. 48; Elliott, *The Apocryphal NT*, 549. Wendland (*Kultur*, 416f.) notes that there was an imperial Roman postal service, but only prominent personages could make use of it. Private citizens had to rely on their own resources.
[2] Haenchen (*Acts* (ET 1971), 581 n. 6) thinks Tychicus and Trophimus are 'probably correctly identified by D as'Εφέσιοι', comparing Acts 21.29; Eph. 6.21; 2 Tim. 4.12.

4.12 he is said to have been sent to Ephesus, while Tit. 3.12 speaks of
either him or Artemas being sent to Titus in Crete. Eph. 6.21 closely
parallels our present verse: ἵνα δὲ εἰδῆτε καὶ ὑμεῖς τὰ κατ'ἐμέ, τί
πράσσω, πάντα γνωρίσει ὑμῖν Τύχικος ὁ ἀγαπητὸς ἀδελφὸς καὶ
πιστὸς διάκονος ἐν κυρίῳ. It is worthy of note that there is not one
reference to him in the major letters. The view that he shared Paul's
last journey to Jerusalem, and subsequently the journey to Rome,
depends on the assumption that all those mentioned in Acts 20.4
made these journeys; but some of them are not mentioned again.

As already noted, the description of Tychicus finds an almost exact
parallel in Eph. 6.21, which omits only καὶ σύνδουλος, but also inserts
τί πράσσω between τὰ κατ'ἐμέ and the following πάντα. Cf. also 1.7,
where some of these terms (ἀγαπητός, σύνδουλος, πιστός, διάκονος)
are used with reference to Epaphras. Lindemann ('Gemeinde', 127 n.
65) notes that Tychicus' relation to the community is confined to the
limited commission (v. 8) of bringing news about Paul and 'encouraging their hearts'; the same holds for Onesimus (4.9) and in another
way for Mark (4.10), whereas the others mentioned appear to have no
connection at all with the community.

In this passage it is at several points necessary to rearrange the
word order if we are to obtain a reasonable English translation: τὰ
κατ'ἐμέ πάντα (lit. 'all the things concerning me') is the object of
γνωρίσει, and Tychicus the subject, but the description following
Tychicus' name complicates matters, and is best made into a separate
sentence. Similarly in vv. 10–11 the verb ἀσπάζεται comes at the
beginning, followed by the three names Aristarchus, Mark and Jesus
Justus, each with a qualification, and then by a rather complex
construction which is again best taken separately. Translation is not
always a simple matter of substituting one English word for each
word in the original: we have to determine the meaning of the
original text, and then try to find the appropriate English idiom.

**8. ὃν ἔπεμψα πρὸς ὑμᾶς εἰς αὐτὸ τοῦτο, ἵνα γνῶτε τὰ περὶ
ἡμῶν καὶ παρακαλέσῃ τὰς καρδίας ὑμῶν** ἔπεμψα here (like
ἀνέπεμψα in Philem. 12) is an example of the 'epistolary' aorist: the
writer puts himself in the position of the addressee, for whom the
sending is a thing of the past. It is normally to be rendered by an
English present, 'I am sending'. This verse in effect repeats what was
said in the preceding verse (τὰ κατ' ἐμὲ πάντα γνωρίσει ὑμῖν
Τύχικος; cf. the further repetition in v. 9, πάντα ὑμῖν γνωρίσουσιν
τὰ ὧδε), but makes clear that the specific purpose of Tychicus'
mission was first to convey this information and secondly to
encourage the readers. Several manuscripts here (P46 אc D1 1739 et
al.) have a variant reading, ἵνα γνῶ τὰ περὶ ὑμῶν, which is the
reading of the Textus Receptus and hence lies behind the King James
Version 'that he may know your estate, and comfort your hearts'. On
this reading, the purpose of the mission was not to convey
information but to obtain it, not to inform the Colossians about
Paul but to find out how things stood with them; but this seems at
variance with the preceding εἰς αὐτὸ τοῦτο (cf. BAGD 123, §1h).

Metzger (*Textual Commentary*, 626) observes that the reading adopted above 'is adequately supported by good representatives of the Alexandrian, Western and Eastern types of text' (he lists A B D* G P 33 81 it[d, g, 61, 86]syr[pal]cop[sa] arm eth Ephraem *al*), and 'best explains the origin of the other readings'. All we need to assume is an accidental substitution of ὑμῶν for ἡμῶν, a common error, and a false reading of ΓΝΩΤΕ as two words (γνω τε) rather than one, or accidental omission of the τε before the following τα. Scribes may also have expected some different form of expression in this verse, rather than a repetition. For παρακαλέω in the sense of 'comfort, encourage', cf. 2.2 above (pp. 184f.).

9. σὺν Ὀνησίμῳ τῷ πιστῷ καὶ ἀγαπητῷ ἀδελφῷ, ὅς ἐστιν ἐξ ὑμῶν· πάντα ὑμῖν γνωρίσουσιν τὰ ὧδε Onesimus is introduced as 'the faithful and beloved brother', which is how Paul in Philem. hopes he will be received, but is scarcely how he would have been known in Colossae before the coming of Paul's letter. It is, however, clear that Tychicus would be the main speaker when it came to delivering their message, and presumably a part of his task would be to explain the situation with regard to Onesimus; but such points still raise questions about the connection between the letters. Some scribes evidently felt that something was missing at the end, and supplied πραττόμενα after ὧδε; it is not necessary in Greek, although it is naturally supplied in English.

10. ἀσπάζεται ὑμᾶς Ἀρίσταρχος ὁ συναιχμάλωτός μου καὶ Μᾶρκος ὁ ἀνεψιὸς Βαρναβᾶ (περὶ οὗ ἐλάβετε ἐντολάς, ἐὰν ἔλθῃ πρὸς ὑμᾶς, δέξασθε αὐτόν) Verses 10–14 convey the greetings of members of Paul's company, and here we may compare Philem. 23–24: the same five names (Aristarchus, Mark, Epaphras, Luke and Demas) appear in both, but in a different order (in Philem.: Epaphras, Mark, Aristarchus, Demas, Luke). It is not easy to see why Epaphras should be given greater prominence in Philem.: in Col. he is already mentioned at 1.7 (see p. 94ff. above) as 'a faithful minister of Christ on our behalf', and there is no other reference to Aristarchus in this letter. Nor is it easy to explain why Mark should be second in both lists, or why Luke and Demas should change places. The order in Col. is clearly determined by v. 11: the first three named are all Jewish Christians, and identified as the only Jewish Christians among Paul's 'fellow-labourers for the kingdom of God'. In Philem. 23–24 Epaphras is described as ὁ συναιχμάλωτός μου ἐν Χριστῷ Ἰησοῦ (the last three words an addition to what we read in Col.), the other four simply as οἱ συνεργοί μου, without reference to the kingdom. Since Epaphras is described as σύνδουλος at 1.7, it may be that we should count all five as συνεργοί, but there is still nothing about the kingdom.

One notable difference between the lists is the inclusion in Col. of Jesus Justus, and it has been suggested that his name could be restored in Philem. (see p. 367 below); but the scope for conjectural emendation in a New Testament text must be regarded as limited, in view of the number of extant manuscripts. Without any manuscript support, conjectures must be regarded as doubtful. In Philem. the

names are simply listed, whereas here each (except for Demas) has a
brief description added. That is a second notable difference, and
must raise questions about the relation between the two letters: if
both were by Paul himself, and he had written these brief descriptions
in Col., he might well have decided to list only the names in the other
letter. This also assumes, of course, that Col. was the first to be
written. If, however, Col. was written by a later disciple, one must
ask where he got his additional information: if he was drawing on
Philem. for the names, what was the source of the material in his
descriptions? We may probably assume that Paul's co-workers were a
fairly close-knit group, and well known to one another, so that our
author might well have added these descriptions from his own
knowledge; but that is still an assumption.

In Col. Aristarchus is described as Paul's συναιχμάλωτος (cf. also
Rom. 16.7), generally translated as 'fellow-prisoner', but in Philem.
this title is given to Epaphras, here described as ὁ ἐξ ὑμῶν, δοῦλος
Χριστοῦ 'Ἰησοῦ.[3] Strictly, an αἰχμάλωτος was a captive, a prisoner of
war, classed according to BAGD (27) 'with beggars, blind men and
oppressed as examples of misery' (Luke 4.18, quoting Isa. 61.1). That
Paul was not, and Moule (137) observes, 'It is hard to believe that
both Aristarchus and Epaphras were, or had been, literally fellow-
prisoners with St Paul, not to mention Andronicus and Junias'
(Rom. 16.7). He therefore sees reasons for taking the word
metaphorically: they are prisoners *of Christ*, as Paul also was. Cf.
G. Kittel, *TWNT* i. 196–97, who notes that elsewhere Paul describes
himself not as αἰχμάλωτος but as δέσμιος.

Aristarchus is first mentioned in Acts 19.29, as caught up in the
riot in Ephesus; he was from Thessalonica (Acts 20.4), and according
to *Beg.* (iv. 253) 'it is an attractive supposition that the group of
disciples mentioned here were the representatives of Paul's churches',
i.e. charged with conveying the great collection to Jerusalem. The
only other reference in Acts is at 27.2, where he embarks with Paul
and his companions at the start of the voyage to Italy, but nothing is
said as to how far he travelled. Lightfoot (*Philippians* (1894 edn), 35)
thought that he parted from Paul at Myra, because he was on his way
home, but later rejoined Paul in Rome.[4] The only evidence that he
was with Paul in Rome, however, is in Col. and Philem., and rests on
the traditional view that these letters were written during Paul's last
imprisonment. The final verdict must therefore be a rather unsatisfactory 'not proven'.

Mark is first mentioned in Acts at 12.12: his mother's house was
the meeting place to which Peter went on his release from prison by

[3] Lightfoot (302) writes: 'In Philem. 23 this honourable title is withheld from
Aristarchus and given to Epaphras.'
[4] On this view, the original plan was to make for Macedonia, and then via the
Egnatian Way to Dyrrhachium, leaving only a short sea crossing to Italy. It was the
chance finding of 'an Alexandrian ship bound for Italy' (Acts 27.6) that led the
centurion to change the plan and risk the long sea voyage at that time of year, with, as
it proved, disastrous results. It all fits together, but it is impossible to be certain.

the angel. He is linked with Barnabas and Saul at 12.25,[5] and went with them on the first missionary journey to Cyprus (13.5), but returned to Jerusalem from Perga in Pamphylia (13.13). This was later to lead to a disagreement between Paul and Barnabas, as a result of which they parted company (15.37–39), but the reference to him here and at Philem. 24 suggests that a reconciliation had been effected (cf. also 2 Tim. 4.11). According to Papias (quoted in Eusebius, *HE* iii.39,15), he became the 'interpreter' of Peter (at 1 Pet. 5.13 'my son Mark' sends his greetings) and wrote down in his Gospel all that he remembered of Peter's teaching.[6] Koester (*Trajectories*, 152) writes, 'Mark's basic concept of the "gospel" is Pauline, and it is probably not only a coincidence that we find a "Mark" in Paul's company', and adds in a footnote that the tradition that connects Mark with Paul is much older than that which finds Mark in Peter's company.[7]

ἀνεψιός (BAGD 66) is another of the hapax legomena in this letter, and means a cousin, although in very late writers it came to be used for a nephew (cf. Lightfoot's note, 302–03, for details; hence the AV 'sister's son to Barnabas'). According to Acts 4.36, Barnabas was a native of Cyprus, which made that island a very natural target for the first missionary journey. In the disagreement which resulted from Mark's defection at Perga,[8] Barnabas naturally sided with his kinsman, and the two went back to Cyprus, while Paul and Silas went to Syria and Cilicia (Acts 15.39–41). As noted above, the references to Mark here and in Philem. 24 indicate that a reconciliation had been effected. If Philem. was written from Ephesus, it could have been much earlier than if the letter was sent from Rome; in any case, the claims of Christian ἀγάπη would have made such a reconciliation imperative. Moreover Paul himself was indebted to Barnabas, who had given him his support when Paul first came back to Jerusalem after his conversion (Acts 9.26–27), and later brought him back from his exile in Tarsus when the Gentile mission began in Antioch (Acts 11.25–26). The bonds of friendship may have proved stronger than any ill-will resulting from the disagreement over Mark.

11. καὶ Ἰησοῦς ὁ λεγόμενος Ἰοῦστος, οἱ ὄντες ἐκ περιτομῆς, οὗτοι μόνοι συνεργοὶ εἰς τὴν βασιλείαν τοῦ θεοῦ, οἵτινες ἐγενήθησάν μοι παρηγορία The third member of this first group is Jesus Justus. As already noted, he is missing from the list in Philem. According to Pratscher (*Der Herrenbruder Jacobus* (1987), 115 n. 43),

[5] On the problems in this verse cf. Haenchen, *Acts*, 387; Barrett, *Acts*, i. 593–97. Barnabas and Saul were sent from Antioch to Jerusalem on a relief mission (Acts 11.30). At 12.25, having fulfilled their mission in Jerusalem, they return to Antioch, taking Mark with them.
[6] The various forms of this tradition differ as to whether Mark wrote during Peter's lifetime, or after his death; according to some versions he wrote with Peter's knowledge and approval.
[7] His inference regarding the place of origin for Mark's Gospel (Asia Minor and Achaia, or perhaps Antioch, rather than Rome) is perhaps more doubtful.
[8] Cf. Luke 9.62. Paul could not, of course, have known Luke's Gospel, but he might have known the saying from oral tradition.

the 'Justus' is a name, not a title: had it been a title, we should have expected δίκαιος. Lightfoot (304; cf. BAGD 380) notes that it was 'a common name or surname of Jews and proselytes, denoting obedience and devotion to the law'. Two other bearers of the name are mentioned in Acts: Joseph called Barsabbas, 'who was also known as Justus', one of the two candidates nominated to replace Judas Iscariot (Acts 1.23), and Titius Justus, a σεβόμενος in Corinth, whose house was next to the synagogue; it was there Paul went when the Jews refused to hear his message (Acts 18.7).

The construction in the remainder of the verse is not altogether easy to follow, but the sense is clear: these three are 'of the circumcision', i.e. they are Jewish Christians, which implies that the others named are Gentiles.[9] It is at first sight strange that Aristarchus, from Thessalonica, should be one of them, but he could of course have been a Jew of the diaspora. Further, only these three Jewish Christians are among Paul's fellow-workers for the kingdom of God.[10] It is clear from Paul's major letters (esp. Rom. 9–11) that he was deeply disappointed at the refusal of many Jewish Christians to accept his gospel for the Gentiles, which did not require a Gentile to become a Jew first, before he could become a Christian. His great collection for the saints in Jerusalem was not just a humanitarian project, but also a gesture of solidarity, an effort to promote reconciliation, although doubts have at times been raised as to whether it was actually accepted by the Jerusalem church. But outright rejection would have been a humiliating rebuff.[11] At all events, what Paul writes in Romans leaves no doubt as to his deep concern for his people, and his firm and confident expectation that God in time will find a way to bring about their conversion: 'if their stumbling means riches for the world, and if their defeat means riches for Gentiles, how much more will their full inclusion mean! ... If their rejection is the reconciliation of the world, what will their acceptance be but life from the dead!' (Rom. 11.12, 15)

Something of this concern comes out in the final words of this verse: these three 'have become a comfort to me'. παρηγορία (BAGD 626) is another of the hapax legomena in this letter. In view of the

[9] Moule remarks (137) that this is the chief evidence that Luke (v. 14) was a Gentile. One might speculate on the significance for the Synoptic Problem of the fact that both Mark and Luke appear here among Paul's companions: did they ever exchange notes, or discuss the life and teaching of Jesus? But this would take us into the realm of pure conjecture.

[10] Davies (*PRJ* 295f.) observes that Paul very rarely speaks of a βασιλεία τοῦ Χριστοῦ: 'Whenever Paul speaks of a kingdom that is to come he thinks of a βασιλεία τοῦ θεοῦ (1 Th 2.12; 2 Th 1.4, 5; Gal 5.21; 1 Cor 6.9–10; 15.50; Col 4.11). ... The only text which explicitly makes mention of a βασιλεία τοῦ Χριστοῦ (i.e. Col. 1.12–13) regards that kingdom as already a present fact' (296). In other words, Christians have already been delivered from the power of darkness and translated into the kingdom of God's Son (1.12–13), but they still await the final manifestation of the kingdom of God.

[11] Bockmuehl for example (*Revelation and Mystery*, 131 n. 14) finds Dunn's argument that the collection was refused 'perhaps less convincing', citing Acts 24.17.

largely hostile attitude of both Jews and Jewish Christians to his Gospel for the Gentiles, it was a source of comfort and of strength to have these three all readily giving their support.[12]

12. ἀσπάζεται ὑμᾶς Ἐπαφρᾶς ὁ ἐξ ὑμῶν, δοῦλος Χριστοῦ [Ἰησοῦ], πάντοτε ἀγωνιζόμενος ὑπὲρ ὑμῶν ἐν ταῖς προσευχαῖς, ἵνα σταθῆτε τέλειοι καὶ πεπληροφορημένοι ἐν παντὶ θελήματι τοῦ θεοῦ This is the second reference to Epaphras in the letter (cf. 1.7). Lindemann notes ('Gemeinde', 127) that in contrast to Tychicus (4.7) the emphasis here is not so much on Epaphras' personality, but rather on his function as the founder and protector of the community. Lindemann sees a special significance in the ὁ ἐξ ὑμῶν, which indicates that Epaphras belongs to Colossae, because vv. 12f. lay stress on his connection not only with Colossae but also with Laodicea (and Hierapolis). This does not necessarily mean that he was the founder of all three churches, but it does suggest that he had taken an active part in the life and work of all three communities.

At 1.7 Epaphras is described as 'our beloved fellow-servant', the title σύνδουλος given above (v. 7) to Tychicus, but found nowhere else in the Pauline corpus. The description here is also quite distinctive: Paul speaks of himself as δοῦλος Ἰησοῦ Χριστοῦ at Rom. 1.1 (cf. also Tit. 1.1; Jas. 1.1; 2 Pet. 1.1; Jude 1), but nowhere else is this title given to any individual, except for Timothy at Phil. 1.1 (Παῦλος καὶ Τιμόθεος δοῦλοι Χριστοῦ Ἰησοῦ). As Lightfoot says, this 'probably points to exceptional services in the cause of the Gospel on the part of Epaphras'. That of course assumes that Col. is an authentic letter by Paul, but this verse presents a certain difficulty for the view that it was written by a later disciple. As the above references indicate, other writers were to follow the example set by Paul in Romans, but why should our author have gone so far as to accord this title to Epaphras? James, Peter and Jude all rank as apostles. We can only assume that Epaphras was known in the Pauline school to have rendered singular service in the area of Colossae, Laodicea and Hierapolis.[13]

The parallel with Paul is carried further in the following words, πάντοτε ἀγωνιζόμενος ὑπὲρ ὑμῶν ἐν ταῖς προσευχαῖς κτλ.[14] The verb ἀγωνίζομαι and the noun ἀγών have both been used of Paul's labours for the gospel at 1.29; 2.1–2; πάντοτε appears in close association with προσευχόμενοι at 1.3 (cf. also 1.9); the goal of Epaphras' labours, 'that you may stand perfect and fulfilled in all the will of God', recalls 1.9, 'that you may be filled with the knowledge of

---

[12] Lightfoot (304) takes the μόνοι to mean only these three of the Jewish Christians in Rome, referring for 'this antagonism of the converts from the Circumcision in the metropolis' to his *Philippians*, 16ff.; 'The words however must not be closely pressed, as if absolutely no Jewish Christian besides had remained friendly.'

[13] There is some variation in the manuscript tradition: a few witnesses read Ἰησοῦ Χριστοῦ, while others (P⁴⁶ D F G *et al.*) have only Χριστοῦ. The text printed above is that of ℵ A B C *et al.*

[14] Davies (*PRJ* 140) refers to Luke 21.36; 13.24; Matt. 5.48.

his will', and 1.28, 'that we may present every man perfect in Christ'; the participle πεπληροφορημένοι echoes the noun πληροφορία at 2.2.[15] We may add that the phrase ὑπὲρ ὑμῶν appears as a variant reading in the description of Epaphras at 1.7, although it must have been a very weary scribe indeed who introduced it there, if this was the passage that influenced him (but some scholars prefer that reading; see pp. 95–96 above). If Paul himself wrote this letter, these verses make clear his high personal regard for Epaphras; if it was written by a later disciple, Epaphras was known to and remembered in the Pauline school as a significant figure in the evangelizing of this area.

13. μαρτυρῶ γὰρ αὐτῷ ὅτι ἔχει πολὺν πόνον ὑπὲρ ὑμῶν καὶ τῶν ἐν Λαοδικείᾳ καὶ τῶν ἐν Ἱεραπόλει This verse rounds off the tribute paid to Epaphras, again with an echo of an earlier passage: at 2.1 our author writes, θέλω γὰρ ὑμᾶς εἰδέναι ἡλίκον ἀγῶνα ἔχω ὑπὲρ ὑμῶν καὶ τῶν ἐν Λαοδικείᾳ (a few witnesses add καὶ τῶν ἐν Ἱεραπόλει, but they are very few, and probably influenced by the present verse). Some manuscripts indeed read ἀγῶνα here, but they are few in number; others have κόπον, πόθον or ζῆλον, but the weight of evidence (א A B C et al.) favours πόνον.[16] As already indicated, Laodicea is mentioned above at 2.1, but Hierapolis for some reason only here.

14. ἀσπάζεται ὑμᾶς Λουκᾶς ὁ ἰατρὸς ὁ ἀγαπητὸς καὶ Δημᾶς The final greetings are from Luke, here described as the beloved physician, and Demas, who in Lightfoot's words (308) 'is dismissed with a bare mention and without any epithet of commendation'. The only other reference to him in the New Testament is at 2 Tim. 4.10: 'Demas, in love with this present world, has deserted me and gone to Thessalonica.' The name appears again in a medieval legend, the *Narrative of Joseph of Arimathaea*, as the name of the penitent robber who was crucified with Jesus (Elliott, *The Apocryphal NT*, 218, 220; in the *Gospel of Nicodemus* (ibid. 176–77) he is called Dysmas). That of course has no relevance for our Demas here, but in the *Acts of Paul and Thecla* (ibid. 364–66) two of Paul's travelling companions are Demas and Hermogenes, 'who were full of hypocrisy and flattered Paul as if they loved him', only to turn against him later.[17] Epiphanius (*Pan.* 51) classifies Demas among apostates from the faith.

[15] πεπληροφορημένοι is read by א A B C D* and other witnesses. Lightfoot (306) notes, 'The reading of the received text here, πεπληρωμένοι, must be rejected as of inferior authority'. It happens to be the reading of P46 D2, but even papyri are not always free from error. The echo of πληροφορία must also be borne in mind.

[16] Lightfoot observes that the word πόνος is very rare in the New Testament (it occurs only here and in Rev. 16.10, 11; 21.4), and was therefore likely to be changed. Cf. Metzger, *Textual Commentary*, 626.

[17] We may recall that there are three men in Acts who bear the name of Ananias: the husband of Sapphira in ch. 5, the disciple in Damascus in ch. 9 who was sent to Paul after his conversion (cf. also 22.12–16), and the high priest in Jerusalem (23.2; 24.1). It may be dangerous to assume that the same name always indicates the same person, unless there are other reasons for making that assumption.

2 Tim. 4.10 mentions not only the desertion of Demas but also the departure of two other members of Paul's company, Crescens to Galatia and Titus to Dalmatia; v. 12 adds that Paul has sent Tychicus to Ephesus. In between, v. 11 says 'Only Luke is with me', and urges Timothy to bring Mark with him. The letter may be pseudepigraphic, but it does convey a vivid picture of the comings and goings of Paul's fellow-workers during his imprisonment in Rome. How accurate it is, we cannot tell, but Paul is portrayed as the commanding officer, with his agents ceaselessly arriving and departing on their various missions. It is interesting to see so many of the names in our present list cropping up again elsewhere.

Luke is mentioned by name only three times in the New Testament (Col. 4.14; 2 Tim. 4.11; Philem. 24), but he is traditionally identified as the author of the Third Gospel and of Acts. If the 'we' passages in Acts are drawn from his own travel diary, as some have assumed,[18] then he was one of Paul's companions on several of the journeys reported in Acts 16–28. Here he is described not only as a doctor,[19] which implies some degree of education and training, but also as ὁ ἀγαπητός, a title extended to only a few individuals (Epaphras, 1.7; Tychicus, 4.7, cf. Eph. 6.21; Onesimus, 4.9; Philem. 16; Philemon, Philem. 1), although it is regularly used in addressing the readers of a letter.[20] It implies a warm affection, a close relationship, a firm and enduring friendship.

15. ἀσπάσασθε τοὺς ἐν Λαοδικείᾳ ἀδελφοὺς καὶ Νύμφαν καὶ τὴν κατ' οἶκον αὐτῆς ἐκκλησίαν The author now asks the readers to greet the neighbouring church in Laodicea (presumably conveying his greetings at the same time), making specific mention of one particular member and the group who gathered at his or her house. Two textual problems arise, first in relation to the name, and second with regard to the following pronoun which refers back to it. The name may be accented either as Νύμφαν, from the feminine nominative Νύμφα ('Nympha'), or as Νυμφᾶν, from the masculine nominative Νυμφᾶς ('Nymphas'), and the pronoun must be either the feminine αὐτῆς or the masculine αὐτοῦ to agree with it.[21] The masculine is the reading of the Textus Receptus, and hence of the

---

[18] For discussion, cf. *Beg.* ii. 520, index, *s.v.* 'We-passages'; Haenchen, *Acts*, 737, index, *s.v.* 'Travel-journal'; Barrett, *Acts*, ii. pp. xxv–xxx.

[19] On Luke 8.43 J. M. Creed writes: 'According to the reading BD syr.sin Lk. omits from Mk. the statement that the woman had expended all her livelihood upon physicians without profit. If the writer is Luke the physician, it is natural that he should do so' (*Luke*, 123). But (1) NA[27] now includes the words ἰατροῖς προσαναλώσασα ὅλον τοῦ βίου (against the previous edition); (2) Matt. 9.20 also omits the reference to doctors. Professional loyalty may have had nothing to do with it.

[20] This makes the frequency of its occurrence in Rom. 16 all the more striking (for Epaenetus, Ampliatus, Stachys, Persis).

[21] The plural αὐτων, favoured by Lightfoot (322), is probably due to some scribe taking the pronoun to refer to the brethren as well as to Nympha. Modern commentators seem to prefer the feminine (e.g. Pokorný 194–95; Dunn, 274 n. 6), but Lightfoot (308) and Moule (28 n. 1) read the masculine, considering a Doric form (against the commoner Νύμφη) to be unlikely. For Lohse (174) the question 'cannot be decided with certainty' (cf. Aletti, 269; Metzger, *Textual Commentary*, 627).

Authorized Version, but is open to suspicion, since scribes might not have believed that a woman could hold so prominent a position (but there are other cases of women prominent in the leadership of the early Church, e.g. Phoebe, Prisca, Junia, Tryphaena and Tryphosa, and Persis in the list at Rom. 16).[22]

Some scholars (e.g. Aletti, 269; Kümmel, 337 (see p. 7 above)) assume that Nympha's house was the meeting-place of the Christian community in Colossae, but the run of this sentence suggests rather that it was in Laodicea. The location of this house church depends on whether we see a break between the two parts of the verse, or take the whole together. If Nympha and the church at her house were in Colossae, our author would probably have needed to make that clear. For Lindemann ('Gemeinde', 121 n. 46) 'all text-critical probability speaks for the originality of the female name Nympha', and she belonged not to Colossae but to Laodicea (124).

At 1.18, 24 the word ἐκκλησία clearly refers to the Church universal (cf. BAGD 241, §4d); elsewhere it can be used of the local church, 'the totality of Christians living in one place' (§4b). Here the reference is to those members of the community in Laodicea who met in the house of Nympha. We have to remember that in the early days there was no such thing as a church building in our modern sense. Christians gathered where they could, in Rome for example in the catacombs, elsewhere in the house of some member who had room enough to accommodate them. The house church situation is still reflected in some of the apocryphal acts, e.g. in the *Acts of Andrew* the community at Patras meets in the house of the governor Aegeates, without his knowledge.[23] Presumably that would be known as the church in the house of Maximilla, since her husband was an implacable foe of the apostle. This in turn would tell against objections to reading the names of Nympha above, or Junia in Rom. 16.7, on the ground that women would not hold positions of such prominence: if the wife made her home available while her husband remained pagan, it would be natural to use her name rather than his.

16. καὶ ὅταν ἀναγνωσθῇ παρ᾽ ὑμῖν ἡ ἐπιστολή, ποιήσατε ἵνα καὶ ἐν τῇ Λαοδικέων ἐκκλησίᾳ ἀναγνωσθῇ, καὶ τὴν ἐκ Λαοδικείας ἵνα καὶ ὑμεῖς ἀναγνῶτε On the reading of letters in public worship, W. D. Davies (*Background*, 129) remarks, 'That Paul could expect his own Epistles to be read in the services points to much flexibility' (he is writing in criticism of Carrington's *The*

---

[22] 'Much work has been done by socio-historians in the last two decades that shows the wide-ranging roles of women in first-century Jewish and Greco-Roman culture' (L. Belleville, *NTS* 51 (2005), 248). Women, particularly wealthy women, could occupy positions of prominence and enjoy certain privileges, so that the commonly accepted picture of male dominance may require some revision. We should not, however, reject that accepted picture altogether: the situation may have varied in different areas and at different periods, not to mention different levels of society.

[23] See Schneemelcher, *NT Apocrypha*, ii. 136, 138–39; also in the *Epitome* of Gregory of Tours §§6, 13 (Elliott, *The Apocryphal NT*, 246, 248).

Primitive Christian Calendar). In a footnote he cites this verse and 1 Thess. 5.27: ἐνορκίζω ὑμᾶς τὸν κύριον ἀναγνωσθῆναι τὴν ἐπιστολὴν πᾶσιν τοῖς ἀδελφοῖς, but warns against making too much of this point. Wendland (*Kultur*, 346) notes that these verses show how such letters were disseminated (cf. also L. Hartman, 'On Reading Others' Letters', *HTR* 79 (1986) 137–46; B. Oestreich, 'Leseanweisungen in Briefen als Mittel der Gestaltung von Beziehungen', *NTS* 50 (2004), 224–45, esp. 237ff.). This verse presupposes close and cordial relations between the two neighbouring communities, and takes it for granted that each would be ready and willing to share with the other.

As to the letter from Laodicea, it remains something of a mystery. As noted in the Introduction (pp. 3–4 above) Ephesians was included under the title of Laodiceans in Marcion's canon, and there have been some who have thought this the correct solution to the problem. The extant *Letter to the Laodiceans*, included among the New Testament apocrypha, is no more than a pastiche of extracts from genuine letters, and was probably composed to make good an apparent deficiency. Modern scholars would be most inclined to assume that if there ever was such a letter, it has now been lost. If Col. is by some later disciple, it is quite possible that there never was such a letter. In that case, the fiction would be of some significance as showing the cordial relations that were expected to prevail among early Christian communities.

17. **καὶ εἴπατε Ἀρχίππῳ· βλέπε τὴν διακονίαν ἣν παρέλαβες ἐν κυρίῳ, ἵνα αὐτὴν πληροῖς** Archippus is mentioned in the opening salutation of Philem., along with Philemon and Apphia, and is most naturally to be thought of as a member of the family, although whether he was Philemon's son or a brother we simply do not know. He is there called συστρατιώτης, a fellow-soldier, a title given at Phil. 2.25 to Epaphroditus. Since this is a title of honour (BAGD 795), it is most unlikely that we should think of an elderly Paul striking up a friendship with the small son of the house, and playfully calling him his fellow-soldier, and the reference here to the service which Archippus has undertaken would finally rule out any such idea. What that service was, we simply do not know, although inevitably attempts have been made to supply suggestions. The Marcionite Prologues, for example, understand the διακονία of Archippus as his ministry to the Colossians, who had received the word from him (cf. Moule, 22 n. 1 for the text; trs. in W. G. Kümmel, *The New Testament: The History of the Investigation of its Problems* (ET 1972), 14; see Introduction, p. 21); but other references in the letter would seem rather to suggest Epaphras as responsible for the evangelizing of the area. Lightfoot (42f.) sees this verse as a warning, and notes the coincidence with Rev. 3.19, the more striking if 'the common view' is correct, that the angels of the seven churches are the chief pastors; but in *Philippians* (199f.) he rejects this common view.

If Paul wrote this letter, Archippus would know well enough what was required of him, but we do not. All we can say is that the fact that Archippus is said to have received the charge ἐν κυρίῳ suggests that it had something to do with Christian service.

18. ὁ ἀσπασμὸς τῇ ἐμῇ χειρὶ Παύλου. μνημονεύετέ μου τῶν δεσμῶν. ἡ χάρις μεθ᾽ ὑμῶν When a person has a letter written, or dictates it to a secretary, it is very natural that he or she should append a signature, perhaps with a few postscript personal comments, as a token of authenticity. That is what we should normally think of here—the author taking the pen from the scribe to add his personal greeting. The usage in the Pauline letters is, however, by no means consistent, and it is open to question whether we may really speak of 'the apostle's usual practice'. In Rom. there is no such signature, and the only indication that the letter was dictated comes in the words inserted by the scribe Tertius at 16.22 (cf. Cranfield, *Romans*, 2–5). 1 Cor. 16.21 has exactly the form of words used here, which might indicate either that this was Paul's normal usage, or that our author derived it from 1 Cor. 2 Cor. again has nothing, while at Gal. 6.11 Paul writes ἴδετε πηλίκοις γράμμασιν ἔγραψα τῇ ἐμῇ χειρί, usually taken as a humorous comment on the contrast between his own large letters and the small neat hand of the scribe (but Duncan, *Galatians*, 189 concludes that Paul wrote the whole letter himself: 'Style and contents alike proclaim that, from first to last, Galatians was not dictated, but came direct from the hand of the apostle'). Phil. again has no signature, nor does 1 Thess., but 2 Thess. 3.17 once again has exactly the formula of 1 Cor. and Col., with the addition ὅ ἐστιν σημεῖον ἐν πάσῃ ἐπιστολῇ· οὕτως γράφω (cf. E. Best, *Thessalonians*, 347f., who notes that the 'sign' is the fact that it is Paul's handwriting, and raises the question of a possible attempt to guard against forgeries).

Were all three letters indisputably authentic, we should have here an example of Paul's usual practice; it would be the omission in other letters that would require to be accounted for. However, the fact that doubts have been raised on other grounds regarding Col. and 2 Thess. means that we cannot be certain that their authors have not borrowed from 1 Cor.[23] In that case the addition in 2 Thess. might appear to be an attempt to bolster the authenticity of the letter (we may recall a line from Shakespeare's *Hamlet*: 'The lady doth protest too much, methinks'). The reference to his bonds fits very well with both Pokorný's suggestion of reminiscences of the apostle and Bockmuehl's interpretation of 4.3f. 'Paul speaks here of a

[23] Cf. Pokorný, 16: 'Only in 2 Thess. 3:17 does the signature clearly have the function of identification over against the false letters of Paul (2 Thess. 2:2). But it is precisely this that causes problems for the immediate Pauline origin of 2 Thessalonians. ... In Colossians the handwritten signature (4:18) does not have a specifically identifying function. It is especially intended to evoke reminiscences of the apostle. Its specific motive may have been to underscore the exhortation addressed to Archippus. Consequently, Col. 4:18 cannot be used as an argument in support of the authenticity of Colossians, nor can it be used against the latter, as is the case in 2 Thess. 3:17.' Cf. also Wendland, *Kultur*, 361.

demonstration of "the mystery of Christ" by way of his own bonds' (*Revelation and Mystery*, 192).

ἡ χάρις μεθ' ὑμῶν This farewell greeting is unusual, in that all the indisputably genuine letters have the fuller form 'the grace of the Lord Jesus Christ be with you' (or 'with your spirit'); cf. Rom. 16.20; 1 Cor. 16.23; Gal. 6.18; Phil. 4.23; 1 Thess. 5.28; Philem. 25. 2 Cor. 13.14 expands the formula into a threefold benediction, while 2 Thess. 3.18 has 'with you all'. Eph. 6.24 also has a fuller version: ἡ χάρις μετὰ πάντων τῶν ἀγαπώντων τὸν κύριον ἡμῶν.

'The Textus Receptus adds the liturgical ἀμήν, with ℵ^c D K P Ψ 88 614 1739 Byz Lect it^{d, 61, 86} vg syr^{p, h, pal ms} cop^{bo mss} goth *al*. If the word were present originally, however, it is impossible to account for its deletion from such early and varied witnesses as ℵ* A B C G 048 33 81 1881 it^g syr^{pal ms} cop^{sa, bo mss} arm eth^{ro} *al* (Metzger, *Textual Commentary*, 627).

EPILOGUE

Reference was made at an earlier point (p. 232) to the view expressed by Martin Hengel, that in the present state of our knowledge the problems of Colossians cannot be resolved. That is not a desperate admission of defeat, a counsel of despair, simply a frank acknowledgement of the facts of the situation. There are many questions we should like to ask, but we do not have the resources to provide the answers. Inevitably, attempts have been made to fill the gap, for example to identify the precise nature of the problems which our author sought to resolve, the nature of the Colossian 'heresy', but many of them have been but short-lived, and soon replaced by yet another theory. Such theories, however, are better presented in a monograph, where the possibilities can be discussed at the author's discretion. A commentary, working through the text verse by verse, does not lend itself to the development of new theories, so no such attempt is made here. A commentary should provide the reader with the information he or she requires for the understanding of the text, and some guidance regarding the theories which have been advanced, with at least some indication as to which are the most likely, but always with due recognition of the limitations of our knowledge.

In his famous Cambridge inaugural, C. H. Dodd wrote: 'The ideal interpreter would be one who has entered into that strange first-century world, has felt its whole strangeness, has sojourned in it until he has lived himself into it, thinking and feeling as one of those to whom the Gospel first came and who will then return into our world and give to the truth he has discerned a body out of the stuff of our own thought.'[1] These words have often been quoted, but they deserve not only to be quoted but also to be pondered, reflected on, given the

[1] Quoted in F. W. Dillistone, *C. H. Dodd: Interpreter of the New Testament* (1977), 141.

fullest consideration. It is all too easy to read a passage of Scripture with the eyes of today, as if it were written yesterday, and accept or reject it because it suits, or does not suit, our modern pre-conceptions.[2] The world of the twenty-first century is vastly different from the world of the first: we need only to think of the things we today take for granted, which did not exist even fifty years ago. We need first of all to try to see what the text meant for the original readers, in the context of their life and times, against the background of current thought and ideas. Only then can we begin to think of relevance for today, of seeking to apply our author's message in our own time, in terms appropriate to our own situation.

One of the major differences, of course, lies in the area of technology, which has seen some remarkable developments even within the past fifty years. Back in the thirteenth century, Roger Bacon 'is said to have been condemned by the General of the Franciscan Order for "suspect novelties" and "dangerous doctrine"' (*ODCC* 143)—including the suggestion that it might be possible to construct a machine which could reproduce the human voice. One wonders what Bacon's contemporaries would have thought of the telephone, television, computers, to say nothing of modern transport. Presumably they would have put it all down to magic in some form or other. Since the Industrial Revolution there have been enormous changes in the lifestyle, habits and working conditions of people in the western world, with the increasing use of machines of one kind or another to remove the need for human effort.

Here, however, we must pause and reflect that these advances in large measure affect only certain parts of our modern world: North America, Europe, Australia, New Zealand, Japan. In large areas of South America, Asia and particularly Africa, the areas commonly described as 'the Third World', people are still living in conditions very far removed from those of 'the affluent west'. Our author is concerned for good relationships within a fairly small community: what would he have said about concern for others in the 'global village' that our world has now become? At 3.17 he bids his readers, 'whatever you do, in word or deed, do everything in the name of the Lord Jesus, giving thanks to God the Father through him'. If Christ is supreme in creation, as the Colossian 'hymn' affirms, what implications does this have for ecology, our concerns for the planet earth and the people who live on it? Floods in Bangladesh, earthquake in Turkey or Nicaragua, famine in Ethiopia, and just recently a tsunami in the Indian Ocean—these may be remote from our experience, but what is our responsibility towards those who have suffered?

In the west, the increasing use of machinery in one form or

---

[2] A journalist once wrote something about the Church's theology being 'the same yesterday, and today, and forever'. That is in the first place a misquotation of Scripture (Heb. 13.8), and in the second place simply is not true: there is variety of theology even within the New Testament itself.

another has largely eliminated the drudgery of human existence, and the need for slavery. But there are still parts of our world in which slavery is a part of life; and there are areas even in 'the affluent west' where relationships between masters and workers may lead to tension. Also there are tensions between groups of people of different racial or religious background, Israeli and Palestinian in the Holy Land, Hindu and Muslim in the Indian subcontinent, Protestant and Catholic in Northern Ireland, white and non-white in America and South Africa—examples could easily be multiplied. Here our author's call for tolerance is highly relevant: it is not a matter of one side gaining the mastery over the other, but of each learning to respect the other, of learning to work together, to collaborate rather than be constantly in opposition. The problem is complicated further when other faiths are involved: what can the Christian do?

The emancipation of women also belongs here, although in some societies there is still a long way to go. But acceptance that women have a right to independence, and to their own proper place (not just with children and the kitchen!), does not necessarily mean that there should no longer be clubs and societies reserved for men alone: there are many such groups reserved for women only, or with men relegated to a subordinate position. The point here is equality of opportunity, and this applies also in many other areas. In all such cases the primary concern must be for tolerance and cooperation, over against rivalry and hostility, bigotry and hatred.

One of the problems facing the Church today is the indifference and apathy, the lack of enthusiasm, shown by all too many members. It is often said that there are people outside the Church who are as good as, or even better than, many professing Christians. What is not always realized is that secular humanism is as much a religion as Christianity or Judaism or Islam—a matter of faith, of belief and conduct. Moreover, some of the arguments regularly advanced against Christianity were originally directed, by the Sophists around the time of Plato, against the worship of the gods of Olympus. The deficiencies of any system based on pure reason begin to emerge when some teenager asks the simple question 'Why should I?'[3] In a 'permissive' society, anything goes. There are no standards by which the individual may be guided—he may do as he pleases. But down the centuries all societies have set their norms and standards of what is considered to be acceptable conduct, from the 'unwritten laws' of the ancient Greeks onwards. For the Christian, the primary standard is obedience to the will of God, who has revealed his love in the

[3] Many years ago, the students in a Moral Philosophy tutorial were required to discuss the proposition 'That the pleasures of a Socrates are superior to those of a pig'. Naturally they opted, one and all, for the pleasures of a Socrates, only to have their arguments shot down in flames by their tutor (no religious sanctions were permitted; it all had to be on the basis of pure reason). The session ended in some hilarity when he pointed out that whatever they might say, it would be quite impossible to convince the pig.

sending of Jesus Christ his Son. As already noted more than once, the old packman Patrick Walker (see p. 88f. above) had it exactly right.

As to the content of the letter, a few things have emerged which can be considered fairly well established. For one, the question of authenticity probably does not merit the attention often devoted to it: attitudes in the ancient world were different, and there may have been reasons, of which we know nothing, for an author to write under an assumed name. It is the letter itself that is important, as coming from the earliest days of Christianity, and from an author who, if he was not Paul himself, was endeavouring to present Paul's theology in response to a new situation. He may not always have adhered strictly to Paul's teaching, as presented in the major epistles, but that is because he was not merely parroting what he had been taught; he was capable of thinking for himself and adapting to new conditions.

Reference has also been made (p. 60f.) to Ernst Käsemann's shrewd judgement with regard to the date of the letter: 'if genuine, as late as possible, because of the content and the style; if not genuine, as early as conceivable'. Were it by Paul himself, we should have to place it near the end of his life, during his imprisonment in Rome; but this leads to problems of various kinds. Would Epaphras have made the long journey to seek Paul's help, and left the community to its own resources? Was the problem really so serious? There is after all a marked difference from Galatians, where Paul is fighting for his life, and quite literally for all he stood for. If we assume that the letter was written by a Pauline disciple, it must have been fairly soon after the apostle's death, very plausibly in a situation where there was no leading authority within the Church, i.e. before the emergence of the monarchic episcopate. As K. M. Fischer put it (see Introduction, n. 23), he who wished to speak to the world could not do so in his own person, but only under the name of those who possessed an authority rooted in the past. Only as 'Paul' or 'Peter' could one hope to find a hearing. We have to consider what Timothy for example could have done at that time and in such a situation.

As to the Colossian 'heresy', there have been numerous suggestions: an incipient form of Gnosticism, links with the mystery religions, a temptation to revert to Judaism, influence from magic or from some local cult, associations with the heavenly ascent in Jewish apocalyptic, influence from Greek philosophy, whether Stoic, Cynic or Platonic. The problem here is that no one theory has commended itself as the sole and sufficient answer, to the exclusion of the others. There was certainly 'a kind of *gnosis*' in the air in the first Christian century,[4] but we have a long way to go before we reach the developed systems of the second-century sects. Quotations in the Nag Hammadi texts show that Col. was known to and used by the

---

[4] Cf. C. H. Dodd's discussion of 'the higher paganism', e.g. in *The Johannine Epistles* (1946), pp. xvi–xxi.

Gnostics later, but that does not make this letter Gnostic. As for a temptation to revert to Judaism, we have only to compare Paul's reaction in Galatians—and recall that evidence for the presence of Jews in Colossae itself appears to be very slight (but if the real target was some other city such as Laodicea, things might be very different).

All of the factors mentioned may have their significance. We need to take them all into account, and ask ourselves how far each one of them may have contributed to the background of thought and ideas in Colossae and its neighbourhood. We are not dealing simply with abstract ideas, but with thoughts in the minds of people. What did they bring with them from their earlier life, before their conversion? How far did these earlier ideas still shape their beliefs and guide their conduct? When we begin to ask these questions, then we begin to realize the magnitude of our problem. For that matter, despite all the differences between the first century and our own day, it is a sober and sometimes sombre fact that human nature remains very much the same. All too often in the course of history man's inhumanity to man has been only too apparent.

One thing is clear: that a major part of the problem as our author saw it was an inadequate conception of the significance of Christ. This leads him to develop the Christological 'hymn' of the first chapter, and to emphasize the completeness and sufficiency of Christ's death and resurrection as the means of salvation. In their conversion, his readers have entered into a new life, and are summoned to live accordingly, no longer bound to the things of this world only but looking forward in hope and expectation to the glory that is to come.

Mention of the 'hymn' recalls Moule's observation (58) that these 'stupendous words' apply to one who had been ignominiously put to death only some thirty years before. As he says, 'the identification of that historical person with the subject of this description is staggering, and fairly cries out for some explanation'. It is easy enough to say that the early Christians were more credulous than people of today; it is also superficial. It is admittedly no longer possible to accept all that is in the Scriptures as literal historical fact, but people do not face up to persecution and even martyrdom for a mere fiction. We have to take account of the reception their message was likely to meet with in a hostile world. They faced opprobrium and ridicule, and some of them were thrown to wild beasts in the arena, or were put to death by excruciating forms of torture. What made them do it? What gave them the courage to endure? Not only that, we have not merely the description of Paul's conversion in Acts, but also his own words in 1 Cor. 15.9: 'I am the least of the apostles, unfit to be called an apostle, because I persecuted the church of God.' What could have happened to change a persecutor into an outstanding missionary for the cause he once sought to destroy? There is an element of the legendary in the development of the portrayal of Jesus, as also in the story of Paul's journey to Damascus, but where legends grow up, as even in modern times, there is usually something to set them going.[5] There is more substance to our Christian faith than is often allowed for.

Another thing that is clear is our author's emphasis upon the qualities of the Christian life, the things that make for good relationships within the community, qualities that are as relevant today as when he wrote centuries ago. Much has changed in two thousand years, but human nature remains the same. People have to learn to accept their responsibilities, as well as enjoy their privileges.

[5] We need only to think of the use of the term 'legendary' by sports commentators to describe personalities of a bygone age: Babe Ruth in baseball, Muhammad Ali in boxing, and any number of famous players in association football, to say nothing of other fields. They achieved their 'legendary' status because of their prowess in their sports, and without that prowess they would not be remembered. A 'legend' of the cinema screen has recently objected to the use of the word to describe an actress half her age, who is certainly famous, but as yet scarcely a legend. What was it about Jesus of Nazareth that led to the growth of the legend that has endured for so many centuries?

PHILEMON

INTRODUCTION

Philemon is unique in the main corpus of the Pauline letters (excluding the Pastorals) in that it is addressed not to a community but to an individual. It is also unique among the accepted Pauline letters in that there is no evidence for it at the earliest stage in the development towards a New Testament canon, in the writings of the Apostolic Fathers.[1]

This in a sense places it on the same level as the seven disputed writings which were the last to be accepted into the canon (Hebrews (which is, however, cited in *1 Clem.*), James, 2 John, 3 John, 2 Peter, Jude, Revelation), but is easily accounted for: nobody had any occasion to mention it. There is no doctrinal content which might have led to its being quoted, no contribution to the development of Paul's theology, or of Christian theology in general.[2] Jülicher (125) notes that the Tübingen School denied its authenticity, but rejects their reasons, suggesting that nobody would have doubted but for the close association of the letter with Colossians and Ephesians, which were already suspect.[3] Kümmel (1966 ed., 246) writes that 'Only "tendency criticism" could doubt the authenticity of this epistle, which already stood in Marcion's canon' and the general consensus of scholars would regard it as genuine.[4]

The occasion for its writing, it would seem, can easily be deduced from the contents of the letter itself: Philemon, to whom it is addressed, was probably a convert to Christianity during Paul's ministry in Ephesus; at any rate, if we give credence to Acts, Ephesus is the nearest point to Colossae at which Paul stayed for any length of time on his missionary journeys, and Colossae is generally regarded as Philemon's place of residence, although this is not actually mentioned in the letter. He had a slave named Onesimus who absconded, probably stealing some of his master's property when he left (cf. v. 18). Later Onesimus came in contact with Paul, and was also converted to Christianity. This placed Paul in something of a dilemma: he would have preferred to keep Onesimus with him (13),

---

[1] Schenk ('Der Brief des Paulus an Philemon', 3440) sees the earliest evidence for use of Philem. in Col., and notes that there are links in Ignatius, *Eph.* 2–6 (n. 3).

[2] On the canonical history cf. Schenk, 3441 n. 4; on the history of the interpretation of Philem. cf. Barth, *Philemon*, 200ff. Swete remarks in his edition of Theodore of Mopsuestia's Commentary that it was 'vigorously attacked' in the fourth century, because the subject matter was considered trivial and unworthy of an inspired book—hence Theodore's 'lengthy disquisition on the utility of the Epistle' (ii. 261).

[3] Cf. Guthrie *NT Introduction*, 250 n. 2: 'It was its close connection with Colossians, which was deemed to belong to the second century, that forced the Tübingen school of criticism to reject Philemon' (cf. also Schenk 3442 n. 5). By way of contrast, Moffatt (164) quotes Renan: 'Paul seul a pu écrire ce petit chef-d'oeuvre'. 'Genuinely Pauline' elements of style and language are listed by Schenk, ibid. 3443–45.

[4] The phrase 'tendency criticism' goes back to F. C. Baur, but was 'taken up by his opponents and used with opprobrium' (Francis and Meeks (eds), *Conflict at Colossae*, 4).

but legally Onesimus was still Philemon's slave, and Paul was bound to send him back. This letter is Paul's way of dealing with the situation. He might have commanded Philemon, by virtue of his apostolic authority (Philemon after all owed him much, v. 19), but prefers to appeal to him (8f.), indeed to do nothing without Philemon's consent (14). It is clear from the content what he would wish Philemon to do—to receive Onesimus back 'no longer as a slave but more than a slave, a beloved brother' (15 NRSV)—but the decision must be made by Philemon.

Thus far all is clear enough, but this is not the only possible reconstruction of the situation, and there are numerous questions to which we have no real answer. We do not for example know the outcome of Paul's appeal, although the preservation of the letter would seem to suggest that it was successful. Again, the suggestion that what Paul really wishes is the emancipation of Onesimus goes beyond the evidence at our disposal; there might conceivably be a hint in v. 21 (εἰδὼς ὅτι καὶ ὑπὲρ ἃ λέγω ποιήσεις), but it is never explicitly stated. Further, Paul writes as 'a prisoner for Christ Jesus' (1, 9), which implies that this is a 'captivity' epistle, but there is nothing to indicate either the place of writing or the date. His use of the word πρεσβύτης in v. 9 has led some scholars to think that he was now advanced in years, which might favour the Roman imprisonment near the end of his life; others, however, regard the word as either a corruption of or a colloquial spelling of πρεσβευτής (see Commentary *ad loc.*), and translate 'ambassador'. In the latter case the question of the place of writing would be much more open. Of the alternatives, Caesarea is probably the least likely, but a case could be made out for Ephesus, which for one thing would be much nearer to Colossae. Runaway slaves notoriously made for Rome, but any large city might have served, and Marxsen (70) notes that the Temple of Artemis at Ephesus was one of the places of refuge for runaway slaves. At v. 22 Paul asks for accommodation to be prepared for him, and seems to anticipate a visit in the near future; that would be easily accomplished from Ephesus. In Rom. 15 however he writes as if his work in the east has been completed, and speaks of going to Spain. His plans could of course have been altered, but a visit to Colossae from Ephesus would certainly seem more likely than one from Rome. Against Ephesus, on the other hand, is the fact that we have no real evidence for any imprisonment in that city (on the Ephesus theory, cf. the Introduction to Colossians above).[5] According to Acts (19.29) Aristarchus (cf. Col. 4.10) was with Paul in Ephesus, and indeed was caught up in the Demetrius riot there; later (Acts 27.2) he shared the voyage to Italy, so

---

[5] Fitzmyer (10) notes that the Marcionite Prologue to Col. states: 'Apostolus iam ligatus scribit eis ab Epheso', and comments, 'So Ephesus as a place of Pauline imprisonment is not a modern concoction.' He prefers Ephesus as the place of writing (11), but adds, 'that locale remains problematic, being only inferred from the Pauline passages noted'.

presumably was with Paul in Rome. Timothy, named in the opening salutation both in Philemon and in Colossians, was sent from Ephesus to Macedonia before the riot (Acts 19.22), but is not mentioned in Acts after 20.4, which would suggest that he was not with Paul in Rome; the conclusion that he was is an inference based on the assumption that both Philemon and Colossians were written from that city (but arguments from silence are dangerous, and in this case there is an element of circularity as well). Here, of course, much depends on our estimate of the historical reliability of Acts, but this evidence, so far as it goes, would strengthen the case for Ephesus.

On the other hand, if the 'we' passages indicate Luke's own presence then he was in Rome, at least for a time (Acts 28.16); there is, however, no 'we' between 16.17 and 20.4, which would imply that he was not in Ephesus.[6] Demas is not mentioned in Acts, but Mark (cf. Col. 4.10) presents a problem: according to Acts 15.37–40, he was the cause of a 'sharp contention' between Paul and Barnabas because of his defection at Perga (Acts 13.13), and Barnabas and he now went off to Cyprus while Paul and Silas went to Syria and Cilicia. Colossians and Philemon would suggest that a reconciliation had taken place, but we do not know when or where. If Philemon was written from Ephesus, it would be sooner than might have been the case if the letter was written from Rome.[7] Altogether the issue is rather finely balanced. Schenke (*Einleitung*, 154ff.) opts for Rome, regarding the addressee's connection with Colossae as an erroneous deduction by the author of Colossians (cf. Schenk, 3481–83, who argues for Pergamum as the home of Philemon; but Fitzmyer (13) considers this 'a far-fetched view, which has little basis in the Letter to Philemon itself'); Lohse (188) thinks the letter was written from Ephesus in the mid-fifties.[8]

A further question relates to the persons named in the address: Apphia has frequently been regarded as Philemon's wife, and Archippus is often thought of as his son (cf. H. Cowan in *DAC* i. 86, 89), but this is not expressly stated in the text; Apphia might have been a sister, and Archippus a brother of Philemon. The ἀδελφή of v. 2, however, proves nothing, since this was a common term for a sister in the faith (cf. BAGD 15, *s.v.* ἀδελφή §3). Archippus is addressed in v. 2 as συνστρατιώτης, and in Col. 4.17 is charged to look to the διακονία which he has received. This would seem to imply some

---

[6] On the 'we' passages, see Koch, 'Kollektenbericht'. It can no longer be taken for granted that they indicate Luke's presence (cf. already Haenchen, *Acts*, 84ff.).

[7] 'Probably the mention of Mark and Luke (Col. 4.10, 14; Philemon) means that Paul was a prisoner in Rome' (Grant, *Historical Introduction*; 172, cf. 191). Moffatt (163) draws the same conclusion from the presence of Luke and Aristarchus, referring to Acts 28.16. Vielhauer (173) thinks Ephesus more probable, noting that Timothy is with Paul, as at the writing of Philippians; Paul's travel plans are, however, different, and so are the fellow-workers around him, so that we must assume a different time of writing. That would be quite possible if the imprisonment was prolonged. Koester (ii. 131, 134f.) assigns both Philippians and Philemon to an imprisonment in Ephesus.

[8] Cf. Dunn, 307–08, with further references.

degree of seniority, which in turn would mean, if he was Philemon's son, that Philemon himself would be fairly well on in years. Lightfoot (375) suggests that Archippus was a presbyter, or perhaps 'belonged to the order of "evangelists"', and locates his ministry at Laodicea; but this is inference, and once more not explicitly stated in the text.[9]

One point which calls for mention is the way in which inferences from Colossians are used to fill out the picture. Onesimus is described in Col. 4.9 as ἐξ ὑμῶν, which provides Lightfoot (370) with a basis for claiming that Philemon was a native, or at least an inhabitant, of Colossae ('This appears from the fact that his slave is mentioned as belonging to that place'). Again, the fact that in Col. 4.17 Archippus is mentioned immediately after the salutation to the Laodiceans leads Lightfoot (375) to the view that he was connected with Laodicea, even though his parents lived in Colossae. Now these deductions are not impossible, and the letter to Philemon is certainly closely connected with Colossians; but are the connections such that we may use the one to amplify and elucidate the other, or are they of a different kind? It used to be commonly assumed that Colossians is the prior letter, and that Philemon is, as it were, a kind of appendage, which creates all manner of problems when doubts are raised about the authenticity of Colossians (see Introduction to Colossians). Does this not cast doubt on the authenticity of Philemon also? And why should this one personal and private letter have been preserved at all?

These questions take on a wholly different complexion if we reverse the order: Philemon is the letter generally regarded as authentic, and Colossians the one about which doubts have been expressed. But if the letter to Philemon provided the impulse for some later disciple of Paul to construct Colossians, applying his master's teachings to meet a new and dangerous situation, and the two were put into circulation together, that would provide an explanation for the retention of this letter in the Pauline corpus (see Schenke, 154, 167f.). Should it be objected that this still does not explain why this letter to Philemon should have been preserved in the first place, there was at least one person involved who had every reason to have an interest in its preservation—the slave Onesimus. If Paul's wishes were fulfilled, he owed to this letter his restoration to the household of Philemon, possibly even, on one interpretation of v. 21 (see above), his liberation, and certainly the removal of that threat of punishment that must for ever have haunted any runaway slave. If the letter failed of its purpose, its preservation becomes all the more enigmatic.

John Knox in a number of publications has attempted to go further, and develop a very far-reaching hypothesis: the intended recipient is actually not Philemon but Archippus, who is the real

---

[9] In the subscription to some mss he is identified as deacon of the church in Colossae (see NA[27]), but these subscriptions clearly bear witness to a growing text. This one is probably an inference from Col. 4.17. The oldest read only πρὸς Φιλήμονα.

master of Onesimus.[10] Philemon is a prominent member of the community in Laodicea, where Tychicus and Onesimus are to make a halt on their journey from Ephesus to Colossae.[11] He is to be given the letter, and then use his influence with Archippus as an advocate for Onesimus. The letter to Philemon is in fact the 'letter from Laodicea' mentioned at Col. 4.16, and the ministry (διακονία) which Archippus is to fulfil according to Col. 4.17 is the service which Paul requests with regard to Onesimus, i.e. to send him back to assist Paul in the work of the gospel.[12] In a further development, Knox builds on a hypothesis first advanced by E. J. Goodspeed to explain the origin of Ephesians: Onesimus later became bishop of Ephesus (cf. Ignatius, *Eph.* 1.3; 2.1; 6.2), and was responsible for the collecting of the Pauline corpus, to which he prefaced the letter to the Ephesians.[13]

The theory is both ingenious and superficially attractive, but builds upon too many dubious assumptions. Certainly Onesimus, as already noted, had every reason for gratitude to Paul, for interest in the preservation of this letter, and perhaps even for the collection of the Pauline corpus (the original Goodspeed theory). But we have no cogent reason for assuming that the bishop mentioned by Ignatius was the Onesimus of this letter, and as Lohse (187) observes, 'The letter to Philemon itself offers no basis whatsoever for the position that Archippus, not Philemon, was the recipient of the letter'. Nor are there any real grounds for the assumption that this is the 'letter from Laodicea'. In a survey published in 1989 Harry Y. Gamble writes, 'this conception of the origin of the corpus has found little favor and has been rightly criticized for an excess of ingenuity, an inadequate comprehension of Ephesians, and incompatibility with

[10] See esp. his *Philemon Among the Letters of Paul* and 'Philemon and the Authenticity of Colossians', *JR* 18 (1938), 144–60. For criticism cf. Greeven, *TLZ* 79 (1954), 373–78; Kümmel, *Introduction* (1975 edn), 349; Guthrie, *NT Introduction*, 247–50; Moule, 14–18; O'Brien, *Thanksgivings*, 47 n. 4; Lohse, 186–87, who writes (187): 'Knox's hypothesis collapses when one enforces the methodological rule of first trying to understand a writing in the light of its own statements before drawing on other documents for purposes of comparison'. In a footnote he adds: 'This principle must be maintained in all circumstances, no matter how one answers the question whether Col. is Pauline or deutero-Pauline. If one opts for the latter position, all the presuppositions on which Knox builds his case crumble away'. See further Fitzmyer, 14–17, who writes (15), 'the main contentions of Knox's interpretation are quite tenuous'. Cf. also R. P. Martin's commentary, 139ff.; Schenk, 3443 n. 15, with further references.

[11] Tychicus is not mentioned in Philemon. The view that he was the bearer of the letter is an inference from Col. 4.7–8, which is reasonable enough if Col. is authentic and both letters were written at the same time, but out of the question if Col. is pseudonymous. He is mentioned in Acts 20.4 as Ἀσιανός, also in 2 Tim. 4.12 and Tit. 3.12, but only at Eph. 6.21 and Col. 4.7 is he described as ὁ ἀγαπητὸς ἀδελφός.

[12] Moffatt (157) already notes the view of Soltau, 'that the ministry which Archippus is to fulfil (4[17]) is to look after the interests of Onesimus!' (exclamation mark in original).

[13] E. J. Goodspeed, *The Meaning of Ephesians* (1933); and *The Key to Ephesians* (1956). This theory, without Knox's further development, was taken up by C. L. Mitton, *The Epistle to the Ephesians* (1951) and *The Formation of the Pauline Corpus of Letters* (1955). V.P. Furnish ('Pauline Studies', 327) observes that to many, 'at least in Britain and America', Goodspeed's hypothesis 'has seemed compelling', but that there are serious difficulties with this theory, and it 'simply does not do justice to the actual contents of Ephesians. It is much more than a potpourri of Pauline thoughts and sentences'.

the documentary evidence'.[14] In contrast he takes a much more favourable view of the theory sketched by H. M. Schenke,[15] who 'regards the redaction of various letters, the production of Pauline pseudepigrapha, and the gathering of Paul's literary legacy as the work of a "Pauline school" whose aim was to preserve and propagate Pauline Christianity in the historic mission-field of Paul after the apostle's death'.[16]

Another alternative has been advanced by Sara C. Winter ('Paul's letter to Philemon'), who differs from the traditional interpretation on four major points: (1) it is not a personal letter, but written to a congregation of which the person addressed is a member; (2) Onesimus did not run away, but was with Paul because he was sent 'by the individual addressed in the main body of the letter (probably Archippus)' on behalf of the church in Colossae; (3) Paul's request is that Onesimus be released from obligations in Colossae for work with Paul in Christian ministry; and (4) 'Paul makes clear that Onesimus is no longer to be considered a slave within the Christian community, and separately suggests Onesimus be manumitted'. The last point is at least possible: Onesimus is to be received no longer as a slave but as a beloved brother, indeed as Paul himself (16–17), and there have been adherents of the traditional view who have thought that Paul is asking for Onesimus' manumission; but this gives rise to a number of problems (see below). The first point is, however, difficult to accept, in that after the first three verses all the relevant verbs and pronouns, with three exceptions (ὑμῶν, ὑμῖν, v. 22; ὑμῶν, v. 25), are in the singular, not in the plural: after politely including Apphia, Archippus and the congregation in the opening salutation, Paul addresses the remainder of the letter to Philemon. The argument for the public nature of the letter, it is claimed (p. 2), 'is supported by the observation that Philemon contains an unusually large number of commercial and legal technical terms, characteristic of a public document rather than a private letter'.[17] These will require to be examined in the Commentary, but the fact that they may be technical terms in a given context does not mean that they are always to be so understood; in any case the purpose of the letter may have made a somewhat more formal language necessary. The assumption that the letter is actually addressed to Archippus is open to the criticism

[14] Gamble, 'The Canon of the NT', 206.
[15] Schenke, 'Das Weiterwirken des Paulus'.
[16] Gamble, ibid. 207

[17] εἰς Χριστόν (8), παρακαλῶ [τινὶ περί τινος] (9, 10), ἀνέπεμψα (12), κατέχειν (13), ὑπὲρ σοῦ (13), γνώμης (14), ἀπέχῃς (15), ἐχωρίσθη (15), κοινωνόν (17), ἠδίκησεν (18), ὀφείλει (18), ἐλλόγα (18), ἀποτίσω (19), προσοφείλεις (20). There are also 'a number of philosophical terms relating to ethical questions of a public nature again suggesting public discourse': παρρησίαν (8), τὸ ἀνῆκον (8), γνώμης (14), κατὰ ἀνάγκην (14), κατὰ ἑκούσιον (14). For all of these, see Winter's notes to justify the description as legal, commercial or philosophical. Her case is weakened by the fact that at least some of them are not *exclusively* legal or commercial or philosophical terms. G. P. Wiles, however, (*Paul's Intercessory Prayers*, 216) can speak of 'the half-playful use of commercial terms throughout the letter'.

directed against the theories of Knox, from whom this point is derived. Apart from this, the second and third points would seem to merit consideration, but against the second we must ask if in such circumstances a master would be likely to send a slave whom he knew to be ἄχρηστος (v. 11).[18] That Paul had found Onesimus useful, in whatever capacity, is evident from the letter; that he wished to have Onesimus back to assist him is perfectly plausible, even on a traditional interpretation.

Yet another reconstruction is put forward by Wolfgang Schenk (3439–95; see esp. 3460): Apphia, Archippus and others had become Christians, but Philemon was not merely not a Christian, he was an oppressor, and Archippus in particular had suffered at his hands. However, Philemon became a Christian, and placed his house at the disposal of the Christians for their assemblies (hence τῇ κατ᾽ οἰκόν σου ἐκκλησίᾳ, v. 2; had it been a family group we should expect ὑμῶν); it was this act of generosity that 'refreshed the hearts of the saints' (v. 7). Philemon then sent his still non-Christian slave Onesimus to Paul with news of a special benefaction, and finally Onesimus was converted to Christianity by Paul. If Col. is pseud-onymous, it is no longer possible to use material from it to fill out the picture in Philem., but the latter was probably written from imprisonment in Ephesus, or some town in Asia Minor (3481). Philemon's home was probably somewhere on the route to Philippi and Corinth, in Smyrna, Pergamum or Troas (3482). Slavery, Schenk claims, was not of such fundamental significance in the ancient world as is often thought, particularly in the east; Rome with its *latifundia* was another matter, and even there slavery was in decline in the imperial period. The only Hellenistic kingdom in which slave ownership played any large role was Pergamum (3483, citing Koester, *Einführung*, i.59–62; cf. n. 28 below). Pergamum is therefore more likely as the home of Philemon and the others, and Onesimus, than Colossae.[19] The letter is a request to have Onesimus seconded

[18] Dunn (303 n. 8) aptly quotes Barclay's comment ('Paul, Philemon and the Dilemma of Christian Slave-Ownership', 164) that a non-Christian regarded by his master as 'useless' 'is hardly the sort of person whom Philemon or his church would commission to serve or assist Paul'. For Winter (ibid. 4) the leap from ἄχρηστον to the conclusion that Onesimus stole from the household and ran away is unwarranted: Paul's use of the word is justified simply by the play on Onesimus' name. 'The η in ἄχρηστον and εὔχρηστον would have been pronounced as ι. Thus Paul is saying: although Onesimus was formerly "onesimus" (from ὀνίναμαι, hence "useful"), he was not truly useful (εὔχρηστος) because he was ἄχρηστος (that is α-Χριστός). Now, however, he is in Christ, in other words εὐ-Χριστός, that is εὔχρηστος, hence truly "onesimus"'. This is of course possible, but one wonders if Paul would have indulged in such word-play in a formal 'public' letter marked, as Winter claims, by considerable use of legal terminology. Lightfoot already wrote, 'Any such allusion (i.e. to χριστός), even if it should not involve an anachronism, is far too recondite to be probable here. The play on words is exhausted in the reference to Onesimus.'

[19] But cf. Dunn, 300 n. 2: 'Schenk 3482–83 surprisingly argues for Pergamum as the location of the addressees, chiefly on the grounds of correlation between v. 22 and 2 Cor 1:8 and 2:12.'

for the service of the gospel. Schenk suggests in a footnote that he might have had some connection with the famous library at Pergamum, and therefore be a highly qualified person and very useful for Paul's purposes. Against this reconstruction, v. 19 is often taken to indicate that Philemon owed his conversion to Paul himself; moreover, in v. 1 Philemon is described as Paul's συνεργός, which is difficult to explain if Paul only learned of Philemon's conversion from Onesimus. These verses, and the letter as a whole, suggest that Philemon was personally known to Paul, and that their relationship was close and friendly (cf. however, Schenk, 3460 n. 58: he admits some of these points but rejects others).

This is not the place to argue in detail the merits of these theories, which are based on acute analysis and contain numerous points of interest and relevance. They are cited here merely to indicate that the background to Philem. is not so clear as we might wish, and that the 'traditional' view which has held the field so long is not the only possibility to be considered. If, however, the purpose of the letter was simply to have Onesimus seconded for service with Paul, why was it preserved? There would seem to be grounds for adhering in broad outline to the traditional view, with due recognition of the difficulties which have prompted these alternative suggestions.

Further problems arise when we ask how and why Onesimus came to be with Paul in the first place: was it merely a chance encounter, and if so when and where? In Rome, according to Acts (28.30), Paul was apparently under some kind of house arrest, but able to receive all who came to him. If Onesimus fled to Rome, he could thus have sought out Paul; but we should then have to ask why he did so. If he was already a Christian when he came to Paul, he might conceivably have hoped to enlist Paul's help, knowing him to be a friend of his master Philemon; but this must remain conjecture. If he was not already a Christian, the mystery deepens: why then did he come to Paul? On this assumption it would seem more likely that their meeting was indeed a chance encounter, and in that case it might not have been in Rome, but in some other city. Obviously, much would depend on the rigour of Paul's imprisonment: was he perhaps confined to a separate cell and closely guarded? That would make contact difficult, and we must also consider whether a prisoner such as Paul and a captured runaway slave would be incarcerated together.[20] At Philippi, however, according to Acts (16.24), Paul

---

[20] For Winter (ibid. 2), the number of companions Paul mentions and his expectation of imminent release indicate 'a minor imprisonment or loose house arrest, probably in Ephesus'. Similarly Rapske ('The Prisoner Paul', 191) writes: 'Paul's imprisonment was, in the light of the evidence of Philemon and in keeping with his status as a Roman citizen, not harsh; probably a loose form of confinement (libera custodia). Onesimus, on the other hand, as a non-citizen and captured fugitivus, would have faced a far stricter form of custody'. This certainly fits with Paul's imprisonment in Rome as described in Acts 28.30f., but the imprisonment at Philippi (Acts 16.23–24) presents a different picture.

and Silas were confined to the innermost cell, but the other prisoners could hear the hymn they sang (v. 25). The point is that these are questions for which we have no firm answers.[21] Conjecture is legitimate enough, in the attempt to reconstruct the background to the letter, but it has to be remembered that it is no more than conjecture; in particular, it is highly dangerous to build hypothesis upon hypothesis, for the result can be no stronger than the original conjecture upon which the whole is based.

Winter's suggestion, mentioned above, would seem to call for some fuller explanation of the circumstances leading to the seconding of Onesimus for service with Paul: we have no real knowledge of the origins of the church at Colossae, or the contacts between Paul on the one hand and Philemon and the others mentioned on the other. How did it come about that Onesimus was seconded for service with Paul? On this hypothesis it would seem to be a necessary presupposition that Onesimus was already a Christian when he first came to Paul; but for this, once again, we have no real evidence. On the other side, it would be perfectly possible to construct a theory that Onesimus was converted to Christianity only after his meeting with Paul, and is now prepared to demonstrate the reality of his conversion and the sincerity of his repentance by returning to Colossae, with all the undoubted personal risk which that would involve; but all we know is that he is going back, with a letter from Paul to plead his cause.

As to the suggestion, often advanced, that Paul is really asking for the manumission of Onesimus, J. M. G. Barclay[22] has shown the practical implications of such an act on Philemon's part: what would be the reactions of the other slaves in Philemon's household? And in an age when one's social standing depended to some degree on the ownership of slaves, what effect would it have on Philemon's own status? For that matter, what of the financial implications? Barclay observes that while the letter 'is skilfully designed to constrain Philemon to accept Paul's request', it is 'not at all clear what exactly Paul's requests are' (172), and suggests that one reason for his vagueness is 'that *he did not know what to recommend*' (175; italics original). 'If we think about the situation in practical terms we will see that there were immense difficulties in *either* of the two main options open to Philemon—to retain Onesimus as a slave or to manumit him—and it was, perhaps, his awareness of these problems which prevented Paul from being able to give a clear recommendation to Philemon' (175).

It was suggested above that if Onesimus was already a Christian when he came to Paul, he might conceivably have hoped to enlist Paul's help, knowing him to be a friend of his master Philemon; but it

---

[21] Cf. further Dunn's discussion (301–07).

[22] Barclay, 'Paul, Philemon and the Dilemma of Christian Slave-Ownership'; on the problems relating to the view that Paul is requesting the manumission of Onesimus, see esp. 176–77.

was added that this must remain conjecture. Since that was written, another recent article has put a rather different complexion on the matter: after reviewing the various possibilities which have been suggested, and finding them unsatisfactory, B. M. Rapske[23] takes up and develops a suggestion first put forward by Peter Lampe[24]: a slave who took refuge with a friend of his master to seek his intercession was not regarded as a runaway, a *fugitivus*, if it was his intention to be reconciled with his master. Thus, far from being a *fugitivus*, Onesimus 'is in fact purposefully running to a friend of the master in the hope that, through the friend's intervention, he might be happily restored to his master' (195f.). Rapske cites two cases outside the New Testament, and on the basis of these makes two observations: first, 'that the prospect of a happy return is increased if a slave goes to an *amicus* who is well known to the master' (198), and second, 'that the prospect of a happy return is increased if the slave ... goes to an *amicus* who has *greater power and authority and a higher social rank than his offended master*' (200, italics original). As it happens, one of the examples quoted involves the emperor Augustus, but the *amicus* need not necessarily have been of such exalted status, provided that he was in a position to influence the master. Rapske writes (202): 'That Onesimus is correct in presuming Paul to be fully capable not only of bringing pressure to bear in his case but also of commanding Philemon and expecting Philemon's obedience is confirmed by hints that the apostle drops at Phlm 14, 8 and 20f. respectively. The evidence available to Onesimus is clear and encouraging: Paul, as an *amicus domini*, has far more than Philemon's ear.' There is one problem here which calls for further investigation: the terms quoted, *fugitivus* and *amicus*, are in Latin, and thus presuppose Roman law. How far can it be assumed that this held in other areas, such as Asia Minor? It may have been so, but this cannot be simply taken for granted.

What can be affirmed with some degree of confidence is that Paul is a prisoner, perhaps in Rome but probably in Ephesus (in view of his hope to visit Philemon in the near future). Onesimus, having got himself into trouble, somehow finds his way to Paul and enlists his help. From his own experience Paul has found Onesimus useful, and would like to keep him at his side, but that would be impossible without Philemon's knowledge and consent. Indeed, if Onesimus was a *fugitivus*, that would entail serious consequences for both if he did not return to Philemon. This letter is Paul's way of dealing with a somewhat delicate situation. The details, of course, would be well enough known to both Paul and Philemon, so that much could be

---

[23] Rapske, 'The Prisoner Paul'. Bartchy ('Philemon', 307f.) holds that Onesimus was not a *fugitivus*. This view is accepted by Dunn (304ff.), who quotes 'the much cited parallel of Pliny's letter to Sabinianus' (*Ep.* ix.21) on behalf of one of the latter's freedmen, adding that another letter (ix.24), also to Sabinianus, shows that the plea was successful. Fitzmyer (20–23) also accepts this view.

[24] Lampe, 'Keine "Sklavenflucht" des Onesimus'.

left unsaid. Our problem is that we do not know enough of these details to enable us to reach a completely satisfactory reconstruction of the background of the letter and the situation with which Paul is trying to deal.[25]

On the surface, the letter to Philemon must appear very simple and straightforward, presenting no real problems; the reconstruction outlined above at the beginning of this discussion would seem to cover everything. However, when we begin to ask questions and try to find the answers the limitations of our knowledge soon become apparent. There are in fact many questions for which we have no real answers, because the necessary evidence is not at our disposal. In the circumstances we are often reduced to speculation and conjecture, and must weigh the possible alternatives against one another to select the most plausible. Speculation in itself is legitimate enough, and without some measure of conjecture it would be difficult in the extreme to fill the gaps in our knowledge. As already noted, however, we must constantly bear in mind what is conjecture, and what is solid fact for which we have evidence. In particular we must beware of the danger of piling conjecture upon conjecture to build an elaborate construction which is in fact devoid of any real foundation.

One aspect of the letter which has sometimes been disturbing to modern readers is Paul's apparently complaisant acceptance of slavery as an institution: in an age which has seen much campaigning for 'civil rights', for proper consideration of the needs and interests of ethnic and other minorities, for the elimination of any form of discrimination on grounds of race or class, sex, creed or colour, it may seem almost self-evident that the Church ought from the beginning to have spoken out with all the emphasis at its command against so great a social evil.[26] Such an attitude, however, completely fails to appreciate the situation in which Paul found himself, and in which the early Church had to live and work, and there are other factors which require to be taken into account. For one thing, our

[25] For Fitzmyer (24), 'The Epistle to the Colossians seems to show that Paul's Letter to Philemon achieved its purpose, because it reveals that Philemon did the "more" at which Paul hinted: he set Onesimus free to become a coworker of Paul.'

[26] In point of fact, this is not merely a modern concern of recent years, since the question is discussed in the older commentaries. Cf. for example Lightfoot, 385–95; Oesterley, *EGT* iv. 207–09; Scott 99–100; *DAC* ii. 213; 509–12. On slavery in the ancient Near East cf. Dandamayev, *ABD* vi. 58–65, and for the New Testament Bartchy, ibid. 65–73; also Gnilka, 54–81 (further references in Dunn, 302 nn. 5–7). The three points made by Scott put the whole matter in a different perspective: early Christians could not have lodged any protest without the danger of incitement to riot and the consequent violence. Slave revolts such as that of Spartacus were ruthlessly suppressed. In addition, those who hold that Paul is really urging the manumission of Onesimus should consider the effect of such an action on the other slaves of Philemon's household: if the runaway was given his freedom, others might be tempted to follow his example; at the very least there would be jealousy and ill-will. Even Paul's suggestion that Onesimus be received back 'as a beloved brother' was in the circumstances of the time a very considerable request to make. On the whole question see Barclay, 'Paul, Philemon and the Dilemma of Christian Slave-Ownership'.

modern attitude is inevitably coloured by recollection of the slave trade, the transportation of black slaves from Africa to America to labour in the plantations, which was by common consent an evil and an injustice; but slavery in the ancient world is not entirely comparable. On the view usually taken (*pace* Koester and Schenk—see n. 28 below), slavery was in fact an integral part of the social structure of the ancient world, and without it the Roman Empire would have been reduced to chaos.[27] It was slaves who carried out most of the menial tasks, the tilling of the land, domestic service, secretarial and other duties, and to replace them by paid labour would have had far-reaching economic effects. Moreover the life of a slave was not necessarily one of hardship.[28] Admittedly he was deprived of freedom, had no rights of citizenship, no part in the control of affairs of state or city; but he could earn, and save his

[27] 'In the first half of the first century C.E., slavery was an essential and for all practical purposes unchallenged element of the Roman Empire's culture and economy' (Barth, *Philemon*, 2; see his extended discussion of the social background, 1–102).

[28] Oesterley, however, (ibid. 209), after noting that the Hebrew laws regarding slavery were 'exceedingly humane', observes that the Roman system was utterly different: 'The Roman system was, practically, the antithesis of the Jewish'. Moule (34ff.) cites a notice relating to two slaves who had run away (*Pap. Par.* 10, from Wilcken, *Urkunden der Ptolemäerzeit*, i. 556ff. (no. 1211)): it gives a description of each, and of property thought to be in his possession, and intimates the rewards offered for information leading to their recovery. These rewards have subsequently been increased by a second hand: the lowest rate is for information that the slave is in asylum at a temple, the next for someone bringing him back, the highest for information that the slave is with some person of means, who was liable to penalty for harbouring a runaway. Dodd (*Abingdon Commentary*, 1292) cites an Oxyrhynchus papyrus (vol. xiv (1920), no. 1643, dated AD 298) which includes the words: 'When you have found him you shall place him in custody, with authority to shut him up and whip him, and to lay a complaint before the proper authorities against any persons who have harboured him, with a demand for satisfaction'.

According to Koester, slavery played only a subordinate role in the Seleucid Empire and in Egypt. He presents a somewhat different picture from that usually put forward: 'That the ancient economy was able to function only because of the institution of slavery is nonsense' (i. 61; cf. the whole discussion, 59–62). He speaks of a marked decrease in the numbers of slaves in the imperial period: there were few wars of conquest, and the supply of new slaves dropped noticeably, while manumissions also led to a marked decrease in numbers (59). Rome was much more dependent on slaves (than other areas) during the second and first centuries BC. Public opinion vacillated between rejection and indifference (62). As to the attitude of the new religions, including Christianity, 'It would have been too much to expect these religions to have advocated the abolition of slavery as an institution (although some of the church fathers indeed demanded just that) ... among the Christians, the manumission of a slave was considered to be a good work' (62). Barth (*Philemon*, 13) notes three factors relevant to the decrease in slave numbers after 'about 50 BCE': the diminished supply of slaves under the imperial Pax Romana; enlightened criticism of cruel slave treatment; and the fact that slave labour became more expensive than the work of free persons. Schenk (3470 n. 70) argues that the decisive difference between freemen and slaves was political, in that the slave had no part in the running of the community, which was reserved to the free citizens; he also notes the variety of occupations undertaken by slaves, who might even themselves be slave-owners.

earnings towards the eventual purchase of his freedom, and he had food and drink and shelter. In some respects indeed he might be better off than the poorer classes in the free population.

Another fault of this modern attitude is a failure to appreciate the facts of history. The New Testament nowhere condemns slavery,[29] and in the nature of the case it is not likely that any condemnation would have had much effect;[30] but the Old Testament legislation already contains some mitigation of the evils of slavery (cf. Exod. 21.1–11; Lev. 25.39–55; Deut. 15.12–18),[31] and the New Testament sets out principles which were eventually to lead to the abolition of the institution: in Christ, says Paul, there is 'neither Jew nor Greek, bond nor free' (Gal. 3.28; cf. 1 Cor. 12.13; Col. 3.11), and both Ephesians (6.5–9) and Colossians (3.22–4.1), as well as Philemon itself, seek to inculcate a new attitude among both slaves and masters, a spirit of Christian charity, since both are servants of the same Lord. This spirit was to spread with the growth of the Church, and led in time to mitigation of slavery in the later Roman Empire and to its eventual disappearance in the western world by the time of the Renaissance. The slave trade to the Americas was a new development under wholly different circumstances, and cannot in any way be condoned: apart from captives taken in time of war, there was no wholesale transportation of slaves in the ancient world, and certainly not across hundreds of miles of ocean to a lifelong servitude, for themselves and for their descendants. We should not too readily transpose our legitimate condemnation of the trade to the Americas back into the

[29] In 1 Tim. 1.10 ἀνδραποδισταί (a hapax legomenon in the NT) appear in a list of evildoers (see Harrill, 'The Vice of Slave-Dealers'). But 'Rather than being a text proving that early Christians condemned slavery, the passage actually reinforces cultural stereotypes present in the ideology of ancient slavery' (120).

[30] Guthrie (252 n. 2) cites H. M. Carson (Tyndale Commentary (1980), 21–24) as firmly rejecting 'any suggestion that the early Christians refrained from attacking this evil system through motives of expediency. Rather by inculcating a sense of responsibility on the part of masters and a sense of self-respect on the part of slaves, Christianity removed the main moral evils of the system'. Cf. Vielhauer (172f.), who like Koester (ii. 135) thinks the letter written to secure the liberation of Onesimus; such a request is not expressly mentioned, 'but it stands clearly enough between the lines'. Koester indeed takes vv. 18f. as an undertaking to meet any costs involved. See, however, Barclay 'Paul, Philemon and the Dilemma of Christian Slave-Ownership', and note his conclusion: Paul 'neither attacked slavery nor explicitly defended it. The most that can be said ... is that he struggled with it, recognising more or less consciously the tension between the realities of slavery and the demands of brotherhood' (186). A footnote (185 n. 93) draws attention to the role of Christianity in sanctioning slavery in the West Indies and the Americas and 'the cogent biblical arguments that could be mounted *against* abolition' (cf. S. A. Marini in Metzger and Coogan, *Oxford Companion to the Bible*, 701–02). John Newton, author of some familiar Christian hymns, was at one stage in his career a slave-runner.

[31] See Barth, *Philemon*, 53–83 for discussion of OT and later Jewish traditions.

ancient world, where the factors which forced people into slavery could have been entirely different.[32]

This question has some relevance for some other problems of modern times. There have been cases in quite recent history in which it has been said that the Church, or church people, ought to speak out in the name of justice and righteousness against some abuse or other; but when they do, they are often accused of meddling in politics, and bidden to confine themselves to their proper task of preparing souls for the world to come. It is as if the Christian faith had nothing to do with the practicalities of everyday living! As it is, there are some areas in which the Church and church people simply do not have the influence or the power to effect any direct change, to bring about any immediate amelioration of the current situation. In that respect we are in much the same situation as Paul was centuries ago. It may be that the real task of the Church, and Christians generally, is to seek to spread more widely in our own day that same spirit of Christian charity which was eventually to bring about the abolition of slavery. What matters here is not the promulgation of doctrinaire statements as to what 'society' (or some other body, but usually somebody other than the speaker!) ought to be doing; it is what we ourselves are prepared to do, in obedience to Christ our Lord and Master, in our dealings with other people. There can be no evasion of responsibility.

On slavery in the ancient world see further Fitzmyer, 25–33, with bibliography at 45–49; M. I. Finley, *Ancient Slavery and Modern Ideology* (1980); J. A. Harrill, *The Manumission of Slaves in Early Christianity* (1995); J. A. Glancy, 'Obstacles to Slaves' Participation in the Corinthian Church', *JBL* 117 (1998), 481–501. For the trade to the Americas cf. Thomas, *The Slave Trade: The History of the Atlantic Slave Trade 1440–1870* (1997).

[32] 'Slavery arises from two main causes, viz. *Want* and *War*. Privation and famine compel a man, a family, or a clan to accept terms of service and maintenance from others to which under normal circumstances they would never submit. War, a yet more potent cause, brings in its train foreign captives who are forced to enter a lot of subjection to the will of their conquerors' (O. C. Whitehouse, in *HDB* iv. 461; see the whole article, 461–69, also Barth's discussion of 'Ways into Slavery', *Philemon*, 5–8). In some areas, children could be sold into slavery in times of economic hardship, and redeemed when the family circumstances improved (see A. Passoni Dell'Acqua, 'Prassi greca e costume egiziano nel negozio giuridico di una donna ebrea di Alessandria', *Aegyptus* 70 (1990), 123–72). Cf. also J. S. Clemens in *DAC* ii. 509–12; I. Benzinger in *EncBib* (cols 4653–58) concentrates entirely on the OT and ignores the NT completely, contrasting Christianity unfavourably with Israel and Islam (col. 4658); further references in Barclay's article (e.g. 162 n. 6).

COMMENTARY

I
SALUTATION
(1–3)

[1]Paul, a prisoner of Christ Jesus, and Timothy our brother, to Philemon our beloved fellow-worker [2]and Apphia our sister and Archippus our fellow-soldier and the church that is in your house; [3]grace to you and peace from God our Father and the Lord Jesus Christ.

The salutation follows the pattern usual in Paul's letters, ending with the characteristic expansion of the greeting into χάρις ὑμῖν καὶ εἰρήνη ἀπὸ θεοῦ πατρὸς ἡμῶν καὶ κυρίου Ἰησοῦ Χριστοῦ (cf. Rom. 1.7; 1 Cor. 1.3; 2 Cor. 1.2; Gal. 1.3; Phil. 1.2; in Col. 1.2 the last four words are missing, although they are supplied by certain mss, probably through assimilation to normal Pauline usage). Timothy is associated with Paul in this letter, as in 2 Cor. 1.1; Col. 1.1, where as here he is described as ὁ ἀδελφός (cf. Sosthenes in 1 Cor. 1.1); at Phil. 1.1 he and Paul are δοῦλοι Χριστοῦ Ἰησοῦ, while in 1 and 2 Thess. Silvanus and Timothy are mentioned without any description. According to Acts (19.22) Timothy was sent from Ephesus to Macedonia shortly before the riot instigated by Demetrius the silversmith, and must therefore have been with Paul at the beginning of his sojourn there. He is not further mentioned after Acts 20.4, which leaves his presence during Paul's imprisonment in Rome at least an open question.

Dodd (1293) remarks, 'It is a little surprising to find Timothy's name at the head of a purely private letter; no doubt there were good reasons of which we can know nothing.' The point might perhaps be taken to add support to Winter's theory, outlined above, that this was not a purely private letter but written to a congregation; but this would depend on our assessment of the theory as a whole. There are, however, other possibilities: for Lightfoot, Timothy 'could hardly have failed to make the acquaintance of Philemon' during Paul's sojourn in Ephesus, which might mean that he is mentioned simply out of friendship. G. C. Martin (12f.) thinks Timothy had a share in the founding of the church in Colossae, and retained 'a deep personal interest' in its progress; but this is no more than pious conjecture. On the other hand, the reference to Timothy may indicate that this is more than a 'purely private' letter: it is a formal request on behalf of Onesimus, and Timothy would then be mentioned as adding support, just as Apphia, Archippus and the household of Philemon are mentioned as recipients because they too are in some respects involved.[1] But the letter is to Philemon, not to a congregation: as noted in the Introduction above (p. 322), after v. 3 all but three of the relevant verbs and pronouns are in the singular, not in the plural (the exceptions can readily be explained: see below). Moreover, if it is a formal request (which might account for the 'legal' terminology listed by Winter), it is still a cordial and friendly letter, indicating a close and amicable relationship between the correspondents.[2] ἀδελφός (see on Col. 1.2) is not a title of office, but refers simply to membership in the Christian community (cf. BAGD 16a; TWNT i. 145f.); in v. 7 and again in v. 20 Philemon is addressed as ἀδελφέ, and at v. 16 he is urged to receive Onesimus no longer as a slave but as a brother in Christ; we may compare Paul's frequent use of ἀδελφοί in addressing his readers (e.g. Rom. 1.13; 7.1; 1 Cor. 1.10; 2.1; Gal. 1.11; Phil. 1.12; von Soden in TWNT ibid. notes that Paul uses the word in this sense some 130 times. It is the more remarkable that, as Schweizer observes, this form of address does not occur at all in Colossians.).

An unusual feature here is that Paul does not describe himself, as in other letters, as ἀπόστολος or δοῦλος (1 and 2 Thess. have no such title at all); he is δέσμιος Χριστοῦ Ἰησοῦ, 'a prisoner of Christ Jesus'.[3] The phrase appears again in v. 9, but the only other occurrence in the NT is at Eph. 3.1, ἐγὼ Παῦλος ὁ δέσμιος τοῦ Χριστοῦ Ἰησοῦ; cf. however Eph. 4.1; 2 Tim. 1.8 (it appears also in the apocryphal 3 Cor.). References to Paul's 'bonds' are frequent in Phil. (1.7, 13, 14, 17; cf. Col. 4.18), but not in the other major letters; nor does δέσμιος appear there. This is not quite the same as 'a prisoner for Christ Jesus' (so RSV), although that is certainly also true: his imprisonment is for the sake of the gospel. The point, however, is that he is Christ's prisoner, carried along in Christ's triumphal parade (cf. 2 Cor. 2.14); his sufferings are for the gospel, and this gives him a certain moral authority, to which he appeals again in v. 9.

[1] Hübner (28) argues from the list of addressees that it is not a private letter, but addressed to a community, and therefore has comething of an official character. Whether the ἐκκλησία, as here, is only a small house church, or a somewhat larger community as in Corinth, it is always a matter of responsible action within this ἐκκλησία and before this ἐκκλησία, and so ultimately of action coram Deo. This would seem a more satisfactory explanation than that proposed by Winter (see Introduction, p. 322f. above). For Fitzmyer (81), 'The inclusion of Apphia, Archippus, and the house-church means that this is hardly a private letter.' Paul is concerned that the whole community be involved.

[2] Cf. Schubert, Form and Function, 172f.: the introductory thanksgiving formula 'was proper only on a noticeably high level of function, intimacy and form', and was 'used with propriety only where genuine feeling (personal as well as religious) is involved'. This would suggest that Philem. is certainly a very personal letter, whatever else it may be. The salutation is addressed to three people and 'the church in your house', but the main body of the letter is directed to Philemon himself. Cf. Schenk (3440 n. 1) on Deissmann's 'anachronistic' distinction between personal and literary (or official) letters. On the form of Paul's letters cf. also Petersen, Rediscovering Paul, 83 n. 66, 85 n. 74.

[3] The few mss which have these terms (ἀπόστολος, D*; δοῦλος, 323 945 pc) only illustrate the tendency of scribes to insert a familiar or expected word. The ἀπόστολος δέσμιος of 629 is an obvious conflation.

This authority, however, is not linked with apostleship (cf. Best, 'Paul's Apostolic Authority'; Schenk 3464, n. 62). Paul's avoidance of the apostolic title here is in keeping with the whole tone of the letter: as he hints (8f., 19, 21 (ὑπακοή)), Paul might have commanded Philemon to do what he wished him to do, but throughout he tactfully avoids any assertion of authority. The decision must rest with Philemon.

Philemon[4] is described as ἀγαπητός, 'dear, beloved', a term indicating a close relationship which is often used by Paul (e.g. Rom. 16.5ff. of Epaenetus and others; 1 Cor. 10.14; 15.58 in addressing his readers; in Col. 1.7 it is used of Epaphras, in 4.7 of Tychicus, in 4.9 of Onesimus; see BAGD 6). In such cases the word does not carry the special significance which it has in the Gospels (Mark 1.11, 9.7 and parallels, and perhaps 12.6), where it is used of an only son (cf. the use in LXX of Abraham's only son (Gen. 22.2, 12, 16) and Jephthah's only daughter (Jud. 11.34); cf. Robinson, *Ephesians*, 229ff.). Strictly, ἀγαπητός is here used with the article, as a substantive, and co-ordinated with συνεργός by the καί; thus NRSV renders it 'our dear friend and co-worker' (cf. NEB). The RSV rendering, followed above, is less paraphrastic and has the advantage of preserving the literal meaning of the word. συνεργός (BAGD 787b) is often used by Paul with reference to those who helped in the work of spreading the gospel, e.g. Rom. 16.3, 9, 21; Phil. 2.25; it is used again in v. 24 below of Mark, Aristarchus, Demas and Luke.[5] Philemon is thus not only a friend but a fellow-labourer, and must have had some share in bringing the gospel to his own region, even if Epaphras was chiefly responsible.[6] This would seem to tell against Schenk's suggestion (see above, pp. 323–24) that he was a comparatively recent convert.

As noted in the Introduction above, Apphia is frequently thought to be Philemon's wife, and Archippus his son, but while it is very natural to think of a family this is not expressly stated in the text.[7]

---

[4] The name was 'relatively common in Phrygia' (Fitzmyer, 86). It was the name of a famous character in Greek mythology, in the tale of Philemon and Baucis, who entertained the gods Zeus and Hermes unawares (see Ovid, *Met.* viii.611–724).

[5] Dunn (311) speaks of 'that select and important band whom Paul designates as "fellow workers"' (with further references).

[6] Cf. Dunn's description (300f.): probably a successful businessman, converted through Paul's ministry (not necessarily directly) and close to Paul, one who owned several slaves and was probably a leader in the church which met in his house.

[7] As Lohse (190 n. 18) observes, following Lightfoot, the opinion that Archippus was the son of Philemon and Apphia was already held by Theodore of Mopsuestia; but Lightfoot (374 n. 7) adds that Chrysostom and Theodoret held other views. 'Speculation about Archippus' position in Philemon's household is idle' (Dibelius and Greeven, quoted by Lohse, ibid.). The same should perhaps be said of Lightfoot's comments regarding 'the apprehensions which the Apostle seems to have entertained respecting Archippus' and his view that 'they were suggested by his youth and inexperience' (376); this is of course possible, but we have no real evidence on which to build. Oesterley (211) suggests that Archippus may have occupied a more important position than Philemon (cf. Col. 4.17), which would be most unlikely if the latter was his father.

Apphia could, for example, have been Philemon's sister, and Archippus a younger brother; and there might also be other possibilities. Here, however, we should not rely on the τῇ ἀδελφῇ which follows Apphia's name, for this, like the masculine ἀδελφός, was a term in common use to describe membership in the Christian community (the Byzantine text reads ἀγαπητῇ, probably by assimilation to the term used of Philemon; some mss combine the two readings to form ἀδελφῇ τῇ ἀγαπητῇ, cf. v. 16). Moreover, had Apphia actually been Philemon's sister, Paul could have removed any ambiguity by writing τῇ ἀδελφῇ σου. On the whole, in view of the following reference to 'the church which is in thy house' (this is a case where the archaic form of the second person singular could have its advantages, although normal modern usage has been followed in the translation above; the pronoun in the greeting formula is the plural ὑμῖν), it is probably better to think of a family group. The lady of the house would of course be directly involved where household slaves were concerned. Lightfoot notes (372ff.) that the name occurs frequently on Phrygian inscriptions, 'and is doubtless of native origin'. Lohse (190 n. 12) refers to a tomb inscription commemorating an Apphia, wife of Hermas, from Colossae.

συστρατιώτης The only other occurrence of this word in the NT is at Phil. 2.25, of Epaphroditus (τὸν ἀδελφὸν καὶ συνεργὸν καὶ συστρατιώτην μου). As this combination of words indicates, it is a term of honour applied to certain of Paul's co-workers (BAGD 795b). If we thought simply in terms of a family group, it might be possible to conceive of an elderly Paul (πρεσβύτης, v. 9) striking up a friendship with the small son of the house and playfully calling him his 'fellow-soldier'; but this would owe more to imagination than to anything in the text, and is ruled out by the other occurrence of the term. Exception is sometimes taken to the use of military terminology, for example in Christian hymns, as inappropriate for people who should be concerned for peace; but as Ephesians reminds us, our warfare is 'not against enemies of blood and flesh, but against the rulers, against the authorities, against the cosmic powers of this present darkness, against the spiritual forces of evil in the heavenly places' (6.12 NRSV). The Christian has 'a constant war to wage with sin'.[8]

τῇ κατ' οἶκόν σου ἐκκλησίᾳ For the phrase cf. Rom. 16.5; 1 Cor. 16.19 (both with reference to Aquila and Priscilla, and therefore with the plural); Col. 4.15 (Nympha or Nymphas). The early Christian communities did not have separate buildings for worship, but met in private houses (cf. Acts 12.12), a situation still reflected in some of the apocryphal acts of apostles (e.g. in *Act. And.* 6, 13 etc. the brethren meet in the house of Maximilla, wife of the governor Aegeates, but without his knowledge; in *Act. Paul. Thec.* 7, Paul preaches in the house of Onesiphorus). The nucleus of these

---

[8] Cf. C. E. Arnold, *3 Crucial Questions about Spiritual Warfare* (1997). Dunn (312) remarks, 'Paul does not use military metaphors for Christian service as much as is sometimes assumed.'

communities would be formed by the household, the family and slaves, of some prominent convert; cf. Acts 16.15 (Lydia); 18.8 (Crispus); at 1 Cor. 1.16 Paul speaks of having baptized 'the household of Stephanas'. On the 'house churches' cf. Gnilka, *Philemonbrief*, 17–33; Stuhlmacher, 70–75; Barth, 260–64; further references, collected by A. D. Jacobson, in R. A. Piper (ed.), *The Gospel behind the Gospels* (1995), 380 n. 57.

Barclay (171) sees the mention of 'the church which is in your house' as part of the pressure applied by Paul 'in all sorts of subtle and significant ways'—Philemon will feel himself answerable not only to the distant Paul but also to the Christians who come regularly to his house. It is, however, open to question whether 'pressure' is quite the appropriate term: as already noted above, Paul deliberately avoids any exercise of apostolic authority, although he hints that he could command obedience. There are times when persuasion is a better course than open imposition of authority, and this was certainly one of them. Paul is using his influence in favour of Onesimus; whether we should speak of his exerting pressure is to say the least more doubtful.[9] Verse 14 expressly says that Paul wishes Philemon to act of his own free will, not under compulsion.

II
THANKSGIVING PERIOD
(4–7)

It is advisable to have the Greek text of this passage available in full for reference, since the passage, as will appear, presents certain problems. The translation in this case must follow the discussion, as it will depend upon the elucidation of these problems.

[4]Εὐχαριστῶ τῷ θεῷ μου πάντοτε μνείαν σου ποιούμενος ἐπὶ τῶν προσευχῶν μου, [5]ἀκούων σου τὴν ἀγάπην καὶ τὴν πίστιν ἣν ἔχεις πρὸς τὸν κύριον Ἰησοῦν καὶ εἰς πάντας τοὺς ἁγίους, [6]ὅπως ἡ κοινωνία τῆς πίστεώς σου ἐνεργὴς γένηται ἐν ἐπιγνώσει παντὸς ἀγαθοῦ τοῦ ἐν ἡμῖν εἰς Χριστόν. [7]χαρὰν γὰρ πολλὴν ἔσχον καὶ παράκλησιν ἐπὶ τῇ ἀγάπῃ σου, ὅτι τὰ σπλάγχνα τῶν ἁγίων ἀναπέπαυται διὰ σοῦ, ἀδελφέ.

---

[9] Hartman ('On Reading Others' Letters', 144) doubts that Paul widens the address in order to put pressure on Philemon; 'the apostle's personal support of Onesimus would be sufficient'. But is this support given by Paul as Paul, or as apostle? The title does not occur in Philem. On the question of Paul's 'apostolic authority' cf. Best, 'Paul's Apostolic Authority'. Petersen (*Rediscovering Paul*, 266ff.) has no doubts about Paul's putting pressure on Philemon, and speaks of 'threats of administrative consequences should Philemon choose to be disobedient' (267). Philemon, he writes (269), 'is on a very public spot'.

For the structure, cf. Schenk, 3461, although this scheme may require some modification in point of detail.[1] Other thanksgivings are more elaborate, or present variations,[2] but this one 'shows the essentially identical structural skeleton'—a principal clause followed by two participial constructions retaining the subject of the finite verb, then a relative clause dependent on one of the objects of ἀκούων (Schubert, *Form and Function*, 12; for the form εὐχαριστῶ ... ἀκούων σου τὴν ἀγάπην he compares PGiessen 21, λίαν ἐχάρην ... ἀκούσασα, ibid. 177). It can therefore serve as a model of the typical Pauline thanksgiving period.

Wendland (*Kultur*, 413f.) already noted affinities with fixed forms of the ancient letter (e.g. the εὐχαριστῶ and particularly the 'favourite periphrasis' μνείαν ποιούμενος (414 n. 2)). For μνείαν ποιουυμέος cf. Rom. 1.9; Eph. 1.16; 1 Thess. 1.2 (see Schubert, table II, pp. 54–55); it occurs already in PLond. 42 (168 BC; Schubert, 160ff.). G. Milligan (*Thessalonians* (1908), 5) cites a papyrus from the second century AD and remarks that the phrase occurs frequently in inscriptions. It could mean 'remember' (so e.g. Fitzmyer, 93), but Moule (141) thinks (following Lightfoot) that the balance of probability favours 'mention' (so also Milligan, ibid.): it is a remembrance through mention in intercessory prayer.

As with Colossians, there is a question as to where the thanksgiving period ends. Most commentators treat it as extending from v. 4 to v. 7, but this is not strictly correct: the thanksgiving proper extends from v. 4 to v. 6, and v. 7 is 'a smooth and effective transition from the specific style and thought of the thanksgiving to the quite different style and thought of the main section of the letter' (Schubert, 5).[3] Verse 4 as it stands is ambiguous, since the πάντοτε could be taken either with εὐχαριστῶ τῷ θεῷ μου or with the words which follow (Wendland, 413f. in fact cites the phrase as πάντοτε μνείαν σου ποιούμενος); but usage elsewhere (cf. on Col. 1.3) suggests that it goes with the preceding words: Paul constantly gives thanks when he remembers Philemon in his prayers. Once the construction of the πάντοτε is recognized, this verse presents no real problems, but there is a difficulty of another kind: the phrase μνείαν σου ποιούμενος ἐπὶ τῶν προσευχῶν μου occurs in the plural (ποιούμενοι ... ὑμῶν) in 1 Thess. 1.2 (cf. also Rom. 1.9), as well as here in the singular, and is therefore perfectly Pauline; it is almost exactly paralleled in the ὑπὲρ ὑμῶν μνείαν ποιούμενος of

---

[1] Cf. Wiles, *Intercessory Prayers*, 215–25; O'Brien, *Thanksgivings*, 47–61. On the thanksgivings in Colossians and Philemon cf. Mullins, 'Thanksgivings'.

[2] Cf. Dunn's table of the parallels (315), which show 'that in the thanksgiving Paul fell into a well-established pattern of his own: thanks to God, assurance of frequent remembrance in prayer, commendation of their faith and love'.

[3] 'The thanksgiving as a whole is closely linked to the body of the letter by the repetition of key words: "love, beloved" (vv. 5, 7, 9, 16), "prayers" (vv. 4, 22), "sharing, partnership" (vv. 6, 17), "the good" (vv. 6, 14), "hearts" (vv. 7, 12, 20), "refresh" (vv. 7, 20) and the vocative "brother" (vv. 7, 20)' (Dunn, 316, with further references).

Eph. 1.15–16, whereas Col. 1.3 has the shorter equivalent περὶ ὑμῶν προσευχόμενοι (Eph. also changes the order of the participial constructions, and reads ἀκούσας for ἀκούων). Here again the simplest explanation would seem to be that these letters are all by the same author, who has merely varied the formulation for reasons of his own, and this might count in favour of the authenticity of Col.; but as noted in the Introduction to that letter there are other factors which tell against any such conclusion. Moreover, a glance at a concordance will serve to show that while Paul frequently employs the verb προσεύχεσθαι with reference to prayer he nowhere in the major letters uses the present participle with περί or ὑπέρ in connection with intercession for his readers.[4] The phrase περὶ ὑμῶν προσευχόμενοι must therefore be added to the dossier of factors which tell against the authenticity of Col.

If, however, Col. is pseudonymous, the author, despite the influence from Philem. which is otherwise noted, has substituted the περὶ ὑμῶν προσευχόμενοι, and the author of Eph., though apparently drawing on Col., has gone right back to the form which appears in Philem. This only serves to show the problems which attend any attempt to develop a 'scissors and paste' theory of the growth of the Pauline letter corpus. We do not know the reasons which led the writers of Col. and Eph. to their choice of a particular formula, and it is almost certainly a mistake to think of them sitting with copies of Paul's letters at hand and deliberately copying now one phrase and now another. They were indeed influenced by Paul, but they were independent authors in their own right.

Verse 5 provides the reason for Paul's thanksgiving: he has heard of Philemon's faith and love, possibly from Epaphras (so Lightfoot and others), but perhaps from Onesimus (Schenk, 3451 and n. 44). The name of the informant is not stated, and in that respect much depends on our reconstruction of the background to the letter: v. 10 suggests that Onesimus has been with Paul for some considerable time, while v. 23 speaks of Epaphras as Paul's fellow-prisoner; there is nothing to indicate which was the more recent arrival.[5] On the traditional view, it may have been the coming of Epaphras that prompted Paul into action: the case of Onesimus might have been delayed thus far, but now, delicate as it was, it had to be dealt with.

As Moule notes, the 'apparently simple expression' τὴν ἀγάπην καὶ τὴν πίστιν κτλ 'presents difficulties when it is analysed'. Are both the love and faith directed towards both the Lord Jesus and the saints,[6] or is there another possible construction? We should note at

[4] The one exception is 2 Thess. 1.11; περὶ ἡμῶν appears at Col. 4.3; 1 Thess. 5.25; 2 Thess. 3.1.
[5] Dunn (317) sees here 'evidence of the network of communication among the Pauline churches which ensured that news of developments (and crises) was quite quickly spread to others'.
[6] So Dunn (317): 'There is no reason why Paul should not have thought of both love and faith as the sum of the Christian lifestyle and therefore of both as related to both "the Lord Jesus" and "all the saints"' (citing Vincent, 178–79; Gnilka, 35–36).

once that the prepositions differ: πρὸς τὸν κύριον Ἰησοῦν and εἰς πάντας τοὺς ἁγίους. Lightfoot remarks that the change 'seems to arise from the instinctive desire to separate the two clauses, as they refer to different words in the preceding part of the sentence' (but he adds that 'some good copies' read εἰς in both clauses; cf. Schenk, 3458 n. 55, who claims this as the original text). O'Brien (*Thanksgivings*, 51ff.) notes three solutions which have been advanced, but like Lightfoot, Moule and others (refs. in Schenk, 3459 n. 56) prefers to take this as an example of chiasmus; as Moule says, 'chiasmus is common enough in St Paul' (cf. Jeremias, 'Chiasmus in den Paulusbriefen', *ZNW* 49 (1958), 145–56, repr. *ABBA* (1966), 276–90: πρὸς τὸν κύριον relates to πίστις, εἰς πάντας κτλ to ἀγάπη (279 n. 5). On this view the faith is directed to the Lord Jesus, and the love extends to all the saints; the thought is spelled out more clearly in Col. 1.4: ἀκούσαντες τὴν πίστιν ὑμῶν ἐν Χριστῷ Ἰησοῦ καὶ τὴν ἀγάπην ἣν ἔχετε εἰς πάντας τοὺς ἁγίους.[7]

The crux of the passage comes in v. 6, 'notoriously the most obscure verse in this letter' (Moule, 142). As Riesenfeld says, 'Few passages in the New Testament have been interpreted and translated in so many different ways'.[8] He sets out four examples (from RSV, NEB, the Good News Bible and the Jerusalem Bible),[9] from which he draws the conclusion 'that there is not the slightest consensus about what Paul really wants to make known to his friend Philemon in this single sentence'. Moule (143), after discussing a whole series of questions, drily comments: 'Unless and until further ἐπίγνωσις is given to Christian interpreters, the answer to these questions must remain obscure'.

There is to begin with a textual problem. According to Lightfoot, the second person plural ὑμῖν has 'somewhat better' ms support (P61 ℵ G P 33 1739 etc.), but Lightfoot thinks the first person ἡμῖν (A C D Ψ etc.) more expressive, and in this he is followed by Metzger (*Textual Commentary*, 657) and others; Riesenfeld (256f.) and Schenk among other scholars prefer the second person plural. A second person plural, however, would look rather strange after the

---

[7] Hübner (30) demurs, claiming that the first part, referring to love and faith towards the Lord, makes good sense; it is the addition of καὶ εἰς πάντας τοὺς ἁγίους that creates the difficulty. Paul right at the outset is referring to the love which characterizes Philemon's Christian way of life, a love inspired by faith in Christ, and this love will be at the basis of his appeal later in the letter. Barth (106) notes that in some witnesses the sequence 'love and faith' is adapted to that in Col., while Fitzmyer (95f.) prefers this reading.

[8] Riesenfeld, 'Faith and Love Promoting Hope', 251. Cf. also Schenk, 3456f. (extensive bibliography at 3486–95, from which, however, Riesenfeld's article is missing).

[9] Dunn (318) adds some more, noting that 'The puzzle is whether κοινωνία is something objective (the fellowship brought about by faith) or subjective (the experience of shared faith), and likewise whether πίστις is objective (the fellowship of a shared confession) or subjective (the shared experience of believing).' He decides for the subjective sense in both cases. See further below.

sequence of singulars which precede it.[10] In terms of meaning there is, on the traditional interpretation of the letter, no very great difference: in the first person, Paul would be speaking of the good that belongs to 'us', including himself, and indeed all Christians; the second person would restrict the possession of this good to Philemon and the local community, 'the good that is in you'.

Confusion of these pronouns is a very common cause of variation in the mss, and it is sometimes difficult in the extreme to determine the original text.[11] Here it is on the whole perhaps more likely that Paul is thinking of the good that is ours as Christians; but that is just the kind of judgement that might have prompted some early scribe to substitute the first person for the second in the text he was copying!

One question which immediately arises is that of the connection between v. 6 and what precedes: is it to be linked with the μνείαν σου ποιούμενος ἐπὶ τῶν προσευχῶν μου as conveying the substance of Paul's intercession (so most commentators), or with τὴν ἀγάπην καὶ τὴν πίστιν ἣν ἔχεις, as indicating the outcome of Philemon's faith and love (so most recently Schenk, 3457 n. 52)? Lightfoot (401) already rejected the latter view, observing that 'even if ὅπως could bear this meaning, such a connexion is altogether harsh and improbable'; but Schenk can appeal to Bauer (= BAGD) for an example of this usage, which he also sees in Gal. 1.4. ὅπως may be used with the subjunctive to indicate purpose (BAGD 576, s.v. ὅπως §2a), but this verse is not there listed under this head; instead it is suggested (BAGD 577, §2b) that it may be a case of the use of a ὅπως clause in place of the infinitive after verbs of petition, 'praying that': 'So perhaps also Phlm 6, where ὅπως could be thought of as depending on προσεύχομαι derived in sense from vs. 4, unless ὅπως here = ὥστε.' It is this last suggestion, that ὅπως here = ὥστε—i.e. that the clause is not final but consecutive—which is taken up by Schenk, who argues that the reference is not to the future but to a specific event in the past, i.e. to Philemon's recent conversion and his generosity in making his house available for the meetings of the local Christian community; ἐνεργὴς γένηται is then not a prayer that something may become effective, but a statement that it has become effective. Philemon's participation in the Christian faith has borne its fruit. As already noted, however, the description of Philemon as Paul's συνεργός would seem to suggest that he was not a recent convert, but a friend and collaborator of fairly long standing; it is in fact difficult to think of this letter as written to someone who was not personally known to Paul. Moreover, if the reference were indeed to Philemon's new-found participation in the faith we should expect a different order of the words: ἡ κοινωνία σου τῆς πίστεως (or does

[10] Cf. Fitzmyer (98), who finds a second plural 'questionable at this point in the letter, where the second singular otherwise predominates'.

[11] Cf. Metzger, *Text of the NT*, 191f.: 'So widespread is this kind of scribal error that the testimony of even the best manuscripts respecting personal pronouns is liable to suspicion, and one's decision between such variant readings must turn upon considerations of fitness in the context.'

the σου govern the whole phrase ἡ κοινωνία τῆς πίστεώς taken as a single unit?). Again, we have to consider the function of this verse in its context. If it is linked with μνείαν σου ποιούμενος ἐπὶ τῶν προσευχῶν μου, and taken as depending on a προσεύχομαι 'derived in sense from v. 4' (cf. quotation from BAGD above; in Eph. 1.16–17 an ἵνα clause follows a similar μνείαν ποιούμενος ἐπὶ τῶν προσευχῶν μου), then it can readily be understood as expressing the content of Paul's intercession; thus Moule (142) observes that it 'no doubt indicates the substance of the apostle's prayer (v. 4): "... praying that ..."' (versions which follow this interpretation, such as NEB, RSV, NRSV, supply the necessary verb, as Moule does).[12] Lohse (192, 193 n. 18) cuts the knot by taking the ὅπως clause as an independent sentence stating the content of the petition.

The prayer then is that something may be effective ἐν ἐπιγνώσει of all the good that is ours εἰς Χριστόν, but what that something is has still to be considered. ἡ κοινωνία τῆς πίστεως σου has been interpreted in several different ways: is it Philemon's sharing, his participation, in the faith, or his sharing of his faith with others? κοινωνία (BAGD 438f.; TWNT iii. 798–810; cf. Taylor, Forgiveness and Reconciliation, 131–34) is one of a group of words denoting fellowship or association: the verb κοινωνέω means to share or participate (cf. Rom. 15.27; Heb. 2.14, where it stands in parallel with μετέχω; 1 Pet. 4.13), but also to give a share (cf. Rom. 12.13; Gal. 6.6; Phil. 4.15); in Luke 5.10 the sons of Zebedee are described as κοινωνοὶ τῷ Σίμωνι, partners with Simon in business (cf. also συγκοινωνούς in Phil. 1.7). And of course there is the familiar benediction of 2 Cor. 13.13, with its ἡ κοινωνία τοῦ ἁγίου πνεύματος, variously rendered 'the communion of the Holy Spirit' (NRSV), 'the fellowship of the Holy Spirit' (RSV; NEB 'fellowship in the Holy Spirit') or 'participation in the Holy Spirit' (RSV footnote). Each of these renderings conveys a slightly different nuance. For present purposes the most telling case occurs in the thanksgiving period of Philippians: ἐπὶ τῇ κοινωνίᾳ ὑμῶν εἰς τὸ εὐαγγέλιον (1.5), which refers to the congregation's collaboration with Paul in the work of the gospel, their support of his missionary effort (cf. F. W. Beare, The Epistle to the Philippians, (1959), 52f., who translates it 'your fellowship in the furtherance of the gospel'). It is not just their 'sharing' in the gospel (so NRSV), but their active 'partnership' (RSV): they not only participate in the blessings which the gospel brings, but have also contributed to its furtherance by the support which they have given to Paul. The term κοινωνία in fact covers a whole complex of ideas and associations which cannot easily be brought under a single English equivalent: participation in the faith

[12] Cf. Fitzmyer (96f.): 'The prayer has to be understood as dependent on the second part of v. 4, Paul's mention of his constant remembrance of Philemon in prayer, because this verse otherwise lacks a main verb. Paul now prays that Philemon's faith may be always active and efficacious in its manifestation of love toward Christians who depend on him.'

creates a *fellowship* inspired by love, which is marked not only by a *sharing* in the blessings of the gospel but also by a reaching out in *united effort* for its further propagation. In the present case, however, some of these associations are not entirely relevant. The prayer is for Philemon, not for the congregation or the wider Church; it is not that his sharing of his faith may benefit the wider community, but that his participation in the faith may prove effective for him ἐν ἐπιγνώσει παντὸς ἀγαθοῦ τοῦ ἐν ἡμῖν εἰς Χριστόν.[13]

As to ἐπίγνωσις (BAGD 291; *TWNT* i. 688–719), this is a term common in Col. (1.9–10, (cf. pp. 100–02) above 2.2; 3.7; see Dunn, 319, who adds 'see also particularly Phil. 1.9'). Lightfoot (204, on Col. 1.9) claims, 'The compound ἐπίγνωσις is an advance upon γνῶσις, denoting a larger and more thorough knowledge'; so here (402) he translates it 'in the perfect knowledge of every good thing', noting that the word involves 'the complete appropriation of all truth and the unreserved identification with God's will'. Armitage Robinson, however, in a special note (*Ephesians*, 248–54) rejects the view that ἐπίγνωσις refers to a fuller and more perfect γνῶσις: 'γνῶσις is the wider word and expresses "knowledge" in the fullest sense: ἐπίγνωσις is knowledge directed towards a particular object, perceiving, discerning, recognising: but it is not knowledge in the abstract: that is γνῶσις' (254). Bultmann more recently (*TWNT* i. 707) sees no distinction between the terms: ἐπίγνωσις in some passages corresponds to the use of γνῶσις in others. It may be natural enough in English to think of a deeper and fuller knowledge, but that is interpretation deriving from the context, and is not necessarily inherent in the word itself. BAGD, it may be added, offers the alternative 'recognition' (cf. Robinson above). As Bultmann puts it, 'The faith which Philemon shares is to be effectual in his recognition of all that is given to the believer and of what must foster union with Christ when it is expressed' (tr. G. W. Bromiley).

Lightfoot, however, is correct in speaking of 'unreserved identification with God's will'. Lohse (194 n. 24) notes that 'According to Jewish understanding, knowledge of the good means knowledge of the divine will' (citing 1 QS 4.26; 1 QSa 1.10f.); moreover, this knowledge entails obedience to the will of God, an obligation to conduct one's life in accordance with that will. Thus at Col. 1.9 the intercession is 'that you may be filled with the knowledge of God's will in all spiritual wisdom and understanding, so that you may lead lives worthy of the Lord, fully pleasing to him' (NRSV; Lohse (25f.) illustrates this with ample references to the Qumran documents. Cf. also W. D. Davies, *Christian Origins and Judaism*, 119–44). At one

[13] Cf. Dunn (318): 'For Paul it primarily denoted common participation in or sharing of something' (see references there supplied). He concludes that what Paul had in mind here 'is almost certainly the subjective experience of a faith shared in common'. Fitzmyer (97) prefers to render it 'that the participation (of others) in your faith may be(come) effective', taking the σου as modifying only πίστεως; 'The sense would be that others (i.e. God's dedicated people, of v. 5) may come to share in Philemon's Christan faith.'

stage the prominence of references to 'knowledge' in the Scrolls was among the factors which led scholars to think in terms of a pre-Christian Gnosticism, but examination of the nature and content of this 'knowledge' soon disclosed the differences from the Gnostic γνῶσις (cf. Davies, *Origins*, 134–41, esp. 137; Reicke, 'Traces').

The final words of this verse are sometimes translated 'in Christ' (so AV, RSV; NEB renders it, 'all the blessings that our union with Christ brings us'), and it is certainly natural to think of the blessings which we enjoy as Christians. Here, however, it is necessary to enter a caveat: 'all the good that is ours' may be a fairly adequate rendering of παντὸς ἀγαθοῦ τοῦ ἐν ἡμῖν, and that good is certainly 'in Christ'; but the text reads not ἐν Χριστῷ but εἰς Χριστόν. Moule (142) comments: 'it seems to yield the best sense if εἰς Χριστόν is taken to mean something like "bringing us into (closer) relation to Christ", and is connected either with ἐνεργής ("active in bringing us" ...) or with παντὸς ἀγαθοῦ ("every good thing that brings us ...") or, possibly, with ἐπιγνώσει ("a recognition ... which brings")'.[14] NRSV recasts the whole clause: 'when you perceive all the good that we may do for Christ' (cf. NEB footnote: '*Or* that bring us to Christ').

Verse 7 in contrast presents little or no difficulty, and sums up the content of the thanksgiving period: Paul has derived (lit. 'had') much joy[15] and comfort from the reports he has received of Philemon's Christian love, because through him the hearts of the saints have been refreshed. **Παράκλησις** (BAGD 618; *TWNT* v. 771–98, esp. 790ff.) is derived from the verb παρακαλέω, which occurs in vv. 9 and 10, and like it has a range of meanings: encouragement or exhortation; appeal or request; comfort or consolation (in Acts 4.36 the name of Barnabas is translated υἱὸς παρακλήσεως, son of consolation). Our choice of rendering must often be determined by the context, and sometimes the context does not lead to any decisive conclusion: at Heb. 13.22, is the λόγος τῆς παρακλήσεως a word of comfort, of exhortation, or of encouragement? These are not exactly the same thing! Here in Philemon the sense is clearly that of comfort or encouragement.[16]

σπλάγχνα (BAGD 763; *TWNT* vii. 548–59, for Philem. esp. 555) originally meant the inward parts, the entrails (cf. AV 'the bowels of the saints'), but since these were thought of as the seat of the emotions it was not difficult for the term to be used in a figurative

---

[14] Dunn (320), after noting the possibility of 'an eschatological thrust', continues, 'More likely it is a variant on ἐν Χριστῷ, perhaps reflecting the influence of a train of thought on faith .... At all events, its basic force is clear: all that is spoken of in the rest of the verse has its validity and effectiveness because of their relation to Christ, or perhaps more specifically, by "bringing us into (closer) relation to Christ"' (citing Moule, Dibelius (103) and Wiles, *Intercessory Prayers* (225)).

[15] 'For χαράν the received text (Steph. but not Elz.,) reads χάριν, which is taken to mean "thankfulness" (1 Tim. i. 12, 2 Tim. i 3); but this reading is absolutely condemned by the paucity of ancient authority' (Lightfoot, 402).

[16] Citing Schmitz and Schlier, Lohse (195) writes: 'The noun παράκλησις conveys more the meaning of comfort and encouragement, than of admonition and request.'

sense, as we in modern usage speak of the heart. The word occurs three times in this short letter, an indication as Koester notes (*TWNT* vii. 555) of Paul's deep concern for the situation. At v. 12 he speaks of Onesimus as 'my very heart'; at v. 20 he picks up the language of the present verse and urges Philemon to 'refresh my heart'. **ἀναπαύω** (BAGD 58–59; *TWNT* i. 352–53) means to give rest or refreshment (cf. the noun ἀνάπαυσις, which later became something of a technical term in Gnostic circles; cf. P. Vielhauer in Eltester and Kettler (eds), *Apophoreta*, 281ff., who sees it as a specifically Gnostic concept, almost alien to the NT (found only in Matt. 11.28–30 and Hebrews, esp. 3.7–4.11; but the actual word there used is κατάπαυσις); but it does occur in a literal sense in Matt. 26.45; Mark 6.31; 14.41; Luke 12.24; Rev. 4.8; 14.11. Cf. also Barth's excursus, 'Rest' (297–301); J. Helderman, *Die Anapausis im Evangelium Veritatis* (NHS XVIII)). For the phrase used here, cf. 2 Cor. 7.13, ἀναπέπαυται τὸ πνεῦμα αὐτοῦ ἀπὸ πάντων ὑμῶν.

One small point might give rise to discussion: who are the 'saints' here who have been thus refreshed? Hübner (31) suggests that they may be the members of Philemon's household community, who have been in some way unsettled and disturbed, possibly through something connected with the flight of Onesimus. In that case, Philemon has contrived to restore peace and harmony within the community. It is, however, also possible that there is a wider reference and that news of some generous act on the part of Philemon has 'refreshed the hearts' of Christians over a broader area.[17] Paul and Philemon would know very well, but once again our information is not sufficient for any final judgement. We may conjecture, but we do not really know.

In the light of this discussion, the whole passage may be translated as follows:

> [4]I give thanks to my God at all times when I make mention of you in my prayers, [5]since I hear of your love and the faith which you have towards the Lord Jesus and to all the saints, [6]that your partnership in the faith may prove effective in the knowledge of all the good that is in us which leads towards Christ.[18] [7]For I have derived much joy and comfort through your love, because the hearts of the saints are refreshed through you, my brother.

[17] Cf. Dunn (321): 'The tense of the verb (ἀναπέπαυται, perfect) indicates some past ministry of Philemon which had had enduring results.' He suggests various possibilities.

[18] W. L. Lorimer (*The New Testament in Scots* (1983), 370) renders this passage, 'I pray that the brotherly kindness that faith has bred in you may be the means of your knowing ever better every blessing that is ours who believe in Christ' (I have Englished Lorimer's Scots translation), with the footnote 'Dear kens what this verse means!' Barth (280) renders it 'I ask that your faith communion be a source of energy to recognize all the good that is found in your congregation, in expectation of Christ'; see his detailed discussion (280–91).

At Acts 4.36–37 we are told that Barnabas 'sold a field that belonged to him, then brought the money and laid it at the apostles' feet'; that must certainly have 'refreshed the hearts of the saints' in Jerusalem. At Acts 9.36 the widows mourning for Dorcas showed to Peter the tunics and other garments she had made for them while she was with them. These are but two examples recorded in Acts of generous and kindly deeds wrought by early Christians for fellow-members of the Christian community. There must have been many others: alms for the poor, concern for the sick, hospitality to fellow-Christians who came on a journey. Some would be known only within a particular community, but others might well have been more widely reported, and so 'refreshed the hearts of the saints' over a wider area. What it was that Paul is referring to here we do not know, although he and Philemon knew very well, so Paul had no need to spell it out.[19] Nor can we tell whether it was something that would be known only within Philemon's own community, or some more striking deed that would arouse more widespread admiration.

What is clear from the salutation and thanksgiving period is that Paul and Philemon are friends of fairly long standing. They have worked together in the past (συνεργός, v. 1), probably during Paul's mission in Ephesus, before Philemon returned home to Colossae and made his house available for the meetings of the community there. If Epaphras was chiefly responsible for the evangelizing of the area, he was no doubt grateful for Philemon's support; but in this letter he is mentioned only as sending his greetings (v. 23).[20]

This very friendship, however, made Paul's position all the more delicate: it was bad enough to harbour a runaway slave, which would expose both to penalty under the law of the empire. The Old Testament legislation regarding slaves was much more humane,[21] and Paul as himself a Jew would be inclined to follow that; but we have no indication that Philemon was other than a Gentile, and the rule in Asia Minor would be the imperial law rather than the Jewish, which might have prevailed in Palestine. That the fugitive was the slave of a friend only made things the more difficult. Paul says expressly in v. 13 that he would have liked to keep Onesimus with him, but Onesimus had to go back, despite the uncertain prospect that lay before him. Even a Christian master could not be expected to extend a cordial welcome to a slave who had run away, especially if, as v. 18 suggests, Onesimus had been guilty of some offence.

[19] Lohse (195) notes that as far as v. 7 Paul 'has spoken of Philemon's conduct in words that could be applied to every true Christian. Now, however, he indicates that he has learned of one particular deed by which Philemon has helped the community', and from this report he derived 'much joy and comfort' (cf. 2 Cor. 7.4, 7, 13). The text, however, speaks only of Philemon's ἀγάπη.

[20] The fact that there is no indication here that Epaphras was responsible for the founding of the community provides a basis for Koester's view (see p. 7 above) that Philemon was its founder. The evidence for the activity of Epaphras as evangelist for the area is drawn entirely from Col.

[21] See Exod. 21.1–11; Lev. 25.39–55; Deut. 15.12–18; also *HDB* iv. 461–69; *EncBib* 4653–58; *ABD* vi. 58–73. For runaway slaves, see Deut. 23.15f.

These opening sections prepare the ground for what is to follow. The phrase *captatio benevolentiae* suggests itself, but it is important to add that this is no calculated rhetorical device: salutation and thanksgiving period both bespeak a warm and cordial friendship. Paul is about to plead for Onesimus (who has not yet been mentioned), but he does so with confidence because of his warm friendship with Philemon and what he knows of Philemon's character and conduct. As he says below, he would be perfectly entitled to command, to exert his authority; as v. 19 indicates, Philemon is in his debt. Instead he entreats: the decision must rest with Philemon (v. 14).

III
THE PLEA FOR ONESIMUS
(8–20)[1]

[8]Because of this, although in Christ I have every confidence to command you to do what is fitting, [9]for love's sake I rather entreat, old man that I am, and now also a prisoner of Christ Jesus. [10]I entreat you on behalf of my child, whose father I have become during my imprisonment—Onesimus, [11]who once was useless to you but now is truly useful both to you and to me. [12]I am sending him back to you, that is to say my very heart.

[13]I wanted to keep him with me, that he might serve me on your behalf during my imprisonment for the gospel, [14]but I did not wish to do anything without your consent, that your good deed might not be done under compulsion, but of your own free will.

[15]Perhaps it was for this reason that he was separated from you for a time, in order that you might receive him back for ever, [16]no longer as a slave but more than a slave—a brother beloved, especially to me and how much more to you, both in the flesh and in the Lord.

[17]If then you hold me a partner, welcome him as you would me. [18]If in any way he has wronged you, or owes you anything, put it down to my account. [19]I, Paul, write with my own hand: I will repay—not to speak of the fact that you owe to me your very self. [20]Yes, brother, I would have this benefit from you in the Lord. Refresh my heart in Christ.

The conjunction διό ('wherefore, for that reason': BAGD 198b) marks the transition to the main body of the letter, with its appeal for Onesimus.[2] It is in the light of what he has just written, because of

[1] Dunn (324) notes that the length of this section is disputed, but after listing various opinions concludes: 'However, the thought of the letter is sufficiently integrated for such disagreements to be of little consequence.'
[2] διό 'is not Paul's normal transition to the body of a letter (usually γάρ or δέ). But the expression of appreciation and commendation in v. 7 has already laid the ground for the central appeal of the letter, so that διό is entirely appropriate' (Dunn, 324, referring to J. T. Sanders, *JBL* 81 (1962), 355).

what he knows of Philemon's character and conduct, and particularly because of the recent news of some act by Philemon that has 'refreshed the hearts of the saints' (v. 7), that he makes this appeal. He is fully aware that he could command Philemon, and expect to be obeyed (v. 8), but that could leave Philemon (and his household, especially the other slaves) resentful at such cavalier treatment. It would not be a sound foundation for future relationships, within the community or between Paul and Philemon; and Paul clearly values Philemon's friendship. The passage, however, leaves no doubt as to what Paul would wish Philemon to do: he presents his appeal in the strongest possible terms, short of actual command.

8. διὸ πολλὴν ἐν Χριστῷ παρρησίαν ἔχων ἐπιτάσσειν σοι τὸ ἀνῆκον The word **παρρησία** (BAGD 630; *TWNT* v. 869–84)[3] means 'frankness, plainness of speech' (e.g. Mark 8.32, παρρησίᾳ τὸν λόγον ἔλεγεν, 'he said this quite openly'), but also 'courage, confidence, boldness', especially before people of rank. Here it is clearly the latter meaning that is required: 'in Christ', i.e. as a Christian, within the sphere of Christ's authority, Paul has every confidence of his right to command Philemon; he shows awareness of his apostolic authority, but declines to presume upon it (on the rendering of πρεσβύτης as 'ambassador' in v. 9, which would in some sense do so, see below).[4] **ἐπιτάσσω** (BAGD 302a) means to order or command, but is never used in the major Pauline letters, although Paul does employ the noun ἐπιταγή (Rom 16.26; 1 Cor. 7.6, 25; 2 Cor. 8.8, usually in the phrase κατ'ἐπιταγήν) and the cognate verb διατάσσω (1 Cor. 7.17; 9.14; 11.34; 16.1; Gal. 3.19; cf. *TWNT* viii. 37, 35). **τὸ ἀνῆκον** (neuter sing. participle of ἀνῆκω, used as a substantive) is what is proper, right or fitting, in other words one's duty. The only other occurrences of this verb in the NT are at Col. 3.18 (of the conduct that is fitting for wives ἐν κυρίῳ) and Eph. 5.4 (of things which are not appropriate). Lohse (158 n. 23) observes that the expression 'gained entry into Christian exhortation from Hellenistic popular philosophy as mediated through the Hellenistic synagogue', referring further to Schlier, *TWNT* i. 360; iii. 440–43 (τὸ καθῆκον). This term might lend some credence to Winter's claim, mentioned in the Introduction (p. 322), that this letter contains 'a number of philosophical terms relating to ethical questions of a public nature'; but we must ask whether these terms are specifically philosophical, or capable of other use. παρρησία for example was taken up by various schools of

[3] Cf. further W. C. van Unnik, 'The Christian's Freedom of Speech in the New Testament', *BJRL* 44 (1962), 466ff., also *Med. Ned. Akad.* 25 (1962), 585ff., *Mélanges Mohrmann* (1963), 12ff.

[4] 'The appeal here is not to Paul's apostolic authority vis-a-vis Philemon .... As one equally "in Christ", Philemon could be expected to acknowledge that an "in Christ" obligation transcended all others' (Dunn, 325). This last sentence is certainly correct in terms of the letter as a whole; but at this point Paul is renouncing any claim to authority over Philemon. On the use of the ἐν Χριστῷ formula in Philemon cf. Petersen, *Rediscovering Paul*, 174 n. 14, 180 n. 53.

popular philosophy, particularly the Cynics (Schlier, *TWNT* v. 872, A3), but this does not make it a specifically philosophical term. In the same way, other words she lists may be legal or commercial within a particular context, but they are not thereby always legal or commercial. After all, one may discuss what is right and proper in a perfectly ordinary conversation.

9. διὰ τὴν ἀγάπην μᾶλλον παρακαλῶ, τοιοῦτος ὢν ὡς Παῦλος πρεσβύτης νυνὶ δὲ καὶ δέσμιος Χριστοῦ Ἰησοῦ Paul prefers to entreat 'because of (the) love' or 'for love's sake'. The nature of this love is not here specified: it could be Philemon's love, mentioned in v. 7, which has 'refreshed the hearts of the saints';[5] but it could also be more general, the love that should mark the relationship of Christians one to another, and perhaps more particularly the mutual affection which obtained between Paul and Philemon. At any rate it has constrained Paul to refrain from any assertion of authority; he prefers to entreat. **παρακαλῶ**, like the cognate noun παράκλησις, which appears earlier in v. 7, is a word with a wide range of meanings (BAGD 617; *TWNT* v. 771–98—for the NT see 790ff.; see also C. J. Bjerkelund, *Parakalô* (1967)): to call to one's side, call for help (cf. the cognate παράκλητος, one called in to help, an advocate or helper); to appeal, exhort or encourage; to request or entreat; to comfort or console. Lohse (198 n. 12) quotes Schmitz (*TWNT* v. 792 n. 166): 'That παρακαλεῖν has the note of "entreaty" even when it means "to admonish" may be seen from Phlm 8f., where it is expressly distinguished from "to command" (ἐπιτάσσειν) and is an outflowing of love.'

τοιοῦτος ὢν ὡς Παῦλος is literally 'being such a man as Paul' (cf. BAGD 821, §2b: *since I am the sort of person* (who presumes to give you orders); Lohse, 196 n. 15: 'since that is what I am'). English versions frequently resort to paraphrase, e.g. 'I, Paul, an ambassador' (RSV); 'I, Paul, ambassador as I am' (NEB); 'and I, Paul, do this as an old man' (NRSV). Adherence to the literal meaning is not always possible, or compatible with English usage.

πρεσβύτης As the translations just quoted show, there is difference of opinion as to this word (also used at Luke 1.18; Tit. 2.2, where there is no ambiguity). Bentley in the eighteenth century, like others after him (cf. Lightfoot, 404), conjectured πρεσβευτής, 'ambassador', first because in Acts 7.58 Paul is described as νεανίας at the time of Stephen's martyrdom, and the lapse of time did not seem sufficient to justify a description now as an 'old man'; and secondly because in 2 Cor. 5.20; Eph. 6.20 Paul describes himself as an ambassador, using the verb πρεσβεύειν. For Lightfoot (405) the second is the main reason for this interpretation, and he questions whether any change is necessary, holding that 'there is reason for thinking that πρεσβύτης may have been written indifferently for

[5] So for example Dunn (326), and before him Dibelius-Greeven; cf. Lohse (198–99 and nn. 13 and 14), who prefers a reference to 'the love which governs the Christians' dealings and association with one another'.

πρεσβευτής in St Paul's time' (404).[6] His interpretation of
πρεσβύτης as meaning 'ambassador' has been widely followed, but
there are other factors to be considered. In LXX, πρεσβύτης is used
in the sense of 'ambassador' in 2 Macc. 11.34; 2 Chron. 32.31 (B); 1
Macc. 14.22; 15.17 (ℵ), but here we have to reckon with the
possibility of scribal error, the more particularly when both forms
are used in different manuscripts in the same context. It may be
dangerous to argue from phenomena in later manuscripts to the
usage of Paul's day. Discussing our present text, J. N. Birdsall
('Πρεσβύτης in Philemon 9', 628) notes 'the unanimous manuscript
attestation of πρεσβύτης throughout the whole tradition of whatever date' and the fact that 'the ancient versions show a like
unanimity in rendering this Greek ... by words bearing the meaning
of "old man"'. In the light of all this, conjectural emendation must
in any case be considered precarious.[7] A more important point is
that Paul in these verses expressly declines to assert his apostolic
authority, and rather appeals to Philemon. The authority is certainly
there, and Paul is conscious of it, as v. 8 shows; but he does not
presume upon it; to introduce his status as ambassador for Christ
would strike a wrong note. As to Bentley's first point, according to
Hippocrates, quoted by Philo (Op. M. 105), νεανίσκός describes the
fourth of the seven ages of human life, up to 28 (ἐς τὰ τετράκις
ἑπτά; BAGD, however, says 'from about the 24th to the 40th year'),
and πρεσβύτης the sixth, between 49 and 56 years of age (ἄχρι
πεντήκοντα ἕξ, ἐς τὰ ἑπτάκις ὀκτώ).[8] If Stephen's martyrdom is
dated about AD 35, this pattern would certainly make Paul a
πρεσβύτης at the time of the Roman imprisonment in the early
sixties; if the letter is dated to an imprisonment in Ephesus in the
fifties it might be more difficult, yet not entirely impossible. Since we
do not know the date of Paul's birth, we cannot deduce his age at
this time with any certainty.[9] In the light of all this, the translation
'old man' is to be preferred.

Cf. Lightfoot, 405f.; Lohse, 199; Moule, 144; Bornkamm, TWNT vi. 672f.; BAGD
700b; Metzger, Textual Commentary, 657; Schenke and Fischer, Einleitung, 156, 157 n.
1; Schenk, 3463 n. 61; Birdsall, 625–30; Dunn, 322 n. 3, 327. On the other side cf.
Petersen, Rediscovering Paul, 125–28, who declares (128) that in the light of the
evidence he produces ' "old man" is simply not a viable interpretation of presbytes'; for
Barth (107; cf. also 321–23) 'The context encourages the version "ambassador".'
Contrast Fitzmyer (105f.), who bluntly says that Bentley's conjecture 'should be
deleted from the apparatus criticus of N-A²⁷'.

[6] Bornkamm (TWNT vi. 683) notes that both forms were current, so that conjecture
is not necessary.
[7] There is in any case a vast difference in this respect between the NT and classical
literature: classical works are often extant in only a few mss, and conjectural
emendation may be essential to the restoration of the text; as noted earlier, however, in
the NT it is probable that the correct reading is somewhere in the great number of
extant manuscripts and versions, so that conjecture is rarely called for.
[8] The four earliest stages are allotted seven years each, but ἀνήρ is assigned 21, i.e.
from 28 to 49; after 56 a man becomes a γέρων.
[9] There has recently been discussion in the letters column of a daily newspaper as to
when one attains to middle age!

The phrase δέσμιος Χριστοῦ Ἰησοῦ clearly picks up the formula used in the salutation at v. 1: it is as now Christ's prisoner that Paul makes his appeal, not as apostle or ambassador. The sufferings he has endured in the ministry of the gospel (cf. 2 Cor. 11.23–33) would certainly add to his authority in Christian circles, but once again he does not presume upon this; he appeals διὰ τὴν ἀγάπην.

10. παρακαλῶ σε περὶ τοῦ ἐμοῦ τέκνου, ὃν ἐγέννησα ἐν τοῖς δεσμοῖς, Ὀνήσιμον Paul now comes to the crux of his appeal, repeating the verb παρακαλῶ and introducing the name of Onesimus for the first time.[10] He has carefully prepared the ground, tactfully reserving the name until now; 'Only after the Apostle has affirmed the close ties that join him to Onesimus, does he mention Onesimus' name' (Lohse, 199). The clause ὃν ἐγέννησα ἐν τοῖς δεσμοῖς suggests that the slave's conversion took place during Paul's imprisonment (cf. Barclay, 'Paul, Philemon and the Dilemma of Christian Slave-Ownership', 163), which would rule out any theory that when they first met he was already a Christian, seconded to Paul by a Christian master for Christian service. Paul has found him useful, as will appear, but that was after his conversion. His conversion was, as it were, a new birth, with Paul his father 'in Christ' (for this figurative use of the verb γεννάω cf. BAGD 155, §1b; there is another example at 1 Cor. 4.14–15, where Paul calls the Corinthians τέκνα μου, adding ἐν γὰρ Χριστῷ Ἰησοῦ διὰ τοῦ εὐαγγελίου ἐγὼ ὑμᾶς ἐγέννησα. Verse 17 then refers to Timothy, ὅς ἐστίν μου τέκνον ἀγαπητὸν ἐν κυρίῳ).[11] Lightfoot observes, 'The name Onesimus was very commonly borne by slaves' (376; cf. his discussion, 376ff., also BAGD 570b). It means 'useful' (cf. the play on words in v. 11).

Lightfoot already notes the references in the letters of Ignatius to a bishop of Ephesus bearing the name (*Eph.* 1.3; 2.1; 6.2), and also that another Onesimus prompted Melito of Sardis to make a collection of extracts from the Old Testament (Eusebius, *HE* iv.26.13f.), and concludes, 'Thus it would appear that the memory of the Colossian slave had invested the name with a special popularity among Christians in this district.' That is of course possible, but there may be a danger here of the fallacy *post hoc, ergo propter hoc*: the very

[10] Standing in apposition to τέκνου, the name should strictly be in the genitive. Presumably it has simply been attracted into the case of the preceding relative ὃν (cf. Moule, 145; Lohse, 200 n. 31).
[11] At Gal. 4.19 the metaphor is cast in terms of a mother in travail: τέκνα μου, οὓς πάλιν ὠδίνω μέχρις οὗ μορφωθῇ Χριστὸς ἐν ὑμῖν. (Barth (332) writes: 'In the NT, the word *gennao* denotes the mother's act of giving birth much more frequently than a man's contribution to procreation'. See his excursus on 'Inclusive Language of Procreation' (329–35), where he argues (334) that only an inclusive translation might be really adequate.) Cf. also *TWNT* i. 663–71, where reference is made to the use of the metaphor in the mystery religions (667ff.); but both Rengstorf (666) and Büchsel (671) warn against laying too much emphasis on the mysteries.

frequency of the name must prompt to caution.[12] We cannot assume
without more ado that the bishop is in fact the slave of this letter, as
in Knox's theory (see pp. 320–22); and the frequency of the name
must make it doubtful that later occurrences are due to the memory
of our Onesimus. Trebilco notes that while the name is found in the
NT and in Christian inscriptions in Asia Minor it is also found in
pagan inscriptions, and 'is not an indication of a Christian, nor of a
Jew' (*Jewish Communities*, 215 n. 51); it appears in two inscriptions
which he cites (pp. 70, 138), and the second at least is unlikely to be
Jewish.

Barclay (165) remarks that in sending Onesimus back Paul is
acting 'in direct contradiction of Deut 23:15–16!': 'Slaves who have
escaped to you from their owners shall not be given back to them.
They shall reside with you, in your midst, in any place they choose in
any one of your towns, wherever they please; you shall not oppress
them' (NRSV). Paul's own instinct would naturally have been to
obey the Jewish law, but while that might have obtained in Judaea
this was Asia Minor, where such matters would presumably be
governed by imperial law. Moreover there is no indication that
Philemon was other than a Gentile, or that he would have felt himself
bound by Jewish law. Paul's appeal is not on any legal basis, but on
grounds of Christian love and fellowship.

This question takes on a different complexion if we follow the
suggestion of Lampe, Rapske and others (see p. 326 above and cf.
Hübner's discussion, 33–35). If Onesimus was not a *fugitivus*, but
seeking the intervention of a friend of his master, the situation would
be very different, even under Roman law; but he could never presume
upon the reaction of his master. Paul's plea on his behalf had to be
very tactful.

**11. τόν ποτέ σοι ἄχρηστον, νυνὶ δὲ καὶ[13] σοὶ καὶ ἐμοὶ
εὔχρηστον** Lightfoot (378) writes of Onesimus, 'There was absolutely nothing to recommend him. He was a slave, and what was
worse, a Phrygian slave; and he had confirmed the popular estimate
of his class and nation by his own conduct.' This, however, as the
context and footnotes show, owes more to the portrayal of slaves in
Roman comedy than to what is actually said in the text (although
Phrygian slaves were notoriously unsatisfactory). This verse says
only that once Onesimus belied his name: he was not 'useful' but
worthless, but now he is a changed man, truly useful both to Paul
and to Philemon. **ἄχρηστος** (BAGD 128b, which notes a similar
word-play in Plato, *Rep.* 411a) occurs only here in the NT,

[12] Fitzmyer (107) notes that A. L. Connolly has listed about sixty instances in
inscriptions, about a third from Ephesus and others from Asia Minor (Horsley and
Llewelyn (eds), *New Documents Illustrating Early Christianity*, iv (1987), 179–81).

[13] Lohse (200 n. 33) observes that this καί is omitted by some mss, 'but is adequately
attested by ℵ* G 33 al vg syᵖ'. His translator adds that it is omitted in the translation
'for stylistic reasons'—failing to recognize the use of a double καί in the sense of 'both
... and' (BAGD 393, §6). Barth (341) presents arguments in favour of its omission, and
translates 'useful to you and especially to me'.

εὔχρηστος (BAGD 329b) also in 2 Tim. 2.21; 4.11; both appear in LXX (Lightfoot). Lohse (200 n. 35) lists other examples of the contrast, particularly from *Shepherd of Hermas*. As noted in the Introduction (p. 323 n. 18), Winter would carry this word-play further: the η in these words would be pronounced ι, suggesting that Onesimus was 'useless' because he was non-Christian, but now is 'useful' because he is a Christian (so earlier Lohse, 200; Barth (345) traces this back to F. C. Baur). Lightfoot, however, long ago wrote (406) that any such allusion, 'even if it should not involve an anachronism, is far too recondite to be probable here. The play on words is exhausted in the reference to'Ονήσιμος'. There is certainly a play on the slave's name (i.e. on 'useful' and 'useless'), but whether we should go further and assume a play on Χριστός and χρηστός is more doubtful; Hübner (35) thinks it possible, but that ultimately the question is unanswerable.[14]

12. ὃν ἀνέπεμψά σοι, αὐτόν, τοῦτ' ἔστιν τὰ ἐμὰ σπλάγχνα
The verb form ἀνέπεμψα is 'demonstrably an "epistolary" aorist, to be rendered by an English present' (Moule, 145, referring to Col. 4.7–9, where the simple verb is used in the aorist in v. 8).[15] The word can be used in a figurative sense of referring a case to a higher or more appropriate authority (cf. Luke 23.7, where Jesus is sent to Herod as belonging within his jurisdiction; Acts 25.21, of Paul being referred to Caesar); but at Luke 23.11, 15 the reference is clearly to Herod sending Jesus back to Pilate, and this is most probably the meaning here (cf. BAGD 59a). This is another of Winter's 'legal and commercial' terms (cf. above, p. 322), but once again it is not exclusively legal or commercial.

Lohse (201 n. 40) observes that 'the manuscript tradition has no uniform reading for this verse'. The text above is that of ℵ* A 33, which according to Metzger (*Textual Commentary*, 657) 'best explains the origin of the other readings'. Other mss insert σὺ δὲ after σοι, or substitute it for σοι, and add προσλαβοῦ (from v. 17). Variations in the placing of this last word suggest interpolation. The scribes were puzzled by the accusative αὐτόν, and tried to complete what they thought a defective sentence; but in so doing they anticipated the content of later verses. Lightfoot (408) already notes, 'The words thus supplied doubtless give the right construction, but must be rejected as deficient in authority.' He explains it as a suspended accusative, the sentence in effect being completed only with the προσλαβοῦ αὐτόν in v. 17. Moule (145) suggests that it might be a Semitism (redundant pronoun following a relative; cf. Mark 7.25), or inserted to pick up the relative before the sentence continues: 'when I say (I am sending) him, I mean my very self'.

[14] Cf. also Barclay, 164 n. 17, who thinks it possible; but Lohse's references to Justin and Tertullian, to which Barclay refers, may be rather late as evidence for the pronunciation of η and ι in the first century. There is also, however, the famous passage in Suetonius (*Claud.* 25), 'Judaeos impulsore Chresto assidue tumultuantes Roma expulit', which is usually taken to involve in some form a confusion of Christus and Chrestus (cf. Lightfoot, *Philippians*, (1894) 16 n. 1).
[15] Cf. Moule, *Idiom Book* (12): 'an understandable idiom—and a rather gracious one, though it causes more ambiguity than the English—whereby the writer courteously projects himself in imagination into the position of the reader, for whom actions contemporaneous with the time of writing will be past'.

13. ὃν ἐγὼ ἐβουλόμην πρὸς ἐμαυτὸν κατέχειν, ἵνα ὑπὲρ σοῦ μοι διακονῇ ἐν τοῖς δεσμοῖς τοῦ εὐαγγελίου Paul would have wished to retain the services of Onesimus, and tactfully suggests that the slave would in fact have been acting as his master's representative (ἵνα ὑπὲρ σοῦ μοι διακονῇ); but as the following verse shows, he is unwilling to do so without Philemon's consent. As Lightfoot (407) notes, the change of tenses is significant: the imperfect ἐβουλόμην here is tentative (cf. Acts 25.22, where Agrippa expresses a wish to hear Paul, a wish in this case granted); the aorist ἠθέλησα in the next verse 'describes a definite and complete act. The will stepped in and put an end to the inclinations of the mind.'[16] There is also a slight nuance of difference in the meaning of these verbs; βούλομαι (BAGD 146; *TWNT* i. 628–31) is indicative of wish or desire, while θέλω (BAGD 354b–55b; *TWNT* iii. 43–52) relates more to will or intent. The latter occurs much more frequently in the New Testament.

κατέχω (BAGD 422b–23a; *TWNT* ii. 828–30) means in general to hold back, restrain or check (cf. Luke 4.42, where the crowds wanted to prevent Jesus from leaving them: κατεῖχον αὐτὸν τοῦ μὴ πορεύεσθαι ἀπ᾽αὐτῶν), but there is a fairly wide range of meaning; here it is quite simply to retain. Lohse notes that this verb, like its cognates, was used as a technical term 'in the context of the sacral rights and duties of asylum', the refugee being considered as 'detained' by the deity to whose temple he had fled, but appropriately cites L. Delekat's statement, 'there is no doubt that Πρὸς ἐμαυτὸν κατέχειν in the context of Paul's letter can only mean "to retain with me"' (*Katoche, Hierodulie und Adoptionsfreilassung* (1964), 7). Since the verb could be translated 'hold back, prevent from leaving', Dunn (330) sees here a suggestion that Onesimus was anxious to return, but Paul, 'far from pushing him to do so, was delaying his departure as long as he could because he found Onesimus so useful'. This may, however, be to press things a little too far: Paul on his own admission had found Onesimus useful, and would have liked to keep him, but that is all we can say with any confidence. Quite apart from any legal aspects, Paul's friendship with Philemon would have made it incumbent upon him to send Onesimus back.

διακονέω (BAGD 184; *TWNT* ii. 81–87) means 'to serve', originally of waiting at table, but also of other forms of service. It is very natural to take it as referring to personal services rendered to Paul during his imprisonment (it is often used of such services in the Gospels and Acts), but Hübner (36; see his discussion) notes that Ollrog (*Mitarbeiter*, 101–06) argues from the use of the word in the accepted Pauline letters that the reference must be to service in the Christian mission, adding that this interpretation has been followed by Wolter (265ff.) and Winter ('Paul's letter to Philemon', 9). Of the four occurrences of the verb in the accepted letters (the cognate noun appears rather more often), διακονῶν τοῖς ἁγίοις in Rom. 15.25

---

[16] Cf. Winter's discussion ('Paul's Letter to Philemon', 8): 'v. 13 expresses an ongoing plan whereas v. 14 expresses a single act of resolve'. See also Schenk, 3468 and n. 70.

refers fairly obviously to Paul's great collection for the saints in
Jerusalem (cf. Cranfield, *Romans*, 770; διακονία occurs in the
context, in v. 31), and the same would hold for 2 Cor. 8.19, 20;
but 2 Cor. 3.3 presents something of a problem (cf. Thrall, *2
Corinthians*, 225). The noun appears in this connection in 2 Cor. 8.4;
9.1, 12, 13, but at 1 Cor. 16.15 would seem to refer to a more general
form of ministry (cf. Barrett, *1 Corinthians*, 393f.); at 16.1, 2 a
different word, λογεία, is used for the collection.

Hübner also notes that Dunn (330f.) has defended the older
position, arguing that Ollrog and others have ignored the pronoun
μοι, but this he finds unconvincing. Instead, he points to ἐν τοῖς
δεσμοῖς τοῦ εὐαγγελίου: Paul is imprisoned for the gospel, and it is
for the gospel that Onesimus is to serve. This in turn, however, raises
problems in regard to the ὑπὲρ σοῦ in this verse: was Philemon too
expected to serve in the ministry of the gospel? The answer to that
must be that all Christians are expected in some way to serve in the
Church's mission: the commendation of the household of Stephanas
in 1 Cor. 16.15 only singles out a particular example. Moreover we
must ask if this is not a case where we should not attempt to decide
between two alternatives, since both may be valid: Paul has found
Onesimus useful in the course of his imprisonment, probably both in
terms of personal service and also in the service of the gospel. On
both accounts he has acted as Philemon's representative, and Paul
would wish that to continue.

ἐν τοῖς δεσμοῖς τοῦ εὐαγγελίου Apart from this letter, Paul
speaks of his bonds only in Phil. 1.7, 13, 14, 17, but the theme is
picked up in Col. 4.18 and 2 Tim. 2.9. Neither δεσμός nor δέσμιος
appears in any of the major Pauline letters. There is, however, a
question as to how much weight should be placed on this coincidence
between Phil. and Philem.; Paul was no stranger to imprisonment.
The classic passage regarding Paul's sufferings for the gospel mission
is of course 2 Cor. 11.23ff., which speaks of 'far more imprisonments'
than those endured by others, particularly the false brethren he is
opposing, and 'countless floggings'. Moule (146) comments:
'Whatever were the immediate causes of imprisonment, St. Paul
was clear that it was ultimately due to his activity as an apostle.'[17]

14. χωρὶς δὲ τῆς σῆς γνώμης οὐδὲν ἠθέλησα ποιῆσαι, ἵνα μὴ
ὡς κατὰ ἀνάγκην τὸ ἀγαθόν σου ᾖ ἀλλὰ κατὰ ἑκούσιον As just
indicated in the preceding verse, Paul would have liked to retain
Onesimus for service, but he is unwilling to do so without Philemon's
consent (χωρίς, according to BAGD 990b, is 'the most typical
Hellenistic word for "without" '). Dodd (1292) writes that Paul 'does

[17] Dunn (331) sees in this phrase 'another not too subtle attempt to remind Philemon
that Paul's need (of Onesimus) was greater than Philemon's since Paul was in prison in
chains; Onesimus could make up for some of Paul's lack of freedom of movement.'
This, however, is open to the same criticisms as suggestions that he is trying to put
pressure on Philemon.

not request Onesimus' emancipation; but, on the other hand, he does hint (v. 14) that if it were to occur to Philemon to send Onesimus back to him, it would be greatly appreciated. Philemon would doubtless like to be of use to his friend. He cannot be with him in prison; perhaps he would like Onesimus to act as his deputy'. Reading the letter as a whole, however, one has the feeling that this is perhaps the least that could be said. Emancipation certainly is not mentioned, but there is more than a gentle hint in Paul's words; the letter is a very powerful plea on behalf of Onesimus. The important point is that Paul nowhere oversteps the line: he does not stand upon his authority, his prestige as an apostle; he appeals. But the decision must rest with Philemon.

γνώμη (BAGD 163a; *TWNT* i. 717), like many other words, has several shades of meaning—purpose, intention, opinion, judgement—but here the nuance required is that of consent (see BAGD §3 for other examples. Lohse, 202 n. 51, aptly cites POx. 10.1280, 4–6: ὁμολογῶ ἑκουσίᾳ καὶ αὐθαιρέτῳ γνώμῃ συντεθῖσθαί με πρὸς σέ: 'I acknowledge that I have of my own free consent made a contract with you'). θέλω, as indicated above, is in some respects close to βούλομαι in meaning, but here has more the sense of purpose or resolve (BAGD 355, §2). The aorist gives expression to the act of decision, although of course Paul's unwillingness to act without Philemon's consent would be of lasting duration. His reason is expressed in the following words: that Philemon's good deed (τὸ ἀγαθόν σου) might not be done under compulsion, as of necessity (κατὰ ἀνάγκην, BAGD 52, §1 at end), but of his own free will (κατὰ ἑκούσιον, BAGD 240; the reference to Num. 15.3 and Thucydides viii.27 goes back at least as far as Lightfoot. Note also ἑκουσίᾳ ... γνώμη in POx. 10.1280 above; further references in Lohse 202 n. 53).

Dunn (333) observes that the language here 'constitutes a gentle acknowledgement from Paul that if things went wrong he would be unable to bring any finally effective compulsion to bear on Philemon. Should Philemon respond positively to Paul's appeal it would be an act of goodness on his part.' This serves to explain the tentative nature of Paul's approach: he could not assert his authority, could not command Philemon, without endangering the whole appeal. The decision must rest with Philemon.

15. Τάχα γὰρ διὰ τοῦτο ἐχωρίσθη πρὸς ὥραν, ἵνα αἰώνιον αὐτὸν ἀπέχῃς 'A tactful letter of appeal written on behalf of a runaway might well avoid referring directly to the offending facts, and in this light it is easy to see why Paul should use the vague expression ἐχωρίσθη in v. 15, especially as the passive carries connotations of the divine will' (Barclay, 164); the 'divine passive' suggests that the initiative belongs to God, that what happened came about in accordance with his will and purpose. The verb (BAGD 890a) means to divide or separate, and in the passive to separate oneself or be separated (e.g. in divorce, cf. 1 Cor. 7.10–15: §2a), or more generally to be taken away or depart (cf. Acts 1.4; 18.1, 2, the latter referring to Claudius' edict ordering the Jews to depart from

Rome: §2b). Here it is used in a tactful suggestion that the separation was only temporary (πρὸς ὥραν: see BAGD 896, §2aβ and cf. John 5.35; 2 Cor. 7.8; Gal. 2.5). In the New Testament τάχα (BAGD 806) appears only here and in Rom. 5.7, in both cases with the indicative, whereas elsewhere the predominant usage is with ἄν and the optative. It introduces a cautious and tentative suggestion: 'perhaps'.

αἰώνιος (BAGD 28ab; *TWNT* i. 208–09) This word is very common in the New Testament, particularly in the phrase ζωὴ αἰώνιος, eternal life, so common in 1 John and the Fourth Gospel.[18] Here, however, it does not necessarily carry the sense of 'eternity' as in other contexts; rather it contrasts with πρὸς ὥραν, and means simply 'for ever', as in Exod. 21.6; Deut. 15.17, where LXX has εἰς τὸν αἰῶνα for לעלם (cf. also John 8.35). The two Old Testament passages relate to the regulations for voluntary slavery, where a slave declines to accept his freedom in the seventh year of his service: he is of his own free will to remain a slave for life. This of course does not apply to Onesimus, who has not been offered his freedom, but as the next verse shows Paul's hope is that he will be received back no longer as a slave but as a Christian brother. The admonitions regarding the relationships of masters and slaves in such passages as the *Haustafeln* of Col. (3.22–4.1) and Eph. (6.5–9) show very clearly that these relationships could be, and indeed were expected to be, very different within the Christian community from what might obtain in the world outside. Masters and slaves had responsibilities one to the other, because they were brothers in Christ.

ἀπέχῃς The first meaning listed for this word in BAGD (84, §1; cf. also *TWNT* ii. 828) is as a commercial technical term: *receive a sum in full and give a receipt for it*. This lends a certain grim finality to the ἀπέχουσιν τὸν μισθὸν αὐτῶν uttered by Jesus at Matt. 6.2, 5, 16: the people concerned have not merely 'received their reward', as the phrase is commonly rendered in English versions—they have received payment in full, signed a receipt, and have nothing more to look forward to. Paul's use of the word at Phil. 4.18 is rather different: 'I have been paid in full and have more than enough' (NRSV); that is a thankful acknowledgement. We need to take due note of the nuances conveyed by the context. In our present verse this word need not carry its full technical sense; rather it means simply to receive back. This is another case of a term which may be technical in certain contexts, but is not always and of necessity technical.

16. οὐκέτι ὡς δοῦλον ἀλλ᾽ ὑπὲρ δοῦλον, ἀδελφὸν ἀγαπητόν, μάλιστα ἐμοί, πόσῳ δὲ μᾶλλον σοὶ καὶ ἐν σαρκὶ καὶ ἐν κυρίῳ This verse brings Paul's plea to a climax. His hope is that Onesimus will be received 'no longer as a slave but more than a slave, a brother beloved'. Moule (147) notes that 'ἀδελφός, or its Semitic equivalents, was common enough even before the Christian era as a term of

[18] On this cf. Dodd, *Interpretation*, 144–50; Hill, *Greek Words and Hebrew Meanings*, 186–201. It is not simply a question of long duration, an endless life; the phrase implies a new quality of life, the life of the age (αἰών) to come.

fellowship or comradeship, upon a racial or religious basis', citing references in support. 'But a quite new depth and intensity was given to the word by Christianity, as is indicated, e.g., by Rom. viii. 29 εἰς τὸ εἶναι αὐτὸν [i.e. Christ] πρωτότοκον ἐν πολλοῖς ἀδελφοῖς. Hence, ἀδελφός(-η) came to be equivalent to "a Christian", as in I Cor. v. 11 ἐάν τις ἀδελφὸς ὀνομαζόμενος ... "... if someone who is called (or calls himself?) a Christian ...", ix. 4 ... ἀδελφὴν γυναῖκα, "... a Christian wife" (cf. v. 2 above).' He adds: 'When a slave became a "brother" to his master, there were bound to be problems, as is indicated by I Tim. vi. 2 (Christian slaves not to take liberties with Christian masters). In the present passage the matter is viewed from the other end.'[19]

It has to be remembered that even if Onesimus was given his freedom, as some have argued, that freedom was not absolute: 'the freedman was still bound to the former owner in a variety of ways' (Bartchy, 'Slavery', 71). The oft-quoted letter from Pliny to Sabinianus is actually a plea on behalf of one of the latter's freedmen. As noted in the Introduction (p. 329), the slave had food and drink and shelter; the freedman, unless he was able to accumulate resources of his own, was also dependent on the goodwill of his former master. In some respects the slave might be more comfortably provided for than the poorer classes of the free population. The fact that some freedmen attained to high office in the Roman Empire should not blind us to the realities of the situation: some freedmen were certainly among the poorer classes.

It should perhaps be added that in 1 Cor. 7.21–24 Paul appears to regard earthly conditions as no longer relevant: 'whoever was called in the Lord as a slave is a freed person belonging to the Lord, just as whoever was free when called is a slave of Christ'. On this basis, Paul would not be greatly concerned whether Onesimus was given his freedom; what mattered above all was that he was now a Christian brother. The matter of manumission may not have been so vital for Paul as it has seemed to some of his modern interpreters.

Paul's hope is that Onesimus will be received as a beloved brother, but the Greek word order ('a brother beloved') allows a further development: beloved especially to me, and how much more to you. He has already indicated his own affection for Onesimus (τὰ ἐμὰ σπλάγχνα, v. 11), and now he suggests that Philemon may come to have even greater cause for affection. It is not simply a question of the relationship between Philemon and Onesimus: Paul too is an interested party, since he is a friend to both. His desire is that they may be reconciled, and in Christ enter into a new relationship. μάλιστα (BAGD 488) is strictly a superlative, 'most of all', but this would not fit well with the following πόσῳ δὲ μᾶλλον: the sense required is 'especially' or 'particularly'. The fact that the slave has

---

[19] On the use of the word in this context cf. Barth's excursus, 'Dimensions and Limitations of the Term "Brother"' (423–46).

won Paul's affection should lead Philemon also to welcome him back in a Christian spirit.

καὶ ἐν σαρκὶ καὶ ἐν κυρίῳ This combination occurs only here in Paul, although the two parts are common enough separately.[20] It succinctly describes the new relationship: Onesimus is to be a beloved brother 'both as a man (ἐν σαρκί) and as a Christian (ἐν κυρίῳ)' (BAGD 744, §6; Lohse, 203 n. 62 cites Dibelius-Greeven for this rendering; cf. Conzelmann, *Outline*, 174). σάρξ (BAGD 743a–44b; *TWNT* vii. 98–151—for Paul see 124–35) has a fairly wide range of meaning: the actual flesh which covers the bones of a body, the body itself, or a person of flesh and blood; in a transferred sense it can refer to human nature with its limitations, the outward side of life as seen by human standards. Here ἐν σαρκί clearly relates to Onesimus' status on the ordinary human level, while ἐν κυρίῳ describes his new status 'in Christ' (the phrase frequently appears as an equivalent for ἐν Χριστῷ).

17. εἰ οὖν με ἔχεις κοινωνόν, προσλαβοῦ αὐτὸν ὡς ἐμέ In the light of what he has said (οὖν), Paul now makes his request: if you consider me a partner, welcome him as you would me. κοινωνός (BAGD 440, §1d; *TWNT* iii. 798–810) recalls the κοινωνία of v. 6 above; it means a partner or participant in some business or enterprise (cf. Luke 5.10). Lohse (203 n. 65) quotes Lightfoot *ad loc.*: 'Those are κοινωνοί who have common interests, common feelings, common work', and adds some examples from the papyri. Hauck (*TWNT* iii. 808), following Dibelius, remarks that the thought is scarcely just that of the bond of friendship; it includes the spiritual bond of a common faith: 'The appeal is to what Paul and Philemon share in common *as Christians*, and not as those legally bound to each other' (Dunn, 337; italics original). Since Onesimus too is now a Christian, this in Paul's view sets the whole question on a different basis; so he asks Philemon to 'receive him as you would me'.

προσλαμβάνω (BAGD 717, §2b) in the middle voice is used of God or Christ accepting the believer (Rom. 14.3; 15.7b), and more particularly for our present purposes of Christians receiving one another (Rom. 14.1; 15.7a; cf. also Acts 28.2, where 'the barbarians' showed no common kindness in their reception of Paul and his companions, shipwrecked on Malta).

18. εἰ δέ τι ἠδίκησέν σε ἢ ὀφείλει, τοῦτο ἐμοὶ ἐλλόγα There was one further factor which might have presented an obstacle to the success of Paul's appeal. A runaway slave was likely to have been guilty of some misdemeanour, which led him to take flight in the first place, and it was common enough for a fugitive to steal some of his master's goods when he left; or Onesimus might have been in debt to Philemon, or have embezzled funds entrusted to him. Nothing is said of the details, so that we are left to conjecture, but Philemon would know very well what Paul meant. Presumably Paul was precisely informed by Onesimus as to what had happened when he made his

---

[20] Barth's discussion, including excursuses, runs to 24 pages (450–73).

confession and sought Paul's intercession. The 'if' at the beginning of the verse does not indicate any doubt on Paul's part; this is simply a tactful way of raising a rather delicate subject. Onesimus had in some way wronged Philemon (ἠδίκησέν; BAGD 17, §2b: *if he has caused you any loss*) or was in debt to him (ὀφείλει; BAGD 598, §1); restitution had to be made if there was to be any basis for a real and lasting reconciliation. So Paul asks Philemon to charge the debt to his own account (ἐλλόγα; BAGD 252: it is a commercial technical term[21]), underlining his commitment in the following verse. Dunn (339) observes, 'This is an astonishing guarantee for someone with as little independent means as Paul, not to mention that he was in prison at the time.' He takes it to mean that Paul could call upon wealthy backers, or alternatively that he could not believe that Philemon would call in the debt. Scott before him had noted (111) that there are indications that in the later part of his career Paul had funds at his command (e.g. in Rome, according to Acts 28.30, he lived for two full years in his own hired house, or at his own expense; cf. p. 365 n. 5 below; Scott thinks the letter written from Rome); he also notes the suggestion made by Ramsay, that Paul might have inherited some wealth from his family. We may further recall Paul's reference in Philippians (4.15ff.) to the gifts sent to him by the congregation at Philippi; other congregations too may have offered their support. All such suggestions are, however, no more than speculation; we do not know Paul's financial circumstances, and the most we can say is that Paul here undertakes to meet any costs involved. Philemon for his part might well have renounced any claim, but here again we have no evidence. We cannot assume that Paul is relying on Philemon's generosity.[22]

19. ἐγὼ Παῦλος ἔγραψα τῇ ἐμῇ χειρί, ἐγὼ ἀποτίσω The phrase τῇ ἐμῇ χειρί occurs at four other points in the Pauline corpus (1 Cor. 16.21; Gal. 6.11; Col. 4.18; 2 Thess. 3.17), and is often taken as an indication that Paul, having dictated the main body of the letter to an amanuensis, is now taking up the pen to write the final salutation in his own hand. Matters are complicated by the fact that in three of these cases (1 Cor., Col. and 2 Thess.) the formula is identical: ὁ ἀσπασμὸς τῇ ἐμῇ χειρὶ Παύλου. Both Col. and 2 Thess. have been considered deutero-Pauline, and it has been suggested that their authors drew the phrase from 1 Cor. (see p. 15 above).

However that may be, the present case is not entirely similar: Paul is not taking over for the final salutation at the end of the letter—he is interrupting the scribe's writing to put down in his own hand a solemn undertaking which serves to underline and confirm the offer he has made in the previous verse. Some scholars have seen here a

---

[21] The form is irregular (cf. BAGD), but is in the oldest mss, א A C D* etc. Later mss (D² Ψ 1739 etc.) 'correct' to ἐλλογεῖ.

[22] 'He would obviously have been bitterly disappointed if Philemon had accepted this offer from the man who had brought him to Christ' (Dodd, 1294). We might well wish to think so, but other scholars have not thought it so obvious.

half-playful use of legal terms (e.g. Scott, 112, who speaks of 'this little jest'), but that is to miss the point.[23] Set down thus in writing this is a serious and binding commitment (note the emphatic use and repetition of the pronoun ἐγώ); Lohse (204) speaks of a promissory note.[24] In this context the legal terms are deliberately used with a legal purpose, but as already noted, in some other cases the usage is more general. ἔγραψα is another case of the epistolary aorist (cf. ἀνέπεμψα in v. 12).[25]

ἀποτίνω (BAGD 101) is another legal term, meaning to make compensation or pay the damages. Lohse (204 n. 72) cites an example of its use in POx 2.275, 24–28. It occurs in the New Testament only here.

ἵνα μὴ λέγω σοι ὅτι καὶ σεαυτόν μοι προσοφείλεις This is probably not to be understood as an 'imperatival' use of ἵνα; it is one of a number of cases which 'can plausibly be explained by an antecedent verb, stated or implied, of saying, wishing, etc., and therefore permit the ἵνα to be more or less consciously *final*' (Moule, *Idiom Book*, 145). Lohse (204) notes that these words pick up the thought of v. 18: if it is to be a question of debts, Paul can lodge a counter-claim, for Philemon is even more indebted to him. προσοφείλω occurs nowhere else in the New Testament; it means to owe besides or in addition (cf. examples from papyri quoted by Lohse), 'though it is often scarcely possible to find any special force in the preposition and to differentiate the compound from the simple verb' (BAGD 717). Here the preposition does have its force: Philemon's debt to Paul, commonly taken as referring to his conversion, outranks any claim that Philemon might have against Onesimus.

20. ναὶ ἀδελφέ, ἐγώ σου ὀναίμην ἐν κυρίῳ The adverb ναί is used 'in emphatic repetition of one's own statement *yes (indeed)*' (BAGD 533, §3, referring to Matt. 11.26; Luke 10.21; 11.51). Having made his request and formally pledged his word in the preceding verses, Paul now reverts to a more cordial and friendly tone, addressing Philemon again as ἀδελφέ (cf. v. 7 above). ὀναίμην is one of the rare examples of the optative in the New Testament, and the only case of a first person singular (cf. Moule, *Idiom Book*, 23, 136). The verb (BAGD 570) is the one from which the name Onesimus is derived, and Dodd remarks, 'Paul was hardly unconscious of the word-play (cf. v. 11)'. This view was already considered 'not unlikely' by Lightfoot (411) and is adopted for example by Dunn (341), who notes that the verb is unusual for Paul, and indeed occurs in the New Testament only here; but Dunn also cites Lohse (205, quoting Blass-Debrunner §448, 1b), Gnilka (87 n. 30) and O'Brien (302) as taking

[23] Cf. Dunn, 339 n. 35.

[24] 'Paul was not content to make promises and provide mere reassurances; rather, he undertakes the formal legal responsibility to make good whatever wrong Onesimus has done Philemon' (Dunn, 340).

[25] 'Whether the whole epistle was in St Paul's hand (as Lightfoot held) is another matter. It would be hard to prove' (Moule, 148).

an opposing view. Perhaps the most that can be said is that it is certainly possible; but the word-play is much clearer and more apposite in v. 11, and it may be a little difficult to think of Paul introducing a rather more remote and recondite word-play here. The verb occurs several times in the letters of Ignatius (*Eph.* 2.2; *Magn.* 2; 12.1; *Rom.* 5.2; *Pol.* 1.1; 6.2); in each of these cases the form is the optative ὀναίμην, as here, and in *Eph.* there is a reference to the bishop Onesimus in the context, which leads Dunn to comment, 'Ignatius probably intended the same pun in *Eph.* 2.2, since he had in mind at that point their bishop Onesimus.' Again it is possible, but when Ignatius uses the word five times in other letters without reference to Onesimus, and moreover there are others mentioned in the context (Burrhus, Crocus, Euplus, Fronto), the possibility should perhaps be considered rather more remote.

ἐν κυρίῳ is paralleled by ἐν Χριστῷ in the following clause, and clearly refers to the sphere within which the favour is to be bestowed. The basis of Paul's plea is quite simply their common standing 'in the Lord' (Dunn, 341 refers back to v. 16). Incidentally, this phrase is added at the end of v. 19 in D*, and substituted for ἐν Χριστῷ in the following clause by D² and the Majority text (cf. AV); but the witness of the older mss weighs against these readings.

ἀνάπαυσόν μου τὰ σπλάγχνα ἐν Χριστῷ This clause picks up the words of v. 7 above. There Paul speaks of Philemon having 'refreshed the hearts of the saints'. Now he asks him to refresh his (Paul's) own heart. 'There is clear reference to the fact that in Christ the relationship of human beings to one another has been radically renewed so that slave and master are one in Christ (Gal 3:28; 1 Cor 7:21–24; 12:13). Thus at the end of the two short sentences that comprise v. 20 Paul places the phrases "in the Lord" (ἐν κυρίῳ) and "in Christ" (ἐν Χριστῷ). The Kyrios demands that all, who are one in Christ, deal with each other in "love" (ἀγάπη)' (Lohse, 205).

There is much that we can never know about the background to this letter: where and when it was written, where Paul was imprisoned, what earlier contact he had had with Philemon (presumably leading to Philemon's conversion), what were the offences of which Onesimus was guilty, how he came into contact with Paul, whether he was actually a fugitive or seeking the intervention of a friend of his master to effect a reconcilication. On such questions we can only have recourse to deduction and speculation. But from the letter itself one thing is crystal clear: it is a plea on behalf of Onesimus, a slave who has in some way wronged his master, but has now become a Christian and is seeking forgiveness and reconciliation.

Paul has no doubt of his own status and authority. He could, if he so wished, assert his authority as an apostle, as presumably Philemon's 'father in God', as an ambassador for Christ, and as one who had suffered in the cause to which he was dedicated. Indeed, he more than once hints at such a possible course of action. Had he done so, he might have prevailed, but at the risk of jeopardizing the

whole enterprise, arousing the anger and hostility of his friend
Philemon, and almost certainly creating jealousy and enmity towards
Onesimus among the other slaves of the household.

What he does is to appeal, in the strongest possible terms, but at
the same time leaving the final decision in the hands of Philemon; and
the basis of his appeal is their common allegiance to Christ. To speak
of bringing pressure to bear on Philemon, as some have done, is to
miss the point: Paul is not trying to compel Philemon to obedience
(although he does use the term ὑπακοή; see below). It was a situation
of extreme delicacy, compounded by the fact that the offended
master was also a personal friend. In purely legal terms, Paul had no
option but to send Onesimus back, and leave him to Philemon's
mercy. But Paul does more than that. He shows due respect for the
rights of Philemon, as the injured party in the case; but he puts
forward a strong plea for Onesimus. Onesimus too is now a
Christian, and a changed man. Paul has found him useful where once
he was worthless, learned to trust him, developed an affection for
him; and he is confident that if Philemon will receive Onesimus back,
he too will find him useful. The fact that all three are Christians
makes a fundamental difference to their relationships: all three are
bound by a common fellowship in Christ. Onesimus may remain a
slave, or if he is given his freedom he would remain Philemon's
freedman, and to some extent under obligation to him; but their
common Christian fellowship had to make a difference to their
relation one to another. Obedience to Christ required that Onesimus
be welcomed no longer as a slave but as a brother in Christ.

This new situation was bound to present problems, but these still
lay in the future: Onesimus, for example, could not be allowed to
presume upon his new status, and slaves had responsibilities towards
their masters. But the new Christian spirit of fellowship in Christ and
love for all the saints carried with it a new attitude and outlook with
regard to all human relationships, which in the course of time was to
bring about the end of slavery in the ancient world. As Lightfoot put
it long ago (411, on v. 21), 'Slavery is never directly attacked as such,
but principles are inculcated which must prove fatal to it.' It is the
more to be regretted that this Christian spirit has not been more
seriously put into practice in some aspects of our modern world.

IV
CONCLUSION AND GREETINGS
(21–25)

[21]Confident of your obedience, I am writing to you, knowing that you will do even more than I say. [22]At the same time, make ready a guest room for me; for I hope that through your prayers I will be restored to you.

[23]Epaphras, my fellow-prisoner in Christ Jesus, greets you, [24]as do Mark, Aristarchus, Demas and Luke, my fellow-workers.

[25]The grace of the Lord Jesus Christ be with your spirit.

There is some difference of opinion as to where the conclusion of the letter begins. NRSV, for example, takes v. 21 as the close of the plea for Onesimus, whereas NEB links it with v. 22 as part of the conclusion. Commentators also differ: Scott, Lohse and Dunn all link v. 21 with v. 22, whereas Hübner takes both vv. 21 and 22 as part of the main body of the letter, leaving only vv. 23–25 with the final greetings and benediction as a postscript (cf. the UBS Greek New Testament, which separates the last three verses as 'Final Greetings'; NA[27] has vv. 21 and 22 together, with vv. 23–24 in a separate paragraph, and then the final benediction).

The words ἅμα δὲ καί clearly link v. 22 to the preceding verse, so that these belong together; but there is no connecting particle in v. 21 to link it with what precedes. Moreover, when throughout the main body of the letter Paul has studiously avoided any assertion of rank or authority or status, any attempt to compel Philemon into any course of action against his will, it would be wholly out of keeping for him to end his appeal by speaking of obedience, as if he expected Philemon to comply with his wishes. The word ὑπακοή therefore presents something of a problem (see below). With regard to the structure of the letter, there is cogency in Dunn's comment (343): 'v. 20 brought the thought back to the same point reached at the end of the thanksgiving (v. 7); and the lack of a linking particle at v. 21 implies a break and a fresh start, with the letter's second ἔγραψα also marking the beginning of the final autograph section'.

In that case we may think of Paul here following what appears to have been his usual practice (cf. 1 Cor. 16.21–24; Gal. 6.11–18),[1] and taking up the pen himself to add the conclusion and final greetings. Lightfoot (410) argued from the epistolary aorist ἔγραψα in v. 19 that Paul himself wrote the whole letter (so also Oesterley, 215 and

---

[1] At Rom. 16.22 the scribe Tertius inserts his own greetings, and it would seem that Paul here did not take over. As already noted, the greeting at Col. 4.18 and 2 Thess. 3.17 is identical with that of 1 Cor., which suggests that their authors may have copied from that letter (but the words which follow differ).

others), but while this is possible it would be very difficult to prove
(cf. p. 359 n. 25). On the other hand, it would be rather unusual for
Paul to interrupt the scribe at v. 19 to insert his solemn pledge, and
then allow him to continue the writing for just one verse more before
penning the final greetings himself. Verse 21 is however a more
appropriate point for the beginning of the conclusion than v. 19.

**21. πεποιθὼς τῇ ὑπακοῇ σου ἔγραψά σοι, εἰδὼς ὅτι καὶ ὑπὲρ ἃ
λέγω ποιήσεις** The form **πεποιθώς** is the perfect participle of the
verb πείθω, and is used with a present meaning: *depend on, trust in,
put one's confidence in* (BAGD 639, §2a; cf. also *TWNT* vi. 5–7, *s.v.*
πέποιθα). The perfect tense of this verb is quite frequently used in
Paul's letters to express his confidence in his readers (2 Cor. 2.3; Gal.
5.10; Phil. 1.6, 25 (cf. also v. 14; 2.24); 2 Thess. 3.4).[2] Here it clearly
expresses Paul's confidence, based on his knowledge of Philemon's
character and conduct from their past dealings, that Philemon will in
fact respond to his request in the spirit in which that request is made.
It does not mean, however, that he is taking that response for
granted: the final decision, as is clear throughout the letter, must rest
with Philemon.

In this context the word ὑπακοή must present something of a
problem. According to BAGD 837 it means 'obedience' such as a
slave owes to his master (§1a; cf. Rom. 6.16), and is used (§1b)
'predominantly of obedience to God and his commands' (e.g. Rom.
15.18; 16.19), but also of 'obedience to God's chosen representatives,
the apostle and his emissaries'. The references under this last head are
2 Cor. 7.15; 10.6, for both of which this meaning is appropriate
enough, and our present verse, where in the light of the letter as a
whole it appears quite out of keeping. 'Since he has expressly
disclaimed (ver. 8) any wish to exercise his apostolic authority, it is
not Philemon's obedience to himself on which he relies' (Scott, 113).[3]
Oesterley (216) sees here 'a hint regarding the authority which St
Paul has a right to wield', which may be true enough; but the whole
point is that Paul does not exercise that right. To take this word here
in its normal literal sense, as signifying obedience to the apostle's
demands, is manifestly wrong.

According to Kittel (*TWNT* i. 225) the word is very rare and late in
non-Christian Greek, and in the New Testament, apart from this
verse (which he takes to mean 'ὑπακοή gegen die Weisung des
Apostels'), is always associated with religious commitment, i.e. with
obedience to God. Dunn (344) notes that some scholars have sought
a solution by understanding the clause as a call for obedience to the
will of God, but objects that this 'would be even more manipulative

[2] It is also used with reference to a false confidence at Rom. 2.19; 2 Cor. 1.9
(πεποιθότες ἐφ' ἑαυτοῖς); Phil. 3.4.
[3] Cf. also Best, 'Paul's Apostolic Authority', on that question. Dunn (344) adds
further references, but some of these relate to 'the obedience of faith', not to apostolic
authority.

in effect'; 'More in tune with the mood is Gnilka's suggestion (87–88) that the objectiveless "obedience" will here denote "the obedience of faith", obedience to the gospel, which is also the obligation to the practice of love (cf. v. 6).' Fitzmyer (121f.) thinks the word here 'seems to be less strong, while subtly expressing Philemon's willing compliance, for which Paul hopes'. He translates by 'acquiescence'.

Paul's confidence is not grounded in any authority of his own, such as might command Philemon's obedience, nor in his status as an apostle (the word is never mentioned in this letter), nor in any special standing he might have, whether as one who has suffered in the service of Christ or as Philemon's 'father in God'. He more than once hints that he could exercise such an authority, but explicitly declines to do so (v. 8). His confidence rests on his knowledge of Philemon's character and conduct from their past dealings, and is rooted in their common fellowship in Christ. He is convinced that Philemon will recognize what is his duty as a Christian in these circumstances, the more particularly since Onesimus also is now a Christian, and therefore a brother in the faith. The obedience of which Paul speaks must be obedience to Christ's command.

Paul, however, goes further: εἰδὼς ὅτι καὶ ὑπὲρ ἃ λέγω ποιήσεις. He is convinced that Philemon will do even more than he asks. What is meant is not spelled out, but many have seen here a hint that Paul is hoping that Onesimus may be given his freedom,[4] and perhaps sent back for further service in the ministry of the gospel (cf. the references in Dunn, 345 nn. 6 and 7). This is of course possible, and we today should perhaps like to think so. Indeed, the very preservation of this letter may indicate that such was the case, but as Lohse says (206), 'not a single word is devoted to the question whether the slave should be given his freedom. How Philemon will concretely express "love" (ἀγάπη) to his returning brother, is his responsibility.'

Fitzmyer, who dates Col. some fifteen years after Philem., writes (24), 'The Epistle to the Colossians seems to show that Paul's Letter to Philemon achieved its purpose, because it reveals that Philemon did the "more" at which Paul hinted: he set Onesimus free to become a coworker of Paul.' A similar view was already advanced by Stuhlmacher, arguing from Col. 4.7–9, but is criticized by Barth (492–93): if we assume the authenticity of Col., or accept Schweizer's view that Col. was written by Timothy on Paul's commission, 'the

---

[4] Cf. Petersen, *Rediscovering Paul*, 97: 'The "even more" would therefore refer to Philemon's bringing the legal aspect of his worldly relationship with Onesimus into conformity with the social structural ground of their new churchly relationship, presumably by legally freeing Onesimus.' But Petersen himself goes on to note that Col., Eph. and 1 Tim. all *affirm* 'the social structure of the master–slave relationship' and address rather 'the quality of Christian behavior appropriate to masters and their slaves'. These three letters may be pseudepigraphic, but we may also recall 1 Cor. 7.21–24 (cf. Barrett, *1 Corinthians*, 170–72). In any case, whatever Paul may have hoped for, the decision had to rest with Philemon. Cf. also Barth's excursuses 'Why No Plea for Manumission?' (368–69) and 'Does Paul Ask for Manumission?' (412–15).

chronological position of Colossians after Philemon is not as certain'
as Stuhlmacher holds. If, however, Col. was written by some later
member of a Pauline school, that view becomes entirely possible.

**22. ἅμα δὲ καὶ ἑτοίμαζέ μοι ξενίαν· ἐλπίζω γὰρ ὅτι διὰ τῶν
προσευχῶν ὑμῶν χαρισθήσομαι ὑμῖν** Paul now has a further
request to make. He expresses his hope that, through the prayers of
the community (the second person pronouns here are in the plural,
although ἑτοίμαζε in the singular is still addressed to Philemon
alone), he may soon be released and able to be with them. So he asks
Philemon to have a guest room in readiness. This of course implies
that the house was large enough to accommodate guests. Since it
could serve as a place of meeting for the Christian community, and
moreover Philemon was the owner of a number of slaves, this
provides some indication that he was a man of some substance.
ξενία is most often used of hospitality, the entertainment shown a
guest, and less frequently the place where the guest is lodged, but in
the two cases in which the word is used in the New Testament (Acts
28.23 and here) the second meaning is perhaps the more probable
(BAGD 547; cf. also *TWNT* v. 18 n. 137).[5]

This verse provides a measure of support for the view that this
letter was written from Ephesus, rather than from Rome. Paul might
well have thought of visiting Colossae after his release, if his
imprisonment was in Ephesus; on the other hand a journey from
Rome would have been very considerably longer, not to mention the
fact that in Romans (15.18–24) he writes as if his work in the east was
complete ('from Jerusalem and as far round as Illyricum') and
expresses the hope of coming to Rome 'when I go to Spain'. There is
also the further point that in this letter to Philemon he calls himself
δέσμιος (vv. 1, 9), a term nowhere used in his major letters, and
speaks of his bonds (vv. 10, 13), a word otherwise employed only in
Philippians (1.7, 13, 14, 17), Colossians (4.18) and 2 Timothy (2.9).
According to Acts, his imprisonment in Rome would appear to have
been a kind of *libera custodia*; would he then have been in bonds?
There would seem to be at least some grounds for thinking that his
present incarceration was not in Rome; but of this we cannot be
certain.

Dunn (346) remarks, 'Whereas ἐλπίς has a strong meaning,
denoting full confidence in the future, ἐλπίζω, particularly where
Paul is talking of his travel plans (Rom 15:24; 1 Cor 16:7; Phil 2:19,
23;[6] cf. 1 Tim 3:14), seems to have something of the tentativeness of
the more regular Greek usage' (referring to LSJ and Bultmann,
TWNT ii. 516–17). Lohse (207) on the other hand says, 'Paul is quite

---

[5] Lake and Cadbury (*Beg.* iv. 546) take ξενία in Acts 28.23 in its usual sense of
hospitality, but see too e.g. Haenchen, *Acts*, 723 n. 4. There is difference of opinion
also in regard to μίσθωμα in Acts 28.30, since the meaning 'hired house' is not found
elsewhere. Hence the translation 'at his own expense' (e.g. NEB, NRSV). Cf. already
Lightfoot on the present verse and in *Philippians*, 9.
[6] Strictly speaking, the Philippians references do not relate to Paul's own travel
plans: he is hoping to send Timothy.

confident that he will soon be released from prison.' At all events,
when it was a question of release from prison any hope was bound to
be tentative, and might often be disappointed. Whether Paul actually
did visit Philemon on his release, we do not know.

Paul spoke in v. 4 of his prayers for Philemon. Now he looks for
the prayers of the community on his own behalf, that he may be
'granted' to them.[7]

Χαρίζομαι means *to give freely or graciously as a favour*, of God
(BAGD 476). At 1 Cor. 2.12, for example, it is used of 'the gifts
bestowed on us by God', while at Phil. 1.29 Paul writes ὑμῖν
ἐχαρίσθη τὸ ὑπὲρ Χριστοῦ, οὐ μόνον τὸ εἰς αὐτὸν πιστεύειν ἀλλὰ
καὶ τὸ ὑπὲρ αὐτοῦ πάσχειν (NRSV: 'he has graciously granted you
the privilege not only of believing in Christ, but of suffering for him
as well'). So here the 'divine passive' suggests that Paul's release will
be an act of God's favour in response to the prayers of the
community (Dunn, 346 criticizes the 'popular translation "restored"'
(used in the translation above) as missing an important nuance).
Lohse (206 n. 9) aptly cites *Test. Jos.* 1.6: 'I was in prison, and the
Saviour restored me' (ἐχαρίτωσέ με; cf. also Eph. 1.6). For Paul to
be released and restored to their company will be an act of divine
grace.

23–24. ἀσπάζεταί σε Ἐπαφρᾶς ὁ συναιχμαλωτός μου ἐν
Χριστῷ Ἰησοῦ, Μάρκος, Ἀρίσταρχος, Δημᾶς, Λουκᾶς, οἱ
συνεργοί μου By switching to the second person plural in v. 22,
Paul includes Apphia and the others: he looks for the prayers of the
whole community, and hopes to be restored to them. Here he reverts
to the singular: the greetings are addressed to Philemon in particular.
The verb ἀσπάζομαι (BAGD 116) is frequently used in such
greetings formulae (cf. Commentary above on Col. 4.10). With five
names following, we should expect the plural, which is found in D[1]
and the Majority text, but this is quite obviously a scribal
'correction'; the older mss (‭א‬ A C D* etc.) have the singular, as at
Col. 4.10. It is by no means unusual for a writer to use the singular in
such cases, thinking only of the first name in his list; moreover, in this
case those mentioned are divided into two groups, which may have
contributed to the choice of the singular: Epaphras alone is described
as συναιχμαλωτός (see again the Commentary on Col. 4.10), the
others as συνεργοί (Philemon is so addressed in v. 1 above; cf. also
Rom. 16.3 (Prisca and Aquila), 9 (Urbanus), 21 (Timothy); Phil. 2.25
(Epaphroditus); 4.3 (Clement and others); 1 Thess. 3.2 (Timothy
again)). All five names listed here are included, with some variation
of order, in the somewhat fuller greetings paragraph of Col. 4.10–14,
which supplies further information about them (see notes in
Commentary there). If we may draw upon Col., the obvious reason
for the prominence of Epaphras is his connection with the church at

[7] Paul in other letters frequently asks for the prayers of the community, or mentions
their prayers on his behalf: 1 Thess. 5.25; 2 Thess. 3.1; Rom. 15.30; cf. 2 Cor. 1.11; Phil.
1.19; Eph. 6.19; Col. 4.3.

Colossae, but if Col. is drawing upon this letter we can only assume that he was a companion of Paul who was known to Philemon.

Jesus Justus, who is mentioned in Col. 4.11, is not included here, but we can only speculate about the reasons for his absence. It has, however, been noted (cf. Lohse 207 n. 16) that this is the only place in the letter where Paul uses the form 'in Christ Jesus'. Elsewhere he employs either 'in Christ' (vv. 8, 20) or 'in the Lord' (vv. 16, 20). If we punctuate after ἐν Χριστῷ here, and assume the accidental omission of the last letter of the name Ἰησοῦς, then it is possible to restore him to the list (the conjecture goes back to Zahn). As Lohse says, 'The name Jesus was surely not yet considered a "sacred name" (*nomen sacrum*) at the time when Phlm was written and avoided for that reason' (but cf. Dunn, 343 n. 2). This is of course possible, but no more: as already noted, there is rarely any call for conjectural emendation in New Testament textual criticism, and without any manuscript support any emendation must be considered doubtful.[8] Also, it is difficult to see why Justus should be placed before Mark here, and after him in Col. On the whole it seems better to adhere to the traditional text.

Dunn (348) remarks: 'Only two explanations for the striking similarity of the lists can command our real support: either the letters were written within a short time of each other, so that those close to Paul were the same, with only Jesus Justus having come or departed in the interval between; or the writer of Colossians derived his list from that in Philemon, with some random and imaginative changes.'

25. ἡ χάρις τοῦ κυρίου Ἰησοῦ Χριστοῦ μετὰ τοῦ πνεύματος ὑμῶν The final benediction follows the pattern usual in Paul's letters (cf. Rom. 16.20; 1 Cor. 16.23; 1 Thess. 5.28; 2 Thess. 3.18; on the problems relating to Rom. 16.24 see Cranfield, *Romans* 5–11, 803f.), with the substitution of μετὰ τοῦ πνεύματος ὑμῶν for the μεθ᾽ ὑμῶν at the end (as in Gal. 6.18; Phil. 4.23; cf. 2 Tim. 4.22a). 2 Cor. 13.13 expands into a rather more elaborate trinitarian blessing, while Eph. 6.24 extends the grace to 'all who love the Lord Jesus Christ'. Col. 4.18 with its ἡ χάρις μεθ᾽ ὑμῶν is almost curt in its brevity (perhaps significantly, the closest parallels are in the Pastorals: cf. 1 Tim. 6.21 and 2 Tim. 4.22b; Tit. 3.15 (like Heb. 13.25) has μετὰ πάντων ὑμῶν).

There are numerous minor variations in the formulae of different letters—the presence or absence of ἡμῶν after κυρίου, the inclusion or omission of Χριστοῦ—and the situation is complicated by variants in the manuscript tradition, but the basic pattern is the same. Here ἡμῶν is found in A C D and other mss, but omitted by ℵ P and others. Some mss add ἀμήν at the end.

The substitution of μετὰ τοῦ πνεύματος ὑμῶν for the simple μεθ᾽ ὑμῶν makes no real difference to the sense. πνεῦμα here signifies 'the representative part of the inner life of man' (BAGD 675, §3b); indeed, 'it can mean simply a person's *very self* or *ego*' (675b). As Schweizer puts it (*TWNT* vi. 433), 'πνεῦμα ὑμῶν in the final greetings

[8] Standhartinger (*Studien*, 81 n. 85), considers the conjecture plausible. Fitzmyer (124) on the other hand thinks it 'highly arbitrary'.

(Gl 6, 18; Phil 6, 23; Phlm 25) means exactly the same as ὑμεῖς (1 Thess 5, 28).' Cf. Dunn, 349 (citing *TDNT* vi. 435 and Stuhlmacher, 56): 'The thought is more Hebraic, with "your spirit" meaning "you", but "you" as spiritual persons, "you" as open to the grace (and Spirit) of God in and through your spirit (cf. Rom. 8.16), that is, precisely by virtue of the fact that you function as persons in a spiritual dimension as well as in the material and everyday dimension of reality.'

The salutation in v. 3 wished for Philemon and his household 'grace and peace from God the Father and our Lord Jesus Christ'. Now the final benediction wishes them 'the grace of the Lord Jesus Christ'. The pronoun is again the plural ὑμῶν, as in v. 22 above, which indicates that they too are in some way involved, although the body of the letter is addressed to Philemon alone. This suggests that this is not a 'purely private' letter: it would be read in the presence of the whole community, and as Hübner notes (see above, p. 332 n. 1) the response would have to be in the presence of the community, and therefore ultimately *coram Deo*. The decision as to the fate of Onesimus will have to be made by Philemon, as the injured party, but in some sense the other members of the community will also be involved: how will they react to a cordial reception for this prodigal son? We need only recall the reaction of the elder brother in the parable to realize that there were problems to be resolved, not only by Philemon himself but by the others in his household. It is no wonder that Paul in his letter is so circumspect; but his last words are cordial and friendly: he is hopeful of the final outcome.

As already noted (p. 360), there are many questions about this letter for which we have no answers: when and where it was written, where Paul was in prison, when and why Onesimus took flight, when and how he came into contact with Paul, whether he was a *fugitivus* or seeking the aid of a friend of his master to plead his cause, and so on. On the other hand, some things emerge quite clearly from the letter itself: that Philemon was a friend of Paul, and one of fairly long standing, indeed one whom Paul could call a fellow-worker; that Paul's knowledge of him was such that he could confidently expect a positive response to an appeal in a very delicate situation; that Onesimus was converted after meeting with Paul. The traditional view outlined at the beginning of the Introduction still has its merits, although we have to recognize the points at which we have no real evidence, and beware of treating our speculations and conjectures as established facts.

Some of the points at issue are not altogether important: it does not greatly matter that we cannot reconstruct the whole situation down to the last detail. What is really important is the letter itself and its message. It was beyond question a difficult situation, and one which if not properly handled might have had disastrous and far-reaching consequences. The story of Naaman in the Old Testament (2 Kgs. 5) provides material for comparison. On receiving the letter brought by Naaman from the king of Aram, the king of Israel exploded: 'Just look and see how he is trying to pick a quarrel with me' (v. 7). He did not, of course, have the background information available to the reader, but fortunately wiser counsels prevailed. Had Paul presumed upon his authority, and tried to command Philemon's obedience, he might have provoked a similar reaction.

The letter of James has a passage about προσωπολημψία, a word translated in AV as 'respect of persons', in NEB as 'snobbery', and in NRSV as 'acts of favouritism' (BAGD 720: *partiality* named as a sin):

> if a person with gold rings and in fine clothes comes into your assembly, and if a poor person in dirty clothes also comes in, and if you take notice of the one wearing the fine clothes and say, 'Have a seat here, please', while to the one who is poor you say, 'Stand there', or, 'Sit at my feet', have you not made distinctions among yourselves, and become judges with evil thoughts? (NRSV)

Today we should speak of discrimination, as something to be avoided, and rightly so. The 'respect of persons' here referred to has no place in a Christian community. The letter to Philemon, however, reveals another aspect: respect *for* persons. Paul shows respect for Philemon (who is after all the injured party) by declining to impose his authority. But Onesimus also, though a slave, is also a person in his own right, and deserving of respect. Moreover, as a Christian like Paul and Philemon, he is their brother in Christ. The fact of their fellowship in Christ, their common allegiance to Christ, makes a very great difference. Paul in the circumstances of his time, and the early Church as a whole, had to accept slavery as an institution. It was part of the very fabric of society, and there was nothing that they could do about it. But in Christ there is neither Jew nor Greek, slave or freeman, male or female (Gal. 3.28; cf. Col. 3.11): the old differences and distinctions have been swept away and are no longer relevant.

The situation in our own day is very different, but this letter still has a message: about relationships between people, about the way they deal with one another, about the resolving of conflicts and disputes. Those who preserved this letter were wiser than they knew, and we may still learn from it.

INDICES

INDEX OF ANCIENT SOURCES

INDEX OF MODERN AUTHORS

This index does not include a number of the more frequently quoted authors of commentaries, such as Aletti, Barth, Dibelius, Dunn, Fitzmyer, Hübner, Lightfoot, Lindemann, Lohse, Moule, Peake, Pokorný, E. F. Scott and Schweizer, since the entries might then have become unwieldy and unhelpful; nor does it list the editors of *Festschriften* and similar volumes. Among other frequently cited authors not included are: Arnold, Barrett, Best, Bultmann, Cranfield, Davies, Dodd, Foerster, Hoppe, H. Koester, Kümmel, Metzger, Moffatt, Pearson, H. M. Schenke, Thrall, Vielhauer and Wedderbum. The reader is not likely to relish having to hunt through ten or a dozen entries (or even more!) in search of the one entry he or she is looking for.